THE UNIVERSITY
OF BIRMINGHAM

INFORMATION SERVICES

This item must be returned promptly if
recalled by another borrower, otherwise by

Regulation, Deregulation, Reregulation

The Future of the Banking, Insurance, and Securities Industries

ALAN GART

JOHN WILEY & SONS, INC.
New York • Chichester • Brisbane • Toronto • Singapore

Copyright © 1994 by John Wiley & Sons, Inc.

Library of Congress Cataloging-in-Publication Data

Gart, Alan.
    Regulation, deregulation, reregulation: the future of the
banking, insurance, and securities industries/Alan Gart.
        p. cm.
    Includes bibliographical references and index.
    ISBN 0-471-58052-X (alk. paper) 2138101/
        1. Financial services industry—United States—Deregulation.
    I. Title.
    HG181.G374 1993
    332.1'0973—dc20   931-13920

Printed in the United States of America

10 9 8 7 6 5 4 3 2 1

Acknowledgments

I wish to express my sincere gratitude to Larry G. Brandon and Robert Gibbons (Insurance Institute of America), Ricardo Mejias (Loan America Financial Corp.), Michael Conn (Michael Conn Associates), James Ross (Radford University), Michael Elliot (American Institute for Property Casualty Underwriters), George Stasen (First City Bankers), Joseph DeSipio (Vector Capital Management), Paul Shalita (lawyer and real estate entrepreneur), Steve Meyers (Federal Reserve Bank of Philadelphia), Alex Anckonie III (905 Associates), and John W. Spiegel (SunTrust Banks) for their insightful comments on earlier drafts. Ron Needleman (Nova University) and Gene Brady (University of Bridgeport) provided valuable editorial assistance, while friends such as George Head and Connor Harrison (Insurance Institute of America), Richard Krassen (independent insurance agent), and Bud Rowell and Larry Brown (Provident Mutual) offered salient suggestions and ideas germane to the problems and future of the insurance industry. Kim Holston, librarian at the Insurance Institute of America, and the acquisition librarians at Nova University went out of their way to be helpful in acquiring the latest books and materials to aid this project.

Deedy Gart, my lovely wife, deserves a special note of thanks for tolerating my long absences in interviewing people, extensive library research, and teaching away from home, as well as an untidy office and guest room for well over a year.

ALAN GART

Huntingdon Valley, Pennsylvania
and Ft. Lauderdale, Florida
September 1993

Contents

Introduction   1

PART ONE.   OVERVIEW AND HISTORY OF FINANCIAL
REGULATION   11

1   The Financial Services Industry   13

Diversification and Regulation   16
Deregulation   16
Distribution Systems   19
Mergers, Acquisitions, and Demutualizations   20
Technological Change   21
Banks and Insurance   22
Trends   23
Problems in the Financial Services Industry   24
Prognosis   29

2   History of Bank Regulation   31

The Depression and Financial History   33
The New Deal Legislation   37
Miscellaneous Commentary   55

3   Securities and Investment Regulation, 1940–1979   59

Investment Company Act of 1940   59
Investment Advisers Act of 1940   60
The Bank Holding Company Act (1956) and the
   Douglas Amendment   60
Branch Banking Outside the United States   61
Bank Merger Act of 1960   62
1966 Amendment to the Bank Holding Company Act   63
Interest Rate Control Act of 1966   63
1970 Amendment to the Bank Holding Company Act   64
Fine and Hunt Commissions   65
National Credit Union Administration (1970)   71

Consumer Protection Regulation: Social Responsibility Laws of
    the 1960s, 1970s, and 1980s   72
Regulatory Reform in the Securities Industry   74
Securities Investor Protection Corporation Act of 1970   75
Securities Acts Amendments of 1975   76

4   Mainframe Bank Deregulation   81
The Depository Institutions Deregulation and Monetary
    Control Act of 1980   81
SEC Rule 415: Shelf Registration   83
The Garn-St. Germain Depository Institutions Act of 1982   84
"Nonbank Banks"   86
1986 Tax Reform Act   87
The Competitive Equality Banking Act of 1987   88
Financial Institutions Reform, Recovery, and Enforcement
    Act of 1989   89
Securities Enforcement Remedies Act of 1990   94
The Comprehensive Deposit Insurance Reform and Taxpayer
    Protection Act of 1991 and the RTC Refinancing, Restructuring,
    and Improvement Act of 1991   94
Comments on the Deposit Insurance Reform and Taxpayer
    Protection Act of 1991   97

5   Regulation of the Insurance Industry   103
Background   103
Insurance Regulators Mount Attack   108
Possible Dingell and Metzenbaum Legislation   109
Risk-Based Capital Requirements   112
Other Issues   113
Worldwide Regulatory Trends   113

PART TWO.   FINANCIAL DEREGULATION AND
CONTEMPORARY FINANCIAL ISSUES   115

6   Contemporary Banking Issues   117
Bank Capital Issues   117
History of Bank Capital Standards   118
Risk-Based Capital Standards   120
Comments on Interstate Banking and Merger Activity   130
Stimulus for Regulatory Reform   131
Decline in Role of Banking in the U.S. Financial System   131
Loan Guarantees   132

Expanding Bank Activities 133
E. G. Corrigan: Banking Commerce Controversy 133
Universal Banking 137
Other Types of Banking Entities 139
Source-of-Strength Policy and the Double Umbrella 139
Multiple Regulatory Agencies 140
Issues of Payment System Safety 143

7   Deposit Insurance and Bank Failures   147

Bank Early Warning Models 147
Too Big to Fail: Double Standard 154
Bank Accounting Systems 157
What Happens When an Insured Bank Fails? 158
Failures at Continental Illinois and the Bank of
   New England 159
The Potential Failures 163
Good Bank, Bad Bank 166
Deposit Insurance 167
Excessive Risk Taking 173
Potential Solutions 174

PART THREE.   INDUSTRY TRENDS AND
STRUCTURAL CHANGE   179

8   Structural Change in the Insurance Industry   181

Life Insurance 181
Property and Casualty Insurance 184
Consumer Confidence in the Industry 187
Mutual Benefit Life and Executive Life 190
Downgrades in Ratings for Life Insurers 195
Other Troubled Life Insurance Companies 198
Salient Issues 205
Exploring Some of the Problems 206
The Thrift Industry-Insurance Industry Analogy 240
Conclusions 243

9   The Investment Banking and Securities Industry   249

Early Investment Bankers 251
Consequences of Glass-Steagall and the
   Securities Acts 252
Role in Underwriting Syndicates 253
Rise of Salomon Brothers and Merrill Lynch 253

Going Public   255
Foreign Partners, Globalization, Financial Conglomerates, and
    Consolidation   256
The Rise and Fall of Drexel Burnham Lambert   258
Salomon Brothers Scandal of 1991   259
Money Market Mutual Funds   263
Discount Brokerage   264
Consequences of Shelf Registration on
    Underwriting Spreads   265
Money Management   265
Corporate Finance   266
Venture Capital and Real Estate   268
The Shifting Role of Research Departments   268
Diversification Efforts   270
Structural Strains and Consolidation   271
Quality of Management   272
Other Managerial Issues   273
Investment Banking and MBAs   275
Securities Industry Structure   276
Classification and Strategies of Securities Firms   276
Shifts in Sources of Revenue   277
Technological Change   281
Where Is the Industry Headed?   283

10   Structural Change in the Banking Industry   289

Balance Sheet Changes   291
Bank Returns on Assets and Equity   303
Foreign Competition in U.S. Banking Markets   307
Shift from Relationship Banking to Price Banking   315
Banking's Role in Securitization   318

11   The Consolidation of the Banking Industry   321
Regulatory Changes   323
What Does the Future Hold?   324
The Era of Consolidation   326
A Megamerger: Chemical Banking Corporation · 328
Why Should Mergers Work?   330
Another Megamerger: BankAmerica and
    Security Pacific   331
Other Money-Center Banks   333
Impact of Mergers   338
The Rise of the Superregionals   339
Superregionals and Investment Banking Activity   353
Merger Activity and Other Potential Mergers   353

Foreign Banking Mergers   356
Financial Conglomerates or "Boutiques"   356
Specialized Banking   357

PART FOUR.   PROSPECTS FOR REREGULATION AND
DEREGULATION IN THE FINANCIAL SERVICES INDUSTRY   361

12   What Do the Experts Say About Reforming
the Banking Industry?   363
Michael Jacobs   364
Jeremy F. Taylor   365
Schumer Plan   365
Pierce Plan   366
McCormick Prescription   366
Bryan's Blueprint   368
Federal Reserve Board Governor John LaWare   369
Charles T. Fischer   369
Irving Leveson   370
David Rogers   371

13   Where Are We Headed?   375
The Rest of the Nineties   376
An Agenda for Reregulation   382
Conclusion   385

Appendix. Major Legislation Affecting U.S.
Depository Institutions   387

Glossary   391

Bibliography   403

Index   407

Introduction

The stock market crash, the revelations of gross misconduct on Wall Street, the failure of nearly 10,000 banks between 1929 and 1933, and the Great Depression of the 1930s generated a pervasive reform of our financial markets and of the institutions that operated therein. However, before that reform could be subjected to the test of time, World War II intervened. The war years and the postwar recovery were so unusual in so many respects, that they prevented a valid test of the efficacy of the revised machinery in a climate of economic "normalcy."

By the 1950s, the chaotic conditions of the earlier period had manifestly settled down. Economic expansion was the watchword of the day. As the economy expanded, and prosperity visited business and individuals alike, the world of finance appeared to be running smoothly—in hindsight, perhaps too smoothly.

Failures of commercial banks and savings institutions were limited in number. Investment companies, investment bankers, and securities brokers were profitable, almost without exception.

Both credit and depository alternatives were limited and straightforward. Secured lines of credit and five- to seven-year loans from commercial banks provided short- and intermediate-term financing for business entities. Mortgage loans from commercial banks were available to fill longer term requirements. For larger concerns, underwritten private placements or public offerings of securities were utilized to raise permanent or semipermanent capital, although the use of this type of financing often was dependent on proper timing within the business cycle and, for the smaller of the larger businesses, the availability of an underwriter.

For consumers, the choices were equally limited and confined. Thrift institutions—that is, savings banks and savings and loan associations—provided most of the residential mortgage financing during this period, which was in truth an orgy of new-house construction. These thrift institutions were able to attract the substantial deposits necessary to service their huge mortgage portfolios only because Regulation Q (which imposed interest rate ceilings on time and demand deposits) assured that

1

they retained the right to offer a rate of interest on deposits of at least 0.25 percent [25 basis points] higher than the rate permitted their competitors. With Regulation Q in place, residential mortgage lending was consistently a highly profitable business for thrifts.

Competition among the various types of financial institutions was severely restricted by law. The transaction function was reserved for the commercial banks because they alone were authorized to offer checking accounts. Even limited competition did not appear until the birth of the negotiable order of withdrawal (NOW) account in 1972. At about the same time, in response to what was by then a generally recognized need, the money market fund was conceived and dedicated as the first device in history to combine payment of a competitive rate of interest on balances and withdrawal of funds on demand. These two innovations provided the impetus that subsequently opened the door to the deregulation of interest rates for small-denominated deposits and culminated in the Federal Deposit Insurance Corporation (FDIC) being pushed to the brink of insolvency. The huge number of bank failures called into question the entire regulatory scheme, which seemed to function effectively for 30 years.

The postdepression regulation led to a segmentation of markets and institutions, with only minimal overlap. Today, the financial services industry is recognized, essentially, as a single industry, although there are obviously a number of interrelated segments within it. Financial institutions, previously limited to only one segment of the market, are presently engaged in expanding their activities across the whole industry spectrum. This broadening of horizons is possible only because of the demise of a substantial portion of the controls imposed by the legislation of the 1930s.

Under the environment established by Roosevelt's New Deal, as practiced in the 1950s, insurance was sold directly by the insurers or through independent agents and brokers. Except for a smattering of involvement by some savings banks and a handful of commercial banks, the buying public had no other market for insurance products.

Brokers and dealers marketed stocks, bonds, and mutual funds. Savings banks and savings and loan associations restricted most of their investment activities to real estate-secured loans, primarily residential mortgages. Commercial banks offered a slightly more varied menu of services, concentrating on short-term business lending, but even they did not often stray across the line into the brokerage or insurance business, much less that of underwriting stocks.

The New Deal legislation provided each subgroup within the industry with an umbrella of protection against unwelcome competition. It also established a highly effective barrier protecting the turf of each group from invasion by potential competitors. Market segmentation by institution proved to be superficially stabilizing.

Because the economy was expanding so rapidly and inflation was low until the late 1960s, each group was able, fairly consistently, to maintain acceptable growth rates and profit margins. Given this set of circumstances, there existed little incentive for any participant to encroach upon the territory of another, or to disturb the "Pax Financus" that appeared to be serving everyone so comfortably.[1]

However, the diamond advertisements notwithstanding, nothing is forever. The caldron that is the American economy never stops boiling. In any given period, events occur or situations develop that underlie a process of change—change which at its inception only a few astute experts anticipate or recognize. The 1950s and 1960s proved to be no exception.

The development of private pension plans and the growth of union-managed retirement programs served to create huge pools of capital that had never previously existed. The necessity to invest these funds brought players into the financial services industry that had never before been involved.

In the early 1960s, Citicorp developed the negotiable certificate of deposit (CD), which acted as a catalyst in changing the nature of banking. The growth and popularity of this new instrument ushered commercial banking into the age of liability management. Most of the large banks shifted from more conservative asset management strategies to more aggressive liability management strategies. Banking became much riskier, as the new philosophy required assumption of liabilities beyond the core deposit base.

The economic expansion of the 1950s slowed in the two decades following. The fiscal pressures resulting from the "guns and butter" philosophy of the Johnson Administration during the Vietnam War brought forth a secular increase in the inflation rate. The accelerating inflation rate rendered obsolete the government-regulated yield on deposits that financial institutions were permitted to offer under Regulation Q. During the period when Regulation Q remained in effect, the inflation rate often exceeded the interest rate ceiling. Under these circumstances, it should have shocked no one that the thrift institutions, the pillars of the residential mortgage market and now the victims of Regulation Q, sustained an immense diminution of their deposit base, which in turn created a shortage of available funds for residential mortgages.

Through the process known as "disintermediation," the withdrawn funds resurfaced in more market-sensitive investments, such as Treasury bills, commercial paper, and money market mutual funds (a new form of investment created in 1972 for the purpose of receiving the gigantic amounts that small savers were in the process of withdrawing from the rate-restricted institutions).

"Disintermediation" also affected larger individual investors and business entities requiring injections of new capital. Always seeking the cheapest available source, large corporations discovered a rate advantage in issuing their own commercial paper directly to the public. Fortune 1000 corporations utilized the commercial paper market rather than the commercial banks for their short-term borrowing because commercial paper rates were considerably lower. The result was an abrupt termination of "relationship" banking and the establishment of what is now commonly referred to as price-sensitive banking. The commercial banks thus lost irretrievably a substantial amount of business from their highest quality corporate customers. To replace the A-1 quality customers, who now borrowed more cheaply in the commercial paper market or in the Eurodollar market, many of the larger banks reached out for lesser quality, high-risk credits in an effort to realize higher returns.

The 1970s added a new and unforseen element to the ferment that was far reaching in both political and economic consequences. Already a net importer of oil, the United States was suddenly and unexpectedly subjected by a political embargo to the deprivation of oil imports from the Middle East. The pervasive inflation that had commenced during the Vietnam War years was thus exacerbated to a point unknown in the memory of those then alive. A phenomenon rarely seen in American economic history suddenly appeared: annual double-digit inflation and short-term interest rates reaching above 20 percent.

Currency exchange rates, which previously had stayed fairly stable under the strictures of the Bretton Woods Agreement, suddenly began to fluctuate wildly. In response, a huge global trading market developed rapidly, Eurocurrency instruments grew in popularity, and London rivaled New York as the center of the world's money and capital markets.

Reacting to this new economic climate and the new opportunities suddenly available, corporate borrowers found it beneficial to expand their internal mechanisms for raising capital. Many of the value-added services, which they had formerly purchased from outside vendors, were now either completely internalized or reduced to pricing or commodity status.

As a result of the 1971 collapse of the Bretton Woods system of fixed currency exchange rates, more volatile and more lucrative interest rates prevailed during the period immediately following. Investors, both individual and institutional, domestic and international, became highly sensitive to interest rate fluctuations and more willing to shift their funds globally in response to investment opportunities. The rapidly developing global markets, made possible in no small part by technological improvements in transoceanic communication capabilities and computers, encouraged every prospective borrower to embark on a worldwide search for even the smallest advantage and every prospective investor to embark on a similar search for the most lucrative return on investment.

To this panoramic quest for financial advantage, the regulator's controls posed only a minor impediment. Regulation Q had no effect whatever on policies of lending institutions in London or in other international financial centers. However, the competition offered by such institutions had a significant effect on their American counterparts, which had to obtain relief from the government controls in order to remain competitive.

In response to these pressures, U.S. financial institutions began to cross over the lines that had previously segmented the financial services industry. Deregulation was in a sense inevitable because of the inherent contradictions of the New Deal package of regulations, which was fundamentally arbitrary and conflicted with the fluidity of the marketplace. Geographic, pricing, and product deregulation were at the center stage of governmental attempts to provide American depository institutions with a more level playing field and the small depositor with a return commensurate with that available to wealthier investors in the money markets. New opportunities seemed to offer growth potential, but in many instances there was growth merely for the sake of growth, without a well-thought-out "game plan" or any real expertise

Table I.1   Market Share of Financial Institutions

Institution	1960	1992
Commercial Banks	34.2%	24.0%
Insurance Companies	21.8	15.0
Other Depository Institutions	17.0	.0
Pension and Retirement Funds	8.8	21.4
Mutual and Money Market Funds	2.6	10.4
Government-Sponsored Agencies and Mortgage Pools	1.7	12.2
Other	13.9	8.0
	100.0%	100.0%

Source: Flow of Funds, Federal Reserve Board of Governors, Third Quarter, 1992.

in areas of new entry. The spectacular failures in the thrift and banking industries are only the most widely publicized of these "growth" disasters. Many banks that have not failed are short of capital and in danger of failure, and the insurance industry is suspect and under intense scrutiny by both state regulatory agencies and some members of Congress.

According to George J. Vojta, executive vice-president of Bankers Trust, "Banks in the traditional form are already obsolete.... If you conduct your business in accordance with the legal definition [of banks], you won't survive." W. Lee Hoskins, former president of the Federal Reserve Bank of Cleveland, adds that "Without reform to deposit insurance and bank regulation, banks will slowly disappear from the financial landscape as unregulated firms take more and more of their business." Less regulated nonbank competitors, such as General Electric (GE), General Motors (GM), Sears, and American Express, now offer a wide array of banklike services. As a matter of fact, banks held 24 percent of financial institution assets in 1992, compared with 34 percent in 1960. Other depository institutions and insurance companies experienced a similar decline. On the other hand, mutual funds (especially money market funds), pension and retirement funds, and mortgage pools experienced big gains in market share between those years. (See Table I.1 and Figure I.1.)

Without question, the collapse of the thrifts is attributable to deficiencies in the legislative scheme and the regulatory controls, which in the 1950s appeared to be working so efficiently and so effectively. The concept of "deposit insurance," originally a reasonable idea, was expanded in the 1950s by an unreasoning Congress to the point where its very presence constituted an invitation to fraud. Budgetary restrictions on oversight agencies and the loose ethics endemic to political lobbying further contributed to such imitation.

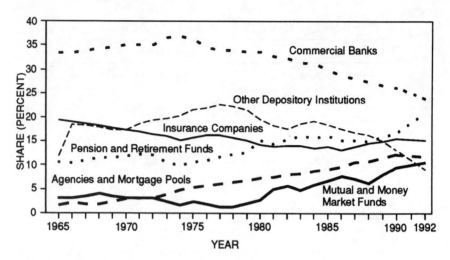

Figure I.1   Shares of Financial Assets, 1965–1992, by Type of Financial Institution. (*Source*: Federal Reserve Board of Governors)

Removed from the jurisdiction of federal regulations, our financial institutions began to be more competitive in the world market. The intensity of this competition caused our regulators to lose control. For example, the Eurodollar market often provided returns that were more attractive than the regulators permitted domestic institutions to offer to depositors. The pressure upon the regulators to level the playing field was immense, but the result was that the regulators now followed the market instead of creating the limits within which the market functioned. In this new game, regulation as the protector of the stability of financial institutions was a total failure.

The new freedom encouraged financial institutions to move across the lines of demarcation that formerly had separated the various segments of the financial services industry. Commercial banks expanded internationally in order to serve their corporate clients, whose own international requirements were growing. The lines between brokers, dealers, and money managers blurred. Thrift institutions offered checking accounts and other services and became commercial banks in everything but name and experience. One-bank and multibank holding companies rose to become cross-state giants of a stature never before seen. Some (KeyCorp, Wachovia, First Union, SunTrust, Banc One, PNC, Corestates, NationsBank, First Interstate, First Bank Systems, and Norwest) have become so large and profitable that they are referred to as regional superpowers.

New financial products were developed. Computerization and other technological advances contributed to the rapidity of the development of new products and services and the rapid global movement of funds. Poor management practices, never uncommon, were now applied to larger and ever-expanding financial giants, particularly within the thrift and banking segments of the industry.

From about 1985 through 1992, the average number of bank failures in the United States exceeded 100 per year, a far cry from the average of only 6 FDIC member banks closed per year between 1945 and 1980. To make matters worse, in 1990-1991, the economy entered a period of recession for the first time in nearly a decade. As the recession appeared, the excesses of the prior years had already eroded the quality of the portfolio of assets held by many of the larger banks to the point that insolvency threatened. Some of the most weakened institutions slipped quickly into failure. For example, one of the largest regional banks in New England failed, and only through mergers were many other banks saved from failure.

It is generally recognized that, given the magnitude of the problem, FDIC reserves are inadequate. Congress and the regulators frequently cogitate over the changes known to be required to ameliorate the deleterious effects of this dilemma.

Whether the banking segment or the insurance segment or both will collapse in the wake of the thrift debacle is presently not known. What is certain, however, is that the financial scene presented in the year 2000 is likely to be radically different from what we have today. It is entirely possible that the retail customer will not be able to tell the difference between the financial products and services offered by Citicorp, First Nationwide, Traveler's, Prudential, Sears, Merrill Lynch, GE, GM, and American Express. It is also possible that the money-center banks will resemble the European universal banks or financial conglomerates. Some of the names of the big New York banks with whom customers have been doing business for decades may disappear as consolidation takes effect to help save a dying industry. The announcement of proposed mergers between BankAmerica and Security Pacific and between Manufacturers Hanover and Chemical Bank could spur other mergers between the megagiants in New York, those in California, and those located in Chicago.

The monumental cost of bailing out the thrift industry, the large increase in nonperforming loans in bank portfolios, the continuing high incidence of bank failures, and the drop in market capitalization of many of the largest banks have focused attention on the urgency of bank reform. This reform will consist of a combination of deregulation and reregulation that is likely to include the following actions:

1. Expanding the powers of banks to permit them to underwrite and sell corporate securities, mutual funds, and insurance products, either along the lines of "universal banks" or through a subsidiary in a financial services holding company.

2. Removing restrictions to geographic expansion that would allow wider diversification of market assets and risks.

3. Easing regulatory burdens, including multiple regulatory agency oversight.

4. Lowering maximum lending limits to any one customer and returning to higher loan-to-value guidelines for all types of real estate lending, as was the case prior to 1982.

5. Closing down more quickly depository institutions with inadequate capital.
6. Providing the FDIC bank insurance fund with the financial wherewithal to survive the current crisis.

In dealing with the insurance crisis, Congress must devise an effective means that would assure the soundness of the banking system, while boistering the competitive strength of financial institutions so that they can contribute to an expanding, low-inflation economy. This book attempts to place into historical perspective the changes that have taken place within the financial services industry, so that we can benefit from looking back at the past and avoid the mistakes of history as we redefine and reregulate the industry for the century that lies ahead. The book explores what the future might hold for members of the industry. The underlying thesis becomes *regulation*, and *deregulation* and the potential need for *reregulation* within segments of the financial services industry. This brings to the forefront six salient questions that must be answered:

- Was regulation of financial markets and institutions called for in the 1930s?
- Was deregulation of financial markets and institutions called for in the 1970s and 1980s?
- Is reregulation of financial institutions called for in the 1990s?
- What has been the impact of deregulation on the financial services industry?
- What changes in regulation and financial structure are likely to take place by the year 2000?
- Don't we really need a more sophisticated type of market-oriented regulation?

Some of the key questions raised for readers interested in the banking industry are:

- Are banks going down the same path as savings and loan (S&L) institutions? Will the FDIC's Bank Insurance Fund (BIF) follow in the same footsteps as the Federal Savings and Loan Insurance Corporation (FSLIC)?
- Why did so many banks and thrifts fail in the last 15 years? Who is to blame?
- What are the key variables that should be monitored to detect bank failures?
- Which banks are likely to fail or to merge?
- Will there continue to be consolidation and increased merger activity within the banking industry?
- Given that most bank mergers in the 1970s and 1980s were not particularly successful, why is the current round of mergers being hailed as a success story by Wall Street analysts?
- Will industrial corporations be permitted to own banks? Will banking powers and products be enhanced? Will more banks be selling insurance products by the end of the decade?

- Why has the role of commercial banking in the U.S. economy declined since World War II?

Some of the key questions pertaining to the insurance industry are:

- If many of the banks are in trouble because of bad commercial real estate loans, why aren't more of the life insurance companies facing financial difficulties?
- How pervasive are the weaknesses that have developed in a few large life insurance companies?
- Are we about to witness the conversion of life insurance mutuals to stockholder-owned companies following the demutualization of Equitable in 1992 and much of the thrift industry in the 1980s?
- Will the distribution system for the sale of personal lines of insurance change over the next decade?
- What are the parallels between the present situation in the life insurance industry and the early stages of the thrift debacle?
- Will there be a new role for the federal government in regulating insurance companies?
- Why have more insurance companies begun to fail, and what are the reasons for their failure?
- What are the prospects for an end to the property and casualty insurance industry underwriting losses of the last decade? Why haven't prices been raised to adequate levels to cover those losses?
- How do insurance company guaranty funds work? Are these consumer "safety nets" really safe?
- What is likely to be the impact of AIDS on insurance companies and on health care costs?

Some of the questions raised about the securities industry include:

- What has been the impact of changes in technology on members of the financial services industry?
- Do investment banking and brokerage firms covet FDIC insurance and greater access to the federal funds market?
- How have the sources of revenues of the securities industry firms shifted since May Day 1975? Prior to May 1975, the New York Stock Exhange required its members to charge fixed (and minimum) commissions. Congress eliminated the fixed commission structure with the passage of the Securities Acts Amendments of 1975. The passage of this Act, which led to negotiated commissions, represented a first step in the deregulation of the financial services industry. The requirement of fixed and minimum commissions was technically price

fixing and therefore illegal. However, the New York Stock Exchange was exempted from prosecution under the antitrust laws.

- What has been the impact of shelf registrations and increased bank underwriting privileges on underwriting spreads?
- What has been the impact of discount brokerage firms on industry revenues?
- What lies ahead for the securities industry? Will there be more mergers, layoffs, or restructurings?

While the primary thesis of this book is concerned with the future of regulation within the financial services industry, the book also deals with important trends, structural change, the impact of technology, and the future of all of the major players within the financial services industry. A busy Wall Street executive, banker, or insurance industry professional may not be interested in regulatory issues that do not affect his or her particular industry. Therefore, the book has been written with that in mind. It can be read like a handbook. For example, an insurance company executive will find two chapters on the insurance industry, while a stock broker or money manager will find one provocative chapter on the securities industry. The banker will find four stimulating chapters on the banking industry. It is not necessary to read the entire book. However, at a minimum, all interested parties should read at least the Introduction, Chapter 1, and the Epilogue, along with chapters related to their professional interests. Readers with broader interests in the banking, thrift, securities, and insurance industries are encouraged to read the text from cover to cover.

ENDNOTE

1. S. Hayes, *Wall Street and Regulation* (Boston: Harvard Business School Press, 1987), pp. 2–3.

PART ONE

Overview and History of Financial Regulation

1 The Financial Services Industry

In May 1988, at a conference at the Federal Reserve Bank of Chicago, Thomas G. Labrecque, president of Chase Manhattan Corporation, mused that Chase could not tell if its bank charter was a blessing or a burden. The firm's concern was based upon two observations. First, Chase found that its most profitable lines of business—credit cards, leasing, real estate, and private banking—did not require a bank charter. Second, Chase believed that doing business under a banking charter prevented it from offering product lines that were necessary to compete globally and serve its corporate customers. Principally, Chase wanted to offer investment banking services to corporate customers.... For this reason, Chase Manhattan and other large U.S. banks were asking Congress to repeal the restrictive legislation and give commercial banks permission to engage in widespread investment banking.

William L. Scott, *Contemporary Financial Markets and Services*

From the post-New Deal era through the mid-1970s, the commercial banking industry was relatively stable. In fact, it was so stable that banks were able to follow the 3–6–3 rule: Pay 3 percent on deposits, lend at 6 percent, and tee off at the golf course at three in the afternoon. Things have really changed since then! The media bombards even the casual observer with reports of failures of banks, thrifts, and insurance companies; mergers; foreign takeovers of U.S. banks or foreign investment in U.S. insurance companies and investment banking firms; taxpayer bailouts of deposit insurance; an ethical decline on Wall Street and the Japanese financial markets; new investment instruments, such as CDs that offer yields tied to the performance of the stock market; conversions from mutuals to stock companies; the takeover of failing banks and thrifts by healthier depository institutions or by the regulators; and proposals to reform the banking and financial system, "clearing away the abuses and faults that stem from an antiquated regulatory framework inherited from a bygone era."[1] There has been a sweeping change in the financial services landscape. With the growth of computers and telecommunications and increasing consumer sophistication, banks now face competition in their traditional markets from nonbank financial institutions, as well as from the money and capital markets.

Banks can no longer be characterized as financial institutions that merely take deposits and make commercial loans. Currently, banks also arrange senior debt, intermezzo financing, subordinated credits, heavily leveraged lending, merger and acquisition financing and advice, cash management activities and sweeps, takeovers, underwritings, securitizations, and the custom design of derivative products. In addition to providing a plethora of new products and services, banks have returned full cycle to a period prior to the Great Depression, when they, along with investment banks, could underwrite corporate securities. (See Figure 1.1.) In the predepression period, banks dominated the financial services industry. However, despite many new products and services and a return to corporate underwriting privileges, banks are no longer "king." Instead, capital has become "king". As a matter of fact, some prestigious banks have fallen on hard times, and some were even forced to close their doors.

The framework of the 1930s was designed to provide financial stability by establishing a system of cartel finance. Financial institutions were divided into three groups: deposit banking, investment banking, and insurance. From the postdepression period until the late 1970s, there was a distinct separation between the functions of these industries. Each industry operated within clearly defined parameters, and companies competed against similar entities on an almost level playing field. Equitable Life competed against New York Life and other life insurance companies for premium income from the sale of life and health insurance and annuities, while Liberty Mutual competed against State Farm and other property and casualty insurers for premium income from auto, homeowner's, worker's compensation and other forms of insurance coverage. On the banking front, Bank of America competed against Wells Fargo and other banking concerns for a share of the market in loans and deposits. In the securities industry, Merrill Lynch competed against Paine Webber and other brokerage firms for stock and bond commissions, while Goldman Sachs competed against First Boston, Salomon Brothers and other investment banking firms for underwriting commissions, merger and acquisition fees, and other sources of fees, as well as brokerage commissions. In other words, all of these companies operated and competed against similar companies within defined, traditional boundaries.

The products marketed by the separate companies within the financial services industry reflected their traditional functions. Brokerage firms dealt primarily with the underwriting and marketing of stocks and bonds and with corporate finance advisory services. Insurance companies sold traditional life, health, annuity, property, casualty, and liability insurance. Banks concentrated on making short-term loans to businesses and consumers, as well as making mortgage loans and accepting demand and time deposits. Thrifts, on the other hand, concentrated on mortgage lending for residential properties and on accepting savings deposits from consumers. For many years, commercial banks were the only firms allowed to issue demand deposits; consequently, they dominated the payments system throughout the United States. Consumer activity was segmented for the most part, with the consumer usually going to an insurance agent for life, property, and casualty insurance needs, frequenting the local bank or thrift to handle checking, savings, and mortgage borrowing needs, and calling a stockbroker when contemplating purchases of stocks and bonds.

For all those years, the respective participants appeared to be satisfied with the specializations of function that existed in the retail financial marketplace. Of course,

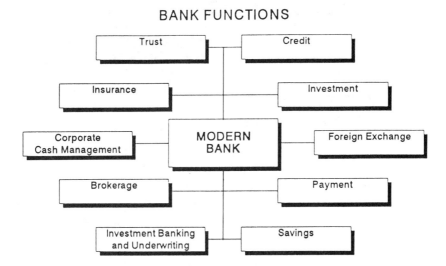

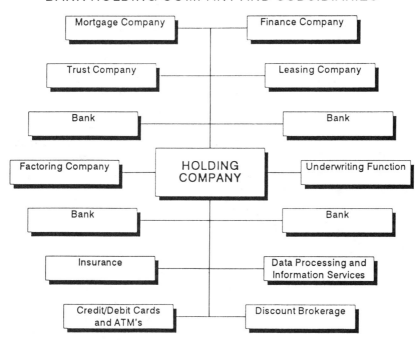

Figure 1.1 Bank Functions/Bank Holding Company and Subsidiaries. (Graph prepared by Ricardo Mejias)

there was a slight overlap in the products and services offered to the public, but it never seemed to create serious problems. For example, savings banks in a few northeastern states offered modest amounts of life insurance to consumers, and most banks offered credit life insurance to customers that was related to their lending activity with the bank.

DIVERSIFICATION AND REGULATION

Depository institutions faced more regulations and restrictions than did brokerage firms or life insurance companies. On the positive side, banks offered depository insurance to customers, but paid no interest on demand deposit accounts. However, banks were prohibited from branching out on an interstate basis, underwriting corporate securities, offering insurance other than credit life, and paying interest rates above Regulation Q ceilings on small deposits. Besides other restrictions, government regulators required cash reserves against deposits, set minimum capital standards, placed limits on the amount of money that could be lent to any one customer, often placed ceilings on interest rates that could be charged on loans, placed constraints on the types of investment that could be made, and restricted the range of products and services that could be offered. In addition, banks and thrifts suffered disintermediation (the withdrawal of funds that were previously invested through financial intermediaries) when market interest rates were higher than ceilings applicable under Regulation Q. Under these conditions, many depositors withdrew their accounts from the rate-capped financial intermediaries and reinvested these funds directly in higher yielding money and capital market instruments.

By the use of laws regulating the degree of competition both within and between financial institutions, the profitability of these institutions could be maintained, despite restrictions and constraints that limited the opportunities and risks banks could take. But it did so only as long as these institutions maintained prudent underwriting standards and did not perpetrate fraud. The safety and soundness of the financial system seemed ensured (at least superficially) for the particular economic environment of the time.

DEREGULATION

Congress continued the general trend toward less regulation and the reduction of competitive constraints by actions taken within the banking industry to deregulate itself. Increased competition and advancing technology made the shadow costs (or losses of efficiency) of continued regulation greater in the 1970s and 1980s. There was also a change in the economy and the political climate that suggested that less regulation could be helpful. Depository rate ceilings were removed, bank holding companies were given increased underwriting activities, and geographic restrictions on the location of banks and their branches were partly removed. The elimination of interest rate ceilings on bank deposits has increased competition for funds. Also, there are now various degrees of interstate banking, which had been forbidden previously. The importance of the growth of superregional banks has been in the forefront of geographical deregulation.

Sharply reduced costs for information and communications, and the globalization of capital markets, together with intense international competition, have all helped play a role in eliminating competitive barriers. A search for new capital and new sources of earnings and ways of diversifying has led to the development of new products and services and foreign financial centers and markets. Over the past decade, there has been a dramatic increase in what is called "off-balance sheet" banking, which includes the issuance of standby letters of credit and commercial loan sales and syndications. We have also witnessed the securitization of bank loan portfolios from mortgage loans to car loans and from credit card loans to LBO loans.

The new world of open competition has destroyed the cartel-like world of old, threatening the viability of many of the formerly insulated financial institutions. Bank regulators are balancing the objectives of promoting efficiency (through deregulation) with maintaining public confidence in the financial system (through regulation). The impact of deregulation varies from bank to bank. The relatively efficient banks should benefit by increasing their market share, while relatively inefficient banks may be forced to merge or may be driven from the industry.

Impact of Deregulation on Bank Performance and Growth

The most important effects of deregulation on banks are:

1. The deposit mix held by banks has shifted away from less expensive deposits (demand and passbook) toward more expensive time deposits linked to current market conditions.

2. The higher average costs of deposits have increased bank operating costs, narrowed profit margins, and slowed the growth of net income through 1991. This has led to cutbacks in dividends and dividend payout ratios.

3. Interest rate risk has increased substantially because of more volatile interest rate movements, while the risk of bank failures has increased because of a decline in the credit quality of loans.

4. Increased competition has induced management to reduce operating expenses. Improvements in computer technology have led management to replace labor with automation or minibranches.

5. Declining profit margins have led banks to seek new ways of increasing revenues. Banks have sought to increase their non-asset-based fee income and are now charging for services that used to be free.

6. Consumers have benefited from the removal of Regulation Q ceilings and a more complete line of products and services.

7. Large money-center banks and other weakened institutions have begun to sell off and restructure their assets in order to meet new risk-based capital guidelines.

8. There appears to be a wave of consolidations and acquisitions taking place within the banking industry.

9. The deregulation trend appears to be taking place worldwide.

10. Deregulation and financial innovation have led to a shift from "relationship" banking to "price" banking.

Deregulation is above all redistributive; it is generally accompanied by intense political maneuvers for favorable legislation, political pressures from trade groups, administrative implementation following long time lags, and judicial review. If the deregulation experience of the airline, trucking, and other industries is any indication, then further consolidation and change are almost certain, as is continued deregulation, followed by reregulation to compensate for the problems caused by the transition itself.

While most regulations were generally designed for the public good, they sometimes created problems because their implications were not carefully analyzed in all economic environments prior to their passage. For example, the existence of deposit insurance creates the moral hazard problem of allowing banks and thrifts to make riskier investments because depositors are less worried about their insured deposits. But regulations that promote stability may also hurt efficiency. Or they may distort incentives in undesirable ways. Regulations are sometimes slow to change and reduce flexibility in responding to changing circumstances. When they stand in the way of profits, bankers have shown considerable ingenuity in circumventing them. For example, bankers utilized the multibank holding company structure and the concept of "nonbank banks" to circumvent restrictions on interstate banking. Overlap and conflict between different regulators and regulations may also create confusion and inefficiency.[2] In addition, there exists what Kane has called the "regulatory dialectic," in which regulators establish regulations that limit the profitability of banks. Then bankers skirt the regulations to improve profits, and regulators respond to the bankers' moves to circumvent the regulations by attempting to close loopholes. After a while, the pattern is repeated.[3]

The distinctions among different types of financial institutions began to blur during the 1980s. For example, commercial banks were no longer the sole source of checking accounts, as savings institutions and credit unions also offered interest-bearing transaction accounts and many nondepository institutions offered money market accounts with a limited checking feature. Nor did the erosion of traditional distinction end with transaction accounts. Legislation permitted savings institutions to enter consumer and business credit markets, offering consumer, commercial, and real estate loans, credit cards, and trust department services. Also, numerous brokerage firms currently offer loans that compete directly with those offered by depository institutions. In addition, some depository institutions began offering discount brokerage services, while many brokerage companies sought to broker customer funds into depository institutions. As mentioned, money market mutual funds were established in 1972, when interest rates reached double-digit levels in the financial markets. Ten years later, banks and thrifts were able to compete on a more equal playing field with money market funds when depository institutions were allowed to offer insured money market accounts without interest rate ceilings. This was a key step in deregulating pricing at banks, which was followed by the removal of the final vestiges of Regulation Q interest rate ceilings on bank deposits in April 1986. The gradual elimination of depository interest rate ceilings began following the passage of the Depository Institutions Deregulation and Monetary Control Act (DIDMCA) of 1980.

During this entire period, insurance companies and securities firms diversified their activities. Both acquired and expanded their money management activities and established or acquired mutual funds, including money market funds. In addition, many Wall Street firms began to sell insurance products and annuities, while a number of large insurance companies purchased stock brokerage firms and investment companies (e.g., Prudential acquired Bache, and Metropolitan Life and Aetna acquired large investment management companies). Also, companies such as Sears, with its purchases of Dean Witter and Coldwell Banker to complement its holdings of Allstate and a savings bank, became bigger players in the financial services industry. Sears also established a "nonbank bank" in Delaware to offer its Discover Card. Other retailers, such as JCPenney, and supermarket chains, such as Kroger and Publix, have become active in the financial services industry as well. Financial service firms have learned from retailers that the more products and services that a firm succeeds in selling to individual customers, the more likely it will be that the customer will stay with the institution. These firms have also learned that it is more expensive and time consuming to acquire new customers than to retain old ones.

DISTRIBUTION SYSTEMS

The system of selling insurance through the "captive" career agency system and independent agents is an expensive means of distribution for many insurance companies. Many have been reevaluating their traditional distribution system through agencies in an attempt to cut the high costs of training and compensation. (The training of an agent is estimated to exceed $100,000, yet three-fourths of all new agents fail within three years.) To improve the efficiency and profitability of their agencies, some insurance companies have realigned their compensation systems. Some have penalized managers whose hiring and training results have been below par, while others have closed agencies that are not cost effective. Most have increased their use of computerized systems to reduce the labor-intensive nature of the selling process. In addition, in an attempt to improve distribution, more insurance companies are aligning themselves with independent agents that represent several insurers (e.g., Allstate sells insurance in many of Sears' retail stores).

Despite the high costs, the life insurance agency system is likely to survive as the primary life insurance network for the remainder of the decade. Since insurance is "sold rather than bought," and since the availability of many new products is confusing to some consumers, a knowledgeable agent can play a key role in clarifying consumers' questions. With the proliferation of investment-oriented products and the growing sophistication of the consumer, well-trained agents are a necessity. However, investment-oriented product and a more sophisticated consumer *have* opened the door for other financial service professionals to compete against traditional insurance agents. Other providers of financial services, such as brokerage houses and banks, can be expected to become increasingly involved in the sale of life insurance products. Still, the tactic of "cross-selling," which has been the impetus for many cross-industry mergers in the financial services sector of the economy, has met with mixed results. Mass marketers, brokerage firms, and banks have attempted to increase their market share at the expense of insurance agents, while insurance companies have battled to hold their market shares, at the same time reducing their distribution costs. Insurers are looking for alternative distribution systems that are more cost effective. Direct marketing (the contacting of prospective customers by mail or telephone) has been experimented with as a low-cost approach to the sale of insurance and has met with varying degrees of success. During this challenging period, the consumer has become more sophisticated, better informed, and more price conscious. Many consumers view insurance as a commodity and tend to buy at the cheapest price.

It appears that the winners in the battle for the consumer dollar within the financial services industry will be those companies with the lowest prices per product, those who offer the best service, and those who can deliver a desirable product efficiently to the consumer. Banks and insurance companies have learned that customer loyalty is typically not toward the financial institution, but toward cost, convenience, and service. It is possible that there will be a thinning of the ranks of insurance agents because of changes in methods of distribution involving telecommunications and other technology, mass marketing, and the sale of personal lines of insurance by banks.

MERGERS, ACQUISITIONS, AND DEMUTUALIZATIONS

Merger activity has gone through spurts of popularity in the banking industry since World War II. There was, of course, the merger activity that helped shape the New York money-center banks in the 1960s and the formation of the multistate banking empires in the west during the period from 1950 through the current period. The takeover of ailing thrifts and banks allowed by the Garn-St. Germain Act in the 1980s helped to broaden the geographic base of some banks. Commensurate with the merger activity that helped gobble up some weak banks was the formation of healthy, well-capitalized superregional banks. During the 1986-1992 period, a series of mergers again helped consolidate some of the wounded banking giants on the east and west coasts.

With both increasing competition and serious problems that have led to a growing number of failing firms within the financial services industry, we can anticipate a plethora of mergers and acquisitions as healthy institutions acquire weaker ones and as firms attempt to expand their customer bases in other geographic regions. J. Richard Fredericks, general partner of Montgomery Securities, has called this period a "Darwinian Age," or "age of the survival of the fittest." The banking industry has discovered that if two banks merge within the same market area, then it is usually possible to reduce noninterest expenses at the smaller institution by as much as 35 percent, while if two banks merge in different geographic regions, it is likely that noninterest expenses can be pared by about 15 percent. Other benefits from a merger with a bank in a different location come from diversifying the portfolio with respect to both a geographic and an industry concentration. The end result is a large number of branch closings and layoffs of employees. The bank consolidation trend has already taken us from an environment of close to 15,000 banks in the mid-1980s to just over 11,000 banks in 1993. Many experts are forecasting that the number of banks will be reduced substantially by the year 2000, to somewhere in the neighborhood of 5,000 to 7,000. Also, the conversion of ailing Equitable Life from a mutual into a stockholder-owned company could act as a harbinger of other shifts in forms of ownership as some of the troubled mutual life insurance companies view such conversion as a method of raising capital and surplus. After all, many of the thrifts converted from mutual to stock companies in the late 1970s and early 1980s, and UNUM, a Maine insurer, had a successful conversion from a mutual to a stock company during the 1980s.

In addition to numerous industry mergers, cross-industry mergers should also increase, as more nonfinancial companies decide to enter the financial services industry because of its growth prospects and as traditional players decide to enter other parts of the industry. The companies that figure out a way to distribute multiple service products effectively and efficiently to a defined market are likely to be among the winners in the highly competitive financial services industry.

Among the numerous examples of cross-industry mergers are the aforementioned Sears acquisitions; the acquisition by American Express of Shearson, Lehman Brothers, and IDS; and the purchases of Tucker Anthony by John Hancock and of DLJ and Alliance Capital Management by the Equitable.

TECHNOLOGICAL CHANGE

Technological developments in computers, communications, and software have provided companies with outstanding on-line information systems or data bases, as well as the ability to utilize this information quickly and cheaply. They have allowed new entrants to come into the financial services industry with only modest costs and to have access to what was once proprietary information, and they have helped make local markets regional, regional markets national, and national markets global. Advances in information technology and communications have reduced the costs of credit evaluations and made the information obtained thereby more available.

Banks and related institutions do not have as much of an advantage as they once did in developing the type of information they need to make a loan. This is one reason why the banking industry has declined in relative importance as a commercial lender. The best bank customers (those with the highest credit ratings) have been lured away from U.S. banks by the commercial paper market, the capital markets, foreign banks, and other competitors that have become more sophisticated. A major effect of technological change and financial innovation is the trend toward direct financing and the movement away from the use of banks and thrifts. Does all of this imply that the institution of banking will some day be a historical artifact, like blacksmiths, or even railroads? The fact is that banks lose market share for a reason; hence, as the conditions of the market change, so will the need for banks. In addition, information technology has allowed creditors to serve large geographic areas and has certainly facilitated the growth of nationwide issuers of credit cards.[4] Advances in technology have also enhanced the development of new products and services, such as derivative products, swaps, and securitization, as well as promoting a secondary market in mortgage-backed securities. Essentially, technological advancement has led to reduced costs for communication, information, and processing, as well as for innovation.

Automated teller machines (ATMs) and point-of-sale terminals have altered methods of approving credit transactions and allowed for the wider use of direct-debit systems. ATMs have also enabled banks to shorten branch hours and build smaller and fewer branches, while giving consumers access to their funds 24 hours a day, every day of the week. As a matter of fact, most ATMs are connected to at least regional, if not national or worldwide, systems, which allow the consumer to access funds while traveling. Systems have also been developed to permit the consumer to pay bills by phone or by personal computer. Home computers can be used for making inquiries about one's bank balance, transferring funds, paying bills, obtaining financial and other information, purchasing securities, obtaining prices on stocks and bonds, and comparing prices on goods and services. A modem attached to the home computer allows subscribers to access a long list of information and news that is available from Prodigy, a videotex systems company owned by Sears and IBM. While the use of videotex systems is still in its infancy, such systems have the potential to play a key role in the future payment, information, and distribution systems within the financial services industry. To see this, all one has to do is consider the possibility of buying simple term, whole life, auto, or homeowner's insurance from a pricing system on your personal computer that would allow you to do comparative shopping for a policy to suit your individual specifications.

BANKS AND INSURANCE

While many of the large banks would like to sell or underwrite insurance, the insurance industry lobby has made every effort to block this practice. Nonetheless, some states permit the sale of insurance by banks, and some banks own insurance agencies or actually sell insurance through their branch systems where the practice is permitted by law. There have been a number of court decisions in the early 1990s that have attempted to rule on whether or not banks can underwrite or sell insurance. These decisions have not been conclusive because different courts have given different opinions on the legality of bank involvement with insurance. Therefore, the issue of whether or not banks will be permitted to sell or underwrite insurance will eventually be decided by a combination of Congress, the Federal Reserve, and the judiciary system. If the sale of insurance by banks is permitted, we will have taken a giant step toward the concept of a financial supermarket for the retail customer, whereby the bank branch network system serves as the linchpin. Banks would then have an advantage over most insurance agents, since people tend to visit their bank branch on a regular basis, while their contact with insurance agents is limited. Banks would also be able to use "statement stuffers" advertising insurance products in their regular mailings of credit card and depository account statements to customers.

TRENDS

The financial services industry has suffered from lax regulation, ineffective congressional action, and a general decline in ethics (e.g., consider the BCCI, Japanese brokerage, and Salomon Brothers Treasury auction scandal and the likes of Ivan Boesky, Michael Milken, Charles Keating, and David Paul).

Other major trends that characterize the financial services industry are deregulation, globalization, securitization, innovation, increased competition, changing relationships of the government to the economy, consolidation, increased merger and acquisition activity, a large number of failures (first at brokerage firms in the mid-1970s, then at thrifts, then at commercial banks, and more recently at life insurance companies), and cost-cutting measures involving large staff cutbacks. Banks and other financial market participants consistently restructured their operations to circumvent regulation, while regulators or lawmakers intervened to impose new restrictions, which market players would once again circumvent. Regulatory response often led to financial innovation, which, in the form of new securities and financial markets, new products and services, new forms of organization, and new delivery systems, has been the catalyst behind the evolving financial services industry and the restructuring of financial markets. The increased securitization of financial assets became one of the salient financial trends of the 1980s, representing a competitive response to problems with the quality of assets, limited capital, and pressures on earnings at banks. In the end, banks substituted fee income for interest income, lowered their capital requirements, and reduced their credit risk by converting loans into marketable securities, while servicing the payments between borrower and lender. It is feared that the combination of deregulation, securitization, globalization, and financial innovation has influenced financial markets and institutions so rapidly, that the aggregate risk of the U.S. financial system and of individual institutions has increased.

The increasing role of governments as risk absorbers (i.e., the socialization of risk) and the increasing role of judiciary systems in writing and enforcing private contracts are among the most important structural shifts that are causing many of the changes in the financial services industry. Another is the dramatic change in exchange rates and international asset prices and the accompanying large and volatile capital flows across national boundaries.

PROBLEMS IN THE FINANCIAL SERVICES INDUSTRY

The following discussion details some of the history of how the financial services industry came to be in the situation it finds itself in today. Banks, thrifts, savings and loan associations, insurance companies, and the securities industry are all examined.

How the Banking Industry Got into Trouble

The banking industry lost some of its most credit-worthy customers to the commercial paper market and some of its other customers to the capital markets, especially the junk bond market. Interest-free demand deposits also declined as a percentage of total liabilities over the last few decades (from well above 50 percent in 1960 to about 10 percent in 1992), while loan-to-deposit ratios of certain classes of banks increased from 60–70 percent in the 1960s to the 90–100 percent range in the 1990s. In most cases, the greater the percentage of loans to assets, the greater was the possibility of default or credit risk. One of the factors that contributed to the decline in demand deposits was the increase in the number of bank failures and the commensurate reduction in respondent non-interest-bearing demand deposit balances at correspondent banks (banks that provide services to other financial institutions and are paid in the form of either deposit balances or direct user fees). The relative loss of demand deposits and the advent of deregulation raised the effective and relative cost of bank interest expense as banks replaced cheaper, dependable core deposits with higher priced, more volatile managed liabilities and borrowed funds. Simply put, borrowing costs increased as depositors converted low-rate savings accounts and demand deposits into deposits bearing market rates. Deposit balances also became less stable because customers were increasingly rate sensitive and moved their accounts to the companies that offered the highest rates. The combination of higher interest expense costs and the loss of their most credit-worthy customers to the money and capital markets and to foreign competition led banks to take greater risks in order to generate higher levels of income. Because loans offer the highest yields, many banks attempted to compensate for declining interest margins by increasing their loan-to-deposit ratios. A large number of banks increased their lending activity in the commercial real estate market and extended loans to companies involved in leveraged buyouts. Some of these banks became overly aggressive in their lending practices and lowered their underwriting standards or were sloppy in their credit analysis and control. There is much anecdotal evidence that loans were made to real estate developers and contractors above the price of land and the cost of development of property and that there was no equity invested by these developers in their projects. Also, many loans appear to have been made with little documentation and with an appraisal value on collateral that was well above true market values.

Deregulation encouraged banks to increase the size of their loan portfolios, which in turn produced greater losses on loans when regional economic conditions deteriorated and agriculture, energy, and real estate problems appeared. From 1982 to 1992, about 1,400 commercial banks failed throughout the United States. The early failures were concentrated in Texas, Oklahoma, and Louisiana (where over 450 banks failed); the next group of failures occurred in the farm belt in Kansas, Iowa, Minnesota, Colorado, and Missouri (where over 275 banks failed); and during the early 1990s, the New England banking industry suffered severely as the economy of the northeast went into a deep recession. In addition, a number of money-center banks remain troubled by a combination of nonperforming Latin American loans, commercial real estate loans, and LBO-related loans. It is interesting to note that fewer than 100 banks failed in the previous decade, which stretched from 1972 to 1981.

In addition to increased competition from the money and capital markets, finance companies, and foreign banks in supplying funds to corporate borrowers, and from finance companies and credit unions in supplying funds to consumers, there has been much competition in the credit card market from the Discover Card (Sears), the Universal Card (AT&T), and the GM and GE cards, as well as from American Express, a long-term credit card player. A consequence of the increased competition is that credit card borrowing rates have been reduced.

Some of the More Obvious Reasons for the Savings and Loan Debacle

The number of thrifts has declined from about 4,000 to 2,000 over the last decade. This consolidation has resulted from both a large number of failures and regulations permitting banks and thrifts to acquire weak or failing institutions in other states. Between August 1989 and November 1991 alone, the Resolution Trust Corporation (RTC), the federal agency handling S&L seizures, closed 583 institutions with assets of close to $280 billion. During 1992 alone, 59 S&Ls with assets of approximately $48 billion failed.

Most obviously the savings and loan crisis could be attributed to (1) in its initial stages, a combination of mismatched maturities of fixed-rate mortgages and variable-rate short-term deposits during a period of rising interest rates; (2) the large amount of losses on loans in areas where economies had weakened; (3) fraud by managers or executives of some savings and loan institutions; (4) illiquidity resulting from withdrawals by depositors; (5) poor loan underwriting practices; and (6) excessive exposure to junk bonds during a collapse in that market. At the time of this writing, 5 of the top 10 thrifts—Home Federal Corp., Coast Savings Financial, Glen Federal, Inc., Cal Fed, Inc., and the Dime Savings Bank of New York—were in serious difficulty. At the end of 1991, the Office of Thrift Supervision (OTS) classified some 437 S&Ls as either troubled by poor earnings and low capital or likely to be closed by the RTC. This number represented more than 30 percent of total industry assets. By the end of 1992, the OTS was predicting that at least 19 more S&Ls with $27 billion in assets were almost sure to fail in 1993.

On a more positive note, 86 percent of the thrift industry was profitable in 1991 and more than 90 percent was profitable in 1992. In addition, a decline in interest rates in 1992 helped reduce thrift depository costs and fatten spreads or margins. According to a study conducted by the U.S. League of Savings Associations, the best performing thrifts had a tight focus on originating mortgage loans on single-family residential properties, an excellent quality of assets, good cost control mechanisms, and lower percentage of assets held in office buildings and other commercial real estate.

Similarities in the Problems of Banks, Thrifts, and Insurance Companies

Like the banking industry, the life insurance industry has had its portfolio problems with nonperforming real estate loans and losses in junk bonds as well as with guaranteed investment contracts (GICs) that had faulty pricing related to a mismatch between the durations of assets and liabilities. The problem of nonperforming commercial and mortgage loan portfolios can be resolved only after several years of a slowly growing economy. While there have not been quite as many insolvencies of life insurance companies (70 failures out of 2,600 companies betwen 1985 and 1989) as there were thrift or commercial bank failures, the failure of two of the top 25 insurers during 1991—Executive Life of California and Mutual Benefit Life—brought calls for federal regulation of insurance, reform of guaranty associations, and uniform and higher standards of capital, as well as investment guidelines for the industry as a whole. The weakness of another industry leader, Equitable Life, with its conversion from a mutual to a stock company, has attracted much media and industry attention. The demutualization of Equitable might be a harbinger of what is to become of the remaining 115 mutuals, which now account for close to 60 percent of the assets of life insurance companies.

Because of all of the media attention given to the problems of life insurers, the entire life insurance industry has suffered from a loss of consumer confidence. However, while there has been a large number of staff cutbacks within the life insurance industry in order to improve profitability, the level of merger activity in the industry has not approached that of either the banking or thrift industries. A.M. Best, the well-known insurance industry rating agency, was busy downgrading most of the life insurance companies in 1991, just as Moody's and Standard & Poors had downgraded many of the banks in 1990 and 1991. Consumer demand, which has shifted toward interest-sensitive insurance investment products, coupled with increased competition, has placed more downward pressure on profit margins. This trend has in part led to investigations of more cost-effective methods of policy distribution and administration, which are central to the industry and its future profitability. While cost-cutting measures and increases in the productivity of agents have facilitated an improvement, a shift in the mix of business favoring annuities has also helped, because annuities are relatively inexpensive to market and administer. Further, in 1992, life insurance companies were helped by a direct infusion of external capital or by a sale of assets in the case of troubled insurers, such as Aetna, Travelers, and Equitable, and by declining interest rates, which increased the value of fixed-rate bond portfolios.

Although the property and casualty segment of the insurance industry has not suffered much from real estate loan losses (less than 2 percent of the industry's investment portfolio is in mortgage or real estate loans, compared with more than 20 percent for life insurance companies) or junk bond losses, it has suffered from insurance underwriting losses since 1979. From 1969 to 1990, there were 372 insolvencies. Cash flow underwriting practices have tended to dominate this segment of the market, as insurance companies have relied upon investment income generated from premiums for their profits. Some industry analysts are hoping that the decade-long underwriting losses, coupled with the low interest rates of 1992, will act as a catalyst in bringing the cash flow underwriting practice to an end. Exacerbating the overcapacity problem is the increased presence of alternative markets. In fact, property and casualty companies have lost about 35 percent of their best commercial customers to captive insurance companies (those owned by companies other than insurance companies, for the purpose of self-insurance), and some actuarial consultants expect the captive market share to reach 50 percent by the end of the century. This factor has lowered the overall quality of most property and casualty company underwriting portfolios.

There is evidence that some insurers are not pleased with their return on capital of personal auto insurance and of worker's compensation and have reduced their participation in these unprofitable, inadequately priced lines of business or have withdrawn from them altogether. These moves might stabilize prices for the remaining competitors. However, profits may be difficult to come by as a result of additional charges from state insolvency guaranty funds. As a consequence, some insurers have reallocated resources into (theoretically) higher return, specialized commercial lines. This has resulted in an influx of capital and competition to those markets, adding some downward price pressure.

There has also been a flight toward quality within the reinsurance industry and a consolidation among underwriters. In 1990, the 20 largest reinsurers accounted for more than 80 percent of the premiums written, while the 5 largest reinsurers accounted for 50 percent of the premiums. Since the last down cycle resulted in a high level of reinsurance insolvencies, primary insurance companies are focusing on the collectibility of reinsurance recoverables and are doing business only with the best capitalized reinsurance companies. Amid concern that inadequate state supervision of certain reinsurance activities played a key role in several property and casualty insolvencies, Representative Dingell, chairman of the House of Representatives' Energy and Commerce Subcommittee on Oversight and Investigations, has introducted a plan to license reinsurance companies federally, as part of a larger plan to overhaul the current state-controlled insurance regulatory system. Further, stricter regulation of the life insurance industry is a strong probability, and government is also likely to continue to struggle with longer term solutions to providing health benefits to the uninsured and underinsured.

According to Standard and Poors insurance analysts, health insurance is the area most vulnerable to political and market pressures and will most likely be the first insurance segment to face the need for consolidation. These analysts expect that by the year 2000, the health insurance industry will be dominated by three types of companies: large multiregional players, some market-focused regional companies with an emphasis on superior service, and strong concerns that serve niche insurance businesses. Standard and Poors also opined that while the insurance industry is still struggling, insurance companies remain relatively stronger than other U.S. financial institutions because most life insurers have shifted new investments into higher quality, more liquid assets following on the heels of the mistakes made in commercial real estate and junk bond investments.

How the Securities Industry Has Fared in This Era of Deregulation, Consolidation, and Technological Change

The securities industry was the first industry affected by the general trend toward deregulation in the financial services industry following the May 1975 decision by the SEC to abolish minimum fixed-rate commissions. Numerous firms were unable to adjust to the new environment of negotiated commissions, and failure and merger rates were quite high during the late 1970s. This shift to negotiated commissions led to the establishment of discount brokers such as Charles Schwab, which was once owned by BankAmerica. As a matter of fact, many banks and thrifts offer discount brokerage services to their customers.

The securities industry is susceptible to extreme profit swings from good to bad times. Recently, the industry has benefited from cost containment and refocusing programs that were implemented in late 1989 and in 1990. While profits were substantial in 1991, they followed on the heels of the first industrywide loss in 1990 in almost two decades, when intense competition and overcapacity in the industry were compunded by the anticipation of the Persian Gulf episode and declines in new issues of junk bonds and equities, as well as in merger and acquisition activity. In addition to the decline in the volume of new issues in 1990, underwriting margins continued their decade-long fall. However, while underwriting spreads remained low, volume increased substantially to record levels in 1992, following strong gains in 1991.

The securities industry has directed more attention toward areas such as asset management and mutual funds, as well as on staff reductions, consolidations, and intercompany mergers of back office operations and the relocation of major operations to geographic areas that offer affordable rental space and an adequate and relatively inexpensive supply of labor. By the end of 1990, industry employment had dropped to 210,000 from a peak of 267,000 in the fall of 1987. Some of the brokerage firms, especially those owned by insurance companies, have made an effort to cross-sell annuities and other insurance products. Some of the larger investment banking firms have increased their risk taking by acting as merchant bankers and lending their own funds to clients.

Just as additional capital was being added to the banking and thrift industry to help meet regulatory requirements and to provide a potential war chest for future acquisitions, securities firms raised additional capital to strengthen their balance sheets in an era when capital is considered king. Some capital was raised by selling interests to foreign firms (e.g., Goldman Sachs sold a 12.5-percent interest to Sumitomo Bank), while other securities firms received infusions of capital from their larger parent holding company (e.g., Shearson received a large infusion of capital from its parent, American Express, and also sold a 13-percent interest in its stock to Nippon Life).

While income from commissions rose steadily for almost a decade (except for 1984, 1988, and 1990) its ratio to total revenues declined precipitously for well over a few decades, from 56 percent in 1973 to approximately 16 percent in 1991. On the other hand, income from trading and investment and fees related to the corporate finance advisory function achieved strong growth over the last decade. Underwriting income is cyclical and dependent on new debt and equity activity, while income from commissions is related to the level of stock market activity and the performance of the stock market. Investment bankers who rely on underwriting and the distribution of corporate securities for much of their revenue will likely find more competition and slimmer profit margins in the future as more commercial banks are permitted to underwrite securities.

PROGNOSIS

As we approach the 21st century, deregulation, technological advances, the integration of business, diversification, globalization, and product innovation are among the hallmarks of progress for the financial services industry. Old regulatory barriers and the clear separation of banks, thrifts, insurance companies, and brokerage firms into traditional functions are breaking down. Most of these companies have diversified by product, service, and location whenever and wherever possible. Firms are much larger and better capitalized, yet leaner in terms of overhead, following a massive consolidation within the financial services industry. Competition is keen, and every effort is being made to reduce costs and become more efficient. Although the size of firms has increased dramatically on average, there is still room for the niche or boutique player. Nontraditional players, foreign banks, brokerage firms, and reinsurance companies have helped develop the financial services industry into a global, highly competitive market. The boundaries of financial service markets have become blurred. The carefully segmented domain of banks, thrifts, insurance companies, and securities firms is now crowded with financial conglomerates, industrial corporations, and retailers, such as GE, Sears, Xerox, American Express, Prudential, Kmart, Montgomery Ward, and Primerica, among others. Accompanying the revolutionary changes in markets are new alliances among the old and new players within the financial services industry. Despite an increase in mergers, acquisitions, competition, failures, and new ventures, much of the industry remains fundamentally fragmented, with many companies suffering from poor-quality assets and poor management decision making.

Currently, we need a decision on the part of Congress and the regulators as to whether the banking industry is to remain restricted and partially protected or whether it is to change and become part of an expanded financial services marketplace.

ENDNOTES

1. T. W. Kock, "The Emerging Bank Structure of the 1990s," *Business Economics*, July 1992, p.32.

2. M. Kohn, *Money, Banking, and Financial Markets*, (Hinsdale, IL: Dryden Press, 1991), p. 489.

3. S. E. Hein, "A Re-examination of the Costs and Benefits of Federal Deposit Insurance," *Business Economics*, July 1992, p. 31.

4. *Federal Reserve Bulletin*, March 1992, p. 177.

2 History of Bank Regulation

Historians have made Nero notorious for having fiddled while Rome burned. Future historians may treat Congress and associated federal regulators equally harshly for having diddled while the heat of globalization gradually melted down the U.S. financial industry into a second-rate player in world financial markets.

Edward J. Kane, "Regulation in a Global Market Context"

Regulation arose from public concerns about the safety of financial institutions and the security of people who purchased insurance, stocks, and bonds and who made deposits in banks and thrifts. The regulators sought to promote bank safety, which fosters economic stability, by minimizing economic disturbances originating in the banking sector. Among the broad objectives of federal bank and security regulations was the separation of banking from other business activities, in order to promote soundness in banking and to prevent a concentration of economic power in the hands of large-scale enterprises.

The stock market crash of 1929, thousands of bank failures, and the ensuing depression brought cries of recrimination from elected officials and government appointees and feelings of betrayal from the public. The ire of politicians and the U.S. public was directed principally toward the bankers and financial institutions that were perceived to have orchestrated the debacle. Consequently, Congress produced a slew of regulations destined to change the face and conduct of the banking and securities industries. It should be noted that although it was never established that the bank failures of 1929 and the early 1930s were a consequence of the participation of banks in the underwriting or ownership of securities or in their affiliation with investment bankers, public perceptions were enough to coerce government reform. Some perceived the banking failures of the 1920s and 1930s as being partially attributable to "overbanking," resulting from an excessively lax chartering policy. This led to led to more stringent chartering practices in the reforms that followed. As a consequence, branch banking in the United States became highly restricted in contrast to the practice in most other nations. The widespread bank failures, combined with revelations of unethical activities by commercial banks engaged in investment banking activities, led Congress to pass the Banking Acts of 1933–1934, which separated investment banking from commercial banking and established depository insurance. During the period 1933–1935, the Roosevelt Administration produced the Glass-Steagall Act, the Securities Acts of 1933 and 1934, and the Public Utility

Holding Act of 1935. According to the *Public Papers* of President Roosevelt, a common thread through all these laws was the disclosure of information for the purpose of "letting in the light" to reveal the true facts of issuers' affairs and their overall business health. The wake of the Great Depression produced an elaborate framework of federal and state regulations that restricted bank market entry, limited bank geographical location and product lines, provided deposit insurance and bank balance sheet restrictions, and controlled the prices of some services offered to the public (e.g., rate ceilings on bank deposits).

From about 1960 to mid-1975, additional regulatory objectives emerged that were concerned with social responsibility and consumer protection. Regulations were enacted that encouraged the allocation of credit to community needs, promoted adequate competition, and encouraged the allocation of bank credit into certain areas (e.g., home ownership) defined as desirable for public policy reasons.

The regulation of financial intermediaries can be classified into three major areas: product line separation, regulation of the banking system, and consumer protection and safety. The types of regulation are sometimes classified as *economic regulation, safety regulation, consumer information,* and *protection regulation.*[1]

Although banks, the government, and the public considered the aforementioned regulations acceptable and desirable when they were implemented, most observers and analysts today consider many of them outmoded, superfluous, and in need of modification and reform. While safety was the primary focus of earlier legislation, quality and the price of financial services became the salient issue in the 1970s. By the 1980s, Congress turned toward deregulation or less regulation within the financial services industry. At the time of this writing, the industry is mired in distress and requires additional public policy measures to place both it and the economy on sounder and firmer footing. Before we deal with recommendations for reform, it is wise to review the historical background of regulation in this country, beginning with the post-Depression-era legislation to reform the banking and securities industry.

The development of trusts during the late 19th century provides an illustration of the trade-off between the fears of centralization and risks of decentralization. A group of financial institutions that developed around J.P. Morgan offered financial services as diverse as insurance and commercial and trust banking. New York's First National and National City Banks also moved toward what is currently called universal banking. As the power of a few large banks increased, traditional suspicions of all banking powers became greater. The Pujo Committee, set up in 1912 to investigate the money trusts, denounced them unambiguously. The committee charged that there was

> a community of interests between a few leaders of finance, created and held together through stock ownership, interlocking directorates, partnership and joint account transactions, and other forms of domination over banks, trust companies, railroads and public service and industrial corporations, which has resulted in great and rapidly growing concentration of the control of money and credit in the banks of these few men.[2]

THE DEPRESSION AND FINANCIAL HISTORY

The economic growth following World War I spawned a freewheeling securities market that was accompanied by excesses and fiduciary abuses during the 1920s. There were few federal laws or public policies to regulate the securities industry. The election of reform-minded Franklin Roosevelt led to new legislation to preserve the capitalist system and to create a series of protections for previously abused suppliers of capital to the system.[3]

The situation prior to the Depression was quite different than it is now. While there was no depository insurance, there was a perfectly safe bank for time deposits: the U.S. government's Postal Savings System. This system did not provide small depositors with check-writing privileges, but neither did commercial banks, which for the most part, catered to the needs of businesses and wealthy individuals. Also, most securities were owned by individuals then, as opposed to institutional investors now.

During the Pecora (counsel to the Senate Banking Committee) hearings, which lasted nine days in late winter 1933, the American financial community was totally discredited. One executive after another from the largest banks and investment houses admitted to practices that ranged from negligence to outrageousness, from the use of publicity agents to push stock to self-dealing, from inattention to quality to inadequate disclosure, from manufacturing securities to insider dealings, and from blatant fraud to conflicts of interest, shocking the "moral sense of the nation."[4]

For example, a securities firm hired a University of Chicago professor to advertise "principles of sound investment" on a radio program. The professor relied on scripts written entirely by the brokerage firm that suggested the purchase of stocks and bonds that the company just happened to have for sale. As an example of inattention to quality, there were Peruvian bonds sold despite the fact that the underwriter's own experts had described the Peruvian government as "an adverse moral and political risk." The Pecora hearings found many instances in which reputable invest-ment houses pushed securities on investors without revealing that the securities firm itself held the stock in the investment houses' own inventory position. Investment firms created new product for their growing sales staffs to sell. They formed over 700 investment trusts between 1921 and 1929, most of which served no useful purpose other than to generate fees for the organizers by providing new capital to their operating companies. These trusts were often used as "buyers of last resort" to absorb slow-moving issues underwritten by the sponsors of the trusts. The pipeline of new products was always full, even when the stocks and bonds being brought to market were of little or no value. In the case of worthwhile securities, many institutions maintained preferred lists of customers to whom these securities were sold below the public offering price.[5] In addition, congressional hearings revealed that "stock watering" (baselessly writing up the valuation of assets to rationalize an increase in the number of outstanding equity shares) had become quite common in the 1920s.

Rarely has a group lost so much status and respect so rapidly as had investment bankers in the three years following the great stock market crash. Their badly tarnished public image was to deteriorate still further in 1932 and 1933, as congressional committees probed deeper into their business affairs.[6] Just a few years earlier, Wall Street was looked up to in awe as "the stage whereon is focused the world's most intelligent and best informed judgment of the values of the enterprises which serve men's needs."[7]

From 1929 to 1933, the number of banks declined from about 25,000 to about 14,000 (a 40-percent drop), while the economy plummeted. The unemployment rate at the depth of the recession approximated 25 percent, while the Dow Jones Industrial Average dropped 88 percent from peak to trough. Money and aggregate deposits within the banking system also fell by one-third. The financial system was in a shambles, and many banks were closed for days or even weeks at a time during bank holidays. Depositors lost faith in the banking system and began withdrawals of their funds, having suffered losses of their savings in many cases when the banks failed in domino style. The ratio of currency to total bank deposits rose from 9 percent in 1929 to 19 percent in 1933 (23 percent if the increase in guaranteed postal savings is included as currency). The Great Depression resembled a holocaust: The traumatization of survivors affected public policy in the near term, as well as in decades to come.

The Pecora hearings, the crash of the stock market, the 8,000 bank failures, the huge unemployment figures, the dismal picture for economic growth, and the thousands of Americans who had lost their life savings through no fault of their own, as well as a desire to prevent a total collapse of the banking system, led President Roosevelt to declare a national bank holiday and to draft new regulations to restore confidence and safety to the American financial system.

The regulations that cropped up as a result of this prolonged financial crisis stressed safety and discouraged competition. New features of the U.S. economy were Regulation Q, insurance on bank deposits, restricted entry into banking, the separation of investment from commercial banking, Federal Reserve control of margin requirements, better information for investors, and the regulation of securities markets. The introduction of FDIC insurance in 1934, which may partially be attributed to the failure of the central bank to inject sufficient reserves to offset the currency drain of 1930–1933 and to prevent the money stock from declining, helped stabilize the banking system by allaying fears of a loss of savings.

When rumors circulate regarding the solvency of depository institutions in general, and the public decides to withdraw funds massively from banks (creating a "run" or "contagion effect"), the result can be quite harmful to the banking system and the economy. Sometimes banks may be closed that are otherwise solvent. The "contagion effect" could cause a liquidity crisis at banks, such as the one that occurred during the Great Depression or, more recently, at credit unions in Rhode Island in the early 1990s and thrifts in Ohio in the mid-1980s. Additionally, the U.S. payments system is placed under stress as funds are withdrawn from banks, and banking liquidity is strained.

The economic malaise and the associated financial difficulties continued to deteriorate through the spring of 1933, until President Hoover's term ended in early March. Arthur M. Schlesinger, Jr., described the situation as follows:

> *The White House,* midnight, Friday, March 3, 1933. Across the country the banks of the nation had gradually shuttered their windows and locked their doors. . . . The very machinery of the American economy seemed to be coming to a stop. The rich and fertile nation, overflowing with natural wealth in its fields and forests and mines, equipped with unsurpassed technology, endowed with boundless resources in its men and women, lay stricken. "We are at the end of our rope," a weary President Hoover at last said, as the striking clock announced the day of his retirement. "There is nothing more we can do."[8]

As Schlesinger so eloquently describes, the nation was in a state of despair in 1933. Financial markets had collapsed, the banking system was on the verge of disintegration, unemployment was rampant, and calls for financial reform were heard throughout the country. On March 4, 1933, Franklin Roosevelt was inaugurated. Congress was called into special session the next day, and President Roosevelt declared a four-day national banking holiday, which was later extended indefinitely. Congress passed sweeping legislative measures over the next 100 days, including approval of the president's authority to proclaim a national banking holiday. A framework was provided for reopening closed banks. The reopening procedure called for the U.S. secretary of the treasury to license any member bank whose financial condition was judged to be sound by the district Federal Reserve Bank. State banking authorities could reopen sound nonmember banks at their discretion. Among the sweeping legislative changes were the Banking Act of 1933 (also known as the Glass-Steagall Act) and the Securities Acts of 1933 and 1934, part of President Roosevelt's so-called New Deal.

By early 1933, the bitter facts of economic collapse had become inextricably linked in the public mind with the market crash of 1929 and with the increasingly feverish operations of high finance in the 1920s. Not only was there an enormous loss in paper wealth, but the public's faith in the essential soundness of the whole economic system and in the men and institutions that had long dominated it crashed. Formerly, these members of the financial community had been regarded with a respect that approached awe. Now, people came to understand what the self-appointed stewards of their economic well-being had been doing, they were angered and betrayed by what they saw as gross violations of the ethic of stewardship. There was a perception that the country had been abused by a rapacious banking fraternity. The following priceless quote by H. O. Havenmeyer, then president of the American Sugar Refining Company, captures eloquently the contempt the public felt was emanating from Wall Street insiders: "Let the buyer beware; that covers the whole business. You cannot wet-nurse people from the time they are born until the time they die. They have to wade in and get stuck and in that is the very way men are educated and cultivated.[9]

By the time of the 1933 Act, industry practice appeared to many to be driven less by the desire to make a fair profit from underwriting and distributing sound, well-researched securities to the public than by the need to help keep the pipeline of distribution filled with securities, no matter what their underlying value. The more actively these financial institutions piled assets on a shaky foundation of faith and credit, the less thoroughly they researched or acknowledged the underlying values of those assets. In addition, the State Department had a habit of informally approving the sale to domestic investors of the debt instruments of foreign governments. As the value of these bonds plummeted, it became obvious that the State Department's implied endorsements were misleading the public and that the government had unintentionally lent credibility to these foreign security issues. The more outwardly successful the bankers were, the more they appeared to their critics as little other than huge engines for the collection of fees, charges, and profits. Instances were also plentiful of insider trading, outright fraud, and securities pools to manipulate markets to inflate or deflate securities prices artificially. Easy credit was available to fuel speculation and manipulation. In addition, there were preferred lists through which investment houses rewarded their friends with certain profits on "sweetheart deals."

At that time, Louis Brandeis, associate justice of the Supreme Court, had a deep and abiding suspicion of the great size of modern enterprises. He challenged the "curse of bigness" in the American economy. Brandeis attributed the economy's lack of equity and failure of performance to the domination of large-scale concentrated enterprises in U.S. business.

The challenge facing lawmakers in drafting the Securities Act was to devise a system for channeling capital into economic activity that was most likely to restore and sustain public confidence in itself, while preventing a recurrence of the crisis that had made regulation necessary. The combination of regulation by information (the Securities Act of 1933) and by prohibition (the Glass-Steagall Act), it was believed, would achieve a comprehensive overhaul of the procedures for the public issuance of securities and thus restore economic vitality and public support for the capital-raising mechanism.[10] Additionally, the Roosevelt administration saw a threat to the inviolability of private property in the degree to which a small group of powerful financial interests were dominating the nation's economy and manipulating the value of securities in the stock market. FDR promised to "counterbalance this power" and "protect private property from ruthless manipulation in the stock market and the corporate system. . . . Every effort [will] be made to prevent the issue of manufactured and unnecessary securities of all kinds which are brought out merely for the purpose of enriching those who handle their sale to the public."[11]

According to Paul Gourrich, an early director of the research division at the SEC and chief economist at Kuhn, Loeb, "the ease of selling poor quality and overpriced securities was enhanced by the frequent absence of adequate information for buyers of securities and for security analysts and experts, who might aid buyers in reaching considered judgments. Sometimes the information was not even available to the bankers. . . . In many cases, whether or not the information was available to the firm, it was not disclosed to the public . . . and [there were] the shocking examples of suppression of factual data."[12]

The 1933 Act had one basic objective: to set down the rules by which an issuer could sell new securities to the public. This led to the *registration statement, prospectus,* and *"due diligence" as a fiduciary concept.* (See later.)

Each new piece of regulation enacted by Congress was the product of intense political contention, lobbying, and maneuvering among diverse banking and securities interests, legislative coalitions, and bureaucracies. These new laws established stability through new operating standards, segmented asset and liability markets by type and territory, fixed prices, and introduced depository insurance. Government control and monopoly markets in a cartellike atmosphere resulted.[13]

It is interesting to note that most big banks were opposed to deposit insurance. The smaller banks were in favor of it, along with policies that restricted intercity branching. The smaller banks won the branching battle with arguments to the effect that huge money trusts would destroy competition and drain the countryside of its savings.[14] Senator Glass proposed a bill supporting statewide branching by national banks, but could not even get it out of committee. To get around these branching restrictions, chain and group banks and, later, bank holding companies were formed. Glass also proposed restricting interest rates on interbank demand deposits to prevent drainage of local deposits to money-center banks. This was considered by some bank historians to be the intellectual foundation of the regulation of interest rates on time deposits. The implementation of Regulation Q amounted to the imposition of price controls on the liability side of the balance sheet. Regulation Q created no controversy at the time. However, a few decades later, it combined with high market rates of interest to cause disintermediation at depository institutions. At times during the 1960s and 1970s, the loss of deposits by banks and thrifts lessened the availability of mortgage money. Prior hearings did not consider anything other than a liberal interest rate ceiling on interbank deposits. Senator Glass indicated that the act was intended "to put a stop to the competition between banks in payment of interest, which frequently induce[s] banks to pay excessive interest on time deposits and has many times over again brought banks into serious trouble."[15] An important linkage of all of the New Deal legislation was the disclosure of information for the purpose of "letting in the light" to reveal the facts of issuers' affairs and their overall business health.[16]

THE NEW DEAL LEGISLATION

Establishment of Federal Home Loan Bank System

In 1931, the United States Building and Loan League began intense lobbying of Congress to create the Federal Home Loan Bank Board (FHLBB), whose responsibilities would be similar to those of the Federal Reserve. The board would provide liquidity to thrifts through funds borrowed in the capital markets. In 1932, the

FHLBB was created to stabilize the housing industry through support and regulation of the nation's savings and loan associations, the primary providers of the nation's residential mortgages. The FHLB system included a central credit facility for the nation's savings and loans and served as a source of secondary liquidity to its members in meeting heavy or unusual withdrawal demands. The system linked mortgage-lending institutions to the capital markets by issuing consolidated obligations and discount notes in large denominations. Essentially, the FHLBB and its 12 regional banks provided liquidity for mortgage-lending thrift institutions by issuing debt that had a higher credit rating (because the 13 agencies were federally sponsored) and was more marketable than the secondary securities of the individual savings and loan associations. These funds, which were raised in the capital markets, were lent directly to the individual thrifts; that is, the FHLB system served as wholesale lenders to the thrift industry. The system was organized in a manner similar to the Federal Reserve system. It was composed of the FHLBB, the 12 regional Federal Home Loan Banks, and the member institutions. The FHLBB, located in Washington, DC, chartered and regulated federal savings and loans, while governing the Federal Savings and Loan Insurance Corporation (FSLIC) and the Federal Home Loan Mortgage Corporation (FHLMC). The board was an independent agency in the executive branch of the government and submitted an annual report to Congress. The whole system was governed by a three-person board, with one member selected as chairman. The president, with the consent of the Senate, appointed board members for four-year terms. Operating funds for the system were obtained from assessments on member thrifts. The 12 district banks carried out the functions of the system in dealings with member institutions. Each of the 12 was and continues to be "owned" by its thrift members, who were required to invest capital in their local FHLB. The S&Ls essentially owned the stock of the local FHLB in their district, elected directors, and received dividends. At the same time, the FHLBs were subject to regulation, oversight, and supervision by the Bank Board in Washington. In addition, the Bank Board appointed about one-third of the directors of each FHLB.[17]

Like commercial banks, savings institutions have a dual federal-state system of chartering and supervision. State institutions are chartered under state statutes and are supervised and examined by state authorities. On the other hand, federally chartered institutions are subject to the supervision, regulation, and examination of the FHLBB. The Home Loan Owners' Act of 1933 established the federal chartering of thrifts. While federally chartered S&Ls had to be members of the FHLB system, state-chartered S&Ls had the option of electing to join the system. This is similar to the option confronting state-chartered commercial banks, wherein they may decide whether to become members of the Federal Reserve System.

The FSLIC, an instrument of the FHLBB, was established in 1934 under the National Housing Act to insure deposits at S&Ls. The FSLIC insured all federally chartered savings associations and many of the state-chartered S&Ls, even though some states offered S&L insurance coverage. Federally chartered S&Ls were required by law to have FSLIC insurance, which was optional for state-chartered S&Ls. The maximum insured deposit in 1934 was $5,000. The FHLBB gained supervisory control over the state-chartered S&Ls and mutual savings banks that applied for federal deposit insurance. A parallel system for federal credit unions was created that same year.

The Banking Act of 1933 (Glass-Steagall Act)

The Banking Act of 1933, also called the Glass-Steagall Act (after its key sponsor, Senator Carter Glass, who was also a principal sponsor of the Federal Reserve Act of 1913), was enacted after the Great Depression, widespread bank failures, and a severe loss of public confidence in the economic, financial, and political system in the United States. Politicians were looking for a quick fix to restore confidence in the commercial banking system, to prevent a channeling of funds from "legitimate" commercial uses to "speculative" uses, and to eliminate the conflicts of interest and self-dealing that were perceived to exist in the marriage of investment and commercial banking. Essentially, the National Banking Act of 1933 divided one industry into two by separating the business of receiving deposits and making loans (commercial banking) from that of underwriting or acting as a dealer or market maker (investment banking). Commercial and investment banks were given a choice of being one or the other, but not both. For example, the powerful House of Morgan, one of the most profitable and prestigious financial houses on Wall Street, was split into two firms in order to separate its commercial banking from its investment banking activities. Today, Morgan Stanley is the investment banking outgrowth of the split, while J.P. Morgan is the commercial banking child. The First Boston Corporation was patched together out of the cast-off securities companies of a few commercial banks, one of which was an affiliate of the First National Bank of Boston. They were joined by some key corporate finance experts from the investment banking firm of Harris, Forbes. In addition, Mellon Securities was merged into First Boston in 1946, just about a decade after the original formulation of the corporation.[18] On the other hand, Harris Trust and what are now called Chase Manhattan Bank and Citicorp dissolved their securities affiliates and kept their commercial banking franchises. In the 1930s, it was politically popular to split up a financial powerhouse such as Morgan and to "pin the tail (blame) on the donkey" for the Great Depression and stock market crash on a handy scapegoat. The Glass-Steagall Act barred banks from paying interest on demand deposits. This was done to minimize the cost of funds so that banks would not take excessive lending risks in order to generate profits. Also, besides separating commercial banking from investment banking, the Act restricted the types of assets that banks could own and established the Federal Deposit Insurance Corporation (FDIC) to provide depository insurance. The Federal Reserve System was given the right to impose ceilings on the interest rates banks were permitted to pay on time deposits; this power was subsequently implemented through Federal Reserve Regulation Q. During the era of Regulation Q interest rate controls, thrifts were allowed to pay 1/4 percent more on deposits than commercial banks (a supposed spur to home mortgage lending).

The Glass-Steagall Act prohibited commercial banks from underwriting corporate securities. This portion of the Act was passed because of the fear that investment banking activities were too risky for commercial banks and that underwriting activity might lead to bank failures or bank control of nonfinancial corporations. Historically, the corporate underwriting ban placed upon commercial banks can be traced to congressional hearings held in 1932–1933, during which enough members of Congress were persuaded of the reality of various allegations, among which was the charge that capital losses on inventories of underwritten securities had gotten many banks into trouble. Banks were also accused of dumping securities from an unsuccessful underwriting into the trust accounts of some of their customers. However, abusing trust beneficiaries (a not insignificant indiscretion) does not make a bank more likely to fail.

Historically, Section 16 of the Glass-Steagall Act was interpreted as prohibiting a bank from underwriting (except for private placements, U.S. government bonds, foreign securities, and municipal general-obligation bonds). Prior to 1987, the Supreme Court ruled that the placement of commercial paper and the management of open-ended mutual funds were illegal under the Act.

Investment banks were also prohibited from accepting deposits. The Act called for a separation of banking and bank-related activities from other, so-called nonbanking activities. Commercial banks were prohibited from operating any nonbank-related subsidiaries. This led to the formation of a number of one-bank holding companies by large commercial banks. A holding company would allow the financial entity to engage in a wide variety of business activities that were not denied by the Glass-Steagall Act.

In addition, the Act prohibited banks from sponsoring or distributing mutual fund shares. Traditionally, banks, through their trust departments, have served as transfer agents and custodians for mutual funds, while also providing automatic purchase, dividend reinvestment, computer operations, safekeeping of mutual fund securities, collection of income on securities held for the fund, receipt of payment for shares and investment of payments according to the instruction of the fund, all record keeping related to custodial activities, redemption of shares and making payment to the transfer agent, and registration of shares held as custodian. In the past few years, banks have been providing mutual fund products to their customers or acting as advisers of mutual fund portfolios, while remaining within the spirit, if not the letter, of the Glass-Steagall Act.

The FDIC

President Roosevelt was not really in favor of government deposit insurance, because he felt that it would promote bad banking. However, he agreed to support it because Congressman Henry Steagall, then chairman of the House Banking Committee, told the president that if he wanted to pass the Banking Act of 1933, he had to agree to federal deposit insurance.

The creation of the FDIC was one of the most important acts in the history of banking in the United States, because it helped restore confidence to the banking system by eliminating periodic panics and bank runs. Bank failures and runs were a serious problem facing not only the banks, but the economy as well. With deposit insurance available from the FDIC, depositors no longer needed to fear that the failure of a bank would wipe out their life savings. Currently, about 99 percent of all U.S. banks are insured by the FDIC. When the FDIC was established, its primary goals were to provide deposit insurance to bank customers and to prevent individual bank failures from spreading to other banks. All nationally chartered banks and those state-chartered banks that are Federal Reserve members are required to have FDIC insurance.

The FDIC regulates state-chartered banks that are not members of the Federal Reserve System. In addition, it has the responsibility for liquidating insolvent banks. (See Chapter 7.) The FDIC is managed by a three-person board of directors appointed by the president and confirmed by the Senate. All three board members cannot be members of the same political party. The comptroller of the currency is always one of the three directors, while one of the other two members is appointed chairman. Operating and reserve funds were obtained from insurance premiums based on domestic deposits at insured banks. New tax laws passed in 1991 allowed the Bank Insurance Fund an additional $70 billion in borrowing authority and increased to $30 billion the amount the FDIC could borrow from the U.S. Treasury to cover the costs of depositor claims on the BIF.

While for the most part, government-mandated deposit insurance helped restore consumer confidence in the banking system, it also brought with it some problems. The other three major thrusts of the Glass-Steagall Act—the separation of commercial banking from investment banking, interest rate ceilings on deposit accounts, and not allowing banks to pay interest on demand deposits—are now widely viewed as being counterproductive to the economic development of the United States.

From the beginning, Congress ignored the possibility that insurance premium levels might vary for individual banks or thrifts, depending on the riskiness of their assets. This neglect was based on the belief that tighter federal regulatory procedures would lessen future losses and on the political unwillingness of banks and thrifts to pay what would essentially be higher premiums. "The unwillingness of Congress in the 1930s to treat deposit insurance as a phenomenon that required the application of *insurance principles* was an unfortunate precedent that would continue to be followed through the 1980s."[19] Risk-based deposit premiums were approved by Congress in legislation passed in late 1991 to be implemented prior to 1994.

Although the Glass-Steagall Act may have been necessary at the time it was enacted, money-center banks have been calling for its repeal or amendment since the late 1970s. The Act soothed the fears of the public about an unruly banking industry in the 1930s, but now, in the 1990s, the industry needs expanded powers to compete in worldwide financial markets. Most foreign banks are not tied down with as many legal restrictions as their U.S. banking counterparts. A strong argument for allowing commercial banks into the securities market is the success that overseas banks have had in underwriting securities. Big money-center banks are frustrated at losing business as another form of disintermediation invades the banking system—the replacement of traditional bank debt by securities. With U.S. banks barred from these underwriting activities, foreign banks have a potential profitability edge over their American banking counterparts. The Glass-Steagall Act is partially responsible for keeping U.S. banks from growing and competing in international finance. The Act's bifurcation of securities underwriting and lending powers has had a profound impact on the subsequent development of the public securities sector in the United States. By separating the two financial vendor groups so completely, Congress created a protected industry for the investment bankers—a cartellike public securities business. In addition, investment bankers emerged after World War II as the principal strategic counselors to the U.S. financial sector. In most other nations, the preeminent financial counseling role is held by the commercial bankers, often as part of what we call a universal bank.

During the 1980s, some money-center banks have threatened to forfeit their charters in order to engage more fully in profitable investment banking activities. As a response to the forfeiture suggestions and the need for additional sources of income to aid a faltering industry, in June 1989 the Federal Reserve gave commercial banks the power to underwrite corporate debt securities through their holding company subsidiaries. Having found a loophole in the Banking Act of 1933, the Federal Reserve extended to J.P. Morgan, a well-capitalized commercial bank holding company, the privilege of underwriting corporate equity issues in 1990. In January 1991, Bankers Trust Corporation and two Canadian bank holding companies were also given this corporate underwriting privilege.

Most countries allow their banks to pay interest on checking account deposits. This authority was denied U.S. banks in the Glass-Steagall Act and remained so until the Depository Institutions Deregulation and Monetary Control Act of 1980 (DIDMCA) was enacted to implement such interest payments. Also, money market mutual funds would never have come into existence if the commercial banks had always been allowed to pay competitive rates of interest on demand deposits.

The Securities Act of 1933

The other security laws passed in 1933 and 1934 were more logical and useful than the Glass-Steagall Act and have contributed to the economic power and stability of the U.S. economy. The Securities Act of 1933 (known as the "truth in securities law") guarantees the investor in primary issues with the right to full disclosure of all the relevant information needed to make a decision about new issues of corporate securities. It provides for the *registration* of new issues of securities sold to the public with the federal government, accomplished in the form of a *prospectus.*

The registration statement requires specific information (See Table 2.1) relating to all aspects of the issuer's business—the underwriting agreement and the terms, purposes, and intended use of the proposed financing. Also, the financial statements must be audited by an independent accountant. The issuer is always liable, uncondi-

Table 2.1   Information Required in an SEC Registration Statement

1. A copy of the issuer's articles of incorporation
2. Purpose for which the proceeds of the issue will be spent
3. Offering price to the public
4. Offering price for special groups, if any
5. Fees promised to developers and/or promoters
6. Underwriter's fees
7. Net proceeds to the issuer
8. Information on the issuer's products, history, and location
9. Copies of any indentures affecting the new issue
10. Names and remuneration of any officers receiving over $25,000 per year
11. Details about any unusual contracts, such as a managerial profit-sharing plan
12. A detailed statement of capitalization
13. Detailed balance sheet
14. Detailed income and expense statements for three preceding years
15. Names and addresses of the issuer's officers and directors and the underwriters
16. Names and addresses of any investors owning more than 10% of any class of stock
17. Details about any pending litigation
18. A copy of the underwriting agreement
19. Copies of legal opinions on matters related to the issue

Source: J. C. Francis, *Investments: Analysis and Management* (New York: McGraw-Hill, 1991), p. 71.
Reprinted by permission.

tionally, for a material misstatement or omission, while the underwriters are conditionally liable, unless they can show that they conducted a "reasonable investigation" (known as due diligence, an independent review of the sales material disclosures) of the data, which must appear in the registration statement. Under the due diligence doctrine, the investment banker is legally required to exercise the care "required of a prudent man in the management of his own property." Note that the federal government performs no test or assessment of the *quality* or *riskiness* of the investment. The Securities Act of 1933 does not apply to private placements of securities or to securities trading in the public secondary markets. In addition to the requirements for full disclosure of information, the Act forbids fraud and deception. It also provides remedies such as injunctions to stop fraudulent actions, reimbursement for damages, and eventual prosecution against securities salespersons who disseminate untrue or misleading information about securities.

The Act also contains antifraud and deception provisions. Issuers of securities are liable to both criminal and civil penalties. In addition, federal regulatory authorities received the subpoena power necessary to confirm the accuracy of registration information. Not only did most investment bankers resent the provisions for criminal liability, but they also objected to the 20-day "cooling-off" period designed to defuse the often speculative and feverish atmosphere surrounding new issues. Justice Douglas felt that the Act was inadequate and complained that "there is nothing in the act which would control the speculative way of the American public."[20]

The "sunshine" approach to the prevention of fraud and unethical financial practices—opening financial transactions to public scrutiny—was not new, and proposals for corporate disclosures have been around since the 1880s. Most states had already enacted "blue-sky" laws to register publicly issued securities and to license brokers in an attempt to protect investors from unwittingly being sold fraudulent securities (or pieces of "blue sky"). However, these measures were for the most part ineffective. There was an odd quilt of blue-sky legislation at the state level that had emerged from a morass of legal theory, parochial interest, and administrative practice. Previous efforts at regulation and coordination at the national level had been unsuccessful. The Investment Bankers Association backed off from its initial efforts, while the New York Stock Exchange (dominated by members who were dealers in securities) consistently dragged its feet on reform.[21]

The 1933 Securities Act rejected the concept that required a public agency to pass on the *quality* of the security or its issuer. Rather, the Act's requirements were limited to ensuring a thorough exposure of all facts germane to an investment decision. President Roosevelt did not want overregulation. The investor was left to draw appropriate conclusions. However, when President Roosevelt sent the Act to Congress, he said, "This proposal adds to the ancient rule of caveat emptor, the further doctrine 'let the seller beware.' It puts the burden of telling the whole truth on the seller."[22] The approach of the 1933 Act to *stock watering* (the practice of exaggerating a stock's assets to give it an unrealistic book value) was not to forbid it or to attach criminal penalties for having done it, but to require disclosing it. The failure to disclose watering is unlawful and carries potential criminal consequences. As Roosevelt said, the disclosure requirements shift the common-law burden of "buyer beware" from the purchaser to the vendor. It is also interesting to note that the due diligence requirements gave a big boost to the accounting profession in the United States.

The political motive behind the reform legislation sought to maintain and increase the traditional fragmentation and geographical decentralization of U.S. financial services. However, because of the physical concentration of the securities markets in New York, decentralization was the exception in the securities issuance sector. The combination of the reality of the geographic concentration of the securities industry and the thrust of the Glass-Steagall Act, which separated securities-related activities from lending and deposit-taking activities, had the practical effect of creating a distinct new genre of financial market participant: the nationwide investment bank. There was no historical precedence for the creation of such an institution, because there had been no perceived need to separate a bank's securities activities from its deposit and loan activities. There is some evidence that the framers of the Glass-Steagall Act never intended such a complete separation of investment from commercial banking. As a matter of fact, Senator Glass attempted to introduce legislation that would have allowed commercial banks to reenter the corporate securities industry business. However, the mood of Congress was opposed to any modifications of the 1937 reform legislation, and the senator's effort failed.[23]

The Securities Exchange Act of 1934

After the Securities Act of 1933 was passed, its limitations were recognized, so the Congress passed the Securities Exchange Act of 1934 to extend the provisions of the 1933 Act. The full disclosure of information required by that Act was extremely important, but insufficient; *conduct* also had to be regulated. The objectives of the 1934 Act were to require the provision of adequate information about securities being traded in secondary markets and to establish the Securities and Exchange Commission (SEC), a federal agency that would not only oversee disclosure requirements, but also establish rules of conduct and act as a quasi-judicial administrator of compliance. The Act discourages price discrimination and facilitates the evaluation of securities traded in the secondary market. Trading in securities is actively regulated to prevent "manipulation and control." In addition, the SEC regulates all national securities exchanges. Companies whose securities are listed on an exchange must file reports similar to registration statements and must provide periodic financial reports with both the SEC and the stock exchange. The SEC, in turn, encourages exchanges to "self-regulate" their activities, including the setting of minimum commissions by fixing prices. It is interesting to note that while most cartels designed to limit competition by fixing prices were illegal in the United States, the New York Stock Exchange requirement that member brokers charge fixed minimum commissions for stocks was exempted from prosecution under the antitrust laws. The Securities Exchange Act required the SEC to approve all commission rate changes proposed by the securities exchanges. Also, the SEC has control over the proxy machinery and practice and the regulation of business conduct of broker-dealer members of an exchange.

The Securities Exchange Act empowered the board of governors of the Federal Reserve to control the minimum down payment that buyers make in purchasing stocks and convertible bonds on credit (initial margin requirements) and to set the discount rate for such items. In 1985, the U.S. Treasury Department and the Federal Reserve Board both recommended that the federal law be changed so that control over margin requirements be taken away from the Federal Reserve and turned over to the exchanges. No action has yet been taken on this recommendation. The Securities Exchange Act also forbids price manipulation schemes such as pools, wash sales (prearranged fictitious sales of securities with no real change of ownership), circulation of manipulative information, and false and misleading statements about securities. Some financial economists believe that commercial banks granted too much credit to purchases of stock in the 1920s, fueling the speculative excesses of the period. Many also believed that this extension of credit came at the expense of lending to more productive sectors of the economy. Accordingly, the Securities Exchange Act also limited securities dealers' total indebtedness to 20 times their owners' equity capital. Further, the Act imposed a set of rules aimed at preventing the manipulation of stock prices and fraudulent trading practices. With Judge Landis as a commissioner and Joseph Kennedy as chairman, the SEC enlisted accounting professionals to create standards for financial reporting, while the exchange itself began to implement rules for membership, trading, and brokerage fees.[24] The Act also regulated and controlled trading practices, including transactions by insiders, and attempted to ensure "fair and honest markets." Insiders are forbidden from earning speculative gains by trading in their firm's securities.

Recent common-law cases have established policies that extend the prohibitions against trading beyond those established in the 1934 Act. The latest view is that anyone who has access to special knowledge or material nonpublic information about a company can be considered an *insider,* along with all employees and directors of a company. Insiders are forbidden from earning speculative profits by trading in the company's securities or in engaging in short sales of their company's stock. Every officer, director, and owner of more than 10 percent of a listed corporation's shares must file a statement (an insider's report) of their holdings of that company's securities in every month in which a change in those holdings occurs. This report is public information. A 1975 amendment provides for penalties in the form of substantial fines and/or up to 10 years' imprisonment for earning speculative profits through inside knowledge. Nonetheless, violations of these rules continue to be a major problem. During the late 1980s and early 1990s, Ivan Boesky and Michael Milken received much publicity for their role in securities fraud. Both men were convicted of numerous securities' violations, including filing false documents with the SEC and manipulating markets. Milken received a huge fine and a 10-year initial sentence, while Boesky received a substantial, but more modest, fine and a shorter jail sentence.

Another well-publicized insider trading case occurred in the daily finance gossip column, "Heard on the Street," in *The Wall Street Journal.* R. Foster Winans, a columnist, was fired by the newspaper for conspiring with a group of traders to use the advance knowledge of what was going to appear in the column to take a position in the stocks that were to be featured in the column. If a company received favorable comments in that column, its stock usually rose in price, while a company that received a negative report in the column would usually see a decline in the price of its stock. Winans first admitted his insider trading activities, but later denied them. He was eventually convicted. SEC enforcement actions have escalated in recent years in response to alleged insider activity. However, the SEC has a relatively small investigative and enforcement staff. Also, there is a great deal of difficulty involved in tracking down and proving insider trading violations. Violations of insider trading laws and market manipulation led to the downfall of "junk bond" king, Michael Milken, and of Drexel Burnham Lambert. Martin A. Siegel and Dennis B. Levine, former investment bankers at Kidder Peabody and Drexel Burnham Lambert, respectively, were found guilty of insider trading and sentenced to jail terms of two months and two years, respectively. Both men were part of a secret network of powerful financiers who illegally manipulated the market for their own advantage. The federal government investigation broke up the cozy relationship between takeover specialists, the investment bankers, and speculators who purchased the stocks of companies in play. The investigation of that network has led to fundamental changes on Wall Street, including the adoption of stricter ethical standards, more training for new employees, and tougher government and internal oversight of potentially illegal activities.[25]

Because of the decline in ethical standards within the securities industry, Congress passed and the president signed the Insider Trading and Securities Fraud Enforcement Act of 1988. This Act mandates that every broker-dealer and investment adviser establish, maintain, and enforce written policies and procedures to prevent the misuse of material, nonpublic information. The new statutory requirements for such policies and procedures and the increased civil and criminal penalties set forth have raised concerns about what policies and procedures are adequate to meet the statutory requirements.

Securities and Exchange Commission

There is a popular misconception that regulation of securities resulted from the stock market crash of 1929 and the ensuing years of financial stagnation. While it is true that the final impetus was given to federal laws by these events, attempts at federal control and supervision of securities markets extend to the last two decades of the 19th century. While the federal government was still searching for its role in securities legislation, state governments were making some attempt to bring order to chaotic securities markets. By 1913, almost half of the states had passed laws aimed at regulating the sale of securities. This legislation could be classified into two categories: fraud laws, which imposed penalties if evidence indicated that fraud had been committed in the sale of securities, and regulatory laws, which tried to prohibit securities sales until an application was filed and state permission was granted. These laws were known as blue-sky laws after a judicial decision characterized some transactions as "speculative schemes which have no more basis than so many feet of 'blue sky.' " State laws have rarely proved totally effective in regulatory securities markets, primarily because of the interstate nature of the U.S. economic and financial system and the absence of legislation or the inadequacy of laws in some states.

The securities markets suffered from instability and abuse in the 1920s. Price manipulation was not uncommon. Brokers and dealers were involved regularly in wash sales or in matched orders, in which successive buy and sell orders created a false impression of activity and forced stock prices to increase. This practice permitted those involved to make large profits before the price fell back to its true market value. The issuance of false and misleading statements was another improper practice that was used to make profits at the expense of unwary investors, as was the excessive use of credit to finance speculative activities (buying stocks on margin), which undermined securities markets because there was no limit to the amount of credit that a broker could extend to a customer. A decline in stock market prices could start a chain reaction that would gain momentum when an overextended customer sold out because of the failure to cover a margin call. The situation became critical when the market began to decline dramatically during the Great Depression. The misuse of corporate information by corporate officials and other insiders was yet another practice that led to instability in the securities markets. Insiders would position themselves in stocks before news became public. Executive officers, board members, and other insiders withheld or released information about company activities that caused large changes in stock market prices.

When confidence in the securities market was shaken by the Depression, the restoration of public confidence was viewed as holding the key to economic recovery. The Securities Acts of 1933 and 1934, along with other statutes, were attempts to infuse a new spirit of trust in securities markets, while protecting the public from fraudulent losses. The 1934 Act required a highly specialized body of experts in the securities industry whose sophistication would regulate, but not frustrate, the efficiency of securities trading. The Securities and Exchange Commission (SEC) was created by the Act to fill this role. Disclosures of pertinent information, combined with law enforcement power against fraudulent acts, became the primary objective of the SEC. Even when SEC approval is granted, it does not imply that the securities that are approved are a good investment; it just indicates that the legally required information has been properly disclosed for investors to analyze if they wish.

The SEC was given the duty to ensure "full and fair" disclosure of all material facts concerning securities offered for public investment. The SEC's intent was not necessarily to prevent speculative securities from entering the market, but to insist that investors be provided with the best data and information possible for making sound investment decisions. This, in turn, would lead to more efficient capital markets. The initiation of litigation in cases of fraud and the provision for proper registration of securities are additional objectives of the SEC. It is important to mention that the typical prospectus provides little help to the individual investor. A really "full" disclosure might overwhelm a reader and submerge the truly important facts in minutiae. All of us have seen prospectuses that fit Judge Weinstein's description: "a literary art form calculated to communicate as little of the essential information as possible while exuding an air of total candor."[26]

In general, government regulation of securities trading is designed to ensure that investors receive information that is as accurate as possible, that no one manipulates the market price of securities, and that corporate insiders do not take advantage of their position as officers, directors, or employees to profit in their company's stock at the expense of other shareholders.

The SEC is an independent, bipartisan, quasi-judicial agency of the U.S. government that was established in 1934, in conjunction with the passage of the 1933 and 1934 Securities Acts. The SEC is located in Washington, DC, and has a staff of about 2,000. It also has offices throughout the United States, where interested persons can file complaints about securities law violations or obtain investment information. The organization is directed by five commissioners, not more than three of whom may come from the same political party. The president of the United States appoints members of the commission for five-year terms with the advice and consent of the U.S. Senate. In addition, the president designates one member to chair the commission. The commissioners are assisted by a staff of professionals, including lawyers, examiners, accountants, financial and securities analysts, and engineers. These professionals are assigned to the various offices and divisions shown in the organizational chart of Figure 2.1. The SEC is organized in a manner conducive to authoritative supervision, allowing honest trading in securities while prohibiting deceit, fraud, and manipulation.

The SEC's powers were increased in 1990, when Congress passed the Securities Enforcement Remedies Act, which the granted the commission the authority to impose monetary sanctions and to handle many cases before an administrative judge, rather than to try the cases in the federal courts. In mid-1991, the SEC approved limited after-hours trading for the New York Stock Exchange. There will be an extra hour of trading for individuals from 4:00 P.M. to 5:00 P.M. and an extra 75 minutes of trading for institutional investors. However, the auction market, a salient characteristic of New York Stock Exchange trading during normal nine to four o'clock operations, will not be present in the extra after-hours trading session. All purchases and sales will be at the closing price as of 4:00 P.M. Every individual buy order in this session must be matched with an opposing sell order. The stock exchange will match up trades and execute them at 5:00 P.M. Any unmatched trades would be held for the next morning's session. By the year 2000, it is likely that the New York Stock Exchange and other regional exchanges, such as the Philadelphia Stock Exchange, will oversee trades 24 hours a day. This movement toward expanded trading hours came about, in part, because of (1) a loss of business by the New York Stock Exchange to foreign markets in Tokyo and London that trade U.S.

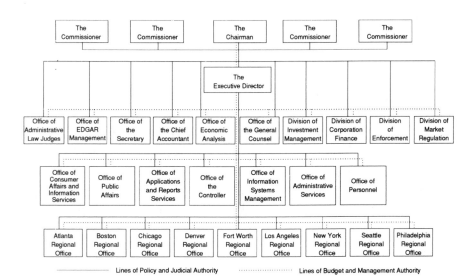

Figure 2.1 Securities and Exchange Commission. (*Sources*: U.S. Securities and Exchange Commission, *The Work of the SEC* [Washington, DC: U.S. Government Printing Office, 1988]; *Federal Securities Law Reports* [Chicago: Commerce Clearing House, Inc., October 1988], § 301)

stocks, (2) money managers who trade on private electronic international trading systems, and (3) third-market trading of stocks.

In sum, the SEC regulates the sale of new and existing securities on the organized exchanges, as well as through the over-the-counter (OTC) markets in amounts exceeding $1.5 million. All publicly offered securities must be registered with the SEC at least 20 days before they are offered. SEC lawyers, accountants, and financial analysts peruse both the registration statement (which provides financial, legal, and technical information about the firm) and the prospectus (which contains a summary of this information for use in selling the securities). If the SEC finds the information inadequate or misleading, the public offering can be delayed or stopped. The securities may be offered once the registration has become effective. However, any sales solicitation must be accompanied by the prospectus. If the prospectus is distributed before the end of the waiting period, it must have a note in red ink on its cover stating that the issue has not yet received SEC approval for issuance as a final prospectus. Such a preliminary document is called a *red herring*. It contains all the salient information that will appear in the final prospectus, with the exception of the selling price. Misrepresentations or omissions of material facts from the prospectus can lead to a lawsuit if an investor suffers a loss. Severe penalties may be imposed on the issuing company's directors, officers, underwriters, appraisers, and other paper entrepreneurs who participated in the preparation of the registration statement.

The Securities Exchange Act requires that annual reports and other periodic reports be filed for public inspection at the SEC offices before the listing of securities for trading in organized exchanges is posted. The Securities Act Amendment of 1964 extended these registration requirements to securities traded over the counter. It also established that companies must provide the SEC with (1) the audited annual 10K report; (2) three quarterly 10Q reports; and (3) the event-oriented 8K report, required within 15 days after a merger, acquisition, resignation of a director, or change in certifying accountants. This report is submitted following the first three quarters of a company's reporting year. Form 10K is an annual report filed with the SEC that contains disclosures relating to a company's business, properties, legal proceedings, matters requiring submission for a vote of security holders, information required by proxy rules to be included in the annual report to shareholders, traditional proxy disclosure relating to directors and executive officers, and management's remuneration, as well as financial statements, schedules, and exhibits not required in the annual reports to shareholders. Form 10Q must be filed within 45 days after the end of each of the registrant's first three quarters. Financial statements, management's discussion and analysis of financial condition and results of operations, legal proceedings, changes in securities, and submission of matters to a vote of security holders are required to be included. Form 8K is submitted to the SEC following the first three quarters of a company's reporting year. The information provided is mostly narrative and is intended to keep prospective shareholders (and the SEC) informed on current developments that have a major effect on the company.

Encouraging Home Ownership

The Federal Housing Administration (FHA) was created in 1934 by the Home Loan Owners' Act of 1933. The FHA provided mortgage insurance for home buyers who did not have a sufficiently large down payment to meet the lending institution's standards. The FHA guaranteed mortgage payments to the lender. This was the first of many federal acts to be passed over the next few decades to encourage home ownership. The "GI Bill of Rights," formally called the Servicemen's Readjustment Act of 1944, authorized the Veterans Administration to offer a similar program for veterans.

Additional government agencies were established to borrow funds and use them to buy mortgages from lenders and originators, thereby increasing the availability or supply of funds for housing and essentially establishing a secondary market for mortgages. The Federal National Mortgage Association (Fannie Mae) was established in 1938, the Government National Mortgage Association (Ginnie Mae) in 1968, and the Federal Home Loan Mortgage Corporation (Freddie Mac) in 1970.

The federal income tax code also allowed home owners to deduct mortgage interest payments and local property taxes when computing their federal income taxes. This provided a substantial subsidy for the ownership of a home. With the passage of the Tax Reform Act of 1986, second mortgages on residential homes became more popular, as the interest deductibility of home equity loans was maintained under the new law, while other interest payments gradually lost their deductibility. Sections of the 1986 Tax Act involving losses from passive activities such as trading in real estate are indirectly responsible for the real estate problems of the 1989–1991 period. The Act ruled that passive losses can be used only to offset passive income.

The Banking Act of 1935

The Banking Act of 1935 increased the influence of the committee coordinating open market operations by moving it to Washington, DC, and renaming it the Federal Open Market Committee. This Act also extended the powers of the Federal Reserve Board, renaming it the Board of Governors of the Federal Reserve System. It gave the board the authority to regulate the discount rates of the District banks and to vary required reserve ratios within prescribed limits. (See Tables 2.2 and 2.3.) In addition, the Board of Governors was given the authority to impose credit controls and to set margin requirements on the purchase of stocks and bonds. The Banking Act of 1935 also extended Regulation Q ceilings to nonmember banks and prohibited nonmember banks from paying interest on demand deposits.

If Congress had scrutinized the operations of the Federal Reserve a little more carefully, it would probably not have received any additional powers. After all, it was the Federal Reserve that tightened credit during the Depression, exacerbating the economic decline. Also, the board made another policy error by doubling reserve

Table 2.2   Reserve Requirements of Depository Institutions[a]

Type of Deposit[b]	Requirements	
	Percent of Deposits	Effective Date
Net transaction accounts [c]		
1 $0 million–$42.2 million..........	3	12/17/91
2 More than $42.2 million[d]..........	10	4/2/91
3 Nonpersonal time deposits[e]..........	0	12/27/90
4 Eurocurrency liabilities[f]..........	0	12/27/90

[a] Required reserves must be held in the form of deposits with Federal Reserve Banks or vault cash. Nonmember institutions may maintain reserve balances with a Federal Reserve Bank indirectly on a pass-through basis with certain approved institutions. For previous reserve requirements, see earlier editions of the *Annual Report* or the *Federal Reserve Bulletin*. Under provisions of the Monetary Control Act, depository institutions include commercial banks, mutual savings banks, savings and loan associations, credit unions, agencies and branches of foreign banks, and Edge corporations.

[b] The Garn–St. Germain Depository Institutions Act of 1982 (Public Law 97–320) requires that $2 million of reservable liabilities of each depository institution be subject to a zero-percent reserve requirement. The board is to adjust the amount of reservable liabilities subject to this zero-percent reserve requirement each year for the succeeding calendar year by 80 percent of the percentage increase in the total reservable liabilities of all depository institutions, measured on an annual basis as of June 30. No corresponding adjustment is to be made in the event of a decrease. On Dec. 17, 1991, the exemption was raised from $3.4 million to $3.6 million. The exemption applies in the following order: (1) net negotiable order of withdrawal (NOW) accounts (NOW accounts less allowable deductions); and (2) net other transaction accounts. The exemption applies only to accounts that would be subject to a 3-percent reserve requirement.

[c] Transaction accounts include all deposits against which the account holder is permitted to make withdrawals by negotiable or transferable instruments, payment orders of withdrawal, and telephone and preauthorized transfers in excess of three per month for the purpose of making payments to third persons or others. However, money market deposit accounts (MMDAs) and similar accounts subject to the rules that permit no more than six preauthorized, automatic, or other transfers per month, of which no more than three may be checks, are not transaction accounts (such accounts are savings deposits).

The Monetary Control Act of 1980 requires that the amount of transaction accounts against which the 3-percent reserve requirement applies be modified annually by 80 percent of the percentage change in transaction accounts held by all depository institutions, determined as of June 30 each year. Effective Dec. 17, 1991, for institutions reporting quarterly, and Dec. 24, 1991, for institutions reporting weekly, the amount was increased from $41.1 million to $42.2 million.

[d] The reserve requirement was reduced from 12 percent to 10 percent on Apr. 2, 1992, for institutions that report weekly, and on Apr. 16, 1992, for institutions that report quarterly.

[e] For institutions that report weekly, the reserve requirements on nonpersonal time deposits with an original maturity of less than 1 1/2 years was reduced from 3 percent to 1 1/2 percent for the maintenance period that began Dec. 13, 1990, and to zero for the maintenance period that began Dec. 27, 1990. The reserve requirement on nonpersonal time deposits with an original maturity of 1 1/2 years or more has been zero since Oct. 6, 1983.

For institutions that report quarterly, the reserve requirement on nonpersonal time deposits with an original maturity of less than 1 1/2 years was reduced from 3 percent to zero on Jan. 17, 1991.

[f] The reserve requirement on Eurocurrency liabilities was reduced from 3 percent to zero in the same manner and on the same dates as was the reserve requirement on nonpersonal time deposits with an original maturity of less than 1 1/2 years (see note 4).

Source: Federal Reserve Board of Governors.

Table 2.3   Federal Reserve Bank Interest Rates, Percent Per Year

Effective Date			Range (or Level)— All F.R. Banks	F.R. Bank of N.Y.
In effect Dec. 31,1977			6	6
1978—	Jan.	9............	6–6.5	6.5
		20............	6.5	6.5
	May	11............	6.5–7	7
		12............	7	7
	July	3............	7–7.25	7.25
		10............	7.25	7.25
	Aug.	21............	7.75	7.75
	Sept.	22............	8	8
	Oct.	16............	8–8.5	8.5
		20............	8.5	8.5
	Nov.	1............	8.5–9.5	9.5
		3............	9.5	9.5
1979—	July	20............	10	10
	Aug.	17............	10–10.5	10.5
		20............	10.5	10.5
	Sept.	19............	10.5–11	11
		21............	11	11
	Oct.	8............	11–12	12
		10............	12	12
1980—	Feb.	15............	12–13	13
		19............	13	13
	May	29............	12–13	13
		30............	12	12
	June	13............	11–12	11
		16............	11	11
		29............	10	10
	July	28............	10–11	10
	Sept.	26............	11	11
	Nov.	17............	12	12
	Dec.	5............	12–13	13
1981—	May	5............	13–14	14
		8............	14	14
	Nov.	2............	13–14	13
		6............	13	13
	Dec.	4............	12	12
1982—	July	20............	11.5–12	11.5
		23............	11.5	11.5
	Aug.	2............	11–11.5	11
		3............	11	11
		16............	10.5	10.5
		27............	10–10.5	10
		30............	10	10
	Oct.	12............	9.5–10	9.5
		13............	9.5	9.5

(Continued)

Table 2.3 Continued

Effective Date			Range (or Level)—All F.R. Banks	F.R. Bank of N.Y.
	Nov.	22............	9–9.5	9
		26............	9	9
	Dec.	14............	8.5–9	9
		15............	8.5–9	8.5
		17............	8.5	8.5
1984—	Apr.	9............	8.5–9	9
		13............	9	9
	Nov.	21............	8.5–9	8.5
		26............	8.5	8.5
	Dec.	24............	8	8
1985—	May	20............	7.5–8	7.5
		24............	7.5	7.5
1986—	Mar.	7............	7–7.5	7
		10............	7	7
	Apr.	21............	6.5–7	6.5
	July	11............	6	6
	Aug.	21............	5.5–6	5.5
		22............	5.5	5.5
1987—	Sept.	4............	5.5–6	6
		11............	6	6
1988—	Aug.	9............	6–6.5	6.5
		11............	6.5	6.5
1989—	Feb.	24............	6.5–7	7
		27............	7	7
1990—	Dec.	19............	6.5	6.5
1991—	Feb.	1............	6–6.5	6
		4............	6	6
	Apr.	30............	5.5–6	5.5
	May	2............	5.5	5.5
	Sept.	13............	5–5.5	5
		17............	5	5
	Nov.	6............	4.5–5	4.5
		7............	4.5	4.5
	Dec.	20............	3.5–4.5	3.5
		24............	3.5	3.5
1992—	July	2............	3–3.5	3
		7............	3	3
In effect April 2,1993			3	3

Source: Federal Reserve Bulletin, May 1993.

requirements in 1936–1937. The consequence of this tightening of monetary policy was to kill the economic recovery before it got a chance to begin. The purpose of mentioning these errors in the actions of the Federal Reserve during and following the Great Depression is to show that most of the economic and financial difficulties were related to policy errors, rather than risk taking on the part of commercial banks.

The Act increased the FDIC's maximum liability per depositor from $2,500 to $5,000. It also authorized the FDIC to assist in merging failing banks into ongoing banks or to engage in purchase and assumption transactions. Thereafter, the FDIC would in effect be able to pay an ongoing bank to take over the assets and to assume the liabilities of a failing bank. (See Chapter 7.)

MISCELLANEOUS COMMENTARY

The high correlation of banking crises with severe depressions in U.S. history demonstrates why banking reform was imperative to the pre-World War I financial and business community and to the post-Depression economic environment. The absence of old-fashioned banking panics in the post-World War II period was a great achievement; it has probably contributed more to the general welfare than most of the widely touted "welfare programs."[27]

Most of the bank runs prior to 1934 were geographically contained, often in rural or agrarian areas, and were usually limited to a small number of banks. These runs involved disruptions to local economies and losses by some depositors. A study by Benston, Eisenbeis, et al. (1986) shows that in the dozen years between 1865 and 1933 identified as crisis years for bank failures, depositor losses averaged only 0.78 percent of total deposits in all commercial banks.[28] One reason for these limited losses is that banks maintained high capital levels, which acted as a cushion or buffer against relatively high loan and security losses. Therefore, fewer banks became insolvent. Benston suggests that most bank runs reflected effective exercises in market discipline that promptly shut down poorly managed, undercapitalized, insolvent banks. During 1988 and 1989, the two worst years for bank failure since deposit insurance was enacted, FDIC losses were about 0.25 percent of total bank deposits, in percentage terms approximately one-third of the depositor losses experienced in the crisis years prior to the Great Depression. It is interesting to note that losses by depositors of the percent of deposits of failed banks from 1930 to 1933 were about 20 percent.[29]

Even if they occur infrequently, the negative effects of bank runs could be considerable and devastating to sectors of the economy or to geographic areas. According to Friedman and Schwartz (1963), during the banking panics of the Depression, frightened depositors lost confidence in the safety of U.S. banks and converted bank accounts into currency.[30] Banks met these withdrawals by liquidating assets, including their reserves. The ensuing decline in reserves led to a multiple decline in deposits because of fractional reserve requirements, followed by a huge decline in the money supply. The Federal Reserve failed to inject reserves into the banking system, which would have offset the panic-induced decline in the money supply. The large number of bank runs in the early 1930s produced a widespread credit crunch that only worsened the momentous decline in aggregate demand. Essentially, Depression-era banking panics imposed large costs on the U.S. economy.[31]

Prior to 1865, Indiana, Ohio, and Iowa required some state-chartered banks to guarantee one another's liabilities. The impact of this mutual system was to coerce the banks in those three states to monitor and control the risks assumed by other banks. The mutual systems that were adopted prevented any losses to depositors and noteholders because individual bankers had an incentive to ensure that other banks were managed prudently. There were only a few bank failures and no losses of deposits when this system was in operation, while in other states such failures and losses were quite common. Eleven states required participating banks to pay into a depositor-protection fund maintained by the state. However, the record of bank failures in these states was poor, and the commingled insurance funds were grossly inadequate. Other state insurance fund failures occurred in 1985 in Ohio and Maryland and again in 1991 in Rhode Island. In addition, the FSLIC fund could not meet its obligations in 1989; however, the federal government was willing to cover the huge obligation that resulted in that instance. The history of clearinghouses in the United States shows that mutual guarantee arrangements among banks are feasible, that they create and sustain essential public confidence, and that they are effective over the long term because they create incentives for supervising banking practices.[32]

The Maloney Act

The Maloney Act, an extension of the Securities Exchange Act of 1934, was adopted in 1938 at the request of OTC securities dealers to provide for their self-regulation. The Act brought the OTC market under the supervision of the SEC. However, it encouraged the OTC market to establish private trade associations for self-regulation, but the SEC was given the authority to oversee and to change the rules of these private associations. The National Association of Securities Dealers (NASD) is the only association of OTC dealers that has registered with the SEC; it has antitrust immunity. The NASD has about 8,000 member securities firms with about 500,000 registered representatives who sell securities in the OTC market. It has established (1) a test that must be passed by any individual wishing to join; (2) a set of rules forbidding fraud, manipulation, and excess profit taking; (3) a uniform practices code standardizing and expediting routine transactions, such as deliveries and payments; and (4) a procedure for disciplining members who engage in illegal or unethical conduct. This procedure is subject to SEC review. The NASD can censure, fine, suspend, or expel its members for unethical behavior. Although the Maloney Act provided for the establishment of other voluntary trade associations to compete with the NASD, none have been formed.

ENDNOTES

1. L. J. White, *The S&L Debacle* (New York: Oxford Press, 1991), pp. 32–33.

2. S. Hayes, *Wall Street and Regulation* (Boston: Harvard Business School Press, 1987), pp. 67–68.

3. Ibid., p. 2.

4. Ibid., p. 16.

5. Ibid., pp. 158–160.

6. V. P. Carosso, *Investment Banking in America* (Cambridge, MA: Harvard University Press, 1970), p. 285.

7. J. K. Galbraith, *The Great Crash* (Boston: Houghton-Mifflin, 1961), p. 59.

8. A. M. Schlesinger, *The Crisis of the Old Order, 1919–1933,* Vol. 1 (Boston: Houghton-Mifflin, 1957).

9. Hayes, p. 5.

10. J. Auerbach and S. L. Hayes, *Investment Banking and Diligence: What Price Deregulation?* (Boston: Harvard Business School Press, 1986), p. 34.

11. F. D. Roosevelt, *Public Papers,* Vol. 1 (New York: Random House, 1938), p. 653.

12. P. B. Gourrich, "Investment Banking Methods Prior to and Since the Securities Act of 1933," *Law and Contemporary Problems* 4 (1937), pp. 44, 52.

13. Hayes, p. 16.

14. Ibid., p. 19.

15. Ibid., p. 20.

16. Roosevelt, p. 653.

17. White, p. 54.

18. D. S. Kidwell and R. L. Peterson, *Financial Institutions, Markets, and Money,* 4th ed. (Hinsdale, IL: Dryden Press, 1990), p. 345.

19. White, p. 55.

20. Hayes, p. 21.

21. Ibid. pp. 21, 132–133.

22. Quoted in T. K. McCraw, *Prophets of Regulation* (Cambridge, MA: Harvard University Press, 1984), p. 172.

23. Ibid., p. 187.

24. Ibid., p. 22.

25. K. Eichenwald, "Why the Wall Street Court Reversal?" *New York Times,* July 12, 1991, pp. D1–6.

26. Hayes, p. 164.

27. Cagan, "Financial Regulation: Comments on Kareken," *Journal of Business* 59, no. 1 (1986), p. 50.

28. G. J. Benston, R. A. Eisenbeis, P. M. Horvitz, E. J. Kane, and G. G. Kaufman, *Perspectives on Safe and Sound Banking: Past, Present, and Future* (Cambridge, MA: MIT Press, 1986).

29. J. A. Neuberger, *How to Close Troubled Banks* (San Francisco: Federal Reserve Bank, December 17, 1990), p. 2.

30. M. Friedman and A. Schwartz, *A Monetary History of the United States, 1867–1960* (Princeton, NJ: Princeton University Press, 1963).

31. Neuberger, p. 3.

32. P. J. Wallison, *Back from the Brink* (Washington, DC: American Enterprise Institute Press, 1990), pp. 6–8.

3 Securities and Investment Regulation, 1940–1979

Today, Wall Street is a magnificent machine; it mobilizes and transfers huge sums around the world at astonishing speed. In many ways it serves society very well indeed. That it does not do a better job is not the fault of the machine, but of individuals—both those who run it and those for whose benefit it is run.

William A. Law, "Wall Street and Public Interest"

INVESTMENT COMPANY ACT OF 1940

The mutual fund industry sustained huge losses in the period 1929–1934. Following these losses, in 1939 the SEC completed a four-year study of investment funds; its recommendations formed the basis of the Investment Company Act (ICA) of 1940. The ICA required registration and detailed financial disclosure of investment companies; SEC regulation of selling practices, capital structure, and accounting practices; and further separation of fund management from other financial entities.[1] The ICA of 1940 and its 1970 amendment

1. Require all closed-ended and open-ended investment companies (commonly called mutual funds) to register with the SEC.
2. Require the investment companies to make prospectuses available to potential investors before securities can be sold.
3. Require that outsiders (nonemployees or owners) be on every board of directors.
4. Require shareholder approval of changes in any management agreements.
5. Require that uniform accounting policies be used.
6. Require that investment companies limit the issuance of debt.
7. Require that investment companies not employ persons convicted of fraud as officers.
8. Forbid fraud.

9. Mandate publicly available statements of every mutual fund's investment goals and expense ratios.

10. Operate the fund for the benefit of shareholders, rather than for the benefit of management.

INVESTMENT ADVISERS ACT OF 1940

The Investment Advisers Act (IAA) of 1940 prohibits fraud and deception by investment advisors receiving pay. The IAA requires that any investment advisors who sell investment advice to 15 or more interstate clients register with the SEC and file information germane to their background and education. However, the law does not require any proof of competence on the part of the advisor as a condition for registering with the SEC. Accordingly, the claim that someone is a registered investment advisor is only a claim of compliance with the law, not a claim of knowledge or ability as an investment advisor. In addition, the IAA forbids investment advisors from entering into profit-sharing agreements with their clients and from assigning investment advisory contracts without the clients' consent. The act also prohibits investment advisers from using selected testimonials in their advertising.

THE BANK HOLDING COMPANY ACT (1956) AND THE DOUGLAS AMENDMENT

The McFadden Act of 1927 and later amendments allow national banks to establish branches only to the degree that states permit state banks to branch. Historically, the McFadden Act and the Banking Act of 1933 prohibited interstate branching by making all branching subject to state authority. However, the McFadden Act left open the possibility of crossing state lines by using bank holding companies. At that time, holding companies were unregulated and could operate in more than one state. Bank holding companies were formed to circumvent the legal restraints in geographic expansion imposed by state laws and the McFadden Act, as well as to gain a tax advantage. Regarding the latter, first, dividend payments from banks to their holding companies are not taxable. Second, bank holding companies can file a consolidated return for the entire organization and save on taxes because losses in one subsidiary can be used to offset profits earned by the bank. Third, a bank can occasionally locate one of its activities in a state or a country where taxes are lower. Since debt is a cheaper source of funding than equity because of interest deductibility, holding companies provide an avenue by which their parents can use debt to fund the purchase of stock in subsidiary banks. Therefore, debt becomes a means by which banks can increase their capital accounts.

As a matter of fact, several large holding companies began to acquire banks in other states, and in response, Congress passed the Bank Holding Company Act in 1956 and, in 1956, the Douglas Amendment to the Act. The provision of the Douglas Amendment accounts for a few large regional organizations, such as First Interstate Bancorp, First Bank System, and Norwest Corporation. The Act had the following objectives:

1. To protect the bank and the public from fraudulent financial dealings.
2. To preserve the integrity of state branching laws and the dual banking system.
3. To prohibit banks from engaging in industrial and other financial activities.
4. To control the future expansion of bank holding companies.

A provision of the Act prohibits bank holding companies from owning voting shares in nonbanking corporations and from acquiring such interests in the future. The Act required all bank holding companies to register with the Federal Reserve, submit to its regulatory actions and periodic examinations, and disclose prescribed financial information.

The Douglas Amendment prohibited a bank holding company from acquiring a bank in another state, unless the state specifically authorized such an acquisition. The Amendment effectively barred interstate banking via the holding company vehicle.

Because the Douglas Amendment restricts commercial banks from setting up branches across state lines, no single bank can control the entire market for bank deposits. Consequently, geographic restrictions effectively limit the concentration of any bank in the lending business, since the bank has limited deposit-accepting capabilities. In addition, the geographic restrictions discourage banks from offering consumer loans or small-business loans outside their boundaries, because the costs of providing these services long distance would not allow the banks to be competitive with local banks. On the other hand, with large commercial loans, the amount of the loan transaction overshadows the cost of long-distance services. The bottom line is that despite the geographical restrictions on branching, the market for large commercial loans is effectively nationwide.

BRANCH BANKING OUTSIDE THE UNITED STATES

If we had unrestricted interstate banking, the number of independent banks would decline because many mergers and acquisitions would likely occur. The number of branches might not change much, but these branches would be owned by a much smaller number of banks. Most industrialized countries do not have branching restrictions that are as limiting as those in the United States. For some of these countries, such as the U.K., France, Germany, Canada, Italy, Switzerland, and Japan, the share of deposits of the five largest banks ranges from 35 to 80 percent, compared with just under 19 percent in the United States.

The number of commercial banks is also considerably smaller in these countries. For example, there are only 11 banks in Canada and 86 banks in Japan, compared with just over 12,000 in the United States.

The number of separately owned banks in the United States is greater than that of most industrialized countries. Also, a branching restriction limits geographic reach and limits the potential for diversification of the bank balance sheet. Costs and regulations are such that our biggest banks all have excellent potential for geographic diversification in their loan portfolios. The degree of diversification depends upon the managerial constraint on geographic reach and on the loan strategy chosen by management. However, the market for loans to the largest corporate and government borrowers is worldwide. Many bank holding companies also have consumer and commercial finance companies and leasing companies throughout the United States and foreign branches or foreign banks in select parts of the world.

Some academic observers argue that branching restrictions, never imposed in either Canada or England, are inconsistent with the desire for bank safety and soundness. It can be argued, by appealing to historical experience as well as to economic theory, that an objective of merger and acquisition policy ought to be a banking industry closely resembling that of England or Canada of the interwar years.

BANK MERGER ACT OF 1960

There were numerous mergers and acquisitions among large New York banks in the 1950s, as well as in the early 1960s. In those days, banks were regarded by most experts as being beyond the reach of the antitrust statutes and, in particular, section 7 of the Clayton Act, as amended by the Celler-Kefauver Act of 1950. Congress responded to the wave of mergers by passing the Bank Merger Act of 1960. The Act made federal bank regulatory agency approval necessary for mergers and acquisitions involving FDIC-insured banks. National banks had to obtain office of the Comptroller of the Currency (OCC) approval, while state member banks needed approval from the Federal Reserve and state-chartered nonmember banks needed FDIC approval. Congress was concerned about possible damage to competition and public service from bank mergers that might reduce the number of competitors. A proposed merger having a substantially adverse impact on competition was likely to be denied. Other factors, such as an increase in services or convenience for the public, the strengthening of a problematic or failing bank, or an increase in the availability of mortgage loan money for underprivileged neighborhoods, were also given strong consideration in the regulatory decision on a merger.

In 1963, the Supreme Court shocked antitrust lawyers by ruling in *U.S. versus Philadelphia National Bank* (374 U.S. 321) that bank acquisitions and mergers were subject to section 7 of the Clayton Act. The Philadelphia National Bank was denied a merger with the Girard Trust Bank (both located in Philadelphia) on antitrust grounds of reduction in competition and too big a local market share, despite the approval of the merger by the Federal Reserve Board.

1966 AMENDMENT TO THE BANK HOLDING COMPANY ACT

The basic response of Congress to the Supreme Court's Philadelphia National decision was the Bank Merger Act of 1966, an amendment to the 1956 Bank Holding Company Act. In the 1956 Act, the Federal Reserve had been given the responsibility of deciding on proposed acquisitions and mergers of FDIC-insured banks. The 1966 Act directed the Federal Reserve also to decide proposed acquisitions and mergers of bank holding companies.

The 1966 amendment allowed subsidiary banks to lend to one another on the same basis as other federally insured banks. The amendment also clarified the evaluation criteria for the acquisition and formation of holding companies. The Federal Reserve was permitted to approve acquisitions that were not anticompetitive. In deciding on any proposed merger or acquisition that might result in a substantial lessening of competition, the agency was to look beyond that effect to the "convenience and needs of the community to be served"; that is, it was to see whether the lessening of competition was clearly outweighed by benefits to the public.

Following the passage of the 1956 legislation, the expansion of bank holding companies took one of two forms: multibank holding companies and one-bank holding companies. Multibank holding companies became a device for geographical expansion. One-bank holding companies, which were explicitly excluded from the bill, were permitted to expand into nonbanking activities. At the time, one-bank holding companies were usually small institutions with no apparent adverse effects on the public interest. Later, this loophole in the law led to a large increase in bank holding companies, from approximately 400 in 1965 to nearly 800 by the end of 1969. The growth of one-bank holding companies was attributable to the perceived synergistic effects of combining bank and nonbank activities, geographic diversification, tax advantages, the desire for profitable investment outlets, and the anticipation of restrictive legislation.

INTEREST RATE CONTROL ACT OF 1966

The prevailing culture of the thrift industry was to invest in long-term fixed-rate mortgages, while funding these mortgages with short-term deposits, typically passbook deposits that could be withdrawn on short notice ("borrowing short and lending long"). As long as interest rates fell, remained stable, or increased only gradually, thrifts made substantial profits. If interest rates increased substantially, a thrift might run operating losses if depository costs exceeded income from the fixed-rate loan and investment portfolios. From the end of 1964 through the fall of 1966, interest rates rose and thrifts began to feel a profit squeeze. If they refused to raise their depository interest rates, S&L customers might invest their funds in higher paying depository institutions or directly in the money and capital markets, where higher interest rates were available (the classic case of *depository disintermediation*). Congress responded to this dilemma by passing the Interest Rate Control Act (IRCA) in the fall of 1966, which placed ceilings on the interest rates that thrifts could pay on deposits for the first time. Regulation Q rate ceilings, administered by the Federal Reserve beginning in 1933, had applied only to commercial banks. The 1966 Act gave the FHLBB the power to set depository interest rate ceilings for thrifts in conjunction with the Federal Reserve. It was agreed that thrifts could pay a modestly higher interest rate than banks on deposits (the differential ranged from an initial spread of 75 basis points in 1966 to 25 basis points in 1973) to compensate their customers because thrifts could not offer them as complete a set of services as commercial banks and to make sure that thrifts would always have funds available for mortgage lending. The Regulation Q "patch" solved the interest rate squeeze problem for close to a decade. Congress provided thrifts with additional help against disintermediation when they increased the minimum denomination of Treasury bills from $1,000 to $10,000. At the time, the average thrift deposit was just over $3,000. During most of the 1970s, the Federal Reserve and the FHLBB engaged in a delicate effort of setting interest rate ceilings on various sizes and maturities of deposit in order to meet the thrifts' need to avoid an earnings squeeze and the banks' need to prevent disintermediation.[2]

The federal regulators and Congress really failed to aid the thrifts, by denying them the right to make adjustable rate mortgages (ARMs), which would have helped solve their interest rate risk problem. These ARMs would have allowed a thrift's income to increase at times of increasing interest rates. While FHLBB officials were not opposed to ARMs, congressional leaders were opposed to the shifting of interest rate risk to homeowners. The recommendations of the Fine Commission and the Hunt Commission during the 1970s that Regulation Q be abolished, that thrifts be permitted to offer ARMs (which were now popular in California and Wisconsin), and that they also be allowed to diversify into other activities were ignored by Congress. The failure to eliminate Regulation Q only delayed the day of reckoning for the thrift industry, because in the late 1970s interest rates rose sharply. Thrifts once again faced a set of choices that led to unavoidable losses, and unfortunately, even the elimination of Regulation Q could no longer rescue the industry.

1970 AMENDMENT TO THE BANK HOLDING COMPANY ACT

The one-bank holding company loophole was closed in the 1970 Bank Holding Company Amendment. The original language of the 1956 Act said that a bank holding company was any corporation controlling at least two banks. Certain bank holding companies were permitted to retain interstate acquisitions under a grandfather clause in the Act. In addition, the Federal Reserve limited nonbank activities to those that could reasonably be expected to produce benefits to the public, such as increased convenience or competition, or gains in efficiency that would outweigh possible adverse effects, such as undue concentration of resources, unfair competition, or conflicts of interest. To be an acceptable activity, the activity would have to be closely related and properly incident to banking. In other words, the criterion used by the Federal Reserve Board to determine the permissibility of an activity would be similarity of process. For example, factoring (the practice whereby a bank or a commercial factor purchases accounts receivable at a percentage of their face value), finance company operations, and mortgage banking are examples of processes that are similar to bank lending. Accordingly, they are among the permissible activities of bank holding companies. In addition, the underwriting of credit life insurance is considered integrable into the lending process and is closely related to banking. Therefore, it, too, is deemed a permissible activity. On the other hand, the underwriting of ordinary life, property, and liability insurance is not part of the lending process, and therefore, each of these activities is denied to bank holding companies.

Table 3.1 shows the permissible nonbank activities for bank holding companies. Table 3.2 shows selected expanded activities that are permitted to state-chartered banks, and Table 3.3 shows permitted services of commercial banks in 11 countries.

Foreign banks were not as tightly regulated as domestic banks, unless they became Federal Reserve members or controlled a subsidiary bank through a bank holding company, in which case they were subject to the Bank Holding Company Act. Foreign banks held a competitive advantage over domestic banks in regard to the extent they were regulated. They were permitted to branch across state lines, and they were allowed to operate security affiliates that could underwrite and sell stocks in the United States. The International Banking Act of 1978 was designed to remove some of the differences that existed between foreign and domestic bank regulation in the nation. Except for those facilities already engaged in interstate banking before passage of the Act, foreign banks presently operate under the same geographical restrictions as their domestic counterparts.

FINE AND HUNT COMMISSIONS

In the 1970s, Congress decided to commission two studies to see what could be done to improve the banking industry and its regulatory structure. The Hunt Commission (frequently referred to as the President's Commission on Financial Structure and Regulation) and the Fine Commission (often called the Commission on Financial Institutions and the Nation's Economy) reached many of the same conclusions. The Fine study urged the repeal of the prohibition of interest payments on demand deposits and recommended easing the restrictions on entry and branching for financial institutions. It also recommended broader powers for thrift institutions (e.g., offering consumer loans, issuing credit cards, maintaining powers of trust, and offering transaction accounts), uniform reserve requirements and equal tax treatment among financial institutions, and the elimination of deposit rate ceilings. Further recommendations were to consolidate regulatory, supervisory, and deposit insurance

Table 3.1 Nonbank Activities for Bank Holding Companies Under Section 4(c)8 of Regulation Y, November 1984

Activities Permitted by Regulation	Activities Permitted by Order	Activities Denied by the Board	Activities Permitted by Order Since 1984
1. Extensions of credit[b]. mortgage banking, finance companies (consumer, sales, and commercial), credit cards, factoring	1. Issuance and sale of travelers checks[b,f]	1. Insurance premium funding (combined sales of mutual funds and insurance)	1. Financial feasibility studies, valuation services, utility rate testimony, credit ratings
2. Industrial bank, Morris Plan banks, industrial loan company	2. Buying and selling gold and silver bullion and silver coin[b,a]	2. Underwriting life insurance not related to credit extensions	2. Tax preparation for individuals
3. Servicing loans and other extensions of credit[b]	3. Issuing money orders and general-purpose variable denominated payment instruments[a,b,d]	3. Sale of level-term credit life	3. Real estate consulting services, personal property appraisals
4. Trust company[b]	4. Futures commission merchant to cover gold and silver bullion and coins[a,b]	4. Real estate brokerage (residential)	4. Credit card loss reporting services, merchant voice transaction verification
5. Investment or financial advising[b]	5. Underwriting certain federal, state, and municipal securities[a,b]	5. Armored car	5. Employee benefits consulting
6. Full-payout leasing of personal or real property[b]	6. Check verification[a,b,d]	6. Land development	6. Municipal securities brokers' broker
7. Investments in community welfare projects[b]	7. Financial advice to consumers[a,b]	7. Real estate syndication	7. Student loan servicing
8. Providing bookkeeping or data-processing services[b]	8. Issuance of small-domination debt instruments[a]	8. General management consulting	8. Consumer financial consulting
9. Acting as insurance agent or broker primarily in connection with credit extensions[b]	9. Arranging for equity financing of real estate	9. Property management	9. Futures and options advisory services
10. Underwriting credit life, accident, and health insurance	10. Acting as futures commissions merchant	10. Computer output microfilm services	10. Operation of collection agency
11. Providing courier services[b]	11. Discount brokerage	11. Underwriting mortgage guaranty insurance[c]	
12. Management consulting to all depository institutions	12. Operating a distressed savings and loan association	12. Operating a savings and loan association[a,e]	
13. Sale at retail of money orders with a face value of not more than $1,000, travelers checks, and savings bonds[a,b,g]	13. Operating an Article XII investment company	13. Operating a travel agency[a,b]	
	14. Executing foreign banking unsolicited purchases and sales of securities	14. Underwriting property and casualty insurance[a]	
		15. Underwriting home loan life mortgage insurance[a]	

(Continued)

Table 3.1 Continued

Activities Permitted by Regulation	Activities Permitted by Order	Activities Denied by the Board	Activities Permitted by Order Since 1984
14. Performing appraisals of real estate[a]	15. Engaging in commercial banking activities abroad through a limited-purpose Delaware bank	16. Investment note issue with transactional characteristics	
15. Issuance and sale of travelers checks		17. Real esate advisory services	
16. Arranging commercial real estate equity financing	16. Performing appraisal of real estate and real estate advisor and real estate brokerage on nonresidential properties		
17. Securities brokerage			
18. Underwriting and dealing in government obligations and money market instruments	17. Operating a Pool Reserve Plan for loss reverses of banks for loans to small businesses		
19. Foreign exchange advisory and transactional services	18. Underwriting and dealing are, to a limited extent, municipal revenue bonds, mortgage-related securities, consumer-receivable-related securities, commercial paper, corporate debt and equity securities		
20. Futures commission merchant			
21. Options on financial futures			
22. Advice on options on bullion and foreign exchange	19. Offering informational advice and transactional services for foreign exchange services		

[a]Added to list since January 1, 1975.
[b]Activities permissible to national banks.
[c]Board orders found these activities closely related to banking, but denied proposed acquisitions as part of its "go slow" policy.
[d]To be decided on a case-by-case basis.
[e]Operating a thrift institution has been permitted by order in Rhode Island, Ohio, New Hampshire, and California.
[f]Subsequently permitted by regulation.
[g]The amount subsequently was changed to $10,000.

Source: Federal Reserve Board.

Table 3.2 State Authorization of Selected Expanded Activities for State-Chartered Banks, May 1990

Insurance Underwriting	Insurance Brokerage	Real Estate Equity Participation	Real Estate Development	Real Estate Brokerage	Securities Underwriting	Securities Brokerage/No Underwriting
Delaware	Alabama	Arizona	Arizona	Georgia	Arizona	Arizona
Idaho	California	Arkansas	Arkansas	Iowa	California[e]	Connecticut
North Carolina	Delaware	California	California	Maine[q]	Delaware	Delaware
South Dakota	Idaho	Colorado	Colorado	Massachusetts	Florida	Florida
Utah[b]	Indiana[n]	Connecticut	Connecticut	New Jersey	Idaho	Georgia
	Iowa[o]	Florida	Florida	North Carolina	Indiana[f]	Idaho
	Nebraska	Georgia	Georgia	Oregon	Iowa	Indiana[f]
	New Jersey	Kentucky	Kentucky	Utah	Kansas[g]	Iowa
	North Carolina	Maine	Maine	Wisconsin	Maine	Kansas
	Oregon	Massachusetts	Massachusetts		Massachusetts	Maine
	South Carolina	Missouri	Michigan		Michigan	Michigan
	South Dakota	Nevada	Missouri		Missouri[h]	Minnesota
	Utah	New Hampshire	Nevada		Montana[i]	Nebraska
	Washington[p]	New Jersey	New Hampshire		Nebraska[j]	New Jersey
	Wisconsin	North Carolina	New Jersey		New Jersey	New York
	Wyoming	Ohio	North Carolina		North Carolina[k]	North Carolina
		Pennsylvania	Ohio		Pennsylvania[l]	Ohio
		Rhode Island	Oregon		Puerto Rico[m]	Pennsylvania[q]
		South Dakota	Rhode Island		Tennessee	Texas
		Tennessee[c]	South Dakota		Utah	Tennessee
		Utah	Utah		Washington	Utah
		Virginia	Virginia		West Virginia	Vermont
		Washington	Washington			West Virginia
		West Virginia	West Virginia			
		Wisconsin[d]	Wisconsin[d]			

Notes:

a   Expanded activities above those permitted national banks and bank holding companies under the Bank Holding Company Act. Extent of practice not indicated.

b   Grandfathered institutions.

c   Banks not allowed to be active partners in real estate development.

d   Wisconsin: enacted expanded power legislation 5/86. New legislation authorized the commissioner of banking to promulgate rules under which state banks may engage in activities that are authorized for other financial institutions doing business in the state.

e   Underwrite mutual funds; law silent on other securities.

f   Underwrite municipal revenue bonds and market mutual funds and mortgage-backed securities.

g   Underwrite municipal bonds.

h   Underwrite mutual funds and may underwrite securities to extent of state legal loan limit.

i   Limited to bonds.

j   Underwrite U.S. government securities.

k   U.S. government, Federal Farm Loan Act bonds and general obligation bonds of state and political subdivisions.

l   Underwrite municipal and mortgage-related securities to extent permitted mutual savings banks.

m   May underwrite bonds of U.S. and Puerto Rican governments, their political subdivisions and instrumentalities, and agencies.

n   Cannot broker life insurance; all other types permitted.

o   Property and casualty only.

p   Banks located in small towns (5,000 or below) may conduct insurance agency activities without geographic limitations.

q   May own or operate brokerage firm established for the purpose of disposing of bank-owned property.

r   May conduct discount brokerage.

Source: Federal Reserve Board of Governors and Conference of State Bank Supervisors.

Table 3.3 Permitted Services of Commercial Banks in 11 Countries

Service	Belgium	Canada	France	West Germany	Italy	Japan	Luxembourg	Netherlands	Switzerland	United Kingdom	U.S.
Insurance:											
Brokerage	Y	N	Y	Y	N*	N	Y	Y	N	Y	N*
Underwriting	Y	N	N*	Y*	N*	N	Y	N	N	Y*	N
Equities:											
Brokerage	Y	Y*	Y	Y	Y	N	Y	Y	Y	Y	Y
Underwriting	Y	Y*	Y	Y	Y	N	Y	Y	Y	Y*	N*
Investment	Y	Y	Y	Y	Y	Y	Y	Y	Y	Y*	N
Other Underwriting:											
Government Debt	Y	Y	Y	Y	Y	N	Y	Y	Y	Y*	Y
Private Debt	Y	Y*	Y	Y	Y	N	Y	Y	Y	Y*	N*
Mutual Funds:											
Brokerage	Y	Y	Y	Y	Y	N	Y	Y	Y	Y	N
Management	Y	Y*	Y	Y	Y	N	Y	Y	Y	Y	N
Real Estate:											
Brokerage	Y*	N	Y	Y	N	N	Y	Y	Y	Y	N*
Investment	Y	Y	Y	Y	Y	N	Y	Y	Y	Y	N
Other Brokerage:											
Government Debt	Y	Y	Y	Y	Y	Y	Y	Y	Y	Y	Y
Private Debt	Y	Y	Y	Y	Y	Y	Y	Y	Y	Y	Y

Notes: N = No; N* = No, with exceptions; Y = Yes; Y* = Yes, but not directly by the bank.
Source: Adapted from American Bankers Association, *International Banking Competitiveness*, March 1990, p. 82. © 1990 American Bankers Association. Reprinted with permission. All Rights Reserved.

functions into a new agency and to permit commercial banks to branch throughout trade areas, such as metropolitan areas, even if doing so meant crossing state boundaries.

In its own words, the Hunt Commission was

> concerned with achieving a regulatory framework that allows adequate freedom for financial firms to adjust to new technological possibilities, encourage new types of financial firms to emerge, and at the same time assume that resulting benefits will flow to the public.

The Hunt Commission also recommended complete regulatory reform. The idea was to free the Federal Reserve to concentrate on monetary policy and to establish a new agency, the Federal Deposit Guaranty Administration, which would assume the deposit insurance functions of the FDIC, FSLIC, and NCUSIF (National Credit Union Share Insurance Fund). The Office of the National Bank Administrator would replace the Comptroller of the Currency and be given supervisory and regulatory responsibility for all federally chartered commercial banks, savings banks, and saving and loan associations whose checking accounts totaled more than 10 percent of their total deposits. In addition, the Office of the Administrator of State Banks would be created to supervise all state-chartered insured commercial banks, savings banks, and savings and loans whose checking accounts totaled more than 10 percent of their deposits.

While few of the Hunt or Fine Commission recommendations were set into law immediately, they provided the foundation for reform and deregulation of the structure of financial institutions during the 1980s. Deregulation could not be stalled totally. Market forces operated to make many of the regulations ineffective. For example, high interest rates provided the incentive to bypass deposit-rate ceilings and restrictions on products, while technical advances in computers and telecommunications, which allowed for instantaneous and inexpensive storage, manipulation, and transferring of information and funds, provided the means to bypass the regulations.

NATIONAL CREDIT UNION ADMINISTRATION (1970)

The National Credit Union Administration (NCUA) was established in 1970 to regulate, charter, and supervise federal credit unions. Before then, responsibility for these credit unions was vested in the Farm Credit Administration in 1934, later shifted to the FDIC, and then transferred to the Department of Health, Education, and Welfare. The NCUA is governed by a three-person board appointed by the president with the consent of the Congress.

Congress also established the National Credit Union Share Insurance Fund in 1970 to provide deposit insurance to credit unions. All federally chartered credit unions must be insured by the NCUSIF, while state-chartered credit unions have an option to apply for such insurance, receive insurance coverage from state insurance agencies, or be uninsured.

Congress established the Central Liquidity Facility in 1978, housing it in the NCUA, in order to provide liquidity to credit unions by making loans to or purchasing assets from them. The Central Liquidity Facility finances its activities by selling debt and also has a $500 million credit line with the U.S. Treasury to meet emergencies.

CONSUMER PROTECTION REGULATION: SOCIAL RESPONSIBILITY LAWS OF THE 1960s, 1970s, AND 1980s

Consumer protection laws were designed to rectify perceived inequalities in the consumer credit-granting process and to deal with the impact banks were having on the quality of life in the communities they served. The salient objectives of these laws were to improve market efficiency by constraining the monopoly power of lenders and to reallocate credit in a more socially desirable manner. The laws forbid discrimination in the granting of consumer credit. For example, usury laws limit the finance charges on installment loans, preventing lenders from charging extremely high prices for credit, and disclosure laws were designed to reduce lenders' market power by making borrowers aware of substitute products. Violations of these laws by banks can result in penalties such as the abrogation of debt or the denial by the Federal Reserve of a bank acquisition on the grounds that a bank holding company had a poor consumer compliance record.

Since 1968, there has been a trend toward legislation designed to protect consumers in their transactions with credit-granting institutions. In 1969, Congress passed the Consumer Credit Protection Act (also better known as the Truth in Lending Act), which made consumers aware of the annual percentage rate and the total finance charges on a loan—that is, the true cost of borrowing money. The basic purpose of the Act was to provide consumers with meaningful and standardized information regarding terms of credit so that they could compare the cost of borrowing among different lenders. The law applies to loans made for personal, family, and household purposes. Agricultural loans and business loans are exempt, as are loans over $25,000 that are not secured by a dwelling or other real property. In 1971, the Fair Credit Reporting Act was passed as an amendment to the Consumer Credit Protection Act, to protect consumers against the dissemination of inaccurate information that might reduce their chances of obtaining credit, insurance, or employment. The Act gives consumers access to their credit files, requires the deletion of obsolete information, and provides for the correction of erroneous data. It protects consumers from inaccurate and unfair billing by presenting them with a detailed description of their rights. The Act states that all customer complaints must be filed within 60 days of purchase of the object in question and resolved within 90 days thereof.

The Equal Credit Opportunity Act (ECOA), passed in 1974, requires that credit be made available to individuals without regard to marital status or sex. Congress broadened the scope of the Act in 1976 to forbid discrimination by creditors based on age, national origin, religion, or race or because they were recipients of public welfare. ECOA focuses on both consumer protection and antidiscrimination. Its consumer protection provisions concentrate on notifying credit applicants of the actions taken on their applications within 30 days of applying for credit, and if the loan is denied, that applicants be told the reason for the denial. However, the act is oriented more toward upholding civil rights than consumer protection. The act applies to banks, finance companies, department stores, and credit card issuers; business and consumer loans are included.

Congress also passed the Fair Credit Billing Act in 1974. This Act required that creditors provide detailed information to consumers on the method the creditors use to assess finance charges. It also required that billing complaints be processed promptly and that customers be given a detailed description of their rights and of the procedures they must follow in making complaints about billing errors.

The Electronic Funds Transfer Act of 1978 (EFTA) deals with the rights, liabilities, and responsibilities of participants in the electronic transfer of funds. The act encompasses ATM transactions, point-of-sale (POS) terminals, direct deposits, preauthorized payments, and telephone transfers in the areas of documentation of transfers, receipt of periodic statements, error resolution, and the issuing of credit cards. In addition, it limits a consumer's liability for unauthorized transfer to $50 if the consumer notifies the financial institution within two business days of the loss or theft of a credit or debit card. The liability grows to $500 if the institution is not notified within two days.

During the 1970s, there was a concern that older, declining urban neighborhoods were being discriminated against (redlined) by mortgage lenders. Congress passed two antiredlining acts, the Home Mortgage Disclosure Act (1975) and the Community Reinvestment Act (1977). The Home Mortgage Disclosure Act requires depository institutions with assets over $10 million and located in standard metropolitan statistical areas to disclose mortgage loans by classification and geographic location. The Act forces banks to demonstrate that their lending policies do not include the practice of redlining.

The Community Reinvestment Act prohibits U.S. banks from discriminating against customers within their trade territories merely on the basis of the neighborhood in which they happen to live. The Act encourages depository institutions to make mortgage loans to low-income borrowers within their community. The lender is not subject to individual causes of action. The pressure for compliance emanates primarily from the desire to remain on favorable terms with the supervisory agencies that make decisions related to a merger or acquisition, a new branch, or a new bank holding company activity. Compliance with this affirmative action law appears to have become much more important to federal regulators, as indicated, for example, by the Federal Reserve Board's denial in February 1989 of an application by Continental Illinois to acquire the Grand Canyon State Bank of Arizona, on the grounds that the Chicago-based bank did not have a satisfactory record following community service guidelines under the Act.[3]

REGULATORY REFORM IN THE SECURITIES INDUSTRY

Regulatory reform in the securities industry was accomplished only after repeated judicial challenges, pressures from the Justice Department, and congressional criticism. The enormous growth of institutional investors and the huge increases in trading volume on the New York Stock Exchange (daily trading volume grew from 3 million shares in 1960 to 21 million shares in 1968) acted as a catalyst in reforming commission rates, providing more protection for investors, and changing some of the rules germane to institutional ownership of a seat on the stock exchange.

For the most part, the SEC was complacent about changing the anticompetitive membership rules of the National Association of Securities Dealers (NASD) and the minimum brokerage or flat rate commissions charged for nearly all sales at the New York Stock Exchange. The fee for a sale of 5,000 shares of stock was 50 times that for 100 shares of the same stock. The pricing schedule bore no relationship to cost and discriminated against large stock purchases by institutional investors. The fixed-rate commission structure cross-subsidizes small transactions by individual investors at the expense of the large trades made by institutional investors. Price competition by exchange members was stifled, and nonmembers were prevented from using the New York exchange as a wholesale market. In addition, fee-splitting between members and nonmembers was forbidden. Further, members were not allowed to take their customers' orders for stocks listed on the exchange to the OTC market, where volume discounts were available. Membership was denied to any publicly held corporation, preventing institutional investors from integrating forward to capture the artificially high commissions on large transactions. After a battle that lasted several years, the SEC staff recommended that members of the exchange be permitted to buy or sell over the counter when OTC dealers offer a better price.[4] This recommendation was made only after a broker complained to the Senate Antitrust Subcommittee. However, faced with strong opposition from members of the stock exchange, the SEC did not implement the recommendation. Several of the regional exchanges sought growth by permitting membership to institutional investors. In 1966, a group of investment companies sued the New York Stock Exchange and four member firms, alleging conspiracy in constraint of trade through price fixing under the Sherman Act. The case was dismissed on the grounds that the SEC had the authority to fix "reasonable" rates. However, Chief Justice Earl Warren dissented because he sensed a discrepancy between "the Exchange rate fixing practice [and] this nation's commitment . . . to competitive pricing."[5] Even if the SEC refused to budge, the Justice Department began to apply pressure for change.

There was enormous pressure for "give-ups" or fee splitting by institutional investors, as an indirect rebate, to another broker who handled the investor's own stock or provided research and consultive services. In a lengthy statement on the SEC's proposed rules against "give-ups," the Justice Department called for the abolition of fixed-rate commissions and new means "for assuring equitable and nondiscriminatory access . . . to the [New York Stock Exchange]" in April 1968. It took seven years to implement these changes fully.

In the meantime, Wall Street was hit hard by a paperwork crisis brought about by increased trading volume and a failure to have automated the back offices of most brokerage firms. Failures multiplied in 1968 and early 1969, despite the hiring and training of thousands of operations clerks as quickly as possible. When the market turned down in 1969, this excess overhead resulted in average losses of just under 3 percent on securities commissions. Over 100 brokerage firms were forced into liquidation.

SECURITIES INVESTOR PROTECTION CORPORATION ACT OF 1970

Congress responded to the problems of Wall Street by passing the Securities Investor Protection Corporation (SIPC) Act of 1970. The Act was established to indemnify clients of brokerage firms by providing insurance for the clients should the firm become bankrupt or close. All registered brokers and dealers and all companies that are members of national securities exchanges must join the SIPC and pay annual dues equal to about 0.19 percent of the company's yearly revenues. That raised an estimated $60 million in premiums for the fund in 1990. The SIPC, a nonprofit organization, functions as a backup form of consumer protection analogous to the protection provided by the FDIC to bank depositors and by insurance funds to insurance policyholders. The SIPC ensures that investors will receive securities that the failed brokerage firm held for their account in street name (i.e., the name of the brokerage firm), up to a limit of $500,000 per customer, including a maximum of $100,000 for cash in customer accounts. The SIPC does not guarantee the dollar value of securities; rather, it guarantees only that the securities themselves will be returned. While the intention is that the fund will be fully supported by assessments made against brokerage firms, backup government pledges of funds are available should the fund ever be depleted. The SIPC can borrow up to $1 billion against the U.S. Treasury. In addition, the SEC can issue promissory notes, and subsequent purchase of such notes by the U.S. Treasury results in funds going to the SIPC.

The SIPC was established as part of an effort to provide greater protection for customers of registered brokers and dealers and for members of national securities exchanges, to restore and improve investor confidence in the capital markets, and to upgrade the financial responsibility requirements for brokers and dealers. Prior to the establishment of the agency, an investor could lose all of the securities or cash held in his or her account if the brokerage firm closed or failed. Although the major exchanges had established their own trust funds for the protection of investors, these funds were probably inadequate to protect customers fully if a large number of brokerage firms or one giant-sized firm were to fail. It is important to note that the SIPC does not protect investors from losses in the value of their securities because of market conditions or fraudulent activities. Restitution for fraud is found only in the federal or state securities laws.

Since 1970, the SIPC has paid out over $180 million to assist about 200,000 investors in recovering more than $1 billion from brokerage firms that failed. When Blinder, Robinson & Co. collapsed in July 1990, it was feared that the resources of the SIPC would be used up (at that time the agency had $570 million in reserves) in paying off 227,000 customers. Fortunately, only $2 million had been paid out by early 1991. Could the SIPC handle the failure of the $64 billion asset-rich Merrill Lynch? After all, brokerage firm failures might have been much worse in 1990 if a number of parent holding companies had not rescued their ailing subsidiaries (e.g., American Express recapitalized Shearson-Lehman, General Electric reinvigorated Kidder Peabody, Prudential Insurance restructured Prudential Bache, and Credit Suisse injected capital into First Boston). The answer is possibly; it would depend on the extent of investor losses. Since the 10 largest brokerage firms now control 60 percent of the industry's $440 billion capital base, compared with only 27 percent of the industry's capital in 1973, the collapse of one or two large brokers could create a serious problem for the SIPC. Richard Breeden, SEC commissioner, has testified before a Senate subcommittee that he would like to see the insurance fund get bigger without turning to the federal government for guarantees or funding. One funding scheme would require stock brokerage firms to purchase Treasury bonds and deposit them with the SIPC in lieu of an increase in payments to the fund. If there were an emergency, the SIPC could cash in the bonds. Another scheme calls for increasing the $500 million line of credit the SIPC has. A third scheme calls for increased insurance premiums.[6]

In addition to offering insurance, the SIPC monitors the financial health of brokerage firms. The agency reviews reports from the SEC, the NASD, and the stock exchanges, which must notify the SIPC whenever a company approaches financial difficulty. If the SIPC determines that the company's customer accounts are at risk, it obtains a federal court order to shut down the brokerage firm and liquidate it. Often, the SIPC tries to arrange a "bulk transfer," in which all the failed firm's accounts are transferred to another brokerage firm.

SECURITIES ACTS AMENDMENTS OF 1975

The Securities Acts Amendments of 1975 legislated the development of a new National Market System (NMS) and eliminated fixed-rate commissions on stock brokerage transactions. Many securities firms failed following the end of fixed-rate commissions. However, by 1980 (a record year), the securities industry's after-tax return was 20 percent, about twice the return of banks. These large profits and the opportunity for functional and geographic expansion attracted new entrants to the industry, especially from banking. While Glass-Steagall prohibited bank entry into corporate underwriting, it did not prohibit brokerage. The new law did not specify the exact form of the NMS, but recommended a big, competitive, centrally administered national securities system that should be made up of the New York Stock Exchange, the American Exchange (AMEX), the OTC, and the organized regional exchanges.

Implementation of the law's objectives has proceeded in stages. A consolidated tape began to report trades in stocks on the New York exchange, the AMEX, the major regional exchanges, and the OTC market using the NASDAQ system and in the fourth market also using the Instinet system. In 1978, the broker became able to rely on electronic equipment to determine the best available terms for a trade, thus avoiding the need for extensive shopping around. Bid and ask prices were made more accessible to those subscribing to quotation services. The Intermarket Trading System (ITS), an electronic network linking seven exchanges (the New York Stock Exchange, AMEX, Pacific, Philadelphia, Boston, Midwest, and Cincinnati) and certain OTC security dealers, was inaugurated in 1978. The system enables brokers, dealers, and specialists at various locations to interact with one another, since the consolidated quotation system provides the bid and asked prices quoted by market makers. The broker can route orders electronically to wherever the best price exists at that moment. In 1988, 1,537 stocks listed on one or another of the exchanges were included in the system. In implementing a single centralized order book, rules must be established concerning the use and disclosure of the book.

The establishment of the totally nationwide electronic central security system mandated by the SEC in 1975 has been delayed by many long-entrenched and powerful institutions and those with vested interests in the securities industry. Numerous issues must still be resolved before implementing the final step. For example, should there be specialists? What requirements should be placed on market makers? And who should operate the central market system?

The New York Stock Exchange finally responded to the increased pressure for abolishing fixed commissions by suggesting a new, but still regulated, rate structure that was more in line with operational costs. The SEC suggested free commissions on transactions over $100,000 and acknowledged in 1971 that fixed commission rates on large transactions were "the source of a number of difficulties."[7] A month later, the New York exchange eliminated commissions on trades over $500,000. The SEC followed a course of "prudent gradualism," lowering the breakpoints for competitive rates through 1974. The Senate Banking Committee completed a detailed investigation of securities markets and concluded that regulation, although essential for protecting investors, was "not an effective substitute for competition."[8] With the Justice Department threatening suit and continued political pressure from just about every trade association in the financial services industry, the SEC's resistance to competition crumbled in 1975.

The 1970s marked the beginning of a general national disaffection with regulation and a basic movement toward deregulation. Although volume discounts for large institutional trades had existed for years, Friend and Blume, at Wharton, claimed that fixed commissions were too high and protected inefficient securities brokers, while efficient brokerage firms made excessive profits.[9] The SEC abolished fixed brokerage commissions on May 1, 1975, but only after repeated challenges by the New York Stock Exchange. Since then, brokers have been free to set commissions at any desired rate or to negotiate with customers concerning the fees charged for each trade. Institutional brokerage commissions fell by 30–70 percent within a few years, and daily trading volume on the New York exchange jumped from 37 million in 1975 to 51 million by 1980. Rates for large trades fell substantially, while broadline full-service firms that provided extensive services to small investors for no additional fee continued to charge commissions similar to those specified in the earlier fixed-commission schedules. As a result of deregulation, commission income moved closer to costs, product lines were unbundled, and the discount brokerage business blossomed. Some brokerage firms were unable to adjust to this new environment and either merged with other firms or closed their doors.

During the 1960s and 1970s, many procedures were utilized to subvert the fixed-commission rates. Third and fourth markets expanded their operations, while regional exchanges invented ways to serve as conduits to return a portion of the fixed commissions to institutional investors. Following the SEC's elimination of fixed commissions, some firms unbundled their services separately from their pricing of execution of orders. Some charged separate fees for research and separate fees for executing orders, while others bundled new services into comprehensive packages. Another group of brokerage firms became discount brokers, dropping most ancillary services while cutting commissions accordingly. Discount firms offered just execution services. In retail brokerage, while full-service national firms increased their commissions for small-investor trades even above the earlier fixed-rate schedules when operating costs increased, retail discount houses such as Charles Schwab and Olde (offering no research or only limited research) captured much of the small-investor business by offering substantial discounts for trades of even 100 shares. By 1980, more than 70 discount brokerage firms held 9 percent of the market share. The result has been greater operational efficiency in U.S. securities markets: While the large institutional investor was the initial beneficiary of negotiated commissions, the small investor also benefited when the retail discount brokerages set up shop all over the United States. Prior to May 1, 1975, small investors had limited bargaining power because brokers didn't lose much commission if a small transaction were taken elsewhere.

The "research boutique" firms that specialized in securities analysis and that depended on soft-dollar commissions, such as Wainwright and Mitchell Hutchins, had the most difficulty acclimating to the new environment. Many such firms were unable to cover their overhead expenses in this deregulated pricing environment and were forced to either merge or liquidate. These firms had given their research reports to clients in exchange for large chunks of their commission business. The proportion of revenue dollars for New York Stock Exchange member firms that was generated by brokerage commissions fell from 53 percent in 1975 to 17 percent in 1990. Also, by the end of the 1980s, institutional brokerage dollars accounted for only 14 percent of revenues among large investment banks, compared with 29 percent in 1980.

ENDNOTES

1. R. H. K. Vietor, "Regulation-Defined Financial Markets," in *Wall Street and Regulation,* ed. S. Hayes (Boston: Harvard Business School Press, 1987), p. 22.

2. L. J. White, *The S&L Debacle* (New York: Oxford Press, 1991), pp. 62–64.

3. P. S. Rose, *Commercial Bank Management* (Homewood, IL: Richard D. Irwin, 1991), p. 533.

4. Vietor, pp. 30–31, 42.

5. *Kaplan v. Lehman Bros.,* 250 F Supp. 562 (1966), *aff'd,* 371 F.2d 49 (1967), *cert. denied,* 389 U.S. 954 (1967).

6. M. Fritz, "How Solid Is SIPC?" *Forbes Magazine,* February 18, 1991, pp. 114–115.

7. *Institutional Investor Study* (Washington, DC: Securities and Exchange Commission, 1971).

8. U.S. Congress, Senate Committee on Banking, *Securities Industry Study,* 92nd Congress, 2nd Session, 1972, Committee Print, p. 2.

9. I. Friend and M. Blume, *The Consequences of Competitive Commissions on the New York Stock Exchange* (Working Paper) (Philadelphia: The Wharton School, University of Pennsylvania, April 1972).

4 Mainframe Bank Deregulation

Deposit insurance and the discount window—the major elements of the safety net—were designed to afford depositors an extra measure of protection from losses and by doing so to shield the aggregate real economy from some of the worst effects of instability in banking markets. . . . [They] made the currency drains that dominated the 19th century and early 20th century banking literature an anachronism. . . . A loss of confidence in the soundness of one or more banks by depositors can engender a contagious withdrawal of deposits—a "run" on banks in general. . . . The United States has not suffered a financial panic or systemic run in the last 50 years.

Alan Greenspan, "Subsidies and Powers in Commercial Banking"

The long trend toward stricter regulation ended in the late 1970s. Rapidly rising and volatile market interest rates combined with major technological innovations in communications and data processing to cause a number of regulations to have harmful effects on depository institutions, putting them at a competitive disadvantage. As a matter of fact, the 1980s and early 1990s may become known as the era of deregulation. There is even discussion of further deregulation, with commercial banks pushing for complete geographic deregulation and more insurance and investment banking privileges.

THE DEPOSITORY INSTITUTIONS DEREGULATION AND MONETARY CONTROL ACT OF 1980

Enactment of the Depository Institutions Deregulation and Monetary Control Act of 1980 (DIDMCA) and the Garn-St. Germain Act of 1982 reduced governmental operating restrictions on depository institutions. These acts were complementary to the deregulation that was occurring in other industries, such as trucking, natural gas, telephone companies, and airlines.

The DIDMCA was one of the most significant financial acts since the Banking Act of 1933. It was a complex act designed to help thrift institutions (by increasing the various sources of their funds and expanding the use of funds by S&Ls), to deregulate financial institutions, to tighten monetary control, and to reduce or eliminate interest rate limitations imposed on the banking system. The Act reduced regulation by eliminating state usury ceilings on residential mortgages and on business and agricultural loans in excess of $25,000 for three years, phased out Regulation Q by April 1986 (except for the zero ceiling on demand deposits), and reduced the restrictions on products that thrifts could offer. It also established uniform reserve requirements for all depository institutions, regardless of whether they were a member of the Federal Reserve. This extension of regulatory power was intended to improve the control of the money supply by the Federal Reserve.

The upward trend in interest rates since World War II gradually coerced the elimination of interest rate ceilings at banks. To help prevent disintermediation from the banks under Regulation Q, the minimum denomination of Treasury bills was raised from $1,000 to $10,000 in 1970. Shortly thereafter, money market funds (a form of mutual fund investing in treasury bills, certificates of deposit, commercial paper, banker's acceptances, and repurchase agreements) were developed to service investors outside the banking industry by offering unregulated market interest rates and liquidity, at first through a toll-free 800 number and later through a quasi-transaction account. It was clear then that Regulation Q was doomed, but it took close to 10 years for banks to be granted an equal playing field related to interest rate deregulation. (Regulations on large deposits were eliminated in the early 1970s.) Most of the ceilings on depository institutions remained in effect until the 1980s because the protected S&Ls feared for their survival without them. The S&L lobby has always been one of the strongest in the United States and was able to delay the removal of interest rate ceilings for a decade. Bank rates were deregulated under the pretense that the small saver was entitled to money market rates of interest that were at that time available only at banks to investors with at least $100,000, to Treasury bill investors with a $10,000 minimum, or to money market mutual fund investors with just $1,000. Deposit rate ceilings were really a protective form of price fixing that had to be removed anyway.

Many banks withdrew their memberships from the Federal Reserve in the 1970s because their reserve requirements were more stringent for members than for nonmembers. However, as mentioned previously, the trend of withdrawing slowed down to a trickle as a result of the passage of the DIDMCA, which created uniform reserve requirements for member and nonmember banks and gradually extended those requirements to all depository institutions with either transaction accounts or time deposit account balances (other than personal).

The actions to broaden the powers of thrift institutions by allowing commercial and consumer loans were made to permit thrifts to balance the maturities of their assets and liabilities better, to help improve their overall profitability, and to diversify their earning asset portfolios away from being dependent on fixed-rate mortgages. Thrifts were allowed to devote up to 20 percent of their assets to consumer loans, commercial paper, and corporate debt securities, up to 5 percent to business loans, and up to 5 percent for education and community development loans. They were also permitted to offer credit and debit cards, as well as trust services. On the deposit side of the balance sheet, thrifts were allowed to offer NOW accounts, which previously had been legal only in selected New England states. Finally, in order to improve confidence in depository institutions as a whole, the DIDMCA raised the FDIC ceiling on depository insurance to $100,000 from $40,000.

In a gesture of evenhandedness, when the Federal Reserve extended reserve requirements to all depository institutions, it offered these institutions services such as borrowing at the discount window, check clearing, safekeeping of securities, wire transfers, automatic clearing facilities, and cash transportation services. Previously, such services were available only to member banks. In addition, all those services that were once free to member banks were now offered at cost to all depository institutions, subject to reserve requirements. In essence, membership in the Federal Reserve lost much of its meaning.

In sum, the main deregulatory provisions of the DIDMCA were:

1. Phasing out of depository ceilings.
2. New lending flexibility for depository institutions.
3. Explicit pricing of Federal Reserve services.
4. Permitting transaction accounts at all depository institutions.
5. Increased competition among depository institutions and between depository and nondepository institutions.

As a consequence of the passage of the DIDMCA, there has been a shift from demand deposit accounts to NOW accounts. Also, consumers have shifted funds from conventional passbook accounts to higher yielding certificates of deposit (CDs). In addition, prior residential mortgage loan restrictions relating to geographic areas and first mortgage lending requirements were removed, and increased authority was permitted in the granting of real estate development and construction loans by federally chartered S&Ls.

The DIDMCA permits greater competition for deposits and greater flexibility in the holding of assets by depository institutions. Consequently, as institutional differences become more blurred, similarities in the their financial management are likely to increase.

SEC RULE 415: SHELF REGISTRATION

In 1982, the SEC began to streamline the process of registering stock and bond issues, allowing companies to register once and for all the securities they planned to issue during the next two years under Rule 415 of the Securities Act of 1933. While the procedure was adopted only on an experimental basis in 1982, it became a permanent option at the beginning of 1984. With such shelf registration, a firm can ask investment bankers to bid competitively for underwriting the issue when the firm wishes to go to market. When the issuer is ready for an infusion of cash, the previously registered issue can be taken off the "shelf" at the SEC and issued to the public without any further disclosures, except for an updating of the company's financial data. The firm can simply refuse to sell the securities if desirable bids are not forthcoming, or it can sell the securities directly to investors without the help of an investment banker. Shelf registration allows a company to time its sales of new stocks or bonds to coincide with the most favorable selling opportunities in the marketplace that occur during the two-year period. Often, once a registration statement has been filed, the issuer will periodically receive calls from underwriting firms offering to purchase the securities at a given price and set of terms. In fact, at times, a de facto competition emerges in the bidding process.

A key purpose of the SEC in allowing shelf registration was to make the issuance of domestic U.S. securities more cost and time effective. The evidence seems to suggest that this has been accomplished. Underwriting spreads are considerably lower today than they were prior to the implementation of shelf registrations for both debt and equity issues. There is greater competition for the underwriting of securities (de facto competitive bidding) and, consequently, lower underwriting fees. Studies show that industrial bond issues sold by shelf registration incur a cost of funds between 20 and 30 basis points lower than the cost of funds for comparable nonshelf offerings. All of these factors had an important impact on the longtime standing (number and size of underwritings) of the major securities firms. For example, Salomon Brothers, which had great expertise in the competitive bid area, increased its share of corporate underwriting activity at the expense of firms like Morgan Stanley, an old-line company with close ties to many corporations that specialized in negotiated underwritings (noncompetitive bidding) for its client base.

By the end of 1984, the shelf registration option had captured about half of the total negotiated debt market. The substitution of the shelf format for negotiated underwriting enhanced competition among a restricted few top-tier investment banking firms and lessened the cost of bringing a new issue to market. While underwriting spreads on shelf registration issues have been relatively thin, the use of bought deals or even small underwriting syndicates can preserve large profits for the participating securities dealers, assuming that the securities are sold quickly to avoid the risk of inventory losses. Since most of the sales of shelf-registered securities are to institutional investors, where underwriters face fixed selling costs, most of the underwriting spread is brought down to the bottom line in the form of profits.[1]

THE GARN-ST. GERMAIN DEPOSITORY INSTITUTIONS ACT OF 1982

Much of the Garn-St. Germain Depository Institutions Act (DIA) of 1982 was shaped by a desire to make S&Ls and savings banks viable. To that end, thrifts were given the scope to become ever so more like banks, but were explicitly exempted from regulation by the Federal Reserve.

The best known provision of the Garn-St. Germain Act was to offer two accounts free of interest rate ceilings: money market accounts (MMDAs) in December 1982 and super-NOW (SNOW) accounts in January 1983. These two deregulated accounts were both insured up to $100,000 and initially had minimum deposits of $2,500. A major difference between them was that the MMDA allowed only a limited number of transactions per month (six, of which no more than three could be checks), while the SNOW account offered unlimited checking transactions. Both gave depository institutions the weapons that they needed to compete against money market funds and other short-term money market instruments. In 1984, the DIA also abolished the interest rate differential under Regulation Q between commercial banks and savings associations.

Garn-St. Germain liberalized further the regulations governing thrift institution earning-asset portfolios, specifically with respect to commercial and consumer loans. Thrifts were also allowed to place up to 3 percent of their assets into a service company that could make equity investments in areas such as real estate development. These service organizations could sell their own debt and invest in a variety of activities. Thrifts were also permitted to offer demand deposit accounts when they were required as a result of business loans that were made and to offer NOW accounts to federal, state, and local governments.

In attempting to maintain a level playing field, the DIA also made service corporations more attractive vehicles for banks. By allowing savings and loans to make commercial loans and accept demand deposits, a salient difference between thrifts and commercial banks was eliminated. The definition of a commercial bank had to be changed from that of a financial institution that made commercial loans and accepted demand deposits to that of a financial institution that was insured by the FDIC. A financial institution that did not make commercial loans or did not offer demand deposits (a nonbank) was not considered a commercial bank and was not subject to regulation by the Federal Reserve. Garn-St. Germain provided emergency powers for three years to the FDIC, FSLIC, and FHLBB to assist troubled thrifts and banks. These powers included the authority to purchase the assets and liabilities of an insured institution, to extend aid in the form of emergency loans and contributions, and to approve the issuance of net worth certificates to improve the capital position of thrifts. The act also authorized mergers of banks with thrifts when either was failing and, under certain circumstances, interstate mergers between banks or between banks and thrifts. This provision was necessitated by the poor financial condition of the FSLIC and the troubled state of the thrift industry in general. The alternative of a payoff of depositors of troubled thrifts was to allow mergers with healthy banks or thrifts. Unfortunately, there were few healthy thrifts with which to merge the weak ones. Therefore, the Act permitted out-of-state or even interindustry mergers. The authority for the FDIC to provide direct assistance was extended to instances in which conditions in financial markets threatened a significant number of banks, a few combined banks with a large total of assets or liabilities, or the FDIC's insurance fund.

A principal focus of Garn-St.Germain was assistance to the thrift industry, which had deteriorated to unacceptably low ratios of capital to net worth. In addition to permitting all depository institutions to issue new MMDAs, the Act authorized

S&Ls to make nonresidential real estate loans and commercial loans and to issue variable-rate mortgages. The MMDA account has proved to be extremely popular with consumers who have reduced their passbook and demand deposit accounts to take advantage of the higher rates and liquidity available in MMDAs.

The insurance activities of bank holding companies were restricted by the DIA because of heavy pressure from insurance industry lobbyists. Holding companies were confined to underwriting and marketing insurance that would protect the loans of their bank and consumer finance subsidiaries. The DIA restricted the authority of the Federal Reserve to decide which activities of bank holding companies were permissible and which were impermissible.

The elimination of Regulation Q prior to changing the deposit insurance policy may have been a mistake, encouraging some weak banks to take greater risks. With no restrictions on rates paid depositors, and with identical insurance premiums for all insured banks, troubled banks often offered above-market rates to maintain deposit levels and made riskier (potentially higher yielding) loans to cover their additional costs. Even banks that were less inclined to take additional risks were coerced to offer above-market interest rates or see their deposit balances bid away.

Thrifts were permitted to buy commercial paper and corporate bonds, to write commercial mortgages, and to have up to 10 percent of their assets in the form of commercial loans. They were also permitted to make consumer loans. In May 1983, regulators allowed federally chartered S&Ls to invest up to 11 percent of their assets in junk bonds. Also, many state regulators broadened the range of allowable assets even more. Some regulators permitted direct investment in real estate, corporate equities, and subsidiary service companies.

"NONBANK BANKS"

A depository institution that provides commercial and consumer loans and offers all types of deposits except demand deposits, or a depository institution that offers all types of deposits, but does not offer commercial loans, was not legally defined as a commercial bank. Therefore, it was not subject to regulations enforced by the Bank Holding Company Act of 1956 or the 1970 amendment to the act.

The concept of a "nonbank bank" or a limited-service bank had been exploited to skirt the Douglas Amendment's restrictions on interstate banking and to provide a way for retail, industrial insurance companies and mutual funds to enter the commercial banking business. (Under the Bank Holding Company Act, they were forbidden to do so.) Commercial bank holding companies (e.g., Citicorp and Chase Manhattan Bank) have often created such "nonbank banks" in an effort to cross state lines and enter new markets. The "nonbank bank" appeared to offer commercial banks an escape route from the geographical and product line restriction that had imprisoned them. Indeed, this route was the means by which insurance, brokerage, and other companies had entered directly into the commercial banking business.[2]

To help slow down the growth of "nonbank banks," in 1984 the Federal Reserve broadened its definition of making commercial loans to include the purchase of commercial paper, commercial notes, and banker's acceptances. It also included interest-bearing checking accounts in the definition of demand deposits. These changes restricted "nonbank banks" and limited-service banks from investing in commercial paper or corporate securities and from offering NOW accounts. Dimension Financial sued the Federal Reserve, challenging its authority to broaden its definition of a bank. Todd Conover, then comptroller of the currency, announced a temporary moratorium on several hundred pending applications, in order to coerce Congress to "foster free and open debate" on the broader issues of deregulation. Paul Volker, then chairman of the Federal Reserve Board, opposed deregulation through "nonbank banks," fearing a loss of control over the money supply. He was supported by the Independent Bankers Association and the Conference of State Banking Supervisors, which feared the "concentration of banking resources in the hands of a few financial giants" and the potential demise of their highly profitable banking franchises. Conover and William Isaacs (then FDIC chairman) defended the "nonbank bank" loophole as a lever to coerce Congress to proceed with deregulation rationally.[3]

In January 1986, the United States Supreme Court ruled that the Federal Reserve had acted outside of its statutory authority in changing the definition of a commercial bank. The court ruled that "non-bank banks" were not subject to Federal Reserve regulation and granted them access to FDIC insurance. Within a few weeks of their authorization, close to a hundred applications for establishing "nonbank banks" were filed. Merrill Lynch, Prudential, Sears, JCPenney, and a few bank holding companies launched their own "nonbank banks" freely. Chief Justice of the Supreme Court Warren Burger stated that "there is much to be said for regulating financial institutions that are the functional equivalents of banks," but it is "a problem for Congress, and not the Board or the courts to address."[4]

1986 TAX REFORM ACT

Prior to 1986, commercial banks were permitted to establish loan-loss reserves as a percentage of their loan portfolio and to deduct allocations to the loss reserve from income. In addition, banks with loan growth were permitted to take deductions in excess of actual loan-loss experience, allowing a form of tax shelter. With the passage of the 1986 Tax Reform Act, all that changed. While banks with assets under $400 million may continue the practice, larger banks may now deduct only exactly what they charge off during a year. The Act also made ownership of municipal notes and bonds by commercial banks less attractive to the banks by limiting deductions to finance these issues. Banks may now deduct only 80 percent of the borrowing costs associated with buying municipal bonds issued for essential public purposes if the municipality issued less than $10 million in securities each year. Commercial banks lost the entire interest deduction on financing costs for new purchases of all other municipal bonds. The result has been that the larger banks, which once were among the major buyers of municipal issues, have chosen to redeploy their assets into other types of securities.

The 1986 Act also eliminated the investment tax credit that made certain types of bank leasing arrangements less attractive. Also, IRAs, a source of stable, long-term deposits for banks, were made less attractive by removing the tax deduction for high-income individuals who are covered by a retirement plan at work.

THE COMPETITIVE EQUALITY BANKING ACT OF 1987

In 1987, Congress passed the Competitive Equality Banking Act (CEBA) to attempt to address the solvency problems of the thrift industry, while placing a moratorium on new activities of banks and other financial institutions. With the rapidly increasing number of failing thrifts and the reluctance of stronger thrifts to acquire weaker ones without federal assistance, it did not take long for the FSLIC to run out of money. This prompted Congress to establish the Financing Corporation and authorize a $10.8 billion recapitalization bonding program to assist the FSLIC. According to some critics, the latter amount was barely enough to dispose of the insolvent thrifts that one would find "along the highway from the airport to downtown Dallas."[5] At the same time, FSLIC insurance rates were increased for thrifts, and FSLIC-insured institutions were forbidden from switching to FDIC insurance for one year. Financial institutions that switched after the one-year moratorium would be assessed a special "exit fee."

The legislation passed was inadequate to beef up the financial resources of the ailing FSLIC. The explanation for the failure to provide the FSLIC with adequate funds was the intense lobbying effort by the League of Savings Institutions, the thrift industry's leading trade association. The cost of these funds would have been borne by the S&L industry. Moreover, numerous technically insolvent S&Ls that were still in business did not want to provide the FSLIC with the resources to close them down. In addition, Congress buckled under to the lobbying pressure by adding a provision to the bill that directed the FHLBB to ease the treatment of troubled thrifts in economically depressed areas. This allowed thrifts that were in the deepest financial trouble to remain open. Of course, it was these institutions that were likely to take the greatest risks and, consequently, that were the most important to close.

Other provisions of the Competitive Equality Banking Act placed much tougher requirements and more restrictions on "nonbank banks," gave credit unions more flexibility in offering mortgage loans, and provided regulators with permanent authority to merge troubled thrifts and banks. The legislation prohibited the creation of new "nonbank banks" for one year and limited the asset growth of existing "nonbank banks" to 7 percent annually. The CEBA also "grandfathered" the existing 160 "nonbank banks" and authorized the purchase by nondepository firms of troubled thrifts with assets of $500 million or more.

Congress put a halt to further "nonbank bank" expansion by subjecting the parent companies of those banks to the same regulatory restrictions that traditional banking organizations face. The Competitive Equality Banking Act also imposed a moratorium on bank expansion into nonbanking activities (specifically insurance, real estate, or securities) until March 1988. The purpose of the moratorium was to give Congress time to review the amount of freedom that commercial banks should be given. Even legislators who opposed allowing banks into the securities business agreed that the Glass-Steagall Act of 1933 was no longer adequate for regulating banks.

A final provision of the CEBA sped up the process of collecting funds in the check-clearing process. Banks were required to make funds available in one day for local checks that were deposited and in no more than four days for nonlocal checks. Some banks were taking an inordinate amount of time to allow depositors access to the checks they deposited. Banks would send the checks through the clearing process, making funds available only upon knowing that the deposited checks were good. However, in some cases, the time lags were inexcusable because banks were using the cleared funds of customers for a few days and earning interest on them without crediting the customers' accounts.

The CEBA plus Federal Reserve interpretations of the law have allowed banks to expand into investment bank underwriting activities (with the exception of underwriting corporate stocks), as long as these activities do not constitute a large portion of their business and as long as they occur in a subsidiary of the bank holding company. Essentially, a "fire wall" must exist between the underwriting activity and the bank depository function.

Finally, Congress redefined a bank as an organization that is a member of the FDIC. The result of this legal maneuvering is to confuse the public over what is or is not a bank. This is especially true since the FSLIC was abolished in 1989, when the insurance of thrift deposits was handed over to the FDIC. Under U.S. law, a bank is defined not by what it does, but in terms of which government agency insures its deposits.

The long delay in the enactment of the CEBA was moderately costly. However, earlier enactment of the bill with much larger sums would not have reduced the costs of the S&L debacle by any considerable amount. This was because most of the bad loans had already been made and the huge losses were already imbedded in the system, but not yet recognized.[6] "As late as 1987 Congress had thought that all thrift operators were Jimmy Stewart in *It's a Wonderful Life*; in 1989 the Congress thought they all were Warren Beatty in *Bonnie and Clyde*."

FINANCIAL INSTITUTIONS REFORM, RECOVERY, AND ENFORCEMENT ACT OF 1989

In 1989, Congress enacted a major overhaul in the system under which thrift institutions had been regulated for more than half a century. Because the problems of many savings and loan associations in the 1980s exhausted the resources of the FSLIC, Congress attempted to rescue the industry through the FIRRE Act. The act tightened capital and supervisory standards, placed the industry's primary regulator, now the Office of Thrift Supervision, under direct control of the U.S. Treasury, located the insurance fund under the administration of the FDIC, allowed bank holding company acquisitions of thrifts, changed the laws governing thrift powers, and authorized the creation of the Resolution Trust Corporation to close or merge problematic S&Ls.

While the DIDMCA and the Garn-St. Germain Act widened the powers of thrifts, the failure of hundreds of savings associations in the late 1980s (in part related to the abuse of these new powers) led to the reimposition of substantial restrictions on assets, through the FIRRE Act. FIRRE provided the most favorable regulatory treatment only to those savings institutions that held at least 70 percent of their assets in approved forms, such as housing and housing-related assets. The Act stipulated that at least 55 percent of an S&L's total assets must be in core assets—housing and mobile home loans, mortgage-backed securities, and certain government agency notes. Noncore assets were limited to 15 percent of assets and included personal and education loans, investments in service corporations, mortgage loans to be resold, and select community development loans. This favorable treatment allowed savings and loans to exclude an 8-percent allowance for bad debts from their taxable income and, consequently, gave thrifts a lower federal income tax rate than commercial banks. Previously, the percentage of assets in "qualified thrift investments" was just 60 percent, allowing for a larger number of qualified housing-related investment instruments. While thrifts still have tax advantages over commercial banks that compensate them for portfolio restrictions, banks have much broader lending powers and investment opportunities that allow for greater diversification of their portfolios. The S&Ls' portfolio restrictions prevent them from employing diversification strategies that actually might reduce the risk of their portfolios. The wisdom of the restrictions is therefore questionable, since it can be argued that a lack of diversification contributed to the problems at many failed S&Ls. In addition, the FIRRE Act banned the purchase of junk bonds by thrifts and called for the gradual elimination of all non-investment-grade bonds from their portfolios by July 1, 1994. An exception is made for mutual S&Ls, which may acquire junk bonds, but only through separately capitalized subsidiaries and only for certain bonds. In addition, a savings and loan association can transfer any junk bonds to a holding company affiliate or to its holding company in return for a "qualified" note.

The FIRRE Act also attempted to strengthen the net worth (capital) requirements of thrifts by requiring them to hold core capital equal to at least 3 percent of their assets in order to remain in good standing with regulators. (Core capital is the sum of common equity, noncumulative perpetual preferred stock, and minority interests in consolidated subsidiaries, minus most intangibles except mortgage-servicing rights and qualifying supervisory "goodwill".) The Act provided for the complete phasing out of all "goodwill" from required capital by 1995. In addition, it required compliance with a new minimum 1.5-percent ratio of tangible capital to assets.

(Tangible capital is core capital minus supervisory "goodwill" and all other intangibles, except qualifying purchased mortgage-servicing rights.) Also, the Act established a minimum risk-based capital requirement for thrifts.

FIRRE established tougher penalties for managers and directors of dishonest thrifts, set tougher appraisal standards, and provided for more vigorous enforcement of regulations and laws related to the operations of insured financial institutions. Under it, regulators can bring civil or criminal suits in response to perceived violations of the rules, and regulators are given the ability to levy civil money penalties for violations.[7]

FIRRE overhauled the thrift industry's regulatory system, tightened up capital and supervisory standards, and placed the industry's primary regulator—the Federal Home Loan Bank Board, now called the Office of Thrift Supervision (OTS)—under direct control of the U.S. Treasury. It was thought that placing the OTS within the Treasury Department would insulate the regulator from industry pressures and from the lobbying efforts of individual congressmen and senators. The OTS charters all federal savings associations and is their principal regulator. Unlike the OCC (which also resides in the U.S. Treasury Department), the OTS retains authority over both federally and state-chartered S&Ls, although the FDIC is authorized to take enforcement action against S&Ls, even over OTS objection. The FDIC was also given the power to terminate insurance for S&Ls. The board of directors of the FDIC was expanded from three to five members, including the comptroller of the currency and the director of the OTS.

The powers of the FHLBB were stripped away because it was subject to extensive influence by the thrift industry and had not adequately protected deposit insurance funds. Many have suggested that the FHLBB's dual roles as thrift chartering agent and overseer of the deposit insurance fund created conflicts of interest that led to a policy that enabled insolvent thrifts to continue to operate and increased the magnitude of the insurance crisis. The $50 billion of funding provided for in FIRRE is likely to be grossly inadequate.

There is another reason given for abolishing the FHLBB. Congress and the Bush Administration were angry at the FHLBB because of the agency's earlier lax regulations, a difference in estimates of the likely cost of the bailout, the agency's coziness with and championing of the thrift industry, and the efforts of particular S&Ls to have individual congressmen and senators intercede on their behalf in specific regulatory matters. Congress was also angry at the thrift industry, whose members they felt were directly responsible for the insolvencies. "The Congress believed it was 'bailing out the thrifts,' rather than being asked to satisfy its obligations on an insurance arrangement that earlier Congresses had either encouraged or willingly ignored."[8] Therefore, Congress expected the thrifts to bear part of the costs and to endure the appropriate punishment. Hence, another part of FIRRE's punishment and revenue-increasing effort was to tax the regional FHLBs' net worth and future dividends.

The FIRRE Act also protected the integrity of the deposit insurance funds by curtailing activities at insured institutions that posed unacceptable risks. The bill gives OTS more authority to restrict activities at undercapitalized S&Ls. For example, OTS can prohibit undercapitalized thrifts from accepting brokered deposits and can circumscribe the growth rate of the assets of those thrifts. These restrictions limit the extent to which an ailing thrift can add to the potential liability of the deposit insurance fund. In the past, regulatory accounting techniques and other means of capital forbearance enabled institutions with zero or negative net worth to continue to operate. However, under FIRRE, new capital standards are to be applied strictly to all thrifts.

The Act consolidated management of the bank and thrift deposit insurance funds under the FDIC. While the administration of the savings association insurance fund and the bank insurance fund were merged, the bank and savings and loan insurance funds were not commingled. The FSLIC was renamed the Savings Association Insurance Fund (SAIF), while the commercial bank insurance fund was renamed the Bank Insurance Fund (BIF). Essentially, the jurisdiction over the thrift insurance fund was taken away from the old thrift regulators at the FSLIC and placed in the hands of the FDIC. In that way, the regulators are less subject to political influence, which was a serious problem at the FSLIC and the FHLBB. In addition, FIRRE broadened the powers of the FDIC to close insolvent thrifts and banks promptly. The Act authorizes the FDIC to step in as a conservator or receiver for any insured bank or savings and loan. While the Garn-St. Germain Act permitted banks to acquire failing thrifts, FIRRE permits banks to acquire healthy savings and loans, encouraging further consolidation of the thrift industry. In addition, the law allows thrifts to convert to commercial banks if they can meet banking standards. The 12 regional Federal Home Loan Banks continue to exist and can still make advances (loans) to their member savings institutions, despite the fact that these regional FHLBs were also subject to extensive influence by local and regional S&L leaders and trade associations.

Passage of the FIRRE Act led to the consolidation and shrinkage of the thrift industry because of (1) forced mergers and closings, (2) the inability of some thrifts to meet the new capital requirements, (3) the prospects of bank holding company acquisitions of thrifts, and (4) the chartering of some thrifts as banks.

FIRRE established housing programs through funding from the regional Federal Home Loan Banks to member institutions for long-term, low- and moderate-income, owner-occupied, and affordable rental housing. Each Federal Home Loan bank was required to subsidize the interest rate on advances to member banks engaged in this activity. These advances must be used to finance home ownership by families with incomes at or below 80 percent of the median income in the member institution's area or to finance the purchase, construction, or rehabilitation of rental housing, of which at least 20 percent of such units will be occupied by or available to low-income households.[9]

The FIRRE Act also established the Federal Housing Finance Board to replace the FHLBB as the regulator and supervisor of the 12 district FHL banks. There are five directors of the board, four of whom are private citizens appointed by the president and subject to confirmation by the Senate. The other director is the secretary of the Department of Housing and Urban Development.

Kane (1989) has argued that the Bush plan from which FIRRE evolved was not based on a comprehensive theory of how the thrift industry losses occurred and that inaction and inadequate FSLIC reserves allowed the losses to grow large. Because FIRRE failed to correct the incentive-incompatibility problems in the current deposit-insurance contract that caused the thrift crisis, says Kane, there is a high probability that taxpayers will be faced with another deposit insurance crisis and an additional huge tax burden to bail out the weakest members of the thrift industry.

Providing more money to continue the closure and disposal of insolvent thrifts was vital, but limiting the borrowing to $50 billion was an error. The Bush administration should have educated the Congress to the fact that the moneys spent to clean up the insolvent thrifts were in reality the honoring of the U.S. government's insurance obligations and had to be spent. They were not discretionary spending on the part of Congress.[10] "The moneys extended were going, and will go, to satisfy the U.S. government's obligation to insured depositors, either directly in liquidation payouts to depositors or indirectly by finding acquirers to assume the obligations to depositors."[11]

An important problem is that the new capital requirements are based on book-value ratios, but in a liquidation or reorganization, book values are irrelevant. The cost to the insurance fund in a liquidation is the difference between the prices the S&L's assets and liabilities can be sold for in the market. An emphasis on book value increases the likelihood that S&L portfolios will appear fine on paper, while concealing weak market-value net worth and huge potential claims on the deposit insurance fund. Although FIRRE makes it easier for the FDIC and OTS to close thrifts that are insolvent according to their book value, clever accounting may make it possible for thrifts that are insolvent according to their market value to continue to operate, pursuing high-risk strategies that entail growing liabilities for the deposit insurer. Also, the growth limits, asset restrictions, and other sanctions contained in FIRRE are all based on book-value measures of capital deficiency. Hence, they suffer from the same weaknesses as the closure rules. These problems with book valuation implicitly allow even S&Ls that are insolvent according to their book value to continue to operate, since, at the discretion of the director of the OTS, a thrift that violates the new capital standards may be granted an exemption from the asset growth and activity restrictions of FIRRE by filing an acceptable "capital plan." While this plan must, of course, deal with the need for additional capital at the S&L and must describe the methods that the insured S&L will use to raise new funds, the provision leaves the door open to continued capital forbearance.[12]

The thrift industry has been undergoing a process of conversion from the mutual form of organization toward that of a stock company since the 1960s. This movement accelerated during the 1980s, as did the shift from state-chartered to federally chartered thrifts.

In an interesting move, the FSLIC retained warrants equal to about 20 percent of ownership in the transfer of some insolvent thrifts in 1988–1989. These warrants have multiple benefits for the insurer. First, they will give the insurance fund a 20-percent share in any gains earned by the thrifts. Also, they should reduce the expected gains from any risk taking on the part of thrifts and may even reduce somewhat their incentives to take risks.[13] The issue is presented here only to show that not all regulatory actions were bad.

Still, one of the major culprits in the S&L crisis was the structure of the federal deposit insurance system. By failing to reform that structure, FIRRE increased the probability that taxpayers would be called upon to share in excessive losses. The act also increased supervisory and regulatory constraints on activities for both weak and strong financial institutions. This, in turn, has boosted costs and lowered the profitability of some institutions and has put some money-center banks at a competitive disadvantage with respect to less regulated non-U.S. banks and other financial institutions. For example, the recently introduced risk-based capital standards are practically unrelated to portfolio risk and so should increase the costs of capital to risky as well as more conservatively run depository institutions. The long-run issue that is not adequately addressed by FIRRE (with the exception of requiring higher capital levels) is how to restructure the system in order to eliminate the incentives to take on more risk.[14]

SECURITIES ENFORCEMENT REMEDIES ACT OF 1990

In 1990, Congress approved the Securities Enforcement Remedies Act, which gave the SEC the authority to impose monetary sanctions and to handle many cases within the agency that previously had been taken to the federal courts. The legislation allows the agency to hear a wider variety of actions, including illegal, insider trading cases and cases of stock manipulation. It has led the SEC to write procedures to permit the administrative judges to consider cases traditionally reserved for federal district judges. Historically, most cases before the administrative judges have been smaller actions involving securities dealers, brokers, and investment advisers accused of such offenses as churning accounts and not keeping books and records in proper order. In the past, the SEC's lawyers fared much better before the administrative law judge, where they almost always have won, than they did in the federal courts, where they succeeded in only two-thirds of the cases adjudicated in 1990.

THE COMPREHENSIVE DEPOSIT INSURANCE REFORM AND TAXPAYER PROTECTION ACT OF 1991 AND THE RTC REFINANCING, RESTRUCTURING, AND IMPROVEMENT ACT OF 1991

After much haggling between the U.S. Treasury and Congress and between and among various congressional committees, internal warfare among the various bank trade associations and between big and small banks, and opposition from insurance, securities, and consumer groups, Congress refused to adopt the Bush administration proposals to overhaul the banking industry. The bill passed by Congress would not allow banks to establish branch offices nationwide, to affiliate with commercial companies, to expand their ability to underwrite securities, or to increase their powers to underwrite and sell insurance. Also jettisoned was a Senate amendment to slash credit card interest rates. However, the new banking legislation bolstered the bank deposit insurance fund, tightened bank regulation (requiring regulators in many cases to seize weak banks before they failed), gave the Federal Reserve new authority to monitor and control the operations of foreign banks in the United States, limited the FDIC's ability to reimburse uninsured deposits over $100,000 after 1994, and gave brokerage firms access to the discount window. While the bill was stripped bare of key measures to boost bank profits, the banking industry was able to fend off some of the hostile legislation and most feared proposals: reduced levels of FDIC insurance coverage; restrictions on existing authority to sell insurance, bonds, and stock; and caps on credit card interest rates. Despite the passage of a banking bill, however, Congress did not address the root causes of the industry's decline or the failure of more than 1,000 banks in the period from 1985 to 1991.

The legislation gave the bank deposit insurance fund an additional $70 billion in borrowing authority and increased the amount the FDIC could borrow from the U.S. Treasury to cover the cost of bank failures to $30 billion from $5 billion. The principal of the loans, plus interest, would be repaid by premiums that banks pay on domestic deposits over the next 15 years. In addition, the legislation permits the FDIC to borrow about $45 billion for working capital needs. The borrowed funds and the interest would be repaid from the sale of the assets of failed banks. The bill requires that the FDIC build reserves of at least $1.25 for each $100 of deposits. To help in this task and to help repay the loans, the FDIC raised insurance premiums to a minimum risk-based premium of 23 cents for each $100 of domestic deposits. (See Chapter 7.)

The FDIC's ability to impose the "too big to fail doctrine," whereby the agency can reimburse uninsured depositors with over $100,000 and foreign depositors, would be sharply limited after 1994. The Federal Reserve's ability to keep banks alive with extended loans from its discount window would also be restricted. Additionally, only the best capitalized banks would be able to offer insured brokered deposits and insured accounts established under employee pension plans. The bill also gave the Federal Reserve Board new authority to police foreign bank activities in the United States. This section of the legislation was in partial response to the problems encountered with Bank of Credit and Commerce International (BCCI). The Federal Reserve will now have the power to review the establishment of any branch, agency, or commercial lending unit of a foreign bank. It will also supervise representative offices, as well as full subsidiaries or branches. The agency will be able to close foreign bank offices for violating the law or for unsound practices. In addition, it will have the power to approve any purchase of more than 5 percent of the shares of a U.S. bank by a foreign bank, even if the foreign bank operates only an agency or a branch in the United States. Also, overseas banks that accept deposits of less than $100,000 in their U.S. branches will be required to set up separate subsidiaries, which would require their own capital, rather than drawing on the capital of the parent.

In order to offer banks an incentive to conduct safer lending and investment practices, the FDIC will charge higher premiums to banks engaged in risky lending practices, compared with banks engaging in safer practices. A new system of risk-based insurance premiums, rather than flat premiums based upon domestic deposit levels, must be in operation by 1994.

Regulators will be required to set five capital levels or ratios by means of which to classify banks and thrifts, from critically undercapitalized to well capitalized. Regulatory action would be required as capital levels fell to an agreed-upon ratio or category. The bill also requires regulators to perform annual, on-site bank examinations, place limits on real estate lending by banks, tighten bank auditing requirements, and disclose clearly and uniformly the interest rate, fees, and other terms of savings and transaction accounts. In addition, regulators must draft a new set of noncapital measures of bank safety, such as underwriting standards on loans, by December 1, 1993.

The new legislation also protected the accounts held by charitable organizations at Freedom National Bank of Harlem and Community Bank of Staten Island with depository insurance, even though the deposits exceeded $100,000. In addition, the federal government would provide loan guarantees to assist depositors at Rhode Island credit unions and banks that collapsed and were not FDIC insured. Further, the bill insured that securities fraud lawsuits, like those against Charles Keating and Michael Milken, that were filed before a June 1991 Supreme Court ruling restricting the statute of limitations would not be affected by that ruling. A truth-in-savings provision was aimed at providing consumers with uniform and conspicuous disclosure, in plain language, of all fees and interest rates paid. Under the Act, the FDIC must give low-income people the first chance to purchase repossessed homes inherited from failed banks.

The legislation relaxed the "qualified thrift lender test" for savings and loan associations by allowing them to invest more of their funds outside of housing-related areas. On the insurance front, the Act protected the rights of Citicorp's Delaware Bank and two affiliates of Bankers Trust in Delaware to continue to underwrite insurance, while barring other bank holding companies from establishing new affiliates to do the same. The bill overrode Delaware law by scaling back the powers of state-chartered banks to those of national banks, which can underwrite credit, title, and debt cancellation insurance, as well as annuities. While the new legislation did not provide blanket authority to broker insurance that many had asked for, it also did not roll back existing powers. The 15 states that permitted banks they charter to sell insurance could continue to do so. The comptroller of the currency had previously opened the door for national banks to sell many types of insurance products, such as fixed-rate annuities.

Congress also approved a further $25 billion for the savings and loan bailout. Since 1989, the RTC has spent $80 billion to pay off 19 million depositors in nearly 600 thrifts in 45 states. As many as 300 additional savings and loans still must be closed. Because of a lack of funds, the RTC had slowed down its liquidations of S&Ls, adding substantially to the ultimate cost of the bailout. Legislators recognized that additional moneys would be required to help fund about \$220–\$300 billion in losses, plus billions more in interest expenses, but took no additional funding action prior to the election in the fall of 1992. The 1991 legislation also streamlined the top-heavy bureaucracy of the RTC, combining two separate boards into one seven-member board called the Thrift Depositor Protection Oversight Board, with the secretary of the U.S. Treasury serving as chairman. Other board members included the chairmen of the Federal Reserve Board of Governors and the FDIC, the director of the OTS, the chief executive officer of the RTC, and two members from the private sector. The bill provided for government financing for low-income buyers of homes held by the RTC and gave nonprofit groups and local governments the first right to buy some RTC real estate. A final item would permit state-chartered savings banks to continue to make some investments in equities if state laws allow it. Such investments were banned under the 1989 savings and loan bailout bill. As of year-end 1991, as many as 300 additional S&Ls had to be closed. The bill also increased borrowing for working capital, to \$160 billion from \$125 billion. Unlike the S&L bill, the banking measure is not a direct taxpayer bailout, since the FDIC is required to pay back the borrowed funds within 15 years.

COMMENTS ON THE DEPOSIT INSURANCE REFORM AND TAXPAYER PROTECTION ACT OF 1991

Despite the backing of the Bush Administration, the Treasury banking reform bill was chewed apart on its way through Congress by lobbyists for the insurance and securities industries, who feared the likes of the money-center banks and the big west coast banking giants. In addition to the opposition from nonbank financial organizations and trade associations, there was much division within the ranks of the bankers. Many of the smaller banks were opposed to nationwide branch banking. The small independent banks also felt that much of the bill (e.g., powers to trade in securities and insurance underwriting) was irrelevant to them. The grudging congressional mood was predictable after the thrift debacle and the powerful lobbying efforts by nonbankers to protect their own turfs. Also, the small regional banks had such an effective hold on their local representatives that they were able to get members of the House to block the Senate proposal for branching across state lines.[15]

Some representatives felt that the additional powers sought by banks brought the possibility of additional risk and the creation of new opportunities to lose money. Others felt that increased deregulation could lead the banks to suffer the same consequences as the thrifts, which have proved to be a regulatory and congressional embarrassment. For some, the banking bill was viewed as a potential "son of savings and loan debacle."[16] There was the fear that passing the administration bill with its enhanced banking powers could lead to a taxpayer bailout of the BIF similar in magnitude to the savings and loan fiasco. Representatives kept overlooking the fact that banks needed the additional powers to make more money and thus stem the losses that led to taxpayer bailouts. According to Rep. Barney Frank (D-MA),

"Voting the money was so controversial that what we thought was the engine driving the train turned out to be the anchor dragging down the ship."[17]

The Bush Administration did a poor job of selling the need for a broad, comprehensive bank overhaul, even though banking reform was called its "top domestic priority." Congress was never told why it should vote to pass the bill. The administration also failed to convince representatives that the new proposals would permit banks to grow stronger and that this would eventually lead to a strong economy, eliminating many of the problems associated with the BIF. For example, Treasury officials never pointed out that nationwide banking provides a wider geographic spread that should lead to less cyclicality in earnings through geographic and industrial diversification of the loan portfolio, which should in turn strengthen the health and stability of the banking industry. They also never pointed out to Congress that J.P. Morgan, which is a AAA-rated, extremely profitable money-center bank, has transformed itself into a European-style universal bank. J.P. Morgan combines investment and commercial banking and trading functions in a highly successful banking operation. The following salient question was not even considered: "What type of financial system would make our nation more competitive?"[18] The Treasury assumed that the need to recapitalize the BIF would act as a catalyst to modernize the banking system, allowing strong banks to set up nationwide branch systems, become financial superplayers, and affiliate with commercial or industrial companies.

In the background of the political battle was a longstanding hostility toward banks in the U.S. According to Robert Litan of the Brookings Institute, "Banks have historically never been popular creatures in American society. . . . And the rising costs of bank failures make banks look increasingly like savings and loans. Savings and loans are skunks. So banks become more skunk-like."[19] Big banks have few friends and are often seen as hostile institutions that refuse to lend to ordinary individuals, while freely making loans to third-world countries, real estate speculators, and takeover artists.[20]

While the Federal Reserve Board opposed some parts of the Treasury plan, Board Governor John LaWare testified before Congress in April 1991 that the agency believed that the proposal to allow bank affiliates to enter the insurance and securities businesses and to operate nationwide branch systems "would strengthen the ability of U.S. banks to serve the public more effectively." He also indicated that the board supported the thrust of the Treasury's proposal to limit the scope of deposit insurance and to strengthen bank regulation by placing more emphasis on higher levels of bank capital or net worth. LaWare cautioned that reductions in deposit insurance might cause a modest movement of funds by some particular risk-sensitive large depositors from small banks to large banks thought to have more government protection.

Banking experts Karen Shaw, Edward Furash, H. E. Heinemann, and Charles Peabody were all critical of Congress' failure to pass substantial and much needed banking reform. According to Shaw, president of the Institute for Strategic Development, "This legislation creates a system of arbitrary, Draconian and inflexible criteria designed to ensure that no bank will ever fail again. . . . In pursuit of this Quixotic goal, the legislation will ensure that few banks will ever fail, none will ever prosper."[21] Furash, a banking industry consultant, felt that the efforts of Congress represented "A Darwinian solution—only the strongest will survive. . . . The bottom line is the bill doesn't help the outlook for banking one bit. It ignores 20 years of decaying earnings. . . . Congress walked away from the worst financial crises the country has faced since the 1930s. Congress said, 'We're so scared of the public reaction to bank failures and the possibility of a bailout and a replay of the thrift industry fiasco that we don't want to give you anything . . . it's survival of the fittest. . . .' All this is not going to help the economy. A healthy economy requires healthy banks . . . but you can't reform the banking system until you reform Congress."[22] Furash is joined by Heinemann, Ladenburg Thalman economist, who said that "it's really a tragedy because it's very clear that fundamental reform is essential."[23] Heinemann also felt that the moral hazard problem associated with deposit insurance remained: "With no reason to worry about the safety of their deposits . . . Americans have no reason to reward good bankers and punish bad ones." According to Peabody, Kidder Peabody bank stock analyst, "You're going to find that these rules and regulations are going to force banks to think a lot more about whether they want to fund high-risk credits. The problems in the real estate industry may be compounded as there may be increased difficulty in rolling over existing loans or obtaining new credit. Bankers are likely to become more gun-shy about taking risks, desiring to avoid errors of the 1980s. This could dampen economic activity in the first half of the 1990s."[24]

While Robert Litan agreed with Peabody about the impact of tighter credit standards by banks and the potential damage to short-term economic growth, he felt that the legislation would strengthen banks over time: "As taxpayers we should feel that this is better than nothing at all. We got new legislation to promote sounder banking."[25]

The new law will force regulators to move more rapidly in dealing with undercapitalized banks. Supervision will increase as a bank's capital declines. Regulators will move more quickly to suspend dividend payments and to change the management of troubled institutions. Banks will be closed when their capital falls below 2 percent of assets, rather than waiting until they are insolvent. Government regulators can freeze or place caps on growth, stop or reduce dividend payouts, and curb executive salaries and bonuses if a bank falls short of certain requirements for capital, asset quality, and earnings. This would prevent government dithering, which at times has permitted bad situations to get worse. Also, weaker banks will be looking for stronger merger partners if they are unable to raise new equity capital, which will add to the consolidation trend in American banking. The problem, oddly enough, is that federal bank regulators (as opposed to S&L regulators) have a decent track record of allowing shaky banks to rejuvenate themselves without tapping the bank insurance fund. Leonora Cross, OCC official, points out that if these tougher standards had been in effect when BankAmerica got into trouble in the mid-1980s, that bank would not be here today. BankAmerica is now one of the best run and most profitable banks in the country. Some analysts plead for a little more regulatory flexibility or discretion. On the one hand, we don't want laws that are too rigid for a new era of financial services. On the other, the bill's structure makes sense in curbing the Federal Reserve's lending to ailing banks through the discount window. Federal Reserve Chairman Alan Greenspan has agreed that if the Federal Reserve wants to lend money to a bank for more than 60 days, either he or the bank's top regulator must certify that the bank isn't failing. If the bank fails, the Federal Reserve would have to reimburse the FDIC for any losses caused by discount window loans. The impact of this agreement could force the Federal Reserve to back away from its "too big to fail" stance of keeping the largest banks alive at all costs.[26]

Frederic S. Mishkin, of the Columbia University Graduate School of Business, felt that the Treasury plan did not go far enough in advocating comprehensive market-value accounting information that would let regulators know quickly whether a bank was falling below its capital requirements so that prompt corrective action could be taken. This strategy would also prevent losses to the insurance fund and taxpayers, deter "bet-the-bank" strategies of excessive risk taking, and make it harder for regulators to hide insolvencies. Mishkin also felt that the Treasury did not pay enough attention to the incentives of regulators to engage in regulatory forbearance. He favored a rule-like regulatory scheme that would coerce regulators to take corrective action as soon as a bank's capital declined below a trigger level. Mishkin believed that the positive factors of the Treasury plan were the provisions to strengthen the role of capital in bank regulation, improve supervision, implement risk-based deposit insurance, remove impediments to nationwide banking, and reduce risk taking on the part of depository institutions. He stated that "even if some or most of the provisions are not passed by Congress, the Treasury plan should stimulate debate that hopefully will lead to a healthier, more efficient banking system."[27]

ENDNOTES

1. S. Hayes, *Wall Street and Regulation* (Boston: Harvard Business School Press, 1987), p. 131.

2. Ibid., p. 49.

3. Ibid., pp. 50–51.

4. Ibid., p. 51.

5. L. J. White, *The S&L Debacle* (New York: Oxford Press, 1991), p. 147.

6. Ibid., p. 261.

7. Ibid., pp. 218–219.

8. Ibid., pp. 180–181.

9. J. R. Barth, *The Great Savings and Loan Debacle* (Washington, DC: American Enterprise Institute Press, 1991) p. 84.

10. White, p. 183.

11. Ibid., p. 160.

12. J. A. Neuberger, "How to Close Troubled Banks" (Federal Reserve Bank of San Francisco, December 7, 1990), p. 2.

13. White, p. 219.

14. A. Eisenbeis, "Restructuring Banking," in *Restructuring the American Financial System,* ed. G. G. Kaufman (Boston: Kluwer Academic Publishers, 1990), pp. 28–29.

15. *Financial Times,* November 29, 1991, p. 18.

16. Ibid.

17. K. H. Bacon, "Cracking Down: The New Banking Law Toughens Regulations, Some Say Too Much," *The Wall Street Journal,* November 29, 1991, p. A8.

18. M. C. Jacobs, *New York Times,* November 8, 1991, p. 15.

19. Bacon, p. 1.

20. Ibid.

21. Ibid.

22. Ibid.

23. H. E. Heinemann, *Heinemann Economics* 7, no. 12 (June 10, 1991), pp. 7–8.

24. Bacon, pp. A1, 8.

25. Ibid., p. 1.

26. C. Yang and M. McNamee, "Reform or a Crackdown on Banking," *Business Week,* July 15, 1991, p. 123.

27. F. Mishkin, "An Evaluation of the Treasury Plan for Banking Reform," *Journal for Economic Perspective* 6, no. 11 (Winter 1992), pp. 133–151.

5 Regulation of the Insurance Industry

The case for federal regulation of insurance company solvency is not compelling. Federal intervention could set the stage for significant, inefficient expansion in government guarantees of insurer obligations. What would promote efficiency is the greater reliance on market discipline that would be induced by reducing guaranty fund protection for commercial insurance buyers. Holding the line on guaranty fund protection, and, if possible, reducing its scope, is probably the single most important step that can be taken to ensure the financial integrity of the insurance industry.

Additional government control over insurance rates is not needed. It would be likely to produce significant inefficiency, including higher claim costs. Instead, rates should be deregulated, and insurance affordability problems should be addressed by measures that reduce claim costs in efficient ways. Finally, changing the insurance industry's antitrust exemption will not reduce insolvencies, make insurance more affordable, or dampen volatility in prices and availability. It could make these problems much worse.

R. W. Kopcke and R. E. Randall, "Public Policy and Property-Liability Insurance,"
The Financial Condition and Regulation of Insurance Companies

BACKGROUND

The first insurance company, in what is now the United States, was founded in Charleston, South Carolina, in 1735. The insurance industry grew rapidly and haphazardly during the 1800s. There was little regulation. In the early years of the 19th century, state regulation of life insurance in the United States had been almost totally unknown. In the 1840s, Elizer Wright, a Massachusetts schoolteacher, newspaper editor, and abolitionist, became concerned with the rather arbitrary methods used by most life insurance companies in calculating their reserves. Wright compiled a series of net valuation tables that showed what reserves should be held at the end of the year during the life of various policies. Wright argued that life insurance companies should be legally obligated to maintain adequate reserves, and he lobbied this version of his legal reserve principle through the Massachusetts legislature. This, plus Wright's appointment in 1858 as head of the Massachusetts state insurance department, marks the beginning of effective state regulation of life insurance in this country. Within a decade, 35 states had established special insurance departments or delegated the supervision of insurance to an official specifically appointed for that purpose.

A system of independent insurance agents developed along with intense price competition. The price competition seemed to contribute to the volatility of earnings among property/casualty insurers and the instability and frequent insolvencies that characterized the industry. A combination of unrestricted growth, frequent failures, price fixing, and unethical practices increased public dissatisfaction with the insurance industry. This attracted the attention of some "muckrakers." During the summer of 1905, the Armstrong Congressional investigation revealed numerous improprieties, mismanagement, and influence peddling in the life insurance industry. Many industry leaders were shamed when interrogated by Charles Evans Hughes. New York and several other states responded with legislation that increased the responsibilities of insurance commissioners. A few years later, the Merritt Commission investigated problems of fire insurance in New York State. Consequently, New York passed a law to permit "action in concert in the fixing of fire insurance rates." The problem with the legislation was that it protected insurance companies from excessive competition more than it protected consumers from excessive insurance premiums.[1]

Under state regulation, the practice of price fixing by private rate bureaus became widespread, and immunity from antitrust persecution was assured. However, the Supreme Court ruled in 1944 that insurance contracts were interstate commerce and that price fixing violated the Sherman Act. Congress and President Roosevelt quickly approved the McCarran-Ferguson Act (Public Law 15) in 1945 (under intense insurance industry lobbying and state insurance regulatory pressures). The law assured cartelization, endorsed the status quo, and provided federal antitrust authority. Eventually, 44 states adopted prior approval laws that permitted coordination of rate setting for liability insurance under state supervision.[2]

Lower Cost Underwriters

Direct-writing insurers, such as State Farm and Allstate, used their lower distribution costs to underprice competitors and grow rapidly during the 1960s. However, they needed freedom from the rate bureaus. They were joined by other low-cost underwriters who desired to have rates more responsive to inflation and loss experience. As inflation increased in the late 1960s, insurance rates began to climb, leaving most state insurance commissioners dissatisfied with the system of prior approval. Although property/casualty insurers appeared to have excess capacity, the inflexible pricing that was related to standard, average operating margins contributed to localized shortages of various types of higher risk coverage, such as medical malpractice insurance and liability insurance for members of certain types of corporate boards of directors. Surprisingly, the property/casualty industry's return on net worth was still lower than either industrials or utilities.[3]

California, New York, and Massachusetts

California had never adopted the prior-approval model of regulation; although rate bureaus existed to pool data, more than 50 percent of the California insurers offered prices below bureau rates. In addition, the frequency of insurance failure was no greater in California than in other states. New York adopted a competitive pricing law in 1969 on a four-year trial basis. It still regulated maximum rates, but declared concerted rate fixing by the companies to be illegal. New York State insurance prices did not jump up, profits did not increase relative to those of other states, and the industry did not become significantly more concentrated. As a matter of fact, prices started to fall in real terms. In addition, the rate of nominal increases dropped below rates of prior-approval states, and the availability of insurance coverage improved, as did product quality.[4]

The National Association of Insurance Commissioners (NAIC) issued a report in 1974 that contained the statement that "the insurance industry [was] earnestly advocating the enactment of open competition laws . . . a classical reversal of historical positions."[5] The success of the New York State experiment led to a wave of conversions to competitive rate making. Open competition prevailed in 17 states by 1984, including Illinois, which had full property and casualty insurance pricing deregulation since 1971.[6] Most states maintained rate bureaus, but could deviate from the established rates with regulatory approval. However, in Massachusetts, the state regulatory agency still sets rates. Since underwiting profits in automobile insurance are at unacceptable levels to most insurers in the state, there has been a movement by insurance companies to withdraw from that marketplace.

Rationale Behind Government Regulation

The principle that the business of insurance is "affected with the public interest" has been established for decades. Statements appealing to it have appeared frequently in judicial decisions and often are repeated by state legislatures in explanation of the purpose of insurance regulation. Consequently, the insurance business has found itself the object of thorough supervision and regulation by the several states exercising their police power germane to the health and safety of their citizens. Statements of regulatory philosophy have repeatedly reflected an endorsement of reasonable governmental supervision. As early as 1871, New York State Insurance Superintendent, G.W. Miller, made the following statement: "The true object and aim of the government supervision should be to afford the fullest possible protection to the public, with the least possible annoyance or expense to or interference with the companies."

The two basic objectives of governmental regulation have been to ensure the stability and financial soundness of the insurance carrier and to ensure the reasonable and fair treatment of prospective and existing policy owners, insureds, and beneficiaries by both the insurer and the insurance agent. The latter objective is achieved by establishing specific standards in the solicitation of insurance and in the formulation of contractual provisions relating to the rights and benefits under an insurance policy. The former is achieved by promoting conditions leading to the insurer's successful operation, which is concerned primarily with the preservation of the insurer's capital, reserves, and investments, which provide the funds for the distribution of benefits in the future.

A number of present-day statutory requirements concerning an insurer's financial soundness and a policy owner's rights appeared for the first time almost two centuries ago: the filing with the legislature (Massachusetts, 1807) or with a state official (New York, 1829) of an insurer's periodic reports of financial condition and a statement of its affairs; the recognition of an insurable interest in the life of the husband or father, for the wife and children, respectively, along with an exemption from the claims of creditors of proceeds payable to them if annual premiums did not exceed $300; and licensing requirements for out-of-state insurers (Michigan and Wisconsin, late 1850s). To implement these regulatory statutes, it became necessary to establish a form of state agency. New Hampshire, Massachusetts, Rhode Island, and Vermont established insurance supervision boards in the 1850s, while the first separate insurance department was created in Massachusetts in 1853 and the first full-time insurance commissioner was appointed in New York in 1859.

The NAIC was organized in 1871 as a voluntary group of chief supervisory officials of several states. It has been an important force in influencing the regulation of insurance, promoting and encouraging uniformity in insurance legislation among all the states.

Because insurance is considered interstate commerce, it could be subject to federal regulation. However, as a result of Public Law 15, regulation has been left to the individual states. Each state creates its own laws and regulates companies selling insurance within state boundaries, often forcing national insurance companies to face 50 different sets of state regulation. Specific rules vary from state to state, but the areas of licensing of insurers, examination, solvency, investment policy, premium rates, reserves, competency of agents, contract provisions, and finance are regulated in all states. Federal regulation is limited to matters such as fraud and antitrust. While insurers are regulated primarily by the states in which they are incorporated, they are also subject to extraterritorial regulations by other states in which they conduct business. Although each state maintains its own regulatory procedures, there has been a trend in the last decade toward uniform legislation among states.

Since corporations and individuals do not want to buy insurance from a company of questionable financial strength, agents and brokers have an obligation to place insurance with financially sound insurance companies. At a minimum, agents and brokers should make a reasonable inquiry as to the financial condition of an insurance company with which they do business. They may also have a fiduciary responsibility to fund loss payments or return unearned premiums to a company or individual if the insurance company with which they have placed coverage becomes insolvent. State regulators attempt to ensure the solvency of insurance companies by establishing and monitoring capital and surplus requirements, regulating rates, setting forth investment guidelines and regulations, formulating statutory accounting rules, establishing financial reporting requirements, examining insurance companies, and applying diagnostic tests to company financial data.

State insurance department examinations generally attempt to accomplish the following:

1. Identify those insurance companies that are experiencing financial trouble or are engaging in unlawful or improper activities;
2. Confirm that the companies are operating and reporting in accordance with uniform accounting instructions promulgated by the NAIC;
3. Develop information needed for appropriate regulatory action.

Role of Federal Government

The federal government has provided flood and storm insurance coverage where the private sector has been unwilling to take the risk and has set up social security, unemployment benefits, medicare, and other retirement benefits. The federal government established the FDIC to protect depositors in banks and thrifts. Although the government doesn't explicitly guarantee the funds of small depositors in FDIC-insured institutions, there is an implicit guarantee and expectation of government backing. From time to time, there has been talk of offering uniform insurance benefits for worker's compensation and unemployment compensation, but this is unlikely to take place before the year 2000. Also, state guaranty funds vary in their capacity to provide policyholders the payments due from insolvent insurers. In the 1980s and 1990s, state guaranty funds covered credit union and thrift deposits in Ohio, Maryland, and Rhode Island with inadequate reserves to cover their depository insurance losses when these institutions failed.

It is likely that the seizure of large U.S. insurers like Mutual Benefit Life and Executive Life will raise the issue once again of imposing new federal guidelines on the insurance industry. The collapse of the junk bond market, in which Executive Life had invested heavily, acted as a catalyst in its demise. The Dingell committee, which was a subcommittee of the House Committee on Energy and Commerce, held hearings on the solvency of the insurance industry and the adequacy of state regulation through 1991. However, the issue does not have a champion in the U.S. Senate. Senators are already grasping with the highly unpopular rescue of S&Ls and the potential bailout of the nation's banks. They are presently in no mood to create another federal bureaucracy for insurance.

The thrift debacle has had a traumatizing effect on Congress, regulators, the media, and the public. Among policymakers and the media, there is an understanding of the high price paid by those who failed to acknowledge or understand the emerging problems of the thrift industry. Since solvency strains are increasing in the insurance industry, that sector is being placed quickly under the microscope for further scrutiny. The thrift crisis has sensitized the entire nation to the risk of insolvency of financial institutions. No representative wants to be accused someday of missing the same boat twice.[7]

Although federal regulation remains a possibility, it is not likely in the near future. The stronger likelihood is setting national standards that would be enforced by state regulators. The federal government might impose new national solvency standards and accredit and monitor state regulators who would enforce these standards. (Up until a few years ago, only 24 states required audited financial statements from insurance companies.) The NAIC Annual Statement blank now requires audited financial statements.

A new study by the General Accounting Office (GAO) that was released in mid-May 1991 asserted that state officials cannot adequately police and regulate the insurance industry. However, lawmakers at a House Energy and Commerce subcommittee hearing remained divided on whether Congress needed to set minimum solvency hearings, create a new federal regulatory body, or try to fix the state system. The GAO favors enforceable national standards.

The NAIC has tried to respond to the industry's troubles (43 life and health insurance companies went out of business in 1989) by developing a national system of solvency regulation. The NAIC asked Congress to pass legislation that would make insurance fraud a federal offense. Although in 1992 the U.S. Senate included criminal penalties for insurance fraud in a broader anticrime bill, S1242, this legislation was not considered by the House. Insurance fraud is expected to be considered again by the new Congress. The GAO claims that the NAIC proposals would not work. The NAIC does not have the power to compel states to adopt or enforce standards. Forty-four states have considered parts of the NAIC system, and 20 states have enacted laws in the last year. The GAO report also claimed that state insurance regulators are usually late in taking formal action against financially troubled insurers. For example, regulators did not take formal action in 71 percent of the cases of failed insurance companies on which they obtained data until those insurance companies became insolvent. In at least 36 cases, insurance companies continued to write policies after regulators identified them as financially troubled.[8]

INSURANCE REGULATORS MOUNT ATTACK

Insurance regulators and rating agencies are mounting attacks on the controversial financial technique of using surplus relief reinsurance that many life insurance companies have utilized to increase their capital. Employed properly, reinsurance is a way of limiting risk. Reinsurance agreements permit one insurance company to take on or share some of the risks of another insurance company, in exchange for part of the insurance premium. Some types of reinsurance transactions, called surplus relief reinsurance, also increase an insurer's capital, either through the income they generate or by permitting an insurance company to lower its liabilities. The concern on the part of the regulators and rating agencies is that some of these agreements permit an insurance company to increase its capital without reducing its risk.

Companies such as Equitable, Connecticut Mutual Life, First Capital Life, First Executive Life, and Monarch Life Insurance are among the users of this financial technique to boost their capital. Many regulators and rating agencies feel that the technique artificially inflates the capital of an insurance company and is being used to hide or mask other problems. The NAIC is discussing whether to eliminate these types of insurance agreements on a nationwide basis. The agency unveiled a new compliance formula that would require a life insurance company to set aside reserves for losses on real estate, as well as reserves for interest rate risk in the bond portfolio. Insurance companies with real estate losses would have to build reserves over a few years to meet numerous requirements determined by a complicated formula. Prior to this action, an insurance company had not been required to establish its real estate reserves for regulatory reporting purposes. Doing so would bring insurance company practices closer in line with those of banks. The insurance industry reserves would be lower than those typically required in the banking industry because insurance industry spokesmen claim that their real estate loans are performing better than the construction and development loans of the banks. In this contention, they are correct: Most insurance company loans provide permanent real estate financing to developed properties, whereby many bank loans are often for more speculative construction financing. While insurance companies always maintained reserves for possible bond and stock losses, they had not experienced large defaults in mortgages prior to the 1990–1992 real estate recession. On the subject of interest rate risk, insurance companies would be required to set aside reserves for fixed-rate bonds when interest rates increased, but they would be permitted to decrease reserves when interest rates declined.

The proposed measures are partially in response to pressure from lawmakers who have criticized insurance company reporting and accounting practices for real estate. They also represent part of an insurance industry campaign to head off federal legislation pertaining to the insurance industry.

The American Institute of Certified Public Accountants issued an auditing rule that forces all insurance companies to disclose more about their investment risks, particularly the quality and concentration of their investments. Generally, the new rule will require both mutual and stock insurance companies to tell more than they have in the past about their investments and pensions.

POSSIBLE DINGELL AND METZENBAUM LEGISLATION

A key premise of *Failed Promises,* published in 1990 by the House Subcommittee on Oversight and Investigations, which was chaired by Representative Dingell (D-MI), and a frequent refrain of congressional criticisms, has been that the state insurance departments were unable, unwilling, or unprepared to regulate the business of insurance effectively. In mid-1991, Congress began to pay more attention to federal involvement in guaranteeing and perhaps even regulating insurance companies. There are members of Congress, as well as members of the insurance and academic communities, who would support proposals for government standards dealing with investment selection guidelines, minimal policy coverage, the availability and affordability of insurance to all, and a federal insolvency plan. A federal plan similar to the FDIC would appear to offer greater security to the public than the current wide array of state insolvency plans. According to John Chesson, counsel to the Subcommittee on Oversight and Investigations, House Committee on Energy and Commerce, there is a certain amount of logic for a national guaranty fund, but he felt that the bad experience with S&L and bank federal guarantees on savings would minimize the probability of enactment of such federal legislation in the near term. Chesson also pointed out that the guaranty funds could establish a stronger financial base if insurance companies that contribute to the funds switched to a prefunded, risk-based financing system. He found fault as well with the facts that the funds are not really guarantees and that states provide different coverage and exclusions.[9]

Representative Dingell and Senator Metzenbaum (D-OH) announced proposals in August 1991 before their respective legislative bodies that would create a federal agency endowed with powers over state regulators in traditional insurance activities and in the traditionally unregulated area of reinsurance. Dingell has proposed statutes that would create a Federal Insurer Solvency Corporation. This corporation would set minimum hurdles—likely higher than existing standards in many states—for a wide range of matters concerning the financial health of insurance companies. Metzenbaum's proposal parallels that of Dingell, but adds a national insurance guaranty fund, superseding existing state guaranty mechanisms. The potential liabilities of such a fund in the face of FSLIC and FDIC government obligations could prove a considerable political drawback. Both bills call for direct federal regulation of reinsurance. The major difference between the two bills is that the Metzenbaum legislation would create a national guaranty fund and a National Insurance Guaranty Corporation, while Dingell's would continue the current state guaranty fund system.

The purpose of the Federal Insurance Insolvency Act of 1992 proposed by Dingell is "to employ the good offices of the federal government to make sure that insurance promises, which have sometimes been failed promises, will be kept."[10] The bill creates a voluntary system by which insurance companies may choose to come within the federal regulatory orbit or stay with the current system. Federally certified insurers would become members of a National Insurance Protection Corporation, so that in case a member fails, the policyholders will be protected. However, this corporation will not be backed by the U.S. government. Rather, the member insurers themselves will pay all claims. The essence of the bill would establish certificates of solvency for insurance companies through the Federal Insurance Solvency Commission. The commission would establish standards for certification that would include capital and surplus requirements and would also monitor the financial condition of certified insurers and their compliance with these standards. The commission would be authorized to suspend or revoke a certificate for failure to comply with the standards. In addition, the commission would help create a self-regulating organization dealing with insurance brokers and agents and would set federal standards and procedures for the rehabilitation and liquidation of federally certified insurers. The Dingell bill also calls for federal regulation of reinsurance companies, including the establishment of significant financial standards, jurisdictional requirements, and reporting obligations on these entities. This new legislation should encourage financially sound international insurance and reinsurance companies to enter the U.S. market and continue to provide such essential coverage as medical malpractice, environmental liability, war risk, aviation and marine hull, and cargo and catastrophe reinsurance protection.

While the exact nature of the final passage of an insurance bill is uncertain, by the end of the decade we are likely to see either tighter, more uniform insurance regulation on the state level or federal standards being placed on the industry. Future legislation might impose new disclosure and auditing requirements, put limits on the proportion of assets that could be committed to any one investment vehicle or type of investment (e.g., junk bonds), establish risk-based capital and surplus requirements to cushion against unforeseen financial shocks, and impose regulation on foreign insurance companies and reinsurance companies.

While insurers have been generally exempt from the full-disclosure requirements of the Investment Company Act of 1940, now that many life insurance companies sell investment products, there is likely to be a requirement of greater disclosure. Under prodding from the NAIC and industry spokesmen, states have been moving to preempt federal legislation.

Many states have passed laws or regulations aimed at uniform standards for financial statements, bond evaluations, portfolio investment guidelines and limitations, and sanctions for troubled companies. The NAIC requires larger reserves against losses in the bond or stock holdings of insurance companies and has also developed model laws for the states and insurance departments to adopt regarding establishing limits and diversification requirements on insurance company investments and establishing reserves for their investments in securities, the size of which is a function of asset quality.

Congress is also discussing more effective regulatory barriers and the setting up of a nationwide data base to curtail certain abuses by foreign-based firms that fraudulently exploit the reinsurance market. An attempt is being made to weed out corruption in this market. At a minimum, there is likely to be stricter oversight of companies incorporated offshore.

"Only the federal government has the power to make and modify trade agreements with other countries and apply sanctions to those who nurture fraudulent reinsurers by promoting veils of secrecy, tax havens, and easy incorporation. . . . [There should be] federal minimum capital and surplus requirements for alien reinsurers, checks of assets and financial records, and federal sanctions for violations of the requirements," claims Sandra Autry, the director of the Unauthorized Insurance Division of the Texas Insurance Commission.

In the 1992 budget proposal of the president, it was suggested that the tax-deferred buildup of certain types of annuities be eliminated in order to generate additional tax revenue. Current law allows for deferring the taxes on earnings in annuities during the accumulation phase, after which the customer can decide how to receive the money—either as a lump sum or a series of periodic payments. The president's proposal would have ended this tax deferral, unless the customer elected to receive a lifetime income stream based upon life expectancy during the payout phase. That election would have to be made when the policy was purchased, which might be decades before retirement. The proposal would raise about $1.7 billion in additional tax revenues over a five-year period. An earlier attempt to do this in 1986 resulted in the institution of a 10-percent tax penalty for withdrawals from annuities before age 59 1/2. If this law is passed, annuities would be less attractive to investors, and there would be a reallocation of savings to alternative investment vehicles. Joseph Belth argues that taxation of the inside interest would have a "devastating impact on the life insurance industry and would threaten its very survival."[11]

RISK-BASED CAPITAL REQUIREMENTS

The NAIC has been developing a set of risk-based capital standards for insurers. The key concept in them is to bolster solvency regulation by requiring companies that write riskier business or that make riskier investments to have larger amounts of surplus in proportion to the size of their operations. The implementation of risk-based requirements in the insurance industry could contribute to a lowering of insurance company insolvencies, as well as a greater focus and discipline on the part of regulators. It should encourage prudent business practices and limit activities of undercapitalized insurers.[12] It might also lead to increased consolidation within the industry as undercapitalized companies are forced to seek merger partners. It is uncertain how much additional capital will have to be raised by insurance companies to support the current book of business and what impact this might have on the market price of insurance.

In December 1992, the NAIC adopted the life risk-based capital model, which creates a national standard to measure the financial well-being of life and health insurance companies for all 50 states. The uniform formula contrasts sharply with the old system in which each state had its own criteria for rating insurance companies and taking action against troubled insurers. This model adds an evaluation of how well companies score according to a formula that measures the adequacy of a company's capital. Under the plan, life insurance companies will be rated on how much capital they have as a percentage of the risk-adjusted capital required to buttress the risk inherent in their operations and in their investment portfolios. Life insurers will have to report this information in their 1993 annual statements. A score of 100 or better will suggest that a life insurance company is healthy because it has met or surpassed its risk-based capital requirement. Those companies that score below 11 will be subject automatically to regulatory action. Under the system, insurance companies with capital levels equal to 35 percent or less of their risk-based requirement would be put under regulatory control. Those scoring above 35 percent but below 50 percent could be seized by state regulators. Companies scoring at least 50 percent, but less than 75 percent, would be issued a regulatory order mandating specific actions to improve their financial condition. Those life insurance companies scoring at least 75 percent, but under 100 percent, would have to file a plan with their state insurance regulators indicating how they will improve their capital-to-surplus position.

The NAIC is researching a similar model to be used by property and casualty insurers. The model is not expected to be ready until 1994. As a result of these new risk-based capital standards, it is likely that insurance companies will begin to examine their businesses according to how much capital they will require and will begin to wean themselves away from riskier assets such as junk bonds and commercial real estate. The new standards should intensify the flight toward quality and should lead to an increase in the number of insurance company mergers and acquisitions.

OTHER ISSUES

With regard to the debate over the repeal of the McCarran-Ferguson Act, the National Association of Insurance Brokers came out in favor of repealing the industry's antitrust exemption, while Franklin Nutter, president of the Reinsurance Association of America, condemned efforts to repeal the law.

It is interesting to note that California's Proposition 103 acted as a catalyst in generating rate-cutting bills in other states. The act was quickly followed by rate-cutting bills for auto insurance premiums in New Jersey and other states. This wave of state regulation is one of the key events in the new social cycle that is likely to intensify and last a long time.[13]

WORLDWIDE REGULATORY TRENDS

There has been a general trend throughout Europe and the United States to encourage consolidation within the financial services industry. A number of countries' policies have shifted toward concentrating on technology-driven, cost-based efficiencies of scale. Declining information technology costs and public policy shifts are combining to introduce unprecedented complexity into management, analysis, and regulatory supervision of financial service companies. Another shift is a greater willingness to subordinate regulatory sovereignty of a state or a country for common global or regional standards. This shift goes beyond the strides made by the Basle Accord on bank minimum risk-based capital standards and by various European Community directives, and similar moves are underway in the securities industry and among state insurance regulators in the United States. There has also been a willingness to accept the continuing blurring of the boundaries within and between the highly regulated financial sector and the commercial sector. A final development is a greater insistence that, in general, providers of risk capital and liabilities absorb losses in the event of failure.

ENDNOTES

1. S. Hayes, *Wall Street and Regulation* (Boston: Harvard Business School Press, 1987), pp. 10–11.

2. Ibid., pp. 23–24.

3. Ibid., p. 40.

4. Ibid., pp. 40–41.

5. National Association of Insurance Commissioners, Monitoring Competition: A Means of Regulating the Property and Liability Insurance Business (New York: NAIC, 1974), p. 65.

6. Hayes, p. 41.

7. O. Kramer, *Rating the Risk* (New York: Insurance Information Institute, 1990), p. 105.

8. S. Kirchoff, "GAO States Oversight of Insurance Is Inadequate," *Philadelphia Inquirer,* May 23, 1991, p. C13.

9. D. Foppert, *Best's Review, Life/Health Insurance,* October 1991, pp. 18–24.

10. Subcommittee on Oversight and Investigations of the Committee on Energy and Commerce, U.S. House of Representatives, *Failed Promises: Insurance Company Insolvencies* (Washington, DC: U.S. Government Printing Office, February 1990).

11. J. Belth, *The Financial Condition and Regulation of Insurance Companies,* Proceedings of a Conference Held in June 1991 by the Federal Reserve Bank of Boston, p. 40.

12. "Risk-Based Capital Requirements Could Help to Ease Insurer Insolvencies, Focus Regulators," *The Insurance Accountant,* June 1, 1992, p. 3.

13. I. Leveson, *Financial Services: The Next Era* (Marlboro, NJ: Author, 1991), p. 195.

PART TWO

Financial Deregulation and Contemporary Financial Issues

6 Contemporary Banking Issues

Inadequate bank capital is like pornography. You can't accurately define it. You simply know when you have seen it.

Anonymous Bank Regulator

BANK CAPITAL ISSUES

The adequacy of bank capital has become a salient issue in the 1990s in the United States, following the insolvency of the FSLIC in 1989, the near insolvency of the Bank Insurance Fund at the FDIC in 1991–1992, and, in general, the huge volume of troubled real estate and other loans of the 1990s, which seem likely to lead to continued high levels of bank failures at least through 1993. The OECD refers to the problems in the worldwide banking industry as "financial fragility," the deterioration of bank balance sheets as a result of a lower quality of assets and declining profitability. It has often been argued that the generous deposit insurance in the United States has been a major cause of the weak position of many banks and thrifts. But, while deposit insurance has indeed weakened the need for self-control on the part of both depository institutions and their clients, it is only one cause that has been contributing to financial fragility. Other contributing factors have been a narrowing of interest margins, an increased exchange rate risk, inadequate cost control, and regulatory restrictions and laxity, especially in allowing ailing banks and thrifts to remain open too long.[1]

Congress demonstrated its displeasure with the capital forbearance policies of thrift regulators, which cost taxpayers billions of additional dollars, when it passed legislation in late 1991 to close banks and thrifts when net worth–to–asset ratios fall below 2 percent and to require the FDIC to institute risk-based deposit insurance premiums by 1994. Banks with capital well in excess of minimum requirements will be eligible to engage in new nonbank financial services. However, banks whose capital drops below minimum levels will be subject to corrective action, which could involve cuts in dividends, sales of assets, or, as a last resort, forced sale or closing of the bank.

The role of capital in banking is no different from its role in most other businesses. Capital reflects a base of funds permanently employed in the business that affords a sense of financial stability to the firm and the wherewithal to deal with financial adversity. The role of capital in an insured bank is to provide a cushion that protects the FDIC (and other uninsured liability holders) from decreases in the value of the bank's assets. In addition to furnishing funds for the growth and development of new programs, facilities, and services, capital functions as a regulatory constraint on unjustified expansion of assets. Capital also promotes public confidence and reassures creditors of the bank's financial strength and long-term viability. Yet another benefit is that stockholders and holders of capital notes and other forms of subordinated debt monitor bank performance closely and impose a degree of market discipline on the bank's senior management. Capital markets also provide access to financial markets and can help prevent liquidity problems caused by outflows of deposits. However, relatively inexpensive capital is available only to banks with high-quality assets and a strong capital base; it is not unusual for weak banks to be denied access to the capital markets. Unfortunately, until capital became king in the 1990s, deposit insurance created incentives for banks to hold less capital and to take on more risk in their operations than they would have without deposit insurance. For example, bank capital ratios declined from 15 percent in the mid-1930s, when deposit insurance was created, to 7 percent in the current banking environment. This represented more than a 50-percent decline in the capital-to-asset ratio. Another example of increased risk at banks is the large increase in loan-to-deposit ratios over the same period.

HISTORY OF BANK CAPITAL STANDARDS

While the historical data are distorted by many factors, the average bank in the United States had an equity capital-to-asset ratio of about 50 percent in 1840. While generally declining over the next 75 years, equity ratios were still about 12 percent prior to the Great Depression. Such high equity capital ratios were not the choice of bankers, but the result of market pressures to make depositors comfortable about the ability of banks to fulfill their obligations. By the mid-1970s, equity capital ratios of the largest banks had fallen below 4 percent. The salient forces that allowed equity-to-asset ratios to decline from 50 percent in the mid-1800s to about 7 percent at year-end 1992 were the statutory and regulatory changes that lowered risk to depositors.[2]

Regulators had always had some sort of capital adequacy standards for their constituent commercial banks. Before the 1980s, however, commercial banks were not required to meet an explicit capital-to-asset ratio. Instead, regulators used "moral suasion" to persuade banks they considered undercapitalized to increase their capital ratios.

During the 1960s and 1970s, the Office of the Comptroller of the Currency moved away from any formula type of analysis toward consideration of the following factors: (1) the quality of management; (2) the liquidity of assets; (3) the history of earnings and their retention; (4) the quality and character of ownership; (5) the reliability and profitability of the bank's deposit structure; (6) the quality of operating procedures; and (7) the capacity of the bank to meet the present needs of its trade area, considering the bank's competition. However, later in the 1970s, the OCC, FDIC, and Federal Reserve Board agreed to use trends and peer group comparisons of the following selected ratios to determine capital adequacy: (1) equity capital to total assets, (2) total capital to total assets, (3) loans to total capital, (4) classified assets to total capital, (5) fixed assets to total capital, (6) net rate-sensitive assets to total assets, (7) reserve for charge-offs to net charge-offs, (8) net charge-offs to loans, and (9) asset growth rate to capital growth rate.[3]

Although this method worked well for many years, it failed to prevent a gradual decline in capital-to-asset ratios at large banks. One of the reasons for this decline at such banks was related to the fact that asset growth was higher than the rate of equity retention—that is, profitability was too low to support the asset growth. The regulators imposed formal capital requirements in 1981 to reverse the trend. At first, capital requirements varied by the size of the bank and differed among the three federal regulators. Finally, in 1985, the regulators got around to defining capital more formally and specifying capital adequacy standards more precisely. The regulators adopted common capital requirements that utilized two measures of capital. *Primary capital* consisted of equity, loan loss reserves, perpetual preferred stock, and mandatory convertible debt. *Total capital* included subordinated debt and limited-life preferred stock. The first measure was intended to reflect a bank's cushion against unforeseen losses, while the second was intended to help limit the FDIC's losses in the event of the bank's failure. In setting guidelines, the regulators placed banks in one of three categories: multinational, regional, and community banks. For multinational and regional banks, the minimum acceptable level of primary capital was 5 percent. For community banks, it was set at 6 percent.

Between 1985 and 1989, the minimum ratios of capital to assets were 5.5 percent for primary capital and 6 percent for total capital, and the regulators could require a bank to exceed these minimums if the bank was considered unusually risky. An additional benefit of minimum capital requirements is that the owners of equity and intermediate- and long-term debt impose market discipline on bank managers because they monitor bank performance carefully. On the other hand, a perverse effect of mandating minimum capital levels is that some banks might reach for riskier assets in order to generate higher returns that might eventually allow those banks to increase their profitability and, consequently, their internally generated capital. At this stage in the development of capital adequacy guidelines, the regulators still lacked control over the risk of the asset portfolio.

While the aforementioned capital requirements helped reverse a decline in bank capital in the aggregate, they did not prevent an increase in overall risk in the banking industry or help stem the increase in commercial bank failures. The capital standards had the undesirable effect of increasing the risk profile of banks because capital requirements were the same for a Treasury bill as for a corporate loan. To offset the cost of capital, banks often sought to increase the profitability of the assets supported by the capital, offering a built-in incentive for the banks to gravitate toward higher yielding, riskier assets. Banks shifted away from default-free U.S. Treasury securities toward much riskier loans in highly leveraged transactions and commercial real estate. Accordingly, the rate of delinquencies and charge-offs increased sharply when the economy softened. At the same time, the quality of most bank loan portfolios suffered as the better lending risks shifted most of their short-term borrowing to the commercial paper market, where the cost of borrowing was generally significantly cheaper than at the banks.

To increase fee income and to avoid capital requirements, banks turned to off-balance-sheet activities or credit substitutes, such as standby letters of credit or commitments, which did not have to be supported by capital. In addition, banks substantially increased their interest rate and foreign currency swaps. Hence, off-balance-sheet items began to grow rapidly. At some money-center banks, they exceeded total on-balance-sheet items.[4] These off-balance-sheet instruments often exposed the bank to significant default risk, which led the regulators to seek capital requirements that would control risk better. This in turn led to the foundation of today's risk-based capital requirements. The new plan took several years to develop. Regulators from the United States and 11 other industrial countries (known as the Basle Accord and comprising the United Kingdom, Canada, Belgium, Sweden, Switzerland, Germany, France, Italy, Japan, the Netherlands, and Luxembourg) began to work on the plan in 1986 under the auspices of the Bank for International Settlements. The need to make the playing field equal for banks from different countries and the increased integration of financial markets across countries led in June 1988 to the Basle Agreement to standardize bank capital requirements. The purposes of the agreement were (1) to link a bank's capital requirements systematically to the riskiness of its activities, including off-balance-sheet risk exposure, and (2) to coordinate the definitions of capital, risk assessment, and capital adequacy standards across nations.[5]

RISK-BASED CAPITAL STANDARDS

By the end of 1990, U.S. banks were required to maintain minimal capital levels equal to 7.25 percent of risk-weighted assets, of which at least 3.25 percent had to be core, or tier 1, capital. By the end of 1992, the minimum capital requirement rose to 8 percent, with core capital of at least 4 percent of risk-adjusted assets. Bank regulators have allowed certain types of debt to be counted as part of regulatory capital. In particular, 2 percentage points of the capital requirement of 8 percent can be in the form of subordinated debentures. Summaries of the proposed risk weight and risk categories, credit conversion factors for off-balance-sheet items, treatment of interest rate and exchange weight contracts, and proposed definition of capital appear in Tables 6.1, 6.2, 6.3.

Table 6.1   Summary of Risk Weights and Risk Categories

Category 1: 0 Percent
1. Cash (domestic and foreign).
2. Balances due from, and claims on, Federal Reserve banks.
3. Securities (direct obligations) issued by the U.S. government or its agencies.
4. Federal Reserve Bank stock.

Category 2: 20 Percent
1. All claims (long and short term) on domestic depository institutions.
2. Claims on foreign banks with an original maturity of one year or less.
3. Claims guaranteed by, or backed by the full faith and credit of, domestic depository institutions.
4. Local currency claims on foreign central governments to the extent that the bank has local currency liabilities in the foreign country.
5. Cash items in the process of collection.
6. Securities and other claims on, or guaranteed by, U.S. government-*sponsored* agencies (including portions of claims guaranteed).[a]
7. Portions of loans and other assets collateralized by securities issued by, or guaranteed by, U.S. government-sponsored agencies.
8. General-obligation claims on, and claims guaranteed by, U.S. state and local governments that are secured by the full faith and credit of the state of local taxing authority (including portions of claims guaranteed).
9. Claims on official multilateral lending institutions or regional development institutions in which the U.S. government is a shareholder or a contributing member.
10. Securities and other claims guaranteed by the U.S. government or its agencies (including portions of claims guaranteed).[b]
11. Portions of loans and other assets collateralized by securities issued by, or guaranteed by, the U.S. government or its agencies, or by cash on deposit in the lending institution.[c]

Category 3: 50 Percent
1. Revenue bonds or similar obligations, including loans and leases, that are obligations of U.S. state or local governments, but for which the government entity is committed to repay the debt only out of revenues from the facilities financed.
2. One- to four-family residential mortgages, with borrowing of 80% or less than value.
3. Credit equivalent amounts of interest rate and foreign exchange rate related contracts, except for those assigned to a lower risk category.

Category 4: 100 Percent
1. All other claims on private obligors.
2. Claims on foreign banks with an original maturity exceeding one year.
3. Claims on foreign central governments that are not included in item 4 of Category 3.
4. Obligations issued by state or local governments (including industrial development authorities and similar entities) repayable solely by a private party or enterprise.
5. Premises, plant, and equipment; other fixed assets; and other real estate owned.
6. Investments in any unconsolidated subsidiaries, joint ventures, or associated companies, if not deducted from capital.
7. Instruments issued by other banking organizations that qualify as capital.
8. All other assets (including claims on commercial firms owned by the public sector).

[a]For the purpose of calculating the risk-based capital ratio, a U.S. government-*sponsored* agency is defined as an agency originally established or chartered to serve public purposes specified by the U.S. Congress, but whose obligations are not *explicitly* guaranteed by the full faith and credit of the U.S. government.
[b]For the purpose of calculating the risk-based capital ratio, a U.S. government agency is defined as an instrumentality of the U.S. government whose obligations are fully and explicitly guaranteed as to the timely repayment of principal and interest by the full faith and credit of the U.S. government.
[c]Degree of collateralization is determined by current market value.

Source: G. H. Hempel, A. B. Coleman, and D. G. Simonson, *Bank Management: Text and Cases,* 3rd ed. (New York: Wiley, 1990).

Table 6.2   Credit Conversion Factors for Off-Balance-Sheet Items

100-Percent Conversion Factor
1. Direct credit substitutes (general guarantees of indebtedness and guarantee-type instruments, including standby letters of credit serving as financial guarantees for, or support for, loans and securities).
2. Acquisitions of risk participations in bankers acceptances and participations in direct credit substitutes (e.g., standby letters of credit).
3. Sale and repurchase agreements and asset sales with recourse, if not already included on the balance sheet.
4. Forward agreements (i.e., contractual obligations) to purchase assets, including financing facilities with *certain* drawdown.

50-Percent Conversion Factor
1. Transaction-related contingencies (e.g., bid bonds, performance bonds, warranties, and standby letters of credit related to a particular transaction).
2. Unused commitments with an original maturity exceeding one year, including underwriting commitments and commercial credit lines.
3. Revolving underwriting facilities (RUFs), note issuance facilities (NIFs), and other similar arrangements.

20-Percent Conversion Factor
1. Short-term, self-liquidating trade-related contingencies, including commercial letters of credit.

0-Percent Conversion Factor
1. Unused commitments with an original maturity of one year or less or which are unconditionally cancellable at any time.

Source: G. H. Hempel, A. B. Coleman, and D. G. Simonson, *Bank Management: Text and Cases*, 3rd ed. (New York: Wiley, 1990), p. 284.

The impact of these new capital requirements will of course vary from bank to bank. However, banks engaged in risky lending and investment practices will face a higher capital requirement, while banks engaged in safer activities will face a lower capital requirement. The risk-based plan should affect enough banks in the desired way to improve the regulation of bank risk taking. According to the Federal Reserve, at midyear 1993 the majority of banks already met the tougher year-end 1992 standards. However, a few banks needed to raise their capital levels or shrink their assets in order to meet the tougher standards, especially for loans other than residential mortgages. (See Figure 6.1.)

The plan attempts to relate banks' capital requirements to their estimated credit risk. All assets are allocated to one of four risk categories, each with a different weight that is related to the assessment of the degree of credit risk. U.S. government securities and mortgage-backed securities directly guaranteed by the Government National Mortgage Association (Ginnie Mae) have no default risk and are placed in a category with a capital weight of 0. The next category has a weight of 20 percent and includes assets such as interbank deposits, general-obligation municipal

Table 6.3 Definition of Capital

Capital would be composed of two parts (tiers 1 and 2). Beginning December 31, 1992, all national banks would be expected to maintain a capital to risk-weighted asset ratio of 8.0%, of which at least half must consist of tier 1 capital. In other words, tier 2 capital elements will qualify as part of a bank's total capital base up to a maximum of 100% of that bank's tier 1 capital.

Definition of Capital

Tier 1:
- Common stock
- Surplus
- Undivided profits, capital reserves, and
- Minority interests in consolidated subsidiaries

Tier 2:
- Perpetual and long-term preferred stock
- Perpetual debt and other hybrid debt-to-equity instruments
- Intermediate-term preferred stock and term subordinated debt (to a maximum of 50% of tier 1 capital)
- Loan loss reserves (to a maximum of 1.25% of risk-weighted assets)

Deductions from Capital:
- All intangibles except mortgage servicing rights
- Loans classified as loss by regulators
- Investments in unconsolidated banking and finance subsidiaries
- Reciprocal holdings of the capital instruments of other banks

Source: Adapted from G. H. Hempel, A. B. Coleman, and D. G. Simonson, *Bank Management: Text and Cases*, 3rd ed. (New York: Wiley, 1990), p. 285.

bonds, and mortgage-backed securities guaranteed by the Federal National Mortgage Association (Fannie Mae) or the Federal Home Loan Mortgage Corporation (Freddie Mac). The category that follows has a 50-percent weight and includes municipal revenue bonds, first mortgages on homes, and half of the unused portion of a home equity line of credit. The final category carries the maximum weight of 100 percent, lumping together all remaining securities and loans, including standby letters of credit backing a customer's commercial paper. With the exception of mortgages and government-guaranteed instruments, there is virtually no attempt to distinguish among the risks associated with different types of private sector claims.

The final step is to add the sum of assets and off-balance-sheet credit exposures, with each item then weighted by the risk for its category (0%, 20%, 50%, 100%). The requirement is computed as a percentage of the bank's risk-adjusted assets. (See example in Table 6.4.)

Federal regulators, backed by Congress, are nudging bank capital standards higher, increasing bank insurance premiums, and coercing banks into increasing loan loss reserves. Improvements in bank capital positions have been encouraged

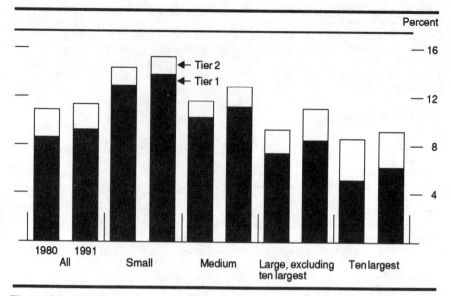

Figure 6.1 Risk-Based Capital Ratios at Insured Commercial Banks by Size of Bank, Fourth Quarter, 1991 and 1992. (*Source: Federal Reserve Bulletin,* July 1993)

and sometimes required by regulators, rating agencies, and even the stock market. Better capitalization of the banking system protects the Bank Insurance Fund and creditors of banks, while giving management leeway to pursue a broader range of potentially profitable business.

The cumulative effect of these moves raises the cost of capital and lowers near-term earnings per share. This makes it even more difficult for relatively weak banks to raise capital. In fact, it may be in the best interests of the banking system as a whole to coerce inefficient, poorly run banks to exit from an industry already suffering from overcapacity. The global push among regulators for more capital is an understandable response to rising risk levels in the banking system and should lead to a reduction in the number of banks.[6]

The original Basle plan focused on the risk of counterparty failure and on credit risk, while ignoring market risks such as interest rate risk, liquidity risk, foreign exchange risk, and positional risk. The coverage of such risks by capital standards is being considered in the Basle Committee on Banking Supervision. For example, there is no differentiation in the capital requirement for a loan to the Ford Motor Company, to Nigeria, or to the corner grocery store. However, residential mortgage lending is placed in a less risky lending category. In addition, there is great risk at a bank when future changes in interest rates affect the value of the bank's assets differently than they affect its liabilities. It would seem desirable to require banks that were highly exposed to future interest rate changes to hold more capital. The Federal Reserve responded to this possibility by implementing a system to measure

Table 6.4   AG National Bank: Risk-Based Capital ($ Thousands)

	Assets Dec. 31, 1993	Risk Weight	Risk-Weighted Assets
Category 1: 0 Percent			
Cash and Reserve	$ 104,000	0	$ 0
Trading Account	900	0	0
U.S. Treasury and Agencies (GNMA)	50,000	0	0
Federal Reserve Stock	6,000	0	0
Category 2: 20 Percent			
Due from/in Process	300,000	20	$ 60,000
U.S. Treasury and Agencies (collateralized repos)	325,000	20	65,000
U.S. Agencies (Government-Sponsored)	412,000	20	82,400
State and Municipalities Secured Tax Authority	87,000	20	17,400
C.M.O. Backed by Agency Sec.	90,000	20	18,000
Domestic Depository Institution	38,000	20	7,600
Category 3: 50 Percent			
C.M.O. Backed by Mortgage Loans	10,000	50	$ 5,000
State and Municipalities/All Other	70,000	50	35,000
Real Estate; 1–4 Family	324,000	50	162,000
Category 4: 100 Percent			
Loans: Commercial/Agency/Institutional/Leases	2,000,000	100	$ 2,000,000
Real Estate, All Other	400,000	100	400,000
Allowance for Credit Loss	(70,000)	0	0
Other Investments	170,000	100	170,000
Premises, Equity, Other Assets	200,000	100	200,000
Total Assets	4,516,900		3,222,400
Off-Balance-Sheet Items			
Loan Commitment > 1 Year	$ 364,000	50	$ 182,000
Futures and Forwards	50,000	100	50,000
Contingencies	$ 414,000		$ 232,000
Assets and Contingencies	$ 4,930,900		$ 3,454,400

Requirement

Tier 1 Capital: $.04 \times (\$3,454,400.) = \$138,176$
Total Capital: $.08 \times (\$3,454,400.) = \$276,352$

interest rate risk. But the plan also measures default or credit risk imperfectly. No distinction is made between loans to highly creditworthy borrowers and loans to borrowers with little credit history or little collateral. Also, a highly diversified portfolio is treated the same as a portfolio of loans concentrated in one industry or in one part of the country. A diversified portfolio also carries less risk than the sum of its parts. However, a mechanistic formula that measures risk on an asset-by-asset basis cannot capture the total portfolio risk. Regulatory systems that rely on rigid arithmetic formulae in defining the relative riskiness of different assets may find that the rules may not conform to economic reality. In addition, the Basle plan relies on book value measures of soundness, because it ignores changes in the market value of assets and liabilities.

This risk-based system ignores many important concepts in risk management diversification by geography and type of loan, use of futures contracts and other derivative securities, interest rate swaps, fixed- versus variable-rate loans and securities, and other methods of controlling risk, such as the use of corporate separateness to isolate risky activities in subsidiaries. A major shortcoming of the Basle plan was its failure to address interest rate risk. Interest rate risk is the risk that fluctuations in interest rates may harm an institution's financial condition. Banks assume this risk whenever the interest rate sensitivity of their assets does not match the interest rate sensitivity of their liabilities or off-balance-sheet positions. Banks can profit from mismatched maturities when interest rates change favorably, but the antithesis is also true. Bank earnings and capital can suffer from maturity mismatches when interest rates move in the wrong direction. The purpose of the interest-rate risk measurement is to ensure that banks with high levels of interest rate risk have enough capital to cover their loss exposure.

A provision in Section 305 of the FDIC Improvement Act of 1991 required federal regulators to incorporate interest rate risk into bank capital standards by the middle of 1993. The original Federal Reserve proposal (June 1992) to measure interest rate risk required information germane to the maturity structure of bank assets and liabilities.

Banks would be required to assign on- and off-balance-sheet assets and liabilities to one of six time bands, based either on the maturity of the instrument in the case of fixed-rate instruments or on the length of time until the interest rate adjusts in the case of variable-rate instruments. The 1992 proposal also required banks to assign each asset to one of the following categories:

Amortizing—assets make periodic payments of both principal and interest.

Nonamortizing—assets pay interest only, delaying principal repayment until maturity.

Deep discount—assets make neither interest nor principal payments, but instead are sold at a deep discount from their face value and then repay the principal at maturity.

In the 1992 proposal, every bank would be required to report its dollar position in each of the time band categories for the three different types of assets and for liabilities. The reported positions would then be multiplied by risk weights derived from the durations of the corresponding assets and liabilities. The risk weights are expressed in percentage terms and represent the change in the value of an instrument that would follow from a 100-basis-point change in all interest rates. The end result would be a series of risk-weighted positions that measure the change in the value of the bank's reported holdings that would follow a 100-basis-point change in interest rates. In the final step, total risk-weighted liabilities would be subtracted from total risk-weighted assets to arrive at the next risk-weighted position of the bank. Expressed in dollars, this number represents the change in the net worth of the bank that would occur as a result of a 100-basis-point shift in interest rates. Expressed as a percentage of total assets, the interest risk of different banks could be compared, just as we compare bank capital ratios.

The Federal Reserve's 1992 proposal suggests that any bank with a net risk-weighted capital position equal to 1 percent of assets or less would not be required to hold additional capital over and above the existing risk-based capital requirements. Banks with interest risk exposures of more than 1 percent would require additional capital, which would be equal to the amount in excess of the 1-percent exposure. Although the Federal Reserve's measure of interest rate risk is far from perfect, it is a step in the right direction in identifying banks that take large interest rate risk exposure.

The Federal Reserve's 1993 alternative would result in continuing to include interest rate risk in the overall assessment of a bank's capital adequacy, but there would be no requirement for a minimum capital charge. Interest rate risk would be assessed on a case-by-case basis considering the measured level of exposure and other factors. The 1993 proposal would set up a three-stage supervisory process for measuring interest rate risk. The first step would be to apply a quantitative screen for exempting potentially low-risk institutions from additional reporting documents. The second step would apply a bank's internal risk measurement model if that process were deemed to be adequate. A basic supervisory model would be utilized where internal models were unavailable or insufficient. The Federal Reserve also proposed two criteria to use in determining whether a bank can be exempt from the proposal. The total notional principal amount of all off-balance-sheet interest rate contracts could not exceed 10 percent of total assets. In addition, 15 percent of the sum of fixed- and floating-rate loans and securities with maturities longer than five years could not exceed 30 percent of capital.

The Federal Reserve did not propose explicit formulas for calculating the risk of concentrating loans in one industry or in one geographical location, or in one type of loan category (e.g., HLT loans). The agency did say that it certainly could identify classes of concentrations and recognize large exposures. The Federal Reserve also did not propose a formula for calculating the risk of entering nontraditional activities, such as commodity-based transactions and sophisticated currency and interest rate hedges. These situations will be reviewed on a case-by-case basis rather than by a quantitative formula. The agency proposed to amend existing capital rules to make a bank's ability to manage such risks a factor in determining capital adequacy.

The new risk-based capital plan was adopted to stem an increase in the overall risk of the banking industry and a decline in capital-to-asset ratios. The plan's requirements should improve control over risk taking by rewarding banks for taking less risk and by discouraging risky banks from increasing their asset growth by more than the growth rate at safe banks. In order to minimize the raising of equity and long-term debt in the capital markets, some banks will restrict their balance sheet growth, limiting their expansion plans. Some banks will reduce the size of their assets through the sale of assets that do not generate enough of a return for the capital required. Others will shift their holdings toward assets deemed less risky and requiring less capital. For example, some banks have begun to shift toward adding more agency and Treasury securities and residential mortgages to their portfolios. Of course, these instruments have lower capital requirements. Other banks have reduced or eliminated their dividends and sold real estate or subsidiaries at a considerable profit in order to strengthen their capital position. Financial institutions have also begun to encourage the continued development of fee-based income, for which there are, for the most part, no regulatory capital requirements (e.g., trust fees, cash management fees, underwriting fees, safe deposit fees, bond trading income).

While most of the large banks in the U.S. met the minimum capital requirements established by the Basle Accord by midyear 1992, a few of the large Japanese banks had less than the amount of capital needed. This is partially because the Bank of Japan had for years set its capital standards differently than the regulators in other countries. Another problem for Japanese banks is that a substantial portion of their capital is in the form of common shares on the Tokyo Stock Exchange, and these values had fallen by about 55 percent from their peak at the time of this writing, as the Japanese stock market collapsed. Also, Japanese banks do not generally write off debts if there is a possibility of eventually recovering a loan, even if that recovery is several years away. This practice accounts for the discrepancies between estimates of problem loans and the provisions for loan losses on their balance sheets.

There is one positive effect and one negative effect on other global banks of a shortfall among some large Japanese banks in meeting capital adequacy standards. The positive effect is that the Japanese are trying to raise new capital (it has proved to be difficult in a falling equity market). On the other hand, the Japanese banks are calling in foreign loans and are refusing to make new loans. Without competition from the Japanese in international lending, margins have risen. The negative effect is that a shortage of liquidity from Japanese banks is causing difficulties for some large borrowers (e.g., the U.K.'s Eurotunnel).[7]

An extra burden imposed by the new capital ratios in the United States is that they are tied to "CAMEL" ratings by regulators. (See Chapter 7 and Table 6.5.) If a bank is not given the top CAMEL rating, it must maintain a capital ratio between 100 and 200 basis points above the minimum equity capital requirement. In addition to the risk-based minimum capital requirements, and regardless of the composition

Table 6.5   Composite CAMEL Bank Examination Ratings

Composite 1:	Banks in this group are sound institutions in almost every aspect.
Composite 2:	Banks in this group are also fundamentally sound institutions, but may reflect modest weaknesses correctable in the normal course of business.
Composite 3:	Banks in this group exhibit a combination of weaknesses reflecting conditions ranging from moderately severe to unsatisfactory. Such banks are vulnerable and require more than normal supervision.
Composite 4:	Banks in this group have an immoderate volume of asset weaknesses or a combination of other conditions that are less than satisfactory. A potential for failure is present, but is not pronounced.
Composite 5:	Banks in this group possess an intensity and nature of weaknesses that require urgent aid from the shareholders or other sources. The probability of failure is high for these banks.

Note: CAMEL stands for Capital, Asset quality, Management, Earnings, and Liquidity.
Source: Federal Reserve Bank of New York.

of its assets, every bank must operate with a minimum equity-capital-to-total-asset ratio of at least 3 percent. Also, banks with poor CAMEL ratings must meet a minimum 4-percent ratio position.

Besides capital adequacy, bank regulators are also concerned with a growing number of accounting techniques that often confuse analysts and have the effect of concealing problems in bank loan portfolios. The biggest controversy centers on the issue of *restructuring,* an accounting practice that allows banks to transform nonaccruing loans into accruing loans by granting more favorable terms to the borrower, even though these terms may involve below-market interest rates that actually lose money for the bank. The way in which banks classify a loan often determines how much they have to put aside for possible credit losses. Regulators will have to come up with guidelines for all banks in handling the loss reserves of restructured loans. One problem lies with the fact that regulators were lenient with the money-center banks and allowed those with restructured LDC loans to get away with this accounting "magic," and now banks want to use that "magic" once again on restructured real estate loans.

A bank does not want to hold excessive capital. For example, if a bank earned a net profit of $1.5 million and had capital equal to 10 percent of its assets (say, $10 million), then the bank's stockholders would have earned a return of 15 percent on the equity capital ($1.5 million/$10 million = .15 = 15%). However, if the bank had capital equal to only 5 percent of total assets ($5 million) and the same earnings, then its return on equity (ROE) would be equal to 30 percent ($1.5 million/$5 million = .30 = 30%). Bank management must weigh the costs of having a smaller cushion of capital against the much higher returns on equity that are earned when that capital is smaller.[8]

The smaller a bank's equity base, the greater are its financial leverage and equity multiplier. High leverage converts a normal return on assets (ROA) into a high ROE. Banks with more capital tend to be able to borrow at lower rates, make larger loans, and expand faster, either through internal growth or through acquisitions. The adequacy of a bank's capital is a function of how much risk the bank assumes. Banks with lower quality assets, limited liquidity, and major mismatches in the durations of assets and liabilities should be required to hold more capital, while lower risk banks should be allowed to increase their financial leverage.

COMMENTS ON INTERSTATE BANKING AND MERGER ACTIVITY

The decade of the 1980s produced the interstate regional merger, the regulatory acceptance of the hostile merger (Bank of New York with Irving Bank), and the rise of powerful superregional banks, such as NationsBank, Wachovia, Fleet Financial, PNC, Corestates, Banc One, First Union, SunTrust, and Barnett. In testifying before the Senate Banking Committee in February 1988, Alan Greenspan, chairman of the Federal Reserve Board, made the following comments on the Bank of New York's hostile takeover bid for Irving Bank:

> Let's remember when we talk about hostile takeovers, the hostility is between the managements of the two organizations, not between the shareholders of either. In fact, the problem that exists is that too often, in my judgment, the managements try to protect themselves from, in effect, their own shareholders, who are essentially their bosses.

By early 1991, 48 states had enacted provisions allowing some form of interstate banking on their books, while 33 states had enacted some form of nationwide interstate banking. These regional interstate banking laws were a major boost to large banks in the regional financial centers and acted as a catalyst in the formation of superregionals—giant non-money-center banks that have expanded across state lines. Many of these superregionals almost approach the money-center banks in the size of their assets, but often exceed them in profitability. The difficulties of the money-center banks in their competition with the strong regional banks were compounded by a shortage of capital brought about by heavy losses in loans to Latin America, commercial real estate loans, and heavily leveraged loans. This capital shortage handicapped the money-center banks in making acquisitions.

The arguments against interstate banking appear to be parochial. They appeal to the siphoning of deposits out of the community, to be invested in other geographic locations. But why would a bank holding company want to pay a premium to acquire a bank and then thumb its nose at the community? The community's reaction would be to find another bank or to charter a new bank. The bank that was doing the siphoning would certainly not be supported by the community and would not be in business for long.[9]

Nationwide banking improves the integration of the financial system and the mobility of funds, so that deposits generated in one state could easily be used to fund projects in other states. Meir Kohn, of Dartmouth College, has concluded that although the movement toward interstate banking has led to increased concentration nationally, there are reasons to believe that competition should actually increase in local banking markets. He also says that interstate banking should result in a more efficient allocation of funds nationwide, by allowing the supply of deposits to be matched to the demand for loans over a larger regional, or even national, market. Further, interstate banking should result in a safer and more stable banking system because of better geographic and industry diversification of loans and deposits.[10]

STIMULUS FOR REGULATORY REFORM

There is widespread consensus that the regulatory framework inherited from the Depression era of the 1930s is no longer adequate in the global and high-technology financial marketplace of the 1990s. The stimulus for financial reform comes from the following sources:

1. The erosion of the traditional roles of financial institutions.
2. The development of many new types of financial instruments; for example, the increase in securitization led to direct lending in credit markets at the expense of bank lending, and the development of the money market fund led to major decreases in bank depository liabilities and a higher cost of funds.
3. The globalization of financial markets, which has increased competition.
4. The problems with the thrift industry.
5. The large increase in bank failures, and the weakening of the banking industry brought about by an increase in loan losses related to commercial real estate and Latin American loan problems.
6. The importance of limiting systemic risk. A key objective of the financial regulation should be the protection of the financial system as a whole against the possibility of destabilizing accidents, multiple bank runs, and market crashes.
7. Technological advances and economic forces that eventually undermined the basis of the system by reducing the market share and profitability of some institutions.
8. The inherent anticompetitive structure of existing regulation.

DECLINE IN ROLE OF BANKING IN THE
U.S. FINANCIAL SYSTEM

In 1991, an FDIC staff study concluded that the changing structure of the U.S. financial system had diminished the role of banks and threatened their financial stability, that the separation of banking and commerce had no inherent historical basis, and that Glass-Steagall was an overreaction to the problems of commercial and investment banking linkages in the 1930s. L. William Seidman, former FDIC head, concluded that Glass-Steagall and much of the Bank Holding Company Act could be eliminated if an effective supervisory wall could be constructed around banks to protect them from their affiliates.

The major effect of financial innovation on the financial system is a trend toward direct financing, a movement away from the use of banks and thrifts. Because of technological improvements in both information systems and communications, banks and related institutions do not have as much of a comparative advantage as they once had in developing the type of information they need to make loans. This is one of the main reasons why bank profitability has declined throughout the 1980s.[11] The best (i.e., most creditworthy) bank customers have been lured away from U.S. commercial banks by the commercial paper market, foreign banks, the capital market, and other competitors. A growing number of businesses no longer limit their search for funds to their domestic market, while internationally active banks compete for customers globally.[12] This has left the banking industry with much less creditworthy customers.

Kane feels that many of the problems cited by depository institutions are less the product of economic and technological change than of inappropriate regulatory behavior. He accuses regulators of subsidizing inefficient or harmful behavior to defend their turf or expand their political influence.

LOAN GUARANTEES

There has been a growing trend toward loan guarantees both in the U.S. and abroad. The federal government, either directly or though its agencies, is probably the largest provider of financial guarantees in the world. Deposit insurance is, of course, the best known of the guarantees, along with loans to small businesses. The Pension Benefit Guarantee Corporation (PBGC) provides limited insurance for corporate pension plans, while many remember the government guaranteeing loans to corporate giants such as Lockheed and Chrysler when they were in financial difficulty. The government also guarantees residential mortgages and farm and student loans.

There can be much risk in government guarantees, especially when most of them do not appear in the budget. "Off-budget" guarantees tend to be overused, as elected officials and regulators have a habit of issuing a guarantee, but not recording the value of any expected losses as an expense. Expenses are realized only if there is a loss. Charges deferred into the future do not appear in the budget and are sometimes denied by government officials or regulators. The thrift debacle represents a prime example of the long delay in admitting the existence of savings and loan losses. A way that loan guarantors can reduce the value of their loan-guarantee liabilities is to join more frequent monitoring of the company with the contractual right to seize the company's assets (or its equity interest) whenever the value of those assets is below the value of its guaranteed debt. Public or private guarantees remain viable only by controlling losses. Controls might consist of restrictions on the assets that can be held by the company whose debt is guaranteed, monitoring the value of assets more frequently and carefully, seizing assets swiftly and efficiently when necessary, or charging adequate fees for guarantees. A viable guarantee system might require a combination of these actions and might change with changing economic conditions.[13]

EXPANDING BANK ACTIVITIES

Reducing the barriers that separate banking from other activities may worsen the deposit insurance dilemma. *Insured banks* have a competitive advantage over other financial institutions in that depository insurance enables banks to obtain deposits at a risk-free rate. If investment banks and commercial banks compete in underwriting, the investment banks will probably have to pay a risk premium on the funds they use, in contrast to the insured commercial banks. If investment banks gain access to insured deposits, then the deposit-insurance subsidy will be extended to a whole new range of activities.[14]

Banks have pressed for expanded underwriting powers through creative interpretation of Glass-Steagall and have been quite successful in accomplishing their objectives. The argument for expanded bank underwriting activities is that these additional opportunities should augment the potential for increased bank profits, while enhancing the stability of the banking system.

A key concern about ending the separation of commercial from investment banking is the potential for conflicts of interest. For example, suppose that a company is close to default on a bank loan. If the bank arranges an underwriting of a debt issue, with the proceeds used to pay off the bank loan, then the default risk is shifted away from the bank to unsuspecting investors. Of course, the bank will likely be less than forthcoming with information pertaining to the company's problems. A second example might involve an unsuccessful underwriting of securities by the bank so that the bank sells the securities to trust department customers. Alternatively, it might offer a bank loan with a reduced interest rate to encourage the purchase of the unsold securities. The bank would avoid a loss by selling the securities for more than they were really worth, as well as making an underwriting profit. These were concerns prior to the passage of Glass-Steagall. It is apparent now that such abuses were not widespread.[15]

There is also the question whether banks can be insulated from the problems of affiliated companies and how that insulation might be accomplished effectively. Some scholars are concerned with the possibility of increased concentration of economic power if a revised regulatory structure permitted the development of large financial and commercial conglomerates, such as the universal banks of Europe or the trading or holding companies of Japan.

E. G. CORRIGAN: BANKING COMMERCE
CONTROVERSY

Current U.S. banking law prohibits commercial firms from owning commercial banks and vice versa. E.G. Corrigan, president of the Federal Reserve Bank of New York, is opposed to combinations of commercial and banking organizations, but remains unopposed to combinations of banking and securities firms. Corrigan believes that there is no strong evidence that a linkage of banking with commerce would have significant economic benefits. He is also skeptical that banking could be effectively insulated from commercial firms. Corrigan concluded that the risks of merging banking with commerce outweighed the benefits. On the other hand, he feels that combinations of banking and securities firms, which are the rule throughout the industrial world, keep well within the spirit of congeneric financial corporations. Even within the limits of Glass-Steagall, banks are actively engaged in a wide range of securities activities in the United States.[16]

Corrigan feels that it would be a huge mistake to eliminate the barriers Congress has constructed between banking and commerce. He argues that "(1) when firewalls are needed most, they will not work; (2) it is inevitable that at least parts of the supervisory system—if not the safety net—will be extended to commercial owners of banks; (3) the risks of concentration of economic resources and power are great; and (4) the potential benefits that might grow out of banking-commercial combinations [are] remote at best and illusory at worst."[17]

Another question is whether a commercial business entity should be allowed to own and control financial institutions that, in turn, have direct or indirect access to the federal banking safety net. The mere fact of permitting commercial firms to own and control banking organizations carries with it at least the implicit transfer of some elements of the safety net to such firms. "It is worth pondering what would have occurred in 1980 had Chrysler owned a family of commercial banking institutions having access to the safety net. Similarly, what might have happened if Texaco were in a similar position at the time of the Pennzoil litigation? It is also worth keeping in mind that the corporate landscape is currently littered with dozens of fallen 'angels,' many of which might well have owned banks in happier times."[18] The risk is of the contagion effect—the danger that problems in any one part of a business will adversely affect other parts of the business, despite fire walls or legal separations between particular business units within the firm as a whole. Walter Wriston, former chairman of Citicorp, once said, "It is inconceivable that any major bank would walk away from any subsidiary of its holding company. If your name is on the door, all of your capital funds are going to be behind it in the real world. Lawyers can say you have separation, but the marketplace is persuasive, and it would not see it that way."[19] Essentially, there is always the danger that problems in one part of an entity cannot, in market terms, be contained and isolated from other parts of that entity.

The reality of the contagion effect gives rise to another set of risks associated with the combining of banking and commerce: There is the danger that such combinations bring with them the likelihood that at least some parts of the safety net will be extended to owners of banking institutions, especially in times of stress. This brings up the issue of systemic risk (the clear and present danger that problems in financial institutions can be transmitted rapidly to other institutions or markets, inflicting damage on those institutions, their customers, and, ultimately, the economy at large). It is the systemic risk phenomenon that makes banks different from department stores or furniture manufacturers. It is this factor that constitutes the fundamental rationale for the safety net arrangements that must evolve. Even though we have both legal and structural firewalls to separate various activities, "the acid test of firewalls arises in the context of adversity to the banking institution itself, a cross-stream affiliate, or the parent. . . . The obvious danger is that in times of stress, firewalls become walls of fire. . . . It seems . . . that the evidence is overwhelming that firewalls and corporate separateness do not stand up well in the face of adversity and that the contagion risks are very real indeed.[20] In fact, "there is no system of firewalls that is failsafe . . . problems in one part of a family of institutions simply cannot be isolated from the family as a whole."[21]

Corrigan feels that the case for allowing commercial firms to control banking institutions should be based on some affirmative public policy reasons. Why would commercial firms want to control banks? Because they may conclude that (1) the rate of return on banking investments is larger than is available on alternative investments, (2) banking investments provide a vehicle for diversification, (3) there are synergies between the core business of the company and some aspect of the banking business, (4) there are advantages to having indirect access to one or more elements of the safety net, and (5) they desire to leverage further their own capital positions.[22] Current laws allow any company to make sizable passive investments in one or more banking institutions. "If control is sought or achieved, or if the investment is motivated by perceived synergies or by a desire to gain indirect access to the safety net, then, it must follow that concerns about conflicts of interest, unfair competition, concentration, and the extension of the safety net must be present. . . . If the firewalls are fail-safe, the synergies must disappear, and if the synergies disappear, the central economic argument that public benefits will flow from such combinations is rendered moot."[23]

Corrigan feels that if we were to allow commercial companies to control banks, the potential dangers in terms of the concentration of economic resources and economic and political power—with all of the implications for compromising the impartiality of the credit-making decision process—could become serious. (However, experience from the nonbank banks suggests that tie-ins would not be a problem: All three financial subsidiaries owned by the big three U.S. automakers make loans for their competitors' products.)[24] This concentration of economic and political power could also have subtle, but serious, implications for monetary policy. Moreover, if commercial bank ownership of banks resulted in an additional increase in overall leverage, the fragility of both the financial and the nonfinancial sectors could increase further.[25] The potential benefits that might grow out of combining commercial and banking organizations seem remote at best and illusory at worst under present conditions.[26] However, some benefits must be recognized. By expanding the field of owners, new capital might be brought to undercapitalized banks from outside the banking industry. Also, there are claims that the combination of banking with commercial firms may lower the cost of providing services through economics of scale or scope. What is more, there are claims that revenue synergies will accrue. Unfortunately, empirical support for these arguments appears to be lacking in the literature.[27]

Perhaps related to Corrigan's argument is the fact that the largest German banks control access to or have a near monopoly on brokerage to the stock exchange in Frankfurt. Under this arrangement, small firms were kept from issuing equity, thus remaining captive loan clients. Large German companies have traditionally relied more on bank credit and bonds than on equity to finance their growth. The integration of banking and commerce in Germany helped contribute to this reliance. German banks, "through their equity holdings, exert significant ownership control over industrial firms."[28]

Henry Kaufman, former Salomon Brothers partner and now head of his own money management company, warned against the association of financial with commercial firms (he wanted to keep separate the functions of lending, underwriting, and equity investment) because of the fiduciary role of financial institutions, their role in payment and credit allocation mechanisms, and the dangers of the extension of the federal safety net. He also suggested that deposit insurance be used to strengthen the financial system by requiring that insured deposits be invested in creditworthy assets.[29] This is similar to the suggestions of Pierce, Litan, and Kareken, who feel that an institution receiving federal deposit insurance should be only a limited or narrow bank, restricted to short-term assets (similar to a money market fund) or a quasi-money market fund, including short-term commercial loans.[30]

While Corrigan has many supporters who also wish to keep commerce and banking separate, others feel that this separation is a history of a principle gone wrong, since these laws were originally designed to protect commercial firms from banks at a time when banks were so large that they seemed to threaten free competition in the business world. Some analysts believe that allowing banks to associate with other financial and nonfinancial firms should lead to a better solution to bank capital adequacy problems, as well as offer cost savings. There are cost advantages in the form of economies of scope and synergies in the joint production of financial and nonfinancial services that should result in increased economic efficiency, lowering costs to the consumer.

Currently, banks are considered weak and laws are being utilized to protect them, not to restrain them. Kenneth Whipple, president of Ford Financial Services Group, raises the issue that the separation of banking from commerce restricts competition and shuts the banking industry out from sorely needed capital. He points out that while some worry that commercial firms might be covered by the "too-big-to-fail" (TBTF) safety net, it is the opposite that has occurred. In the case of Ford's First Nationwide subsidiary, Ford contributed $1.5 billion in capital, actually reducing the taxpayer burden of the thrift crisis. Whipple also points out that the fire walls that protect the separate businesses of Ford Motor Company and its subsidiaries do work. Ford watches itself and the regulators watch them, to ensure that there is no impropriety. The company is also watched by the markets, the rating agencies, and investors buying the debt of Ford's subsidiaries. Whipple points out that not only could financial resources be brought into the industry, but so could planning concepts and managerial talent: "Commercial firms could bring new ideas and life to banking because they are experienced in planning for the long term, developing innovative products, listening to the voices of the customer, and managing complex organizations for strategic advantage."[31]

A. W. Clausen, former chairman of BankAmerica, contends that even though industrial corporations are not permitted to own banks, we have a bastardized system of financial entities in the United States. For example, GM is the second largest servicer of home mortgages and a new player in the credit card market, offering discounts on its cars as a reward for using the company's credit card. Similarly, American Express owns an FDIC-insured bank, as well as a brokerage firm and insurance company. And AT&T is rapidly closing ranks on the largest credit card issuers, while bank holding companies cannot even engage in most areas of vertical integration.

The validity of many of the arguments for or against allowing commercial banks and commercial firms to mix often depended on the ability of regulators to control possible abuses of the financial system by its participants. However, as banking reforms, such as risk-based deposit insurance premiums and limits on "TBTF" are implemented, the prohibitions against commercial firms' owning banks and banks owning commercial firms should be reconsidered.[32]

UNIVERSAL BANKING

Countries in which investment banking and commercial banking are combined have what is commonly called a *universal banking system.* Universal banks (a term believed to have been coined by Deutsche Bank) are usually domiciled in the United Kingdom (e.g., Barclays Bank, National Westminster, Midland Bank Group, Lloyds Bank) and in continental European countries that have no effective regulatory barriers to comprehensive product and geographic coverage of all major customers. Typically, these banks have both large capital bases and special distribution advantages. For example, the "Big Three" Swiss universal banks (Union Bank of Switzerland, Swiss Bank Corp., and Credit Suisse) have placing power within the accounts they manage for individuals, while the German universal banks (e.g., Deutsche Bank and Dresdner Bank) have large stakes in most institutional investors. The universal banks have already benefited from the full-service investment and commercial banking relationships that combine corporate finance fee-based income with lending opportunities. Also, the large banks are able to obtain some economies of scale in investment banking businesses such as government bond trading and swaps, while having lower funding costs than investment banks.[33]

Some disadvantages to the universal banking structure are personnel recruitment problems involving salary differentials between investment and commercial bankers, the establishment of necessary lines of communication, and the management of capital to contain losses and enhance returns. Another cultural difference may be in response time in decision making: Most universal banks may take a longer time to respond to environmental shifts than their investment banking counterparts because of the substantial bureaucracies with which universal banks control their lending and other credit services. In order to deal with these issues, most universal bankers who operate investment banking units segregate these units from their commercial banking activities and separate them physically in order to preserve the required entrepreneurial atmosphere. This geographic separation is particularly true of the continental banks, wherein the investment banking arm is located in London, while the lending function might be headquartered in Frankfurt, Brussels, or Zurich.[34]

The European Community issues a single license that permits banks to expand their networks throughout the community, governed by their home country's regulations. Since banking powers are determined by the rules of the home country, banks from countries with more liberal banking laws should have a definite advantage over their domestic competitors. Under these conditions, it is likely that the most efficient form of banking will prevail. Countries with more fragmented banking systems will have to change if they wish to compete with universal banking on an equal playing field in the markets served. In addition, as financial service companies in Europe begin to operate with fewer restrictions, there will be competitive pressure on the United States and Japan to remove barriers that exist in those countries between investment and commercial banking.[35]

According to Benston, of Emory University, financial stability is more likely under universal banking than under specialized banking because universal banks are more diversified and therefore can better withstand the effects of unexpected economic changes. The regulators can largely alleviate the detrimental effects of failures by requiring all depository institutions to hold adequate amounts of capital and by following a policy of expeditious closure of failing institutions. Systemic collapse is not a function of financial market structure, but of actions that the central bank takes or does not take. In addition, Benston found that economies of scale were not likely to be achieved through specialization, while economies of scope may be foregone if banks are prevented from offering an unrestrained range of products and services. Benston concluded that most of the charges of conflicts of interest against banks in the United States that engaged in securities operations prior to the passage of Glass-Steagall remain unsubstantiated. He also concluded that economic development is likely to be enhanced if banks can offer companies a full range of financing alternatives and that concentration of power has not been a consequence of universal banking. As long as antitrust laws prevent banks from cartelizing an industry, there is no reason for concern about bank ownership of nonbanks. However, there is reason to believe that specialization is conducive to the development of coalitions that acquire the political power to transfer resources to their members from other people. Benston found that universal banking did not reduce competition and in fact expanded consumer choice. Tie-in sales are not abusive practices, except when a bank might force companies in which it invests to take the bank's services at above-market prices. This abuse has not occurred in West Germany, according to Benston. In addition, in a large-scale study of possible conflicts of interest among West German banks, the Gessler Commission found no evidence of actions that were detrimental to the interests of consumers. Benston's overall conclusion is that universal banking can provide considerable benefits and pose few problems for the economy. Specialized providers of financial services (e.g., investment banks) would still exist and in some cases do things better than universal banks.[36]

OTHER TYPES OF BANKING ENTITIES

The historical legislative separation of investment banking from commercial banking in the United States and Japan is quite unusual. In most European countries, universal banks can accept deposits, make loans, underwrite securities, engage in brokerage activities and insurance, and perform most investment banking and corporate financial activities.

There is also a fuzzy line of demarcation between global investment banks (e.g., Salomon Brothers and Nomura Securities) and universal banks. Global investment banks are securities firms that offer a comprehensive array of services associated with the public securities markets. While not nearly as large as their universal banking competitors, global investment banks are substantial organizations with a wide variety of products and services in multiple geographic markets around the world. They provide brokerage, investment management, research, money and capital market activities, private placement activities, corporate financial advice and counsel, merger and acquisition activities, deal making, and investment or merchant banking activities that might include underwriting and bridge financing, as well as trading activities. Their strengths and benefits come from a system of interconnecting lines of business that provide vital market intelligence in addition to economies of scale, an entrepreneurial environment, and a quick response time.[37]

In addition to universal banks and global investment banks, there are global niche investment banks that specialize in some segment of the international investment banking market. The niche of one of these banks can take the form of a specialized knowledge base or a unique access to a customer or a client group, or the bank may be on the cutting edge of technology, with constantly innovative new products and services. Lazard Freres and Wasserstein, Perella are examples of niche firms or boutiques that focus on mergers and acquisitions, facilitation of corporate finances, and, in the case of the latter firm, leveraged buy-out structuring and restructuring.[38]

SOURCE-OF-STRENGTH POLICY AND THE DOUBLE UMBRELLA

After reviewing existing banking law, James Pierce concluded that sufficient protection already existed in permitting bank holding companies to offer a wider range of financial services if bank regulators have the will to enforce existing regulations.[39] He also agreed with analysts who suggested that firewalls might be strengthened. For example, the holding company should be a source of strength to its subsidiary banks, standing ready to provide additional capital in times of financial stress.[40] In the absence of a *source-of-strength policy,* holding companies could be tempted to ask their banks to remit excessive dividends, could charge unwarranted management fees, or could loot the banks in other ways. The holding company might also cut loose subsidiary banks that did not perform up to expectations. If a subsidiary encountered difficulties, it would be permitted to fail. The FDIC would be left to pay off depositors, while there would be no penalty to the shareholders of the holding company; therefore, regulators must be careful of the insulation policy and of separateness carried to the extreme. Federal Reserve Board Governor H. Robert Heller supports the double-umbrella concept for bank holding companies. The financial services holding company would have to commit itself to being a source of strength to its bank subsidiary in return for the right to own a bank that has access to the federal safety net and payment system. Heller would also permit commercial companies to own financial services holding companies, with the proviso that they serve as a source of strength to the financial services holding companies. This would provide the banking system with a double umbrella of protection, which should enhance financial stability in periods of upheaval.[41]

It is important to point out that insulation is a two-way sword. In addition to protecting depositors, legal fire walls between banks and affiliated companies help to deny those companies access to low-cost funds that might otherwise give them an advantage over companies that are not associated with banks.

MULTIPLE REGULATORY AGENCIES

Under the dual banking system, banks and thrifts may choose the regulator who is most favorable to their needs. Since regulators often competed with each other to have more members, on occasion they may have lost sight of the common goal of bank safety. In other words, in the past, regulators sometimes attracted depository institutions by offering less onerous regulation—in effect, the regulators were competing in laxity.

Some critics claim that the system of multiple regulatory agencies and overlapping jurisdictions leads to confusion and wasted resources, since federal and state regulations often duplicate each other. In addition, federal regulators do not adequately coordinate their rules and decisions. Others claim, however, that multiple regulatory agencies foster innovation and flexibility. (See Figure 6.2 and Table 6.6.) Banks often can and do play one regulatory agency against another. For example, if one regulatory agency is unwilling to permit a bank to engage in certain business activities, sometimes another regulator will.

One example of innovation was the introduction of adjustable-rate mortgages in California. Initially, federal regulators were unwilling to allow state-chartered S&Ls to issue variable-rate mortgages. These mortgages have now become an important and popular factor in the residential mortgage market.

In 1979, Congress tried to establish better coordination of bank regulatory agencies by creating a council of all the federal regulators of depository institutions,

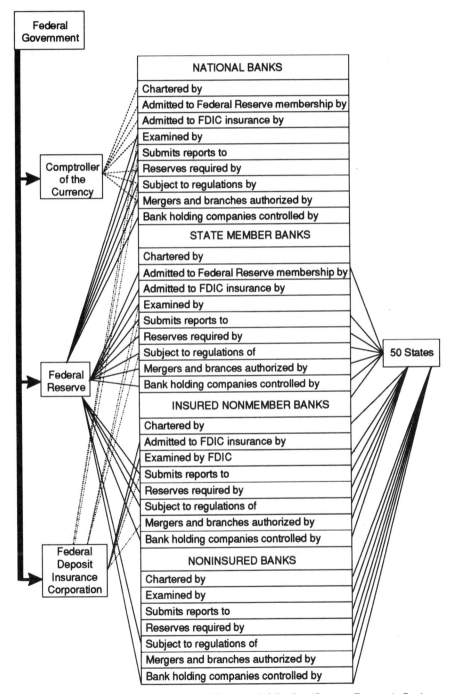

Figure 6.2 Regulation and Supervision of Commercial Banks. (*Source: Economic Review,* Federal Reserve Bank of Atlanta, December 1982, p. 46)

Table 6.6 Depository Institutions and Their Regulators

The regulatory structure for depository institutions is based on a dual banking system, in which both states and the federal government can issue charters. A single institution may be supervised by the state and by several federal regulators, depending on the activities in which it is engaged.

	Chartering and Licensing	Branching — Intrastate	Branching — Interstate	Mergers, Acquisitions, and Consolidations — Intrastate	Mergers, Acquisitions, and Consolidations — Interstate	Reserve Requirements	Access to the Discount Window	Deposit Insurance
A. National Banks	Comptroller	Comptroller	[a]	Federal Reserve and Comptroller	[d]	Federal Reserve	Federal Reserve	FDIC (BIF)
B. State Member Banks	State authority	Federal Reserve and state authority	[b]	Federal Reserve and state authority	[d]	Federal Reserve	Federal Reserve	FDIC (BIF)
C. Insured State Nonmember Banks	State authority	FDIC and state authority	[b]	FDIC and state authority	[d]	Federal Reserve	Federal Reserve	FDIC (BIF)
D. Noninsured State Banks	State authority	State authority	[c]	State authority	State authority	Federal Reserve	Federal Reserve	None or state insurance fund
E. Savings Banks — Federal Mutual [a]	OTS	OTS	OTS	OTS and FDIC	[d]	Federal Reserve	Federal Reserve	FDIC (SAIF)
E. Savings Banks — State Mutual [b]	State authority	FDIC and state authority	FDIC and state authority	FDIC and state authority[d]	[d]	Federal Reserve	Federal Reserve	FDIC (BIF) or state insurance fund
F. Savings and Loan Associations — Federal [a]	OTS	OTS	OTS	OTS, FDIC and state authority	[d]	Federal Reserve	Federal Home Loan Bank and Federal Reserve	FDIC (SAIF) or state insurance fund
F. Savings and Loan Associations — State [b]	State authority	OTS and state authority	OTS and state authority		[d]	Federal Reserve	Federal Home Loan Bank and Federal Reserve	
G. Credit Unions — Federal [a]	NCUAB	[a]	[a]	NCUAB	[d]	Federal Reserve	Central Liquidity Facility and Federal Reserve	NCUSIF
G. Credit Unions — State [b]	State authority	State authority	State authority	NCUAB and state authority				NCUSIF or state insurance fund

[a] Federal credit unions are not required to receive approval from the NCUAB before opening a branch.
[b] While the McFadden Act prevents interstate branching by national and state member banks, banks can provide certain services on an interstate basis.
[c] While the McFadden Act's interstate branching restrictions are not applicable to insured state nonmember and noninsured state banks, state laws generally prohibit branching by out-of-state banks.
[d] The McFadden Act prevents interstate branching by national and state member banks.

Source: Federal Reserve Board of Governors.

called the Federal Banking Regulator. The council has not resulted in the formation of a single regulatory agency for depository institutions, but the regulators have begun to develop more uniform regulations and regulatory procedures. In 1980, there was a proposal to consolidate the regulatory web. The Federal Reserve was to be the single surviving regulator, carrying out both monetary policy and bank regulation. These proposals were never formally introduced into legislation, because of lobbying efforts by the regulatory agencies then in place and because regulators rarely agree to go out of business.

The Bush Administration suggested a change in the bank regulatory function in February 1991. Under this proposal, the FDIC would no longer regulate state-chartered nonmember banks. Instead, the Federal Reserve would be responsible for the regulation of all state-chartered banks, while the Department of the Treasury would regulate all nationally chartered banks and S&Ls. The proposal did not become legislation, and the regulation of depository institutions still follows an entangled web, as can be seen from Table 6.6. In 1992, the regulators did agree that the OTS, part of the U.S. Treasury Department, would be the primary regulator of federally chartered S&Ls. However, the FDIC would also examine weak S&Ls—institutions that were candidates for potential insolvency.

If Congress cannot consolidate regulation by combining state and federal agencies to create a superregulator, then the next best initiative would be to keep the different regulatory bodies, but have them focus their oversight activities either on different functional areas, such as size and market, or on specific business activities. However, major congressional action on this issue is unlikely in the near future because Congress has not been able to reach a consensus.

ISSUES OF PAYMENT SYSTEM SAFETY

One of the major reasons why there is a safety net for depository institutions is that failures of banks or thrifts can produce systemic risk. Unchecked systemic risk can impose major costs on the entire economy of the United States, as well as on other nations in the case of the failure of a large, global money-center bank.

Every bank assumes some risk by participating in the payments system. These risks were developed in an environment in which there was no interest charge on interday credit and, until recently, no constraints on the magnitude of intraday credit. While there have been no losses to date resulting from the daylight credit exposures, the risk is recognized by all.

In addition to the Federal Reserve's concern with the stability of the financial system is the parallel responsibility for the safety of the payments system, particularly the wire transfer systems of Fedwire and CHIPS. The Fedwire's problem is *daylight overdraft* during the business day, while the CHIPS problem is *systemic risk,* that is, risk relating to the possibility that the failure of one bank will cause the failure of other banks. The Federal Reserve is exposed to considerable credit risk with daylight overdraft exposures. If a bank that has an overdraft outstanding fails, the

Federal Reserve might be left with a bad debt. However, the risk of substantial losses related to Fedwire is ultimately borne by the FDIC and the taxpaying public.

Payments on CHIPS are provisional; they are finalized only at the end of the day, when clearing occurs. The risk is that a CHIPS participant will fail during the day. In that case, its payment would have to be canceled and the net position of the other banks would have to be recalculated. Some banks would have large "uncoverable" deficits, which could lead to a domino effect and the collapse of a number of banks. Would the Federal Reserve step in and prevent a collapse? Would it also help foreign banks who use the CHIPS system?

In 1982, the Federal Reserve suggested that banks reduce their daylight overdrafts to no more than a given multiple of their equity capital. In 1989, the Federal Reserve proposed a charge of 25 basis points for daylight overdrafts in excess of a deductible of 10 percent of the institution's capital.[42] Another proposal would require additional reserve balances at those banks which regularly overdraw their reserve accounts during the day. The Federal Reserve would pay interest on these reserve balances at a rate just under the federal funds rate.

The objective of a policy change is to reduce the risk of the Federal Reserve without creating the risk that a failure of one bank will cause the failure of other banks, thus disrupting the operation of the payments system. A major goal of the Federal Reserve is to improve the safety of the payments system, in which both daylight overdrafts and systemic risks are serious concerns. Wayne D. Angell, Federal Reserve Board governor, feels that the Federal Reserve must introduce a system for pricing daylight overdrafts (an above-market rate) as a means of controlling the problem and reimbursing the Federal Reserve for some of the credit risk it assumes. He also would allow Fedwire to operate 24 hours a day. The latter would provide more timely payment for institutions throughout the world, as well as allowing less pressing domestic transfers to be conducted during off-peak hours.[43]

ENDNOTES

1. *Banks Under Stress* (Paris: OECD, 1992), pp. 9–10.

2. A. Greenspan, "Subsidies and Powers in Commercial Banking," *Game Plan for the '90s,* Proceedings of Conference on Bank Structure and Competition, Federal Reserve Bank of Chicago, May 9–11, 1990, p. 2.

3. G. Hempel, A. Coleman, and D. Simonson, *Bank Management: Text and Cases,* 3d ed. (New York: John Wiley & Sons, 1990), pp. 278–279.

4. T. Koch, *Bank Management,* 2d ed. (Hinsdale, IL: Dryden Press, 1992), pp. 808–809.

5. F. Mishkin, *The Economics of Money, Banking, and Financial Markets* (Hinsdale, IL: Dryden Press, 1992), p. 234.

6. O. Kramer, *Rating the Risk* (New York: Insurance Information Institute, 1990), pp. 107, 123.

7. "Danger at the Frontier," *Financial Times,* May 20, 1992, Sec. III, p. 1.

8. Mishkin, p. 234.

9. J. M. Leggett, "Interstate Banking Concept Outlines Many Years of Criticism," *American Banker,* May 30, 1991, p. 8A.

10. M. Kohn, *Money, Banking and Financial Markets* (Hinsdale, IL: Dryden Press, 1991), pp. 199–205.

11. J. B. Taylor, "Commentary, the Financial System and Economic Performance," *International Competitiveness in Financial Service* (Boston: Kluwer Academic Publishers, 1990), p. 308.

12. G. P. Driscoll, "Comment on Bank Insulation," *Governing Banking's Future: Markets vs. Regulation,* ed. C. England (Boston: Kluwer Academic Publishers, 1991), p. 112.

13. R. C. Merton, "The Financial System and Economic Performance," *International Competitiveness in Financial Service* (Boston: Kluwer Academic Publishers, 1990), p. 308.

14. Kohn, pp. 498–499.

15. Ibid., p. 498.

16. E. G. Corrigan, "A Perspective on Recent Financial Disruption," *Quarterly Review,* Federal Reserve Bank of New York, Winter 1989/1990, p. 12.

17. Corrigan, "The Banking-Commerce Controversy Revisited," *Quarterly Review,* Federal Reserve Bank of New York, Spring 1991, pp. 1–2.

18. Ibid., p. 10.

19. W. Wriston, Testimony before The Senate Committee on Banking, Housing and Urban Affairs, Financial Institutions Restructuring and Services Act of 1981, 97th Congress, First Session, 1981.

20. Corrigan, "The Banking-Commerce Controversy Revisited," pp. 7–8.

21. Corrigan, "Balancing Progressive Change and Caution in Reforming the Financial System,"*Quarterly Review,* Federal Reserve Bank of New York, Summer 1991, p. 3.

22. Corrigan, "The Banking-Commerce Controversy Revisited," p. 6.

23. Ibid., pp. 6–9.

24. L. J. Meister, "Banking and Commerce: A Dangerous Liaison?" *Business Review,* Federal Reserve Bank of Philadelphia, May/June 1992, p. 24.

25. Corrigan, "Balancing Progressive Change," p. 3.

26. Corrigan, "The Banking-Commerce Controversy," pp. 10–11.

27. Meister, p. 20.

28. C. Pavel and J. N. McElravey, "Globalization in the Financial Services Industry," *Economic Perspective,* Federal Reserve Bank of Chicago, May/June 1990, pp. 3–18.

29. H. Kaufman, "Overview," *Restructuring The Financial System,* A symposium sponsored by the Federal Reserve Bank of Kansas City, August 1987, pp. 234–235.

30. J. L. Pierce, "Can Banks Be Insulated from Nonbank Affiliates?" *Governing Banking's Future: Markets vs. Regulation,* ed. C. England (Boston: Kluwer Academic Publishers, 1991), pp. 59–77; R. Litan, *What Should Banks Do?* (Washington, DC: Brookings

Institute, 1987); J. H. Kareken, "Comment on Insulating Banks," *Governing Banking's Future.*

31. K. Whipple, "Debate," *Harvard Business Review,* July/August 1991, pp. 155–156.

32. Meister, p. 28.

33. S. L. Hayes and P. M. Hubbard, *Investment Banking* (Boston: Harvard Business School Press, 1990), p. 332.

34. Ibid., pp. 332–333.

35. Pavel and McElravey, pp. 3–18.

36. G. Benston, *The Separation of Commercial and Investment Banking* (New York: Oxford University Press, 1990), pp. 212–213.

37. Hayes and Hubbard, p. 333.

38. Ibid., p. 334.

39. Pierce, pp. 59–75.

40. C. England, ed., *Governing Banking's Future: Markets vs. Regulation* (Boston: Kluwer Academic Publishers, 1991), p. 6.

41. Ibid., pp. 13, 14.

42. Kohn, pp. 504–505.

43. England, p. 7.

7 Deposit Insurance and Bank Failures

The short-run issue is how to finance the elimination or reduction in the number of economically insolvent institutions from the system. Most of the past policies, such as forbearance, were really temporary responses to the financing problem. Insolvencies were financed by permitting insolvent institutions to continue operating rather than closing and paying them off or warehousing their assets elsewhere. Such policies shift the burden to future taxpayers and are bound to fail because they do not address the incentive problems in the system ... The long-run issue is how to restructure the system to eliminate the incentives for institutions to take on more risk and to eliminate the incentives for regulators and politicians to game the tax payer.

Robert A. Eisenbeis, *Restructuring Banking: The Shadow Financial Regulatory Committee's Program For Banking Reform*

There has been considerable discussion about the relatively poor performance of commercial banks in recent years. The names of problematic or failed banks, such as SeaFirst, Continental Illinois, First City Bancorporation, Texas Commerce Bancshares, First Republic Banks, Bank of New England, and Southeast Bank, have become well known to financial analysts and the public. As a matter of fact, First City Bancorporation has the dubious distinction of having become a two-time loser. The bank was among a group of major Texas banks that collapsed in 1988. Then, the bank holding company was seized by federal regulators on October 30, 1992, and filed for chapter 11 bankruptcy protection following massive loan losses that wiped out most of the institution's tier 1 capital. Congress was also warned that the Bank Insurance Fund at the FDIC was near insolvency and would require an infusion of capital in late 1991 or early 1992. The problems at the FDIC were in part related to the huge number of bank failures of the 1980s and early 1990s and the inadequacy of insurance premiums. (See Table 7.1 and Figure 7.1.)

BANK EARLY WARNING MODELS

The aim of early warning models is to identify those banks which are likely to experience financial problems. If the models do a good job in identifying problem

Table 7.1   Banking Failures

Year	Number	Total Deposits ($ Billions)
1945–1954	44	
1955–1964	47	
1965–1974	60	
1975–1981	75	
1982	42	$9.9
1983	48	5.4
1984	79	2.9
1985	120	8.1
1986	138	6.5
1987	184	6.3
1988	200	24.9
1989	206	24.1
1990	169	14.8
1991	127	53.8
1992	122	N.A.

Source: FDIC annual reports.

banks, they are extremely useful to banks, mutual funds, investors, and regulators. Obviously, banks that signal problems would be avoided by investors and depositors, as well as by other banks in the federal funds market. A good model would also reduce the total costs of bank supervision by allowing regulators to allocate examination resources more efficiently and enabling them to identify and resolve problems more quickly. Regulators would be able to take the steps necessary to minimize the drain on the deposit system. Among the salient variables that have been useful in forecasting bank insolvency are changes or variability in net worth, measures of asset risk (e.g., a concentration of loans in real estate, in commercial and industrial enterprises, or to lesser developed countries), and a major decline in the price of a bank's stock. A problem with the use of the last of these is that the loss in net worth already may be irreversible by the time the stock price declines. Also, asset composition alone is not sufficient to distinguish healthy from unhealthy banks, because the riskiness of various categories of assets changes over time, as does the extent to which the risks might offset one another.[1]

Other important financial ratios that have proved helpful in detecting problematic banks are return on assets (ROA), loans to assets, capital to assets, net occupancy expense to net income, nonperforming loans to total loans outstanding, gross charge-offs to net operating income plus provision for loan losses, and purchased funds to assets. For example, a low ROA and a high charge-off ratio indicates a higher probability of failure than does a high ROA and a low charge-off ratio. Similarly, a low capital ratio and large purchased funds increases the likelihood of failure, as does a large ratio of nonperforming loans to total loans outstanding. Banks that fail tend to exhibit most of these ratios at unfavorable levels, though not any one alone.

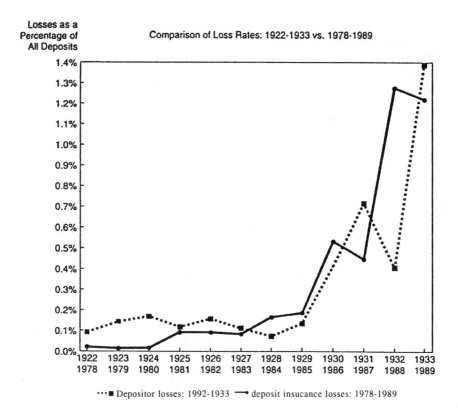

Figure 7.1   Comparison of Loss Rates: 1922–1933 vs. 1978–1989. (*Source:* Federal Deposit Insurance Corporation)

Also, banks that are prone to failure tend to have an aggressive position in brokered deposits. Although brokered deposits are not a major source of funding at these "soon to fail banks," there is a virtual absence of such deposits among the top-performing banks.[2]

The CAMEL Ratings

Although the question of FDIC regulatory powers is undergoing debate, the FDIC remains the provider of depository insurance coverage for banks and S&Ls. While poor management and fraud are the most common causes of bank failures, there is no reliable measure of poor management. Bank failures had averaged only 10 per year through a 40-year period following the Great Depression, but the 1980s represented a period where bank failures exceeded 200 in some years. The FDIC has a failure–to–quality rating model that rates banks on the basis of five characteristics:

Capital adequacy	C
Asset quality	A
Management	M
Earnings	E
Liquidity	L

These five characteristics make up the CAMEL ratings, the acronym that identifies the first letters of each of the five key components of the safety and soundness examination process.

Capital

Capital represents the funds invested in the bank by its owners. Those funds act as a buffer to shield the bank from losses in the value of its assets. The higher the level of capital adequacy (capital divided by assets), the more easily a bank can absorb potential losses, enhancing the probability of its survival. Consequently, banks with higher capital ratios are assigned a higher capital adequacy ratio. When capital is deemed inadequate, the regulator may recommend that the bank raise more new capital or raise new uninsured subordinated debt; or the regulator may recommend the closing or merger of the bank into a healthier bank. The regulators will in any case make a "capital call" to a bank that is deficient in capital. The bank must then submit a plan describing how and when it will increase its capital to meet the established requirements. If the bank is unable to raise additional capital, the regulators can impose severe limitations on management in documents such as memoranda of understanding. These restrictions may limit the amount of dividends the bank can pay, reduce its freedom to attract insured deposits, or induce the bank to curtail its risk-taking behavior. The regulators can also issue cease-and-desist orders as the net worth of a bank approaches zero. The regulators take the action that they deem most appropriate on a case-by-case basis.

It must be mentioned once again that all banks are required to satisfy a system of minimum risk-based capital requirements. Above these levels, regulators may exercise some discretion regarding the level of capital a bank should hold. They can permit banks with strong composite CAMEL ratings to hold less capital than banks with lower CAMEL ratings.

Asset Quality

In addition to evaluating capital adequacy, the FDIC also evaluates the quality of the bank's assets. The quality, type, liquidity, and diversification of assets are all vital factors in determining the adequacy of capital as well as the quality of management. Regulators are concerned with whether management is too slow in charging off bad loans and whether the reserve for loan losses is adequate. An appropriate examination of a bank's loan portfolio not only assesses whether borrowers are current on loan repayments, but whether events in the future (e.g., a recession, higher interest rates, or an anticipated corporate bankruptcy) will lead to loan defaults and, consequently, a bank failure. Troubled loans are often categorized as substandard or doubtful, depending on the expected ability of borrowers to make scheduled interest payments and repayments.

Banks fail when earnings are consistently negative, which can occur from too many loan losses and an inadequate capital base. Regulators often suggest increases in bank loan loss reserves commensurate with a rise in nonaccruing loans, thus providing for potential future loan losses. Banks usually take these loan loss provisions from the current net income of the bank or against capital if income proves insufficient. A bank with a high level of nonperforming loans to total loans and inadequate loan loss reserves or capital is a potential candidate for failure.

It can be extremely difficult to judge the quality of a bank's assets, and the regulators sometimes err in assessing the quality of a portfolio. When an examiner has found a bank with "too many" bad and suspect loans, or a bank in trouble, the examiner must advise the bank as to what to do. Often, such a bank will be told to increase its equity capital or capital-to-asset ratio or to adopt a new and less risky loan policy—for example, to tighten internal credit controls or to stop making loans to insiders.

The catch-22 is that the problematic banks would have to become much sounder financially before they could raise sizable amounts of capital, but if they were to succeed in increasing their capital substantially by paying a market premium, would they not increase their portfolio risks commensurately?

There are also examples of an unwillingness on the part of regulators to see or blow the whistle on certain banks, as was certainly the case in the failure of The United States National Bank of San Diego in the 1970s and many S&L failures in the late 1980s and early 1990s. In the words of Kareken, "There is an inevitable closeness between the [regulatory] agencies and the banks, a closeness that nurtures tolerance or a sympathetic appreciation of bankers' problems—too sympathetic an appreciation."

Further, there is an inability to quarrel with success, as in the cases of Continental Illinois, First National Bank of Seattle, and Bank of New England. Suppose that there are two loan strategies, X and Y, and that policy Y is held to be riskier than policy X. The examiner observes a bank following policy Y that achieves an exceptional rate of return for several years. In the face of the record, will the examiner doubt his or her judgment about the riskiness of policy Y? Doubt prompted by success is only a failure of will. Can you imagine the regulatory agency deciding to be tough on the bank that follows policy Y or even issuing a cease-and-desist order after a half dozen years of superior earnings performance? Could that agency persuade a court that an exceptional rate of return that is sustained over a long time can be attributed to bad management? Could it prove that strategy Y must produce a disaster in the future, having so far produced only an exceptional rate of return? It is likely that if the regulatory agency had gone to court in early 1981 or before to get Continental Illinois or Penn Square to change its loan policy, it would not have been successful.[3]

It must also be remembered that loan charge-offs and nonperforming loans increase substantially during recessions; poor asset quality and the lack of diversification in bank loan portfolios often lead to writing off assets in an economic slowdown.

Management

Rating bank management is subjective and, again, difficult to accomplish. In many ways, a bank's management rating is dependent upon its earnings performance, portfolio diversification and risk level, liquidity, and adequacy of capital, as well as upon its administrative skills, technical competence, leadership ability, ability to comply with existing regulations, and ability to cope with a changing environment. Credit controls, asset-liability management, control of noninterest expense ratios and management information systems are other factors that enable regulators to judge the quality of management.

Earnings

Earnings are rated with consideration given to the ability to cover losses and provide for adequate capital and for the rate of growth of retained earnings.

The return on assets at a bank is usually considerably lower than at an industrial corporation; however, the return on equity of a high-quality bank is often higher than that of an industrial corporation. This is because of differences in capital structure and the fact that many banks have a ratio of equity to total assets of less than 7 percent.

In general, banks with a consistent return on assets above 1 percent and a return on equity above 15 percent are performing exceptionally well. On the other hand banks with a consistent return on assets below 0.3 percent and a return on equity below 5 percent are performing considerably below average. Of course, these financial ratios vary over time; banks must also be compared with other banks in the same peer group.

Liquidity

Liquidity is rated in relation to the volatility of deposits, degree of reliance on interest-sensitive funds, frequency and level of borrowings, availability of assets readily convertible into cash, and access to money markets or other ready sources of cash.

Regulators prefer that banks do not expand much beyond their core deposit base and that they limit their borrowings either in the federal funds market or from the discount window of the Federal Reserve Bank. Most banks keep considerable cash on hand and hold at least 15 percent of their funds in investment portfolios to act as a secondary liquidity reserve. Banks also depend on the federal funds market and the discount window to maintain their liquidity. However, if there is fear of a bank failure, it may not be possible to borrow from either of these sources. Banks that rely heavily on borrowed funds are more likely to experience a liquidity crisis. Sometimes depositors sense a banking crisis and withdraw their funds, compounding the problem. This is often referred to as a *run* on a bank. Banks that lack a large base of core deposits and that rely heavily on borrowed funds or institutional negotiable certificates of deposit can become illiquid if there are either large loan losses or rumors to that effect. The problems of Continental Illinois National Bank and Trust Co. in 1982 are an example of this situation. During and immediately after the regulatory rescue of Continental, we were reminded of how stringent Illinois branching restrictions were. If Continental had all along been freer to branch, then it would have had a larger base of consumer core deposits and would not have been dependent upon so much "purchased money."

Because of the practice of paying on demand, a bank's liquidity is extremely important. Depositors do not know whether a particular bank's illiquidity implies that it is insolvent; they simply want to avoid the inconvenience of the immobilization of their funds. Whenever the liquidity of a depository institution is suspect, many customers will withdraw their funds posthaste, creating a run on the bank. Runs can spread easily to other institutions that may initially be liquid by ordinary standards, but will subsequently be put in danger. The end result is often financial stringency and economic contraction. Although illiquidity does not appear to be the proximate cause of a bank's financial problems, it is usually the bank's inability to meet liquidity needs that causes its ultimate demise.

Each of the CAMEL characteristics is rated on a scale of 1 to 5, with 5 representing a poor rating and 1 an excellent rating. (See Table 6.5.) The CAMEL composite rating is not necessarily the mean rating of these five characteristics. Banks with composite ratings of 1 or 2 are considered to be in good condition, while those with a rating of 3 are weaker than desired and probably deficient in some areas covered by the rating process. Banks with composite CAMEL ratings of 4.0 or more are considered problem banks. These banks are monitored closely, since their level of risk is perceived to be high. The FDIC publishes a list of problem banks periodically. When a bank has a composite rating of 4 or more, it appears on the list. Although CAMEL ratings have been helpful to regulators, several banks have failed during the 1980s that were not on the problem list until immediately before their failure. Other rating systems, involving accounting ratios and stock returns, or risk-adjusted stock returns of banks, appear to have improved upon the CAMEL rating system as predictors of failure. While the absolute number of problematic banks has declined gradually from the high levels of 1987, the total assets of failed (insured) banks has increased dramatically. In 1987, the total deposits of the 184 failed institutions amounted to $6.3 billion, while in 1988 and 1989, the deposits of failed banks amounted to $24.9 and $24.1 billion, respectively. The 169 bank failures in 1990 had $14.8 billion in deposits, while the 127 bank failures in 1991 had $53.8 billion in deposits. The failure of larger banks has put an enormous strain on the Bank Insurance Fund.

In the CAMEL system, it is desired that banks maintain sufficient capital to absorb unanticipated losses, make loans and investments whose risk of default is acceptable, exhibit sound and ethical management practices, generate enough earnings to build capital, and maintain sufficient liquidity to absorb unanticipated loan losses.

Uniform Bank Performance Rating System

In addition to the CAMEL system, some federal bank examiners evaluate a bank's loan portfolio, assigning a numerical rating based on the quality of the bank's asset portfolio, including all of its loans. Like the CAMEL system, this Uniform Bank Performance Rating System rates banks from 1 (highest) to 5 (lowest). The higher a bank's rating, the less frequently the bank is reviewed and examined by federal regulators. The exact ratings are:

1   strong
2   satisfactory
3   fair
4   marginal
5   unsatisfactory

In sum, the Uniform Bank Rating System is an attempt to assess the condition of a bank by rating the quality of its loan portfolio and other aspects of the bank's operations. Regulators investigate carefully the cause of a bank's deterioration when the bank is classified as problematic. When possible, the regulators discuss with management possible remedies or corrective actions to cure key problems. Often they suggest a delay in expansion plans, an increase in the bank's capital, tighter credit controls, the sale of assets, or diversification of the loan or investment portfolio. Regulators have the authority to remove key officers and directors of a problematic bank if they feel that such a step would enhance the performance of the bank. Also, they have the right to take legal action against a problematic bank that does not comply with their suggested solutions to problems.

If regulatory corrective action fails to improve the bank's situation, further deterioration may lead to a failure. If the bank is insured, the FDIC has to decide whether to liquidate the bank's assets or search for another bank that may be willing to take control of the failing institution.

The surveillance systems of the federal agencies are made up of three components: computer screening to identify outlying financial organizations that fail certain ratio tests; analytic reports that allow an examiner to perform a detailed analysis of a financial entity; and corrective action and follow-up of problems identified through the screening process.

The primary objectives of the computer screening systems are to identify changes in the financial condition of institutions that they regulate, in order to prevent their failure, and to identify financial institutions whose financial conditions warrant special supervisory attention. Once the analytic effort confirms that a serious financial problem exists, corrective action is initiated. Nonregulatory predictors of corporate and bank failures also offer insights into the general problem of insolvency.

TOO BIG TO FAIL: DOUBLE STANDARD

The "Too Big to Fail" Doctrine was formalized following the liquidity crisis at Continental Illinois Bank in 1984. The objectives of the doctrine were to preserve public confidence in banking institutions and to avoid the systemic problems associated with large bank failures and commensurate interbank activities. As a matter of fact, the regulatory agencies did try to find a merger partner for Continental Illinois, but they were unsuccessful. When Continental suffered massive losses of funds, the Federal Reserve rushed in with temporary loans, and the FDIC ultimately supplied billions of dollars to keep the bank from closing its doors. While depositors were fully protected, shareholders received nothing.

The "Too Big to Fail" doctrine is not unique to the banking industry: Lockheed was rescued by a $250 million government loan guarantee in 1971, and Chrysler received $1.2 billion of U.S. government loan guarantees when it teetered near bankruptcy in 1981. The justifications given for the Lockheed guarantee included the company's status as an important defense contractor and the desirability of increasing competition in the commercial airframe industry. The justifications for the Chrysler guarantee included a desire to avoid the impact of a company failure on unemployment, as well as a wish to maintain competition in the domestic automobile industry. Both companies survived their financial and operating difficulties, remaining viable, but weakened, firms. Stockholders retained a significant ownership interest in the firms.[4]

Under the "too big to fail" doctrine, uninsured deposits at large banks have often been protected in full, while those at smaller banks have generally faced a greater risk of loss. Although the Board of Governors has expressed discomfort with regulatory policies that discriminate largely on the basis of size, it has also indicated a need to insure all deposits at the troubled big banks because of repercussions that might occur within the entire banking system if they would not take those protective actions. The reason that it may sometimes be necessary to protect certain uninsured creditors or delay normal regulatory actions is systemic risk—the possibility that the financial difficulties at one bank may spill over to many more banks or even the entire financial system. The failure of a large bank can cause a ripple effect of liquidity and solvency problems for smaller banks. In addition, the failure of a large correspondent bank can lead to settlement and clearing problems for customers of other banks that depend upon the services of the larger correspondent. Also, a major source of systemic risk relates to foreign exchange contracts: If one of two parties fails before the settlement of a foreign exchange contract, the other party would be exposed to substantial losses on its transactions should exchange rates move unfavorably. An even greater risk arises because of the practice of paying foreign currencies in the settlement of foreign exchange contracts before the completion of counterpayments in U.S. dollars. Because of this, participating banks face a temporary risk exposure equal to the full amount of the foreign currency that was paid out prior to the receipt of dollars. Other sources of systemic risk include the classic run on a bank and the potential damage to the operations of either the municipal market or the mortgage-backed securities market if a major player in that market were suddenly to collapse.[5]

The policy of not allowing large banks to fail while permitting smaller banks to fail raises an issue of fairness. The FDIC has operated with a double standard and has been tougher on the resolution of failures of small banks. While all deposits at the $27 billion First Republic Bank of Dallas were protected, prior to the collapse of First Republic, 3,000 depositors lost over $58 million when a number of small Texas banks were liquidated. A consequence of this regulatory action has been a shift of deposits out of small banks that are candidates for insolvency and into larger banks that have implicit 100-percent insurance.[6]

In testimony before Congress, John LaWare, of the Board of Governors of the Federal Reserve System, indicated that the board was sensitive to the arguments of equity and efficiency that have been advanced for eliminating "too big to fail" policies and that the board felt that regulatory policy should be equally applicable to banks of all sizes. He said:

> It is desirable that no bank should assume that its scale insulates it from market or regulatory discipline, nor should the depositors with uninsured balances in a large bank assume that they face no risk of loss should that institution fail. For these reasons the Board supports those provisions of the Treasury proposal that would enhance the accountability of, and tighten the criteria used by regulators in resolving failed banks. . . . However, we believe strongly that it would be imprudent for Congress to exclude all possibilities of invoking the too-big-to-fail doctrine under any circumstances. One can contemplate situations in which uninsured liabilities of failing institutions should be protected, or normal regulatory actions delayed, in the interests of macroeconomic stability. Such a finding typically would be appropriate only in cases of clear systemic risk involving, for example, potential spillover effects leading to widespread depositor runs, impairment of public confidence in the broader financial system, or serious disruptions in domestic and international payments and settlement systems.[7]

A banking debacle will be avoided as dividends will be cut, layoffs will continue, and weak institutions will either downsize (by selling off major blocs of assets) or merge. Beyond formal government safety nets lies an even more powerful source of support: the shared recognition among regulators, policymakers, investors, and players in the financial marketplace that the actual failure of a large money-center bank or superregional bank could have calamitous effects on the financial system and the shared commitment to avoiding such a failure. Hence, should such a bank head toward insolvency, the system would intervene.

In November 1990, Freedom National Bank, a relatively small, minority-owned, Harlem-based bank became insolvent as a result of numerous speculative loans that went bad. The FDIC decided to close and liquidate the bank using the "payoff method" because the failure of the bank would not have any serious repercussions on the rest of the banking system. Large customers received about 50 cents on the dollar for deposits in excess of $100,000. Charitable organizations, such as the National Urban League and the Negro College Fund, and several churches suffered losses. William Seidman, then FDIC chairman, testified before Congress that "My first testimony when I came to this job was that it's unfair to treat big banks in a way that covers all depositors but not small banks. I promised to do my best to change that. Five years later, I can report that my best wasn't good enough."[8] It is interesting to note that legislation was passed by Congress in late 1991 to eliminate "too big to fail" operations by the FDIC beginning in 1994.

BANK ACCOUNTING SYSTEMS

One of the more controversial issues in banking concerns the choice of an accounting system for banks. Recent proposals would have banks abandon their traditional accounting system, based on historical costs of assets and liabilities, in favor of a market-value system. Comprehensive proposals would have banks value all bank assets, liabilities, and off-balance-sheet items at current market prices. The movement toward market accounting is motivated primarily by changes in financial markets, greater volatility of interest rates, and increased bank failures. Current bank accounting systems do not measure capital accurately. For example, if the fall in the value of an asset causes the true value of capital to decline (as in the case of interest rate risk, foreign exchange risk, or credit risk), an accounting system should not have rules that allow discretion on whether or not the decline is recognized in measured capital. Many analysts believe that by overcoming the limitations of the current system, market-value accounting would give bank owners, creditors, and regulators better information for making investment and regulatory decisions to the extent that market values provide a more accurate measure of a bank's health. Most bankers, however, oppose market-value accounting. They feel that it is unnecessary and would have undesirable side effects, in addition to being inaccurate, costly, and difficult to implement. They also feel that until better valuation models for outstanding loans are developed, full market-value accounting might not provide accurate measures of bank capital. On the other hand, most bankers favor partial market valuation of at least the investment portfolio, because the market values of tradeable securities are easily obtained. Morris and Sellon conclude that market-value accounting is conceptually attractive, but that the proposals that urge its adoption have important practical limitations that must be balanced against their benefits.[9] In fact, many assets and liabilities of banks cannot readily be marked to market.

Morris and Sellon feel that financial institutions would be subject to greater market discipline by the use of market-value accounting and public disclosure of their finances. Litan has expressed his concern that expanded activities out of the bank or through a bank subsidiary could still impair capital. (The regulatory fire walls now in place require capitalization of underwriting subsidiaries in the bank holding company separate and distinct from the bank depository function.) Litan also was fearful that too much faith was being put in the ability of supervision and regulation to minimize the dangers of new bank activities. He questioned whether such an approach could result in overregulation that could eliminate the scope of economies of diversification.

WHAT HAPPENS WHEN AN INSURED BANK FAILS?

When a bank fails, the FDIC has a number of alternatives to use in resolving the problem. One way is to pay off the insured depositors, take over the failed bank, and liquidate the bank's assets. The failed bank is dissolved and the assets are sold, with the intention of recovering as much of the original asset value as possible. If sufficient funds were not realized under a payoff policy, the insured depositors would be paid up to $100,000 per deposit. Following that, if the insolvent bank had total assets worth less than the total value of its liabilities, the depositors might receive an additional settlement when the assets of the bank were liquidated.

A second solution is for the FDIC to permit another bank to enter into a purchase and assumption (P&A) agreement, in which the bank would purchase the failed bank and assume all of its liabilities. Under this scenario, the FDIC might provide financial assistance to the acquiring bank by relieving the weak bank of all of its bad assets in order to induce the new buyer to assume the failed bank's liabilities. It is sometimes less costly for the insurance fund to provide financial assistance than to liquidate the failed bank. Also, no depositor would lose any money if all the liabilities were assumed by the acquiring bank. The majority of the FDIC's transactions in the last decade have been in such an "assisted" manner. Another type of assisted transaction (in addition to P&A) is the "modified payoff" transaction. The modified payoff is aimed at combining the economies of the P&A with the discipline-encouraging aspects of the payoff. With a modified payoff, the FDIC arranges for another bank to assume only the insured deposits of a failed bank. Uninsured depositors receive an immediate credit for the amount of their claims that the FDIC has estimated will be eventually recovered. The acquiring bank pays a premium, and the acquired bank's office usually remains open as a branch of the acquiring bank. Uninsured depositors suffer a smaller loss than in the ordinary payoff, because they have immediate use of some of their uninsured funds.

Until the Continental Illinois problem in 1984, the FDIC always appeared reluctant to liquidate large banks to avoid having to pay off depositors. A third policy, nicknamed "too big to fail," provided 100-percent deposit insurance for the 11 largest banks; that is, it was a policy of all depositors being paid off in full. This policy was discriminatory against smaller banks, for which depository protection in the case of failure remained at only $100,000 per deposit.

FDIC treatment of failed banks has made the legal limits of coverage of minimal importance. In 861 of the 1,086 bank failures during the 1980s, the FDIC either found another bank to take over the operations of the failed bank through a P&A or provided financial assistance to give the bank time to recover or arrange a merger. In these instances, no depositors lost any money, regardless of the size of their deposits. Accordingly, these depositors would have little incentive to impose market discipline on the banks that held their deposits. In the remaining 225 failures, insured deposits were transferred to another bank or were paid off up to the $100,000 limit of coverage. Those with balances in excess of this limit may have suffered losses. In almost all of these cases, small banks with assets under $100 million were involved. No failed commercial bank with more than $500 million in deposits was resolved through an insured deposit transfer or payoff in the 1980s or early 1990s. Of course, small banks derive less than 10 percent of their deposits from accounts with balances in excess of $100,000, whereas large banks have nearly one-third of their deposits in large accounts. Consequently, without a change in the treatment of bank failures, small banks would bear the brunt of any adjustment to a lower insurance limit. Depositors in these banks who were less than completely insured would demand higher interest rates or would shift their funds to larger banks, where total protection would be more likely. Apparently, then, there is little to gain from reducing the deposit insurance coverage limit to under $100,000. Little additional depositor discipline is gained, except possibly at small banks. Recommendations for lower insurance coverage seem to overlook a major benefit of deposit insurance: the elimination of the threat of destabilizing bank runs. Since instability in the banking system is potentially extremely costly, the case for lower insurance coverage is quite weak.[10]

FAILURES AT CONTINENTAL ILLINOIS AND THE BANK OF NEW ENGLAND

Continental Illinois

During the early 1980s, Continental Illinois was the seventh largest bank in the United States, with assets of close to $40 billion. It was considered a model wholesale bank located in Chicago that operated out of two skyscraper buildings without a domestic branch system. The deposit base of the bank was corporate, institutional, and governmental in nature, as opposed to a consumer-oriented depository base such as that of BankAmerica or Wells Fargo. Continental had embarked on an aggressive lending campaign in which it purchased more than a billion dollars worth of energy loans from a smaller bank in Oklahoma called Penn Square. Continental also sold loan participations from this portfolio of purchased energy loans to some of its respondent banks. Continental collapsed when most of these loans proved worthless and when large corporate depositors withdrew over $6 billion as their certificates of deposit matured. Carelessness and dishonesty on the part of the originating bank threatened the solvency of all the banks that purchased energy loans from Penn Square. However, that was not an excuse for the less than meticulous examination that was made of the loans and oil and gas reserves by the credit and lending groups at Continental. Nor was it an excuse for the failure to demand proper documentation. As a matter of fact, the officer in charge of energy lending was later indicted for accepting in excess of one-half million dollars in kickbacks.

The failure of Continental Illinois focused attention on the interdependence among banks in deposits and in loan syndications, as well as on the importance of a consumer core deposit base. When Continental collapsed, it was unable to honor the standard gentlemen's agreement on respondent loans. Consequently, many of its respondents took enormous losses. Continental was not the only bank to fail because of Penn Square. It was joined by Seafirst of Seattle, a bank that was taken over by BankAmerica when Seafirst failed because of its participation in $400 million worth of bogus energy loans from Penn Square.[11]

Rumors of impending financial difficulties in early May caused large depositors to withdraw billions of dollars of deposits from Continental Illinois in both the domestic and Eurodollar markets. By mid-May, the FDIC announced that it would guarantee all of Continental's deposits. In addition, the FDIC sought to arrange $7.5 billion of loans to the bank with the Federal Reserve and several money-center banks. The FDIC then decided to use the purchase and assumption method to handle the failure and searched unsuccessfully for merger partners. The outflow of deposits from Continental Illinois continued and had reached over $10 billion by mid-July, despite over $5 billion in discount window loans from the Federal Reserve. With the situation now hopeless, the FDIC announced in late July that it would rescue the bank and protect all depositors. The FDIC assumed $3.5 billion of the debt Continental owed to the Federal Reserve in exchange for $4.5 billion of the bank's problem loans. This enabled the bank to strengthen its balance sheet. The FDIC also purchased $1 billion of Continental's preferred stock to shore up the bank's net worth, making it the owner of 80 percent of the bank. Although the bailout plan was in the spirit of the P&A method, it involved the unprecedented FDIC purchase of ownership in a failed bank; that is, the FDIC assumed the role of a merger partner. Federal assistance was given despite the widespread belief that the bank's top management, all of whom were later removed from office, was responsible for the bank's financial condition because of careless credit controls.[12]

Generally, in these kinds of cases, there is an implicit understanding (a gentleman's agreement) that the correspondent will guarantee the loans to its respondents. Many of the respondents took substantial losses upon the FDIC's refusing to honor unwritten agreements when the loans proved to be worthless. When Continental collapsed, it had about $6 billion in uninsured deposits and liabilities from over 2,000 banks. In 113 banks these deposits exceeded 50 percent of their capital, while at 66 banks the deposits exceeded their total capital. Depending upon the extent of their losses, many of the small respondents would have failed. One can now see why the Federal Reserve, the comptroller of the currency, and the FDIC did not allow all uninsured depositors to lose their funds. In September 1984, the comptroller of the currency stated in congressional testimony that the 11 largest banks would not be allowed to fail—that is, in the event of insolvency, no depositor or creditor would suffer a loss, because the FDIC would intervene and guarantee all deposits. These 11 banks became known as the "too-big-to-fail" banks.[13]

It is ironic that a few years before the collapse of Continental, the bank was selected by *Forbes Magazine* as one of the five best managed companies in the United States. "Roger Anderson (Continental chairman) and Continental were viewed as paragons by the banking world. Continental was often described as the best run bank in the country, the most feared bank, the most dynamic. It was doing all those things that analysts and the media prize: posting steadily increasing earnings, a burgeoning return on equity, and a rapidly expanding share of the commercial and industrial loan market."[14] In August 1984, Anderson saw his picture with the words "Banker of the Year" on the cover of *Institutional Investor*. The article's headline pointed out that "the excesses of his regime brought ... the bank to the brink of collapse—and symbolizes all that has gone wrong with banking today."[15]

In 1974, almost 10 years prior to the Continental Illinois drama, there was a similar, but smaller, incident. The public had learned in May 1974 that Franklin National Bank (then the 20th largest bank in the nation) had suffered large losses on bad loans and in foreign exchange. Large depositors began to withdraw their deposits, and the failure of the bank was imminent. It was feared that the immediate failure of Franklin might set off a chain reaction of bank failures. Accordingly, the Federal Reserve announced that the discount window would be open to Franklin so that no depositors would suffer any losses. Finally, the Franklin Bank was merged into European American Bank in October of 1974. By then, the Fed had lent Franklin $1.75 billion (total deposits were nearly $3 billion prior to the problem), close to 5 percent of the total reserves in the banking system. The Federal Reserve's action succeeded in preventing any other bank failures related to the problems of Franklin.[16]

Bank of New England

The Bank of New England's failure is likely to be the third most costly loss to the Bank Insurance Fund of the FDIC, behind only the failures of Continental Illinois National Bank and First Republic Bank of Dallas. The failure occurred because of huge losses in the bank's real estate portfolio (over 30 percent of New England's loan portfolio was in commercial real estate), following almost 10 years of unprecedented growth and profitability. The bank suffered from a lack of diversification of the loan portfolio, sloppy credit controls, a serious downturn in the New England economy, and a consumer run. The Boston-based bank had total assets of nearly $14 billion, while its sister banks within the holding company had assets of just over $7 billion (Connecticut National Bank) and $1 billion (Maine National Bank) at year-end 1990. The combined banks saw their assets shrink from $36 billion in 1989 to $22 billion by the time they were closed.

All three banks had agreed to comply with the February 1990 cease-and-desist orders from the Office of the Comptroller of the Currency that, among other things, mandated that they improve their real estate lending procedures and tracking systems. In addition, the banks were told to increase their capital positions. Unfortunately, losses continued throughout 1990, as the banks were unable to resolve their problems or to raise enough capital to offset continuing losses, despite the sale of a leasing subsidiary for $613 million, the securitization of automobile loans, and the securitization of more than $1 billion in credit card loans, mortgage loans, and other loans.

On January 4, 1991, the Bank of New England indicated that it expected to report a fourth quarter loss of $450 million, which followed on the heels of losses of $123 million in the third quarter, $33 million in the second quarter, and $46 million in the first quarter. The fourth-quarter loss exceeded the bank's capital of $255 million. Consumers, made skittish by the closure of 45 financial institutions (mostly credit unions) in neighboring Rhode Island and the failure of another bank in Massachusetts, withdrew $1 billion in deposits from the bank in the two days following the announcement of the anticipated loss. A large percentage of the depository withdrawals were made through ATMs. The surge in withdrawals contributed to the FDIC's decision to take action on January 6, 1991. The Bank of New England, Connecticut National Bank, and Maine National Bank were declared insolvent by the OCC and placed in receivership at the FDIC. The FDIC also indicated that it would protect all deposits—including those that exceeded $100,000—because of financial problems in the New England region and because of heavy interbank deposits. While the loss to the FDIC was substantial, none of the depositors lost money.[17] Once again, the "too big to fail" provision was invoked. The FDIC also infused $750 million in capital into the bank as part of the rescue effort. The OCC then set up bridge banks to take over the assets and liabilities of the failed banks, with the FDIC running the bank until a buyer could be found. In this "purchase assumption method," the FDIC and the buyer of the bank put additional capital into the bank over time; eventually, the acquirer would buy out the FDIC share. Bank of Boston, Fleet, and BankAmerica made bids for the failed bank, which was eventually awarded to Fleet (with headquarters in Rhode Island) and its partner, Kohlberg Kravis Roberts & Co. (KKR), an investment firm specializing in buy-outs and takeovers. There is some controversy involving the winning bid, as on paper, BankAmerica made a higher bid. However, when adjusted for "whatever" fudge factor pleased the FDIC, Fleet was declared the winner.

Fleet obtained a $15-billion-asset, 330-branch company, without $5.5 billion in bad loans that forced it out of business. The FDIC remained responsible for any existing Bank of New England loans that turned sour through 1994. The Bank of New England's failure will cost the government between $2.3 billion and $2.5 billion, the difference between the value of the bad loans and the amount the FDIC expects to recover by selling bad assets, such as repossessed real estate. Fleet will manage the sale of the assets. The company paid $625 million for the Bank of New England—a capital infusion of $500 million in the failed bank and a $125 million premium payment to the FDIC. Fleet financed the purchase by raising a total of $708 million: $283 million in convertible preferred stock that was sold to KKR, $175 million through the sale of common stock, $150 million from the sale of subordinated debentures, and $100 million in a publicly sold preferred stock offering. The salient factor the FDIC considered in selecting a winning bidder was the cost to the bank insurance fund during the time it would take the winning bidder to assimilate the Bank of New England.

Then-Chairman Seidman of the FDIC emphasized that KKR would be only a passive investor in the acquisition by Fleet. This marked one of the first times that a nonbanking concern had been permitted to inject substantial capital into a major U.S. bank.

Another interesting development was the unprecedented use of government funds borrowed from the Federal Financing Bank by the FDIC to carry the Bank of New

England's troubled loans on its books after it sold the bank to another institution. This strategy was designed to lower the government's cost of salvaging the failed bank, while also lowering the acquirer's cost of managing Bank of New England's troubled assets. The acquiring bank (Fleet) was still to manage the Bank of New England's troubled assets for a fee. In previous government-assisted mergers of large banks, the FDIC reimbursed the acquiring banks for funding the troubled assets.

Many observers and analysts feel that slack government supervision played a role in the collapse of the bank. Despite citing the bank in 1986 and 1987 for underwriting problems, insufficient loan loss allowances, and poor quality of assets, regulators never pressed the bank's board of directors to take actions such as limiting growth or diversifying the portfolio. An example of lax underwriting standards could be found in the bank's policy of lending up to 100 percent of appraised real estate value on commercial real estate loans, requiring no equity or down payment by the borrower.[18]

Former Comptroller of the Currency Robert Clarke had softened regulatory policies on banks early in his tenure, helping fuel excessive real estate lending by banks. By mid-1990 and early 1991, the regulatory philosophy had changed: Bank examiners became too restrictive, helping to create a near credit crunch.

Because the Bank of New England was insolvent (real estate loan losses wiped out its equity capital), Connecticut National Bank was unable to recover the full value of nearly $1.5 billion that it had lent to the bank, which left it with an equity capital deficiency of $49 million. The closure of Maine National Bank was triggered by cross-guarantee provisions in FIRRE, which makes an insured bank liable for any loss the FDIC anticipates in connection with the default of a commonly controlled depository institution. The FDIC demanded an immediate payment of its anticipated loss, and the bank was unable to comply.

THE POTENTIAL FAILURES

In a research study by Michael Light of Bear Stearns titled "What If," published in early 1991, a "quick and dirty" analysis was made of the largest 59 banks to see how they would weather a severe recession.[19] It was assumed that in such a recession every bank's construction loan portfolio would suffer a 40-percent loss, commercial mortgages 20 percent, highly leveraged loans 10 percent, lesser-developed country (LDC) loans 50 percent, and all other loans 3 percent. These loss figures were subtracted from the institution's equity and reserves to arrive at what the hypothetical equity number would be in a depressed economy. Total assets were also reduced by 15 percent to arrive at the equity-to-assets ratio. In this "quick and dirty" study, two salient conclusions were reached:

1. Almost all the major bank holding companies would have a positive equity position.
2. Many of the bank holding companies would not meet the new capital guidelines established for the end of 1992.

It is doubtful that the regulators will force all banks to adhere to these guidelines, but adequacy of capital will probably be used as a carrot in approving debt and equity underwritings and geographic expansion. Also, pressure may be applied to merge banks and obtain cost benefits that will lead to adequately capitalized, healthy banks.

Among the banks that achieved healthy ratios of adjusted equity to total assets in excess of 3 percent were Bankers Trust, First Bank Systems, Banc One, Zions Corp., First Tennessee, Northern Trust, Boatman's Bankshares, Harris Bancorp, Republic, National City Corp., West One Bancorp, NBD Bancorp, First Wachovia, Fleet (prior to acquiring the Bank of New England), SunTrust, Shawmut, Amsouth Bancorp, Norwest Corp., Mellon, First Chicago, and PNC Financial. Four banks—Wells Fargo, Midlantic, Barnett Banks, and First Empire—achieved negative adjusted equity–to–asset ratios, while just over a dozen banks achieved anemic ratios that were under 1.5 percent (but positive). These were Southeast Banking Corp., Chase Manhattan, South Carolina National Bank, BB&T Financial Corp., Marine Midland Banks, Citicorp (which received a large infusion of capital after the study, but also was a major lender in the Olympia & York bankruptcy), Signet, Continental, Bank of Boston, Riggs, MNC Financial, Valley National, C&S/Sovran Corp., and Michigan National Bank. Despite selling off many of its northernmost Florida branches to raise cash, Southeast could not obtain enough capital to remain independent. The bank was closed in September 1991 because it was illiquid, inadequately capitalized, and suffering from too many bad loans. In addition, it was unable to pay back a large Federal Reserve loan. The FDIC selected First Union to take over Southeast, rejecting bids from Barnett and SunTrust. From the Bear Stearn list of banks with capital-to-asset ratios under 1.5 percent, South Carolina National merged with Wachovia, C&S/Sovran merged with NCNB, Valley National merged with Banc One, and NationsBank purchased MNC.

The surprises included the poor showing of Wells Fargo, an extremely well-thought-of bank, and the relative strength of New England–based Shawmut, whose large real estate and leveraged-buyout (LBO) portfolios suggested doom and gloom with nonperforming assets of 6.1 percent of total assets outstanding. Wells Fargo had one of the largest real estate and highly leveraged buy-out loan portfolios in the country as a percentage of assets on the books. Its commercial real estate loans outstanding on December 30, 1991, as a percentage of assets, were 29.0 percent, while highly leveraged transactions accounted for 5.3 percent of total loans outstanding. Its nonperforming assets, including real estate owned, reached 5.3 percent of total assets at year-end 1991, wiping out all but $21 million in earnings for the year. Bank earnings rebounded in 1992, but the bank still had $13.6 billion in commercial real estate loans (the most of any bank in the United States) with about 11.5 percent delinquent or so troubled that full payment was not expected. Wells Fargo was not alone on the west coast with potential problems with real estate loans and highly leveraged transactions: Security Pacific, BankAmerica, and First Interstate also had large exposures. (See Table 7.2.) Wells Fargo and BankAmerica are better reserved and have higher percentages of capital-to-assets than the other banks in the table.

Table 7.2   Commercial Real Estate and Highly Leveraged Transaction Exposure, December 31, 1991

	Commercial Real Estate % of Asset	Highly Leveraged Transactions % of Loans	Nonperforming Assets % of Assets
Wells Fargo	29.0	5.5	4.5
Security Pacific	19.0	5.6	5.7
BankAmerica	10.5	2.1	3.1
First Interstate	18.7	1.5	3.2
Citicorp	7.5	3.2	6.4

Source: Federal Reserve, FDIC, company annual reports.

If the current weakness in California commercial construction and real estate markets does not turn around with the business cycle, Wells Fargo could become a serious problem. Deflationary bear markets in commercial real estate (e.g., New York in the 1930s and Texas in the 1980s) are often as long lived as they are destructive. Real estate values could continue to fall, and banks could continue to pay for their boom time exuberance.[20] Prior to having these real estate problems, Wells Fargo had been regarded as a paragon of strong management that specialized in good cost controls and good quality of credit. Now it belongs on our list of banks to watch as a potentially troubled bank that has a not so well diversified portfolio.

To replace their falling shares in consumer and business credit markets, banks moved aggressively to increase their presence in nonresidential mortgages and heavily leveraged transactions. Some heavily leveraged acquisitions depended on the combined good fortune that there would continue to be no recession and no decline in asset prices in order to service debt obligations without difficulty. In the real estate market, banks were willing to lend on the basis of optimistic assumptions for real estate prices based on the real estate boom of the preceding eight years. The pace of nonresidential construction doubled between 1980 and 1985, increasing the supply of commercial buildings much faster than demand. As a result, vacancy rates increased sharply. By 1991, only 2 of the 25 largest metropolitan areas had vacancy rates under 15 percent, and returns on investment were negative.[21]

According to an FDIC report, there were $610 billion of assets associated with troubled banks that had CAMEL ratings of 4 or 5 at the end of 1991. Despite this number, bank closings slowed down in 1992. The slowdown could be related to the influence of a presidential election year, wider net interest margins resulting in a lower cost of funds, or even a lack of adequate reserves in the Bank Insurance Fund of the FDIC. Lower interest rates have also played a key role in slowing down the pace of bank failures, and a fresh influx of capital has rescued a handful of banks.

According to the FDIC, banks with assets over $100 million that were on the edge of failure included the World Trade Bank, which was insolvent as of March

31, 1992, and the following banks, which had leverage ratios (tier 1 capital to assets) under 2 percent: Howard Savings Bank (NJ), First National Bank of Houston (TX), River Bank America (NY), First Citizens (TX), Heritage Bank for Savings (MA), Attleboro Pawtucket Savings Bank (MA), Eastland Savings Bank (RI), First City Texas (TX), Plymouth Five Cents Savings Bank (MA), First Guaranty Bank (LA), Martha's Vineyard National Bank (MA), Bradford National Bank (VT), and Guardian Bank (FL).

GOOD BANK, BAD BANK

On quite a few occasions during the late 1980s and early 1990s, holding companies chose to clean up the balance sheets of their subsidiary banks by collecting nonperforming loans and spinning them off into a new entity, sometimes referred to as a *bad bank* or self-liquidating trust. Simultaneously, the spin-off allowed the holding company to create a healthier balance sheet for the primary or *good bank*. The formation of a good bank or bad bank spin-off starts with a perception by management that nonperforming loans are imposing a particularly heavy burden on the bank. In addition to a low price-to-earnings multiple, the burden of carrying impaired loans often includes costly workout efforts (renegotiating a schedule of loan repayment) within the bank that can distract loan and credit officers from servicing good loans or developing new business.[22]

What is the value of segregating the problem loans from the primary bank? Is it more cost effective to establish a separate corporation, to pool questionable assets, and to concentrate workout efforts outside of the primary bank? Proponents of this approach feel that segregating good from bad assets enables the banking firm to manage the bad assets more efficiently by taking advantage of economies of "management specialization," concentrated in the bad bank. Another reason is that there exist groups of long-term investors (who can afford to ride out temporarily distressed conditions in real estate and other markets) to whom the assets of the bad bank have appeal at the right price. Also, a bank alleviates some regulatory pressures by cleaning up its loan portfolio, selling problematic assets to the new entity, and replenishing its capital. Since the holding company may be a minority shareholder in the bad bank, the holding company may not be required to include the activities of the bad bank in the consolidated balance sheets and income statements. Further, information asymmetries in financial markets may be clarified: When the good and bad assets are combined in one bank, it may be difficult for investors to value the bank accurately; with a spin-off of the bad assets into one bank and a clean portfolio in the good bank, it should be easier for investors to make more accurate assessments of risk and expected return.[23]

In principle, the holding company has a variety of options in funding the bad bank spin-off. It can issue new equity and spin off ownership of the bank to (new and old) shareholders through a stock dividend in the form of shares in the bad bank. It can also sell various forms of debt to investors, the proceeds of which will pay for purchasing the assets of the bad bank, capitalizing the bad bank, and rebuilding the capital of the good bank. Or, the holding company can completely divest itself of the bad bank by selling it to outside investors. Recall that the bank sells the problem loans to the bad bank at a price that may be substantially below book value. Consequently, the sale usually involves substantial losses on the part of the good bank. Some of this loss is absorbed by the bank's loan loss reserve. However, if the reserve is insufficient to absorb all of the loss, the bank's capital may be depleted, and the bank may need to obtain additional funding to restore the loan loss reserve to a level that is acceptable to regulators.[24]

DEPOSIT INSURANCE

Federal deposit insurance was designed to (1) protect the small depositor from loss related to the failure of a depository institution, (2) prevent the occurrence of systemic bank runs, and (3) protect the payments mechanism. At the time of the establishment of this insurance, it was felt that problems in these areas plagued the U.S. financial system.[25]

President Franklin D. Roosevelt opposed deposit insurance because he felt that it would undermine market discipline. Despite Roosevelt's objections, the deposit insurance system was enacted, although initial coverage was limited to $2,500 per account in order to protect small savers against loss during the Depression. It was not contemplated then that the system would be changed to protect all depositors against any loss, regardless of its size.[26]

While depository insurance was once regarded as a competitive advantage, as well as a multi-billion-dollar government subsidy to the banking industry, it has shielded the industry from market discipline. According to John G. Medlin, chairman of Wachovia Corp., because deposit insurance has enabled institutions that were near insolvency to attract small deposits as easily as healthy banks or thrifts do, it has allowed and encouraged indirectly the deterioration of credit quality, loan pricing, and capital cushions within the financial system.[27] Worse, the health of the banking industry and the FDIC may be more precarious than the regulators admit. Most banks have probably overstated their capital positions, because they carry assets at original cost rather than at current market value. In a depressed real estate market and in an economy that is recovering ever so slowly from a recession, it is highly likely that the actual market value of most real estate loans is considerably lower than original cost. The insurance fund would show a huge multi-billion-dollar deficit if marked-to-market valuations were utilized. Still, the plight of the banks is not nearly as gruesome as that of the thrifts, because banks are better run, regulated, and capitalized for the most part. Also, real estate prices are highly cyclical in nature and should recover over time in most parts of the country. Further, increased deposit insurance premiums should net an additional $10 billion per year for the fund, since regulators boosted the rate for depository coverage from $0.19 to $0.23 per $100 in deposits on July 1, 1991.[28]

In May 1992, the FDIC proposed to boost the premiums that banks and S&Ls pay for deposit insurance. Under this new risk-based premium schedule, institutions judged to have the smallest risk of failure would pay premiums of $0.25 for each $100 of domestic deposits, while the weakest institutions would pay $0.31. The gap would widen over time because the weakest institutions would face semiannual premium increases until their risk status improved. This change was designed to repay FDIC borrowings from the Treasury, to build insurance deposits to 1.25 percent of insured deposits within 15 years, and to give depository institutions an incentive to boost their capital or to seek merger partners. Supporters of the increase claim that it strengthens the insurance fund, which was in the red and at its lowest level since its creation during the Depression. The fund, which stood at $18.3 billion in the mid-1980s, has been battered by the failure of 885 banks since then, costing more than $26 billion. At year-end 1992 the fund had a $100 million deficit, compared with a $7 billion deficit at the end of 1991. Failing in 1992 were 122 banks with $44.2 billion in assets, down from 127 bank failures with $63.2 billion in assets in 1991.

Deposit Insurance and the Moral Hazard Problem

The potential drawbacks of generous deposit insurance that gives depositors a legal right of reimbursement have been described as a *moral hazard:* In choosing a bank, depositors lose the incentive to consider factors other than the highest rate of return offered. Also, the banks themselves are encouraged to engage in excessively risky investments, which they might otherwise be inclined to avoid. Consequently, the insurance protection scheme subsidizes weak and risky banks.[29]

A salient implication of the current safety net is that some banks with relatively low capital ratios have funded riskier assets at a lower cost and on a much larger scale than would have otherwise been possible. The exploitation of this moral hazard has been encouraged by the increased ability of prime corporate customers of many banks to raise funds directly in the money and capital markets. Consequently, customers have migrated away from the banks, eroding the traditional value added from the intermediation of their credit. In turn, some banks have sought to boost returns on assets by reaching for higher-yielding, riskier loans, increasing their probability of failure.[30]

While bank regulation has been relatively successful in protecting deposits, FDIC insurance protection and the deregulation of interest rates have sometimes encouraged excessive risk taking by depository institutions, creating another moral hazard. Although most analysts regard FDIC deposit insurance as positive, there remains some controversy surrounding it. Unlike the failure of a chain of appliance stores or a local grocery store, a bank failure is frequently viewed as "contagious"—able to cause other bank runs and the potential failure of otherwise solvent banks. The fear that a bank might be in trouble can also be a self-fulfilling prophecy. Haunted by the succession of bank failures that occurred during the Great Depression, regulators are still wary of letting banks—especially large banks—fail. One of the justifications of federal insurance of deposits is simply that depositors will no longer have an incentive to pull their money out of a bank that is merely rumored to be insolvent.

Because of the failure-resolution policies that have been applied to large banks, such as Continental Illinois and First Republic, the perception exists that some banks are "too big to fail" and that all deposits in these banks are, in effect, insured. This factor works to reduce the disciplinary action of depositors.[31]

Still, a salient argument in favor of deposit insurance is that banks are not like other businesses: They are special, because bank failures can cause undue hardship in a particular geographic area. Also, the economy depends on the safety and security of the banking system, which could be upset if some larger banks were to fail. On the other hand, the closing of a steel mill or a paper mill in a one-mill town would be just as devastating as the closing of the community's only bank.[32]

A major problem resulting from the provision of deposit insurance is that it reduces the incentive of depositors to monitor the health of the financial institutions in which they deposit their funds. As a matter of fact, there is little incentive for insured depositors to withdraw their funds from a potentially insolvent bank. This is a moral hazard in the sense that the insured individual is less careful when a bank is insured. Deposit insurance can also create a moral hazard for the managers of depository institutions. The fact that deposit insurance protects depositors means that the threat of withdrawals by most individuals no longer exercises discipline on the managers of depository institutions. The fear is that deposit insurance induces institutions systematically to take inappropriate risks with their assets at the potential expense of the U.S. Treasury and its taxpayers. For example, prior to the passage of FIRRE, some insured problematic banks and thrifts offered depository rates well in excess of competitive market rates. These higher cost funds were channeled into higher yielding, riskier loans. Eventually, this led to greater loan losses and an increase in bank failures. The banks paid the higher rates for deposits simply because they could not attract funds at conventional rates. Many of these institutions used "brokered deposits." For example, the bank might hire Prudential or Dean Witter to sell insured certificates of deposit to their brokerage clients. Since the regulators often practiced capital forbearance, these depository institutions would not be closed. As the net worth of unhealthy depository institutions declined, the incentive to pay high rates for deposits and to take on higher levels of risk increased.

The lack of market discipline poses a particularly serious problem for banks or thrifts with low or negative net worth. These financial institutions have an incentive to undertake risky investments, since their owners enjoy the benefits when the investments do well, yet bear little or none of the costs when the investments fail, because the personal liability of bank and thrift owners is legally limited to the value of their investment.

Risk-Based Deposit Insurance

While most academics and insurance experts laud risk-based insurance premiums, the bottom line is that although it is desirable to have them, it may not be practical to charge banks different fees for FDIC insurance based on the riskiness of their assets. The details remain a bit sketchy at this time, but the Comprehensive Deposit Insurance Reform and Taxpayer Protection Act of 1991 mandates that a system of risk-based insurance premiums be established by 1994. On a preliminary basis, the FDIC has suggested that the riskiness of deposits would be graded by means of a grid or matrix. Each institution would be placed in one of three categories corresponding to its capital levels and one of three categories corresponding to its financial strength. The regulators' judgments would be based upon examination reports and other measures of management. The capitalization levels would be defined as follows:

- *Well capitalized.* Banks would have a ratio of tier 1 capital to total assets of at least 5 or 6 percent and ratios of total capital to risk-weighted assets of at least 10–12 percent.
- *Adequately capitalized.* Banks would have a tier 1 capital-to-asset ratio of at least 4 percent and a ratio of total capital to risk-weighted assets of at least 8 percent.
- *Less than adequately capitalized.* Banks would have a ratio of tier 1 capital to total capital of less than 4 percent and a ratio of total capital to risk-weighted assets of less than 8 percent.

The supervisory levels would be defined as follows:

- *Healthy.* Financially sound institutions with few minor weaknesses.
- *Requiring supervisory concern.* Banks that demonstrate weaknesses which, if not corrected, could result in significant deterioration.
- *Requiring substantial supervisory concern.* Banks for which there is a substantial probability that the FDIC will suffer a loss in connection with the institution, unless effective action is taken to correct the area of weakness.

For 9,115 banks, or about 75 percent of the industry, the premium for 1993 remained at $0.23 per $100 paid in 1992. For the weakest 222 banks, the rate increased to $0.31. The remaining 2,703 insured banks will pay premiums somewhere in between these two extremes, depending upon their capital position and risk structure. The new premium structure should bring in an estimated income of $6.35 billion in 1993, compared with $5.75 billion in 1992. If the board had stuck to a proposal that it had endorsed prior to the unexpected death of FDIC Chairman William Taylor, it would have raised an additional $600 million in 1993 premium income. While the more modest increase in premium rates satisfied the banking community and the Bush Administration, it may prove inadequate to cover future bank losses. The theory behind the new risk-based insurance system is that it would reward the best managed depository institutions and would deter other institutions from risky lending practices.

Many banks are likely to increase fees on services such as checking and safety deposit boxes, to make up for the increased fees for deposit insurance. Some analysts feel that Congress fell short in its reform of the system by not lowering deposit insurance limits. Prudence is left, not to depositors, but to the regulators and the banks themselves. The disincentive for depositors to have concern for the lending policies of their bank eliminates an important source of market discipline on banks.

If Congress ever decided to seek private insurance coverage instead of FDIC insurance coverage for bank deposits, an advantage of such a shift would be to take the federal government out of the banking business and allow market forces to assess the riskiness of bank portfolios and the price for deposit insurance coverage. Another solution is that banks be required to raise large amounts of unsecured and uninsured subordinated debt. Simply put by Horvitz in 1984, if all insured banks had such debt capital, then the FDIC would be better protected against loss than it currently is.[33] With this added long-term subordinated debt, the FDIC would have a greater margin for error; it could still be late in closing a bank, yet experience no loss. Also, another virtue of increasing the use of subordinated debentures as regulatory capital is that investors in these bonds will have a strong incentive to monitor the condition of the banking firm. Even today, the marketplace asserts some discipline by charging large premiums over riskless rates for subordinated debentures by undercapitalized banks. To be effective as a market disciplinarian, the subordinated debentures must have a claim on the bank that is *junior* to the claim of the insurance fund.[34]

Both debt and equity exert market discipline on bank behavior. Shareholders may vote to change the bank's management, or creditors can reorganize by initiating bankruptcy proceedings. The risk of loss disciplines the bank to alter its behavior. Also, if banks are required to hold larger levels of both debt and equity capital, risky banks may face some difficulty raising the necessary external funding. Thus, outside funding can also exert market discipline on bank behavior.[35]

Private Insurance Plans

Some scholars have suggested replacing FDIC insurance with private-sector depository insurance. Private insurance would likely compel risky banks to pay higher insurance premiums than banks with higher quality assets. The problem with private insurance is that it might not work if a myriad of banks were to fail simultaneously. The failure of a single large bank could result in other bank failures, which, in turn, could lead to thousands or even millions of claims that might overwhelm a private insurance company. Also, if any increases in risks are disclosed to the public, depositors may become frightened and begin to withdraw their deposits en masse, creating a run on a bank—the very thing the FDIC was created to prevent. The salient challenge is how to price deposit insurance fairly and efficiently so that risk is managed and the government is not coerced into using excessive amounts of taxpayer funds to support private risk taking.

Voluntary deposit insurance may be a practice worthy of consideration. While such insurance might not be free to individuals, the massive multibillion dollar deposit insurance bailout now being funded by U.S. taxpayers demonstrates clearly that the current system of deposit insurance is not without its costs.

There are assorted private deposit insurance plans that are usually state sponsored and that typically cover industrial banks, thrifts, and credit unions. Many of these plans failed in the 1980s; for example, the Nebraska Depository Guarantee Corporation and the Thrift Guarantee Corporation of Hawaii failed in 1984, while the Ohio Deposit Guarantee Fund and the Maryland Savings Share Insurance Corporation failed in 1985. The Ohio Deposit Guarantee Fund was depleted by losses from the failure of Home State Savings Bank because of bad loans to a securities firm that was engaged in fraudulent activities. While the private insurance fund that insured Home State was unable to bail out the bank's depositors, the run on Home State spread to other S&Ls insured by the Ohio Deposit Guarantee Fund. The governor of Ohio declared a bank holiday, temporarily closing 70 savings institutions. The institutions were reopened later, when they were able to obtain help from the FHLBB and the Federal Reserve, and after they obtained federal deposit insurance. A similar panic occurred in Maryland two months after the Ohio thrift crisis, when losses at two S&Ls exceeded the reserves of the private Maryland Savings Share Insurance Corporation, which had insured them. Runs by depositors began at other institutions insured by this fund.[36]

A larger bank panic followed the failure of the Providence-based Rhode Island Share and Deposit Indemnity Corporation in 1990–91 after an examination failed to catch the embezzlement by the president of Heritage Loan and Investment Company. Governor Sundlun of Rhode Island shut down 45 of the state's small banks and credit unions because of the failure of the insurance fund on his first day in office (January 1, 1991). This failure of private insurance was brought about not only by the failure of the Providence institution, but also by heavy loan losses experienced at other credit unions. The result was the freezing of $1.3 billion in nearly 360,000 accounts and a serious blow to the local economy in a state with approximately one million people. Although the state did not own or back the failed deposit insurance company, it decided that it had a moral obligation to protect depositors. It was felt that the name of the failed institution and the advertising of local financial institutions created an appearance of state backing. This represented a major challenge to state officials who were required by law to keep the state budget in balance. The initial bailout proposal by the governor amounted to no more than $12,500 in cash to each depositor at a failed institution, plus non-interest-bearing state scrip that would be paid back over a period of several years. A second and more substantial cash payment was made in 1992. The delay in payments was needed so that the state could create a special corporation called the Rhode Island Depositors Economic Protection Corporation, or Depco, which could raise money for depositors by selling bonds. To provide money to repay the bonds, the state raised its sales tax from six to seven percent. According to the state's plan, 90 percent of every deposit over $4,000 would be paid to depositors from the bond receipts. The remaining 10 percent would be paid in 15 annual installments beginning in 1998. While they were waiting for this remainder, depositors would earn 5 percent annual interest. The money for the remaining 10 percent would come from assets of failed institutions that Depco was selling, money from insurance companies or lawsuits, and Depco's share of sales tax receipts that exceeded what it needed to pay bondholders.

At the time of this writing, all but a dozen of the closed institutions have reopened with National Credit Union Administration (NCUA) Insurance. A government study of the Rhode Island crisis revealed numerous cases of fraud, imprudent loan underwriting standards, poor documentation of loans, lending to cronies, friends, and business colleagues, and lax supervision by management and the board of directors.

The failures of private funds led the states of North Carolina, Massachusetts, and Rhode Island to ask institutions to seek federal insurance whenever possible. Wisconsin, Connecticut, New Mexico, Utah, and Virginia stopped allowing private deposit insurance altogether. Several state-related private insurance funds still operate in California, Maryland, Florida, Georgia, Texas, and Washington. In addition, the Mutual Guaranty Corporation of Chattanooga insures $2 billion in deposits in five states (Kansas, Missouri, Tennessee, Indiana, and Iowa), while the National Deposit Insurance Corporation of Columbus, Ohio, insures about $5.4 billion in deposits at 420 credit unions in 22 states.In California, all 19 members of the California Credit Union Guaranty Corporation voted in 1991 to convert to federal insurance coverage.

Since the Rhode Island crisis, 11 of 21 states with private credit union insurance have announced plans to eliminate or restrict such insurance. In addition, 185 credit unions abandoned private insurance and obtained coverage from the NCUA. An additional 300 credit unions have applied for NCUA insurance. Mutual Guaranty Corporation is negotiating with the NCUA to accept 120 credit unions from Kansas and Missouri into their share-draft insurance system. Currently, the company is talking to federal regulators about converting all of its 317 members to NCUA status.

Attempting to capitalize on the FDIC's new policy of not covering the uninsured deposits of failed banks, the General Reinsurance Corporation announced that it was willing to insure bank deposits exceeding $100,000 in all states where permitted by law. (Seven states, including New York, California, and Florida, forbid such coverage.) The deposit insurance policies offered by a General Re subsidiary will cost 25 to 30 cents for each hundred dollars of insurance for the minimum $200,000 policy. General Re will limit its risk at any one bank to no more than $5 million of insurance and will only offer insurance coverage at about 9,000 of the nearly 11,400 banks.

EXCESSIVE RISK TAKING

Managers of troubled institutions have an incentive to gamble. If the gamble is unsuccessful, the managers can gamble again, hoping that the gambling process will obscure their loan losses, buy them more time as managers, and give their depository institutions a chance to grow out of their difficulties. Deposit insurance makes this gambling possible, as it allows remotely generated deposits to be funneled to the gambling depository institution by brokers (for a fee), even if local depositors become wary of an institution that is taking too many risks. (The passage of FIRRE in 1989 eliminated the use of brokered deposits by unhealthy institutions.) Even if a bank is insured and risky, it usually can continue to issue certificates of deposit to obtain funds at much the same rate or at a slightly higher rate than less risky institutions can get them. It can do so because most deposit holders do not share the risk of loss with the FDIC. If the bank and its managers do not bear the full cost of their risk taking, management may be encouraged to take more or even greater risks than they would if they could issue only uninsured deposits.

Robert P. Black, erudite president of the Richmond Federal Reserve Bank, has stated that "risk may be systematically underpriced in the U.S. economy because deposit insurance reduces the risk premium that depository institutions have to pay when they compete for deposits. Loan rates may therefore not reflect adequately the risk associated with particular loans. . . .Too many economic resources are being drawn to relatively high-risk ventures and away from lower-yielding but economically more defensible projects. The apparent excess supply of office buildings and condominiums in many parts of the country currently suggests that there may have been a significant misallocation of capital in the United States over the last decade. Deposit insurance may have contributed to this misallocation."[37]

POTENTIAL SOLUTIONS

There have been numerous proposals to reform the deposit insurance system. Some analysts favor abolishing deposit insurance altogether, in the hope of enlisting depositors as a source of market discipline on banks and thrifts. Some suggest lowering deposit insurance limits, while others propose narrowing sharply the powers of depository institutions in order to create inherently "safe" banks that would pose no risks of insolvency. These banks might resemble conservative money market funds. Another group of analysts would impose stringent, market-value capital standards on depository institutions, closing or reorganizing any institution failing to meet those standards.[38]

There is general agreement that broader disclosure and better, more timely, and more comparable information on asset quality is now considered important in helping corporate treasurers choose their banking relationships. In general, however, banks are chosen on the basis of services offered, availability of financing, and convenience. Financial analysis of their banks by corporate treasury officers is often cursory.[39]

Purchase and assumption and "too big to fail" policies only aggravate moral hazard problems, because they completely break the linkage between greater risk and higher costs that exists in most companies. For example, a bank with an excessive number or amount of bad loans may fear that it will have to write off these loans. As a consequence, the bank may become insolvent and be liquidated by the regulators. The bank managers would then lose their jobs. Therefore, they might continue to issue more insured deposits, make more loans at high rates, and charge hefty loan origination fees. They might then be able to report enough profits on the bank's newly expanded loan portfolio that it would be able to absorb the losses on past loans and still appear to be profitable. This strategy can work only if losses appear on the new loans with a lag, while the income from loan origination fees and higher rates on loans immediately increases reported profits. Such a "profitable" institution can continue to operate. If the new loans are sound, the management may have true profits and survive the crisis. However, most banks that have followed this strategy have failed as soon as a recession develops or when the quality of their loans deteriorates. Weak institutions will have to grow still faster, so that reported earnings from new loans will grow faster than reported losses on old loans. The process becomes further complicated by the new risk-based capital guidelines.

The Danish government has relied upon an aggressive bank soundness policy to limit public and depositor liability. The policy relies on market valuation of bank portfolios and prompt closure of any bank with impaired capital, even when the bank has a positive net worth. Danish regulators permit capital-impaired banks a short time to raise capital. If the bank is unsuccessful, the institution is closed promptly. This policy tends to minimize the public costs of bank rescues by ensuring that liquidation of assets provides sufficient funds to redeem most obligations to depositors. In sum, despite a highly competitive environment and powers greater than those of U.S. banks, the Danish system was able to operate essentially without deposit insurance until 1988 and still operates today without runs and with orderly failures of banks. Most Danish banks also maintain capital-to-asset ratios averaging 9.5 percent.[40]

New legislation passed by Congress in 1991 calls for the FDIC promptly to close banks with inadequate capital-to-asset ratios.

ENDNOTES

1. M. Levonian, "Early Warning System," *Weekly Letter,* Federal Reserve Bank of San Francisco, November 12, 1990, pp. 1–4.

2. G. Hempel, A. Coleman, and D. Simonson, *Bank Management: Text and Cases,* 3d ed. (New York: John Wiley & Sons, 1990), pp. 94–97.

3. J. H. Kareken, "Restructuring the Financial System," *Economic Review,* Federal Reserve Bank of Kansas City, August 1987, p. 23.

4. R. C. Moyer and R. E. Lamy, " 'Too Big to Fail': Rationale, Consequences, and Alternatives," *Business Economics,* July 1992, pp. 19–21.

5. Ibid., pp. 21–22.

6. M. Kohn, *Money, Banking, and Financial Markets* (Hinsdale, IL: Dryden Press, 1991), p. 466.

7. *Federal Reserve Bulletin,* July 1991, p. 549.

00

8. K. H. Bacon, "Failures of a Big Bank and a Little Bank Bring Fairness of Deposit-Security Policy into Question," *The Wall Street Journal,* December 5, 1990, p. A18.

9. C. S. Morris and G. H. Sellon, Jr., "Market Value Accounting for Banks: Pros and Cons," *Economic Review,* Federal Reserve Bank of Kansas City, March–April 1991, pp. 5–17.

10. M. Levonian and H. Cheng, "Checking the $100,000 Deposit Insurance Limit," *Weekly Letter,* Federal Reserve Bank of San Francisco, May 10, 1991, pp. 1–3.

11. Kohn, p. 466.

12. F. Mishkin, *The Economics of Money, Banking, and Financial Markets,* 2d ed. (Glenview, IL: Scott Foresman, 1989), p. 191.

13. Kohn, p. 466.

14. S. L. Hayes and D. M. Meerschwam, *Managing Financial Institutions* (Hinsdale, IL: Dryden Press, 1992), p. 207.

15. "Banker of the Year: Roger Anderson of Continental Illinois National Bank," *Institutional Investor,* August 14, 1984, pp. 68–69.

16. Mishkin, p. 377.

17. *BNA's Banking Report,* January 14, 1991, pp. 44–47.

18. K. H. Bacon, R. Suskind, and P. Thomas, "Financial Casualty: U.S. Recession Claims Bank of New England as First Big Victim," *The Wall Street Journal,* January 7, 1991, p. 1.

19. M. Light, *What If?* Bear Stearns Research Department, January 2, 1991.

20. J. Grant, "The Olympia Ordeal: It Won't End Soon," *New York Times,* May 24, 1992, p. F11.

21. *Annual Report, 1991,* Federal Reserve Bank of New York, pp. 8–14.

22. J. A. Neuberger, "Is a Good Bank Always Bad?" *Weekly Letter,* Federal Reserve Bank of San Francisco, May 1, 1992, p. 1.

23. Ibid., p. 2.

24. Ibid., p. 3.

25. S. Hein, "A Re-examination of the Costs and Benefits of Federal Deposit Insurance," *Business Economics,* July 1992, p. 30.

26. O. Kramer, *Rating the Risk* (New York: Insurance Information Institute, 1990), p. 114.

27. C. Yang, H. Gleckman, and others, "The Future of Banking," *Business Week,* April 22, 1991, p. 75.

28. C. Yang and M. McNamee, "Reform or Crackdown on Banking?" *Business Week,* July 15, 1991, p. 123.

29. K. H. Bacon, "FDIC Seeks Rise in Premium for Insurance," *The Wall Street Journal,* May 13, 1992, p. A3.

30. A. Greenspan, "Game Plan for the '90s," in *Proceedings, Annual Conference on Bank Structure and Competition, May 1990,* Federal Reserve Bank of Chicago, pp. 2–3.

31. *Banks Under Stress* (Paris: Organization for Economic Cooperation and Development, 1992), p. 134.

32. C. T. Carlstrom, *Bank Runs, Deposit Insurance, and Bank Regulation, Part I* (Federal Reserve Bank of Cleveland, February 1, 1988), pp. 1–3.

33. P. M. Horvitz, "Subordinated Debt Is Key to New Bank Capital Requirements," *American Banker,* December 31, 1984.

34. Carlstrom, pp. 1–3.

35. R. J. Pozdena, "Recapitalizing the Banking System," *Weekly Letter,* Federal Reserve Bank of San Francisco, August 3, 1991, pp. 1–7.

36. J. A. Neuberger, *Weekly Letter,* Federal Reserve Bank of San Francisco, December 1, 1990, p. 1.

37. L. J. Meister, "Banking and Commerce: A Dangerous Liaison?" *Business Review,* Federal Reserve Bank of Philadelphia, May–June 1992, p. 26.

38. H. E. Heinemann, *Heinemann Economics* 7, no. 12 (June 10, 1991), p. 8.

39. J. G. Ehlen, "A Review of Bank Capital and Its Adequacy," in *Dynamics of Banking,* eds. T. M. Havrilesky, R. Schweitzer, and J. T. Bookman (Arlington Heights, IL: Harlem Davidson Press, 1985), p. 383.

40. Pozdena, pp. 1–4.

PART THREE

Industry Trends and Structural Change

8 Structural Change in the Insurance Industry

Glorification of the "pluribus" at the expense of the "unum" does not enhance the prospects for national health insurance.

Victor K. Fuchs, *National Health Insurance Revisited*

There are about 6,000 insurance companies in the United States. The industry is divided into two broad categories: property and casualty insurance and life and health insurance. The insurance industry provided more than 2.2 million jobs and had responsibilities for more than $2 trillion in assets at the end of 1991.

LIFE INSURANCE

The U.S. life insurance industry, with $1.55 trillion in assets, had almost $10 trillion of life insurance in force in the United States by the end of 1991. During 1991 alone, the industry had premium receipts of about $264 billion. (See Table 8.1.) Almost half of those premiums were related to annuity considerations. Of the industry's assets, 40 percent were in corporate debt obligations, 17 percent in mort-

**Table 8.1   U.S. Life Insurance Industry
($ Millions)**

Year	Assets	Premium Income
1970	$ 207,254	$ 36,767
1980	480,572	92,624
1990	1,404,888	266,234
1991	1,520,225	263,860

Source: A.M. Best Aggregates and Averages: Life/Health (Oldwick, NJ: A.M. Best Company, 1992), pp. 11, 40.

This chapter was written in collaboration with Lawrence Brandon, executive vice-president of the Insurance Institute of America.

gage loans, 17 percent in Treasury and agency securities, 11 percent in common stock, 4 percent in policy loans, 3 percent in real estate, and 7 percent in miscellaneous assets. (See Table 8.2.)

According to Michael Conn, president of Michael Conn Associates, the life insurance industry as a whole has undergone much structural change since the end of World War II. After the war, the industry shifted from an emphasis on whole life policies to term and group-oriented insurance. This phase lasted until about 1970. From that year through 1986, many new products were introduced as the demand for traditional life insurance products appeared to falter in a changing economic environment. Since 1987, life insurance sales grew more slowly, partially because of lower income and employment growth in the economy, as well as a shift toward lower cost term insurance. There were also greater demands for investment-based products from the late 1970s through the early 1990s. To deal with a declining demand for traditional and highly profitable whole life insurance policies, life insurers began offering universal life, variable universal life, single-premium whole life insurance, various annuity alternatives, and other investment-type products. (See Table 8.3.) These products proved to be less profitable and poorly managed. Combined with the added expense of developing and introducing the new products, the shrinking profitability and poor management resulted in a deterioration in the return on equity for life insurance companies during the 1980s. Essentially, there was a subtle shift away from the mortality- and morbidity-based risk of traditional life insurance products toward more balance sheet risks in investment-based products. Today, annuities account for the largest percentage of the life industry's total premium—almost 48 percent in 1990, compared with only 14 percent in 1975. (See Table 8.4.) Like other life insurance products, annuities have been sold as investment vehicles, offering tax-deferred inside buildup in a market environment in which many other noninsurance investment products no longer shelter income from taxes.[1] However, if federal tax rates are increased, the demand for products that combine insurance and investments may increase because of the tax advantages those products offer.

The continued announcements of large investment losses throughout 1990 and 1991 by some major life insurance companies created additional problems for the industry and led to an increase in life insurance company insolvencies. (See Figure 8.1.) A few companies suffered losses when they underpriced health insurance or mismanaged guaranteed investment contracts (GICs) while others failed because of severe losses suffered in their junk bond or commercial real estate portfolios. In addition, illiquidity of assets became a serious problem at several troubled life insurance companies. A combination of all of these problems acted as a catalyst in influencing Equitable Life to shift from a mutual to a stock company in order to replace lost capital and to provide opportunities for growth in the future. Problems in the junk bond portfolio led to the seizure of Executive Life of California following a run by investors to cash out of annuities, while nonperforming real estate loans and the illiquidity of policy loans were the primary reason for the seizure of Mutual Benefit Life.

Table 8.2 Life Insurance Industry

Statutory Balance Sheet

	\$ Billion		% of Total	
	1990	**1985**	**1990**	**1985**
Assets				
Bonds	\$ 699	\$ 365	49.8%	43.9%
Preferred Stocks	10	10	0.7	1.2
Common Stocks	50	34	3.5	4.1
Mortgage Loans	266	167	18.9	20.1
Real Estate	32	20	2.3	2.4
Policy Loans	62	55	4.4	6.6
Cash, Short-Term and Other Invested Assets	73	44	5.2	5.3
Premium Receivables	16	15	1.1	1.8
Accrued Investment Income	20	13	1.4	1.6
Other Assets	18	21	1.3	2.5
Separate Accounts	160	87	11.4	10.5
Total	\$1,405	\$ 832	100.0%	100.0%
Liabilities				
Policy Reserve	\$ 832	\$ 500	59.2%	60.1%
Policy Claims & Dividends	35	26	2.5	3.1
Premium & Deposit Funds	208	40	14.8	4.8
Mandatory Security Valuation Reserve	15	11	1.1	1.3
Other	64	112	4.5	13.5
Separate Accounts	158	86	11.3	10.5
Total	\$1,312	\$ 775	93.4%	93.3%
Capital and Surplus	93	57	6.6	6.7
Total	\$1,405	\$ 832	100.0%	100.0%

Statutory Summary of Operations

	\$ Billion		% of Total	
	1990	**1985**	**1990**	**1985**
Revenues				
Premium Income	\$266.2	\$155.5	66.9%	67.4%
Net Investment Income	103.3	62.7	26.0	27.1
Other Income	28.4	12.7	7.1	5.5
Total	\$397.9	\$230.9	100.0%	100.0%
Expenses				
Benefits (including Dividends)	\$210.9	\$101.9	55.4%	45.9%
Change in Reserves	78.2	55.7	20.6	25.3
Commissions	23.3	18.2	6.6	8.3
Expenses	30.9	23.5	8.1	10.6
Other Disbursements	37.1	22.0	9.3	9.91
Total	\$380.5	\$220.6	100.0%	100.0%
Net Gain before Taxes	\$ 17.4	\$ 10.3		
Federal Income Taxes	3.8	3.1		
Net Gain after Taxes	\$ 13.6	\$ 7.2		

Source: Best's Aggregates and Averages (Oldwick, NJ: A.M. Best Company, 1991), pp.16,41.

Table 8.3   Market Share of New Premiums

Type	1980	1991 (est.)
Whole Life	82%	64%
Term	18	20
Universal Life		11
Variable Life		1
Variable Universal		4

Source: Based on data in *1992 Life Insurance Fact Book* (Washington, DC: American Council of Life Insurance, 1992), p. 11.

Table 8.4   Premium Receipts of Life Insurance Industry ($ Millions)

	Life Insurance	Annuities	Health Insurance
1980	$40,829	$22,429	$29,366
1990	76,692	129,064	58,254
1991	79,301	123,590	60,900

Source: 1992 Life Insurance Fact Book (Washington, DC: American Council of Life Insurance, 1992), p. 5.

PROPERTY AND CASUALTY INSURANCE

Property and casualty insurance companies had just under $600 billion in assets at year-end 1991 and had collected $223 billion of insurance premiums that year. Despite self-insurance programs and higher deductibles, premiums have grown with increased litigation and the growth of large jury awards. Of the total funds available for investment, 19 percent were invested in corporate bonds, 23 percent in Treasury and agency securities, 36 percent in municipal bonds, 20 percent in common and preferred stocks, 1 percent in real estate and mortgages, and 1 percent in miscellaneous assets. (See Table 8.5.)

Among property and casualty insurance companies, premiums were still being chased to generate investment income as an overabundance of capital led to aggressive price cutting. There have been net underwriting losses in this sector of the insurance industry since 1979. (See Figure 8.2.) In fact, the industry has shown profits on underwriting operations in only 5 of the last 25 years. However, in all but 3 of the last 25 years, investment income exceeded these underwriting losses, allowing for positive combined net income before taxes for the property and casualty industry as a whole. Nonetheless, some companies occasionally had severe problems. The property and casualty industry joined the banks, thrifts, and life insurance companies with declining returns on equity during the 1980s. As a matter of fact, return on equity was only 3.7 percent in 1992, after hovering around 10 percent in the 1980s. With a statutory accounting mechanism, returns on equity for property

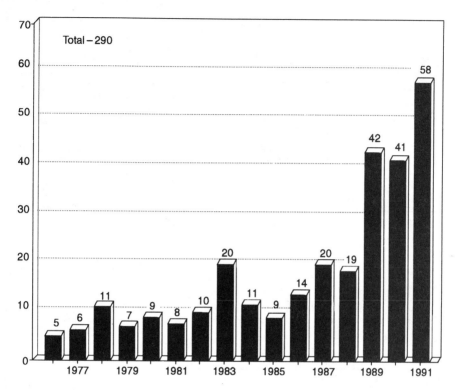

Figure 8.1 Annual Number of Life/Health Financially Impaired Companies 1976–1991. (*Source:* A.M. Best Company, *Best's Insurance Management Reports,* July 1992, p. 4)

Table 8.5 Investments of Property and Casualty Insurance Companies

Type	1991	1986	1981
U.S. Government and Agency Bonds	22.8%	21.7%	12.5%
Municipal Bonds	36.0	39.2	48.1
Stock	19.7	21.7	23.6
Corporate Bonds, Notes, & Paper	18.7	15.0	14.2
Mortgages	1.4	1.6	0.8
Miscellaneous	1.4	0.8	0.8
Total	100.0%	100.0%	100.0%

Source: The Fact Book 1993: Property Casualty Insurance Facts (New York: Insurance Information Institute, 1993), p. 21. Copyright © 1993 Insurance Information Institute.

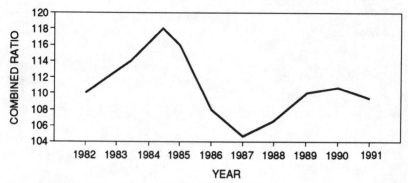

Note: 1991 estimated based on first half of year.

Figure 8.2 Property and Casualty Insurance Cycle Combined Ratio, 1982–1991. (*Source:* A.M. Best Company)

Table 8.6   Property and Casualty Underwriting Results

Year	Underwriting Gain/Loss[a]	Net Investment Income	Pretax Operating Income
1970	$ −426	$ 1,976	$ 1,550
1971	826	2,309	3,135
1972	1,062	2,662	3,724
1973	6	3,094	3,100
1974	−2,645	3,604	959
1975	−4,227	3,905	−322
1976	−2,189	4,594	2,405
1977	1,112	5,816	6,928
1978	1,296	7,290	8,586
1979	−1,301	9,279	7,978
1980	−3,334	11,063	7,729
1981	−6,288	13,248	6,960
1982	−10,290	14,907	4,617
1983	−13,332	15,973	2,651
1984	−21,268	17,660	−3,609
1985	−25,288	19,508	−5,780
1986	−16,613	21,924	5,312
1987	−10,620	23,960	13,340
1988	−11,800	27,723	15,923
1989	−21,093	31,207	10,114
1990	−21,856	32,901	11,046
1991	−20,930	34,247	13,317

[a]After dividends to policyholders; all data are in $ millions.
Source: A.M. Best Averages and Aggregates: Property/Casualty (Oldwick NJ: A.M. Best Company, 1992), p. 61.

and casualty insurance companies declined from 13.3 percent in 1981 to 8.8 percent in 1991. With GAAP accounting, returns on equity declined from 11.8 percent to 8.7 percent during the same period. Table 8.7 shows net income after taxes as a percent of equity for property and casualty companies, as well as for other members of the financial services industry.

The decline in property and casualty ratios (e.g., capital-to-asset ratio) can be attributed in part to both underpricing and a shift from property to liability lines. Liability claims take longer to be paid, permitting a longer earning period, and therefore build up more assets. This does not necessarily mean that insurers are riskier, at least as long as their loss reserves are adequate. Currently, the property and liability industry is not sufficiently profitable to support its capitalization.[2]

Just as many of the highest quality corporate customers deserted the banks when it came to short-or intermediate-term borrowing, many of the best liability risks appear to have left the primary insurance market for self-insurance and participation in risk retention groups. By the late 1980s, the alternative market accounted for nearly 35 percent of commercial liability premiums. The movement toward the alternative market was brought about by rapidly rising insurance premiums related to increased tort costs in the primary insurance market and an attempt by corporate risk managers to reduce insurance costs. As with banks that lost their best customers, liability insurance underwriters were also left with a more risky book of business. The resulting "adverse selection" increased the riskiness of the portfolio because the more desirable lines of coverage, such as commercial property, went to the captive insurers, while the less desirable catastrophe layer remained largely in the hands of the traditional industry.[3] Essentially, the property and casualty insurers have failed to recognize that theirs is a commodity business.[4]

The major risks facing property and casualty insurance companies is, of course, the danger from a natural disaster and the fear that regulators in some jurisdictions will suppress rates (insurance premiums) while the courts impose unforeseen liability awards on the insurance industry. Increasingly, rates have fallen, while a revolution in modern tort law has greatly expanded liability.[5] Orin Kramer has suggested that an irreconcilable tension exists between the regulatory goal of affordability and the need to preserve the solvency of insurance companies. The biggest threat to the solvency of insurers, however, may not be from bad loans or imprudent investments; rather, it may be because society chose to socialize the costs of some of its priorities through private insurance companies, which may eventually run out of capital. For example, the risks from a major earthquake or another environmental catastrophe are great, and the desire to have the insurance industry pay a substantial share of the huge costs of cleaning up hazardous waste are large.[6]

Table 8.8 lists the largest property and casualty companies in 1990, together with their market share of net written premiums.

CONSUMER CONFIDENCE IN THE INDUSTRY

The well-publicized failures of a few major life insurance companies have concerned over 156 million people in the U.S. who are anxious and frightened about whether

Table 8.7 Annual Rate of Return: Net Income After Taxes as a Percent of Equity

Year	Property/Casualty Insurance[a]		Non-Property/Casualty Insurance Industries[b]				
	Statutory Accounting	GAAP Accounting[c]	Diversified Financial[d]	Commercial Banks	Utilities	Transportation	Fortune 500[e]
1982	9.3%	8.5%	10.0%	12.0%	12.5%	7.9%	10.9%
1983	9.1	8.1	11.7	12.5	13.3	11.6	10.7
1984	1.7	1.9	9.3	12.6	13.4	13.6	13.5
1985	2.8	3.9	9.4	13.0	13.0	11.5	11.6
1986	13.9	13.5	15.9	12.8	13.3	7.7	11.6
1987	13.2	15.8	16.3	11.1	12.8	9.7	14.4
1988	13.2	13.4	12.8	14.6	12.7	11.6	16.2
1989	9.1	10.2	13.0	13.6	12.4	11.7	15.0
1990	8.5	8.4	12.7	9.9	11.5	11.0	13.0
1991	8.9	8.7	13.9	11.9	11.5	5.1	10.2

[a] Property/casualty insurance data: GAAP accounting, Insurance Services Office; statutory accounting, calculated by Insurance Information Institute from A.M. Best data.

[b] Non-insurance industry data for 1981 through 1983 are industry averages; for 1984 through 1990 they are medians. Both the averages and the medians come from Fortune Magazine. Data for 1991 are not comparable to prior years. The 1991 figure is the return on common stock only. Data for prior years include the return on preferred stock.

[c] 1982–1989 revised by Insurance Services Office because of revisions to GAAP adjustment procedure.

[d] Composed largely of companies engaged in property and casualty insurance with or without life insurance and other financial services.

[e] Median for Fortune 500 U.S. Industrial Corporations.

Table 8.8   Property and Casualty Industry, 1990 Market
Share ($ Billions)

Groups	Net Premiums Written	Market Share
State Farm	$24.5	11.2%
Allstate	14.0	6.4
AIG	7.4	3.4
Aetna Life & Casualty	7.4	3.4
Farmers Group	6.5	3.0
Liberty Mutual	6.5	3.0
CNA	6.4	2.9
Nationwide	5.8	2.7
Hartford	5.1	2.3
Travelers	4.4	2.2
Total	$88.4	40.5%

Source: INSURSTAT. Copyright © 1992 Insurance Information Institute. Property and casualty insurance data: GAAP accounting, Insurance Services Office; statutory accounting, calculated by Insurance Information Institute from A.M. Best data. Non-insurance industry data for 1981 through 1983 are industry averages; for 1984 through 1990, they are medians. Both the averages and the medians come from *FORTUNE* magazine.

or not they can really count on their life insurance companies for retirement, health, disability, annuity, and death benefits. After all, life insurance companies had been thought to be paragons of safety and conservative investment. The rise in life insurance insolvencies has shot a hole in the age-old expression, "Once a life insurance company gets to be a certain size, malice might hurt it, but sheer stupidity can't." Consumer confidence in insurance companies has declined as a result of the failures of a few large life insurance companies. Such a failure exposes even healthy insurance companies to the danger of a run, and the integrity of life insurance products may be called into question, deterring their purchase. In addition, the thrift debacle and the problems of the banking industry have sensitized legislators, regulators, and the public at large to the risk of insolvency of other financial institutions. While most analysts do not equate the degree of insurers' problems with that of banks or thrifts, they do suggest that supervisory restraints on excessive risk taking are equally appropriate in insurance companies and depository institutions.

There has been a call among some members of Congress for federal regulation of insurance. The insurance industry as a whole is not about to collapse, as did the commercial banks in the 1930s and the savings and loans in the 1980s. However, more insurance companies are likely to fail in the 1990s than in either the 1970s or 1980s.[7] During Senate hearings in December 1990, Senator Howard Metzenbaum stated, "The warning signs of the S&L crisis were clear, but unfortunately they were ignored. We must not ignore the same signs in the insurance industry—lax regulation, outdated accounting methods, overvalued assets, and, in some instances, low capital requirements." There is a lesson to be learned from the thrift crisis for insurance regulators: Do not let happen to the insurance industry what happened to the S&Ls. Regulatory forbearance raised the cost of resolving the thrift debacle considerably and, consequently, should not be repeated in the case of insurance companies.[8]

MUTUAL BENEFIT LIFE AND EXECUTIVE LIFE

While the U.S. public was used to the announcements of thrift and bank failures during the 1980s and 1990s, it seemed shocked when two major life insurance companies were seized by regulators in 1991. Both companies suffered from illiquidity of assets, as well as nonperforming or suboptimal investments.

Mutual Benefit Life

The July 1991 seizure by New Jersey regulators of Mutual Benefit Life Insurance Company, the 18th largest life insurer in terms of assets in the United States, prevented the largest failure of an insurance company in U.S. history. New Jersey regulators acted after successive reductions of Mutual Benefit's credit rating in 1990 and 1991 had precipitated a flood of withdrawal demands and a drain of cash through surrenders of policies—equivalent to a run on a bank.

Mutual Benefit joined Monarch Capital, Executive Life of California, First Capital Life, and Fidelity Bankers Life Insurance as major life insurance company casualties during 1991. Following on the heels of the Mutual Benefit Life seizure, New Jersey Life Insurance Co., a much smaller insurer with about $161 million in assets was prohibited from selling new policies in both New Jersey and California by the respective insurance commissioners when studies showed that the company had inadequate reserves. This action was taken after the courts refused to allow the New Jersey insurance commissioner to seize New Jersey Life (which had protested the commission's seizure attempt).

Merger talks between Mutual Benefit Life and Metropolitan Life, as well as other potential investors, earlier in 1991 were unsuccessful. Money managers had been pulling their funds out of Mutual Benefit in a flight toward quality. The company was being forced to sell off money market instruments and bonds in order to meet policyholder and investor demands for cash. Mutual Benefit ran into liquidity problems soon after, with 27 percent of its admitted assets at year-end 1990 in the form of policy loans and with an even larger portion in mortgages (in a declining real estate market). The problem of illiquidity of assets was symptomatic of structural change within the life insurance industry.

The state rescue plan called for the separation of the company's profitable group insurance operation, headquartered in Kansas City, from the rest of the operation. This was accomplished in fewer than 60 days when Amev Holdings, Inc., a U.S.

subsidiary of Belgium's Groupe AG and Dutch insurer N.V. Amev, purchased the group health business for $500 million. This approach is similar to a plan sometimes used by troubled banks and thrifts in which a company is split into two parts, known as the "good bank" and the "bad bank." Other parts of the plan established market values for the assets of the company. Mutual Benefit also reached an agreement in principle to form a joint venture with the Hartford Insurance Co. for the corporate-owned life insurance business, which would enable Mutual Benefit Life to retain an interest in future profits on existing business, as well as profits from new business within the corporate-owned life insurance sector. However, state regulators were unable to obtain an agreement from a group of the country's largest life insurance companies to foot the entire $800 million bill to bail out Mutual Benefit in 1992. New Jersey regulators and the insurance industry did reach a tentative agreement to provide policyholders with all of their money if funds were not withdrawn over the next seven years. State guaranty funds would furnish most of the money, with private insurance companies providing the remainder. Although state guaranty funds are financed through assessments on insurance companies, the companies get to subtract the amount paid into the fund from their state tax bill. This provided a partial subsidy from taxpayers in states where Mutual Benefit Life policies were written. The ultimate cost to the insurance industry will depend on which classes of policyholders are covered by the state funds. Negotiations on this key issue were continuing at the time of this writing. The plan would run for five years and provide policyholders with about 88 percent of the cash values of their policies, with the balance of the funds coming from guaranty funds and the insurance industry. An examination of Mutual Benefit's investment portfolio showed that nearly 40 percent of its funds were invested in mortgages and real estate, while only 3 percent were invested in junk bonds. Unfortunately, Mutual Benefit had seen its net worth fall steadily as a result of a large increase in bad real estate loans. The insurer's nonperforming or nonaccruing loan percentage approximated 10 percent of its real estate loans at the time of this writing and appeared to be rising. Real estate loans at peer insurance companies were between 20 and 30 percent of assets, with nonperforming loans less than a quarter of that at Mutual Benefit Life. Mutual Benefit's troubled real estate portfolio consisted of rather large loans and equity investments in big projects. When problems arose with these nonaccruing projects, Mutual Benefit, hoping to profit from its equity stake, continued to lend even more money to the projects.

New Jersey imposed an immediate freeze on all cash withdrawals, making it impossible for policyholders to withdraw money that they had invested through life insurance policies or annuities. The court put an end to further policy cash-ins, loans against policies, and other "nonessential" conversions and redemptions. However, death, disability, pension, and health insurance benefits, as well as interest to annuity holders, would still be paid. This could have a ripple effect on the industry if bad publicity about the industry grows, as investors might begin to increase borrowings against their cash value in whole life policies, withdraw funds from annuities and investment contracts, and generally move their cash away from life insurance products altogether. In addition, the ability to raise funds and the cost of available funds for many insurers will most certainly be affected.

Mutual Benefit Life is also a participant in the financial guaranty market for tax-exempt bonds and collateralized mortgage obligations. The insurer guaranteed about $750 million in municipal revenue bonds—many of which are "putable" to the insurance company at full face value—and $650 million in collateralized mortgage obligations. With the demise of the insurance company, many of these bonds (which will trade in the secondary market at about $0.60–$0.70 on the $1.00) will certainly be put back to the insurance company, since the company has guaranteed the principal of those bonds. Given the state's freeze on payments, however, the ability of the insurer to honor its obligations on the bonds remains doubtful. This issue has raised questions about certain municipal bonds that carry financial guarantees from insurance companies. Investors who purchase insured municipal bonds will have to pay more attention to the quality of the security itself, along with the quality of the guarantor.

The rehabilitator, Mutual Benefit, and Metropolitan Life have reached an agreement regarding Mutual Benefit's non-tax-sheltered allocated annuities whereby Metropolitan Life will replace Mutual Benefit's guaranteed certificate account with Metropolitan's subfund account. The account will become a part of Mutual Benefit's new separate account. Mutual Benefit will invest this account in a funding agreement issued to the account of Metropolitan Life. The account principal will be guaranteed by Metropolitan's assets. Also, the account will be treated as if it is insulated from the claims of other Mutual Benefit creditors and will be unaffected by restrictions on withdrawals.

Executive Life Crisis

Executive Life took an investment perspective on its products, guaranteeing good returns on tax-deferred annuities. The company was a leader in the industry shift away from the classical insurance risk-taking business to the asset-risk business.

Executive Life was seized by California regulators in April 1991 when the value of its $7 billion junk bond portfolio declined sharply, prompting a run of investors to cash in their policies. California Insurance Commissioner John Garamendi called for all interested parties to place bids with his office for taking over the insolvent insurer.

California insurance regulators announced that they had received eight offers for Executive Life Insurance Company (with 208,000 life insurance policyholders and 164,000 annuity holders) before an established bidding deadline set by state regulators in a court-supervised auction. The bids promised that policyholders would initially receive between 81 and 89 cents per dollar of policy cash value. The various state guaranty funds would then chip in additional money so that policyholders would eventually receive between 95 and 100 cents on the dollar. A decision on the winning bid was to be made by Insurance Commissioner Garamendi, subject to state court approval.

In late August 1991, the insurance industry announced that it had agreed to pay as much as $2 billion in coming years to make up losses suffered by Executive Life customers through state guaranty funds. This arrangement was coordinated through the National Organization of Life and Health Insurance Guaranty Associations (NOLHGA). The deal was motivated by the desire of the members to restore public confidence in the life insurance industry and by the desire to head off calls for federalizing insurance regulation. Commissioner Garamendi conditionally approved a takeover by NOLHGA. However, the conservator pointed out serious legal issues that affected the safety and certainty of the NOLHGA bid. The conservator also required NOLHGA to fulfill numerous financial and legal conditions. California finally rejected the NOLHGA offer to acquire Executive Life because the industry's bid did not overcome all the financial and legal hurdles set by the state insurance department.

Commissioner Garamendi then selected the French consortium led by Altus Finance on the second go-round to acquire failed Executive Life of California. Garamendi indicated that the French group's revised bid promised a higher return to the 372,000 policyholders. It also severed Executive Life's huge portfolio of junk bonds from the company's insurance operation. The French consortium would rename the insurance company Aurora National Life Assurance Co. Garamendi indicated that under the latest French bid, all policyholders would receive close to 90 cents for every dollar invested in annuities and other insurance policies and that 97 percent of policyholders would suffer no loss at all, because industry-financed guaranty funds would make up the shortfall on all policies up to $100,000 in most states. This type of policyholder settlement could be expected as long as the state court ruled in a separate decision that $1.85 billion of municipal bonds backed by Executive Life were subordinate to conventional insurance and annuities. Mr. Garamendi had held that so-called funding agreements issued by Executive Life to back municipal bonds and notes weren't conventional insurance business and would rank as subordinate creditors in a position reserved for suppliers and other unsecured creditors.

Following Garamendi's recommendation that Executive Life be awarded to the French consortium, a California state court ruled that holders of municipal bonds guaranteed by Executive Life have a claim to the failed insurer's assets that is equal to the claims asserted by the holders of its conventional insurance policies and annuity contracts. Garamendi's restructuring of Executive Life had assumed that the claims by the bondholders were subordinate to the insurance and annuity policies. If Judge Kurt Lewin's ruling is upheld, it would sharply reduce recoveries at Executive Life for big policy and annuity holders to approximately 73 cents on the dollar from an expected 90 cents on the dollar. It could also add about $1 billion to the industry's cost, through its guaranty associations, of clearing up the Executive Life fiasco. Although California insurance regulators had determined years ago that Executive Life's obligations backing the bonds were "unauthorized," the insurance department made no effort to stop the issuance of the bonds. Judge Lewin ruled that the regulators failure to act provided a trap for unwary investors.

Following Judge Lewin's decision, bank trustees for $1.85 billion of municipal bonds backed by the failed Executive Life Insurance Co. said that they would ask a California state court to order that more than $100 million in back payments be made to bondholders. Most insurance and annuity claimants at Executive Life have been receiving interim payments equaling 70 percent of amounts otherwise payable. However, the holders of municipal securities guaranteed by Executive Life had received nothing because their claims previous to the judge's ruling were deemed subordinate to those claims.

In November 1992, California's state appeals court upheld the lower court ruling that the holders of the municipal securities backed by Executive Life have the same claim on company assets as do policyholders of conventional life insurance and annuities issued by the company. The appeals court ruling was a setback to Commissioner Garamendi and the state life insurance guarantee associations. The decision would lower the overall settlement for policyholders to about 70 cents on the dollar from 89 cents.

Under the new agreement, the guaranty associations would once again cover the losses of most policyholders. The cost to the guaranty associations (and ultimately the life insurance industry) is estimated at $1.9 billion, or $1 billion more than before the court ruling on municipal bonds. The revised plan also called for real estate owned by Executive Life to be placed in a trust and eventually sold for the benefit of policyholders whose losses were not fully covered (those with annuity contracts exceeding $100,000) and, possibly, to generate partial repayment to the guaranty associations.

One stumbling block in the settlement of Executive Life of California's insurance claims was removed in early 1992, when the IRS accepted a disputed income tax claim for $73 million for the years 1981–1990. However, the municipal security claims hurdle has not been settled, and Commissioner Garamendi has filed appeals to reverse the lower court ruling that the municipal securities claims should rank equally with all other insurance claims at Executive Life. Should these appeals fail, Garamendi has proposed to deny inordinate returns to those who bought bonds after the default date. His proposal calls for a much lower payout to speculators than to long-term bondholders.

In the spring of 1993, a California court ruling struck down Garamendi's plan to sell Executive Life to Mutuelle Assurance Artisinale. While Garamendi has publicly said that he hopes to salvage that deal, there were rumors at the time of this writing that talks were in progress to sell Executive Life to Pacific Mutual Life Insurance Company.[9]

In dealing with a sister company in New York State, insurance regulators in New York announced a rescue plan that should pay 118,000 customers of Executive Life of New York 100 cents on the dollar. However, insurance customers wishing to cash out immediately might have to pay surrender charges. Also, some customers who continue in the plan might receive a lower rate of interest than they had received before Executive Life of New York was seized by state regulators in the spring of 1992. The state plan calls for Metropolitan Life to provide bookkeeping services for Executive Life policyholders who are receiving current payments and for Metropolitan to take over the rest of Executive Life's business in deferred annuities, whole life policies, term policies, and universal life policies. Executive Life policies would be cancelled, and former policyholders would be issued new contracts by Metropolitan Life.

DOWNGRADES IN RATINGS FOR LIFE INSURERS

The crisis of confidence surrounding the life insurance industry became worse in mid-1991, following the First Executive Life and Mutual Benefit Life crises, when Moody's downgraded its ratings on John Hancock Mutual Life to Aa-2, Massachusetts Mutual Life to Aa-1, Mutual Life Insurance Company of New York (MONY) to Baa-1, New England Mutual Life to Aa-3, Principal Mutual Life to Aa-1, Aetna Life Insurance Company to AA-2, Crown Life Insurance Company to A-3, Kemper Investors Life Insurance Company and Federal Kemper Life Assurance Company to A-2, Home Life Insurance Company to A-3, and Travelers Corp. to A-2.

At the end of 1991, the Aetna Life and Casualty Corp. (with assets of $92 billion) identified $1.4 billion in bad real estate loans and $975 million in foreclosed properties of mortgage loans. Aetna's reserve for possible mortgage losses stood at $533 million on September 30, 1991, up from only $312 million at the end of 1990. In addition to real estate investment problems, Aetna has been troubled by guaranteed investment contract problems. To become more liquid, Aetna invested new funds in the money markets and sold its American Re-Insurance Co. subsidiary, the third largest U.S. reinsurance company, to KKR in a deal valued at $1.21 billion. The deal offered Aetna the advantage of reducing its underwriting risks while raising much needed capital to help strengthen the company's reserves. Aetna also laid off 10 percent of its work force, saving about $200 million per year beginning in 1994. Troubled loans held by the life insurance company rose to a record 7.3 percent in the second quarter of 1992, up from 6.2 percent in the first quarter of the year. Office building delinquencies increased to 9.49 percent in the second quarter of 1992 from 8.05 percent in the first quarter, and retail store delinquencies rose to 5.75 percent in the second quarter from 4.14 percent in the first quarter. Aetna estimated that problematic loans could grow by another $1.2 billion in 1992.

The life insurance industry as a whole held more than $15.6 billion in past due loans on June 30, 1992, a sign that its commercial real estate woes had intensified and spread to older properties. In numerous instances, tenants were vacating to offices where landlords offered cheaper rents. Of the past due loans, those in foreclosure accounted for 3.39 percent.

Actually, the number of problematic real estate loans is understated because many troubled loans are restructured, with their maturities often lengthened or their interest rates reduced before they show up as delinquent on the books. Loans taken back in foreclosure also may not appear on the books as delinquent or troubled.

Travelers Insurance Company has suffered from problems with real estate (a $19 billion portfolio) and guaranteed investment contracts. The trouble began early in the 1980s, when Travelers began chasing the business of pension funds by selling guaranteed investment contracts. To be a successful player in these contracts, the insurance company sought anticipated high yields in real estate investments in Texas, Colorado, Utah, and California just prior to the real estate crash in those regions. It invested too much in the overbuilt commercial office building market and also lent too much to too few borrowers. Despite all of these problems, Travelers generated profits of $318 million in 1991, following a loss of $178 million in 1990. While not a candidate for failure, Travelers has suffered from a flight by nervous pension customers to the safety of higher rated competitors. Also, gross insurance premiums fell in 1991 as the company retrenched. While Travelers seems to have a lot more problems than some of its competitors, the company has given the impression of being able to identify and manage its problems. Travelers raised $300 million in the capital markets in early 1992 and later sold $300 million in preferred stock, as well as some of its subsidiaries, such as Dillon Read.

In an effort to improve its financial health, Travelers Corp. received an infusion of $550 million in cash as an investment from Primerica Corp. and agreed to eliminate at least 3,500 jobs during 1992–1993. Primerica gained four seats on Travelers' board of directors, along with a 27-percent stake in Travelers' stock. Under the agreement, Travelers will get a 50-percent interest in Primerica's Gulf Insurance Co. unit, a property and casualty insurance company, and a 100-percent interest in certain health insurance operations of Primerica's Transport Life/Voyager Group. The deal raised Travelers' common equity by $722.5 million and brought to $1.2 billion the amount of capital that Travelers raised in 1992. Primerica paid about one-half of book value for its 27-percent ownership position, a fair price given the great concern over the insurer's real estate portfolio. On June 30, 1992, Travelers had $13.8 billion in real estate properties and mortgages ($5.2 billion of which were producing losses or poor returns) out of a total company investment portfolio of $45 billion.

By recapitalizing, Travelers avoided another downgrade by Moody's, which had already downgraded it to Baa–1. Following the Primerica announcement, Moody's placed Travelers Corp. on review for a possible upgrade. Low ratings for an insurance company are anathema because they may lead to a general loss of business in annuities, guaranteed investment contracts, etc. The cash infusion should give Travelers added financial flexibility to ride out the real estate recession. In the meantime, the company has assembled a new management team, eliminated thousands of jobs, and withdrawn from unprofitable markets. In the process of restructuring, Travelers eliminated almost half of its personal and commercial policy agents. While Aetna and Travelers are both profitable, they have been weakened considerably and face the potential threat of cancellations, surrenders, or withdrawals by policyholders and annuity holders if there is a further loss of confidence in the quality of either company.

Following the downgrade in rating of MONY, the commercial paper rating of the company was lowered to P–3. The lower rating by A.M. Best reflected the size of the company's problematic real estate losses and the potential for further write-downs. MONY's large portfolio of non-investment-grade bonds also contributed to

Table 8.9   Moody's Rating Changes

Company	Assets (S Billions)	Old Rating	New Rating
Aetna Life	$ 52.3	Aaa	Aa–3
Home Life	4.4	A–1	A–3
John Hancock Mutual	33.7	Aaa	Aa–2
Kemper Investors Life	6.1	Aa–3	A–2
Massachusetts Mutual	27.2	Aaa	Aa–1
MONY	18.0	A–2	Baa–1
New England Mutual	17.1	Aa–1	Aa–3
Principal Mutual	27.5	Aaa	Aa–1
Travelers	33.0	A–1	Baa–1

the "contingent" rating. (See Table 8.9.) MONY, the country's 13th largest life insurance company in terms of assets, with large amounts of troubled real estate loans (mortgages represent 40 percent of the firm's invested assets, compared with an industry average of 27 percent), has been holding discussions with other insurance companies, such as Metropolitan Life, about joint ventures or other transactions that would boost its capital. MONY's troubled real estate portfolio, including foreclosures and problematic mortgages, totaled $426 million at mid-year 1991, equal to almost 60 percent of its $730 million of surplus. Only a handful of other life insurance companies had a larger amount of bad real estate as a percentage of capital at year-end 1990. Hoping to prevent the kind of withdrawals (runs) that have hurt other life insurance companies, MONY took out full-page newspaper advertisements to reassure policyholders and pension clients. MONY even set up an 800 number to answer their questions. In late October 1991, MONY announced that it planned to transfer up to $1.3 billion of its pension business to Metropolitan Life, signaling the probable end of merger talks between the two insurance companies. This action represents a partial solution to some of MONY's problems. The transaction will boost the company's capital ratio slightly, giving it and its policyholders a bigger cushion against losses. The transaction will also remove the pressure on MONY from pension managers who had requested withdrawals of hundreds of millions of dollars in guaranteed investment contracts, threatening to strain the company's liquidity. Since the seizure of First Executive Life and Mutual Benefit Life, pension managers are acting more quickly to withdraw funds from insurance companies at the first sign of trouble. The key attraction for pension fund managers is that the contracts are backed by AAA-rated Metropolitan Life and that pension managers will not have to settle for a lower interest rate, as they would have if they had withdrawn their contracts from MONY. Under the agreement, the pension funds will receive the current rate on their guaranteed investment contracts through 1992. Additionally, Metropolitan Life and MONY have agreed to a reinsurance transaction, in which Metropolitan will share the risk on $300 million of MONY's business.

Following downgradings by the rating agencies, 10 large insurance companies received capital infusions from their parent holding companies to help blunt the effect of junk bond and real estate losses. Some insurers supplied funds to prevent downgrades and to maintain the confidence of policyholders and agents. Some insurance companies received additional capital because growth in their businesses, rather than investment losses, had stretched their capital.

The growing uncertainty as to whether an insurance company is able to pay out claims has begun to terrify policyholders. The downgradings were particularly worrisome because of increased concern about policyholder runs on low-rated companies. Those companies with a heavy amount of corporate pension business and tax-deferred annuities can be most vulnerable. In addition, many independent insurance agents rely heavily on a company's ratings, and many will sell only policies of companies with top ratings. Finally, some purchasing companies have contracts that specify minimum insurance rating levels for their policies.

Unfortunately, insurance rating agencies like A.M. Best do make mistakes. For example, Best did not change its A+ rating on Mutual Benefit Life until 10 days before the seizure of the company by state regulators. Also, two different rating agencies proclaimed Executive Life healthy until it announced a large write-off on its portfolio of junk bonds. Rating agencies are simply going to have to do a better job of monitoring changes and increased risk exposure in the insurance industry. As a matter of fact, Best has indicated that it will change its analysis of an insurance company's financial strength by implementing a "policyholder confidence factor"—that is, whether an insurer could be exposed to a run by its policyholders. This factor will attempt to address the unprecedented environment caused by the combined effects of a recession, a depressed national real estate market, a decline in consumer confidence in financial institutions, and new legal pressures on pension fund managers. Best has said that in this current economic environment, "a solvent company's liquidity problems, which in the past were manageable, can develop into a liquidity crisis."[10] In January 1992, Best announced that it was refining its current rating system and would increase the number of different ratings to 15 from 9. The new system will assign grades of A++ through F, replacing the previous ratings of A+ through C-. Contingent ratings, which indicated a modest decline in financial performance, but not enough of a decline to warrant a reduction in rating, will be eliminated.

In November 1991, a new Standard & Poor's survey indicated that more than 500 insurance companies, accounting for about 3 percent, or $7 billion, of the total of premiums written, were financially vulnerable. The rating company utilized sophisticated models that weighed profitability, liquidity, cash flow, and quality of assets, among other factors. In making public its announcement, S&P indicated that 23 companies were given credit downgradings through the first 10 months of 1991, but no companies fell below investment-grade status.

OTHER TROUBLED LIFE INSURANCE COMPANIES

While the vast majority of life insurance companies are healthy, a *USA Today* study of 1,269 companies found 91 that could face financial risk at the end of 1991.[11] In

1988, state regulators took control of 13 life insurance companies, as opposed to 32 in 1990 and 34 in the first nine months of 1991. How do the problems of the insurance industry compare with those of the savings and loan and banking industries? According to Stephen Brobeck, executive director of the Consumer Federation of America, a Washington lobbying group, "The good news is that the insurance industry is far more solvent than the S&Ls and more solvent than the banks. . . . The bad news is that insurance companies made some of the same investments that other financial institutions did and that are causing other financial institutions serious problems."

In 1992, the average life insurance company had a much larger cushion of net worth (8.8 percent of assets) than did the thrifts (less than 2 percent of assets) during the 1980s. This cushion gives both life insurance companies and policyholders greater protection from investment losses.[12] Several hundred life insurance companies out of a total of several thousand have suffered large losses of surplus, and it is likely that many of these companies will not survive the 1990s, unless their problems of nonaccruing commercial real estate loans are resolved through a pickup in economic activity. Some life insurers are guilty of chasing higher yields offered by higher risk assets, such as junk bonds and partially leased real estate.

Those companies with the largest exposure of junk bonds to adjusted net worth are Exceptional Producers (1,355%), Guarantee Security (1,355%), Executive Life (1,344%), Presidential Life (1,241%), and Investors Equity Life of Hawaii (1,217%). On December 31, 1990, for the industry as a whole, life insurance companies held an average of under 5 percent of their assets in junk bonds. Of that total, 19.6 percent of the junk bonds were in higher risk, lower quality speculative bonds. The figures on junk bond holdings are lower now, as many insurance companies took advantage of a large rally in the junk bond market during 1991 to sell substantial portions of their junk bond portfolios.

Those companies with the largest ratios of nonperforming or nonaccruing mortgage loans to net worth are Chicago Metropolitan Mutual Assurance (506%), Supreme Life of America (228%), Kentucky Central Life (162%), Travelers (124%), and UNUM Pension (115%). Mutual companies with substantial holdings of nonperforming and foreclosed properties as a percentage of their assets include Fidelity Mutual (4.6%), Mutual Benefit Life (3.6%), and Mutual Life of New York (3.6%) at year-end 1990. Stock insurance companies with a high percentage of nonperforming mortgage loans to total mortgage loans as of December 31, 1990, include Lincoln National (7.0%), USLIFE (6.5%), and UNUM (4.1%). Among multiline insurers, as of March 31, 1991, those with a high percentage of nonperforming mortgages to stockholders' equity include Travelers (107%), Aetna (36%), CIGNA (27%), and Lincoln National (15%).

For the life insurance industry as a whole, insurers had 17 percent of their money invested in mortgages at year-end 1991. Ninety-two percent of these mortgages were commercial mortgages. Of that total, 5.9 percent were in repossessed properties and mortgage payments that were either 90 days late or in default. Figure 8.3 shows the soaring delinquency rate on commercial mortgages. This means that for the next

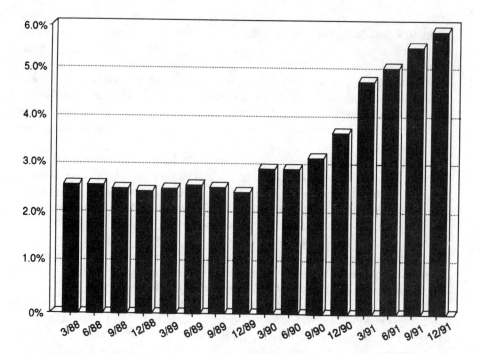

Figure 8.3 Life and Health Industry Commercial Mortgage Loan Delinquency Rates (Including Loans in Process of Foreclosure), End-of-Quarter Data. (Based on companies reporting and accounting for 87% of mortgages held by U.S. life insurance companies.) (*Source:* American Council of Life Insurance)

few years, life insurers will continue to be plagued with large losses stemming from foreclosures, restructurings, and divestitures. Also, accounting rules may conceal the depth of the real estate problem, since insurers do not have to write down the value of their own properties when local real estate prices collapse. That is, insurance companies can avoid showing a paper loss on a defaulted mortgage until the foreclosure on the mortgage.

The weakest life insurance companies had nonaccruing junk bonds and nonperforming real estate far exceeding industry averages. For example, Mutual Benefit Life had nearly 10 percent of its $5 billion in real estate mortgage holdings in default or 90 days past due. And Executive Life had 82 percent of its $10 billion bond portfolio invested in junk bonds.[13]

In November 1992, about 16 months after the failure of Mutual Benefit Life, Pennsylvania insurance regulators seized Fidelity Mutual Life Insurance Company. The Pennsylvania Insurance Department took over the management of the company and ordered an indefinite moratorium on policy cancellations and loans to customers following a sudden run on the company's assets. The move by the regulators blocked

Table 8.10   Ratios of Junk Bonds and Nonperforming Mortgages to Net Worth, Selected Large Life Insurance Companies, December 31, 1991

Company	Ratio of Junk Bonds[a] to		Ratio of Problem Mortgages[b] to	
	Assets	Adj. Net Worth	Assets	Net Worth[c]
Aetna Life Ins. Co. (CT)	2%	44%	6%	119%
Equitable Life Assurance Society of the U.S. (NY)	7%	186%	2%	73%
John Hancock Mutual Life Insurance Co. (MA)	6%	101%	2%	38%
Mutual Life Ins. Co. of New York (NY)	8%	125%	5%	101%
Phoenix Mutual Life Insurance Co. (CT)	4%	55%	5%	83%
Travelers Insurance Co. (Life Dep't) (CT)	3%	37%	11%	161%

[a] Junk bonds are non-investment grade (speculative) bonds which carry Standard & Poor's Ratings of BB, B, CCC, CC, C, or D.
[b] Problem mortgages consist of (1) mortgages on which interest is overdue more than three months and are not in the process of foreclosure, (2) mortgages in the process of foreclosure, and (3) properties acquired in satisfaction of debt.
[c] Net worth does not include the mandatory securities valuation reserve, which covers potential losses from bond and stock investments but not from mortgages. Adjusted net worth is net worth plus the bond and preferred stock component of the mandatory securities valuation reserve.
Source: The Insurance Forum, Ellettsville, IN, 47429, July 1992.

100,000 customers from taking their money out of the company. However, the company continued to pay annuities and death benefits. At the end of 1991, nearly 43 percent of Fidelity Mutual's investment portfolio was in mortgages and real estate investments. By then, problem mortgages had risen to $78 million, or 146.5 percent of the company's surplus capital.

Table 8.10 compares the ratios of junk bonds and nonperforming mortgages with assets and net worth at some of the larger, better known life insurers. Among the 10 largest life insurance companies, nonperforming real estate holdings equaled 20 percent of capital, surplus, and reserves at the end of 1990.

Real estate problems at depository institutions are probably more severe than those at life insurance companies because banks and thrifts have a history of lending for development and construction, while life insurance companies tend to have a reasonable geographic distribution of real estate loans and tend to lend on fully tenanted properties with cash flows already arriving. However, insurers are finding that in a weak real estate market, tenants are being lured away from buildings that were once 80–100-percent occupied by cheaper leases at competitive properties, a phenomenon known as *tenant migration.* Through tenant migration, a 90-percent leased building can slide quickly into a 50-percent leased situation. A concern among financial analysts is that some life insurance companies have not put aside enough reserves to cover their potential real estate losses. Accounting standards germane to potential real estate losses are not quite as rigorous as those established by bank regulators, in part because they lack a federal regulator. But the insurance industry is slowly moving toward stricter disclosure. The NAIC has adopted a regulation that will be phased in during 1992 and fully implemented by 1994 to force insurance companies to set aside reserves for real estate losses and to require that all insurers be audited. However, reserves would be based upon past default experience and not on the quality of the current loan portfolio. Publicly held insurance companies will also have to disclose the market value of their real estate holdings. Large write-downs would mean reduced capital, which could drive weaker institutions into mergers and cause some to fail. In the early days of lending to lesser developed countries (LDCs), when it became apparent that Latin American and other less developed countries could not pay the large debts they owed the banks, the banking regulators tacitly agreed to let the banks carry their LDC loans at unrealistically high levels, so as not to wipe out their stated capital levels. In the current environment, some bank regulators are arguing that real estate should not be given the same break, while state insurance regulators have until recently been "out to lunch" on this issue. Although capital forbearance seemed to work on the LDC issue, it caused more losses to taxpayers when it came to the thrift debacle. The forbearance issue germane to real estate is yet to be resolved at banks or insurance companies. If regulators push for write-downs, financial institutions could be involved in more bankruptcies, bailouts, and mergers before too long. If regulators exercise forbearance, the lenders could be drained slowly, as were the money-center banks in their LDC loan exposure. Since real estate has an enormous cyclical element, the problem could fade over time if a sustained and strong economic recovery takes hold.[14]

Even though a mortgage loan may become a problem, there is a reasonable likelihood that the recovery rate on principal will be relatively high. The company may lose some income, but the insurer will usually get back much of its principal over time, provided that prudent underwriting standards were employed and that the economic recovery which follows the cyclical decline is sustainable. The long-term liabilities of the life insurance industry have traditionally been a source of strength. The longer liability structure has allowed the industry to sit and hold nonperforming or depressed assets. This advantage is available today only as long as policyholders with discretionary withdrawal options are comfortable with the prospects of their company. It is interesting to speculate on whether or not Mutual Benefit Life could have waded through the depressed 1989–1993 real estate market if policyholders had decided not to surrender their policies.

Note that not all junk bonds are going to default. Indeed, up until 1989, only a yearly average of 3.5 percent of all junk bonds outstanding had defaulted. However, the default rate for 1990 approximated 11.5 percent. Junk bond issues such as those of RJR Nabisco and Kroger are not in danger of defaulting, as they were issued by reasonably healthy, well-run companies following a leveraged buyout. In addition,

Table 8.11   Commercial Real Estate Assets, Selected Life Insurance Companies, Dec. 31, 1991

Life Insurance Companies	Commercial Real Estate Assets		
	Total[a] ($ Millions)	Total as Percent Policyholders' Surplus	Nonperforming Loans and Foreclosed Properties
Prudential	$26,221	402%	$ 811
Metropolitan	23,780	499	1,676
TIAA	21,928		1,581
Aetna	18,546	1,000	1,920
Travelers	12,283	600	3,190
Equitable	10,717	968	715
John Hancock	9,186	581	460
Connecticut General	9,834	656	587
Northwestern	6,864	415	122
New York Life	6,900	263	417

[a] Does not include real estate held in joint venture or in separate accounts managed for customers.
Source: FORTUNE, Source: Company Data, ©1992 Time Inc. All rights reserved.

some bonds classified as junk were actually privately placed debt securities of solid midsized companies that are in no danger of defaulting. Also, because real estate is a highly cyclical investment (see Table 8.11), some of the troubled real estate loans could recover much of their full value as the economy improves. What is necessary in the short run is that the insurance companies holding many of these issues have staying power and be able to sustain or prevent a run on the company, by regaining the confidence of their policyholders and investors.[15]

Other criteria that regulators and consumers can utilize to help them evaluate life insurance companies are the risky asset ratio, the surplus ratio, and the adequacy of investment income. Adequate investment income shows whether an insurance company earns enough from its investments to meet the "required interest" to maintain its reserves and to make interest payments to customers. An insurance company with sufficient investment income has 25 percent more than it needs, or investment income in excess of 125 percent of "required interest." The surplus ratio is the percentage of surplus to the total assets. A higher ratio offers policyholders greater protection than a lower ratio. A salient barometer of financial health is whether a life insurance company's financial cushion—called *adjusted surplus*—is large enough to cover nonperforming assets. These assets include mortgages more than 90 days overdue or in foreclosure, repossessed property, and a portion of lower quality bonds, while adjusted surplus consists of capital, surplus, and state-mandated investment reserves. If an insurance company has nonperforming assets of $10

Table 8.12 Selected Ratios of 10 Large Life Insurers,
Year-End 1991

Insurance Company	Risky Asset Ratio	Surplus Ratio	Adequate Investment Income[a]
Prudential	105.9%	8.5%	Yes
Metropolitan	66.3	6.1	Yes
TIAA	151.6	6.7	Yes
Aetna Life	135.0	6.1	No
New York Life	59.5	7.5	Yes
Equitable Life	199.2	4.7	No
John Hancock Life	129.8	6.1	Yes
Northwestern Life	50.5	8.1	Yes
Travelers Life	182.5	7.3	Yes
Connecticut General	138.0	6.5	No
Industry Average	85.5	8.0	

Risky Asset Ratio = total of all non-investment-grade bonds
+ mortgages 90 days overdue
+ mortgages in foreclosure
+ foreclosed real estate
/ capital & surplus + Mandatory Security Valuation Reserve
Surplus Ratio = capital + Mandatory Security Valuation Reserve
/ total assets - separate accounts
Adequacy of Investment Income = net investment income (except
capital gains/loss)
/ interest credited on policy and contract funds
[a]Yes implies ratio is greater than or equal to 125%.
Source: Michael Conn Associates.

million and an adjusted surplus of $20 million, its nonperforming asset ratio is 50 percent. The lower the ratio, the better is the financial cushion.[16] (See Table 8.12)

Following the seizure of Mutual Benefit Life, Phoenix Mutual Life Insurance Company and Home Life Insurance Company, both with large real estate portfolios, announced plans to merge. This combination represents the first merger of major mutual life insurance companies. The new company, called Phoenix Home Life, has about $10 billion in assets, ranking it among the country's 25 largest life insurance companies. In addition, Metropolitan Life Insurance Co., the second largest insurer in the U.S., with assets of about $144 billion, considered merging with Mutual Life Insurance Co. of New York (with $18 billion in assets, but troubled by real estate loans and junk bonds). However, the two companies decided against a formal merger. Analysts say that Metropolitan represents to the life insurance industry what J.P. Morgan represents to the banking industry. While other insurance companies were mired in investment problems and lack of profitability during 1990–1991, Metropolitan's total capital increased by 14 percent to $6.3 billion, and sales for all lines of business to individuals rose by close to 40 percent, as consumers were drawn to the safety and security of an insurance company rated AAA. Metropolitan also acquired part of the pension business of MONY and the annuity business of Executive Life of New York.

In another example of an acquisition of one property and casualty mutual insurance company by another, Nationwide Insurance took over the management of segments of Wausau Insurance Company's businesses several years ago. Industry analysts feel that troubles in the insurance industry and rising doubts among policyholders about the safety of insurance companies could lead other mutual insurers —especially those with a diminished capital base—to seek merger partners or convert to a stock company. A proposal from the NAIC that would require insurance companies to conform to so-called risk-based capital guidelines similar to those in the banking industry could coerce some companies to find a merger partner. On the other hand, a number of companies have taken immediate steps to boost capital through an infusion of funds from their parent firms. For example, in an effort to calm worries and improve the confidence of its policyholders, Kemper Corp. pledged the full strength of the parent company behind the operations of its insurance companies by injecting $125 million in capital into its two life insurance companies, which had potential problematic real estate loans in their investment portfolios. Other insurance companies have attempted to assure investors and policyholders of their financial soundness by running full-page advertisements in financial newspapers and magazines.

Most analysts do not expect the current problems with the quality of assets in the life insurance industry to reach the proportions of those of savings and loans or banks, as most life insurance companies have conservatively managed asset portfolios. However, those problems, as well as undetected insolvencies, have raised questions about the ability of state authorities to regulate insurance companies adequately and to identify and correct problems in a timely fashion. The unexpected deterioration of Mutual Benefit Life and Executive Life set off policyholder runs that removed vast amounts of funds that further weakened these companies. The shock waves caused fears that indiscriminate runs on other life insurers might occur and damage their otherwise sound financial condition. The issue of the capability of state insurance regulators to detect problems is particularly important because many life insurance companies are mutual institutions that are not subject to careful monitoring by investors in the financial markets. Also, accounting practices at life insurance companies can obscure the market values of assets and often do not signal nonperforming assets. Given this concern, state regulatory authorities have sought a unified approach to regulation through the NAIC. For example, the NAIC has instituted surveillance models for predicting financial problems at life insurance companies and has issued uniform standards for evaluating the performance of those companies.

SALIENT ISSUES

There appear to be close to a dozen salient issues that must be discussed in regard to the future of the life insurance industry. These include insolvency, the accessibility and affordability of health insurance, insuring the uninsured, bank entry into insurance, the extent of federal regulation of insurance, public versus private sector insurance, demutualization, consolidation, globalization, insurance industry guaranty funds, and the impact of the increasing numbers of patients with AIDS on life and health insurance carriers.

Losses from the liability lines have beset property and casualty insurance companies, as has severe price competition, which has led to underpricing some insurance risks. At the same time, many customers of insurance companies have rebelled against soaring automobile insurance rates. In a public referendum, citizens of California sought a rollback of as much as 30 percent in those rates. The California Insurance Department has been attempting to implement a reduction in automobile insurance premiums. Some insurance companies have announced their withdrawal from markets for automobile insurance that have unfavorable pricing. Also, some corporations are bypassing property and casualty insurance companies in favor of self-insurance on certain property and casualty lines. Finally, regulators have a conflict between promoting the solvency of an insurance company and keeping insurance premiums affordable to the customer.

The political clout of the industry appears to be weakening. State insurance commissioners and legislators are no longer comfortably in the back pockets of the industry. Insurance commissioners have become more independent, the health market has become dysfunctional, and millions of people cannot afford coverage. There is even the possibility that this market may be increasingly assumed by state and federal insurance mechanisms. Price competition has become vicious, with premiums still being chased to generate investment income in the industry. In addition, critics are seeking to abolish the insurance industry's antitrust immunity, which would leave small property and casualty companies essentially without pricing information.[17]

As two experts have said, "The problems that have already emerged in the insurance industries are similar in certain respects to those that have emerged in the banking industry. These common experiences demonstrate that supervisory authorities can avert problems only if they have the ability and the authority to prevent insurers from assuming excessive risk at an early stage, well before economic events entail future losses. . . . If . . . risk concentrations are allowed to develop, and conditions transform these risk exposures into actual problems, supervisory authorities can do little except to manage the resolution of damaged institutions. At that point, supervisors have little opportunity to materially decrease the magnitude of losses to individual companies."[18]

EXPLORING SOME OF THE PROBLEMS

The traditional reliance of life insurance companies on high-quality private placements and other highly rated investments was reduced and partially replaced with junk bonds at some companies. The issuance of high-yielding guaranteed investment contracts required life insurance companies to offer higher returns. Companies began to lose money on these contracts because of nonperforming investments or a mismatch in the maturity of assets and liabilities that eventually left the companies earning less on their funds than they were paying out on the contracts. When interest rates fell from their lofty levels and "credited" interest rates could not be adjusted, serious losses occurred. In some instances, the marketing department of the insurance company did not coordinate its efforts with the investment department in setting rates on guaranteed investment contracts. In another development, heightened price competition forced down industry rate levels for term insurance, leading to lower margins on such insurance.

In one case, California regulators took over Western Pacific Life Insurance Co. in late August 1991, a little more than a week after Florida regulators seized its parent company, Guarantee Security Life Insurance Co., the sixth largest life insurance company in the state. Guarantee Security is currently under criminal investigation in Florida. At one time, as much as 90 percent of the company's assets were invested in junk bonds. The California order of conservatorship was sought because of Western Pacific's financial instability resulting from a portfolio of high-risk, high-yield bonds and the insolvency of the parent company. John Garamendi, California's first elected insurance commissioner, put 16 insurance companies into receivership in 1991. In contrast, his predecessor took control of a total of 7 companies in 1990 and 12 in 1989. Of course, economic conditions were more favorable in 1989 and 1990 than in 1991, especially in California.

A fundamental industry problem is insufficient profitability, which has led to greater risk taking and weaker capital ratios. There are also too many insurance companies; it would be wise to remove barriers to consolidation so that mergers could take place more easily. It would be helpful as well to make the demutualization process easier.

Globalization

U.S. life insurers have been geared to serve the domestic market, although there were some early ventures overseas to satisfy the foreign needs of large domestic group or pension clients. On the other hand, Dutch, Swiss, Japanese, and French insurers have shown great interest in the U.S. market, with European capital flowing in to purchase large U.S. insurance companies in order to solidify these countries' global markets. There has been much talk in U.S. board rooms about expansion abroad because of the liberalization and deregulation in markets such as the European Community, Eastern Europe, South America, and the Far East. Another reason for expansion abroad comes from the fact that multinational customers of insurance companies demand insurance company capabilities worldwide. The ability to diversify risks in foreign markets and to free companies from the saturation of the domestic market are yet other reasons given for global expansion. We have not seen a great deal of globalization among U.S. insurers because of problems with adequacy of capital. The acquisitions and joint ventures of strong foreign insurers in U.S. markets might act as a catalyst toward globalizing U.S. insurance companies.[19]

Globalization will present unprecedented challenges to insurance companies, consumers, and regulators. The major thrust toward globalization will be mergers and acquisitions, because of the difficulty of entry and huge start-up costs for a new insurer in a market. Of course, this will favor the larger companies, which have the capitalization and resources to achieve market penetration.[20]

Diversification

Life insurance companies became more performance oriented to meet consumer demand and also introduced many new products, including variable and universal life, during the 1970s and 1980s. Many insurance companies entered into the brokerage business, while some established or purchased families of mutual funds or investment management companies. These companies hoped to cross-sell insurance products and annuities through traditional stockbrokers and to have more investment products for their traditional insurance agents to sell. There was also the feeling that customers of brokerage firms would be in a higher income category than the ordinary insurance company client and would be more amenable to purchasing insurance products from a friendly broker rather than from an insurance agent on a cold call.

Among the insurance companies, Travelers bought Dillon, Read and Keystone Mutual Funds; Prudential purchased Bache; Equitable purchased Donaldson, Lufkin, & Jenrette and Alliance Capital Management; John Hancock purchased Tucker Anthony; Penn Mutual purchased Janney, Montgomery Scott; Provident Mutual purchased Newbold, a small, regional investment banker, as well as a number of money management companies; Aetna purchased large positions in the British merchant bank Samuel Montagu and in Federated Investors, Inc., a large money management company; Metropolitan Life purchased State Street Management Co.; and Sun Life purchased Massachusetts Financial Services, one of the oldest fund managers in the United States. Some of these acquisitions were later sold. On the other hand, several investment banks, such as Merrill Lynch and E. F. Hutton, expanded into products traditionally perceived to be in the domain of the insurance industry, while several hundred depository institutions began to offer discount brokerage.

Insolvency

Generally speaking, an insolvent company is a company without enough assets to pay claims. Before the introduction of guaranty associations, this meant that when an insurance company was liquidated, insureds and claimants were unpaid or underpaid after a long wait.

Since insurance is crucial to the workings of our society and economy, the insolvency of an insurance company is both socially and economically disruptive. Policyholders are hurt most when they are left with unpaid claims, which can amount to considerably more than was paid out in premiums.[21]

Life Insurance Industry

While banks and savings and loans have shared most of the headlines concerning failures, the insurance industry also has made the national headlines, with the junk bond–related failure of Executive Life, and local headlines, with an increasing number of failures of small or regional insurance companies. The industry has become more concerned with the ability of state regulators and the National Association of Insurance Commissioners (NAIC) to detect potential insolvencies. The regulators and insurance company executives wish to improve the models of early warning signals of troubled insurance companies, so that corrective actions can be taken before insolvency occurs. The NAIC has a model of 12 financial ratios that it has used to help determine which life insurance companies are problematic. (See Table 8.13.) A committee of the American Council of Life Insurance studied 68 life insurance companies that became insolvent between January 1985 and September 1989. The committee categorized 17 as failing because of fraud and 30 as failing because of questionable practices; the remaining insolvencies were associated with mismanagement. Sixty percent of the companies examined identified one line of business as the cause of insolvency; of those, 78 percent identified accident and health as the problem line, while single-premium deferred annuities were cited as the second most common line of business figuring in the insolvency. Underpricing of products was a factor in 59 percent of the insolvent companies examined, while unsound investment practices played a role in 46 percent of the cases. New management was a factor in 37 percent of company insolvencies, while excessive use or poor selection of reinsurance companies and general economic conditions were cited as factors in the insolvencies of 13 of the companies examined. Transactions of affiliates were cited as a significant factor in the insolvencies of 47 of the 68 companies. Other common key factors leading to insurance company insolvencies are overdelegation of authority to managing general agents and brokers, unreliable information, insufficient regulation, too rapid expansion into new products or distribution systems, inadequate control of underwriting, poor claims handling and loss control, poor policy and benefits design, theft and fraud, inadequate surplus for the risks, and poor quality or inadequate diversification of assets.

Of particular interest is the fact that only 4 of 60 companies that failed were not identified by the IRIS ratios as potentially troubled companies prior to insolvency. On the other hand, the IRIS ratios and the NAIC review process also identified incorrectly as candidates for insolvency a large number of reasonably healthy companies, thus diluting the effectiveness of the overall predictive process. Efforts are being made to improve the forecasting model and to utilize it on a quarterly rather than a yearly basis in an effort to detect potential problems and to deal with them immediately.

Over the last five years, the number of multistate life and health insurance insolvencies has averaged 11 per year, or 0.5 percent of the 2,300 companies domiciled in the United States. This upsurge in life and health insurance failures can be largely attributed to the escalation of health care costs and lower margins on interest-sensitive products. Figure 8.4 shows the increasing number of financially impaired life and health insurance companies as a percentage of the average number

Table 8.13   Financial and Other Ratios Used by the National Association of Insurance Commissioners (NAIC)

IRIS [Insurance Regulatory Information System] RATIOS (Outside Usual Range) (Industry Average)	1987	1988	1989	1990	1991
Net Change in Capital and Surplus	1.4%	7.1%	10.5%	7.7%	10.8%
Gross Change in Capital and Surplus	4.8	10.3	12.2	10.1	15.7
Net Gain to Total Income	1.9	2.1	2.5	2.8	3.0
Change in Reserve Ratio	8.7	4.6	5.4	−3.9	−1.3
Adequacy of Investment Income	155.5	155.9	157.2	153.4	155.7
Nonadmitted Assets to Admitted Assets	0.6	0.6	0.6	0.7	0.7
Real Estate to Capital and Surplus	51.5	50.6	47.0	47.6	46.5
Investments in Affiliates to Capital and Surplus	53.2	52.7	53.0	52.8	53.4
Surplus Relief	0.8	−0.5	0.2	−0.1	0.2
Change in Premium	7.7	9.7	6.3	9.3	1.1
Change in Product Mix	1.3	0.9	0.4	0.7	0.5
Change in Asset Mix	0.5	0.4	0.2	0.2	0.4
Supplemental Ratios					
Commissions and Expenses to Premiums and Deposits	20.8%	21.4%	21.5%	21.7%	21.1%
Leverage Ratios					
Assets to Adjusted Surplus	13.4%	13.4%	13.2%	13.7%	12.5%
Adjusted Liabilities to Adjusted Surplus	12.4	12.5	12.2	12.7	11.5
Risky Assets to Adjusted Surplus	NA	NA	NA	NA	85.5
Liquidity Ratios					
Liquid Asset Ratio (Current Ratio)	NA	NA	NA	123.1%	133.2%
Liquidity Test (Quick Ratio)	NA	NA	NA	124.9	140.0
Risk-Adjusted Capital Ratio					
Risk-Adjusted Capital Ratio	NA	110.6%	111.6%	103.1%	111.3%

NA = Not available.
Source: Copyright © 1988–1992, Insurance Statutory Analytical Systems, Inc.

of licensed companies from 1976 to 1991. The primary causes of financial impairment during those years are pointed out in Table 8.14.

Property and Casualty Industry

In a separate study of insolvencies within the property and casualty industry conducted by A.M. Best, it was concluded that many of the insolvent insurers failed because of mismanagement, cash flow underwriting, deficient loss reserves, too rapid growth, significant changes in business, alleged fraud, overstated assets, catastrophic losses, and reinsurance failure. The financial stability of the insurance industry

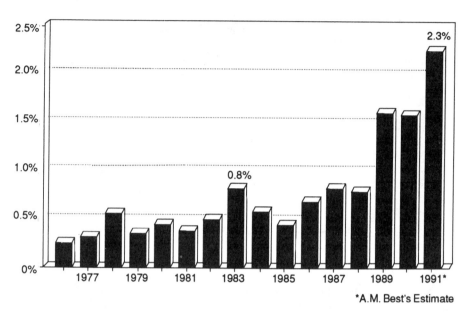

Figure 8.4 Frequency of Financial Impairment of Life and Health Insurance Companies, 1976–1991. (*Source:* State Insurance Departments and A.M. Best Company)

was also challenged by state-mandated rollbacks, increasing guaranty association assessments, the collapse of the real estate market, and proposals to repeal the McCarran-Ferguson Act, the law granting antitrust exemption to the insurance industry. The cash flow underwriting strategy justifies price cutting when the additional cash flow from increased market share provides additional investment income that more than offsets future underwriting losses. High interest rates and excess underwriting capacity often act as a catalyst in cutting prices. A problem with this strategy comes when interest rates decline substantially and the industry's combined ratio rises significantly, as was the case in 1984, when interest rates declined more than 900 basis points and the combined ratio peaked at 118. This led to a record 49 failures of property and casualty insurance companies in 1985. (See Figure 8.5.)[22] Even the combined effects of Hurricanes Andrew and Iniki, tornadoes, hailstorms, the Chicago flood, and the Los Angeles riots, destroying some $22 billion in insured property in 1992, resulted in only 45 insurance company failures. The A.M. Best study shows that the frequency of insolvencies correlates with the property and casualty underwriting cycle, with the peaks coming toward the ends of soft markets. The study also identifies the characteristics of a company that is at high risk of insolvency and makes several recommendations to reduce the number and costs of insurance company insolvencies.

Table 8.14   Primary Causes of Financial Impairment of Life and Health Insurance Companies, 1976–1991

Primary Causes	No. of Companies	Percent of Total Identified
Inadequate Pricing/Surplus	47	23%
Rapid Growth	41	20
Problems with Affiliates	40	19
Overstated Assets	37	18
Alleged Fraud	16	8
Significant Change in Business	15	7
Reinsurance Failure	5	2
Miscellaneous	6	3
Total Identified	207	100%
Unidentified	83	
Total Impaired	290	

While failures have been concentrated among smaller insurance companies, there has been a long-term upward trend in the percentage of companies that fail each year. For example, on average, about 0.3 percent of all property and casualty companies ceased operations involuntarily each year during the 10 years ending in 1981, while about 0.8 percent of all insurers failed each year during the 10 years ending in 1991. (See Figure 8.6.)

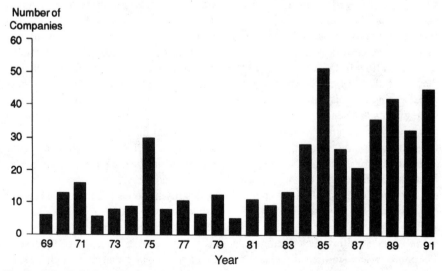

Figure 8.5   Failed Property and Casualty Insurers. (*Source:* A.M. Best Company, by permission)

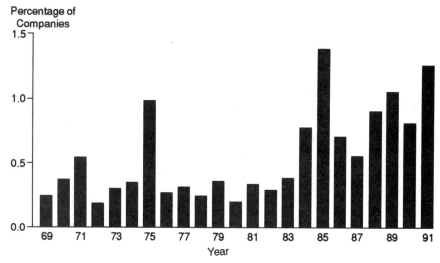

Figure 8.6 Property and Casualty Failure Frequency.

Representative John Dingell of Michigan, chairman of the House Committee on Energy and Commerce, Subcommittee on Oversight and Investigations, released a report in February 1990, entitled *Failed Promises,* on the committee's oversight investigation of six recent insolvencies of relatively large property and casualty insurance companies. The report pointed out the common elements of fraud, mismanagement, and the failure of state regulators to detect warning signs of any of these impending insolvencies. The report also listed several important factors that could bring about the insolvency of an insurance company: rapid expansion, overreliance on managing general agents, extensive and complex reinsurance arrangements, underpricing, problems with cash reserves, incompetence, fraud, greed, and self-dealing. Examples of mismanagement are replete with attempts at quick profits in the short run, with no apparent concern for the long-term well-being of the company. Some managers also treated the reinsurance process as a way to pass loss problems to someone else in exchange for easy premium dollars, rather than as a prudent method of sharing risks with other companies. In addition, the study pointed out parallels between the insurance industry and the savings and loan debacle, but "found no evidence of an overall crisis threatening the existence of the insurance industry at this time."[23] However, the subcommittee did conclude that "the insurance industry is vulnerable to the types of mismanagement and fraudulent activity that led to the savings and loan crisis."[24]

The Dingell Report went on to say that "an insurer's ability to pay—its solvency —must be subjected to proper regulation on a continuing basis, from the time premium payments are accepted until the time all anticipated insured events have occurred. The policyholder must rely on the competence of the regulatory system,

as well as the skill and integrity of the insurer, for protection from insolvency. . . .
Solvency regulation in the U.S. suffers from inadequate resources, lack of coordination, infrequent regulatory examination, poor information and communication, and
uneven implementation."[25] The report also stated that it is too easy to obtain an
insurance license with inadequate capitalization in some states, while other states
do little in the way of background checks or the monitoring of activities of persons
and entities responsible for operating insurance companies.

American Insurance Association President Robert Vagley testified before the
Dingell panel and recommended a number of features that should be included in
any enhanced system of insurance regulation. Among these were removing commercial and excess coverage from guaranty associations, focusing attention and resources
on regulation for solvency, and avoiding duplication and conflicting regulations.
Vagley also mentioned that his association was exploring various federal alternatives
that might enhance state regulation for solvency, including federal minimum standards.[26]

A.M. Best and most insurance commissioners believe that regulation regarding
solvency can be more effectively developed and better managed. However, there
must be a thorough understanding of the nature of past insolvencies, their characteristics, and the economic and underwriting environments in which they occurred. Once
this basis is established, more informed recommendations can be made to minimize
future insolvencies and to contain them within acceptable levels.[27]

Orin Kramer, an insurance consultant and author of a 1991 study of auto insurance
and worker's compensation insurance for the Insurance Information Institute, contends that regulated rates (price controls) are eroding the insurance industry's capacity
to pay out claims. Kramer sees evidence that rate caps have contributed to insolven
cies and that hostile state regulation will become a key factor in insurance failures.
According to Kramer, the rapidly increasing cost of medical and hospital care and
litigation are the salient issues behind accident insurance problems. Until these
problems are dealt with by regulators and lawmakers, the problems associated
with the cost of automobile and workers' compensation insurance coverages will
not disappear.[28]

While it is the duty of the regulator to prevent insolvencies, it is difficult to
accomplish this by early detection and swift action because of the uncertainty about
the extent of liabilities. On the other hand, it is easy to forbear and avoid recognizing
insolvency for several years, thereby escaping responsibility. This perverse incentive
for the regulator increases the risk of even larger losses, according to Richard
E. Stewart.[29]

Numerous life insurance companies reached for riskier assets in the late 1980s
and early 1990s to attract deposit funds in the form of guaranteed investment
contracts by offering high interest rates. These companies invested in junk bonds,
commercial mortgages, and real estate projects to increase their long-term yields.
While problematic mortgages and real estate loans are currently creating capital
losses for some companies, overconcentration of junk bond investments caused the
initial surge of conservatorships in 1991. For example, Executive Life of California,

Executive Life of New York, First Capital Life, and Fidelity Bankers Life held. 83 percent, 68 percent, 46 percent, and 40 percent of their respective bond portfolios in junk bonds at the end of 1990.

Guaranty Funds

The first guaranty or insolvency associations came into existence in the United States in the 1930s for particular lines of insurance. Today, guaranty associations represent an example of private action at the state level throughout the country to deal with the issue of insolvent insurers. As of year-end 1991, all states, as well as Washington, DC and Puerto Rico, had passed property and casualty insurance guaranty fund laws, while all states had passed a life and health insurance guaranty fund law. The present nationwide state guaranty system did not result from public policy debate, but developed out of fear that there was a federal threat to state regulation of insurance. The guaranty associations were established to protect the insured and to forestall the creation of federal regulation. Guaranty associations are essentially a mechanism for pooling money from solvent insurers for the purpose of paying certain claims against an insolvent insurance company.[30] They are nonprofit associations that comprise companies licensed in each state. State laws differ regarding types of policyholder coverage and dollar limits of guaranty association liability. Typically, states protect direct life policies to a limit of $300,000 in death benefits, $100,000 cash or withdrawal value for life insurance, $100,000 in the present value of annuity benefits, and $100,000 in health benefits. If the insurance company cannot pay its claims, the guaranty association collects the money it needs from its other insurance company members. These collections, or assessments, are performed after an insurer is declared financially impaired or insolvent by a court. Member insurers' assessments may not exceed a certain sum each year, set by state law at a percentage of the previous year's premiums written in the state. Essentially, private insurance companies cooperate to increase the financial security offered to the public in the aggregate by all insurance companies. If affected by many insolvencies or one large insolvency, an association may assess its members over a number of years. As long as there were relatively minor insolvencies, there were few problems or complaints, and most insurance companies went along with the assessed payments in an insolvency. However, now that the losses are more significant, some large insurance companies are balking at having to come up with substantial assessments to meet guaranty fund demands. Well-run insurance companies feel that they are being unduly penalized in having to rescue their weak sisters. Is this similar to the savings and loan or weak bank scenario whereby companies are encouraged to take excessive risks because of the safety net when they get into trouble in an attempt to survive?

Critics point out that the guaranty programs are not run or guaranteed by state governments and that they are not true funds because they do not keep money in reserve. There are also the issues of insufficient capacity, unpredictable costs facing guaranty funds, and lack of uniformity in regard to rehabilitation and liquidation, as well as the issue of a corporation's residence, which calls for cooperation among different state guaranty associations to make the system work. The programs are usually state supervised, but privately run, and respond to the failure of an insurance company by assessing surviving insurance companies a certain dollar amount. In some instances, guaranty association money is used to pay policyholders of the failed insurer; in other cases, the money might be used to provide financial guarantees to investors who rescue the failed company.[31]

Following are a few more interesting facts about guaranty funds:

1. Billions of dollars of corporate pension money remain outside the guaranty system, essentially uninsured, because these funds are not in the names of individual investors.

2. It would be theoretically possible to exhaust a few years' capacity with one major insolvency.

3. The capacity of guaranty funds could be enhanced by borrowing among accounts, by borrowing from outside sources, and by gaining early access to the assets of the insolvent insurer.

4. The usefulness of the system has suffered, not from bad design, but from a lack of cooperation between liquidators and guaranty associations in the different states.

5. The 1991 collapse of two major life insurance companies and the concomitant notoriety in the media present a sobering reality to regulators and consumers regarding the potential inadequacy of the safety net set up to protect policyholders when a large insurance company fails.

The majority of guaranty associations date from the late 1960s, when a slew of failures involving small inner-city auto insurers left policyholders with unpaid claims. By the late 1970s, almost all states set up guaranty programs for property and casualty insurance companies. Life insurance programs were slower in developing, because failures of life insurers were infrequent and losses from those that did fail were small. As a matter of fact, the system gives the appearance of assuming that all failures will be of small, insignificant companies. However, when the Baldwin United Corporation collapsed in 1983, policyholders were left with $279 million in losses, as the guaranty funds could raise only $62 million a year. Rather than risk a public relations debacle, insurance companies, led by Metropolitan Life, decided to rescue Baldwin themselves. Nonetheless, many Baldwin policyholders had to wait more than a year for the money they were owed. In addition, interest rates were cut sharply on their annuities. Following the seizures of First Capital Life and Executive Life, the state of California sought a corporate merger or an industry rescue. In the case of First Capital, a marriage was arranged: California Insurance Commissioner Garamendi awarded First Capital to Pacific Mutual Life Insurance Company. The other bidders included Shearson Lehman, Transamerica Life Occidental, Leucadia National Corporation, and creditors of First National Holdings. The plan would guarantee 100 percent of contract values, including interest of at least 4 percent a year, to policyholders who maintain their policies with First Capital for at least five years. Policyholders will also have the option of cashing out their policies for 90 percent of their value. Pacific Mutual indicated that it would reduce the percentage of junk bonds held in the investment portfolio to under 5 percent in five years and would provide $50 million in new capital. Garamendi's decision was supported by Judge Kurt Lewin of Los Angeles Superior Court, who oversaw the conservation of First Capital Life.

Prior to 1991, total assessments since the guaranty system began amounted to less than $500 million. Assessments provide an offset against amounts payable for future state taxes on premiums; therefore, the net burden for insurance companies is lower, since the major burden falls on state revenues and, consequently, on taxpayers. With multibillion-dollar deficiencies expected in 1991–1993, voluntary efforts to cover the excess policy amounts beyond the guaranty fund limits are doubtful.[32]

Interest in the safety of retirement annuities provided by insurance companies was heightened following the collapse of the junk bond market, the real estate market, and several insurance companies during 1990. The Pension Benefits Guarantee Corporation (PBGC) feels that the guaranty of annuities is best left at the state level, and to the extent that state laws are inadequate, the state insurance commissioners and the insurance industry should be encouraged to improve them. The PBGC is also considering standards for administrators to follow in the selection of an insurance annuity provider. Political pressure may be placed on the insurance industry to have the PBGC insure annuities before long if the industry doesn't come up with its own solution. The life insurance industry trade associations felt that, rather than await federal standards, the insurance industry would be in a better position politically if it took the offensive and put forth a set of standards itself that would provide additional protection to participants for whom annuities had been purchased. In a sense, the PBGC and state guaranty funds are competitors: When a company purchases an irrevocable contract for an annuity to cover pension liabilities, the guarantee shifts from the PBGC to a state guaranty fund.

Richard Stewart, former New York state superintendent of insurance and a former president of NAIC, fears a coming wave of large, national, complex, interconnected insolvencies related to general liability insurance. He feels that the state system of liquidation and guaranty associations is ill suited to face this coming event. Only a combination of early detection, prompt action, and guarantees against loss can deal with the coming insolvencies. Stewart suggests five principles to govern the design of a guaranty program: (1) The program should build on current industry structure and regulation; (2) the liquidation of insolvent insurance companies and the guaranty of their obligations should be national in scope; (3) insolvency costs should be charged back to the activities causing them; (4) the system should include close monitoring of the companies' financial positions; and (5) the national program should assign key roles to the state insurance departments and the private insurance industry. Specifically, Stewart proposed that Congress create the National Insurance Guaranty Corporation (NIGC), which would be privately financed by assessing insurance companies and would charge guaranty costs back to carriers in the state and lines of insurance involved. The guarantees would be designed so that policyholders, brokers, reinsurers, and others in the private sector would have financial incentives to maintain close surveillance of insurance companies. The NIGC would serve only as a rehabilitator or liquidator of companies already placed into receivership by the individual states or by the court. The NIGC's guarantee obligations, and its powers to assess members to fulfill them, would extend only to policy claims owed by insolvent companies in liquidation. Stewart's suggestions would combine the strengths that private insurance companies, the state regulatory agencies, and the federal government can bring to this emerging challenge.[33]

An argument against the use of guaranty funds proposes that it is up to the individual or risk manager to be a smart shopper and to be sure that the company from which he or she purchases insurance is in solid financial shape. According to this viewpoint, on occasion, when the customer purchases a policy from the company that has the lowest rate for that particular policy, the inadequacy of that rate to create a pool of money sufficient to pay claims is the cause of that company's insolvency. Companies such as A.M. Best provide help to the consumer in rating the quality or financial health of insurance companies, just as Moody's and Standard & Poor's provide ratings on corporations to assist investors in selecting stocks and bonds. However, rating agencies do make mistakes, as was noted earlier in the case of Executive Life.

Recently, many state regulators have expressed interest in revising the guaranty system for life insurers in light of increases in the number, size, and complexity of insolvencies. At the very least, salient provisions of the NAIC model guaranty funds could be added to the financial regulation standards to ensure that a minimum level of protection is provided to all insurance policyholders and claimants.

In an article in the *New England Economic Review,* Warren Wise acknowledges that the insurance industry is more vulnerable to failure than it once was.[34] He feels that all policyholders should be protected in the case of insolvency and proposes that all interested parties, including insurance sales representatives, policyholders, and state governments, share in losses when an insurance company fails. He believes that guaranty assessments should be based on risk and collected on a regular basis, so that the heaviest impact will fall on those insurance companies which are most likely to fail. Sales representatives should have an incentive to recommend safe companies, and states should have an incentive to devote adequate resources to regulation. State contributions should be in the form of the tax offset for guaranty fund assessments that already exists in a few states. Insurance consumers should share the burden by recovering less than the full amount due them. Both Wise and Scott Harrington (see endnote 8) believe that guarantees reduce policyholders' incentives to buy coverage from safe insurance companies. All of these factors combined might contribute to increased market discipline. Wise would also improve regulation by linking capital requirements to risk, strengthening investment restrictions, improving accounting practices, and placing controls on reinsurance transactions. He says:

> Neither regulation nor guaranty funds necessarily promote safety and soundness. At times, regulations limit either the assets intermediaries hold or the variety of liabilities they issue in a fashion that diminishes their efficiency, perhaps reducing their expected returns more than the potential variability of their returns. At other times, intermediaries reporting substantial current returns (by undertaking a risky investment strategy) may appeal strongly to customers and may not be examined closely by regulators; these institutions also may be allowed to carry less capital or surplus than their competitors. To the degree customers believe that regulated intermediaries bear an "underwriters' laboratory seal of approval," and to the degree that intermediaries are covered by explicit guarantees or by an implicit put option to the government, financial institutions can become less sound, unless regulators can accurately assess their financial strategies.[35]

Demutualization: Conversion from a Mutual to a Stock Company

The primary interest of both mutual and stock life insurance companies is long-term growth and survival. Growth must be financed from surplus and capital. This is related to the long-term nature of life insurance obligations and the maintenance of policies. If an insurance company fails, the consequences to policyholders are obvious. Without growth, expense ratios will increase and inefficiencies may soon become apparent, since the efficient operation of a life insurance company requires considerable economies of scale generated by business volume. Without growth, the necessary business volume may not be met to insure the collective pooling of insurance risks under the law of large numbers. This could expose the remaining insurers to risks and uncertainty, especially in our current unstable economic environment, where real estate and non-investment-grade portfolios have suffered major losses and where stock markets fluctuate considerably. Insurance companies need more permanent capital, which is available in the equity market to ensure growth so that obligations to future shareholders are not exposed to risks and perils.

To provide for future growth and to maintain its ability to meet insurance obligations, an insurance company must generate and maintain sufficient capital to allow it to enter into selected markets and expand and compete in those markets. It is this need for equity capital that has highlighted the structural differences between mutuals and stock insurance companies. Both forms of organization generate capital funds through contributions from their existing and previous policyholders. However, stock insurance companies have a significant alternative source of funds not available to the mutuals—the equity capital market. An insurance company can enter into the equity capital market to raise and retain sufficient capital to assure the safety of competitive pricing, its financial operations, and its future growth.

Equitable Life and Demutualization

Equitable Life, the fourth largest insurance company in the United States, suffered losses well in excess of $2 billion on real estate, junk bonds, and guaranteed investment contracts. By all accounts, the company has suffered nearly $2 billion in losses related to the last of these since 1988. Equitable had a reserve of $230 million against its directly owned junk bond portfolio of $3.2 billion. In addition, nearly $1.7 billion, or over 18 percent, of commercial loans were delinquent, in foreclosure, or restructured. After accounting for a $312 million reserve, the carrying value of Equitable's problematic and restructured commercial mortgages is $1.4 billion, a total equal to more than the company's net worth. The company also owns $6 billion in real estate that is separate from its holdings of commercial mortgages. About 70 percent of this investment is in office buildings, whose value has probably declined at least 25 percent from its peak in 1988. If Equitable were required to dispose of equity real estate in the near term, the company's *Policyholder Information Booklet* warns, "it is likely that for a significant portion of its portfolio, The Equitable would recover substantially less than the related carrying value."[36] Equitable's real estate is carried at $5.8 billion, an amount equal to more than four times the company's net worth. Further, there is the issue of nearly $3 billion in balloon payment mortgages due between 1992 and 1995. "Depending on the condition of the real estate market and lending practices in those years," the Equitable *Policyholder Information Booklet* warned that Equitable "could be required to refinance, restructure, or foreclose upon many of these loans."[37] The concern among analysts is that not all the bad news on commercial real estate may be out, as the recovery from the recession is delayed.[38] (See Figure 8.7)

Equitable's new management team under Richard H. Jenrette and the directors of the company concluded that inadequate capital existed, and they sought to become a stock company. Equitable received a $1 billion infusion of capital from Groupe Axa S.A., a large French insurance company (the eighth largest European insurance company, with $42.6 billion in assets), as a first step in converting to a stock company with a public offering during 1992. Under the latest investment plan, Equitable issued $1 billion in notes to Axa from a newly created holding company, along with preferred shares that can be converted into common equity following a stock offering. Axa wound up initially with a 49-percent equity stake, which could increase to 55 percent in two years following conversion of the preferred shares. The initial public offering of common shares raised $450 million for the company, about $25 million less than originally contemplated. Proceeds of the sale would add little to the company's surplus, since $220 million has been committed to pay dividends at the holding company level, and another $150 million or so was to be paid to policyholders in exchange for giving up their rights as owners of a mutual insurance company. The public would have about a 29-percent stake in the company. This infusion of capital represents the largest single equity investment in the history of the U.S. insurance industry.

The policyholders of Equitable will automatically receive shares in the company. The number of shares received by each policyholder depends upon estimates of how much his or her policy contributes to profits. Equitable has also set aside about $7.4 billion in high-grade bonds and mortgages to assure the payment of dividends to shareholders. Between $600 million and $700 million would be used to write

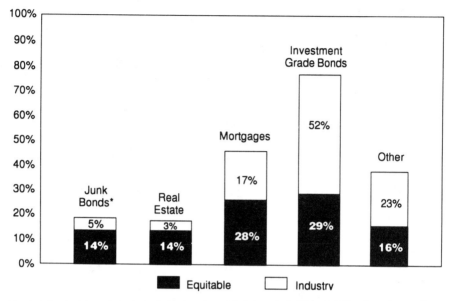

*Equitable's junk bonds include limited partnership interests in high-yield funds and a small of below-investment grade common and preferred stock acquired in connection with the bonds.

Figure 8.7 Distribution of Assets, Equitable Life Assurance Co., March 31, 1992, and Life Insurance Industry, December 31, 1991. (Graph prepared by Ricardo Mejias)

down the value of troubled real estate and junk bond holdings. This move should improve the credit rating of the insurance company. The conversion of Axa debt to equity would add $700 million to Equitable's surplus of $1.6 billion as of March 31, 1992. The capital-to-liabilities ratio would rise a bit from the current 4-percent level. Under the terms of the plan, a new holding company, the Equitable Companies, would be chartered in Delaware. The holding company would be the publicly traded entity, while the insurer will become its subsidiary.

Equitable disclosed that policyholders and holders of annuities withdrew about $2 billion in 1991 in response to the poor earnings performance and bad publicity surrounding the life insurance industry in general and Equitable in particular. The company reported pretax losses from continuing operations of $506 million in 1991 and $308 million in losses in 1990. Particularly troubling to James Grant, author of a respected Wall Street newsletter, is Equitable's heavy exposure in commercial real estate. As a matter of fact, in 1991, only 33 percent of the mortgage maturity payments were paid when due, with an additional 22 percent foreclosed, 22 percent delinquent or in default, and 23 percent extended.[39]

In 1992, Equitable raised an additional $450 million in an initial public offering of common stock and $800 million more from a convertible preferred issue. Equitable was expected to sell at least part of its Donaldson, Lufkin & Jenrette unit in order to generate additional capital.

Equitable's demutualization plan was watched carefully by other mutual insurers. A number of these insurers are also considering a conversion from mutual to stock ownership. Joseph Belth, Indiana University professor of insurance, feels that "the consequences of a negative vote are so serious it seems [that] policyholders are forced to go along."[40] The Axa investment in Equitable follows in the footsteps of other deals by foreign insurance companies in the United States. For example, Dai-Ichi Life Insurance Co. has a 9.6% stake in Lincoln National Corp., while Zurich Insurance Co. of Switzerland bought Maryland Casualty Co. for $740 million, and Alliance A.G. of Germany bought Fireman's Fund Insurance Co. for $1.1 billion. Willis Faber PLC, an English brokerage firm, combined with Corroon and Black.

Even companies that do not contemplate near-term capital needs might undertake conversion to a stock company to achieve structural flexibility. The new structure would allow for the formation of a vertical holding company, merger with other entities, and future access to the equity market if financial needs arise. Also, a stock company is in a better position than a mutual company to retain highly desired executives, by being able to offer stock options.

Participating policyholders have two basic motivating factors in initiating or approving a demutualization. First, they may decide that the stock structure will enhance the company's ability to meet their insurance needs and continue current dividend scales. In addition, they would receive a fair value for the cancellation of their rights to receive dividends, elect directors, and receive the net value of the firm in the case of liquidation. The value received could be paid in cash, increased life insurance benefits, additional dividends, securities, or some other manner.

Demutualization allows former mutual life insurance companies to reorganize as stock life insurance companies and obtain access to the capital markets. The debt mechanisms available to mutual life insurers, such as commercial paper and bank lines of credit, are short term and, therefore, of limited use for long-term development.

Most state demutualization statutes allow for an infusion of equity capital, while simultaneously protecting the policyholders' interests. To the extent that the policy-holders of a mutual have not received payment for their interests at the time of reorganization, a liquidation account is generally established to assure that such payment will eventually be made to the policyholder. Provisions are also made to allow the stockholders of the reorganized companies and the former mutual policyholders to share equitably in the profits of the ongoing company. The types of reorganization may range from a plan with a straight exchange of stock for ownership interest to plans in which the mutual policyholders' interests are paid for at the time of conversion or over a period of years. The reorganized company may become a widely held public company, or it may be merged into another stock company, or it may become part of a holding company system in which the insurance company would be a separate entity. In all of these situations, the reorganized companies would continue as a going concern, without interruption in their activities or management.

A mutual insurance company can enhance its capital by converting to a stock form of ownership. The company obtains additional equity capital in an initial public offering of common stock concurrently with demutualization if the state regulatory authorities permit. Where this is not possible, an insurance company can raise additional capital through the sale of commercial paper, debentures, or preferred stock or through borrowing from the bank and mortgaging or securing its real estate assets.[41]

The advantages of demutualization include the following:[42]

1. The equity base of the insurance company may be expanded.
2. There is greater access to money and capital markets.
3. Expansion through mergers and acquisitions is facilitated.
4. Some federal income tax increases contained in certain proposed congressional legislation may be avoided.
5. A vertical holding company may be formed to participate in business activities outside the purview of the state insurance regulatory agency.
6. The opportunity exists to attract and offer management new equity-linked compensation plans.
7. The opportunity exists to stimulate media attention, which could help a company increase its market share by heightening the degree of recognition of its name.
8. The company may impose a discipline on management.

Among the disadvantages of demutualization are:[43]

1. The managerial strategy and operating results are subject to greater scrutiny.
2. There is a shorter term management focus rather than a longer term focus, because of quarterly earnings reports and shareholder pressures to increase earnings per share.
3. A stock company could become susceptible to an unfriendly takeover.
4. There are costly and complex accounting, actuarial, valuation, legal, and tax issues that must be resolved.
5. A stock company has the additional regulatory burden of complying with security laws and the additional expenses of shareholder reports, communications, and administrative activities.

At the time of this writing, only a handful of insurance companies had demutualized, the largest being UNUM, in Portland, Maine. However, with the conversion by Equitable Life from a mutual into a stockholder company, there are likely to be other companies (e.g., Mutual Life Insurance Company of New York and John Hancock Mutual Life Insurance Co.) converting during the 1990s. Many state legislatures are now considering new laws that would make it much easier for an insurance company to convert from a mutual to a stock company.

Changing Distribution Systems*

In 1982, *World Magazine* quoted Buchan Marshall, chief general manager of General Accident (Perth, Scotland), as saying, "Insurance is insurance is insurance; the product itself never really changes. What does change is the way in which it is sold, and the attitude of those who sell it."[45] If one defines the insurance product as a financial hedge or protection against loss, Mr. Marshall may be correct in saying that the product never really changes. However, that financial protection will expand to new areas of risk and be combined and packaged in new ways in the future. So in that sense, the insurance product will change.

Marshall's statement about what does change—the way insurance is sold and delivered and the attitude of those who sell it—is true. The increased use of computers in the home, combined with more emphasis on the theory of consumer efficiency, demanding greater savings of money, time, and effort in the purchase of products and services, will have significant effects on the marketing of insurance and financial services in the future.

It is estimated that by the year 2035, at least 80 percent of the nation's households will be capable of handling their financial matters from their homes. Over time, a large number of bank clerks, loan officers, insurance agents, and those who provide similar services will be replaced by electronic systems that will be faster and less expensive than humans. Through the use of computer networks, investors are already able to make their own stock purchases, perhaps after seeking the advice of a financial planner in deciding an investment strategy. This same approach is being expanded to the purchase of insurance protection.

Of course, many consumers of goods and services will continue to seek highly qualified professional practitioners to handle their needs. Some people resist changing their habits to accommodate technological change. This was clearly illustrated during a discussion at a seminar for chief executives conducted by the American Institute for Property and Liability Underwriters. One executive claimed never to have used an automated teller machine. In an age of multiple options, organizations would do well to recognize that not everyone will desire to transact business in the same manner.

A large number of consumers will prefer to shop from home, using video screens and computer systems to compare prices. Since insurance tends to be viewed more as an expense than a benefit, consumers are more sensitive to the price of the coverage than they are to the service provided. In the absence of a strong relationship of loyalty and trust between agent and insured, the insured is likely to seek the lowest price, treating insurance as a commodity, such as sugar. The computer permits the insurance buyer to select and reject policies and to purchase only what the buyer

---

*Much of the material in this section comes from Larry Brandon's Book, *Sound a Clear Call.*[44]

wants, and not what the company or the agent wants to sell. With the anticipated intense competition in the financial services area, the client of the future will enjoy all the advantages of a buyer's market.

There are currently several delivery systems operating in the insurance business. Each will be searching for ways to determine the needs of the consumer and how best to meet them. The theory of consumer efficiency suggests that knowledgeable consumers want to save money, time, and effort and also wish to maintain some sort of balance between their needs for insurance and their needs for other financial services. The following analysis describes how each major delivery system is likely to function in the future. Each marketing arrangement will place increasing importance on automation and the computer, in order to achieve maximum efficiency in the delivery of the product to the consumer.

The Agency-Brokerage System

Insurance agents and the companies they represent have become increasingly aware that the traditional system must undergo major changes if it is to survive. Currently, there are about 45,000 independent agencies, but this number is expected to decline to 25,000 by the year 2000, because of acquisitions and mergers and some insolvencies. However, the size of the average agency, now 6–10 people, is projected to be 11–15 by the year 2000. The incomes of the principals of many agencies have been reduced significantly. Agents have suffered severely as a result of unprecedented competition, which has forced down the prices of property and liability insurance. Agency commissions have been reduced, and, unlike companies, agents do not have extensive investment earnings on which to fall back. Additionally, the shift by companies to "cash-flow nonunderwriting" has resulted in the loss of contingency payments (profit sharing) to agencies. Agencies and companies alike have been most reluctant, until recently, to reduce their expenses. Over the past 20 years, premium dollars have been gradually and cumulatively flowing out of the traditional independent agency system and into the exclusive agency companies, direct-selling companies, life insurance companies that have entered the property and liability business, group and trade association programs, the newly formed captives, and the large insurance brokerage firms. The future flow of premium dollars may well go into securities brokerage houses, as well as into banking and savings institutions that currently sell insurance products.

Property and liability insurance companies operating exclusively through independent agents cannot afford to let the independent agency system deteriorate. Companies are being forced to provide whatever support is necessary to ensure that the independent agency system will survive and remain a significant factor among all the different delivery systems. The independent agency system, though, will need to undergo a substantial change. In some instances, this will mean a change in ownership and control: It makes little sense for the "manufacturing" function (the companies) and the "sales" function (insurance agencies) to exist as adversaries, as happened often in the past. They must work together for their mutual survival.

The biggest problem today is the amount of redundancy in the system: Too often, companies and agents are performing the same tasks. There must be a clarification of the roles each segment plays, and then a concerted effort must be made to bring maximum efficiency to those separate roles. The formulation of a clear marketing plan by each company, as well as by each agency, would seem to be the first step. By using more market segmentation and product differentiation, companies and agencies will be able to determine which classes of business they wish to target. These classes of business may be viewed as falling into the following four basic categories:

1. *Personal insurance accounts.* Certain forms of insurance—the fairly standard personal lines coverages, including personal auto, homeowners, and life and health insurance—resemble a commodity. The majority of this business is presently written through the exclusive agency marketing system. A significant amount of premium dollars is also written through direct-selling companies. The home computer may tend to support personal business going to such insurers. The consumer participating in this new technology will tend to be price sensitive and will have direct access to the rates of various companies through a videotex system such as Prodigy. A new type of life insurance has begun to attract attention: the no-load policy, which does not charge agent's commissions. With this policy, insurance is treated like a commodity: The insurance agent is eliminated because the insurer is contacted directly through an 800 number. The net result is lower insurance premiums and a quicker buildup of cash value for whole life policies. The no-load policy is anathema to large insurance companies and their vast sales forces. Most no-load companies are small, but carry top ratings from A.M. Best.[46]

2. *Small-business insurance.* This class of insurance encompasses commercial accounts with annual premiums ranging from about $2,400 to $25,000. Currently, as much as 80 percent of this business may be written through the independent agency marketing system, with the balance going to exclusive agents or direct-selling companies. The national brokers, who have concentrated on "jumbo" accounts, have shown increasing interest in small-business insurance, particularly as they acquired smaller insurance agencies through purchases or mergers. Insurance coverage for small businesses will likely continue to be provided through the independent agency system, although the exclusive agency and direct-selling systems will be taking increasing shares of this market.

3. *Large-business accounts.* These accounts have annual premiums of $25,000 to $100,000 and generate a sizable volume of premium. They have primarily been the domain of very large independent agencies. For the most part, they are attractive risks, and within the independent agency system, there is considerable competition for these accounts, particularly as they increase in size.

4. *"Jumbo" commercial accounts.* These are the largest and most complex commercial accounts, with annual premiums exceeding $100,000. They have

been handled almost entirely by national brokers, with little exclusive agency company or direct-selling company incursion, except in the area of workers' compensation. Customers with "jumbo" commercial accounts are concerned primarily with professional service and protection against catastrophes. Their business is likely to remain with the large brokers, but these brokers will face increasing competition from companies that choose to become more heavily involved in providing service in addition to merely assuming risk.

Each of the foregoing classes of business favors a particular distribution or delivery system. Many companies are attempting to use just one system to reach all four classes. In the future, companies will likely use a variety of marketing systems targeted toward specific classes of business, rather than being bound by tradition to one distribution system.

The strength of the independent agency system lies in its appeal to the smaller-than-"jumbo"-size commercial account and a concerted effort to maintain or acquire its fair share of personal business. Companies will continue to use independent agents as their sales force in these markets. Keen competition will continue, with the result that mergers, acquisitions, and the disappearance of marginal agencies will significantly reduce the number of agencies operating in the future. The smaller number of agencies will also represent fewer companies, in order to achieve a level of efficiency enabling them to be more competitive. The next few years will be critical in determining the future nature, scope, and significance of the independent agency system. Agents will likely assume three distinct characteristics in the future:

1. They will obtain broader authority from their companies in order to function as mini branch offices within a geographical area.
2. They will streamline their operation so that they can get back into the business of selling products and servicing customers.
3. They will represent fewer companies and will concentrate their sales efforts on the distinct expectations each company has of their agents.

Without question, automation will play a fundamental role in whatever work is performed by the agent of the future. Through the use of computers, the agent will be able to:

1. *Make more effective cost comparisons on rates provided by the companies the agency represents.* The computer will allow the agent to obtain premium quotes from among the companies willing to provide coverage.
2. *Program the computer to diagnose clients' needs and prescribe insurance coverages or alternative risk management techniques.* Additionally, a client's business can be continually monitored in order to recommend changes as personal or business conditions change.

3. *Become more oriented toward market planning and market targeting.* Agents will then be able to segment which accounts, territories, types of business, and the like create a profit and which of them operate at a loss. Agents will also be able to perform a more sophisticated "intraaccount" analysis to assist in applying risk management techniques.

4. *Offer a wider range of financial service products (e.g., life insurance, mutual funds, and money market funds).* These added financial services can be built into the computer-based financial analysis program for their clients. Such computer programs will have been prepared through cooperative efforts of various insurance and financial experts and computer specialists. The prescribed package will include items from each of these areas to give balance to the client's array of financial protection. (Already, the Travelers Insurance Company is able to offer its agents a full range of bank money market funds and various finance plans through their affiliation with the largest bank in the state of Connecticut.)

5. *Make his or her offerings available to clients through monthly billing.* Consumers will also be able to pay by credit cards and electronic transfers of cash and payroll deductions.

Those agencies electing to seek greater authority to perform many functions now handled by company branch office personnel will have to increase their staffs to provide more underwriting capability for their companies. For their part, the companies will require the agencies to provide their own staffs of underwriters before granting them greater authority to accept, issue, and deliver policies in a more timely and efficient manner. If the agency underwriters and other personnel do not become more efficient than the companies, neither reductions in redundancy nor streamlined operations will result.

Agents and brokers must become more adept in the principles and practices of risk management to hold their share of the commercial lines market. Corporate buyers are becoming increasingly knowledgeable in risk management and will be able to determine for themselves whether or not they are receiving sufficient professional service from their agent or broker. One choice might result in agents specializing in particular types of risks.

Agents and brokers must also engage more aggressively in selling and providing services for their clients. They will be required to engage in more telephone solicitation, more house calls, and more out-of-the-office selling time on both personal and commercial accounts. As companies and agents work together to eliminate duplicate efforts and sort out responsibilities, based on where the best capabilities are located, the sales function will reside where it should be—as the primary function of the agent. In the future, companies will eliminate the position of "marketing representative" or "special agent," designed originally to assist the agent in making sales. With the gradual disappearance of smaller, marginal agents, the role of the special agent has largely become an unused and unnecessary function. Those agents who are more professional feel that the traditional "service" of a field representative is generally overrated and a waste of human resources. Consequently, company underwriters will be likely to work more directly with the agent on complicated sales and underwriting decisions and will therefore need to become more sales and service oriented. Regardless of whether companies provide individuals known as special agents or underwriters to assist agents on the more complex accounts, some knowledgeable specialist from the company is needed, since agents cannot be expected to have expertise with all types of exposures. The real key to the future of the agents or brokers, given that the adverse underwriting cycle will likely continue for some time, is for them to return to their fundamental activity: selling insurance and professional services to their customers. As an incentive to keep agents selling, future commission contracts will likely give a greater remuneration for the production of new business than for the retention of existing business.

Finally, the changing competitive climate and the changing roles of agent and broker will require these individuals continually to study the business of insurance, intensively as well as extensively, to improve their knowledge of this rapidly changing institution. They will need to be better trained and educated to accommodate the additional products and services flowing through their offices in the future. Future consumers are likely to be more knowledgeable than in the past, and agents and brokers will have to increase their level of professionalism in order to survive. They will also have to increase their command of the basic tools of their trade: salesmanship, initiative, and technical competence. In turn, companies that stand behind these agents will have to make certain that their own personnel keep pace by improving their professional levels of competence and knowledge in their supporting role. Insurance company personnel will need broad-based knowledge of the total insurance environment in order to function effectively as advisors to the agents and brokers.

The Exclusive Agency Marketing System

The exclusive agency system of marketing involves the "exclusive agent" or representative who is "salaried with a bonus" and has been highly successful in the personal lines area and certain areas of commercial insurance. Currently, people involved in the exclusive agency system are making stronger inroads in the commercial lines area.

Companies like State Farm, Allstate, Nationwide, Farmers Insurance Exchange, Liberty Mutual, and Sentry will continue to operate most successfully in the personal lines market. However, like independent agents, they will have to expand their person-to-person selling approach. As independent agents become more aggressive in their sales efforts, aim will be taken at business currently written by exclusive agency companies. Based on past performance, it is not likely that exclusive agents will become complacent, but they cannot afford to slacken their pace of selling insurance in the foreseeable future.

The national advertising programs of exclusive agency companies, which concentrate on low cost, high efficiency, and ease of doing business, have great appeal to consumers. The personal service offered by these firms will continue to grow and may well result in an expansion of their market share of the classes of business in which they now engage.

The trends in regard to package and combination policies are as relevant for the exclusive agency marketing system as they are for the independent agency marketing system. Given the wider range of insurance packages and financial service products that is likely to exist in the future, exclusive agents and their clients will benefit if the agents avail themselves of the education that is now offered by growing numbers of insurance companies. Such training and education should include knowledge of the products sold, as well as such related subjects as economics, accounting, finance, and taxation.

Insofar as automation is concerned, the exclusive agents enjoy a substantial advantage in that they interface with only one company. This advantage serves to ease the process of computerizing their operations. Many of these agents have direct on-line computer connections with their company. Independent agents will find it a much longer, expensive, and tedious process before they are able to interface with all their companies. Eventually, exclusive and independent agents will be able to assemble, market, monitor, and update their package combination offerings. This equal capability within both systems will serve to intensify the competition for a greater market share in a given class of business.

The Direct-Selling Marketing System

Through the direct-selling marketing system, the personal-lines customer is contacted by telephone, television, or mail by a company employee or, sometimes, a computer.

Companies such as USAA, GEICO, Colonial Penn, Amica Mutual, JCPenney, Montgomery Ward, and 20th Century Insurance Company are likely to be in an increasingly advantageous position because of their efficiency and, in some cases, their close ties to affinity groups (e.g., USAA insures primarily military people, GEICO primarily government employees). They are in a much more ideal situation for offering savings of money, time, and effort to a greater degree than are any other systems. Direct selling would appear to be in a preferred position in a highly price-competitive market because of its low-cost delivery of the product. It has no acquisition costs beyond the company's expense that is associated with contacting the customer. In other words, direct-selling companies pay no commission fees to agents and tend to offer standardized, undifferentiated policies that do not require sophisticated analyses or explanations to consumers.

Direct-selling sales personnel will require more intensive and extensive knowledge of their products in the future because otherwise, their prospects for insurance may know as much about the product as they do. To respond intelligently to telephone and mail inquiries regarding coverage, costs, comparative advantages, and the like, and to compete effectively with agents representing other delivery systems, direct-selling personnel must become technically competent if the full potential of this delivery system is to thrive and penetrate existing markets.

Direct selling can and will offer the full range of products. In addition to personal automobile, homeowners, life, and health insurance policies, which have been traditional and quite popular with these companies, it is likely that mutual funds and money market funds will be added. This expansion of offerings will be necessary to compete with other systems and to tie current customers into their organizations.

One advantage direct-selling companies have that will continue well into the future is their ability to be more adventurous and innovative in selecting and moving into or out of markets. These organizations "own" the business they sell, as well as their customer lists, and need not be concerned with adverse effects on producers or on sales of products.

The Direct-Response Marketing System

Successive advances in electronics and communications will make the typical household of the future a financial command center operated by time- and price-conscious shoppers and knowledgeable investors. From their living rooms, people will be able to do business with their banks and their insurance companies and will be able to trade securities on a stock exchange through their broker.

Most of the systems that will make all this possible will require the purchase of a personal computer with a modem. The machines of the future will respond to voice commands and will be able to "talk" to the user by way of a voice modulator. The home computer should prove to be a major factor influencing the manner in which insurance is purchased in the future. The owner of a home computer will be able to join a market system group in which various insurance companies will list their coverages and rates for review by consumers and provide a choice among alternatives.

This direct-response marketing system offers perhaps the best example of the theory of consumer efficiency, providing the maximum savings of money, time, and effort. Home computer users who purchase their insurance directly from the insurance company, thereby circumventing the agent, will most likely force the independent agency companies to offer a secondary marketing system through the direct-response alternative. Otherwise, they would surely lose market share to the exclusive agency companies or to the direct-selling companies (through mail and telephone). Both of these marketing systems will undoubtedly avail themselves of the marketing potential of the home computer.

The direct-response delivery system appears to have the greatest potential for growth during the decade of the 1990s. Despite this, there will continue to be millions of people who will desire to do business with an agent whom they know and trust. The computer will indeed be used in marketing insurance in the future, but not to any truly sizable degree: There is substantial support for the belief that people want to have an agent representing them, especially when a loss occurs. So, while some business will be written through the direct-response system, that system is not expected to make a large dent in the overall market.

Banks and Securities Firms Selling Insurance

Many brokerage firms own their own insurance companies and utilize their stockbrokers primarily to sell life insurance and annuities to their existing client base. The success of these ventures has varied widely. Some insurance companies offer their products to brokerage firms to sell, utilizing the existing base of stockbrokers as an alternative marketing arm. Other insurance companies actually own stockbrokerage firms. Prudential Insurance Co. offers a complete "menu" of insurance products for sale through Prudential Securities, its wholly owned subsidiary. The broker has a theoretical advantage over the insurance agent because the broker has more contact with the typical customer over time than the insurance agent does. However, few stockbrokers have become adept at selling ordinary insurance. Instead, they have been far more successful in selling annuities, an investment-based product.

Banks already sell insurance in many states, either through their branch systems or in envelope stuffers in monthly statements sent to customers. Most participating banks have a relationship with an insurance company or an insurance agency and either have their own internal sales staff or have insurance company or agency personnel at the branches to handle sales. Banks already have extensive customer bases and branch systems that draw a lot of traffic. Accordingly, they should have a definite marketing advantage in offering car insurance, homeowner's insurance, and mortgage life insurance to customers who apply for an automobile loan or a mortgage loan. Banks represent an area of great potential for insurance sales, particularly for the sale of individual lines of insurance as well as annuities. Several of the large banks would also like to underwrite insurance, but so far, Congress and the bank regulators have not given them permission to do so. Citicorp claims that, because of lower distribution costs, it would be able to offer bank customers insurance at premiums 10 to 15 percent below those available at most insurance companies. The sale of life insurance through savings banks in New York State and in several states in New England has been in existence for decades. A number of other states, such as Delaware and South Dakota, have passed legislation allowing banks to sell insurance outside of their state from state-chartered banks within their state. These states hope to attract new banks and new jobs to their local areas.

The decision by the U.S. government in October 1991 not to appeal a court ruling clears the way for Citicorp to underwrite and sell insurance throughout the country through its Delaware-based holding company. A 1990 Delaware law permits banks to sell insurance products nationwide through subsidiaries of bank holding companies that are chartered in the state. However, there are two more roadblocks that Citicorp faces. First, there is the possibility that Congress will override the Delaware law as part of a comprehensive package to overhaul banking laws or that the Supreme Court will hear the case and rule against Citicorp. Second, an additional twist in the insurance battle came when the Justice Department indicated that it would not represent the Federal Reserve before the Supreme Court because it believed that the agency's case was shaky. Furthermore, the Justice Department felt that the suit might prove meaningless if Congress moved to restrict bank activities in insurance.

Following the passage of the Delaware law, the Federal Reserve Board of Governors barred Citicorp from expanding its insurance activities through the Family Guardian Life Insurance Co., a subsidiary of Citicorp's Delaware bank holding company. While the regulatory agency was not opposed to banks having insurance powers, it reserved the right to regulate units of bank holding companies.

In June 1991, the U.S. Circuit Court of Appeals overturned the Federal Reserve's order, ruling that the regulatory agency had no jurisdiction in the matter, since Citicorp's insurance business would be conducted under the auspices of state authorities. The Court ruled that the Federal Reserve could not use its authority under the Bank Holding Company Act to regulate the nonbanking activities of a state-chartered bank owned by a bank holding company.[47] In late 1991, Congress finally passed legislation that allowed already established bank-owned insurance operations in Delaware to continue operating, but forbade the establishment of new bank holding company facilities that would underwrite insurance.

In early 1992, the Supreme Court dealt a blow to the insurance industry's bid to keep banks out of its business when it allowed state-chartered subsidiaries of banks to sell insurance if permitted under state law. The Supreme Court denied an appeal by a number of insurance industry groups of a ruling in June 1991 by a U.S. Court of Appeals in New York. The affirmed ruling was expected to encourage banks to enter the insurance business nationwide. The appeals court ruled that state chartering bodies have the legal powers to determine which nonbanking activities should be allowed banks in their jurisdictions. Previously, the court had stated that the basic federal banking law did not bar bank subsidiaries from selling insurance.

In another decision in February 1992, a federal appeals court in Washington, DC, ruled that national banks have no legal right to sell insurance. This decision overturned 76 years of history and marked a victory for insurance agents, who had long been fighting to stop the incursion of banks into their lines of business. Thousands of banks had been selling insurance in small towns and rural areas under the terms of a 1916 federal statute in which Congress granted national banks "located and doing business in any place the population of which does not exceed 5,000 inhabitants" to act as agents for "any fire, life, or other insurance company." The Comptroller of the Currency expanded this power in 1986 by ruling that U.S. Bancorp of Oregon and other nationally chartered banks could use their rural base to sell insurance nationwide. The 1992 Court of Appeals ruled that a punctuation error invalidated a key section of the 1916 statute. In June 1993, the Supreme Court reversed the lower court decision that said that in 1918 Congress canceled the authority of national banks to sell insurance in small towns. Essentially, the Supreme Court decision resurrected the 1916 provision of federal banking law that formed the basis of the Comptroller of the Currency's policy allowing national banks to sell insurance from their small-town branches to customers nationwide. Currently, more than 100 national banks operate essentially as insurance agencies, offering a range of insurance products. Since 37 states have laws allowing state-chartered banks to exercise the same powers as national banks, the practice could spread even wider. The decision did not address the actual validity of the Comptroller of the

Currency's policy to allow national banks with branches in small communities to sell insurance.[48]

Peter Cooke, chairman of Price Waterhouse's World Regulatory Advisory Practice, notes that "insurance and banking are moving into a closer relationship, with Europe leading the way in institutional ties, while the United States has been the early innovator in risk management. The case in Europe for closer links between banking and insurance is made on grounds of cross-selling opportunities and diversification of profit sources, maximizing the marketing capacity of branch networks. . . . It would be surprising if this trend were not to spread into the United States and become a stronger influence."[49]

In the fall of 1992, J. P. Morgan, Marsh & McClennan, and other institutional investors formed Mid Ocean Reinsurance Company with more than $350 million in capital. The new company hoped to take advantage of deteriorating conditions in the world reinsurance market, which has shrunk dramatically after years of huge losses, including losses from the severe 1992 hurricane and other storms in the United States. Previously, commercial banks had joined with insurance companies, securities firms, and other institutional investors to form insurance companies that offered credit risk insurance for bonds (especially tax-exempt bonds) such as FGIC.

Convenience is still believed to be "king" in the marketplace for retail customers. Any firm that can offer all of its services under one roof will likely control more of the client's assets.[50]

Insurance Companies and the Changing Environment

The insurance companies that are the driving force behind each of the delivery systems will, in some instances, undergo tremendous change in the years ahead. Increasing competition will force more company mergers and the formation of various conglomerates to accommodate the expanding financial services field. There will always be companies that will provide a specialty product or serve a separately defined market or small geographical area, but the distribution of full financial services will be left to a relatively few multiple-function companies. These groups will result from the merger activity that has already occurred and from similar mergers likely to occur in the future. Thus, some insurance companies will provide many of the same services as other providers of financial services, such as banks, savings and loan companies, and securities brokerages. However, this will be an evolutionary development—and a slow one at that.

There will also be companies, like State Farm, that will consciously elect not to change radically from their successful way of doing business. These companies will still be substantially the same in the year 2000 as they are in 1992. Their products will be amended and updated periodically, but they will continue to be insurance companies—clearly distinguishable from banks, savings and loan companies, brokerage companies, etc.—and they will not confine themselves to specialty lines of business or small geographical regions. As John Naisbitt pointed out in *Megatrends,* we are in an era of "multiple options," and we will see insurance companies making very different decisions on how to position themselves for the future.[51] Fortunately, there is room for many approaches.

There will be fewer groups of insurers in the future, but they will be larger in size and will offer a multitude of products and services. The larger groups will be more international in scope and operation. Medium-sized companies of today will either grow larger to survive or maintain their current size to serve a specific segment of the population or a particular geographic area. Small regional companies should do well in the future. Although they will likely be unable to realize as much economy of scale as larger companies, they will be in a position to maintain closer rapport with their agents and customers and respond more quickly and flexibly to needed change than will their larger, more bureaucratic competitors.

Problems of inefficiency will continue to plague all insurance companies. Today, every company is being forced to cut its expenses of operation (distribution of insurance, administration of underwriting, and administration of claims), from as much as 35 percent in some companies to as little as 17 percent in the most efficient direct-selling companies. The first thing companies will be required to do is face the reality that there are many ways to reduce inefficiency and improve operations. Reductions in expenses may be achieved through any of the following means:

1. Additional mass-marketing approaches.
2. Expanded use of direct billing.
3. Increased agency automation and multiple company interfacing.
4. Expanded interdepartmental automation.
5. Increased use of continuous-coverage (automatically renewable) policies.
6. Elimination of duplication of work between company and agency at casualty companies.
7. Payroll deduction or electronic transmission of funds and other ease-of-payment plans for personal lines coverages.
8. Full realization of paperless operation of companies and agencies alike.

Property and casualty insurance companies are trying to become more efficient producers by eliminating excessive paperwork and reducing unneeded personnel. There must be a severe reduction in operating costs if the property and casualty industry is to deliver an affordable, but profitable, product. Buyers of insurance will demand such efficiency; they will expect and receive more of their premium dollars for their insured losses and less for operating the insurance mechanism.

Insurance companies of the future are likely to use multiple delivery systems, rather than a single system, for the sale of personal lines property and casualty insurance. Failure to do business in a variety of ways could place companies in a disadvantageous position in the intensely competitive marketplace of the future. To continue growing, companies must ascertain and then respond to customers' needs and desires. They can no longer afford to rely on their timeworn products, services, and methods of transacting business.

The greatest growth in the service sector of the economy, both domestically and internationally, is expected to be in financial services. In the banking, insurance, and securities businesses, sophisticated data-processing and telecommunications equipment now enables companies and individuals to move money quickly into different credit markets, across state lines, and across international borders. This allows these financial institutions to take advantage of the slightest variation in interest rates. Such technological advances, along with continuing deregulation of financial institutions, will create a new integrated financial services industry. Financial supermarkets will begin to provide a full range of financial services, not only in the United States, but also abroad, for some personal lines of insurance, such as term life and homeowner's insurance. It will, however, take time to change consumers' habits, so this development may not occur as quickly as many predict. Accordingly, there will still be a need for highly trained professionals and specialists to sell certain insurance products. Also, many people prefer the personal services, comfort, and convenience offered by an insurance agent who has earned the faith and trust of his or her client.

The inevitable merging of financial services and the advancing electronic technology supporting those services are having a dramatic impact on the delivery systems of all sellers of financial services. It is imperative that the insurance industry take a firm and objective look at how business is being conducted and adapt its operations to the changes that will continue to occur at a gradually accelerating rate. Agents should seek out more markets and send them a clear, concise message.

The insurance industry was created to provide protection for those who suffered financial loss as a result of unexpected events. It was supposed to conduct business in an honest, ethical way for the public, which has little time or interest in acquainting itself with the technicalities of the business. Today, consumers are becoming more sophisticated, but there will still be a need for persons with integrity to help the client identify needs and choose proper coverage. Moreover, there will still be a need for a knowledgeable underwriter to safeguard the interests of both the company and the client, and there will still be a need for an empathetic and professional claims person to serve when an unexpected loss occurs. No computer can replace the human element in providing professional service; computers can only support competent people, who are then free to perform their functions more effectively and efficiently.

The amount of time, effort, and money being put into automating insurance offices and operations must never be allowed to obscure the greater goal of improved competence and professionalism on the part of the people who design insurance products and services and those who deliver those products and services in the years ahead.

Finally, the industry cannot ever afford to lose sight of its ultimate reason for existence: service to the public, which is in need of an efficient, low-cost method of protection against unforeseen losses. However, the insurance industry can use some help from regulators, who might remove some of the artificial barriers to consolidation and make the demutualization process easier. This would permit mutuals to raise capital. As public companies, they might be more disciplined and profit oriented. Also, consolidation should lead to greater efficiency.[52]

Other Changes

There is a general movement underway to reduce overhead and operating costs. Martin Leshner, managing director for insurance at Hay Group, foresees employee cuts of as much as 15 percent or more in the next several years among life, health, and property and casualty insurers. The main goal is to reduce costs and improve profitability in an industry in which numerous companies have severe financial problems. Insurance companies selling personal lines insurance are going to have to become more efficient producers if they wish to survive and prosper in an era of a more sophisticated, price-conscious consumer shopping for financial services. Just as some New York banks have moved their staffs from high-priced Manhattan to lower priced Brooklyn, some New York–based insurance companies and brokerage firms have moved their processing and computer operations out of Manhattan to New Jersey, where real estate and other operating costs are considerably lower. In addition, there will be a movement toward reducing the costs of marketing and delivering services by moving toward cheaper and more efficient sales techniques than the traditional local sales agent method of generating customers. These techniques include direct mail offerings, telemarketing, and marketing through branch offices of banks and brokerage firms. Mass marketing is popular in selling some forms of property insurance. One method is distribution through employer payroll deductions. The premiums are usually less expensive because of economies of scale and savings in commissions that arise, even though underwriting is still done on an individual basis. Some insurance companies have also reduced commission costs by distributing their products through mass marketing, banks, and brokerage firms. Today, it probably takes five to six cold phone calls to reach one party who is interested in buying life insurance. The success rate in selling that party life insurance following the cold call and a personal interview is only one out of three or four. Some insurance people feel that they can improve the success rate substantially by using private banking customers. After all, French banks sell 30 percent of the life insurance policies in France. There will be more consolidations and mergers within the industry, as there are far too many life insurance companies (2,300 in the United States alone). The financially wounded will seek a partner, while the well-capitalized companies will be looking for a good fit in making an acquisition where costs can be cut and the joint company can be operated at lower cost, becoming a more efficient provider. The number of life insurance companies may shrink from over 2,000 to between 200 and 300 by the time the consolidation process is completed.

A run on an insurance company such as Mutual Benefit Life or the failure of a giant annuity provider such as Executive Life has brought forth another major change—a flight toward quality. Insurance companies have learned that they must maintain sufficient liquidity to withstand the proverbial run. Failure to maintain the necessary degree of liquidity has been the downfall of Baldwin-United and First

Executive. Both firms had to sell assets in a depressed market to meet policyholder demands for funds.[53]

Insuring the Uninsured

The two primary health dilemmas in the United States are expanding access to health care and containing health care costs. Before examining these problems carefully, we must become familiar with a few important health insurance statistics. First, U.S. citizens spend more than 12 percent of GNP on health care, more than any other developed country. Second, an estimated 34 million people in the United States have no health insurance. Third, many people find that their employers are cutting back their health insurance benefits or charging more for them. Fourth, according to pollsters, nearly two-thirds of Americans favor national health insurance, supported by taxes. Fifth, the growing American problems of getting and paying for health care are winding their way through the congressional front in Washington.

The uninsured individual is either unemployed, employed with a low income, or a dependent of an employed person. The uninsured comprise two distinct groups: the insurable and the uninsurable. Many insurable individuals work for companies that do not provide employer-sponsored medical insurance, primarily because of its expense. Uninsured but medically insurable individuals either cannot afford or choose not to buy private insurance. The uninsurable are people who have medical conditions that make it impossible for them either to qualify for health insurance or to purchase insurance at affordable prices.

The plight of the uninsured has received increased media and congressional attention in recent years. President Clinton has promised to come up with a solution during 1993 that could have major consequences for employers, insurance companies, and taxpayers. For example, state governments could encourage employers to introduce or expand health insurance coverage through incentives and penalties. In addition, the federal government could extend Medicaid to low-income individuals with sliding-scale premiums or provide catastrophic health insurance coverage to the uninsured. Potential solutions could entail the use of state risk pools for the high-risk uninsured. Another option involves the development of a national health insurance program similar to those in England and Canada. There could also be a specific program designed for the uninsured that would combine features of the current system while leaving private coverage largely intact. For example, the federal government might provide health care, catastrophic coverage, well-baby/well-child care, and maternity services to low-income individuals, while employers would be required to provide a minimum benefit covering the cost of services between a minimum level and the government's catastrophic coverage level.[54]

Before trying to solve the problem, questions such as the following must be answered: What kinds of coverage do the uninsured need most? Who would administer a program for the uninsured—a private company, such as an insurance company, a newly established organization developed specifically for that purpose, or a state or federal government agency? Would health insurance for the uninsured offer a choice of providers? Would they use a pool similar to assigned-risk auto insurance?

What is the true nature of the underwriting risk? Will increased access to the health care system lead to increased utilization that will create a strain on the capacity of the system? Who should pay for insuring the uninsured? If employers are forced to pay, will that lead to increased prices for products and services, lower wages for employees, or fewer jobs? Will the government impose additional sin or luxury taxes, or even an increase in general taxes, to fund health care for the uninsured? Will the federal government impose a payroll tax on employers or remove the current tax-favored treatment of employee benefits? It will be difficult to find an acceptable solution to the problem of the uninsured because of the complexity of the issues and the divergent interests of insurance companies, governments, employers, providers, taxpayers, and the uninsured themselves.[55]

The advantages of government involvement in insuring the uninsured are that (1) low-income individuals become protected, (2) socially desirable preventive and maternity services would be available to all, (3) everyone is protected against catastrophic expenses, (4) the cost of employer insurance coverage is reduced, making it easier for an employer to provide more affordable benefits, and (5) important elements of the existing private insurance market are maintained. The disadvantages of government involvement in such a system include the creation of administrative problems coordinating employer, government, and individual insurance and the failure to provide an incentive to use less expensive or more efficient providers.[56]

Increasing efforts will be made to contain health care costs, improve access to care, and cover the uninsured. A national health insurance bill will likely retain primary reliance on employers for employee coverage, with mandatory coverage for firms above a minimum size. However, initiatives will increasingly expand the role of government in financing the delivery of national health care.[57] There will likely be a "play or pay" plan, in which companies falling below the threshold size will have an option of either providing coverage or paying into a fund that insures their employees and the remaining uninsured. Such a fund would be financed by public subsidies and by a surcharge on the premiums of all the employees covered by firms whose number of employees was above the threshold level.

In a sharp break from past practice, the board of directors of the Health Insurance Association of America, representing 270 commercial insurers, adopted a policy statement in December 1992 that called for reform through a new federal law that would require health insurance coverage for all Americans, define a basic set of benefits, and attempt to contain health care costs. In the board's policy plan, the government would help define "an essential package of benefits" that all private insurers would agree to provide to all Americans, regardless of their medical history. To hold down costs, the federal government would limit tax-free health benefits and oversee fees charged by doctors and hospitals. The open-ended federal subsidy for health insurance would be curtailed, and benefits exceeding the basic government package would be treated as taxable income. If employers are required to provide health insurance for all employees, it may prove to be an economic burden to some companies.

The Impact of AIDS

The AIDS epidemic represents a challenge to many U.S. life insurance companies. While AIDS is not expected to cause substantial deterioration in the creditworthiness of those companies in the near term, it could reduce the profitability of a number of carriers by the mid-1990s, since experts anticipate AIDS-related claims of about $50 billion during the 1990s. Also, the average health care cost of an AIDS sufferer is approximately $50,000, with the private health care insurer paying about 50 percent. Studies suggest that AIDS has infected 1.0–1.5 million Americans; a report by the Society of Actuaries suggests that cumulative AIDS fatalities could be as high as 2.9 million by the year 2010. Other studies have shown that a disproportionate share of AIDS death claims occurred within two years of the issue date of the policy, suggesting that the insured knew or suspected that he or she had AIDS when the policy was purchased.[58]

Health insurers should be able to pass along most of the additional cost of AIDS through the repricing of group policies. To reduce future exposure, underwriting practices have been tightened for new policies. However, AIDS does not represent a substantial solvency threat to the entire industry, but a few companies may be severely affected by their exposure to the cost of AIDS.[59]

THE THRIFT INDUSTRY–INSURANCE INDUSTRY ANALOGY

While the financial condition of the insurance industry is fragile, insurers are not on the verge of repeating the thrift industry debacle. Insurance companies are vulnerable to interest rate risk and to credit risk, but to a lesser degree than thrifts. Both the insurance and the thrift industries require that products be priced prior to the exact knowledge of the losses that will eventually flow from those products. Both are businesses that offer strong short-term cash flow advantages (in the form of either origination fees at the thrift or advance payment of the insurance premium) to companies which underprice their product or do not provide enough reserves against future losses. Both give imprudent management the opportunity to defer the recognition of loss for at least awhile. Many of the thrift and insurance company failures stem from a common thread: aggressive price cutting and accelerated growth. Each of these factors can lead to superior short-term results and enormous long-term risk. However, while there appear to be some common elements, the risk levels in insurance today are of a lower order of magnitude and are of a different character than those that existed for thrifts as early as the late 1970s. The thrift crisis did not simply emerge full-blown after the 1988 elections; it had a history that combined structural defects in the thrift business, severe errors in policy judgment, a distinctive new breed of entrepreneur, and devastating economic conditions in the southwestern and northeastern parts of the nation. The specific forces that propelled the thrift crisis bear no resemblance to the particular characteristics surrounding the insurance industry.

Analysis of life insurance assets reveals that nearly half of all such assets were in investment-grade bonds and that non-investment-grade bonds accounted for just under 4 percent of assets. Mortgage holdings declined from 31 percent of assets in 1975 to approximately 19 percent in 1990, while real estate dropped from 3.3 percent of assets in 1975 to about 2.2 percent in 1990. Unlike commercial banks and thrifts, life insurance companies shed, rather than added, real estate holdings over the 1980s. Life insurers, commercial banks, and thrifts all have substantial portfolios of real estate mortgages. However, banks and thrifts are more active at the riskiest stage of the real estate process—in construction and lending—as well as in long-term financing. Life insurance companies have tended to focus on lending for commercial properties for which tenants have already signed leases. While every extension of credit involves the risk of default, bank and thrift financing is more heavily weighted toward the higher risk, higher return front end of the development process.[60] Further, while institutions in general can hedge against interest rate risk, and life insurance companies can balance geographic real estate risk with other forms of investment, there is no hedge readily available to most depository institutions against overall economic weakness in a bank's or thrift's lending area.[61]

The property and casualty insurance asset portfolio is even more conservative and liquid than the life insurance portfolio, in order to meet cash flow needs. Nearly 70 percent of property and casualty assets were in government, agency, or investment-grade corporate bonds, while stocks made up less than 15 percent of assets. Non-investment-grade bonds constituted less than 1 percent of assets, while real estate holdings accounted for just over 2 percent of assets.

For property and casualty companies, the major insolvency risks are (1) the risk of a major earthquake or series of hurricanes; (2) the risk that, through reinterpreting contracts, courts may impose enormous unforeseen losses in the form of environmental cleanup costs on the industry (e.g., judicially imposed liability for the costs of cleaning up toxic waste sites); (3) the pressure on operating margins if the cost of claims continues to escalate and the trend in jurisdictions favoring rate suppression continues to spread; (4) difficulties in determining the reserves that will be needed to cover future costs of claims in an uncertain legal environment; and (5) the risk of structural excess capacity, which is holding down premium costs. For life insurance companies, the salient risks are (1) the potential further deterioration in the quality of credit in some asset categories, such as commercial real estate and junk bonds; (2) vulnerability to a major regional downturn for certain companies with geographically concentrated real estate investments; (3) mismatches in the maturity of assets and liabilities (e.g., exposure to risk resulting from fixed-rate, long-term guaranteed investment contracts funded by short-term assets); and (4) the risk of illiquidity for weakly capitalized carriers in a risk-sensitive financial environment in which investors and policyholders cash in their guaranteed investment contracts and annuity contracts early and cancel insurance coverage.[62] However, unless one or more of these factors spiral out of control, there is an extremely low probability that insolvencies will reach the point of creating serious dislocations in the insurance system. For example, the 1989 earthquake in San Francisco destroyed about $5 billion worth of property, but produced only about $600 million in insurance claims. And although the combined losses from Hurricane Hugo (also in 1989) and the San Francisco earthquake created severe catastrophic losses, these losses amounted to only 4.8 percent of the industry's net worth. The potential cost of cleaning up hazardous waste sites and the timing of these potential payments are uncertain. Estimates vary from $100 billion to a trillion dollars when the job is done, or about $75 billion to $213 billion in current dollars. At the end of 1990, the net worth of the property and casualty industry stood at about $135 billion.[63]

An analysis of life insurance company portfolios reveals that insurers are estimated to hold about 30 percent of the total of $220 billion in outstanding non-investment-grade debt and the majority of non-investment-grade bonds is concentrated among a limited number of companies. Of the 2,020 life insurance companies, 159 accounted for 84 percent of the industry's junk bonds, and all of these companies had non-investment-grade bonds equivalent to 100 percent or more of their net worth. Note that not all junk bonds are in default or have market prices under par value. Also, most bonds that are in default are not worthless and may in fact be worth between 10 cents and 40 cents on the dollar. In addition, there was a large rally in the junk bond market in 1991. Most mortgages held by life insurers were for loans on farm, city, and suburban establishments. A few large insurance companies have in excess of 50 percent of their total assets in mortgage holdings. With the softening of the real estate markets nationally, about 4 percent of the mortgages held by the largest 100 life insurance companies were delinquent in 1990. In most states, there are laws which stipulate that real estate investments may not exceed 10 percent of an insurance company's admissible assets. Real estate holdings represent less than 3 percent of the industry's assets, and about 17 percent of real estate investments are in home or field offices. There has probably been some modest increase in the risk of illiquidity with the deterioration of the quality of real estate holdings, since these investments are currently suffering from weak markets. On the subject of guaranteed investment contracts and annuities, most funds were initially invested in treasury instruments or other low-risk instruments. However, in some cases, insurers invested in long-term assets or in assets of lower quality (e.g., junk bonds). In some instances, those assets were not readily marketable. The payout from some annuities was far in the future, and penalties discouraged early surrender of the policies. In many instances, the insurance companies underestimated the asset-liability and credit quality risks associated with these investments. While high-risk scenarios abound, "There is no evidence that the insurance industry faces a systemic solvency crisis, and there is no reasonable probability that the circumstances that might produce such a crisis will, in fact, occur."[64]

While there are, of course, similarities between the insurance and thrift crises, there are similarities across all financial institutions in the kinds of management behavior that induces insolvency. Although the insurance environment appears riskier today than it did a decade ago, industry problems in the aggregate appear less frightening and complex than those of the thrifts; it is difficult to conjure up a likely scenario whereby insurers would replicate the thrift debacle. The fear is that there could be a regulatory overreaction to a report of commonalities between the two industries and that there will be a tendency to paint all institutions with the same broad brush strokes. In the case of the thrift situation, policymakers imposed costs and constraints even on healthy thrifts that will make adequate returns extremely difficult for all but the strongest competitors. Financial regulatory policy always faces a tension between the goal of avoiding large, costly failures and the goal of attracting private capital into a regulated industry. With regard to the thrift crisis, any semblance of balance has disappeared. Congress has certainly reduced the risk of highly expensive savings and loan failures by tightening restrictions on diversifying assets and by increasing capital standards. However, that benefit has been achieved at the cost of a sharp devaluation of the savings and loan franchise. Essentially, the thrifts have been limited to low-margin businesses and will have to endure higher capital costs. As indicated earlier, most savings and loans will not be able to generate returns equivalent to their costs of capital. While there will be fewer enormous thrift failures, many of the healthy thrifts will be unable to raise new capital, leaving thrifts to atrophy slowly, eventually to fade away.[65] In fact, this may even be the unstated intent of the regulations. It is not clear that a thrift industry is needed any longer in the United States now that commercial banks and other lenders are active in the mortgage markets.

CONCLUSIONS

Insurance companies have responded to a changing environment in a number of different ways. Some insurers have merged, raised external capital, sold off assets, or exited select business lines. Others have sought to expand activities such as managed care, money management, or securities brokerages to gain new sources of revenue. Past efforts at diversification appear likely to reshape the companies in the future. The pace of acquisitions—particularly foreign acquisitions of U.S. insurance companies—has increased in the last several years. While some of these companies seek to learn about U.S. methods, products, and markets, foreign insurers in general seem to be pursuing a wide range of business strategies. A foreign presence in the U.S. market should intensify competition and create opportunities for partnerships and capital.[66] Also, a wide range of intertwined computer and communications applications involving everything from protection against viruses and loss of data during the electronic transfer of funds is likely to develop.[67]

In addition, the property-casualty reinsurance business has been undergoing de facto consolidation as the big get bigger and the little companies disappear. The frequency of disasters such as hurricane Andrew has precipitated an extreme shakeout, including the departure of some of the industry's major insurers. On the other hand, this has enabled surviving reinsurers, such as General Reinsurance and National Reinsurance, to bolster their capital bases and form new strategic alliances. As demand for reinsurance from strong carriers increases, the major players and some new players, such as Mid Ocean Reinsurance, have been able to charge higher prices and demand stricter terms.[68]

The lessons that can be learned from the failures of a few large life insurance companies is that there is room for improvement of state regulation of insurance companies. Certainly, financial examinations must be made on a more regular basis. In the case of Mutual Benefit Life, the last record of examination of the company was filed in mid-1990 for the period 1982 to 1987. In the future, we will also see some prefunding of state guaranty funds so that money will be available to policyholders and annuitants more quickly when there is a regulatory seizure of a weakened or insolvent insurer. In the case of Mutual Benefit Life, the company was seized by regulators in April 1991, but as of July 1993, policyholders had not yet been reimbursed.

ENDNOTES

1. "Best's Insolvency Study Life/Health Insurers 1976–1991: Executive Summary and Recommendations," *Best's Insurance Management Reports,* June 1992, p. 2.

2. R. E. Randall and R. W. Kopcke, "The Financial Condition and Regulation of Insurance Companies: An Overview," *New England Economic Review,* May–June 1992, p. 34.

3. R. E. Litan, *The Revolution in U.S. Finance: Past, Present, and Future,* Frank M. Engle Lecture (Bryn Mawr, PA: American College, April 30, 1991), pp. 33–34.

4. F. Danner, "The Incredible Shrinking Insurance Industry," *Institutional Investor,* January 1990, p. 67.

5. B. Malkiel, "Assessing the Solvency of the Insurance Industry," *Journal of Financial Services Research,* May 1991, pp. 168, 178.

6. Ibid., p. 178.

7. B. Light and C. Farrell, "Are You Really Insured?" *Business Week,* August 5, 1991, pp. 43, 80.

8. S. Harrington, "Public Policy and Property-Liability Insurance," *Financial Condition and Regulation of Insurance Companies,* eds. R. Kopcke and R. Randall, Federal Reserve Bank of Boston Conference Proceedings, June 1991, p. 250.

9. "Another Plan for Executive Life," *Business Week,* April 19, 1993, p. 40.

10. "A.M. Best to Change Its Analysis Procedures for Insurance Firms," *The Wall Street Journal,* August 5, 1991, p. B4.

11. A. Saken, "Insurance: Opening the Books," *USA Today,* October 8, 1991, p. B1.

12. P. Wiseman and B. Montague, "Insurance: Opening the Books," *USA Today,* October 7, 1991, p. B2.

13. A. Saken, "Insurance: Opening the Books," *USA Today,* October 8, 1991, p. B2.

14. C. J. Loomis, "Victims of the Real Estate Crash," *Fortune,* May 18, 1992, pp. 76, 78.

15. R. W. Stevenson, "Court Ruling Sets Back Insurers," *New York Times,* June 19, 1991, p. D2.

16. A. Saken, "Insurance: Opening the Books," *USA Today,* November 8, 1991, p. B2.

17. C. Welles and C. Farrell, "Insurers Under Siege," *Business Week,* August 21, 1989, pp. 73–74.

18. R. Kopcke and R. Randall, "Insurance Companies as Financial Intermediaries," *Financial Condition and Regulation of Insurance Companies,* Federal Reserve Bank of Boston Conference Proceedings, June 1991, pp. 42–43.

19. F. D. Marsteller, "Good Hands," *Transition,* January 1992, p. 14.

20. S. S. Shalicky, "Discussion," *Financial Condition and Regulation of Insurance Companies,* eds. R. Kopcke and R. Randall, Federal Reserve Bank of Boston Conference Proceedings, June 1991, p. 196.

21. R. Stewart, "Needed Now: A National Guarantee Fund," *Insurance Review,* April 1991, p. 51.

22. *Best's Insolvency Study: Property/Casualty Insurance, 1969–1990* (Oldwick, NJ: A.M. Best Company, 1991), p. 1.

23. *Failed Promises: Insurance Company Insolvency,* a report on oversight and investigation of the Committee on Energy and Commerce, U.S. House of Representatives (Washington, DC: U.S. Government Printing Office, February 1990), p. 2.

24. Ibid., p. 2.

25. Ibid., p. 1.

26. *The Fact Book* (New York: Insurance Information Institute, 1991), p. 8.

27. *Best's Insolvency Study,* p. 2.

28. P. Passell, "Pricing Insurers Out of Business," *New York Times,* November 20, 1991, p. D2.

29. Randall and Kopcke, *Financial Condition and Regulation of Insurance Companies,* p. 42.

30. M. P. Duncan, "Property-Liability Post-Assessment Guaranty Funds," *Issues in Insurance,* II, ed. E. D. Randall (Malvern, PA: American Institute for Property and Liability Underwriters, 1987), p. 241.

31. E. N. Berg, "Life Insurance Failures Point Up Flaws in Safety Nets of States," *New York Times,* June 24, 1991, p. A1.

32. K. Wright, "The Structure, Conduct and Regulation of the Life Insurance Industry," *Financial Condition and Regulation of Insurance Companies,* eds. R. Kopcke and R. Randall, Federal Reserve Bank of Boston Conference Proceedings, June 1991, p. 93.

33. Stewart, p. 54.

34. Randall and Kopcke, *Financial Condition and Regulation of Insurance Companies,* p. 41.

35. Ibid., p. 23.

36. R. H. Jenrette and J. J. Melone, *The Equitable Policyholder Information Booklet,* Part II (New York: Equitable, March 1992), pp. 78–82.

37. Ibid.

38. M. Levinson, "A Deal They Can't Refuse," *Business Week,* April 29, 1992, p. 60.

39. P. Kerr, "Equitable Takes a Capital Step," *New York Times,* July 1, 1992, p. D8.

40. Levinson, p. 60.

41. A. Gart, *Banks, Thrifts and Insurance Companies: Surviving the Eighties* (Lexington, MA: Lexington Books, 1985), p. 112.

42. *Insurance Company Demutualization* (New York: Merrill Lynch Capital Markets, 1984).

43. Gart, p. 112.

44. Lawrence G. Brandon, *Sound a Clear Call* (Malvern, PA: CPCU Harry Loman Foundation, 1984), pp. 99–112.

45. Light and Farrell, p. 99.

46. "No Load Insurance: A Bigger Bang for Your Buck," *Business Week,* May 25, 1992, p. 134.

47. *Investor's Business Daily,* October 10, 1991, p. 34.

48. L. Greenhouse, "Law Upheld on Bank Insurance Sales," *New York Times,* June 8, 1993, p. D6.

49. P. Cooke, "Pitfalls Await in Any Mergers of Banks, Insurance,"￼ *American Banker,* May 31, 1991, p. 4.

50. "The Prophets of Profit," *Transition,* January 1992, p. 15.

51. J. Naisbitt, *Megatrends* (New York: Warner Books Inc., 1982).

52. J. Cohen, "Discussion of Insurance Companies as Financial Intermediaries," *Financial Condition and Regulation of Insurance Companies,* eds. R. Kopcke and R. Randall, Federal Reserve Bank of Boston Proceedings, June 1991, pp. 55–56.

53. R. Schneider, "Discussion of The Structure, Conduct and Regulation of the Life Insurance Industry," *Financial Condition and Regulation of Insurance Companies,* eds. R. Kopcke and R. Randall, Federal Reserve Bank of Boston Proceedings, June 1991, p. 114.

54. N. E. Felson and R. H. Dobson, "Insuring the Uninsured," *Emphasis,* 1990, pp. 3–5.

55. Ibid., pp. 1–5.

56. Ibid., p. 5.

57. R. Pullen, "Progress Slows on Health Care, Banking Bills; Industry Groups Split on McCarren-Ferguson Repeal," *Best's Insurance Management Reports,* August 5, 1991, p. 1.

58. O. Kramer, Rating the Risks (New York: Insurance Information Institute, 1990), p. 84.

59. Ibid., p. 84.

60. Ibid., p. x.

61. Ibid., p. 19.

62. Ibid., pp. ix, x.

63. Ibid., pp. 164–166.

64. Ibid., p. 9.

65. Ibid., pp. 105–107.

66. I. Leveson, *Financial Services: The Next Era* (Marlboro, NJ: Author, 1991).

67. Ibid.

68. T. Smout, C. Roush, and R. Melcher, "Insurers Scramble to Spread the Risks," *Business Week,* April 1992, pp. 98–99.

9 The Investment Banking and Securities Industry

When Drexel Burnham Lambert announced, shortly after 10:30 in the morning on February 13, 1990, that it was filing for Chapter 11 bankruptcy, the news set off declines in stock and bond prices on Wall Street. It was on that street that Drexel once raised large amounts of capital for firms, principally in leveraged buyout deals involving the issuance of junk debt. In fact, Drexel had originated the junk bond market—with the help of Mike Milken—and was the linchpin of the leveraged buyout market. . . . However, the junk bond business that led to Drexel's rise also led to its fall. . . . The problems began when the junk debt mastermind, Mike Milken, left his reign with Drexel, due to a mounting federal investigation of his allegedly illegal activities in securities. Next came the financial problems of several key LBO [leveraged buy-out] firms and the fall of the junk bond market. This had two harmful effects on Drexel. First, the revenues from LBO deals fell with the junk bond market, since LBO underwritings declined. Second, Drexel itself had a substantial position in junk bonds, so that losses in that market translated to significant declines in Drexel's own income. *

William L. Scott

The term *investment banking* was coined in the United States to distinguish the newly spun-off securities operations (underwriting and securities sales) from their former parents' commercial banking operations (taking deposits and providing loans) following the passage of the Glass-Steagall Act in 1933. Investment banking is now the term commonly applied to the activities of securities firms. These include their traditional function: locating and collecting funds so that clients can finance new or existing ventures. Initially, private bankers did little investment banking or securities underwriting. Investment banking remained a relatively quiet business until there was a need to fund the Civil War and the development of railroads in the United States. There was a dearth of raw materials for a securities business; even government securities were in short supply. This was in part related to the fact the U.S. economy was highly agrarian at the time.

Thomas A. Biddle founded the first investment banking house in the United States, in 1764 in Philadelphia. Shortly thereafter, Alexander Brown set up an

---

* Reprinted by permission from page 440 of *Contemporary Financial Markets and Services* by William L. Scott; Copyright © 1991 by West Publishing Company. All rights reserved.

investment banking house in Baltimore when he left his dry goods business. Many other general store proprietors and merchants who had been advancing credit to their customers in domestic trade made the transition from selling goods to selling credit. They included, among others, Goldman Sachs and Company; Lehman Brothers; Astor and Sons; Kuhn, Loeb, and Company; Morton Hutzler; and Corcoran and Raggis. Hutzler, a member of the Hutzler Department Store family in Philadelphia, joined two Salomon Brothers in a fledgling operation under the name Discount House of Salomon Brothers and Hutzler in 1907.

Until the intensive railroad building in the mid-1800s, financial services had been provided by auctioneers and speculators, foreign exchange brokers, shippers, merchants like Stephen Girard and John Jacob Astor, and unincorporated banks. By the 1840s, some of these individuals became private bankers dealing in securities transactions. Although America's need for capital lured representatives of European houses like the Rothchilds, the Barings, and the Speyers, a number of German-Jewish immigrants with commercial backgrounds, such as the Lehmans, Marcus Goldman, Abraham Kahn, and Solomon Loeb, moved from mercantile activities into private banking. Like the Yankee houses of Morgan and Lee, the Jewish firms prospered because of their access to European capital. The Jewish banking houses enjoyed the advantage of extensive family ties in different geographic locations.

Philadelphia financier Jay Cooke introduced aggressive sales tactics and a nationwide distribution system to help sell government notes to farmers during the Civil War. It was Cooke's idea to tap the universe of potential middle-class investors through a nationwide network of distribution agents supported by mass advertising and his appeal to patriotism. Cooke's willingness to support the price of securities in a secondary market defined a mix of salesmanship and managerial skill characteristic of post–Civil War underwriting. The concept of mass retailing had a distinctly American, rather than European, flavor.[1]

The market for financial services changed to relationship banking during the 1870s. Bankers were actively influencing the policies of client companies through board memberships, supplying technical assistance with new issues and supporting newly issued securities in the aftermarket. Long-term loyalties between banker and corporate client developed, and selected investment houses became "principal bankers" to many companies through these valued relationships. Such relationships created a substantial and ongoing income that helped attract talented people to investment banking.[2]

The richness of U.S. cattle and agriculture enterprises, the discovery of gold in California, and the end of the Civil War created an unprecedented demand for the building of railroads to transport people, mail, and freight. The role of the merchant banker was to supply a steady stream of capital. Later, when the century of railroad building came to an end, merchant bankers recapitalized the industry by refinancing and restructuring existing issues. Railroads formed the seed of American industrialization, becoming responsible for shipping coal, steel, and other manufactured metals that were in growing demand in part because of railroad construction.

Not until the establishment of the Interstate Commerce Commission (ICC) in 1887 to regulate the railroad industry's excesses, prevent exploitation of the public, and secure competition were the practices of the capitalists of the transportation industry restrained. The Sherman Anti-Trust Act, passed in 1890, prohibited the restraint of trade and the creation of monopolies, but did not bar either horizontal or vertical mergers. The Act established a policy whereby all industry would be monitored through the Office of the Attorney General. The passage of the Clayton Act in 1914 enlarged the scope of the initial antitrust initiative and established the Federal Trade Commission (FTC) as a regulatory agency. The FTC was concerned with establishing standards, rather than with resolving disputes between adversaries. The Clayton Act provided for public-interest appraisals of the consequences of lessened competition in markets that were affected by mergers. This new spirit of reform and regulation had a decisive impact on the investment banking industry. From 1898 to 1902, there was a huge wave of horizontal mergers. The period was one of increased activity for the rapidly developing U.S. investment banking industry and created a financial bonanza for investment bankers.[3]

Concurrently with the merger boom, the government sector required substantial funds that were provided by the public marketplace. The United States was a net importer of capital prior to 1900, but became a net exporter of capital by the end of World War I. As an instrument of foreign policy, the State Department encouraged foreign borrowing through U.S. investment bank underwritings. The most important source of both debt and equity capital before World War I had been wealthy Americans. However, the newly established U.S. income tax and other events channeled their capital to alternative investments. During the war, the individual investor of more modest means emerged in the public marketplace, through the Liberty bond campaigns. By the late 1920s, individual investors held the overwhelming share of corporate equities and about 50 percent of public debt securities.

EARLY INVESTMENT BANKERS

The investment bankers of the early 1900s focused on the financial needs of large private corporations and foreign governments and on the banking requirements of the rich. The commercial bankers focused on taking deposits and offering loans. Many commercial banks joined the booming securities business of the 1920s, since there were no laws to restrict them. The traditionally dominant private banks enjoyed the bulk of the underwriting business in the early post–World War I period. However, commercial bank participation in the underwriting of securities picked up substantially during the 1920s. The commercial banks carved out a different market than the investment banks did—one comprised of companies that were new to the public markets and were of a lesser quality than the clients of the private bankers. In the 1920s, the use of underwriting syndicates expanded rapidly to distribute the increased volume of securities being created. Historically, the leading securities firms bought entire offerings of securities and sold them directly or indirectly by forming selling groups comprised of other firms with strong distribution facilities. These issues often took a few months to distribute and added to the underwriting risk. With the dramatic increase in underwritings came lax underwriting standards and the investigation of the 1920s, which would haunt the securities vendors in the 1930s. The unprofessional approaches, blatant excesses, misconduct, and fraudulent activities among securities firms led to a strong congressional reaction during the Great Depression that produced reform legislation known as the New Deal. From 1933 to 1940, the Roosevelt Administration formulated additional reform legislation that featured the disclosure of information for the purpose of "letting in the light" to reveal the true facts about issuers' affairs and their overall business health. New Deal legislation included the Glass-Steagall Act, the Securities Acts of 1933 and 1934, the Public Utility Holding Company Act of 1935, the Trust Indenture Act of 1939, the Investment Company Act of 1940, and the Investment Advisers Act of 1940. An unintended negative consequence of the legislation was the artificial separation of powers and the reduction in the possibilities for effective competition among vendors of financial services.

The industry status quo began to unravel in the 1970s. There was a political shift toward deregulation and an increase in competition among conventional securities firms, as well as incursions by nonconventional U.S. vendors and foreign firms. Developments in telecommunications and computer technology, as well as deregulation, acted as a catalyst to increase competition. By the end of the 1980s, successive assaults on the status quo had altered the playing field dramatically and changed the players in the financial services industry that were set into play by the reform legislation of the 1930s. The Glass-Steagall Act that separated commercial from investment banking began to erode. During the mid-1980s, many bank holding companies were allowed to underwrite mortgage-backed securities, municipal revenue bonds, and commercial paper. By 1989, the Federal Reserve had granted some of the largest U.S. banks the right to establish separately incorporated and capitalized securities affiliates within the bank holding company framework in order to underwrite and trade in all corporate debt instruments. In 1990, four bank holding company subsidiaries were permitted to underwrite corporate equities. These actions by the central bank authorized bank involvement in corporate underwriting for the first time in half a century.

CONSEQUENCES OF GLASS-STEAGALL AND THE SECURITIES ACTS

One of the major consequences of the Glass Steagall Act was the abrupt separation of securities underwriting from deposit taking. This bifurcation had a profound impact on the subsequent development of the U.S. securities industry and, following World War II, on the Japanese securities industry, as a consequence of the U.S. occupation of Japan. Glass-Steagall fundamentally recast the financial services community and led to the establishment of a cartellike environment with specific product and service demarcations that might be characterized as separation of business and, consequently, less competition. As a matter of fact, Congress created a protected industry for the investment bankers, an industry that was effectively safe from any challenge by commercial banks. Other major consequences of the Glass-Steagall Act, the Securities Act of 1933, and the Securities and Exchange Act were the establishment of the FDIC and the SEC. The accounting profession was also a major beneficiary of the passage of the aforementioned acts, especially with the passage of due diligence requirements, as someone had to generate the financial information required under the new legislation.

The securities firms spun off in the aftermath of Glass-Steagall had relatively small capital bases, few employees, and only a limited amount of underwriting and other business because the economic malaise of the Depression lasted almost until World War II began. The extensive postwar economic expansion that began in the 1950s was characterized by robust secular growth, low inflation, a strong dollar, and a favorable U.S. balance of payments. Generally speaking, this was a period of prosperity for U.S. securities firms, which emerged as the principal counselors to the U.S. corporate sector. This development probably occurred because most of the investment banks were direct descendants of the 19th-century private banks that had developed strong relationships with many leading corporations. By controlling the flow of new securities, the investment banks could also exercise substantial influence over the smaller and more fragmented retail securities firms that were developing all over the nation, as the American public became enamored with the stock market. This degree of control emanated from the fact that the small firms had extensive overhead costs and were therefore quite dependent on the commissions that resulted from primary market issues.[4]

ROLE IN UNDERWRITING SYNDICATES

The companies with the most impressive and financially active customer base were in the driver's seat and were regularly accorded the most favored positions in Wall Street underwriting syndicates. Their names always appeared at the top of an underwriting tombstone, even if they were not a managing underwriter. Behind them came about 18 firms that were considered major forces in generating new financing business, and these firms were given major bracket status in tombstones on an alphabetical basis. Next came junior bracket firms that "knew their place" and usually accepted this arrangement in order to share in the available business, which they needed to help cover their relatively high overhead. The "special" bracket firms that dominated public underwritings were Morgan Stanley, First Boston, Dillon Read, and Kuhn Loeb.[5]

RISE OF SALOMON BROTHERS AND MERRILL LYNCH

The 1960s witnessed numerous consolidations among the retail-oriented firms that increased their competitive clout somewhat. During the period, the economy continued to expand, as did profits on Wall Street. The leadership of some of the aspiring retail firms utilized this sustained period of prosperity to challenge the firms that had dominated the apex positions in underwriting since the passage of Glass-Steagall. The institutional investor emerged as a powerful marketing focus for a number of securities firms. The new players included Merrill Lynch; Donaldson, Lufkin & Jenrette; and Salomon Brothers. Donaldson, Lufkin & Jenrette built a major position by producing sophisticated research for institutional investors. Merrill Lynch created an efficient organization to service the retail customer profitably, while building up its research capability. Salomon Brothers progressed from an obscure money broker and marginal player in the securities markets to a world-class underwriter and trader that concentrated on developing its trading and secondary market skills to handle large institutional trades of both stocks and bonds. In the early post–World War II period, Salomon had almost no presence in origination, especially of equities, and no position at all in mergers, acquisitions, and corporate reorganizations. As a matter of fact, neither Salomon nor Merrill Lynch was included among the 17 firms named in the Justice Department's 1947 antitrust suit against the investment banking industry. The omission—and indeed the filing of the suit—reflected the tight clubbish configuration of the American securities industry at that time.[6]

The inflationary pressures of the 1970s, with the accompanying volatility of interest rates, deregulation in the financial sector, growth of offshore markets and globalization, and securitization of formerly illiquid assets and liabilities, created openings for Salomon Brothers. Another door was opened to firms like Salomon Brothers when the SEC required utility companies to use competitive bidding instead of negotiated underwritings to raise debt capital. The ICC required railroads also to use competitive bidding in the public underwriting of debt issues. Salomon aggressively entered the competitive bid side of both utility and railroad underwritings. The company also developed great expertise in the competitive bid market for municipal bonds. Salomon focused its research on debt securities under the direction of Sidney Homer, Henry Kaufmann, and Martin Leibowitz. The research department provided analyses of the institutional investors' market, interest rates and the economy. The department pioneered new research on the duration and convexity of debt markets. The quality of the qualitative and quantitative research by Salomon Brothers' intellectual cadre of Ph.Ds, affectionately referred to as "rocket scientists," who blazed trails in synthesizing new securities and building the information systems needed to establish liquid markets for trading and arbitrage in a variety of new financial instruments. Salomon, Blythe, Lehman Brothers, and Merrill Lynch banded together in 1963 to form the "Fearsome Foursome" underwriting group, breaking away from the established bidding groups, which limited their advancement in syndicated groups, despite their exceptional performance in the distribution of securities issues. The move shocked Wall Street because for years there had existed only two competing syndicates, one led by Halsey, Stuart and the other led by Morgan Stanley (to which the "Fearsome Foursome" had belonged and continued to belong for smaller deals). The "Fearsome Foursome" enjoyed immense success, with Salomon Brothers eventually becoming the leader in competitive bidding for utility and municipal bonds. The new success in competitive bidding and debt underwriting led Salomon to form a bank research group in 1963 and then an industry and stock research department in 1969. As a result of the advances made by both Salomon Brothers and Merrill Lynch, these two distribution-oriented firms were gradually accepted into the charmed circle of the special bracket of U.S. underwriting firms in 1971. Kuhn Loeb and Dillon Reed were demoted to major bracket status because of their inability to keep up with the distribution power of Salomon and Merrill. At the same time, Donaldson, Lufkin & Jenrette was elevated to major bracket status.[7] The placement power of Merrill Lynch among both institutional and retail investors with over 10,000 salespeople is substantial and the envy of many firms. In addition, Merrill developed one of the top equity research departments among Wall Street firms. Merrill Lynch research department analysts have continued to win an above-average number of positions on the coveted Institutional Investor All-America Research Team.

During 1991, Merrill Lynch ranked first in market share of total U.S. debt and equity underwritings, as well as first in global underwritings. Merrill Lynch has also taken the lead among larger firms in automating stock orders. Its system uses a standard IBM personal computer, which sits on every broker's desk. When a client calls to place an order to buy a stock listed on either the New York Stock Exchange or the American Exchange, brokers use computers to place the order directly into the electronic execution system on the appropriate exchanges. They receive a confirmation of trades within seconds. The new system enables stockbrokers to bypass the slower, traditional system of writing tickets that described the transaction to buy or sell a security. Those tickets were then sent to clerks, who wired the order to a broker on the floor of the designated exchange. Merrill expects to save about $400,000–$700,000 per year by using the system, because fewer clerks and floor brokers will be needed. In addition to this cost-saving feature, under the new system branch managers should be able to exert greater supervisory control over salespeople. For example, the computer can be programmed to screen out particular trades and refuse to execute them if management feels that they are too risky. The system could also be used to prevent the execution of trades in which brokers have agreed to give customers a commission discount beyond a fixed percentage.[8]

GOING PUBLIC

Many brokerage firms were overwhelmed during the 1969–70 period by the huge increase in trading volume toward the end of the bull market. The leading securities firms were literally buried in paperwork. The New York Stock Exchange closed each Wednesday in an effort to unclog the processing of stock certificates and broken trades and the mass of record keeping. Some brokerage firms (e.g., Goodbody, DuPont, and Walston) disappeared or merged when their back offices could not handle the increased trading volume. Most surviving firms went public between the late 1960s and the early 1980s as a means of financing growth and raising permanent capital. The balance sheets of wholesale firms grew from a typical $100 million at the beginning of the 1970s to $30 billion by the end of the 1980s. Public issuance of stock on behalf of securities firms broke the prohibition of the New York Stock Exchange that barred member firms from being publicly owned. This public issuance bailed out some senior partners with substantial equity investments who were alarmed by adverse market and industry developments. The raising of public capital also allowed firms to serve the expanding institutional sector better and to cushion themselves from the consequences of volatile swings in earnings. Donaldson, Lufkin & Jenrette; Merrill Lynch; Dean Witter; Paine Webber; Bache; Hutton; and Shearson Hayden Stone went public in the late 1960s and early 1970s.

In the 1980s, several firms decided to go public or to link up with large companies with deep financial pockets. In addition to needing more capital, some owners (partners) decided to go public because prices were extremely attractive to them. Salomon Brothers went public in the 1980s. Before then, the firm had concentrated on building its capital base and had adopted strict rules on withdrawals by partners. Goldman Sachs, which still remains a partnership, also concentrated on capital building during both the 1970s and 1980s.[9]

FOREIGN PARTNERS, GLOBALIZATION, FINANCIAL CONGLOMERATES, AND CONSOLIDATION

The United States is a major center of trading in international securities. Foreign transactions in U.S. markets exceed U.S. transactions in foreign markets by a ratio of almost 7 to 1. This is a result of several factors. First, the United States has the largest and most developed securities markets in the world. Second, U.S. equity markets are virtually free of controls on foreign involvement. Third, SEC regulations on disclosure dissipate much uncertainty concerning the issuers of publicly listed securities in the United States, while less or even inadequate regulation in other countries makes investments more risky in those foreign markets. Finally, the market for U.S. Treasury securities has been attractive to foreign investors; in fact, large purchases of these securities by the Japanese have helped finance the U.S. budget deficit.

Shearson, Goldman Sachs, Paine Webber, Blackstone, and Wasserstein Perella have each invited one major Japanese institutional investor to buy a substantial minority interest in their firm to expand their capital base and make themselves more accessible to foreign investors. (See Table 9.1.) Soon, insurance companies and other financial and retail companies began to purchase securities firms. For example, Equitable purchased Donaldson, Lufkin & Jenrette; Prudential purchased Bache; John Hancock purchased Tucker Anthony; American Express purchased Shearson, and then Shearson purchased Lehman Brothers and E.F. Hutton; GE purchased Kidder Peabody; and Sears purchased Dean Witter Reynolds. Another salient change that affected the securities industry significantly came on May 1, 1975, when the SEC moved to abolish fixed-rate commissions. Commissions declined

Table 9.1 Japanese Ownership of U.S. Investment Banks

U.S. Investment Bank	Japanese Investor	% of Equity/$ Investment
Shearson Lehman	Nippon Life	13.0/508 million
Goldman Sachs	Sumitomo Bank	12.5/500 million
Paine Webber	Yashuda Life	20.0/300 million
Blackstone Group	Nikko Securities	20.0/100 million
Wasserstein Perella	Nomura Securities	20.0/100 million

immediately, to between 40 and 50 percent of the earlier fixed-rate levels. This change brought severe pressure on research "boutiques" that specialized in security analysis and "soft-dollar" commissions. These firms had given their research recommendations to institutions that gave them rich chunks of their commissioned trading business. More consolidations followed, as "boutiques" like Mitchell Hutchins and H.W. Wainwright were unable to cover their overhead expenses and were either liquidated or forced to merge. In addition, corporate clients sought more efficient ways of obtaining the services of Wall Street, and pressure developed on underwriting spreads. Many leading European and Japanese investment banking and securities firms have become extremely active in the U.S. marketplace on their own, without any alliance with a U.S. securities firm. Among the most prominent Japanese and British firms that have done so are Nomura (the world's largest brokerage firm), Nikko, Daiwa, Yamaichi, Hambros, Hill Samuel, Morgan Grenfell, and Kleinwart Benson. This is related to their own clients' interests in the U.S. market, the trend toward globalization in the money and capital markets, the opportunity to become "Federal Reserve recognized primary U.S. government dealers," and the desire to satisfy their own need for market information and deal making in U.S. securities. The Japanese are making a concerted effort to penetrate the U.S. investment banking market, but they have met with limited success. The big four—Nomura Securities, Daiwa Securities, Nikko Securities, and Yamaichi Securities—expanded in the United States in the mid-1980s, but have scaled back personnel due to highly cyclical earnings and occasional unprofitable U.S. operations. Two of the big four—Nomura and Yamaichi—have been trying to model their U.S. operations as identifiable Wall Street companies, and not just subsidiaries of Tokyo firms, by their appointment of Americans to head their U.S. operations. Nomura's strengths have been its primary dealership in U.S. Government securities and U.S. stock trading unit, primarily for Japanese purchase. Nomura's weaknesses, however, are its lack of financial product development and its trading skills.

The Japanese have been more successful in U.S. derivative markets. In April 1988, Nikko Securities became the first Japanese securities firm to acquire a clearing membership at the Chicago Board of Trade (CBOT). Since then, 15 others have joined the CBOT. The Chicago Mercantile Exchange (CME) has 17 Japanese companies as members. Nikko, Daiwa, and Yamaichi are members of both the CBOT and CME.

Three American investment banks, Salomon Brothers, Merrill Lynch, and First Boston, have been able to develop profitable operations in the Tokyo market. All three attribute their success to a well-trained staff, to hiring Japanese college graduates to fill positions, and to being niche players. However, the strength of U.S. firms abroad lies primarily in Europe. U.S. investment banking firms are active in corporate and government underwritings in the Eurocurrency markets and in merger and acquisition work. In the area of securities underwriting, U.S. firms are quite strong. Seven of the top 10 underwriters of debt and equity securities worldwide are U.S. firms; however, only three U.S. firms rank among the top underwriters of non-U.S. securities.

Greater demand for international financing is stimulating important changes in financial markets, especially in Europe. Regulations and procedures designed to shield domestic markets from foreign competition are gradually being dismantled. London's position as an international market was strengthened by the lack of sophistication of many other European markets. Greater demand for equity financing in Europe has been encouraged by private companies and by governments that privatized large public-sector corporations. These measures to deregulate and, therefore, improve efficiency, regulatory organizations, and settlement procedures are a response to competition from other markets and the explosion of securities trading in the 1980s. The changes suggest opportunities for continued underwriting and trading profits abroad. Former communist and socialist countries have begun a transition to largely capitalist economies without the benefit of a modern financial system. There will be large demands for capital from these countries, as well as from third world nations such as Kuwait, Iraq, Iran, and China. Investment banking and commercial banking companies must be poised to respond intelligently to these opportunities.[10]

There is much excitement among investment bankers stemming from the potential of China's equities. Among numerous possibilities are taking Chinese companies public in China and the United States, brokering joint ventures between U.S. and Chinese companies, and teaming up with the Chinese government in making direct investments in infrastructure-related projects, such as building highways, bridges, mass transportation systems, and theme parks. While little has as yet come from investment banking forays into China, Eastern Europe, and the former Soviet Union, the potential is enormous, and U.S. investment banking firms are hoping for a bonanza.

THE RISE AND FALL OF DREXEL BURNHAM LAMBERT

The importance of a firm's capital base was underscored when Drexel Burnham Lambert, the junk (i.e., non-investment-grade) bond and leveraged buy-out star performer of the 1980s, filed for chapter 11 bankruptcy protection in 1990. Drexel took advantage of the opportunities to create new products for a price-sensitive market, exploiting windows of opportunity in the capital markets under the leadership of Michael Milken. Almost single-handedly, Drexel created a primary and secondary market in junk bonds to aid the financing of leveraged buy-outs and mergers. Being innovators in the use of new-issue junk bonds and preempting a commanding position as the leader in this high-margined market led to the initial success of Drexel. However, as bond prices deteriorated and a number of Drexel-aided clients filed for bankruptcy protection following leveraged buy-outs, Drexel's special position as market leader in junk bonds was undermined. In addition, legal difficulties arose, and the value of the inventory of junk bonds was questioned by outside suppliers of capital. As a result, Drexel could no longer fund itself in the commercial paper market or from the commercial banks, and the company was forced into reorganization. Drexel was considered a renegade firm, and no one on Wall Street was willing to rescue it or buy it out. The company was fined $650 million by the government for its trading scandals and other fraudulent activities. Milken was sentenced to a 10-year prison term for violating securities laws in connection with corruption in the junk bond division. He is also certain to be sanctioned by the New York Stock Exchange. Later, Frederick H. Joseph, former chief executive officer of Drexel Burnham Lambert, was censured by the New York Stock Exchange and barred from associating with member firms for two years. Joseph was cited for his failure to carry out proper supervision that might have prevented the scandal that led to the firm's collapse.

Michael Milken and other officials of Drexel Burnham Lambert have negotiated a settlement of civil claims under which they would pay $1.3 billion to savings and loan regulatory agencies, states, and institutional and individual investors.[11] Milken was later sentenced to a long prison term for securities law violations and agreed to pay an additional $700 million to settle other claims. He was released early from his incarceration after serving about a 2-year prison term.

In June 1992, the SEC filed insider trading charges against seven corporate executives and investors, including Edward A. Downe, Jr., husband of an auto heiress and a former vice-director of Bear Stearns, for wrongdoings that occurred in the late 1980s at the height of the trading scandals that brought down Drexel, tarnished Kidder Peabody, and sent Michael Milken and others to jail. According to Columbia University law professor John C. Coffee, Jr., the entire Drexel Burnham Lambert affair "shows that insider trading will always be with us because, by definition, it involves a combination of very high potential profit and relatively small risk of detection compared to other crimes."[12]

SALOMON BROTHERS SCANDAL OF 1991

On the heels of the Japanese brokerage scandal, the drug and money-laundering activities of the Bank of Credit and Commerce International (BCCI) in 1991, the junk bond debacle of Drexel Burnham Lambert in 1989–90, and the insider trading problems of the late 1980s, the admission of improper Treasury note and bond dealings at Salomon Brothers, Inc., in August 1991 could help brand the recent decade as one of vanishing trust in financial markets. According to R. W. Fogel, an economist at the University of Chicago, "Moral issues are increasingly becoming the political issues of our age. . . . Wall Street is one of the arenas in the struggle for a moral life."[13]

Salomon Brothers admitted that it had lied to the government, faked customers' orders to circumvent government rules limiting bidding to 35 percent of the securities offered in Treasury auctions, and violated other rules by illegally bidding in possibly as many as eight Treasury note and bond auctions. Senior management delayed five months in informing the U.S. Treasury that it knew about the last of these, in which the firm bought more than its legal share of Treasury securities. For example, Salomon controlled 94 percent of a new issue of two-year Treasury notes in May 1991. By owning the lion's share of the securities, the firm was able to dictate prices and receive a financial advantage at the expense of other companies.

In August 1991, government regulators launched criminal and civil investigations of Salomon's Treasury activities. Salomon faced possible criminal fines because of the fraudulent customer orders and potential civil damages when shareholders and market dealers sued the firm for fraud. As of year-end 1991, Treasury investors, Salomon stockholders, and competitors had already filed over three dozen civil suits against Salomon, its former top executives, and its board of directors.

Ultimately, Salomon fired the head of government trading and his chief deputy, suspended several employees involved in the auctions, and then announced the resignation of Chairman John H. Gutfreund, President Thomas W. Strauss, and Vice-Chairman John Meriweather. Later, the chief general counsel of Salomon was also forced to resign. Warren E. Buffet, a well-regarded, wealthy investor and owner of a large position of convertible preferred shares of Salomon, was named acting chairman. The government's options included fining the firm, suspending it from further trading of Treasury securities, and/or bringing criminal charges against the firm. Following a 10-month investigation, Salomon agreed to pay $290 million in fines to the U.S. Treasury. The fine is the second largest for wrongdoing on Wall Street, behind the $650 million paid by the now-defunct Drexel Burnham Lambert in the 1980s. The Salomon settlement with the SEC and the Justice Department includes $190 million in fines and forfeitures related to cheating in the Treasury auctions and a $100 million fund to compensate victims who lost money as a result of the wrongdoing. Without admitting or denying wrongdoing, Salomon settled SEC charges of violating antifraud and record-keeping provisions of federal securities laws. However, the Justice Department decided against criminal charges. Otto Obermaier, the Manhattan U.S. attorney, said Salomon was spared criminal indictment because it had cooperated extensively in the investigation and restructured its management to prevent future misconduct. A guilty plea to criminal charges would have made it more difficult for Salomon to do business with certain countries and states. As part of the settlement, Salomon Brothers was suspended from trading with the Federal Reserve Bank of New York for two months beginning June 1, 1992. Also, effective August 3, 1992, the U.S. Treasury lifted sanctions imposed on Salomon in 1991, allowing the firm to resume bids for customers in the Treasury auctions.[14]

Individuals linked to wrongdoing are likely to face stiff penalties and jail terms. Plea bargaining with prosecutors is likely. This appears to be the situation in the case of Paul Mozer, the former chief Treasury trader at Salomon, who has been cooperating with federal investigators in an attempt to strike a plea bargain agreement. As of this writing, Mozer had not yet struck a bargain with prosecutors to provide damaging evidence against his superiors, and he hasn't been able to supply material evidence implicating other securities firms.

Salomon has confirmed that a number of large institutional clients have stopped doing business with the firm because of the scandal and that the firm has lost substantial underwriting business. For example, the United Kingdom removed Salomon Brothers from the position of lead U.S. manager in the partial sale of the UK Telecom Group. Salomon has also found funding to be more difficult and more costly, as multibillion-dollar lines of credit from commercial banks had to be arranged to replace much of its commercial paper. The remaining outstanding commercial paper is backed by bank lines of credit. Faced with higher borrowing costs, Salomon has also been forced to sell large holdings of securities. Despite all of these problems and the severe fine, Salomon officials felt that with the case resolved, they should be able to lure back investment banking clients who shied away from having the firm handle their lead underwriting duties. Even without these clients, Salomon Brothers had its third best quarter ever during the first quarter of 1992.

Because of the uncertainty of Salomon's future, corporate restructuring, and the uncertainty of future bonus money and profit-sharing arrangements, Salomon has lost at least a dozen key executives to other Wall Street firms. Under Buffet, Salomon has also eliminated a few departments, reduced staff in many other departments, and cut overhead.

Once dubbed "the King of Wall Street" by *Business Week,* John Gutfreund spoke of Salomon as the "greatest trading organization the world has ever known" during the mid-1980s. According to Michael Lewis, former Salomon bond salesman and author of *Liar's Poker* (a book that gave an account of the arrogance and power that came to define Salomon in the 1980s), management often acted as if the rules didn't apply to Salomon: "You acquire a sense of being above the rules." Congressman Edward (D–MA), who chairs a house subcommittee that oversees Treasury bond trading, blamed lax regulations for permitting Salomon to display a "cavalier disregard for the rules." Congressman Gonzalez (D–TX), asked that Salomon be barred from its role as a primary dealer of Treasury securities until it has demonstrated an ability to control its operations. Responding to the Salomon Brothers scandal, the U.S. Treasury Department announced that, effective November 5, 1991, government debt auctions were open to all registered securities broker–dealer firms, abolishing the elite club of 39 primary dealers that dominated the purchase and resale of government debt instruments. The new rule allows any registered securities broker–dealer to bid on behalf of customers in U.S. Treasury auctions of bills, notes, and bonds. Another rule change allows bidders to enter auctions without putting up a deposit or guarantee, as long as they have signed a special agreement in advance.

When customers lose trust in an established firm, the firm can be destroyed. Scandals have destroyed established firms such as E.F. Hutton and Drexel Burnham

Lambert. The steps taken by Warren Buffet to come clean and reveal all reduced the government's need to punish the company or its officers, said Bruce Baird, the government lawyer who prosecuted Drexel Burnham Lambert.[15]

We are likely to see some or all of the following changes in U.S. securities laws:

1. The use of false or inaccurate information on Treasury auction bids will be a violation of securities law.
2. Sales practice rules will be imposed on dealers and investors in bonds.
3. Treasury dealers will be required to set up mandatory procedures within their firms to detect bidding or trading irregularities.
4. Large-position traders will be required to report on the positions held by their major clients.
5. The SEC will be given the power to oversee how prices and trading information are distributed in the market.
6. Plans to automate the Treasury auction market will be accelerated.
7. Written verification will be required for large winning bids in the Treasury auction, in order to guarantee their authenticity and to prevent the kind of phony bidding that Salomon said was executed without its customers' authorizations in an effort to corner the market in government bonds.

In mid-September 1992, the U.S. Treasury launched a one-year trial utilizing a Dutch auction to help sell its two-year and five-year notes. Under the old auction rules, each bid was entered by a sealed order submitted to the Federal Reserve, the fiscal agent of the Treasury. The U.S. Treasury then awarded securities to the bidders who offered to take the lowest yields and continued awarding notes to the next lowest bidders. The method created a "winner's curse" that penalized the highest bidders by forcing them to accept yields below what other bidders would take. Under the Dutch auction rules, although the Treasury would still grant the notes to the lowest bidders, it would sell all the securities at the same price—specifically, the highest yield accepted in the auction. It was hoped that firms would bid more aggressively because there was no "winner's curse." The risk of bidding too strongly was eliminated by having bonds awarded at the highest yields. The Dutch auction strategy has led to a larger share of the winning bids going to those who bid less than the highest winning yield accepted by the Treasury. In addition, the Dutch auction has led to a wider distribution of bids accepted by the Treasury than under the old auction system.

While probing the Salomon scandal, Richard C. Breeden, SEC chairman, disclosed that other firms and banks have placed false orders for debt issues and may have intentionally misled other government agencies and federally backed lenders, such as the Federal National Mortgage Association and the Federal Home Loan Mortgage Corporation (Freddie Mac) that sell hundreds of billions of dollars in securities to the public. Freddie Mac imposed the first penalties against the securities industry for abuses in the sale of government agency–sponsored bonds, fining 18 of 25 investment or commercial banks that sell its debt. Freddie Mac announced that it was seeking fines of about $1 million, or 20 percent of the firms' commissions from the government-sponsored agency's debt sales over the past two years, to punish dealer groups that inflated orders or faked written confirmations. Although the size of the fines was not large, it still worried many dealer firms, since the fines might set a precedent for action by other agencies, many of which are several times larger and more important to the dealer community than Freddie Mac. The SEC is also considering taking legal action against members of selling groups of the agencies who cheated their customers out of interest or who falsified their records. Also, overordering by dealers has been a standard practice in the underwriting of Treasury and agency debt, in order to obtain a bigger share of the overall offering of securities.

The U.S. Department of Justice's antitrust division, extending its focus beyond Salomon, is investigating evidence that there may have been widespread collusion and price-fixing by a number of firms that participate in the Treasury securities market. In addition, the SEC has asked Salomon employees many questions about the government trading desk and the firm's relationship with Steinhardt Partners and other securities firms, including questions about whether they attempted to "park" securities temporarily with the understanding that they would later be repurchased. Any such arrangement violates securities laws. The SEC has alleged that to create phony losses, Salomon covered up existing short positions—in which it had previously sold borrowed Treasury securities—by buying Treasury securities from another firm. By prearrangement, Salomon then reestablished its original short positions by selling the same securities back to other firms. These prearranged trades were illegal because they did not entail any investment risk. Consequently, the losses are not real losses for tax purposes. The government alleged that in 1986, Salomon falsely paid lower income taxes by claiming $168 million in fake trading losses. The charge that Salomon had cheated the government on its taxes was the only surprise in the SEC complaint, which accused Salomon of falsifying customers' orders at Treasury auctions, inflating bids, and making false or inadequate disclosures in bidding for both Treasury and Resolution Trust Corporation bonds. In a move that underscores Salomon's changing attitude under Warren Buffet, the firm announced a large management shake-up in November 1991 in which the firm's board of directors and management were replaced. In addition, it appeared as if power would be spread across more Salomon divisions, with cuts coming in equity research, trading, and investment banking. Further restructurings and appointments were made in May 1992, in preparation for Salomon's management in the post-Buffet era.

MONEY MARKET MUTUAL FUNDS

In 1972–1973, the money market mutual fund was spawned. This new financial instrument, which gravely affected depository institutions, gave investors money market yields and liquidity. Check-writing privileges and an 800 telephone number gave investors immediate access to their funds. Double-digit inflation and rising interest rates hurt stock prices and frightened investors out of the long-term bond market. The money market fund proved to be a good place to park money with minimal risk and a money market rate of return, previously limited to large institutional investors or wealthy individuals. While initially a diversion of customer funds from what had been free-credit balances, money market mutual funds grew to be extremely large multibillion-dollar liquidity pools that earned attractive management fees for their sponsoring securities firms. They acted as a catalyst in creating more disintermediation at depository institutions, which were limited in the rates that they could pay on deposits by Regulation Q. Banks and thrifts lost substantial portions of what had been their core deposit bases to these new money market mutual funds. Merrill Lynch's introduction of the cash management account in 1977 was an event that affected the savings patterns of individuals. Every retail brokerage firm rushed to duplicate it, in order to prevent encroachment on their customers' free-credit balances and defection by those very customers. Retail securities firms offered their customers dividend- and interest-collection services and a sweep of these available balances into money market funds that gave current market yields and liquidity. They also offered their customers check-writing privileges. In addition to generating income from management fees, the cash management account gave account executives a good handle on the availability of their customers' funds.

DISCOUNT BROKERAGE

After May 1, 1975, a number of discount brokerage firms sprang up to service retail customers. Initially, the share of the retail market captured by discounters was minimal. However, as banks and insurance companies watched money market funds erode their core deposit bases and the commercial paper market erode blue-chip client lending bases, they pushed quickly into new services and began their campaign to repeal the Glass-Steagall Act. Many bank holding companies began to offer discount brokerage services to their customers. Although profits from these operations have been disappointing and even nonexistent at depository institutions, many banks feel that the continued relationship with the client aids in the cross-selling of many more profitable services.

In addition to standard discount brokerage firms, where discounts range from 40 to 60 percent of the commissions charged by full-line service firms, there are deep discount brokers, where commissions are available for up to 90 percent of the commissions charged by firms such as Prudential or Shearson Lehman. The deep discount brokers offer only execution of buy and sell orders, whereas the standard discount brokers also offer modest amounts of research and newsletters. Most of the discount brokers that are not affiliated with banks or thrifts are highly profitable. It is estimated that discount brokerage firms service approximately 20 percent of the transactions of retail customers.

CONSEQUENCES OF SHELF REGISTRATION ON UNDERWRITING SPREADS

The practices of securitization and shelf registration also played to the strengths of well-capitalized firms such as Salomon, Goldman Sachs, and Merrill Lynch. SEC rule 415 (shelf registration) shifted the market toward big, quick debt financing, which benefited and required underwriters with large capital bases and fast distribution and trading capabilities to handle aggressive underwriting commitments. Salomon capitalized on the innovations of its band of Ph.D.s in developing conventional pass-through securities, variable pass-through securities, the securitization of other mortgages, automobile and credit card loans, zero-coupon Treasury securities, computer leases, and many other new instruments.

The gross spreads or fees on conventional debt offerings came under increasing pressure by corporate issuers, in part related to shelf registrations, increased competition, and the use of the Euromarkets by both U.S. and foreign borrowers, which offered shorter regulatory time delays and lower underwriting spreads and expenses. These spreads became considerably lower than they were five years earlier. In regard to shelf registrations, the offerings did lead to cost savings for issuers and de facto competitive bidding. This benefited Salomon Brothers at the expense of Morgan Stanley, a traditional investment banker. However, Morgan Stanley benefited later from a concurrent renewal of merger-and-acquisition activity. The increase in this activity was spawned by low stock prices and cash-rich buyers. Some companies were selling at prices substantially below the cost of replacing their plant or equipment or below their breakup value. The wholesale securities firms served as financial advisers and strategists in bringing about takeovers and in countering with antitakeover strategies. Drexel Burnham Lambert introduced the use of junk bonds to help finance mergers and acquisitions and in leveraged buy-outs. Drexel fine-tuned the sale of these below-investment-grade debt instruments to public investors, especially pension funds, mutual funds, insurance companies, and savings and loan associations. With junk bond resources as capital, thinly capitalized entrepreneurs launched credible bids for multibillion-dollar companies, enhancing the volume and variety of merger activity during the late 1970s and all of the 1980s.

MONEY MANAGEMENT

While securities firms such as Lehman Brothers had a long tradition of money management, most did not manage large investment funds until the 1970s or later. They restrained from investment management to avoid antagonizing important institutional-investor clients; few people enjoy doing business with potential competitors. Also, few securities firms were staffed to take on money management activities on a large scale.

Many of the retail-oriented securities firms have become heavily involved in portfolio management and the distribution of open-ended mutual funds through their broker network. Morgan Stanley, Goldman Sachs, Salomon Brothers, First Boston, and other members of the investment banking elite now manage money for select institutional customers and wealthy individuals. For example, both Morgan Stanley's and Goldman Sachs's money management activities have increased to over $25 billion in 1991. In addition to standard money management practices some firms have also sponsored takeovers, leveraged buy-outs, mergers and acquisitions, purchases of real estate, and special funds for their clients. This activity has proved to be a new, highly profitable source of income for the securities community.

CORPORATE FINANCE

One of the biggest money-makers on Wall Street has been the leveraged buy-out, restructuring, and mergers and acquisition business. Investment bankers have always dispensed advice on dividend policy, capital structure, acquisitions, and financial structure. During the 1950s and 1960s, investment bankers would counsel chief financial officers (CFOs) on the appropriate mix of debt and equity and would undertake the due diligence investigation required in conventional public securities' issues. It was typical for investment banks to undertake strategy studies and financial structure analyses without charge, in the expectation of attracting management and distribution fees on future debt and equity offerings, for which the banks would be the lead underwriters.[16]

However, during the 1970s, clients sought more innovative financial solutions to their problems, rather than the conventional financial solutions of the previous decade. Corporate CFOs were willing to talk to creative investment bankers, even if they did not have a previous relationship with them. The increased level of competition, combined with a surge in merger and acquisition activity, coerced the wholesale securities firms to expand their corporate finance departments greatly and to develop new in-house skills and greater sophistication in valuation analysis. They also developed capabilities to engineer esoteric financial instruments targeted to the needs of specific clients.[17] The battery of Ph.D.s in mathematics and finance, previously referred to as "rocket scientists," helped develop these new products and the sophisticated software required to analyze potential returns and risk management. While relationship banking has not died, it requires a diversified, sophisticated investment banking or corporate finance team to attract and hold financially active U.S. corporations as clients. The once-dominant generalist (the traditional "gentleman banker" with white shoes) has become an endangered species as securities firms and their clients have turned to specialization and segmentation of corporate finance activities. There are industry specialists, private placement specialists, real estate specialists, derivative instruments specialists, junk bond specialists, leveraged buy-out specialists, merger and acquisitions specialists, and many other kinds of specialists. The broad corporate finance umbrella now houses numerous business niches. The growth in merger and acquisition activity has provided some of the most spectacular profits to the investment banking and corporate finance function.

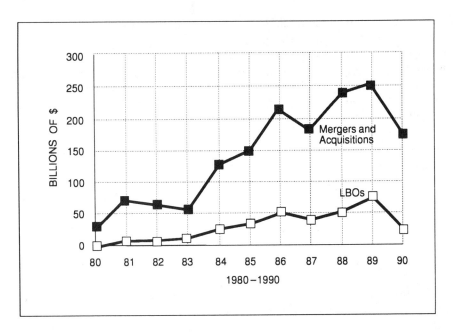

Figure 9.1 Deals in the 1980s. (Graph created by Adam Pollack)

The dollar volume of U.S. mergers grew from $16.4 billion in 1970 to just over $250 billion in 1989, before slumping to approximately $175 billion in 1990, following the collapse of the junk bond market and restrictive bank lending policies. The total value of leveraged buy-outs peaked in 1989 at just under $75 billion before retreating to about $20 billion in 1990. (See Figure 9.1.) The merger and acquisition and leveraged buy-out businesses have also led to the commitment of the securities firms' own funds in the form of bridge loans to ensure that the deals can be consummated. This has brought American investment bankers into the realm of British and French merchant bankers. The role of capital is crucial once again in that one must have the financial wherewithal to make bridge loans. When the investment bank provides the client with its funds for a financial restructuring, the bank has added incentive to raise money for the client in the capital markets in order to retire the bridge loan. A failure in the underwriting of the securities issue means that the bank cannot free up its own investment in the transaction and may face serious losses if the quality of the borrower's credit declines. First Boston and other investment banks suffered such losses in 1990 when the junk bond market dried up before they were able to raise capital for clients.

It is interesting to note that one of the rationales for the Glass-Steagall Act was to prevent conflicts of interest between lenders and underwriters; a bridge loan from an underwriter presents just such a conflict.

Robert Litan of the Brookings Institute fears that, when banks broaden their corporate underwriting activities, prices for underwriting services will come down even further, and profits will decrease. Underwriting margins for corporate bond issues have already dropped from about 1 percent for A-rated securities to 0.5 percent, while spreads on junk bonds have plummeted from 5 to 3 percent. The effect will be most pronounced in merger and acquisition services. Underwriting capabilities are extremely advantageous to the merger business. Banks can now offer advice on mergers and acquisitions, but most are still limited in their underwriting activity.[18] The Federal Reserve has also given permission to NationsBank and Dauphin Deposit Corporation (Harrisburg, PA), in addition to J. P. Morgan and Bankers Trust, to underwrite equity securities.

VENTURE CAPITAL AND REAL ESTATE

A number of securities firms, such as Donaldson, Lufkin & Jenrette have been active in the venture capital market for a long time. Other firms, in a diversification effort, joined the venture capital players during the 1980s. New entrants have looked in awe at the high-margin initial public offering business and decided to help "grow their future clients." Real estate transactions on the part of securities firms is, for the most part, a product of the 1970s and 1980s. Many of these firms have moved heavily into mortgage-backed securities, as well as into investing principal in properties. Morgan Stanley purchased Brooks Harvey, and Goldman Sachs acquired a mortgage banking firm to help speed the parent company's entry into real estate activity.[19]

THE SHIFTING ROLE OF RESEARCH DEPARTMENTS

Since May 1, 1975, Wall Street investment banking and securities firms have found it increasingly difficult to make money the old-fashioned way—by providing investment counsel to customers in return for brokerage commissions. Once brokerage commissions were drastically reduced, the viability of firms specializing in research was in question. The growth of discount brokerage and razor-thin negotiated commissions, in which investors pay three to five cents per share on securities transactions, do not cover the heavy fixed costs of a high-quality research department. This often means that research departments are under increasing pressure to justify their existence by serving the firms' own corporate finance, merger and acquisition, investment banking, or trading interests, rather than concentrating on serving investors. The equity investment departments of institutional investment managers such as managers of pension funds, insurance companies, bank trust departments, and managers of mutual funds had historically footed the bill for Wall Street's stock research. The average Wall Street research department costs between $30 million and $40 million a year to run. Some companies spend as much as $80 million a year for salaries, bonuses, data systems, overhead, publishing, travel, and other costs of their research departments. For example, in 1992, Shearson Lehman employed 113 equity analysts and 30 fixed-income analysts, Merrill Lynch employed 96 equity analysts and 25 fixed-income analysts, Dean Witter employed 49 equity analysts and 4 fixed-income analysts, and Prudential employed 47 equity analysts and 22 fixed-income analysts. Many firms lack the commitment to funding a high-quality research effort. Some have been rethinking their goals and what businesses they want to be in. The result has been that many brokerage firms have cut back their commitment to research. As a matter of fact, most institutional investors feel that there has been a decline in the quality of research and creative investment ideas emanating from Wall Street. This can again be related to the economics of institutional investing, since brokerage commissions for big trades are at low levels. Therefore, it is uneconomical and illogical for brokerage firms to have big research staffs to serve institutional investors.

Research directors warn that increasing pressures on research analysts to serve a company's investment banking or corporate finance needs can lead to a conflict of interest. It is easy to compromise research in pursuit of corporate finance, merchant banking, internal money management, or the threat of a lawsuit. In the well-publicized 1990 case of Donald Trump, the real estate and casino mogul, a negative research report on the Trump organization's Taj Mahal Casino by Marvin Roffman, a research analyst of Janney Montgomery Scott, Inc., a regional Philadelphia brokerage firm, led Trump to threaten to sue Janney over Mr. Roffman's critical assessment. The analyst was put under pressure by the management of the brokerage firm to retract his report on Trump's new casino. He was pressured into apologizing to Trump. Roffman retracted the apology the next day, prompting Janney to dismiss him. Of course, the report was accurate, and problems related to debt coverage at Trump's highly leveraged company occurred within one year of publication of the report. The chief executive of the brokerage firm was forced to step down, and the analyst was rewarded with a $750,000 monetary settlement from Janney by an arbitration panel of the New York Stock Exchange. In addition, Roffman received a handsome out-of-court settlement from Trump, whom he sued in federal district court for defamation of character and for pushing for his dismissal. In a similar case, some former Morgan Stanley research analysts have made public the fact that the firm's investment bankers had pressured the analysts to avoid or alter negative research on its corporate clients, especially those for which the firm did underwriting deals.

It is important to maintain the integrity of research. The research function provides information on issuers and their industries. Research helps salespeople represent investment products to investors. In addition, research analysts can be an important contact with issuing customers, and they certainly help bring in underwriting, merger and acquisition, and restructuring transactions. Research analysts can integrate information on investment banking, corporate finance, sales, and trading.[20] Like other professionals, research analysts are often more loyal to their craft than to their firm, moving frequently from one company to another in response to a more lucrative offer or a long-term contract with job stability. Note that it is possible for a securities firm to buy visibility in research by hiring an All-America Research Team analyst; following along the lines of some sporting publications, *Institutional Investor,* a leading investment banking magazine, publishes an all-star list of such analysts each year.

DIVERSIFICATION EFFORTS

A broad range of activities has given securities firms greater stability than in the single-product days of the 1950s and 1960s. However, earnings are still volatile. A half-dozen firms dominate the marketplace in the most important categories. Their skills in underwriting, trading, merger and acquisition activity, and other corporate finance-related areas are at the cutting edge of the industry. Many foreign securities firms and some of the money-center banks are trying to emulate them. On the whole, the culture of investment banking has not mixed well with the culture of commercial banking, as the heritage of conservatism, bureaucracy, and a wait-your-turn attitude of commercial banking contrasts sharply with the risk taking and faster pace of the star-oriented investment banking climate. There are also major differences in salaries and bonuses. This has been a problem at some commercial banks with investment banking divisions, where commercial bank employees look with awe, jealousy, resentment, and suspicion at their higher paid colleagues on the other side of the wall. The management at J. P. Morgan and Bankers Trust appear to have minimized these problems, but that is not yet true at the other money-center banks.

Brokerage firms have broadened and diversified their activities by developing and marketing their own mutual funds, limited partnerships, leveraged buy-outs, restructuring, merger and acquisition, and other special types of pooled funds to take advantage of investment opportunities. They have also developed many new types of securities, such as mortgage pass-throughs and collateralized credit card and automobile loans. They rejuvenated the junk bond market to facilitate corporate restructurings, invented stripped securities, and developed new forms of swaps to generate additional income. In addition, many brokerage firms sell annuities, life insurance, and broker bank deposits. Even the wholesale firms have begun in-house brokerage activities aimed at wealthy individuals whose needs often compare in size with those of smaller institutional investors. Following the lead of Merrill Lynch's cash management account, just about every brokerage firm offers customers cash management services with check-writing privileges. Some firms, such as Merrill Lynch, issue bank credit and debit cards and own a national real estate brokerage network, a real estate financing company, an international bank, a mortgage broker-age firm, and an employee relocation business. Personnel administering these diversified activities coexist with a brokerage sales force of 11,400 distributed over 510 branches.

Many brokerage firms are becoming "department stores" of financial services. Well-capitalized investment banks have also been willing to put their own capital at risk in leveraged buy-outs and venture capital investments, performing a role similar to that played by the British and French merchant banks. "Boutiques" (e.g., Kohlberg Kravis Roberts and Co.) and full-service securities firms (e.g., First Boston and Lehman Brothers) are taking large positions in the securities of the companies they assist.

STRUCTURAL STRAINS AND CONSOLIDATION

During the 1970s and 1980s, the securities industry was subject to structural strains, including high-volume back-office problems, deregulation of fixed-rate brokerage commissions, major new product innovations, and changes in technology that improved back-office processing procedures and gave brokers access to information on all their investor accounts. The sophisticated automated systems were developed not only to process business, but to help companies compete for and retain clients.

There have been close to 500 security firm mergers within the last 15 years and many failures of brokerage firms. We have also seen the acquisition of primarily retail-oriented securities firms by giant nonbanks such as Sears, American Express, and Prudential.

The total number of branch offices for these firms reached 24,457 in early 1991, down by almost 5,000 branches from the year-end 1989 figure. This consolidation is a function of both cost-cutting efficiencies and the outright failure of some firms. The number of branches is less important than it used to be, since nearly 85 percent of business is done on the telephone today. Fewer people come into an open board room to watch the tape. As a matter of fact, the number of securities firms has declined to an eight-year low of 5,600, reflecting both mergers and closures of entire firms. The industry had reached a peak of nearly 6,700 firms in 1987. Many of the defunct firms were low-priced "penny stock" boiler shops with regulatory problems.

The operating leverage of most securities firms is still high, and earnings are volatile. For example, member firms of the New York Stock Exchange reported their first loss in over 10 years in 1990 and record profits in 1991. Historically, periods of high brokerage transactions have been associated with exceptional profitability, while periods of relatively lower volume can result in substantial losses if overhead has not been adjusted. There has been a trend for the break-even point to increase steadily at most brokerage firms as "permanent employees," leased communications and computer facilities, building rentals, and other fixed costs grew rapidly in the 1983–1987 period. Not until after the mammoth market declines of October 1987 and October 1989 and the subsequent decline in the junk bond market did the securities industry start to cut back on its overhead. Extensive cost cutting resulted from these declines, the end of the leveraged buy-out and megamerger wave, and the reduced volume of private placements. Following the cut in institutional negotiated commissions, the growth of retail discount brokerage forced a reduction in commission rates. This reduction was soon accompanied by a decline in underwriting spreads, leading to a shrinking of margins, which appear unlikely to turn around. However, corporate finance activities have saved the day, generating huge revenues for the best players. It seems as if a firm must be flexible and prepared to benefit from the cyclicality of different parts of the business. At times, the traders are heroes. Sometimes, it is the merger and acquisition group that generates most of the revenues. Or a new product can carry the ball for a few years. Asset management appears to be growing, while underwriting profits are flat, with an occasional great year. Commission income should continue to grow steadily, as stock and bond ownership and volume expand.

QUALITY OF MANAGEMENT

Prior to May 1, 1975, there was a less demanding and less competitive atmosphere than exists today. It was possible to manage a brokerage firm with a few simple informal structures and rules. The brokerage industry has typically suffered from weak management. There was a general view among Wall Streeters that no one could predict what the situation would be like tomorrow, much less next year. Therefore, flexibility was considered crucial. There was a feeling among "high commission producers" that systems and procedures were made to be ignored. The successful brokerage firms were considered by many to be the ones without rules, but with a lot of agility—a tendency to avoid the establishment of systems, priorities, and procedures and an ability to react quickly to changing conditions. In many brokerage firms, there was a focus on finding, spotting, and maintaining a group of "supermen"—elite individuals, exceptional performers, the giants of the industry. The typical Wall street executive had usually been a superstar account executive or trader with limited time for human relations or effective counseling, listening, or team building. He (and it was practically always a he) operated in much the same manner as he was trained, carrying out day-to-day routines with a degree of skill. The failures of this type of executive came from negatives—from not digging into serious operating problems, not confronting personal and performance-related flaws directly, not planning for the future, not coming up with an optimal structure or reporting system for the firm, and not specifying lines of authority. Most firms operated without an effective long-range plan or a real marketing program and with a chaotic organizational structure.[21] This general attitude has often created problems for firms within the securities industry.

Rarely was a top manager cited because he or she was a superlative general manager. The focus on the personalities of individuals was permitted to destroy or obscure the equally important need for policies, procedures, and systems. After all, it is difficult for a basketball team to operate with five great shooters. Who will bring up the ball, who will rebound, and who will play defense? Chaos and failure are the likely result for such a basketball team. A great team cannot be totally effective unless all the players are involved together, focused on the same goals and objectives.

Essentially, management and its tasks have not been given sufficient time at many securities firms because both have been viewed historically as not important. In many firms, management was equated with administration or an advanced form of paper shuffling. Managerial tools such as long-range planning, marketing, market planning, maintaining rational organizational structures, and developing lines of authority have long been viewed as critical to success at the best managed commercial and industrial companies. Yet big brokerage firms resisted formal management structures and procedures until the 1970s and 1980s. Today, these firms are just beginning to utilize planning, market research, and appropriate systems and procedures as managerial tools. Some of the change in philosophy is a function of a recognition of the need for better management, and some has come from the wave of acquisitions of brokerage firms by large insurance companies that were already utilizing planning and appropriate structures and systems as part of their culture and managerial repertoire.[22]

OTHER MANAGERIAL ISSUES

While some foreign and U.S. retail-oriented securities firms have tried to replicate the U.S. wholesale investment banks' skills, they have not been able to challenge the investment banks' market grip on underwriting and corporate finance functions. Only two U.S. commercial banks, J.P. Morgan and Banker's Trust, have made some headway in gaining a small market share in corporate underwriting, as these institutions have begun to shift their emphasis away from commercial banking toward investment banking activities. It is not just a matter of hiring people with *savoir faire* in investment banking; rather, it is a matter of imparting an accumulation of experience and a culture which is distinct from that of other sectors of the financial marketplace. Even the successful investment bankers have run into problems from time to time. Numerous securities firms have failed or have been forced to merge because their managers have not been able to deal effectively with an ever-changing environment, or control costs, or resolve back room problems. Those firms ran with the herd into wrong ventures, were inadequately capitalized, or did not have the flexibility and insights necessary to deal with the complexities, competition, and resourcefulness of other players. They were ill equipped for their environment.

A few of the leading securities firms took advantage of the prosperity of the 1981–1986 period to expand, diversify into other product lines, and set up offices abroad in the financial centers of Europe and Asia, especially London and Tokyo. As a result, the management of these firms became strained. Trading losses in 1987, and the large stock market declines of October 1987 and October 1989, in addition to the increased competition from U.S. and foreign commercial banks, all produced calls for professional management and better control of expenses as the period of sustained Wall Street prosperity appeared to recede.[23]

Securities firms have not always exhibited superior management skills. They continually hire too many people during periods of boom, only to fire them during the lean times. Management in investment banking means managing networks of external ties between the firm and its clients, creating, maintaining, and changing these networks as needed. The complexity of deals, the speed with which those deals are completed, and the financial stakes involved in them require a high level of coordination among the staffers at the investment bank.[24] A distinctive characteristic of the ties between investment banks and their customers is the loose linkage between value provided to the customer and fees earned by the securities firm. Investment bankers provide a continual stream of information, advice, and even special studies for which little or no compensation is received until a deal is completed. Profitability varies substantially by product line and over the business cycle. Low-margin products are often used as a means of maintaining contact with the customer to obtain information that may make it possible for the firm to sell high-margin products as well.[25] The management practices of investment banks that are effective have their roots in the underlying nature of the business. These practices have been developed to manage flexible and continually changing networks of external and internal ties. Among such practices are the process for formulating strategy, the design of the organizational structure, management control systems, the process of determining bonuses, and relationship management. In many ways, investment banks are self-designing organizations, since much of their business is at the grass roots level, that is, driven from the bottom. The self-designing organization gives people throughout the firm a large degree of autonomy. This grass roots process of formulating strategy usually involves a flat, flexible, and complex network. It appears as if structure, systems, and the bonus determination system form a triad of organizational characteristics in which each one compensates for the weaknesses inherent in the others. The management practices at investment banks are a function of the activity, economic characteristics, and production process of the business. When a bank is large, complex, and geographically dispersed, and when its products are diverse, it becomes more difficult to apply these management practices.[26]

The network configuration is also influenced by performance measures put in place by management that complement the self-designing organization. These systems are utilized in the bonus determination process, which is designed to ameliorate some of the negative consequences inherent in the system by including a subjective component in evaluating the performance and contribution of an individual to a firm. Supplementing these practices is the role of the relationship manager, who is responsible for coordinating all of the product specialists from the investment bank who are assigned to a specific client.[27]

Managers at many brokerage firms have concentrated on pruning overhead, merging unnecessary branches, lowering commissions paid to brokers, extending bonuses over several years of employment, and reducing the number of personnel in back offices. As a matter of fact, the number of non-income-producing employees on Wall Street has declined from about 160,000 in the fourth quarter of 1987 to approximately 140,000 in mid-1991. Discussions have also taken place between different brokerage firms regarding the possibility of combining their back office operations in order to reduce operating costs and to become more efficient.

Some Wall Street firms started hiring brokers in mid-1992. However, rather than just hiring recent college graduates and pirating salespeople from other brokerage firms, securities firms began to look for people with experience in other types of business. Salespeople in other industries, bankers, tax lawyers, and insurance and real estate professionals were among the most sought-after personnel.

INVESTMENT BANKING AND MBAs

The investment banking industry attracts some of the brightest talent the United States has to offer because of the stimulating nature of the work and the opportunity to make enormous salaries and bonuses quickly during the best of times. Few fields offer the excitement or the opportunity to become a millionaire in less than a decade. The firms also seek out the best available talent from the finest schools and reward the producers and players handsomely. The industry attracts creative people, self-starters, entrepreneurs, and risk takers. However, since the crash of 1987, Wall Street firms have been contracting in size and reducing employment in order to cut costs and return to acceptable levels of profitability. Tens of thousands of employees have lost their jobs in the securities industry since 1987, and, although the outlook for employment within the investment banking industry in 1992 was better than in the previous few years, it was still nowhere near the golden years of the mid-1980s, when about 30 percent of Harvard Business School graduates went to work for Wall Street firms. From 1988 to 1991, between 11 and 14 percent of Harvard MBAs chose Wall Street firms to start their careers. Now, senior managers have awakened to the need to rein in compensation, especially bonuses. The rookies on Wall Street and newly minted MBAs are finding that securities houses are reviving something that seemed to have died out a long time ago: the apprenticeship. Now it will take a little while longer to join the millionaires' club.

The fast track of investment banking contrasts with the world of commercial banking, where John Meehan, *Business Week's* money and banking editor, character-ized bankers as people who are "good at taking orders and accomplishing well-defined, routine tasks." Sanford Rose, economist, editor, and a distinguished observer of banks, has said that "regulated industries tend not to attract fine minds." Walter Wriston, former chairman at Citicorp, was once quoted as saying that he went into commercial banking because it was a field that had attracted so many mediocre people, giving him a greater chance of success. Of course, the world of commercial banking competes head on with investment bankers for the best talent available today. However, that wasn't always the case. James Tobin, in a Fred Hirsch Memorial Lecture in 1984, confessed to "an uneasy physiocratic suspicion, perhaps unbecom-ing in an academic, that we are throwing more and more of our resources, including the cream of our youth, into financial activities remote from the production of goods and services, into activities that generate high rewards disproportionate to their social productivity."[28]

SECURITIES INDUSTRY STRUCTURE

Five types of organizations compose the securities industry: Investment banks provide the service surrounding a public offering of securities (they also offer brokerage services); registered representatives (brokers or salespeople) arrange the buying and selling of securities; dealers make markets in securities or act as brokers; "boutiques" offer special niche services, such as research into securities, investment management, counsel on mergers and acquisitions, and advice on restructuring; and exchanges provide a place to conduct transactions and a vehicle for setting prices. Investment banks are sometimes classified into two categories: originating firms and distribution firms. Originating firms are the major players in the development of securities offerings, while distribution firms come together in syndication, under the guidance of an originating firm, to underwrite and sell the securities of an issuer. The investment banking community is best known for its ability to underwrite and distribute common stock and new government, corporate, and municipal debt issues; arrange private placements; provide advice on managing funds, corporate finances, and real estate; act as advisers and marriage brokers in the merger and acquisition business; offer advice on defenses against takeovers; and make available whatever services might generate fee income from business and government. Most investment bankers provide brokerage services to institutional and retail clients and make markets in over-the-counter securities, as well as in commodities and foreign exchange. Most are active in both spot and futures markets, hedging activities, and assisting clients in swaps and trades.

CLASSIFICATION AND STRATEGIES OF SECURITIES FIRMS

At the national level, securities firms can be divided into wholesale firms and retail firms. Wholesale securities firms (e.g., Goldman Sachs, Salomon Brothers, and Morgan Stanley) cater primarily to institutional investors and corporate and municipal clients, while retail firms (e.g., A.G. Edwards, Dean Witter, Prudential, Advest, Paine Webber, and Wheat First Securities) cater primarily to individual investors. There are also foreign securities firms with principal offices in New York City and branch offices throughout the country. A myriad of small regional brokerage firms that cater to individual investors exists as well. The wholesale securities firms tend to be the pacesetters because of the business they get from the institutional sector and the lucrative fees they derive from servicing the corporate sector. At the beginning of the 1990s, four of the six dominant securities firms were wholesale oriented (Goldman Sachs, Salomon Brothers, First Boston, and Morgan Stanley). Merrill Lynch and Shearson Lehman, the other two, were primarily retail-oriented national firms that also participated in institutional business. Following the consolidations of the 1970s and 1980s, about 20–25 major securities firms shared more than half the remaining available business. Firms can also be categorized by location: global, national, regional, or local. Some of the full-line service firms are national in scope, while others are regional. There are still many small brokerage shops with a single office that concentrate on retail customers and yet do not have a full range of products. The basic choices of successful investment bankers tend to boil down to one of two strategies: the comprehensive, worldwide coverage of the global investment banking unit or the niche strategy, where only a piece of the pie is digested.[29]

As high-margin products and services mature, they tend to attract increased competition and suffer shrinkage in their margins. Economies of scale may be a remedy for their eroding profits, their size may be important, the amount of capital they have and their reputation are definitely important, and the broader distribution bases they maintain are extremely significant in a large or worldwide underwriting. The ability to control costs often distinguishes well-run from poorly run firms.

Many corporate and institutional users of investment banks have a natural disposition to unbundle services and to have multiple vendors with special pockets of expertise, rather than relying on a single investment banker. The niche vendors have found a role in this scheme of things and have been able to gain pieces of high-margin business from the clients of global investment banks.[30] The investment "boutiques" of Kohlberg Kravis Roberts and Co.; Foresman, Little; Wasserstein, Perella; and Lazard Freres have gained widespread recognition in leveraged buyouts, mergers and acquisitions, corporate pension fund management, and financial restructuring advice. Firms such as John Nuveen have concentrated on municipal bond underwriting and sales, including the formation of unit investment trusts and mutual fund management. They have also gotten involved in secondary market activities.

Securities firms as well appear to follow three basic strategies: overall cost leadership, differentiation, and focus, in the framework of Michael Porter's *Competitive Strategy*.[31] If we redefine Porter's strategies in brokerage terms, the overall cost leadership position might be filled by the discount brokerage firm, the low-cost producer with a small product range. The discounter would sell products to price-sensitive clients who neither require nor want service. A differentiated firm resembles a full-service firm with a large coterie of products and services. These firms are typically technological leaders and have a creative flair and strong marketing abilities. A "boutique," selling a highly specialized, bundled product to a relatively narrow segment of the market, would be classified as a focused firm. Firms that offer money-market funds, hedge funds, or a highly specialized, but limited, number of services are of this variety.

SHIFTS IN SOURCES OF REVENUE

The historic reliance on underwriting by the wholesale firms was reduced over time, while the reliance of retail firms on equity-based commissions was also curtailed, as securities firms diversified their products and services. The normal brokerage commission business no longer produces as large a portion of total revenue as it

Table 9.2   Sources of Revenue for Investment Banks

Activity	Percent of Total Revenues			
	1973	1983	1986	1991[a]
Commissions	56	28	21	16
Trading and Investment	8	26	27	24
Underwriting	9	12	12	6
Margin Lending	13	7	6	6
Commodities	4	3	2	3
Other[b]	10	24	32	45
Total	100%	100%	100%	100%

[a] January–September 1991.
[b] Fees for mutual fund sales and investment advice and counsel, service charges, custodian fees, dividends, interest on term investments, and miscellaneous income.
Source: New York Stock Exchange Fact Book, various editions.

once did, nor is it as profitable as it once was. Fee-based services have become an extremely important source of revenue at brokerage firms, especially the large national and global firms. Both wholesale and retail firms have increased trading and fee income revenues. Much of the latter was generated by a combination of corporate financing, mergers and acquisitions, restructuring, and counsel on leveraged buy-outs. There was also a movement toward merchant banking and bridge financing as investment bankers put their own capital at risk in the deal-making euphoria of the 1980s.

The salient shift in investment banking has been the increasing reliance on advisory services and transactions for generating revenue during the late 1980s and early 1990s. The shift in the sources of gross revenue for member firms of the New York Stock Exchange from 1973 to 1991 shows a major decline in securities commissions as a percentage of total revenues (56 percent in 1973 versus 17 percent in 1991) and major increases in trading and investment (8 percent in 1973 compared with 28 percent in 1991), as well as in other income (10 percent in 1973 as against 37 percent in 1991). Much of the revenue generated in the latter category reflects an increase in income related to mergers, acquisitions, and leveraged buy-outs and in various types of fees related to advice on corporate finance activities. (See Table 9.2.)

Merger and acquisition activity has been extremely profitable at investment banks because of the trend toward consolidation and takeovers. Also, both parties in a deal are represented by at least one, if not two, banking groups, as are major shareholders and board members, and those companies desiring defense strategies against takeovers. While classic underwriting is no longer the main business of contemporary U.S. investment banks, it has grown dramatically in volume and in the diversity of specially tailored instruments. For example, some $235 billion of debt funds were publicly and privately raised on behalf of private-sector businesses in 1990, compared with $43 billion in 1977, while $103 billion was raised for

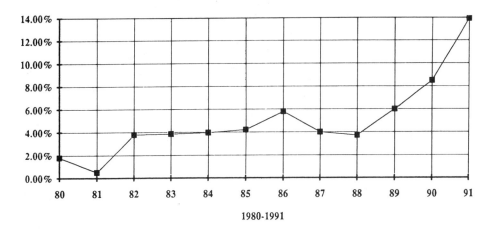

Figure 9.2   Percentage of Junk Bond Companies Defaulting on Bonds, 1980–1991. (Graph created by Adam Pollack)

municipal and nonprofit units in 1990, compared with $36 billion in 1977. Prior to the Tax Reform Act of 1986, which significantly restricted the granting of tax-exempt status to certain financing categories, the municipal debt market reached a historic high when nearly $200 million was raised in 1985. In addition, $58 billion was raised in the equity markets in 1989, compared with $12 billion of new equity that was raised in 1977. While precise numbers were not available at the time of this writing, new equity financing in 1991 exceeded 1989 levels by a substantial amount. Underwriting spreads also declined for "plain vanilla" bonds by nearly 50 percent, from about 7/8 of 1 percent in 1977 to close to 1/2 of 1 percent in 1991. Similar reductions in underwriting spreads occurred in the municipal bond market. The reintroduction of junk bonds, which were used for the most part in leveraged buy-outs during the 1980s, brought underwriting spreads of approximately 300 basis points in their heyday. The failure of numerous highly leveraged companies in the late 1980s and early 1990s led to a major decline in new offerings of junk bonds. The appetite among institutional investors for these bonds shrank when failure rates on junk bonds appeared to have approached double-digit levels, compared with expected losses of between 1.5 and 3.5 percent that were suggested in earlier studies by Edward Altman, of New York University, and by both the Harvard and Wharton Business Schools. These loss rates were later questioned. (See Figure 9.2.)

Underwriter asset-backed securities, from mortgages to auto loans and credit card paper, were among the newer securities offered to the public. Various securities firms have followed different strategies in reacting to changing market conditions. Morgan Stanley and Dillon Reed have been recent entrants into the municipal bond business as a result of positive perceptions regarding long-term profits. On the other hand, Salomon Brothers, which had an exceptionally strong municipal bond franchise

Table 9.3   Leading Underwriters in Each Market in 1991 and 1992

	1991		1992	
Buyer	Amount (\$ Millions)	Top-Ranked Manager	Amount (\$ Millions)	Top-Ranked Manager
U.S. Domestic	589.5	Merrill Lynch	851.2	Merrill Lynch
Straight Debt	200.5	Merrill Lynch	309.2	Merrill Lynch
Convertible Debt	7.5	First Boston	7.0	Merrill Lynch
Junk Debt	10.0	Merrill Lynch	38.0	Merrill Lynch
Investment-Grade Debt	190.6	Merrill Lynch	271.2	Merrill Lynch
Mortgage Debt	250.2	Kidder Peabody	377.3	Kidder Peabody
Asset-Backed Debt	50.1	First Boston	50.9	First Boston
Collateral Securities	300.3	Kidder Peabody	428.2	Kidder Peabody
Preferred Stock	19.9	Morgan Stanley	29.9	Morgan Stanley
Common Stock	56.6	Goldman Sachs	72.4	Merrill Lynch
Initial Public Offerings	25.1	Alex Brown	39.4	Merrill Lynch
International Debt	252.5	Nomura	268.3	Duetsche Bank
International Equity	11.6	Goldman Sachs	13.6	Goldman Sachs
Municipal New Issues	171.1	Goldman Sachs	231.7	Goldman Sachs

Source: IDD Information Services, Inc., and reports of companies listed.

and staff, withdrew from the market abruptly in late 1987. Salomon cited declining underwriting spreads and expectations of greater competition from commercial banks now that these institutions could participate in the revenue bond segment of the municipal business.

After four years of declining, disclosed fees earned by investment bankers in 1991 for underwriting stocks and bonds rose to \$4.64 billion, compared with only \$1.94 billion in 1990. The only year underwriting fees were higher was in 1986, when they totaled almost \$5.1 billion. There were two forces that combined to boost fee income in 1991: a surge in initial public stock offerings and a large boost in seasoned offerings. There was also a modest revival in the underwriting of junk bond issues. Initial public offerings and junk bonds provide investment bankers with the highest underwriting spreads. The rise in underwriting fees more than made up for the decline in merger and acquisition fee income in 1991. During the first nine months of 1992, investment banks generated record underwriting income, smashing the prior full-year underwriting record set in 1991. Low interest rates and a reemergence of initial public offerings in the first half of the year were the reasons for the spectacular results.

Merrill Lynch led all investment banking firms in fee income generated from underwriting new issues of stocks and bonds from 1990 through 1992. Goldman Sachs was in second place. Other major players included Morgan Stanley, Alex Brown, Lehman Brothers, First Boston, Salomon Brothers, Dean Witter Reynolds, Paine Webber, and Kidder Peabody. The top underwriters of U.S. debt and equity in 1991 and 1992 were Merrill Lynch, Goldman Sachs, First Boston, Kidder Peabody, Morgan Stanley, Salomon Brothers, Bear Stearns, Prudential Securities, and Donaldson, Lufkin & Jenrette. Alex Brown was a leader in the underwriting of initial public offerings. (See Table 9.3.) Just as underwriting revenues as a percentage of total revenues had declined until 1991, so had the revenue stream for securities commissions since May 1, 1975. However, while the proportion of revenue dollars coming from brokerage commissions for member firms of the New York Stock Exchange declined from the mid-1970s, the absolute dollar income has tripled because the number of shares traded has risen dramatically over the same time frame. Turnover ratios have risen substantially, and institutional volume has grown rapidly, with the tremendous growth of U.S. pension and retirement money and foreign buying of U.S. stocks, as well as more active management of institutional portfolios. Average daily volume on the New York Stock Exchange grew from 18,551,000 shares traded in 1975 to 178,900,000 shares traded in 1991, a compound yearly growth rate in excess of 15 percent. Still, the importance of organized exchanges has declined relative to the NASDAQ over-the-counter share of the total volume of trades. Bond trading, primarily an over-the-counter activity, has also benefited from the development of many new types of securities and the securitization of assets, as well as from more active management of bond portfolios by institutional investors. These trading activities have had a major impact on the operations and revenues of securities firms, with a big shift toward increased reliance on secondary market trading. The increased capitalization of Wall Street has also given securities firms more opportunities to use their own capital to make trading profits. Market intelligence gained through active secondary-market trading for clients can be used in managing the firm's own trading portfolio. Market making has become an integral part of the overall strength of a handful of investment banks in the public securities markets,[32] especially Salomon, Goldman Sachs, and First Boston.

While revenues generated from the sale of insurance by brokerage firms is not yet significant, some believe that there is potential in generating future insurance product sales, especially annuities, from the cadre of brokers already in place at securities firms. The fact that Merrill Lynch has entered the insurance business and that a half-dozen large investment banking and brokerage firms are owned by insurance companies could eventually lead to greater penetration of the insurance market once brokers become more familiar with the insurance products and are taught cross-selling techniques.

The return on equity for securities firms was quite volatile during the 1980s and early 1990s. Large investment banks seemed to outperform both national full-line firms and the industry as a whole. (See Figure 9.3.)

TECHNOLOGICAL CHANGE

Changes in technology and communications have had an enormous impact on the securities industry, helping to provide better information systems to account

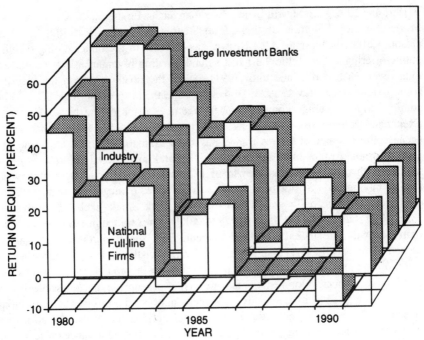

Figure 9.3 Securities Firms' Pretax ROE, 1980–1991. (*Source:* © 1992 Securities Industry Association)

executives, managers, and credit and security analysts. Technological advances have cut back office costs and have led to a significant rise in the effectiveness and productivity of account executives. Computers have aided the "rocket scientists" in developing new products and services, while both computers and advances in communication and information systems have transformed national markets into global markets.

Financial globalization was driven by advances in data processing and telecommunications, a liberalization of restrictions on cross-border capital flows, deregulation of domestic capital markets, and greater competition among these markets for a share of the world's trading volume. Globalization is growing rapidly, but primarily at the intermediary, rather than the customer, level. Its effects are felt at the customer level mainly because prices and interest rates are influenced by worldwide economic and financial conditions, not because direct customer access to suppliers has increased. However, globalization at the customer level will soon become apparent, at least in Europe after 1993, when European Community banking firms will be allowed to cross national borders.

Globalization has affected derivative financial products in two ways. First, it has spurred the creation and rapid growth of internationally related financial products, such as Eurodollar futures and options and foreign currency futures and options, as well as futures and options on domestic securities that trade globally, such as U.S. Treasury securities. Trading hours on some U.S. futures and options exchanges have been expanded to support cross-border trading of Treasury securities and other underlying assets. Second, globalization has led to the establishment of futures and options exchanges worldwide. Once the exclusive domain of U.S. markets, especially in Chicago, financial derivative products are now traded in significant volumes throughout Europe and Asia.

In regard to improved communications and the ability to handle trading volume, the New York Stock Exchange has increased its computer capacity so that it can comfortably handle 800 million shares a day, compared with about 200 million in 1987. Brokerage firms also have developed computerized systems, to get around trading bottlenecks pointed up in the October 1987 stock market crash.

WHERE IS THE INDUSTRY HEADED?

It is likely that most of the barriers that currently separate the players in the financial services industry will be gone before the turn of the century. With this will come increased business opportunities for those who are quick to recognize them and who know how to compete. There will be increased interaction and cooperative efforts among banks, insurance companies, and the securities industry. There may be additional mergers between some of the players across industry lines, and there will certainly be further consolidation within current industry definitions. A shrinking number of regional brokerage firms will continue to be acquired by national broker-age firms and insurance companies. It is also likely that the sections of the Glass-Steagall Act dealing with the separation of commercial and investment banking will be removed gradually, resulting in the sharing of more underwriting revenues with bank holding company subsidiaries. Investment bankers and securities firms will eventually enjoy the advantages of deposit insurance and direct access to the federal funds market. The latter should speed up the firms' access to cash payment for securities sales. Also, prudent management decisions will be forthcoming, lest firms succumb to the temptation to rush into business activities for which they are ill suited or ill prepared. Securities firms will have to learn to exit from low-margin or unprofitable businesses. Finally, the problem of rapid product obsolescence is characteristic of extremely competitive environments: Innovative firms cannot patent their creations and retain market share in a relatively new product, since market share can erode as quickly as copiers and fax machines of competitors can crank out versions of the newly designed product.

There is also likely to be a large increase in the amount of attention and money spent on management, in part related to the recognition that Wall Street and the big money-center banks have suffered from serious managerial problems.

The emerging financial services industry will consist of extremely competitive institutions of all types and sizes. A number of giant-sized financial "supermarkets" or universal banks will coexist with smaller niche or specialty "boutiques." Institu-

Table 9.4   Size of Brokerage Firms, January 1, 1991[a]

Broker	Capital ($ Billions)	Number of Offices	Number of Employees
Merrill Lynch	$9.67	510	39,900
Shearson Lehman	5.41	427	31,003[b]
Goldman Sachs	4.70	21	6,733
Salomon Bros.	4.42	17	8,735
Morgan Stanley	3.38	12	7,172
Paine Webber	1.55	267	13,500
First Boston	1.47	10	4,218
Dean Witter Reynolds	1.41	499	15,866
Bear Stearns	1.39	13	5,558
Prudential Securities	1.22	336	17,000

[a] Except for head count, 1992.
[b] Before merger of Shearson into Smith Barney.
Source: Copyright 1991 by Securities Industry Association.

tional participants will be striving to develop multiple relationships with clients, to tie customers to their firms and to try to increase customer loyalty to one institution. The problem is that many firms have forgotten the impact of Madison Avenue on today's consumers. We have been taught to buy our suits at store W, our shirts and ties at store X, and our shoes at store Z. Do people really want to shop at financial "supermarkets"?

Although many brokerage firms have attempted to diversify into other industries to offset part of their overhead and operating risk, their success has not been tested by either a decline in market volume or a steep recession. Successful national full-line brokers and discounters have added new products and services to augment their previously narrow product lines. These firms have also worked hard to trim costs in order to become more efficient distributors.

We have witnessed a large number of mergers, acquisitions, and consolidations among Wall Street firms. In 1993, Primerica's Smith Barney acquired Shearson (without Lehman Brothers) from American Express to form Smith Barney Shearson. The new firm will have 495 offices, 11,400 brokers, and $62 billion in mutual funds under management, just behind industry leader Merrill Lynch, with 510 offices, 11,800 brokers, and $117 billion of mutual fund assets under management (see Table 9.4). Merrill Lynch, Shearson, and Fidelity Investments have been buying small specialist firms since the stock market crash of October 1987. These specialist firms are able to reduce trading fees and either lower customer commissions or increase firm profitability on each trade. They are also attempting to control the flow of orders, that is, control orders for stock from start to the moment a trade is completed on an exchange, in order to make more money. In buying specialist firms, brokerage houses are also making a long-term bet that they will gain more influence on how stock trading evolves in the future. Brokers want to be on the inside of developments that include making markets both "upstairs" (direct trades between big brokers) and downstairs on exchange floors. Also, specialist firms are now much stronger financially than they were during the 1987 crash. In addition, institutional investors have largely abandoned a controversial trading strategy known as *portfolio insurance,* a technique blamed for feeding the crash. Instead, investors have turned to complex strategies using derivative instruments that allow them to hedge investments without putting direct pressure on falling prices. The use of derivative instruments is huge and largely unregulated. This relatively new area must be watched more carefully by regulators because derivatives could pose new threats that may not be completely understood until the next time the market crashes.[33]

What have we learned about brokerage mergers? Essentially this: It is a lot easier to make a merger than to make a merger work. It is great to talk about synergies, but successful integrations of firms and their philosophies, back office operations, and software systems are a difficult task. If a merger or acquisition is to succeed, it is an absolute necessity to prune costs by closing redundant branches and laying off unnecessary personnel in order to become more efficient.

The industry also appears headed for better and more professional management practices and away from the concept of the superstar. There will be more effective long-range planning, coordinated marketing research and marketing toward the firm's developed goals and objectives, the development of appropriate systems and procedures, full utilization of the latest in computer, information, and communication technology, and better cost controls, as well as respect for professional managers within the industry.

The industry has also emerged from a decade of mergers and acquisitions in a more consolidated and concentrated format. There were rumors that GE would sell or spin off Kidder Peabody, that Xerox would exit from the financial services industry, and that Equitable might take Donaldson, Lufkin & Jenrette, its successful brokerage unit, public. Sears has already sold 20 percent of Dean Witter to the public. Dean Witter itself teamed up with NationsBank to sell stocks and bonds at the bank's branches.

Wall Street firms are currently much larger and better capitalized than they were five years ago. (See Table 9.4.) The additional capitalization can be attributed in part to the injection of fresh capital by the new and larger parent firms, as well as by some external financing. The firms involved in underwriting, leveraged buyouts, merchant banking, and "mezzanine" financing have much greater need for capital than firms that rely on just equity and mutual fund commissions. Additional capital is also required for technological developments, computer hardware and software, and communication systems, as well as for the promotion of new products. Also, firms that have suffered losses on their lending, trading, and investment activities require at least a replenishment of lost capital.

Financial markets and financial services are becoming more globally integrated. As businesses expand into new markets around the world, there is greater demand for financing to follow them. All major areas of international finance have grown far more rapidly than foreign trade in recent years. The trading of securities in U.S.

markets by nonresidents, the trading volume of foreign currency futures and options, and foreign exchange trading have been growing at 40 percent or more a year. This rapid growth of international financial transactions reflects a corresponding growth in cross-border capital flows and suggests high levels of profits for those securities firms that can capture a reasonable market share.

The financial services industry will become more consolidated, with firms from a handful of countries garnering substantial market share. International joint ventures will be common and, often, precursors to outright acquisitions. For smaller firms to survive as global competitors, they will have to find and service a market niche.

As the financial services industry and financial markets become more globally integrated, the most efficient and best organized firms will prevail. Also, countries with the most efficient—but not necessarily the least—regulation will become the world's major international financial centers.

The New York Stock Exchange is wondering what changes are likely to follow from an SEC study entitled *Market 2000*. The last time that the SEC commissioned a lengthy study, it resulted in an end to fixed-rate commissions on Wall Street in 1975. Wall Street pundits are suggesting that the SEC is likely to begin to regulate trading systems, such as Instinet and Posit, that compete with the stock exchange. The SEC is also likely to bring an end to the practice of some trading systems and over-the-counter market makers that pay brokerage firms for directing customer orders towards them instead of the stock exchange. In addition, the SEC has called for commentary on SEC rules 390 and 500. The former protects specialists from competition from member firms of the New York Stock Exchange who are forbidden from trading securities listed on the exchange in the over-the-counter market. If the SEC drops rule 390, benefits might result from the increased competition among markets. Rule 500, which makes it extremely difficult to remove oneself voluntarily from the stock exchange list, curbs competition between markets.[34]

ENDNOTES

1. S. L. Hayes and P. M. Hubbard, *Investment Banking* (Boston: Harvard Business School Press, 1990), pp. 91–92.

2. Ibid., p. 91.

3. Ibid., p. 92.

4. Ibid., pp. 94–95.

5. Ibid., pp. 104–105.

6. Ibid., p. 105.

7. Ibid., p. 235.

8. K. Eichenwald, "New York Merc Chairman May Be Facing Civil Charges," *New York Times,* July 15, 1991, p. D2.

9. Hayes and Hubbard, p. 238.

10. I. Leveson, *Financial Services: The New Era* (Marlboro, NJ: Author, 1991), pp. 141–153.

11. K. Eichenwald, "Broad Outline Described for a Milken Settlement," *New York Times,* January 22, 1992, p. D2.

12. B. Henriques, "A New Insider Trading Case," *New York Times,* June 5, 1992, p. A1.

13. M. Golan, L. Nathans, T. Smart, and D. Faust, "Salomon: Honesty Is the Gutsiest Policy," *Business Week,* September 11, 1991, p. 100.

14. M. McNamee, D. Faust, and L. Nathans Spiro, "The Judgment of Salomon: An Anticlimax," *Business Week,* June 1, 1992, p. 106.

15. Ibid., p. 106.

16. Hayes and Hubbard, p. 130.

17. Ibid., p. 130.

18. Federal Reserve Bank of Chicago, *Weekly Review,* September 10, 1988, p. 124.

19. Hayes and Hubbard, p. 133.

20. R. Eccles and P. B. Crane, *Doing Deals: Investment Banks at Work* (Boston: Harvard Business School Press, 1988), p. 138.

21. D. E. Howard, *Dynamic Planning and Management in the Securities Industry* (New York: New York Institute of Finance, 1987), pp. 11–13.

22. Ibid.

23. Eccles and Crane, p. 1.

24. Ibid., p. 2.

25. Ibid., p. 2.

26. Ibid., pp. 3–5.

27. Ibid., p. 5.

28. J. Tobin, Fred Hirsch Memorial Lecture, *Lloyd's Bank Review,* May 10, 1984.

29. D. Rogers, *The Future of American Banking* (New York: McGraw-Hill, 1993), pp. 9, 307.

30. Hayes and Hubbard, p. 336.

31. M. E. Porter, *Competitive Strategy: Techniques for Analyzing Industries and Competitors* (New York: The Free Press, 1988).

32. Hayes and Hubbard, pp. 336–337.

33. K. Eichenwald, "A Leaner But Not So Mean Wall St.," *New York Times,* October 19, 1992, p. D3.

34. G. Weiss, "Nightmare on Wall Street: A New Rule Book," *Business Week,* December 21, 1992, pp. 76–77.

10 Structural Change in the Banking Industry

Given the obvious "overbanking" problem in this country, a good case can be made that part of the problem in banking and finance may well be that we have too much capital chasing too few good loans.

E. G. Corrigan

The number of insured commercial banks in the United States has declined from nearly 14,000 in the mid-1980s to approximately 11,400 in 1993. (See Table 10.1) As a matter of fact, the number of banks is likely to decline to the 5,000-to-7,000 range by the year 2000. This decline will be aided by new legislation that will permit nationwide banking, as well as by the high failure rate among banks, and the continued trend toward consolidation. While the merger trend is expected to continue, many of the highly touted mergers of the 1980s have not worked out as planned. According to James McCormick, president of FMCG Capital Strategies,

**Table 10.1 Number of Banks and Their Assets,
Selected Years, 1900–1992**

Year	Number of Banks[a]	Total Assets ($ Millions)
1900	13,053	$ 11,388
1920	30,909	53,094
1930	24,273	74,729
1940	15,076	179,165
1950	14,676	230,165
1960	13,999	518,220
1970	13,550	1,532,974
1980	14,163	2,943,000
1990	12,300	3,399,900
1991	12,269	3,748,000(est.)
1992	11,815	NA

Note: NA = not available
[a]Included stock savings banks, nondeposit trust companies, private banks, industrial banks, and nonbank banks. There were 11,419 insured commercial banks at year-end 1992.
Source: Federal Reserve Board of Governors.

"The fate of the typical acquirer was that its stock price four or five years after the acquisition was only about 65 percent of what it would have been without the merger." One of the problems was that the purchasing banks generally overpaid by nearly double what the banks were actually worth. Unfortunately, the acquiring banks could not boost profits enough to recoup their investments. In some cases, acquisitions were made to increase the size of a bank's assets, making it more difficult and expensive for the enlarged bank to be acquired by another bank holding company, hence preserving the power of current management. In other cases, the management of the newly merged institutions did not make enough cuts in overhead and staff to reduce operating costs and maintain adequate levels of profitability.

The relative decline in bank assets during the 1930s and 1940s, compared with the assets of competing financial intermediaries, was caused by inadequate demand for bank loans. Many banks discouraged the growth of deposits at that time by paying low rates on interest-bearing deposits and making only limited marketing efforts to attract funds because they felt that attractive investment opportunities were limited. Even though the demand for loans grew rapidly in the 1950s and 1960s, banks still limited their marketing effort and were content to allow their deposit rates to remain below the rates of competitive institutions. In addition, increasing interest rates encouraged disintermediation and led depositors to minimize their demand deposit balances, which pay no interest. Finally, in the 1960s, banks became concerned about their falling market share and began to utilize marketing efforts to attract more deposits. Banks also began to emphasize compensating deposit balances for lines of credit for corporate borrowers and began to boost their rates on time deposits to the maximum levels permitted under Regulation Q. When Regulation Q was removed, banks responded by paying rates as high as or higher than competing intermediaries. The large banks also began to utilize new types of deposits and deposit liabilities to attract consumer business and public deposits. Negotiable certificates of deposit were introduced in the 1960s to solicit corporate time deposits. Banks also began to utilize longer term saving certificates, deposits with market-oriented rates, and insured money market deposits to attract consumers. Banks and their holding companies increased their use of nondeposit sources of funds as well, such as commercial paper, repurchase agreements, borrowed funds, capital notes, and Eurodollar instruments.[1] Figure 10.1 gives the shares of financial assets held by major intermediaries from 1950 to 1989.

While U.S. commercial banks once dominated lending activity in the country, their role has been reduced substantially. Between 1975 and 1990, commercial and industrial lending more than tripled, but the commercial paper market grew by more than tenfold. Also, foreign banks, insurance companies, finance companies, mortgage companies, and brokerage firms have been responsible for the loss of business by commercial banks. A consumer can now conduct almost all of his or her banking needs without having to set foot in an actual bank. Transactions on government-guaranteed checking and savings accounts can be done by mail at nonbanks like brokerage firms; credit and debit card transactions are available at firms such as stockbrokers, Sears, AT&T, and American Express; mortgage loans are available from mortgage companies and brokers; and corporate loans may be transacted in

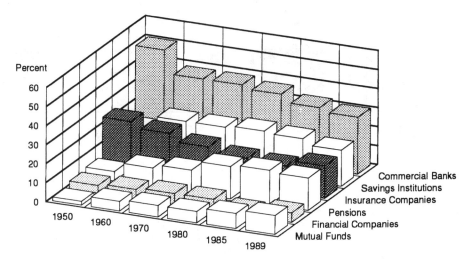

Figure 10.1   Shares of Financial Assets Held by Major Intermediaries, 1950–1989. (*Source:* Board of Governors of the Federal Reserve System, *Flow of Funds Accounts*)

the commercial paper market and the junk bond market and are available from insurance companies, finance companies (e.g., GE Credit), asset-based lenders such as Congress Financial, and brokerage firms, in terms of bridge financing in leveraged buy-outs and mergers. At the end of 1990, banks held only 16 percent of the $3 trillion in residential mortgages outstanding, 44 percent of automobile loans, and only 30 percent of corporate debt among nonfinancial companies. In the last category, businesses have many choices besides banks to meet their financing needs. They range from the commercial paper market to the bond market and the financing arms of GE, Ford, GM, and Westinghouse, which offer loans to businesses and are among the 40 largest financial institutions in the United States. Foreign banks have also gained a 30-percent market share of all loans made to U.S. companies, about the same percentage as that of U.S. banks. In addition, companies such as American Express have infringed on the once exclusive ATM market of banks. American consumers are placing a lower proportion of their wealth into traditional depository institutions and putting more of their funds in mutual funds and pension funds. Furthermore, business borrowers are turning away from banks and borrowing more from finance companies and in the money and capital markets of the securities industry.[2] Put simply, banks face stiff competition from other intermediaries and markets on both sides of the balance sheet.

BALANCE SHEET CHANGES

Asset Shifts

There has been a large shift in allocation of assets by commercial banks over the last few decades. The loan-to-asset ratio has risen steadily since World War II, from

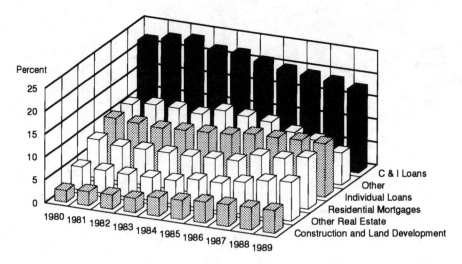

Figure 10.2 Composition of Bank Loan Portfolios as Percentage of Assets, 1980–1989. (*Source:* Barth, Brumbaugh, and Litan, *The Banking Industry in Turmoil.* Copyright © 1991 by The American College. Reprinted with permission. This originally appeared in the 1991 Frank M. Engle Lecture.)

an average of 38 percent in the 1950s to 58 percent in the 1980s and approximately 62 percent in 1990. Within the loan portfolio, the major shift was the growth in commercial real estate, construction, and land development financing in the 1980s. Between 1980 and 1990, total real estate lending rose from 14.5 percent to 23.5 percent of assets. This was overshadowed by the growth in commercial real estate financing, which rose by an average of 25 percent per year between 1986 and 1989. (See Figure 10.2.) As a gauge for what may lie ahead, consider that problems with commercial real estate loans typically tend to appear two to four years after the loan is made. The most significant changes on the asset side of the balance sheet over the last few decades show a smaller proportion of commercial and industrial loans compared with total loans and a large increase in real estate loans. By 1991, banks had a near religious conversion from lax to tight loan underwriting standards as a result of heavy loan losses and regulatory pressure to tighten underwriting controls. Commercial and industrial loans had always been the mainstay of commercial banks, but beginning in 1987, real estate loans surpassed them as the main lending vehicle for such banks. Loans to consumers accounted for almost two-thirds the level of commercial and industrial loans by 1990, after accounting for less than half as recently as 1985.

During the 1980s, real estate loans continued expanding as a share of bank assets, finally becoming the largest category of bank loans. Within the real estate portfolio, the largest category is that of one-to-four-family residences, although as a percentage of total assets, the group has remained relatively constant since 1960. The growing importance of real estate lending at banks was aided by the declining role of thrift institutions and insurance companies in providing residential mortgages and other real estate financing, the relatively more favorable treatment assigned to qualifying residential mortgages under the risk-based capital guidelines, and the increasing popularity of adjustable-rate mortgages. The growth in real estate lending by banks offset much of their losses in corporate lending to the money and capital markets. More important, real estate lending became popular because it offered a high effective yield, including generous fee income, as well as interest rate payments well above the prime rate. There was also a need for banks to deploy excess funds. For some banks, the only alternatives to real estate lending were to accept years of low growth or to focus on activities that offered returns below the cost of capital.[3]

Real estate had been rising in price throughout the 1980s, until the bottom seemed to drop out of the market in New England and in the southwest at the end of the decade. The real estate recession spread to most of the United States by 1990. Particularly in New England, the mid-Atlantic states, and the southwest, banks suffered enormous losses on commercial real estate loans. A large portion of S & Ls, credit unions, and commercial banks failed in those regions. Bad real estate loans also weakened both the money-center banks in New York and California and some eastern regional banks and thrifts. Losses in real estate loans appear to be acting as a catalyst, accelerating the trend toward more bank mergers. In 1990–1991, the composition of real estate lending shifted away from commercial and toward residential mortgages. This shift occurred in response to problems with the quality of loans and overbuilding in commercial real estate markets. Banks had become victims of their own success and became sloppy in their real estate underwriting practices. To put commercial real estate exposure into perspective, the number of commercial real estate loans that were outstanding was 10 times the number of outstanding loans to less developed countries and 4 times the number of loans to heavily leveraged companies. The persistence of commercial real estate and heavily leveraged lending activity through 1989 testifies to the pressure to book high-yield loans. Banks began making seven-year construction loans and began to offer permanent financing when insurance companies backed out of advance commitments to take out construction loans. As insurance companies began to withdraw from the market, banks with substantial excess capacity began relaxing their requirements for permanent financing as a condition for receiving construction loans. Banks were attracted to the higher fees and interest rates they could charge in return for assuming the risk that no permanent financing would be available. Since property values were increasing, the loans seemed more than adequately collateralized, and the problems seemed more theoretical than real. At the end of 1992, 5.6 percent of commercial-property loans were nonperforming, compared with 6.8 percent a year earlier.

The accelerated growth of high-risk lending developed into a prescription for trouble, if not disaster. Rapid growth always entails an eventual reduction in credit standards. Since there is generally a time lag of several years before the costs of excessive growth become apparent, the above-average returns from hefty fee income and lush interest rates reinforce the go-go mentality of the lenders. Additionally, when asset growth exceeds the natural growth rate of the local deposit base, the bank must offer higher deposit rates to capture a larger share of the local core deposit market or part of the national market. A double whammy generally occurs when the costs of excessive growth hit home, with the income statement suffering from delinquent interest payments on loans (a loss of earning assets) and expenses growing as "workout" costs rise, while nonlocal depositors demand higher yields on their certificates of deposit in the face of increased risk. Few tools are more reliable as a leading indicator of future problems than explosive growth in high-risk loans. In assessing the risk of bank insolvency, analysts commonly look at the existing risk-adjusted capital levels relative to assets, the adequacy of capital and loan loss reserves relative to nonperforming loans, the potential exposure level among nonproblematic loans, the ability to generate future earnings, and the ability to raise new capital through the sale of assets or through other means.[4]

Following the passage of the Tax Reform Act of 1986, which phased out the deductibility of interest on most nonmortgage household debt, the growth of home equity loans accelerated. Commercial and industrial loans declined gradually as a percentage of total loans during the decade, as banks lost many of their best credits to either the commercial paper market or the capital markets. In 1970, commercial banks met nearly 90 percent of the short- and medium-term credit needs of corporate America, compared with about 60 percent in 1990. More important than the loss of market share was the loss of the highest quality corporate borrowers to the financial markets. This was the beginning of a period of declining credit quality for bank loan portfolios and declining bank underwriting standards. Loan losses rose exponentially in each decade from the 1950s through the 1980s, while net charge-offs as a percentage of capital doubled each decade. For example, the ratio of net charge-offs to equity and reserves equaled 8.6 percent in 1990, compared with 4.5 percent in the 1970s, 1.2 percent in the 1960s, and 0.5 percent in the 1950s.[5] Loans have also been increasing faster than capital.

A deterioration in the economy and a slowing of merger and acquisition activity in late 1989 and throughout 1990 helped lead to a cyclical decline in commercial and industrial lending at banks. In addition, banks needed to provide more competitive rates for those customers who remained in the banking system. Banks also ran into difficulty with defaults on numerous heavily leveraged loans as the lending euphoria to support the leveraged buy-out activity of the mid-1980s came abruptly to an end. As a matter of fact, three large banks have loan exposures to heavily leveraged companies in excess of twice the size of their equity base,[6] while 14 banks have 5 percent or more of their assets in these loans. The market for loans to heavily leveraged corporations is dominated by the large banks in New York, Chicago, and California. The "lead" banks in loans to heavily leveraged companies have typically sold some of their loans to smaller regional banks. Note that risk exposure in other loan categories is not comparable to that for commercial real estate, for heavily leveraged transactions and for Latin American loans. While losses in the consumer credit business have been more stable historically than in commercial lending, the entry of substantial new capacity into the consumer credit arena has watered down credit standards. Some of the new major players in the consumer credit business—retail chains, telephone companies, finance companies, and auto companies—have a lower cost of funds than do commercial banks because of higher ratings by Moody's and Standard & Poors. These institutions are in an excellent position to bid aggressively for market share. The result of this aggressive competition has been more expansive loan terms and the broader availability of credit. For example, car loans were typically offered for a maximum of 36 months in the 1970s; now they are available for up to 72 months on some of the higher priced models.[7]

During the 1980s, consumer lending was the driving force that sustained the profitability of banks. For large banks that can capitalize on economies of scale, returns on credit cards and home equity loans have frequently exceeded 30 percent. Of course, the recession of 1990–1991 and increased competition are likely to erode these exceptional levels of profitability.[8]

Consumer loans exhibited modest growth during the 1980s, despite the fact that auto finance companies offered below-market rates during much of the period. The growth in loans kept on the books was also slowed by the rapid pace of securitization, mostly in credit card loans during the 1989–1990 period, despite heavy consumer installment borrowing from banks. Consumer banking and credit card operations remain highly lucrative for institutions that can generate economies of scale. However, for many institutions, branch banking produces inadequate returns, and competition for consumers' funds and consumer credit business continues to increase. Since the announcement that risk-based capital standards would be imposed, banks have begun the securitization of consumer loans at a quickening pace. Securitization also accelerated in the credit card market, as several banks and thrifts sold their credit card accounts to larger banks that specialized in securitizing and servicing this type of credit.[9]

U.S. bank loans to foreign addresses, especially in developing countries, declined during the latter part of the 1980s after experiencing good growth in the 1970s and early 1980s. Money-center banks continued their retrenchment in foreign lending and their restructuring of loans to heavily indebted developing countries, whose defaults had been substantial. While U.S. banks have retrenched abroad, foreign banks have expanded rapidly in the U.S. in both wholesale and retail markets. Table 10.2 gives the composition of bank assets in 1985, 1990, and 1991.

As the table shows, there has also been a relative decline in the use of tax-exempt securities and a major increase in mortgage-backed securities in bank investment portfolios. Bank holdings of state and local government securities continued to decline as well, as they have since the passage of the Tax Reform Act of 1986, which limited the tax advantage of holding such securities. In fact, municipal securities as a percentage of total assets declined from 13.6 percent in 1970 to 3.5 percent in 1990 for all banks. The less favorable treatment of municipal securities under risk-based capital guidelines may also have contributed to the recent declines in holdings of these securities. In addition, the poor earnings performance of many banks diminished the demand for tax-exempt securities, as these banks were no

Table 10.2   Composition of Bank Assets, 1985, 1990, and 1991

Balance Sheet Items as a Percentage of Average Consolidated Assets

Item	1985	1990	1991
Loans	59.88	61.16	60.07
Commercial and Industrial	22.02	18.49	17.34
Real Estate	15.70	23.51	24.39
Consumer	10.88	11.23	10.84
Foreign Government	1.56	0.79	0.76
Agriculture	1.51	0.96	1.02
Depository Institution	2.88	1.66	1.50
Other	5.35	4.52	4.23
Securities	15.52	17.25	18.66
U.S. Government and Other Debts	10.58	14.35	16.08
U.S. Treasury	4.53	4.34	4.88
Government-Backed Mortgage Pools	0.95	4.07	4.46
Other	4.00	2.10	2.17
State and Local Government	4.94	2.57	2.23
Other Bonds and Stocks	1.08	2.50	2.49
Trading Account	1.24	1.44	1.78
Gross Federal Funds Sold and Reverse Repurchase Agreements	4.42	4.33	4.40
Interest Deposits	5.53	3.54	3.04
Non-Interest-Bearing Assets	12.61	10.73	10.47

Source: Federal Reserve Bulletin, July 1992, p. 474.

longer in need of sheltering income from taxation. On the other hand, bank holdings of both Treasury issues and mortgage-backed securities grew throughout the decade. The banks liked the attractive yields on mortgage-backed securities, while they continued to increase their investments in Treasury securities because they were safe, were not subject to state taxes, were relatively liquid, minimized capital requirements, satisfied regulators, and were a good substitute for declining loan demand in the early 1990s.[10] The central vulnerability of the banking system is that since 1975, banks have become less liquid and increased their commercial real estate activity, resulting in an increase in the risk of their portfolios.[11] In addition to their increase in real estate lending, banks also increased their holdings of investment securities as a percentage of assets to a greater amount than C & I loans.

There appears to be a greater emphasis on selected lines of business. Several banks with superb financial ratios—including Fifth Third, Wilmington Trust, and State Street—have found a profitable niche and stuck to it.[12]

Bank Liability Shifts

The 1960s were characterized by innovations that included the introduction of liability management that provided banks with new sources of funds, primarily

**Table 10.3   Composition of Bank Portfolios, 1985, 1990, and 1991:
Deposit Liabilities and Equity**

Balance Sheet Items as a Percentage of Average Consolidated Assets

Item	1985	1990	1991
Deposits	60.89	62.50	63.47
In Foreign Offices	12.18	9.16	8.59
In Domestic Offices	48.72	53.34	54.88
Demand Deposits	15.61	12.98	12.77
Other Checkables	4.56	6.22	6.76
Savings (Including Money Market Deposit Accounts)	16.35	16.56	17.45
Small Time	16.33	19.38	20.55
Large Time	11.47	11.18	9.63
Gross Federal Funds Purchased and Repurchase Agreements	7.68	7.75	6.86
Non-Interest-Bearing Liabilities	3.59	4.85	4.79
Loss Reserves	0.80	1.55	1.58
Total Equity Capital	6.18	6.26	6.55

Source: Federal Reserve Bulletin, July 1992, p. 474.

purchased money available in large volume at money market rates. With the introduction of negotiable certificates of deposit and Eurodollars, and with the growth of federal funds trading, commercial banks untied themselves from the apron strings of demand and savings accounts. Now they could turn to purchased money to meet credit demands. The rapid growth of commercial banking made possible by liability management was a mixed blessing: While it was effective in meeting demands for credit, the rapid expansion of loans and investments also meant increased demand for additional bank capital and the beginning of the erosion of returns on assets. The 1980s could be characterized as a decade of aggressive lending practices largely for leveraged buy-outs. In the early 1990s, the opposite seems to be taking place, with corporations adding equity capital and reducing debt.

The money market deposit account, introduced as part of the Garn-St. Germain Act in 1982, represented close to 11 percent of all assets at banks, while demand deposits and other checkables accounted for nearly 13 percent and 7 percent of assets, respectively, at year-end 1991. (See Table 10.3.) Non-interest-bearing accounts represented almost 74 percent of bank deposits in 1954 and were once the principal source of bank funds. While they have eroded over the last few decades, other checkables or transaction deposits, like NOW accounts, have gained ground gradually since their introduction in the 1970s. The decline in the importance of demand deposits is related to the introduction of interest payment on checkables, the introduction of money market funds and money market accounts with check-writing privileges, a period of extraordinarily high interest rates, and a shift away from compensating balances and toward fees to pay for bank services and lines of credit.

PERCENT

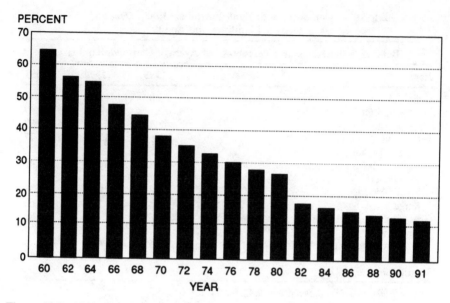

Figure 10.3 Non-Interest-Bearing Deposits as a Percentage of Average Assets. (Graph by S. L. Gart)

While demand deposit accounts were declining relative to time deposits, retail time and savings deposits continued to become a larger source of funding. (See Figure 10.3, Table 10.3, and Table 10.4.) This trend was in part related to the acquisition of thrifts by banks and a shift of consumer funds from thrifts to banks during the well-publicized savings and loan debacle, when households were concerned about the viability of savings and loans. It was also in part a response to a decline in higher deposit rates offered by troubled thrifts. The strength in retail accounts was concentrated in small-denomination time deposits. These inflows reduced the need for banks to issue more costly managed liabilities to fund the growth of their assets. Also, the shift was induced by the increased costs of large time and Eurodollar deposits relative to other interest and deposit rates as investors demanded higher risk premiums for uninsured deposits.[13]

As regards deposits, money market funds have siphoned off much of the low-cost deposit base from banks and thrifts, primarily because they offered higher yields, liquidity, and check-writing privileges. They can offer higher yields because they have a cost advantage over banks in that their overhead is about 80 cents for every hundred dollars in assets, while banks must still pay for multiple branches and tellers as well as depository insurance. With the deregulation of interest rates, banks no longer thrive on subsidies from small savers, who receive less than money market rates on their deposits. The deregulation of interest rates was one factor that led to lower bank profits in the early 1980s.

Table 10.4 Percentage Distribution of Assets and Liabilities of Commercial Banks

Assets	1950	1964	1987	1992
Cash and Monies Due from Banks	24%	18%	13%	11%
Treasury and Agency Securities	37	21	7	18
Other Securities	7	10	11	5
Loans	31	49	64	58
Other Assets	1	2	5	8
Total Assets	100%	100%	100%	100%
Liabilities and Capital				
Transaction Deposits	70%	55%	20%	20%
Time and Savings	22	34	54	54
Borrowings	0	1	14	12
Other Liabilities	1	2	5	5
Capital Accounts	7	8	7	9
Total Liabilities and Capital	100%	100%	100%	100%

Source: Selected FDIC Annual Reports and Federal Reserve Bulletins.

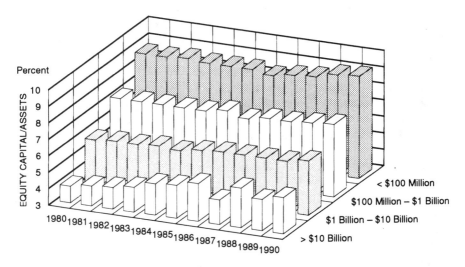

Figure 10.4 Ratio of Equity Capital to Assets of Banks, 1980–1990 (by Asset Size). (*Source:* Federal Deposit Insurance Corporation)

Equity capital-to-asset ratios have risen recently despite bank earnings problems, as banks have raised new equity in the capital markets, cut dividends, and sold off assets in order to prepare themselves for the new risk-based capital requirements. Some banks have added capital to pursue acquisitions in the coming years. (See Figure 10.4.) For every major segment of the financial services industry, capital and operating expenses grew more rapidly than GNP in the 1980s. However, operating expenses for commercial banks grew 50 percent faster than net worth.

From a longer term, historic perspective, the financial solidity of the banking industry has been weakening over much of the 20th century. A century ago, bank equity-to-asset ratios were nearly 25 percent; in the 1920s, they were about 12 percent; by 1974, the ratios for the largest banks had fallen to under 4 percent. The driving force behind this long-term decline in capital ratios has been the strengthening of bank safety nets: deposit insurance, assisted mergers, access to the discount window at the central bank, and the "too big to fail" doctrine. Depositors and creditors have tolerated a reduction in equity capital because the federal government has absorbed more of the risk of loss. The paradox is that the safety nets—in particular, federal deposit insurance—may have weakened the banking system's internal dynamics.[14] However, by year-end 1992, equity-to-asset ratios had risen to 7.06 percent.

Profitability Trends

While nonperforming assets (led by Latin American loans and domestic real estate loans) grew substantially during the 1980–1990 period, causing highly cyclical bank earnings and a deteriorating trend of returns on assets and on earnings for many banks, there were many positive developments on the banking front. Banks began to become more efficient as layoffs occurred throughout the industry and unnecessary branches were closed. For example, cost-cutting efforts and bank mergers contributed to a 1-percent decline in bank employment from year-end 1989 to year-end 1990. As a matter of fact, the nation's 25 largest banks eliminated 44,151 jobs in 1991, more than the combined cuts of the previous three years. Another 50,000 to 100,000 layoffs occurred at the big banks in 1992. Layoffs should remain substantial in the early 1990s as a result of consolidations and an attempt by banks to trim overhead in order to become "meaner and leaner" competitors. For some banks, this may be the only way they can survive. Noninterest income increased throughout the decade of the eighties. There were modest increases in fees for deposit services and in fees earned from credit and debit cards, mortgage servicing, servicing newly issued securities backed by consumer loans, securities processing, corporate cash management, merger advice, leveraged buy-out and mortgage lending, and money management. Fees for underwriting corporate securities are expected to become a new source of income for money-center and large regional banks in the rest of the decade. After the consolidation and cost-cutting period that lies ahead, powerful, profitable, and well-capitalized U.S. money-center and superregional banks will emerge. Some of these banks may have assets in the $300–400 billion range, while many community banks with high returns on assets and on equity will also survive and prosper, as many customers like doing business with the bank president and enjoy service on a friendly, first-name basis.

During 1991, the nation's banks earned $18.6 billion, a 15-percent increase over 1990. Most of the gain came from profits in the investment portfolio that could be

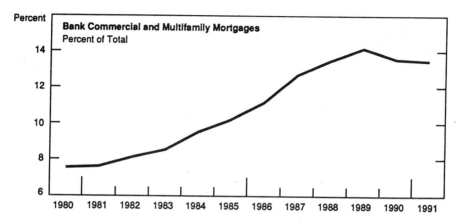

Figure 10.5 Trends in Bank Lending. (*Source:* Federal Reserve Bank of New York)

attributed to declining interest rates. It was the banking industry's best performance since 1988, when banks earned $24.8 billion. The 1991 earnings performance occurred even though 11 of the largest banks lost money. The number of banks on the FDIC's 1991 problem list reached 1,071, with assets at these banks reaching $613 billion. Bank earnings rose even higher in 1992 because of a widening spread between the return on loans and the cost of funds. Higher earnings led to a large decline in the number of banks on the FDIC's 1992 problem list.

The average estimated return on equity for lending to the highest quality corporate customers remaining at commercial banks is 7.5 percent, well below the bank's cost of capital. In the 1980s, prior to the collapse of many highly leveraged companies that had participated in leveraged buy-outs, substantial fees from heavily leveraged transactions masked temporarily the poor returns from "plain vanilla" corporate lending.[15]

The persistence of commercial real estate lending and loans to highly leveraged companies through 1989 testified to the pressure to book high-yield loans. Also, despite clear evidence of softness in property values and a weakening economy, commercial real estate loans grew twice as fast as commercial and industrial lending in 1989. (See Figure 10.2.) Of the portfolio of real estate loans, approximately 7 percent were classified as nonperforming at year-end 1990. (See Figure 10.6.) Also, for the 25 largest lenders, total loans to highly leveraged companies were about equivalent to total stated net worth.[16]

Banks are resorting to dividend cuts, layoffs, branch closings, and the sale of major blocks of assets by weaker banks to help increase profitability, reduce capital financing needs, and improve their overall chances of survival. Some banking giants have chosen to merge (e.g., C&S/Sovran with NCNB and Security Pacific with BankAmerica) in order to deal with the crisis and the need to boost capital. OECD economists refer to these large mergers as *elephant weddings*.

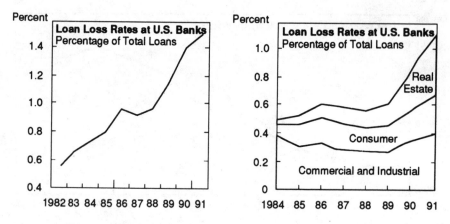

Figure 10.6   The Debt Hangover: Weakened Lenders. (Source: Federal Reserve Bank of New York)

For commercial banks, there remain a number of primary risks:

1. The banking industry's high level of operating leverage.
2. Deteriorating credit quality for banks with high-risk lending profiles, resulting in an enormous drag on income and profits relating to nonperforming and underperforming loans.
3. The vulnerability of banks with a geographically concentrated lending business to regional economic downturns.
4. Increasing capital costs imposed by public policy and the marketplace.
5. Liquidity pressures as investors tend to remove or not renew deposits in response to increasing risk levels or low interest rates.
6. Excess capacity: too many banks chasing too few good business opportunities. This often leads to inadequate returns, encouraging banks to take greater risks in order to generate increased income and revenue.[17] Also, banks with large branch networks are trying hard to make more effective use of their costly distribution systems by increasing the number of products and services that can be sold through these channels.
7. Swaps that may, according to E.G. Corrigan, be "introducing new risks into the marketplace." The lengthy chains of deals that swaps engender worry some critics. Analysts fear that if one transaction becomes unstuck, payments among dozens of other parties could be disrupted, transmitting financial shocks from market to market and country to country at alarming speeds, since most swaps are unsecured and exposed to volatile interest rates, currency, and futures markets. The size of the swaps market eclipses the value of all shares traded on the New York and Tokyo stock exchanges combined.[18]

Table 10.5   Comparative Balance Sheets: Manufacturing Firm Versus Commercial Bank

Manufacturing Company Assets	% of Total	Liabilities and Equity	% of Total
Cash/Securities	5%	Accounts Payable	20%
Accounts Receivable	25	Short-Term Notes Payable	10
Inventory	30	Current Liabilities	30%
Current Assets	60%	Long-Term Debt	30
Plant and Equipment	40	Stockholders' Equity	40
Total	100%	Total	100%
Commercial Bank Assets	**% of Total**	**Liabilities and Equity**	**% of Total**
Cash	5%	Deposits	76%
Short-Term Securities/		Short-Term Borrowings	8
Deposits	16	Current Liabilities	84%
Short-Term Loans	50	Long-Term Debt	9
Current Assets	71%	Stockholders' Equity	7
Long-Term Securities	6	Total	100%
Long-Term Loans	13		
Other Assets	10		
Total	100%		

BANK RETURNS ON ASSETS AND EQUITY

Bank returns on assets (ROAs) tend to be much lower than ROAs at industrial companies. This is because equity as a percentage of total assets is at best no more than 8 percent at most banks, compared with closer to 40–60 percent at industrial corporations. (See Table 10.5.) Banks have substantial liabilities in the form of deposits. While bank ROAs are typically considerably smaller than ROAs at industrial corporations, bank returns on equity (ROEs) are higher, on average, than those at most industrial corporations.

The steady increase in loan losses among banks is the product of greater risk taking, the loss of the Fortune 1000 customers, and the narrowing of spreads on conventional lending business. Figures 10.5 and 10.6 show the increased risks assumed by banks in the larger percentage of loans they make to finance commercial real estate. The charts mask the increased risks at banks in the huge growth in highly leveraged transactions to finance corporate takeovers and other restructurings, since these loans are included in the commercial and industrial category. Many of these transactions have not worked out, and some analysts expect that about 15 percent of all loans for highly leveraged transactions will eventually have to be restructured, compared with just over 5 percent at the time of this writing. Banks might have cushioned the negative effects of their lending mistakes if they had

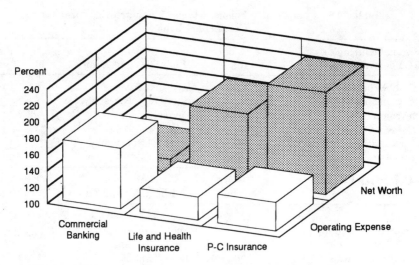

Figure 10.7 Runaway Noninterest Expenses in Banking, 1980–1989. (*Source:* Orin Kramer, *Rating the Risks: Assessing the Solvency Threat in the Financial Services Industry.* Copyright © 1991 Insurance Information Institute.)

Table 10.6 Profits of Insured Banks, By Asset Size, 1985–1991 (Percent)

Type of Return and Bank Size	1985	1986	1987	1988	1989	1990	1991
ROA							
All Banks	.71	.64	.09	.83	.49	.49	.54
Less than $300 million	.75	.58	.62	.72	.85	.79	.82
$300 million to $5 billion	.85	.79	.53	.75	.74	.53	.53
$5 billion or more[a]	.75	.70	-.13	.80	.55	.28	.58
Ten largest banks	.47	.47	-.70	1.07	-.22	.47	.21
ROE							
All Banks	11.29	10.21	2.26	14.41	8.04	8.02	8.09
Less than $300 million	9.40	7.60	7.76	8.08	10.56	9.42	9.67
$300 million to $5 billion	12.98	11.96	10.05	12.96	11.58	7.58	7.50
$5 billion or more[a]	13.34	12.20	-2.44	15.97	9.71	5.82	9.40
Ten largest banks	9.87	9.59	-15.61	22.82	-4.40	10.11	4.26

[a] Excluding 10 largest banks.
Source: Federal Reserve Bulletin, July 1992.

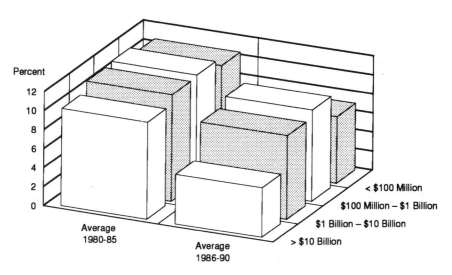

Figure 10.8 Bank Return on Equity by Size, 1980–1990. (*Source:* Barth, Brumbaugh, and Litan, *The Banking Industry in Turmoil.* Copyright © 1991 by The American College. Reprinted with permission. This originally appeared in the 1991 Frank M. Engle Lecture.)

better control of their noninterest expenses, which grew faster than their net worth during the 1980s.[19] (See Figure 10.7.) Bank ROAs and ROEs have been trending downward for almost a decade. While there are still many fine regional and community banks with ROAs in excess of 1.0 percent, there are few money-center banks that exceed that level. Most profitable money-center banks have ROAs clustered between 0.25 and 0.70 percent. (See Table 10.6.) ROAs at these banks have been extremely volatile over the last six years because of heavy losses in Latin American, leveraged buy-out, and commercial real estate loans.

Smaller community banks tend to have higher and more stable ROAs than the larger banks. They tend to utilize only their core deposit base, minimizing the use of more costly funding. There is also a tendency among smaller banks to know their customers well and to be more conservative in their lending practices. Many of these banks have their portfolios concentrated in residential mortgage loans, Treasury securities, and mortgage-backed securities. Many well-run community banks have ROAs in excess of 1.25 percent, with some of the best exceeding 1.5 percent.

The best of the superregionals have ROAs in the range of 1.0 to 1.45 percent. However, most of the big regionals have experienced problems in their real estate portfolios, while those with large participations in loans for highly leveraged transactions have also experienced some difficulties. Few regional banks have suffered from the foreign lending problems of the money-center banks; hence, most regionals have posted higher ROAs than the giant banks. Those regionals that avoided lending

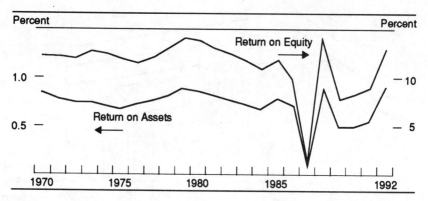

Figure 10.9 Return on Equity and on Assets, All Insured Commercial Banks, 1970–1992. (Based on data from the Board of Governors of the Federal Reserve System)

for highly leveraged transactions and that minimized their commercial lending exposure have outperformed the average bank.

The typical bank in the $300 million-to-$5 billion asset range has an ROE between 7.50 and 13.00 percent, compared with a range of 7.60 to 10.60 percent for the smaller banks. The ROEs for the largest banks are the most volatile and have ranged from -16 percent to 23 percent. The latter return was achieved when some unexpected interest payments from a Latin-American country were made. (See Table 10.6 and Figure 10.8.)

From the duPont formula,

$$ROE = Net\ Income/Equity =$$

$$Profit\ Margin \times Asset\ Utilization \times Equity\ Multiplier,$$

$$(Net\ Income/Revenues) \times (Revenues/Assets) \times (Assets/Equity)$$

and a careful perusal of the numbers in Table 10.6 and Figure 10.9, we see that ROE fell below 3 percent in 1987 (one of the lowest ratios in U.S banking history). This was caused for the most part by low profit margins. Banks were finding their earnings squeezed by increasing expenses and heavy deductions from current revenues to cover loan losses, particularly from energy and real estate loans in the southwest. In 1988, ROEs roared back to average nearly 15 percent, as the industry's profit margin surged upward, with revenues—particularly, noninterest or fee revenues—growing much faster than operating expenses. This caused banking's asset utilization to increase as well. In 1989 through 1991, ROEs declined again, to about 8 percent, as profit margins faltered when losses from loans for real estate, Latin America, and highly leveraged transactions increased. However, in the early 1990s, banks strengthened their financial condition by making substantial provisions against loan losses, improving their capital positions, and reducing expenses through restructuring and consolidaton. Lending spreads also widened in 1992. This helped raise the ROE to 12.80 percent and the ROA to 0.92 in 1992. There were continued increases in noninterest income, including higher service charges on deposits and increased income from credit card fees, consumer banking fees, and fees for processing securities. There were also increased fees from off-balance sheet activities, including fees associated with derivative products, loan servicing, mortgage banking, securitization, and trust activities.

The relatively poor performance of the biggest banks is no mystery, because they suffered the most from the loss of good customers to the commercial paper market, securitization in general, their major role in lending for highly leveraged transactions, and nonperforming Latin American debt. However, most of these giant banks also had bloated staffs, which drove up their noninterest expenses and drove down their profit margins. The money-center banks began to address their high noninterest expenses in 1989–1992 and, for the most part, have announced large cutbacks in personnel and branch systems. While many banks have serious problems, a number of banks have performed exceptionally well. Among the 10 most profitable banks in the United States are Banc One, SunTrust, and Manufacturers National, in the $10 billion and larger category; Mercantile Bancshares of Baltimore, Fifth Third, First Hawaiian, and First Virginia, in the $5-to-$10 billion range; and Wilmington Trust, River Forest Bancorp in Chicago, and Valley National of Clifton, New Jersey, in the $1-to-$5 billion range (See Table 10.7.) These banks are well capitalized, well managed, and powered by strong market niches or strong market share. They are also characterized by good cost controls and excellent credit quality and loss control. Most of them pay strict attention to providing products and services of outstanding quality and perceived value. They also understand how to make a good acquisition without suffering much dilution in earnings per share, and, at the same time, they know how to make the acquisition work. A number of these banks have concentrated on generating increased fee income. (See Figure 10.10.)

FOREIGN COMPETITION IN U.S. BANKING MARKETS

As recently as 25 years ago, foreign banks and U.S. branches of foreign banks accounted for only 1.5 percent of total commercial lending by banks in the nation. However, foreign penetration of U.S. wholesale bank lending in the United States (including offshore lending) reached 45 percent in 1991 and controlled about 22 percent of total U.S. banking assets. (See Tables 10.8 and 10.9 and Figure 10.11.) Assets of foreign bank offices in the U.S. reached $789 billion in 1990, compared with only $198 billion in 1980. A higher level of foreign penetration has been achieved in only one broad industry group: leather goods. In sum, U.S. wholesale banking has gone from an extreme dominance of the domestic market in the 1960s to a position whereby foreign banks are extremely competitive and hold a sizable market share. Much of this gain can be attributed to the growth of Japanese banks in this country and in their participation in large syndicated leveraged buy-out related

Table 10.7 Ten Extremely Profitable Banks

Bank	Assets ($ Millions)	Equity/ Assets	1991 ROAA	1991 ROAE	NPA/EQ + RES	4-YR. AVG ROAA
Banc One	46.3	8.24	1.39	14.29	18.6	1.39
SunTrust	34.5	7.37	1.13	15.17	24.11	1.12
Manufacturers National	13.5	6.15	1.00	15.05	13.97	1.04
Fifth Third	8.8	9.96	1.64	16.24	12.83	1.62
First Hawaiian	6.5	7.65	1.36	17.35	11.86	1.27
First Virginia	6.1	8.83	1.22	13.44	7.50	1.30
Mercantile	5.2	10.46	1.35	12.91	14.27	1.54
Wilmington Trust	4.1	8.51	1.90	22.58	17.81	1.85
Valley National	2.9	6.79	1.28	15.41	17.47	1.67
River Forest	1.3	7.62	1.62	21.21	17.53	1.77

ROAA = return on adjusted assets
ROAE = return on adjusted equity
NPA/EQ = non-performing assets/equity
RES = reserve for losses

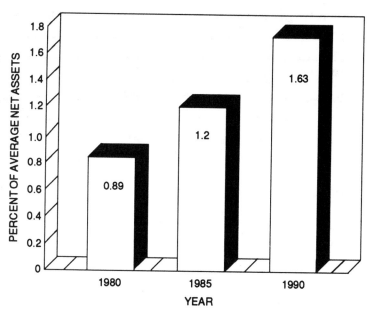

Figure 10.10   Rise in Bank Fee Income in the 1980s (Noninterest Income/Average Net Assets). (*Source:* Federal Reserve data for all insured commercial banks)

**Table 10.8   Foreign Bank Assets Held in United States,
Year-End 1990 ($ Billions)**

Country	U.S. Assets	Foreign Assets
Japan	$435.5	55.3%
Italy	48.0	6.1
Britain	44.1	5.6
Canada	40.2	5.1
France	37.4	4.8
Switzerland	25.6	3.3
Hong Kong	22.4	2.8
Germany	16.2	2.1
Netherlands	12.8	1.6
Israel	10.3	1.3
Spain	10.3	1.3
Ireland	9.2	1.2
Others	75.1	9.5

Source: Senate Banking Committee.

Table 10.9   Foreign Bank Share of U.S. Commercial and Industrial Loan Market, Selected Years ($ Billions)

	1983	1987	1989	1991
Commercial and Industrial Loans to U.S. Addresses	467	654	765	777
Loans by U.S. Banks	381	445	481	428
Onshore	364	431	460	407
Offshore	17	15	21	22
Loans by Foreign-Owned Banks	86	209	284	348
Onshore	66	130	168	196
Offshore	20	79	116	152
Foreign Share %	18%	32%	37%	45%
Onshore	14%	20%	22%	25%
Offshore	4%	12%	15%	20%

Source: Federal Reserve Bank of New York *Quarterly Review,* Spring 1992, p. 54. [Figures subject to round-off error.]

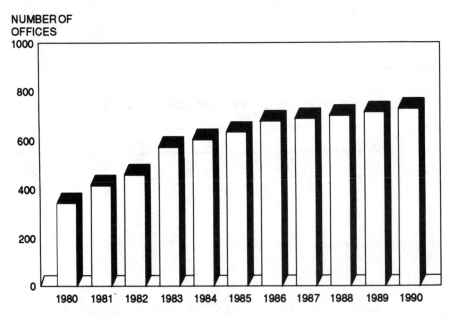

Figure 10.11   Foreign Bank Offices in the United States. (*Source:* Board of Governors of the Federal Reserve System)

loans, in loans to foreign companies doing business in the United States and in the sale of loans by U.S. banks to foreign banks to avoid violating lending limits and to reduce capital requirements. On the other hand, foreign banks play only a limited role in retail banking in the United States. Because of weaker balance sheets and higher borrowing costs at U.S. commercial banks, many U.S. corporations are turning more toward foreign banks and U.S. insurance companies to provide them with external funding. A study by Greenwich Associates showed that more than one-third of 1,150 companies recently surveyed downgraded or terminated a banking relationship because of the financial condition of the bank.[20]

The rapid growth in competition from foreign banking organizations can be explained in part by the continued global integration of the nonfinancial portion of the U.S. economy and increased foreign direct investment in the United States. The rapid growth of foreign banks in the nation can be explained partially by the huge increase in market capitalization of Japanese banks, the removal of Japanese foreign exchange controls and restrictions on capital outflows in 1980, the availability of huge amounts of leveraged buy-out related loans at attractive rates in the 1980s, and the reversals suffered by U.S. banks in the late 1980s and early 1990s. The lifting of foreign exchange controls and restrictions on capital outflows allowed Japanese industrial customers to avoid the banks and go directly to the capital markets for financing. The loss of some of their best customers, along with the regulation of deposit rates and stiffer competition from other types of institutions, reduced bank profits. In order to improve their profitability and to service Japanese nonfinancial companies that had expanded abroad, Japanese banks moved into new markets overseas. It is noteworthy that the largest Japanese banks were four to five times better capitalized than the major money-center banks in New York prior to the 55-percent decline in the Nikkei average in 1990–1992.[21] Japan's share of all foreign assets and liabilities rose from 4 percent in 1982 to more than 15 percent in 1990.

Since Japanese banks are permitted to hold stocks in their investment portfolios, the capital position of many Japanese banks deteriorated substantially as capital gains on stocks that were accumulated (and unrealized) over the years were wiped out at many banks. Under the rules established by the Bank for International Settlements, Japanese banks are permitted to count as capital a portion of unrealized gains on their stock holdings. Now, some Japanese banks no longer meet the Basle Accord minimum-risk-based capital standards required for 1992. If these banks are unable to raise capital to replace the value of their stock holdings, they will have to cut back sharply on lending, especially foreign loans in the United States. Such a cutback could affect the U.S. economy. Also, some Japanese banks needed their former capital cushion to cover huge losses in commercial real estate, estimated to exceed $200 billion. At least one Japanese bank could fail if the economy and stock market of Japan do not improve during 1993–1994, although it is assuring to note that regulators have not allowed a single bank to fail since World War II. A number of weakened smaller banks have been forced into marriages with bigger ones, while the Bank of Japan is working hard to arrange mergers to prevent even a single bank failure. According to a report leaked from the Bank of Japan in April 1992, Japan's banks are holding $215 billion in bad loans. (In other words, about 5 percent of all Japanese bank loans are nonperforming.) Analysts claim that about 8 percent of borrowers from Nippon Credit Bank Limited are not paying interest on loans.[22] There is also speculation that the Finance Ministry may adopt radical reform measures that will force the banks to reveal the extent of their bad loans and allow them to trim their assets by converting their loans to securities and then selling them to pension funds and insurance companies in a newly created secondary market.[23]

Pavel and McElravey sum up the changes that are taking place in world financial markets: "Financial globalization is being driven by advances in data processing and telecommunications, liberalization of restrictions on cross-border capital flows, deregulation of domestic capital markets, and greater competition among these markets for a share of the world's trading volume."[24]

A glance at a list of the largest banks in the world might suggest the misleading conclusion that U.S. banks have been losing their positions of prominence in the international marketplace to the Japanese. A closer analysis shows that the domination of the list by Japanese banks is primarily related to Japan's domestic economic situation, its healthy level of market capitalization, the fact that the largest U.S. banks suffered repeated reverses related to a series of regional downturns, the failure of many lesser developed countries and leveraged buy-out borrowers to repay their loans as scheduled, and the collapse of the domestic commercial real estate market. The retrenchment of U.S. banking abroad reflects the lessening attractiveness of low-return foreign operations as severe loan losses, as well as limited capital, have pressured U.S. banks to reduce their foreign lending and branching activities. By the end of 1990, U.S. banks were operating 819 branches in foreign countries and overseas areas of the United States, a decline from 916 branches at the end of 1985. U.S. banks have also been handicapped in dealing with customers by regulations forbidding banks to engage fully in securities and insurance underwriting and sales. Most foreign banks have no such limitation. Also, U.S. banks earn substantial net revenues from services, rather than from loans and other investments. Therefore, size as such is not as meaningful for them.[25]

Most Japanese and European banks acquired U.S. financial institutions from domestic owners. The number of foreign bank offices in the United States reached 727 at the beginning of 1991, including 370 branches and 224 agencies. Nearly half of the offices are located in New York, with most of the remainder in California, Illinois, and Florida. A similar change of ownership has been observed in countries such as the United Kingdom and Italy, where Japanese or European owners have replaced U.S. owners. Only in 1992 did we observe a change in the opposite direction, when the Bank of New York agreed to purchase Barclay's retail branch network in New York.

Stung by the collapse of BCCI, bank regulators in Europe, Japan, and the United States are tightening their rules for dealing with multinational banks. The U.S.

Congress is expected to adopt a Federal Reserve proposal that will enhance the central bank's powers to police foreign banks operating in the United States. If the central bank is not satisfied with bank supervision and compliance in the home country, the Federal Reserve will be allowed to keep a foreign bank from operating within the United States. While many banks have international operations, only a few are truly international in scope. More than 50 percent of the total banking assets and liabilities in Switzerland, almost 50 percent in the United Kingdom, and more than 25 percent of total banking assets and liabilities in France are foreign. On the other hand, less than 25 percent of the balance sheets of Japanese, German, and U.S. banks consist of foreign assets and liabilities. The United Kingdom (London) and Switzerland (Zurich) have long been international financial centers. For over 100 years, Swiss bankers have been raising money for foreigners, and more than half of all banking institutions in the United Kingdom are foreign owned, while close to 60 percent of all assets of banks in the United Kingdom are denominated in foreign currency. Also, a considerable portion of international banking assets are in unregulated offshore banking centers and in interbank deposits. Consequently, a large proportion of banks' foreign assets and liabilities are claims on or claims of foreign banks. Foreign exchange trading is another important international banking activity, with average daily trading volume estimated to be between $400 and $500 billion.[26]

One of the implications for European banks brought about by the political and economic changes in 1992 was a large increase in mergers and consolidations, as well as in joint ventures. The largest and strongest financial institutions—those with the managerial talent to operate a geographically dispersed organization—have become Euro-wide firms, while smaller firms have a more regional focus. Still, others serve as niche players. In addition, just as state laws have slowed the process of nationwide banking in the United States, language and cultural barriers will slow the process in Europe. As financial service companies in Europe begin to operate with fewer restrictions, there will be competitive pressure on Japan and the United States to remove barriers between commercial and investment banking. The European Community's efforts at regulatory harmonization may hasten the demise of Glass-Steagall in the United States and Article 65 in Japan.[27]

While U.S. money-center banks have suffered for years from their nonperforming loans (see Table 10.10), there may be an unexpected bonanza for several giant banks with the biggest loan exposures to lesser developed countries. Bankers reached an agreement with Argentina in spring 1992 and with Brazil in summer 1992 to swap most of their nonperforming loans to those countries for interest-bearing "Brady" bonds, backed by U.S. Treasury securities purchased by Argentina and Brazil. That deal should eventually translate into earnings gains for the banks involved, because the value of the bonds will be greater than the value of the nonperforming loans. Most banks have already written off between 55 and 90 percent of these loans to lesser developed countries. The Brady bond swaps and the writing off of a large

Table 10.10 Lesser Developed Country Exposure at Money-Center Banks, as of December 31, 1990 ($ Billions)

Bank	Medium- and Long-Term Lesser Developed Country Loans	Lesser Developed Country Reserves	Reserves to Lesser Developed Country Loans (%)	Lesser Developed Country Loans as Percent of Loans	Adjusted[a] Reserves as Percent of Adjusted Lesser Developed Country Loans
Citicorp	7.6	2.4	31	4.9	43
Manufacturers Hanover	4.2	1.4	34	10.3	50
Chase Manhattan	4.0	1.6	40	5.4	59
BankAmerica	3.0	1.5	49	3.5	62
Bankers Trust	1.8E	1.3	72	8.4	N/A
Chemical Banking	1.4	0.9	69	3.1	78
J.P. Morgan	1.3	1.3	100	4.7	100
First Chicago	0.3	N/A	N/A	1.1	74

[a] Net charge-offs added back both to loans and reserves.
Note: NA = Not available; E = Estimated.
Source: Company reports.

Table 10.11   Lesser Developed Country Loan Recovery Potential

Institution	Original Loan Amount	Current Book Value	Postrenegotiation Face Value	Gain
BankAmerica	$1,950	$ 655	$1,268	$ 613
Chase Manhattan	2,030	716	1,320	604
Chemical	3,590	1,285	2,334	1,049
Citicorp	4,020	1,436	2,613	1,177

Source: Company reports.

percentage of Latin American loans will also help to clean up bank balance sheets and free up much of the $4 billion that U.S. banks have reserved against Third-World debt. The banks have two options: They can receive the face amount of their loans in below-market, fixed-rate bonds, or they can forgive 35 percent of their loans in exchange for floating-rate bonds. As of June 1992, Argentine loans were valued at about $0.30 on the dollar, while Brazilian loans were valued at about $0.36 on the dollar. In either case, banks could receive securities with a face value of $0.65 on the dollar after debt forgiveness. The banks could then book the difference as income if they sold the bonds. (See Table 10.11.)

While U.S. money-center banks have suffered large losses from their nonperforming lesser developed country loans, these losses pale in comparison with what analysts expect to see eventually from the commercial real estate market collapse. Commercial mortgages outstanding at year-end 1991 amounted to $373 billion, five times the level of outstanding lesser developed country loans for the U.S. banking industry as a whole. In addition, banks have $425 billion in outstanding real estate loans. While banks have written off approximately $26 billion in lesser developed country loans from 1987 through 1991, they have only written off $18 billion in commercial real estate loans from 1989 through 1991. Since the real estate crisis is not expected to end until the mid-1990s, some bank stock analysts expect commercial real estate losses to eventually dwarf loan losses to lesser developed countries.

SHIFT FROM RELATIONSHIP BANKING TO PRICE BANKING

Relationship banking refers to a banking environment in which financial transactions are seen as part of a continuous, unfolding relationship between banks and their customers. *Price banking* describes financial transactions that are usually price driven. In price banking, it is more likely that funds are moved to another financial partner when prices are attractive, since each transaction is viewed as an independent event.[28] Although prices do play a modest role in relationship banking, what matters in a relationship environment is that current prices generally do not determine the allocation of funds. In such environments, frequent and rapid changes of partners among lenders, banks, and borrowers are less likely than they are in a price-driven environment, where the players are led primarily by the best price or deal. Therefore, in a relationship system, the ability to attract and gain access to funds is partly vested in the relationship itself. The development and maintenance of these relationships in the United States provided long-term banking stability and profitability for many years.[29]

Historically, relationship banking often had roots in old school ties between a treasurer or CEO of an organization and a banker; in regulatory reforms of the 1930s, such as price ceilings on deposits and limitations on the maximum size of a loan; in geographic segmentation; and in market restrictions on products, which limited the alternatives available to suppliers and users of capital. In the market, banks could compete only with a limited number of products, while customers faced limited alternatives or opportunities. Banking was simplistic: Well-defined products were sold to longstanding customers in an environment of regulatory price ceilings.[30]

Following interest rate increases from the middle of the 1960s to 1982, relationship banking began to deteriorate because new price-oriented instruments, developed by financial innovators, attempted to exploit newly identified market opportunities.[31] When banks wanted to accelerate their growth, it was clear that they could do so only if they could attract money beyond that provided by their traditional customers. The older forms of financial transactions, which had been based on simple, established relationships, gave way to more complex and price-oriented dealings. As customers attempted to reach for higher yields, disintermediation occurred, and alternatives to the traditional relationships appeared. The banks countered by becoming more aggressive and innovative. This led to a more complex and volatile financial system in which banks chose the rate at which they wished to grow by pursuing liability management—that is, purchasing the required funds in the wholesale marketplace.

The traditional fundamentals that had permitted and even encouraged the development of relationships were increasingly compromised as the emerging influence of price banking gave banks further opportunities to buy and sell money. Funding opportunities could easily be entered into through price competition, without having to rely on carefully developed relationships. Money began to depend more and more on prices.

Long-lasting relationships had developed because the cost of switching financial partners was high, while alternatives were limited and price competition was lacking. In switching banks, a borrower had to reestablish credentials as the information vested in existing relationships was lost and the mutual noncontractual obligations were dissipated. Regulation Q was supportive of relationship banking, since a ceiling on depository rates offered no incentives to switch banks. Banks were left to compete on service and convenience, which also fostered ongoing relationships because there was no price competition or product differentiation.[32]

The development of the negotiable certificate of deposit and the Eurodollar market, as well as the growth of the commercial paper market, led to the decline of relationship banking. The stability and relative simplicity of relationships, which

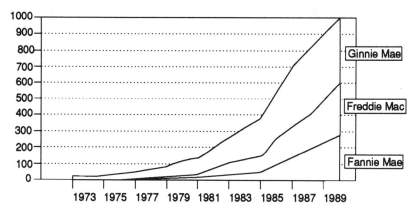

Figure 10.12 Mortgage-Backed Securities, 1973–1990 (Billions of Dollars). (*Source: Federal Reserve Bulletin,* various issues)

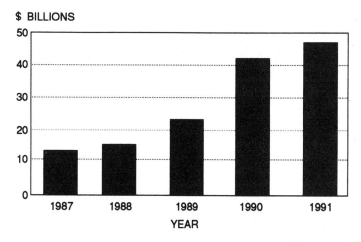

Figure 10.13 The Boom in Securitization: Face Value of Issues of Securities Backed by Loans. (Graph by S. L. Gart)

had depended on a lack of financial alternatives, were replaced by a variety of price-sensitive new financial products and instruments. A large flow of product innovation allowed market participants to avoid relationships and to react to price incentives. Also, the value of customer relationships declined relative to the ability to offer a product at a competitive price.[33]

One implication of a price-driven banking environment is that the largest U.S. banks enjoy a competitive advantage. This is because failures of large banks do not occur without serious disruptions to the entire financial system. It appears as if some "implicit guarantee" may be taken into account by large banks that adopt speculative loan policies. In sum, the shift from relationship banking to price banking evolved during the 1980s, bringing with it product innovation and a reliance on price-competitive markets, which are inherently less stable than traditional relationship banking.[34]

BANKING'S ROLE IN SECURITIZATION

Securitization has been made possible by the increasing availability of information on the quality of customers' credit in computer-managed databases. With this information, loans may be packaged with predictable maturity and credit risks. Many bank loans, such as home mortgage loans, car loans, and credit card receivables are being packaged into actively traded securities. (See Figures 10.12 and 10.13.) The availability of significant information regarding consumer loans and the ability to perform statistical, actuarial, and financial analysis on that information have acted as a catalyst in stimulating the growth of securitization and loan sales. Banks benefit from securitization by earning both packaging and underwriting fees. In addition, banks can remove loans from their books (making room for new loans), reduce their capital requirements, earn fee income, and earn the interest rate spread between the yield on the security and the loan yield. Also, a combination of asset sales and securitization permitted depository institutions to reduce their interest rate risk. Banks and thrifts turned over funds more frequently, financing a greater volume of loans and earning additional fee income. Holdings of securities backed by mortgage pools grew rapidly, accounting for part of the decline in the share of financial assets held by financial institutions in the 1980s.[35]

By allowing lenders to originate and sell off the aforesaid loans quickly, securitization makes it much easier for nonbanks to enter the lending business. For example, half of all home loans in the 1990s were financed with mortgage-backed securities. Securitization has lured other lenders into the mortgage business, which has eroded the need for thrift institutions.

Increases in Off-Balance-Sheet Banking

Together with increasing securitization, the growth of the secondary loan sales market has not brought greater discipline to the commercial lending process. Indeed, it has led to a lowering of underwriting standards.

When forward rate agreements, credit enhancement agreements, and interest rate swaps are made, there is no entry on the balance sheet of the banking institution. These transactions involve either cash flows or contingencies, so they are referred to as *off-balance-sheet items*.

Banks have offered guarantees for decades to help in the open-market funding of obligations. For example, banks have offered standby letters of credit in the issuance of bankers' acceptances and in guaranteeing municipal bonds and commercial paper against default on payment of either interest or principal. Banks have also offered corporate borrowers backup lines of credit for commercial paper issues and have arranged explicit lines of credit with customers. Some of these credit enhancements have enabled corporate borrowers to have wider access to direct markets. Because there is less risk to lenders, corporations can borrow at a lower rate of interest. Banks now earn fee income rather than interest income in this type of transaction.

Off-balance-sheet banking does not mean that assets and liabilities are not subject to interest rate risk. Neither does it mean that credit enhancements and guarantees are without credit risk. Banks writing such agreements may have to assume the debt of a troubled company to which the agreement or guarantee was offered. Holders of securities having such guarantees are also subject to third-party risk—that is, the chance that the bank will default on its credit enhancement.[36]

Banks may avoid reserve requirements and deposit insurance premiums if revenues are earned sans deposit taking and with off-balance-sheet products and services. Also, the development of secondary markets for loans has helped banks sell and securitize loans, shrinking the banks' balance sheets.[37]

ENDNOTES

1. G. H. Hempel, A. B. Coleman, and D. G. Simonson, *Bank Management: Text and Cases,* 3d ed. (New York: John Wiley and Sons, 1990), p. 28.

2. R. E. Litan, "The Revolution in U.S. Finance: Past, Present and Future," Frank M. Engle Lecture (Bryn Mawr, PA: The American College, April 30, 1991), p. 1.

3. O. Kramer, *Rating the Risk* (New York: Insurance Information Institute, 1990), p. 95.

4. Ibid., p. 98.

5. Ibid., p. 91.

6. Ibid., p. xxiii.

7. Ibid., p. 89.

8. Ibid., p. 90.

9. A. D. Brunner, J. V. Duca, and M. M. McLaughlin, "Recent Developments Affecting the Profitability and Practices of Commercial Banks," *Federal Reserve Bulletin,* July 1991, pp. 508–509.

10. Ibid., p. 519.

11. Kramer, p. 44.

12. "The Prophets of Profit," *Transition,* January 1992, p. 5.

13. Brunner, Duca, and McLaughlin, pp. 509–510.

14. Kramer, pp. xxxiii–xxxiv.

15. Ibid., p. xxi.

16. Ibid., pp. xxii–xxiii.

17. Ibid., pp. 4, 11.

18. W. Glasgall and B. Jaretski, "Swap Fever: Big Money, Big Risks," *Business Week,* June 1, 1992, pp. 102–104.

19. Litan, pp. 19–31.

20. F. Bleakley, *The Wall Street Journal,* October 19, 1991.

21. H. L. Baer, "Foreign Competition in U.S. Banking Markets," *Economic Perspectives,* Federal Reserve Bank of Chicago, May–June 1990, pp. 22–29.

22. T. Holden and J. Bernathan, "The Squeeze Felt 'Round the World," *Business Week,* April 27, 1992, p. 56.

23. Holden and Bernathan, p. 57.

24. C. Pavel and N. McElravey, "The Globalization of the Financial Services Industry," *Economic Perspectives,* Federal Reserve Bank of Chicago, May–June 1990, pp. 3–18.

25. G. J. Bentson, "U.S. Banking in an Increasingly Integrated and Competitive Economy," *International Competitiveness in Financial Service,* eds. M. H. Kosters and A. H. Meltzer (Boston: Kluwer Academic Publishers, 1991), pp. 313–335.

26. Pavel and McElravey, pp. 7–8.

27. Ibid.

28. Quoted in D. Meerschwam, "Breaking Relationships: The Advent of Price Banking in the United States," *Wall Street and Regulation,* ed. S. L. Hayes (Boston: Harvard Business School, 1987), pp. 63–65.

29. Ibid., p. 65.

30. Ibid., pp. 65, 90.

31. Ibid., pp. 80–81.

32. Meerschwam, p. 89.

33. Ibid., pp. 90–93.

34. I. Leveson, *Financial Services: The Next Era* (Marlboro, NJ: Author, 1991), p. 199.

35. *Investor's Business Daily,* May 4, 1992, p. 3.

36. W. L. Scott, *Contemporary Financial Markets and Service: Instructor's Manual* (St. Paul: West Publishing Co., 1990), p. 7.

37. Ibid., p. 33.

11 The Consolidation of the Banking Industry

One way out of the banking problem is a massive consolidation of banks. The cost efficiencies that can be realized are huge . . . with fewer players, lower costs and lower risks, [banks] will make more money.

Thomas S. Johnson

Historically, the primary reason for government intrusion into the affairs of banks has been to "insure the safe and sound conduct of such business." Much of the regulatory structure remains oriented toward the "soundness" objective. For example, the major benefit of providing deposit insurance is the prevention of a bank run that will spread to other solvent banks. As another example, Regulation Q was imposed initially to control the prices institutions paid for funds. Later, it also induced banks to take fewer lending risks because their funding costs were limited. In fact, Regulation Q protected banks and thrifts by controlling their cost of funds. On the other hand, with rising interest rates, Regulation Q became a burden for, rather than a protector of, depository institutions. With the introduction of unregulated money market accounts in the early 1970s, classical depository disintermediation occurred when interest rates rose substantially in the mid-1970s and large deposits left the banks and thrifts for higher interest rates in money market funds and Treasury bills. Gradually, Regulation Q was repealed. However, while its repeal stopped the problem with disintermediation of deposits, it proved to be disastrous for many of the thrift institutions, whose short-term cost of depository funds rose above the average yields of long-term mortgages. Many thrifts failed as a result of this unprofitable mismatch of long-term fixed-rate mortgages that were at rates below short-term deregulated deposits. At that time, thrifts did not have the power to make consumer loans (which were short term) and thus could not offer attractive interest rates.

As a matter of fact, if banks and thrifts and their holding companies had been permitted to branch and expand nationwide, many financial institutions would not have failed in the 1980s and early 1990s, when economic conditions soured in the oil states of Texas, Oklahoma, Louisiana, and Arkansas and then later in New England. According to R.E. Litan of the American Enterprise Institute, if nationwide branching or expansion had been in effect, many of the failed depository institutions in these regions would probably have belonged to larger, more geographically diversified organizations whose profits generated from throughout the country would have helped them absorb losses in the regionally depressed areas.[1]

Although Congress did not approve nationwide banking in the 1991 reform bill, in May 1992 the Office of Thrift Supervision gave approval to federally chartered savings and loan associations to open branches in any state. This should allow institutions to diversify their risk, since lenders would be less vulnerable to local economic disturbances and regional recessions. However, savings and loans seeking to expand would still have to apply to federal regulators for permission to open branches across state borders. These thrifts would have to meet certain solvency criteria and would have to comply with the Community Reinvestment Act in regard to lending to all sectors of the community. A key feature of the nationwide branching proposal is that it might add value to the failed thrifts being marketed by the Resolution Trust Corporation. It would permit a buyer to purchase a thrift in one state and then open branches in desirable locations in other states.[2]

In the 1970s and 1980s, a number of new regulatory objectives emerged, including providing for consumer protection, encouraging appropriate allocation of credit to community needs, promoting competition in the banking and financial services industry, and encouraging the allocation of bank credit to certain areas defined as desirable for public policy reasons. With the current sizable problematic loans of many commercial banks, regulation in the early 1990s has been concerned with solvency issues, adequacy of capital, and FDIC insurance reform. Following on the footsteps of a risk-based capital adequacy policy, Congress passed legislation in 1991 requiring the establishment of risk-based FDIC insurance premiums by 1994. In summer 1992, the FDIC responded to this legislation by proposing a formula for risk-based deposit premiums that included an increase in premiums for depository insurance for 1993 only for the bottom quartile of banks with the lowest capital-to-asset ratios.

The regulators are also expected to offer clearer guidelines to banks on how to calculate loan-loss reserves. Regulators may allow a bank that has received a partial payment on a loan to consider that part for which interest payments have been received on time to be excluded from classification as a nonaccrued loan. The combination of depository insurance and bank reregulation has placed an added burden on the marketplace to regulate bank behavior and discourage excessive risk taking. However, there is a tendency to overestimate the incentive and willingness of uninsured depositors to exert an effective and nondisruptive influence on the banking industry. On the other hand, bank money and capital markets have shown some evidence of imposing such discipline, in a nondisruptive fashion, on large multinational institutions that are most dependent on these markets for funding. A hierarchy of quality has arisen in the negotiable domestic market for certificates of deposit, the Eurodollar market, and the interbank Eurodollar market. As a result, on occasion a rate differential is paid by banks for these commodities, based on perceptions of quality, rumors, and reported problems. Generally, banks that are perceived to be of higher quality pay lower rates than banks that are perceived to be of lower quality. There is sometimes a flight to quality in the aforementioned markets when rumors or fears of bankruptcy interfere with normal market developments. However, evidence of the existence and potential of genuine market discipline is not persuasive enough to warrant its substitution for the discipline provided by regulatory agencies. While customers' greater perceived risk of loss from a bank failure could increase incentives to impose market discipline, the behavior of participants in the market will depend mainly on the nature and magnitude of changes in the deposit insurance system.

During the 1950s and 1960s, the banking industry was more stable and had fewer failures than during the 1970s. Continuing the undesirable trend, the 1980s and early 1990s posted the greatest frequency of failures since the Depression. The contrast between the earlier years and the eighties is stark: There was an average of 6 failures per year between 1945 and 1979, compared with 110 between 1980 and 1990. (See Table 7.1.) The greatest changes in the banking environment since the passage of the Glass-Steagall Act occurred during this period of high bank failure rates. The changes brought new competitors to banks, new technology, floating-rate instruments and loans, securitization, deregulation of interest rates, many new banking products and services, increases in interstate banking, increases in fee-based (noninterest) income, movements by banks to provide services such as annuities and mutual funds through third-party marketers, and, in general, a loosening of regulation. Some of these changes were driven by new technology and competition, while others were accelerated by the high rate of bank failures. There seems to be a constant tug-of-war between market forces and the desire for regulation of the U.S. financial sector. Regulations become obsolete, get enforced ineffectively, and sometimes are avoided. Consequently, the alternating potential for deregulation and reregulation seems to be ever present.

REGULATORY CHANGES

In the past decade, banks have challenged the limits of the Glass-Steagall Act to meet growing competition from the nonbank sector and to respond to the changing financial requirements of their customers. Put bluntly, the money-center banks, faced with declining profits and an increasing ability on the part of corporate treasurers to lure funds away from banks, have seen an erosion of their share of deposits and loans from the large corporate sector. On the other hand, although Glass-Steagall still remains in effect, it no longer presents the barrier it once represented. At each step in the deregulation process, banks have usually been opposed by securities industry trade groups. The following are among the key advances banks have recently made:

1. Placing commercial paper without recourse to, and solely upon order for, the account of a customer.

2. Transferring commercial paper to a holding company subsidiary.

3. Issuing, underwriting, and dealing in collateralized mortgage obligations through finance subsidiaries.

4. Offering securities brokerage and investment advisory services to institutional customers through a single subsidiary.

5. Offering and selling units in unit investment trusts solely on order and for the account of the bank's customer through a bank or holding company subsidiary.

6. Making limited investments in an investment bank.

7. Creating and selling interests in a publicly offered common stock trust fund for individual retirement account (IRA) assets.

8. Offering brokerage firm services to the public.

9. Underwriting all debt issues in subsidiaries of the bank holding company, separately from the depository function.

10. Underwriting equity securities, at least in the case of J.P. Morgan and Bankers Trust.

Restrictive regulation provides a basic motivation for financial innovation. To the extent that regulation constrains private initiatives, entrepreneurs will weigh the cost of complying with the regulations against the cost of circumventing them. Free enterprise and customer needs also lead to innovation. Business opportunity and regulation have served as a catalyst for the introduction of new products, new delivery systems, and new organizational forms.[3]

WHAT DOES THE FUTURE HOLD?

Some of the banking restrictions in the United States were finally recognized as archaic and as a hindrance to the financial strength of the nation's banks. Deregulation in the 1970s and 1980s abolished depository interest rate ceilings, diversified bank holding company activities, and removed some geographic restrictions on branching and expansion. On the other hand, the regulatory authorities were strengthened, the bank examination process was made more rigorous, capital standards were raised for all depository institutions, and FDIC insurance premiums were raised to help avert the failure of the FDIC insurance fund. Although reform of the present banking system may be desirable, a growing body of evidence indicates that many of the current financial problems in banking were at least partially the result of the incentive structure created by deposit insurance and by the manner in which deposit insurance was administered.

  U.S. banks have fallen behind in competing with merchant banks abroad because many of these foreign banks are permitted to perform both commercial and investment banking, as well as other services in what is commonly referred to as "universal banking." The regulatory authorities took some deregulatory actions to allow U.S.

banks to be more competitive with the large foreign banks by permitting increased corporate underwriting activities as well as increased possibilities of geographical expansion.

Commercial banks have come a long way toward overcoming the rather outdated barriers presented by Glass-Steagall. Some banks that have challenged the status quo have been richly rewarded. There are few activities that banks cannot pursue today, especially now that they have been given a clear mandate to underwrite corporate bonds and, in at least a few cases, to underwrite equity securities. Banks will continue to push for more powers, such as the right to underwrite insurance or at least sell insurance without the underwriting risk. Even though banks did not receive congressional approval for performing greater insurance and securities activities in the banking legislation of 1991, pressure will once again be applied to Congress by 1993–1994 to reconsider these deregulatory steps.

Many factors have contributed to the banking crisis. The loss of high-quality corporate borrowers to the commercial paper market aggravated the problem. The diminished high-quality customer base forced bankers into new, less familiar, and less creditworthy lines of business to compensate for their loss of customers. The real estate recession of 1989–1992 has lasted longer than expected. Poor management is another reason for the crisis. Money-center bank managers are guilty of abandoning sound credit control practices of lending to borrowers who will repay and loading their balance sheets instead with dubious loans. "Every lending binge—to less developed countries in the late 1970s, to highly leveraged corporations and to real estate magnates in the latest case—has added to the toxic waste on bank balance sheets."[4] In some cases, these banks also failed to diversify their portfolios in pursuit of a 15-percent-per-year asset growth and increased fee income.

It is annoying to see so many banks paying their chief executives between half a million and 2 million dollars a year without expecting sterling performance. Combined with poor performance, these lofty salaries and bonuses raise serious questions about our compensation system, the quality of managers we employ, and the job being done by the directors of the institutions in question. Why aren't more chief executives of poorly managed banks dismissed? Are members of the board of directors literally so handsomely rewarded by the senior management team or on such friendly terms with them that they don't wish to rock the boat? It is perfectly acceptable to pay exceptionally high compensation for exceptional performance; however, there are too many examples of huge compensation and suboptimal performance.

There appears to be a fundamental shift in the philosophy of regulation. After the Depression, rules were formulated to restrict and separate the growth and power of large financial institutions; by contrast, today's view holds that conglomeration is better for the economy and helps the country compete on a global basis. This change in regulatory perspective is the cornerstone of the bank consolidation movement. Of course, the desire for geographic expansion, increased market share, and a recognition of savings in non-interest-related expenses from in-market mergers were all salient factors in furthering the bank merger wave.

THE ERA OF CONSOLIDATION

While the first wave of money-center bank mergers occurred in the late 1960s, the Wells Fargo acquisition of Crocker in 1986 and the 1988 acquisition of Irving Corp. by the Bank of New York acted as harbingers of the merger and consolidation wave that is taking place in the 1990s. The Wells Fargo merger demonstrated that enormous cost savings could be achieved by merging banks in the same geographic locale. Dramatic cost cutting and integration improved profits enormously following both mergers. The merger of the New York banks was a watershed event for both the bank and the industry in that the deal was unsolicited (i.e., it was a hostile takeover) and was a cost-driven, in-market merger at a time when most other banks in the industry were pursuing a strategy of geographic expansion.

Banks eager for similar results have adopted this strategy in ushering in the era of consolidation. In 1991, Thomas S. Johnson, then president of Manufacturers Hanover Corporation, noted in a speech that in California, where only four banks dominate the market (soon to be three, following the BankAmerica–Security Pacific merger), consumer deposit rates are lower and loan rates higher than at New York banks, where there are a dozen competitors. The combined difference is nearly two percentage points, or 200 basis points.[5] For example, rates offered to depositors on NOW accounts on August 13, 1991, averaged 4.03% in Los Angeles, 4.06% in San Francisco, and 4.45% in New York, while two-year personal loans charged an average of 20.25% in Los Angeles, 19.12% in San Francisco, and 18.35% in New York. While bank earnings may benefit from consolidation, the bottom line is that with less competition, customers may receive lower deposit rates and pay more for their loans.[6]

Within a few months after Johnson's remarks, Manufacturers Hanover announced a merger with the Chemical Bank to form Chemical Banking Corporation (with $135.46 billion in assets as of June 30, 1991), making it the third largest bank holding company in the United States. Analysts are suggesting other possible mega-mergers, such as Chase Manhattan with either J.P. Morgan, Marine Midland, Bank of New York, or even a west coast bank; Wells Fargo with First Interstate; and First Chicago with Continental. A few analysts expect some sort of merger activity between Old Kent or First of America and Comerica, NBD, or Michigan National. There is speculation that Marshall and Ilsly, a $7.3 billion Wisconsin-based bank with a ratio of nonperforming loans to total assets of under 1 percent and over $100 million per year in fee revenue from its data-processing business for other banks, is a merger candidate with Key Corp., Northern Trust, NBD Bancorp, Comerica, or Banc One. Another candidate for a takeover is likely to be Ohio-based Huntingdon Bancshares, with $12 billion in assets. Potential acquirers are Banc One, National City, Mellon, and PNC Financial. Bay Banks of Massachusetts is likely to be courted by Bank of Boston, Key Corp., Fleet, or another bank from out of the region. UJB, a New Jersey-based bank holding company, is being courted by First Fidelity, CoreStates, PNC Financial, Mellon, and Bank of New York. First Fidelity and CoreStates are rumored to be interested in acquiring MidAtlantic bank, a troubled

New Jersey franchise. Some analysts feel that if Chase Manhattan doesn't merge with Bank of New York or BankAmerica, it will acquire retail-oriented banks in Connecticut or a savings bank in New York City.

Mergers between banks in the same city or state have a greater potential for cost savings than interstate combinations. The emphasis behind many of the big mergers is to slash costs and solve the capital inadequacy problems confronting many of the large banks that are suffering from enormous losses on commercial real estate loans, lesser developed country loans, and loans made to support leveraged buy-outs and debt-laden mergers.

For sure, the big money-center banks are examining what they would look like paired off with each other. Major issues are the potential for cost savings, capital adequacy, the quality of loan portfolios, and management succession.

Even if potential merger partners can settle their differences, there are still other regulatory and political battles to be fought. For example, the First Interstate Bank System of Montana had its merger with Commerce Bancshares, Inc., in Wyoming, run into a snag with the Federal Reserve after receiving regulatory approval. The issue of redlining came up in a suit against First Interstate under the Community Reinvestment Act (CRA) of 1977, which requires banks to make loans equitably to both rich and poor neighborhoods. First Interstate was accused of discriminating against a local Cheyenne Indian reservation in its lending practices. In addition, the Federal Reserve held up the acquisition by First Union Corp. of Florida National Bank for several months in 1989 after community groups challenged First Union's CRA record. Other challenges to mergers might be categorized into fear over loss of local control of community banks, fear of foreign ownership of U.S. banks, interstate banking issues, and potential job losses from cost cutting. A great fear is that mergers among the big banks in New York will only add to the city's serious unemployment woes. Even without merger activity, many of the money-center banks have announced large layoffs of staff members. It is estimated that almost 40 percent of banking's work force in New York City consists of minorities, adding to the potential for a political backlash. Although consolidation may be necessary for the long-run survival of the banks, it may prove painful for some consumers, employees, and politicians.[7] A frightening thing about the saga of the banking industry is that some highly respected banks may have under-reserved their problem loans, and this is almost impossible to detect by outsiders. It could mean even more loan charge-offs and more banks joining the regulatory lists of troubled banks.

Gary Hector of *Fortune Magazine* feels that (1) bank examiners will be supervising bank loan portfolios and capital adequacy more closely (banks will be closed more rapidly if they cannot meet regulatory guidelines on equity capital); (2) banks with capital in excess of the minimum requirements will be rewarded by the regulators and will be allowed to expand into new businesses such as securities underwriting, brokerage, and interstate banking; (3) banks will be required to disclose what their loans are actually worth; (4) assets will be marked to market; (5) cross-border mergers, but not interstate banking, will be allowed in all states; and (6) banks will be allowed to participate in more securities activities and may even be permitted to own securities firms within the holding company structure.[8] McKinsey and Company, a major consulting firm, forecasts a sweeping consolidation within the banking industry. The company estimates that by the mid-1990s, after curbs on nationwide banking have fallen, the nation's 125 largest bank holding companies, which hold two-thirds of the industry's $3.2 trillion in assets, will be consolidated into 10 to 15 large bank holding companies. Such a consolidation could save the industry $10 billion a year in operating costs. An interesting sidelight is that Fedwire transfer and daylight overdraft problems should diminish as banks expand nationwide, because there will be fewer banks to which funds and checks have to be transferred and cleared.

Banks have chosen to merge because they wish to become bigger in their current market and because they feel that the consolidation of two banks can save up to 35 percent of the noninterest costs of the acquired bank. In addition, they merge to enter an adjoining market in which they expect reductions in expenses of up to 15 percent of the acquired bank's overhead. Banks also merge to enter geographically dispersed markets and diversify their loan portfolios and bases of core deposits. In this case, the cost savings are minimal. In addition, banks merge or buy select assets to become a dominant player in certain products. There are certainly efficiencies of scale here. The First Chicago purchase of Banker's Trust's credit card business is an example of an attempt to become a dominant player in the credit card market.

Banks also merge to take advantage of once-in-a-lifetime buying opportunities. For example, a bank might be tempted to purchase a troubled institution at a minimal price if it were offered government assistance or guarantees. The purchase of the Bank of New England by Fleet is such an example. Finally, banks merge to keep out the competition. The acquisition of First Pennsylvania Bank by CoreStates is an example of this strategy. Such a merger of a weaker bank into a much stronger bank in the same region also allowed for considerable cost-cutting opportunities.[9]

There are two things that slowed down the pace of bank consolidations in 1992–1993: Bank stock prices and price-to-earnings ratios rose in anticipation of a surge in merger activity and a recovery in economic activity. Many banks have been careful to avoid purchasing another bank that will lead to a dilution in earnings per share. However, there have been aggressive bids by some banks which are afraid to miss out on an acquisition, fear that the competition will buy the bank in question, or are betting on a turnaround in the performance of the bank to be acquired.

A MEGAMERGER: CHEMICAL BANKING CORPORATION

The merger of Manufacturers Hanover into Chemical Bank was an example of two wounded giants with an abundance of nonperforming loans seeking cost savings and time to heal from wounds associated with poor asset quality. It was a prime example of troth out of weakness. It was questionable as to whether adequate external capital could be raised by these banks if they remained independent. However, with the promise of enormous cost savings anticipated from the merger, and with the establishment of adequate loan loss reserves, over $1.5 billion of new tier I capital was raised, which easily exceeded minimal risk-based capital requirements and which will allow time for the economy to recover, so as to reduce the amount of money tied up in nonperforming loans substantially.

The merger made sense because the two banks might not have survived on their own. John McGillicuddy, chairman of Manufacturers Hanover, became CEO until 1994, when Gordon Shipley is expected to take over the reins. The new bank, called Chemical Banking, has promised significant cost cutting at headquarters and the closing of 70 redundant branches. Chemical hopes to build "the best broad-based financial institution, a leader in our chosen market."[10] The bank remains widely diversified, with a major presence in retail as well as corporate banking.

In addition, Chemical and, to a lesser degree, Manufacturers Hanover, enjoy major strengths in lending to small business and middle-market corporations, consumer banking, and lending for mergers, acquisitions, and reorganizations under bankruptcy law. Moreover, Manufacturers Hanover is better established with blue-chip companies. The new Chemical Banking has assets that exceed $139 billion. The combined bank has over 9 percent of the New York City area's consumer deposit market, just behind Citibank, but well ahead of Chase Manhattan. It was the hope of the management at both banks that, through a friendly merger, they could cut duplicate costs and recover more quickly from their heavy loan losses. The banks hope to save at least $750 million annually by 1995, rather than the previously anticipated $650 million, about 50 percent more than the combined banks earned in 1990. Unfortunately, at least 6,200 people out of a total employment of 44,000 (14 percent) will lose their jobs in the first round of cost cutting. Besides these job cuts, the new bank eliminated Chemical's credit card operation in Delaware and part of the bank's processing center in Jericho, Long Island, as well as Chemical's old corporate headquarters on Park Avenue in New York City. If the cost savings can actually be achieved, then given its equity capital raised in 1992, the new Chemical Banking Corporation could rebound quickly and regain the dominance among money-center banking powers formerly held by Manufacturers Hanover and Chemical Bank. The new bank should also benefit from an improved financial condition that includes lower relative borrowing costs and a larger market share of interest rate swaps, currency swaps, and other instruments known as derivatives that allow clients to hedge financial risks. An improved credit rating will be crucial to achieving Chemical's ambition to be a major player in these areas. The most successful banks in the swaps and derivative markets carry at least AA ratings, because nervous corporate treasurers are less willing to deal with lower rated banks that pose more of a risk of default. In addition, a higher debt rating can mean cost savings of millions of dollars when a large bank raises money from institutional investors.

In the fall of 1992, the new bank was still saddled with a $2.5 billion portfolio of nonperforming commercial real estate loans. The bank's total nonperforming loans reached $6.16 billion out of a total loan portfolio of $84.24 billion following the merger. By year-end 1992, nonperforming assets declined to 4.4 percent of total assets. While the increased capitalization and efforts at controlling expenses should go a long way toward solving the bank's problems and positioning it for future growth, there are many questions that analysts feel must still be answered. For example, is management up to the task of merging the two former banks' computer systems, check-clearing operations, branch systems, trust operations, international operations and branches, and cash management and lockbox services? Will it shift and fire personnel and merge two different cultures and lending, credit, and cost-cutting philosophies? After all, neither management team was very successful at Chemical or Manufacturers Hanover since 1986. The same executives who presided over the missteps of the past will be holding the reins going forward. If they are up to the task of turning an even larger ship around, and if they get some help from an improving economy and real estate market, then the deal will be one of the great success stories on the merger circuit. If management can achieve its anticipated reductions in expenses, the new bank's return on assets could reach 0.80 percent, up from a return of 0.67 percent in 1992. This would be well above average performance levels of most money-center banks.

In early 1993, Texas Commerce, a unit of Chemical Banking Corp., agreed to acquire First City Bancorp branches in Houston, Dallas, Beaumont, El Paso, and Midland, with combined assets of $6.64 billion. With this acquisition, Texas Commerce will have 126 branches and will become one of the largest branch networks in Texas. Once again, a Chemical Bank subsidiary will face the challenge of slashing $200 million in costs by eliminating 1,700 employees and duplicate operations, while integrating the two banking networks. Chemical incurred a one-time charge of $30 million for severance and consolidation costs in 1993 and indicated that it would raise an additional $150 million in common stock to help finance the hefty acquisition price. Chemical is expected to make another bank acquisition in New Jersey, where it is currently the fifth largest bank in the state.

In a move to keep consumer deposits and maintain customer relations in a low-interest-rate environment in 1993, Chemical has teamed up with a unit of Liberty Mutual Insurance Co. to create a joint venture to expand the range of mutual funds, annuities, and other investment products available at Chemical branches. In addition to maintaining the customer relationship, the sale of mutual fund and insurance products should generate fee income for the bank. An additional source of fee income should come from Chemical's authorization to underwrite corporate bonds. The bank plans to become a major player in the market for junk bonds over the next few years.[11]

WHY SHOULD MERGERS WORK?

Why will a merger work today when there is much evidence that cost cutting failed following most mergers in the 1970s and early 1980s? The reason is twofold: First, a merger is often necessary for survival; and second, the prestige and reputation, if not the jobs, of executives at many banks are on the line if they are not successful. Both the federal regulators and impatient boards of directors have removed members of executive management at the Bank of New England, First Chicago, BankAmerica, Mellon, First Fidelity, numerous Texas banks, and Continental Illinois after varying degrees of mismanagement.

ANOTHER MEGAMERGER: BANKAMERICA AND SECURITY PACIFIC

Following on the heels of the Chemical Bank–Manufacturers Hanover merger announcement, BankAmerica, the second largest bank in the United States, with assets in excess of $185 billion, and Security Pacific, the fifth largest U.S. bank before this merger round, announced plans for the biggest merger in U.S. banking history, a $4.5 billion deal. This move will make the new entity a regional powerhouse throughout the western part of the country, as well as the second largest bank holding company in the nation. The deal will give the bank operations in 10 western states, including dominant positions in California, Nevada, and Washington. The two banks indicated that they expected to produce annual savings of about $1.2 billion over a three-year period, with about 30 percent of the savings expected to come from the California retail system and bank operations, where some 16,000 positions are expected to be cut and where 532 branches out of a total of 1,443 will be closed. The bank would probably need reserves of about $700 million to pay for restructuring to integrate the original banks' facilities, work forces, and systems. BankAmerica will take a $250 million restructuring charge on its books to cover severance and consolidation costs. Purchase accounting adjustments will result in a charge of $175 million after tax in each of the first two years, $150 million in each of the third and fourth years, and $100 million in the fifth year. The bulk of the adjustments is amortization of intangibles at Security Pacific. The BankAmerica–Security Pacific merger announcement came just months after Wells Fargo backed out of an acquisition of Security Pacific because of the latter's large loan losses in California real estate and problems abroad (5.5 percent of assets were nonperforming at year-end 1991).

BankAmerica, which, five years prior to the merger announcement, was one of the most financially troubled of the large U.S. banks, has staged a remarkable recovery to become one of the strongest and most expansive banks. This giant bank recently emerged from a near disastrous struggle with bad foreign loans and escalating operating costs that almost brought it to ruin in 1986. The bank reduced its emphasis on foreign lending, slashed costs, restructured, and concentrated on collecting consumer deposits and making consumer and small to midsized business loans. As a result of the bank's poor performance in the mid-1980s, it was spared the embarrassment of following the herd in lending heavily to commercial real estate customers and those seeking leveraged buy-outs. Ironically, BankAmerica was fortunate that it did not have the capital to become involved in these speculative lending practices.[12]

The new company claimed that it would have more capital, greater pro forma market capitalization, more domestic assets, and the largest branch network of any existing or proposed U. S. bank (over 2,300 branches). The new bank will have a risk-adjusted tier I ratio of 5.9 percent, well above minimum regulatory guidelines. The postmerger BankAmerica has higher levels of potentially risky loans than does the new Chemical Banking Corporation, but fewer than Citicorp. Postmerger problem assets at BankAmerica total $8.6 billion, compared with $10.1 billion at struggling Citicorp. This worked out to be about 4.3 percent of BankAmerica's total assets, compared with 6.4 percent at Citicorp and a 3.4-percent average for the top 25 U.S. banks at year-end 1991. By year-end 1992, nonperforming assets had declined to 3.4 percent of total assets at BankAmerica. The new BankAmerica would have $71 billion in risky categories (commercial real estate, highly leveraged transactions, and loans to lesser developed countries), compared with $8 billion in net tangible common equity and $5 billion in loan loss reserves. That is, risky loans amounted to 5.5 times equity plus loan loss reserves at the time of the announced merger. By comparison, Wells Fargo had a ratio of risky loans to tangible common equity plus reserves of 11 to 1, while Chemical Banking had a ratio of 3.5 times.

BankAmerica's merger application with the Federal Reserve Board indicated a plan to establish a "bad bank" with more than $2.8 billion in problematic loans. The "bad bank" would also include $300 million in performing loans that would serve as a source of cash flow and an enticement to investors. BankAmerica hoped to finance the "bad bank" through stock and debt offerings of between $1.8 billion and $2.35 billion. BankAmerica expects to own about a third of the "bad bank." In the application to the regulators, BankAmerica indicated that it expected to write off about $800 million in loans.

BankAmerica is also looking for an east coast banking franchise; it appears as if Chairman Richard Rosenberg has a vision of retail national banking. So far, his strategy has involved the purchase of troubled thrifts and banks and the implementation of aggressive merchandising initiatives and effective cost controls at the branch level. Rosenberg has stated an interest in additional mergers with retail-oriented banks. As a matter of fact, BankAmerica announced agreements to acquire the second largest bank in Nevada (Valley Capital) and a large thrift institution in Hawaii (HonFed) during the second quarter of 1991, just prior to its announcement that it would merge with Security Pacific. The Nevada and Hawaii acquisitions would add about $10 billion to BankAmerica's asset base.

There was opposition to BankAmerica's merger with Security Pacific in the states of Washington and Arizona, on the grounds that it would produce anticompetitive market conditions. Without any divestiture of deposits, the combined banks would have controlled 49 percent of the deposits in Washington and more than 40 percent in Arizona. BankAmerica agreed to divest itself of 213 branches in Washington, Arizona, Nevada, Oregon, and California with $8.8 billion of deposits to meet antitrust concerns of the Justice Department and of state regulatory commissions. The planned divestitures would reduce the combined banks' control of deposits to less than 30 percent of the total deposits at banks, thrifts, and credit unions in the aforementioned five states. BankAmerica and Security Pacific came to dominate banking in Washington through their purchases in the 1980s of the troubled SeaFirst and Rainier banks, the two largest banks in the state.

Following the merger with Security Pacific, BankAmerica acquired the Dallas-based, insolvent Sunbelt Federal Savings, with 111 branches and $3.7 billion of deposits. BankAmerica then agreed to buy almost all of the 130 Texas branches, $7.5 billion in deposit liabilities, and $6.85 billion in consumer and commercial loans of First Gibraltar Bank FSB. The addition of these two financial institutions would give BankAmerica the state's second largest branch system and make it the fourth largest bank in Texas in terms of deposits. These moves allowed BankAmerica to increase its market share in Texas, while expanding its retail banking empire in an arc from the state of Washington down the west coast and into the southwest.

In the latest round of rumors, BankAmerica's next acquisition would be an east coast retail bank that is ripe for a financial turnaround. After that, there is speculation that the giant will merge with Chase Manhattan if Chase cannot resolve its own problems.

BankAmerica had a return on assets of 0.80 percent and a return on equity of 12.7 percent in 1992.

OTHER MONEY-CENTER BANKS

Bankers Trust

Historically, Bankers Trust was a patrician, establishment bank, much like Morgan Guaranty. In the old days, Bankers was a class-conscious, preppie, skull-and-bones Yale and Princeton institution. Its management emphasized collegiality and gentility, as well as entrepreneurship. However, Bankers Trust transformed itself from an unfocused (wholesale/retail), second-rate, near insolvent commercial bank into a dynamic, well-capitalized, highly profitable merchant bank. The bank's strategy in the late 1970s and early 1980s involved exiting from its retail business and focusing on wholesale business: wholesale banking, the fiduciary business, capital markets, and corporate finance. Its late 1980s and 1990s strategy changed the bank's focus and emphasized merchant and investment banking, global markets, and a group of nonbanking service businesses, which coexist with private banking and investment management. Bankers' management has shown its ability to anticipate deregulation and the squeeze on commercial banking by turning itself into a transaction-driven, fee-driven merchant bank. Bankers Trust executives are smart, extremely competent, nice people who work incredibly hard. While Morgan is still regarded as the class act and Rolls Royce among money-center banks, Bankers Trust is considered more like a Ferrari, with the instincts of an alley cat or street fighter.[13]

Bankers Trust has followed a clear strategy and exemplifies strong and effective leadership. It sold off its branches in 1979 and its credit card operation shortly thereafter to concentrate on investment banking and merchant banking on a global basis and the management of its vast trust department resources. It has also remained a major corporate lender. Seventy percent of the bank's assets consist of liquid securities. This is because the bank tends to originate many loans, but sells off about two-thirds of them in the secondary market after earning generous fees and "cherry picking" the best loans for its own portfolio. The asset composition of the bank is the antithesis of that of the traditional bank, where between 60 and 70 percent of the assets consist of loans.[14] The returns on assets and equity for 1991 were 1.03 and 23.1 percent, respectively, while the 1992 returns were 0.91 and 23.1 percent, respectively, among the highest at money-center banks. Salomon Brothers stock research group has described Bankers Trust as the "The most sophisticated U.S. merchant bank, as well as one of the top merchant-banking providers of global finance in the world."[15]

J. P. Morgan

J. P. Morgan remains closely focused on businesses such as advising corporations, managing cash for pension funds and wealthy individuals, trading in securities and foreign exchange, underwriting, and corporate lending. The firm has only a limited number of so-called consumer accounts, typically belonging to lawyers, professionals, and other wealthy individuals. J. P. Morgan has successfully combined investment and commercial banking, along with aggressive trading and skillful money management, in a large trust department to become the preeminent commercial bank holding company in the United States. Morgan's management is highly respected and extremely competent. The company does not follow the herd instincts of many of its competitors, and it has been among the top performers in the industry throughout its long history. Morgan is a well-capitalized institution and represents the epitome of asset quality and investment banking among commercial banks. Its strengths reflect a distinguished reputation for quality, professionalism, and integrity; relationship banking; its global presence; its conservative balance sheet; its analytic depth; its high-quality personnel; its superior technology; its trading expertise and flow of new products; its collegial culture, fostering teamwork; and its ability to combine commercial with investment banking.

J. P. Morgan's returns on assets and equity were 1.00 and 19.6 percent, respectively, in 1991 and 0.97 and 18.1 percent, respectively, in 1992. Both J. P. Morgan and Bankers Trust have avoided mergers and have concentrated on investment banking and trading activities and the generation of fee income. For example, in 1991, the combined trading and foreign exchange income was 37.9 percent of total revenues at Bankers Trust and 31.0 percent of total revenues at J.P. Morgan. By comparison, in 1988, the numbers were 14.0 and 12.7 percent, respectively. In a 1992 presentation to bank analysts, Bankers Trust indicated that nearly 60 percent of its profits came from trading-related functions. While profits from trading have grown substantially at most money-center banks, they are volatile and may not be sustainable on a year-to-year basis.

Citicorp

A key trend is the shift of acquisitional power away from the money-center banks in New York and toward the superregional banks in the southeast and midwest and on the west coast. Under more normal conditions, the big New York banks would be among the acquirers of out-of-state banks. However, their inadequate capital and poor-quality loan portfolios have them concentrating first on their own survival as independent entities, as well as on exploring within-state mergers.

It is possible that Citicorp, GM, Ford, GE, American Express, or some other commercial or industrial company will buy one of the money-center banks and infuse it with fresh capital. Some observers feel that Citibank and Chase Manhattan could fit nicely in this mold if legislation would allow such a combination. John Reed, Citicorp's chairman, has stated that Citicorp's efforts to cut costs by $1.5 billion and raise $3 billion more in capital will be far more effective than any potential merger and will leave the firm in a stronger position than any of the merged behemoths. However, Reed also indicated that Citicorp might be interested in acquiring a large U.S. or foreign retail-oriented bank, but not a middle market lender. Citicorp could sell 12 to 15 properties or businesses with total assets of $20 billion to help eliminate its capital deficiency. The firm was the only one of the nation's 25 largest banking companies not to meet the minimum capital standard for shareholder equity capital of 4 percent of risk-adjusted assets needed by the end of 1992 at year-end 1991. Citicorp raised $1.0 billion through a preferred stock offering in October 1992 to help strengthen its capital position. In addition, it planned to record an $800 million pretax gain on the sale of nonessential assets, including $600 million in gains from equity stakes of Latin American companies acquired under debt restructuring. Citicorp has also increased its capital by selling AMBAC for a $100 million gain and a 10-percent stake in Saudi American Bank for a $203 million gain. Similarly, it may sell a shopping merchant credit card processing business for about $150 million, and it is expected to sell Capital Markets Assurance, a securities insurer, freeing $200 million in capital. The combined impact of all of these asset sales and stock offerings would be to increase the firm's ratio of equity to risk-adjusted capital to approximately 4.5 percent at year-end 1992.

Citicorp Chairman Reed indicated that global consumer banking "will be the engine of the company going forward."[16] John Leonard, Salomon analyst, has stated that Citicorp's goal is to triple its customer base to 10 million households, while growing to 2,000 branches in the 50 largest metropolitan areas of the United States before the end of the decade.[17] In addition, Reed ruled out a Japanese bank partnership and saw few benefits from a Citicorp merger with a large U.S. bank. On the other hand, if Citicorp were to seek partners, it would likely look toward a European bank or an industrial company. To improve profitability and boost its retained earnings, Citicorp announced the elimination of its dividend through at least 1993 and a 50-percent reduction in interest rates paid on NOW accounts effective December 1991. The move was a harbinger of a New York City–wide reduction in interest rates paid on transaction deposits.

Citicorp suffered substantial losses in the final quarter of 1991 and had weak earnings in the third quarter of 1992. Nonperforming assets exceeded 10 percent of the value of loans and foreclosed real estate at one point during 1992. The delinquency rate on consumer mortgage loans had even reached 5.3 percent of outstandings in 1992. Citicorp appeared to be underreserved for bad loans, especially after the Olympia & York bankruptcy, in which Citicorp had a large exposure, was announced in May 1992. According to NYU professor David Rogers, Citicorp, the bank with the "boardinghouse reach," will require a radical change in its expansionist strategy.[18] It will have to sell off more nonperforming businesses and begin to concentrate on a few core businesses. The "financial supermarket" strategy may have to be abandoned as an unrealistic goal for the present. Citicorp has been unable to maintain consistent profitability, largely because it lost so much money on so many ill-timed, poorly managed acquisitions and new ventures. Numerous new businesses were losers, including Quotron (an information business), AMBAC (a seller of bond insurance), several sick thrift institutions, and Scrimmegour Vickers (an English brokerage firm). Why did all of these problems occur? Both Walter Wriston, the former chairman of Citicorp, and John Reed allowed them to happen by emphasizing an aggressive growth strategy and demonstrating institutional arrogance. Both executives ignored advice from consultants and bank analysts to exit from poorly performing businesses. They refused to recognize the fact that many of these businesses were losers and held onto them far too long.[19]

Without the aforementioned sales of some of its assets, Citicorp would have remained an even weaker competitor, lacking liquidity and resources for acquisitions. According to an early 1992 research report by Keefe, Bruyette, and Woods, among the 50 largest U.S. banks, Citicorp ranked 41st in quality of loans, 43rd in profits, and 10th in risk-adjusted capital. Citicorp achieved a return on assets of 0.23 percent and a return on equity of 6.6 percent during 1992. This performance was well below that of its peer group.

Richard S. Braddock was ousted as president of Citicorp in the fall of 1992. Since then, John Reed has walked a tightrope in maintaining his job as chairman, despite an abundance of problems with credit quality, loose record keeping, and insufficient loan loss reserves. Reed has assiduously cultivated the board of directors and has consistently emphasized to them that while he may not be the best person to lead Citicorp, there is no one else at the bank who could replace him. Professor David Rogers points out that Reed sounds in some ways like a visionary, sophisticated organizational sociologist.[20] Yet he is not adept at implementing his vision, nor does he always use good judgment. Reed astutely contrasts consumer banking, which has a routinized technology and produces uniform and standardized products, with corporate banking, which has a craftlike, research-and-development-oriented technology that must interact with clients who have unique, specialized needs. The two require different management styles, organizational forms, and delivery systems.[21] Says Rogers:

Consumer banking is a little like building cars. Success comes when you routinize things to a point where a group of people at the top build the strategy, drive the creative work, and push new products, while execution takes place relatively effortlessly through good blocking and tackling. . . . Corporate banking is more like delivering medicine. . . . In the corporate bank, we don't have common products that we design and sell. We have relationships and transactions that are specialized and unique. Moreover, our professional competence sits down low in the corporate bank, with the people on the front lines who deal with customers and devise the transactions. We can't develop new products at the center and push them out. Good corporate banks are walking product development departments.[22]

Bank of New York

The Bank of New York, one of the oldest banking organizations in the United States, was founded by Alexander Hamilton in 1784. By year-end 1992, it had just under $43 billion in assets, ranking 6th in the state of New York and 16th nationwide. While considerably smaller than its New York City counterparts, it has been one of the most consistently profitable and well-capitalized banks in the state. A leader in securities processing, it is a niche bank with a relatively large trust department and special strength in communications industry lending, mortgage warehousing, marine transportation, and public utilities. After the 1992 acquisition of 63 branches of Barclay, the company would be the largest branch bank in affluent Westchester County (having as many branches as Citicorp, Chemical, and Chase combined) and among the largest branch banks in suburban New York City. On the other hand, it has only a token presence of 38 branches in all of New York City. Also, Bank of New York showed continued interest in retail banking when it announced an agreement to acquire National Community Bank, a New Jersey holding company with $4.2 billion in assets and 105 branches. Bank of New York paid 2.4 times book value for National Community, a premium over the average price of twice book value being paid for recent bank acquisitions. Another strength of the Bank of New York is that it minimized its mistakes in lesser developed country and commercial real estate lending compared with most of its competitors. As a result of its strong financial position, it was able to acquire Irving Bank Corp. in 1988. The merger was extremely successful, with Bank of New York realizing substantial cost savings.

While Bank of New York has always emphasized wholesale banking, its acquisition of the Barclay, National Community Bank, and American Savings Bank branches has gradually shifted its funding base from purchased money toward a strong consumer deposit base. Its ratio of core deposits to loans is roughly two-thirds. At the same time, there has been a subtle shift in the firm's asset base toward retail and middle market banking. Still, Bank of New York's commercial and industrial loans account for slightly more than 50 percent of all of its loans, while foreign loans account for another 17 percent. Total consumer lending, including residential mortgage loans, account for an additional 21 percent of the bank's lending activity.

Fortunately, Bank of New York is recovering from its asset quality problems much more quickly than most of its peers, because of its relatively much smaller lesser developed country and commercial real estate loan exposures. Its credit problems were chiefly from loans related to leveraged buy-outs. These problems have resolved themselves more rapidly than those having to do with nonperforming commercial real estate loans. Bank of New York's ratio of reserves to nonperforming loans is among the highest in the industry, and its capital base is good in absolute terms and quite strong in relationship to its money-center peer group.

During the second quarter of 1992, some 46 percent of the company's revenues were derived from noninterest income, compared with an industry average of about 34 percent. More important, Bank of New York's noninterest revenue is from more reliable fees income, rather than more volatile trading activities. Of particular importance are Bank of New York's trust and processing operations, the sixth largest such operation in the nation, which produced revenues of $350 million in 1991. The company is among the most efficient in New York, with a ratio of expenses to operating revenues on the low side of its peer group. During 1992, the Bank of New York achieved a return on equity of 12.4 percent and a return on assets of 0.97 percent, well above the performance of most other retail-oriented New York City banks.

The company's strong capital position also enhances its flexibility in pursuing acquisitions. Analysts expect it to acquire some of the smaller or failing institutions in New Jersey or Connecticut or a bank with a large retail credit card operation. There is speculation that Chairman Carter Bacot has in mind a merger with First Chicago, which has a large credit card operation and a good-sized trust operation, as well as being a major presence in wholesale banking and the Chicago area's largest middle market bank and retail branch network.

IMPACT OF MERGERS

The aforementioned mergers are likely to be a harbinger of dozens of similar mergers within the financial services industry over the next few years that should reduce costs substantially and lead to more efficient operations, as well as a massive consolidation of the banking and insurance industries. However, consolidation in and of itself is not the solution to the problems in these industries: A healthy bank or insurance company does not just arise out of the ashes of two or more weak or sick banks or troubled insurance companies that have been combined. Bigger is not necessarily better, as is amply illustrated by the problems of Citibank and Dai-Ichi Kangyo Bank. Mergers may offer a short-term solution to a problem, but without better credit controls by management, greater diversification within the lending and investment portfolios, a carefully designed strategy, an abundance of capital, and improved regulation, the errors of the past are likely to be repeated. The major impediment to bank and insurance company mergers today is the uncertainty of the credit quality of both loan and investment portfolios, as well as concerns over which executives will run the company following the merger. However, as the recession subsides and positive economic growth emerges, mergers will begin to proceed rapidly, with fewer fears that a "black hole" could appear after a deal is completed.

According to Gary Gorton, professor of finance at the Wharton School, the banking industry still has an overcapacity problem, despite a trend toward mergers. Bank managers also appear mesmerized by size and the higher compensation that comes from managing bigger companies. Banks have unwisely replaced their higher quality borrowers with greater risks in commercial real estate loans and highly leveraged transactions. In addition, bankers lack diversification routes or exits toward greener pastures that are available to unregulated companies. Further, the moral hazard problem of depository insurance discourages banks from shrinking their assets because bankers are willing to take on these added risks in the hopes of growing out of their problems without any increase in deposit insurance premiums.[23]

It is interesting to look at a chart of the 15 largest banks in the United States following the announcement of the mergers of Chemical and Manufacturers Hanover, BankAmerica and Security Pacific, NCNB with C&S/Sovran, First Union with Southeast, Comerica with Manufacturers National, National City with Merchants National, and Society with Ameritrust. (See Table 11.1.) Many analysts expect significant changes in this chart in the next few years. By the end of the decade, we may have $300–$400 billion giants that will dwarf today's leaders. There are just too many banks chasing too few high-quality customers. The closing or merging of inefficient banks may restore sanity to competition, but may eliminate some of the higher deposit rates and lower cost loans now available to consumers.

Testifying before the House Banking Committee in 1991, Federal Reserve Governor John LaWare indicated that available evidence suggests that recent mergers have not resulted in adverse affects on the vast majority of consumers of banking services and that we can expect to have 6,000 to 7,000 banks by 2010. Robert L. Clarke, former comptroller of the currency, emphasized that the United States had the least concentrated banking industry among major industrial countries, with about 10 times as many commercial banks per capita as the rest of the major Western European countries all together. Clarke forecasted that the number of banks would be down to 10,000 in 1995, compared with about 12,000 in 1992. He pointed out that intelligently structured mergers promote competition and usually improve prospects for satisfying customer convenience and needs in affected markets.[24]

THE RISE OF THE SUPERREGIONALS

NationsBank and Wachovia

Two banks with relatively unfavorable financial ratios in the Bear Stearns simulation model agreed to merge with stronger superregionals. In 1991, Wachovia acquired South Carolina National Bank, after NCNB acquired C&S/Sovran in 1990. NCNB had previously attempted to acquire C&S in 1989, but was rebuked at that time.

Table 11.1   Top 15 U.S. Banks as of June 30, 1991

Bank Holding Company	Total Assets ($ Billions)
Citicorp	$217
BankAmerica Corp.	113
Chase Manhattan	99
J. P. Morgan	97
Security Pacific	80
Chemical Banking	74
NCNB	69
Manufacturers Hanover	61
Bankers Trust	59
Wells Fargo	54
First Interstate	50
First Chicago	48
Fleet/Norstar	48
PNC Financial	44
First Union	40

After Pending Mergers (1993 E)	
Citicorp	$217
BankAmerica Corp.	190
Chemical Banking	140
NationsBank	118
J. P. Morgan	103
Chase Manhattan	96
Banc One	76
Bankers Trust	73
First Union	58
Wells Fargo	57
PNC Financial	55
First Interstate	52
First Chicago	50
Fleet Financial	48
Norwest	45

C&S/Sovran, mired in real estate problems, was under pressure to seek a merger partner. The C&S merger with Sovran was a classic case of a merger of equals, where nobody was really in charge or willing to make the tough decisions on layoffs, branch closings, and the like. Consolidation moved at a snail's pace. Few cost-cutting advantages were achieved, and the recession acted as a catalyst in the deterioration of the loan portfolio. The NCNB/C&S Sovran merger created a holding company called NationsBank with assets of nearly $118 billion at year-end 1992, making it the fourth largest bank holding company in the United States. Its network of 1,900 branches would extend from Baltimore south to Key West, Florida, and west to El Paso, Texas. It has become the second largest branch network in the United States, behind only BankAmerica. NationsBank has the second largest domestic deposit base of any U.S. bank, the largest number of corporate cash management accounts, and the fourth largest capitalization. In addition, it has become the nation's fifth largest mortgage-servicing company, eighth largest bank card corporation, tenth largest trust group, and third largest factoring operation. NationsBank was granted corporate debt and equity underwriting privileges in 1993.

Hugh McColl, chief executive, realizes that this merger is not without its risks, because of a few billion dollars in nonperforming loans outstanding at the combined banks. By year-end 1992, total nonperforming assets were just below $2 billion, while total assets were at $118 billion. To finance the merger, NationsBank issued $300 million of new common stock, raising its ratio of tangible equity capital to assets to nearly 5 percent, well above the minimum required tier I capital ratio. Earnings per share should not be diluted by the acquisition; return on equity is expected to be between 14 percent and 17 percent. The bank carried forward into 1992 unrealized capital gains of $951 million at year-end 1991 on a securities portfolio of almost $25 billion. NCNB also announced that it had sold off real estate and hotel loans with a face value of approximately $208 million for slightly more than $108 million as part of its restructuring program to clean out nonperforming or underperforming assets.

NationsBank has come up with a cost savings estimate of $450 million a year by year-end 1994 that can be carved out of the combined operations through overlapping functions and the integration of various systems. This figure represents just under 25 percent of the noninterest expense of C&S/Sovran.

McColl's takeover bid for C&S/Sovran in 1991 followed his 1988 takeover of First Republic BanCorp (Texas), which was more than double the size of NCNB at the time of the merger. Huge tax benefits from First Republic losses sheltered earnings, while the FDIC picked up most of the bad loans. In 1991, First Republic accounted for more than half of earnings at NCNB. NCNB would probably have bid for Southeast Corp., the troubled Miami holding company, if it were not occupied with the C&S/Sovran negotiations. NCNB has also applied to the regulatory authorities to operate a merchant bank that would be separate and independent of the commercial bank. The privately capitalized merchant bank would underwrite securities, offer advice on mergers and acquisitions, and sell insurance and mutual funds. While NationsBank's returns on equity and assets for 1991 were only 2.7 percent and 0.15 percent, respectively, they returned to much higher levels in 1992 as the benefits from the merger began to come down to the bottom line. Specifically, for 1992, return on equity was 15.8 percent, while return on assets was a respectable 1.00 percent.

In July 1992, NationsBank announced that it would invest $200 million in MNC Financial, the ailing Maryland banking company with $16 billion in assets and 241 branches throughout Maryland, Virginia, and Washington, DC. The deal gave NationsBank a five-year option to acquire MNC, which it exercised in 1993. The bank also purchased Chrysler First, the automaker's consumer finance unit. The acquisition fits well with NationsBank's existing consumer finance operation. The combined operation will be renamed NationsCredit. In addition, NationsBank agreed to form an alliance with Dean Witter to offer security products and services at branches of NationsBank and other banks. The new company is called Nations Securities. Dean Witter should bring expertise, technology, and financial products to the deal, while NationsBank offers its huge customer base. Further, NationsBank planned to buy Chicago Research and Trading Group, a prominent options, swaps, and financial derivatives firm. The purchase will enable NationsBank to offer complex financial risk management services to corporate clients. In the last two cases, we have another example of the eroding wall between commercial banks and brokerage firms. Also, NationsBank is lobbying hard (along with First Union and Wachovia) to help pass a bill in the North Carolina legislature (as well as in other southern legislatures) that would open the state to reciprocal banking in 1996. Thirty-four other states already have adopted nationwide interstate banking; 20 of them, including California and New York, require reciprocity. NationsBank has expressed an interest in entering the California market. This suggests that the firm's strategy is to become a truly national retail bank, operating in key banking markets in a loop from Maryland to Florida through Texas to California.

On the other hand, the Wachovia/South Carolina National merger would produce the 12th largest bank holding company outside of New York. However, in term of asset size, it would be only about one-third the size of NationsBank. In 1991, Wachovia's return on assets was 0.72 percent, while its return on equity was 9.3 percent, well below the historical profitability ratios for the bank. The decline in these ratios was related to the merger. Wachovia's return on equity and return on assets rebounded to 16.7 percent and 1.36 percent, respectively, as profitability improved because of a decline in nonperforming assets and an increase in the net interest margin.

A key to Wachovia's success has been its reputation for financial strength, pristine balance sheet, abundant capitalization, and overall asset quality. Wachovia did not follow the herd of commercial bankers who took excessive positions in commercial real estate lending and merger-related lending. Instead, the bank pursued its traditional consumer banking and middle-market loan businesses. In addition, Wachovia invested heavily in cash management products that brought in large corporate customers who otherwise might not have been attracted to this North Carolina-based bank. Also, Wachovia has emphasized fee-producing businesses such as administering trusts, servicing student loans, and offering credit cards.

Banc One

Banc One Corp. is an example of an exceptionally well-run superregional bank holding company that has made good use of innovative technology to expand profits. An Ohio-based company, Banc One has been on a merger binge in the 1990s. Between 1990 and 1993, it announced plans to acquire Firstier (Nebraska), Key Centurion (West Virginia), Valley National Corp. (Arizona), Team Bancshares (Texas), First Illinois Corp. (Illinois), Marine Corp. (Illinois), First Southeast Banking Corp. (Wisconsin), Affiliated Bancshares (Colorado), Central Banking Group Inc.

(Oklahoma) Central Trust of Lorain, Central Trust of Canton, Central Trust of Marietta, Central Trust of Newark (all located in Ohio), First Security Corp. (Kentucky), MCorp (Texas), Metropolitan Bank of Lima (Ohio), and Bright Banc (Texas). All of these acquisitions would make Banc One the seventh largest bank holding company in the United States, with $76 billion in assets. The firm's asset base tripled in the last few years as it established key locations in Ohio, Indiana, Illinois, Kentucky, Texas, Wisconsin, Louisiana, Arizona, Colorado, West Virginia, Nebraska, and Michigan. Banc One is now the second largest bank holding company in Texas with 200 branches and $19 billion in assets. It has generally provided remarkable service to customers and has exhibited the uncanny ability to absorb a steady stream of acquired banks smoothly into its multistate system.

While Banc One's return on equity (16.6 percent in 1991 and 16.3 percent in 1992) and return on assets (1.52 percent in 1991 and 1.31 in 1992) have always been among the highest in the industry, the quick succession of takeovers raises some questions among industry followers and analysts about whether Banc One can sustain profitability amidst this rapid growth. While the consolidations it made from 1990 to mid-1992 seemed to work out well, its four most recent acquisitions are in disparate markets throughout the country. Also, Valley National has had significant asset quality problems over the past several years, and its merger into the system would increase the nonperforming assets of Banc One from 2.0 to 2.5 percent. The price paid for Valley National places Banc One under some pressure to improve its near-term earnings per share and maintain high profitability ratios. On the other hand, Banc One has been able to protect itself from big mistakes by eschewing large, risky loan transactions and pursuing middle-market and residential mortgage loans. John B. McCoy, chairman, has followed a strategy of entering markets where his organization can be first, second, or third. Growth for the sake of growth has been of little interest to Banc One. While forging a national identity, Banc One has worked hard to keep management in place at the banks that have been acquired, so that local ties with customers can be maintained. According to bank analyst Dennis Shea, of Morgan Stanley, "There is no better buyer [than Banc One] of other banks in the business."[25] Banc One should be equipped to consolidate management, mesh information systems and back office functions, and market retail products nationally. Following its agreement to purchase Valley National, Banc One outbid Mellon Bank in acquiring Key Centurion Bancshares, a West Virginia–based bank holding company with $3 billion in assets and 54 offices in West Virginia and Kentucky. Key Centurion, a well-capitalized (equity-to-asset ratio of 10 percent) bank with a return on assets of 1.1 percent and a return on equity of 10.5 percent in 1991, concentrated on retail customers and middle-market lending, the same as Banc One.

Banc One's basic strategy includes conservative lending, innovative technology, high-quality customer service in attractive physical facilities, a broad array of products offered at branches, and effective merger plans. The merger formula includes never acquiring a peer bank, buying banks considerably smaller than itself, leaving in place the existing management of any acquired bank, and allowing each bank to make its own decisions in a decentralized structure. Banc One also offers incentive compensation packages for senior managers when growth targets are met. Wherever Banc One goes, it has a formula, a culture, systems, a structure, and a strong executive management group that bear close examination as a model for success. At the time of this writing, Banc One Corporation and Banco Nacional de Mexico (Mexico's largest bank) were exploring a possible alliance to establish a Mexican credit card processing program. There was also the possibility of undertaking a joint venture to provide the service throughout Latin America.

Other strong superregional banks are Fleet Financial, PNC Financial, SunTrust, CoreStates, Norwest, FirstBank Systems, and First Interstate. Some of these are interested in additional acquisitions and appear to be building war chests. They differ from the money-center banks in having adequate capital to pursue mergers because they lack the burden of nonperforming foreign and leveraged buy-out loans in their portfolios. These profitable regional banks have concentrated on local, smaller commercial customers, solid middle-market businesses, and consumer lending. Usually, their lending policies have been more conservative than that of the New York banks. The ability to control costs, make prudent loans, and absorb acquisitions smoothly and without overpaying will be among the keys to which of the superregionals emerge as the industry leaders during the 1990s.

Society Acquires Ameritrust

In September 1991, Society Corp. agreed to acquire cross-town rival Ameritrust Corp. in a stock transaction valued at nearly $1.4 billion. This merger created the largest banking company in Cleveland, with more than $23 billion in assets. Society Corp. will control about 26 percent of deposits in Cleveland, compared with only 15 percent held by National City, the closest competitor. The merger is the third major acquisition for Society, which had previously acquired and successfully "digested" two formerly distressed Ohio banks: Trustcorp, Inc., of Toledo in 1990 and Centran in 1985. Society Corp., about the 25th largest U.S. bank holding company after the merger, will have 550 branch and trust offices in eight states, including Ohio, Indiana, Michigan, and Texas. National City Corp. put Ameritrust up for grabs when it made an unsolicited bid for its cross-town rival.

Society is one of only a handful of banks among the top 50 in the country that have reported 10 consecutive years of increasing earnings on an originally reported basis, or before restating the results of acquisitions. At year-end 1991, Society had a return on assets of 1.09 and a return on equity of 15.4 percent; Ameritrust lost money in 1991. That same year, Ameritrust had nonperforming assets of 4.3 percent, compared with only 1.2 percent at Society. Cost savings from the merger are projected to be $50 to $60 million in 1992 and $130 million in 1993. In 1992, Society achieved a 17.5 percent return on equity and a 1.24 percent return on assets. Analyst Mike Milanovich, of R.W. Baird & Co., said, "I think it's a good deal. . . . Management is good; these people are experienced in correcting a badly defective loan portfolio and cutting costs. Society is in good shape."[26] Aside from the usual advantages of a merger, one of the more significant benefits of this deal was the acquisition of Ameritrust's fee-income-producing trust business. The transaction boosted Society's trust business to $29 billion in assets, placing it among the top 12 banks with over $200 million in annual revenues and managed assets. Prior to the merger, Society's trust business already had a pretax profit margin of 40 percent, relatively high by industry standards. Trust fees now represent about 14 percent of the firm's total operating revenue, compared with 8 percent before the merger.[27] In July 1992, Society also agreed to acquire First Federal S&L ($1.1 billion in assets and 24 offices) of Ft. Myers.

First Union Acquires Southeast and Dominion Bankshares

First Union, a Charlotte-based bank holding company, took over $10.3 billion in assets and 224 branches of the failed Southeast Banking Corp., a Miami-based bank holding company, in late September 1991. Barnett Banks and SunTrust Banks both bid unsuccessfully for Southeast. On the heels of this acquisition, First Union also agreed to buy the $9.4 billion Roanoke-based Dominion Bankshares in 1992 and First American Metro-Corp., a Virginia bank with $4.6 billion in assets. First American had been affected by the 1991 disclosure that a majority of its stock was owned by the Bank of Commerce and Credit International (BCCI), the rogue international bank that was nicknamed "The Bank of Crooks and Criminals." Strategically, the deal expands First Union's geographic presence into Virginia, with 380 offices and close to a 15-percent market share in a state where it previously had no presence. These acquisitions will make First Union the ninth largest bank holding company in the United States, with about $58 billion in assets, and the second largest bank in Florida, as well as one of the largest bank holding companies in the southeastern part of the nation. First Union has an exceptionally strong presence in North Carolina, South Carolina, Virginia, Georgia, and Florida.

Under the terms of the risk-sharing agreement with the FDIC, First Union paid a total $212 million for Southeast. This amount includes a cash payment of $81 million to the FDIC and the establishment of a $131 million loan-loss reserve. The deal calls for the FDIC to bear 85 percent of the losses on bad Southeast loans for the next five years, with First Union accepting the rest. In earlier agreements, the FDIC had given the bank doing the purchasing the right to return all bad loans to the FDIC for up to three years. This new loss-sharing agreement with First Union should help hold down the FDIC's insurance losses.

Southeast had been struggling for two years from loan losses and a sharp decline in large deposits and other funds from institutional investors. The bank had lost nearly $200 million in 1990 and $261 million in the first half of 1991. Southeast was closed in late September 1991, when it was unable to repay a loan of nearly $600 million from the Federal Reserve Bank of Atlanta. Under the terms of the agreement made, no depositor suffered a loss, but the interests of Southeast's stockholders and bondholders were wiped out.

At the end of 1992, First Union had a return on assets of 1.08 percent, a return on equity of 14.7 percent, and nonperforming assets of 2.9 percent. Reserve coverage of nonperforming loans was close to 98 percent. In addition, First Union became the third largest bank in South Carolina when it agreed to acquire South Carolina Federal S&L. The acquisition will add $917 million in assets, 32 branches, and three mortgage-lending outlets to First Union's retail base. The merger should not dilute earnings per share because of significant cost saving.

First Union, with a strong appetite for acquisitions in the 1980s, gave its chairman, Edward A. Crutchfield, Jr., the nickname "Fast Eddie." Crutchfield has certainly lived up to his reputation with the acquisition of Southeast Banking Corp. in 1991, Dominion Bankshares in 1992, and First American in 1993. The acquisitions by First Union, NationsBank, and Banc One reflect the national trend of strong banks expanding their total share of the retail market at the expense of weaker rivals.

Barnett Banks

After losing out in a bid to acquire Southeast Bank in 1991, Barnett Banks, Inc., agreed in 1992 to buy First Florida Banks, Inc. (assets of $5.4 billion) in a stock swap valued at about $810 million. Barnett won a bidding war against competing offers from rivals First Union and SunTrust to capture the last large independent bank in Florida, fortifying its market-share lead in that state. The acquisition will boost Barnett's share of Florida's deposits to 27.4 percent from 23.2 percent. First Union has a 21-percent share of the market, followed by NationsBank with a 14-percent share and SunTrust with a 13-percent share.

As a result of the merger, Barnett will close between 90 and 100 branches, cutting noninterest expenses by $66 million in 1993 and $87 million in 1994. The merger should give Barnett assets of close to $38 billion if the Justice Department doesn't require sales of assets. Essentially, the merger pushes Barnett into the number one position in eight markets in which it has been number two or below, including the Tampa market, where First Florida is based. Barnett was anxious to acquire the nearly $5 billion in trust assets under management at First Florida.

Some analysts feel that Barnett paid a huge premium of twice book value to acquire First Florida Banks. However, Barnett's management feels that the merger will not dilute earnings per share within the first year. Nonetheless, both institutions have real estate loan problems that may have a negative impact on earnings for quite a few years. Standard & Poor's placed Barnett's senior and subordinated debt on its CreditWatch with negative implications after the merger announcement. First Florida lost money in 1990 and 1991, while Barnett was profitable. However, Barnett's return on assets was only 0.33 percent in 1990, 0.35 percent in 1991, and 0.50 percent in 1992, compared with an average return on assets for the company of nearly 0.95 percent from 1983 to 1989. Barnett appeared to have adequate reserves to cover its nonperforming assets. Earnings are expected to rebound in 1993 and 1994, lifting the financial ratios of the firm. If this does not happen, look for Barnett Bank to be acquired by another southeastern bank.

Strategically, Barnett expects to keep its main focus on the consumer sector and the small-business sector, while continuing to reduce its real estate concentration and exposure. The goals of the company include improving credit quality, improving efficiency, strengthening the balance sheet, and improving its financial ratios. Barnett may also be looking for an out-of-state acquisition in the southeastern sector of the country.

Bank of Boston Fails to Acquire Shawmut

After failing to acquire the Bank of New England in 1991, Bank of Boston failed in an attempt to acquire Shawmut Banking Corporation in 1992. This merger would have created a bank holding company with about $46 billion in assets, the largest such company in New England. Bank of Boston's failure to merge with Shawmut was the result of a clash of corporate cultures and an improved tone of earnings at Shawmut, which desired to remain independent.

Bank of Boston raised about $155 million in new equity capital in 1992, boosting the company's tangible common equity to 5.2 percent from 3.5 percent. The earnings of the company are expected to be positive in 1992 and 1993; the bank suffered substantial losses in 1990 and 1991. Bank of Boston had 15.1 percent of its total loan portfolio in commercial real estate, with an additional 12.1 percent in highly leveraged transactions. Nonperforming loans to total assets were 6.5 percent, while reserve coverage of nonperforming loans was 90 percent.

Bank of Boston's improved financial health encouraged the bank's management to make three acquisitions in 1992. The bank acquired the branches and deposits of First Mutual Bank for Savings, the Society for Savings Bancorp, Boston Trade Bank, and Multibank Financial Corp. The last financial institution is a $2.5 billion bank holding company with 75 branches that is based in Dedham, MA. The acquisition expanded Bank of Boston's market share in Massachusetts, particularly in the western part of the state and in Cape Cod. Multibank specializes in small-business loans, an area in which Bank of Boston has not been strong and has been seeking to expand its influence. The Society for Savings Bancorp is a Hartford-based retail savings bank with $2.7 billion in assets and 19 branches in Connecticut. With the acquisition of Society, Bank of Boston will become the fourth largest bank in Connecticut, with 59 branches and $5.1 billion in assets. An attractive feature of the Society acquisition is its subsidiary, the Fidelity Acceptance Corporation, a Minneapolis-based consumer finance company with 102 offices in 23 states. The company specializes in financing late-model used cars and home equity loans. Both the acquisition of Society and that of Fidelity Acceptance were made without federal assistance, the first such unassisted transactions in New England since 1989.

Bank of Boston's acquisitions suggest two things: The bank feels that the New England economy is beginning to recover and the bank's prospects are improving. Otherwise, why would it buy a few banks that had not been profitable for a couple of years and gamble on a turnaround? The acquisitions also suggest a subtle shift in corporate strategy toward consumer and small-business banking, areas with higher margins than wholesale banking and international banking, Bank of Boston's previous areas of concentration. While the Federal Reserve Bank approved the bank's acquisitions, the central bank required Bank of Boston to increase its equity capital.

Comerica and Manufacturers National Corporation

Former Detroit rivals Comerica and Manufacturers National agreed to join forces to create Michigan's 2nd largest bank and the 25th largest in the United States, with $26.8 billion in assets and $20.3 billion in deposits. The merger will allow the banks to cut costs by about 15 percent of their combined cost base and gain the financial muscle they need to survive in an industry shakeout. The banks plan to eliminate 60 of their combined 413 branches and 1,800 of their 13,500 jobs. About $145 million would be saved by 1994, including $95 million from staff cuts, $7 million from occupancy costs, $9 million in equipment, and $34 million in miscellaneous reductions.

The combined banks will be organized under the Comerica name, with their board memberships split evenly between them. A sign of management's earnestness in controlling expenses is that the two companies had a total of 40 directors prior to the merger, whereas after the merger there will be only 14 directors.

This merger differs from recent bank mergers because both banks are financially healthy, are well managed, and have strong capital positions, solid credit quality, and strong franchises. Both Comerica and Manufacturers were highly profitable in 1991, with returns on equity of 15.2 and 15.4 percent, nonperforming asset ratios of 1.4 and 1.6 percent (a fraction of the industry average of 4.3 percent), and tangible common equity-to-asset ratios of 5.7 and 6.1 percent, respectively. Comerica lends more to small and medium-sized businesses and consumers, while Manufacturers concentrates more on midsize to large-size companies. A common trait of the loan portfolios of both banks is that construction lending is just a low 3 percent of loans in each case and has remained consistently at this level for the past few years. Highly leveraged transactions are not a significant issue for either company. Lesser developed country loan exposure at Manufacturers is just over $100 million.

Both banks rely on low-cost consumer deposits and have good records in avoiding bad loans. Comerica is a big lender to automobile suppliers ($800 million) and a nationally recognized lender to automobile dealers ($500 million); Manufacturers National has an extremely profitable subsidiary that specializes in forwarding freight and helping customers move goods through customs. While still smaller than cross-town rival NBD Bancorp, the new Comerica will rank first in consumer and commercial loans among banks in Michigan. Comerica's return on assets was 1.33 percent in 1992, while its return on equity was 17.1 percent. Nonperforming assets were at a low 1.5 percent of related assets, while loan loss reserves to nonperforming loans stood at 136 percent.

A benefit of this merger is that Comerica should be able to post double-digit increases in earnings over the next few years, even if there is little or no loan growth. Comerica also acquired the Texas bank that formerly belonged to Hibernia, the weakened Louisiana bank holding company. It is anticipated that, following the merger, NBD might acquire Michigan National or merge with another strong regional bank based in another city. The latter move would not provide as much in the way of cost savings as the Comerica-Manufacturers deal, but it might avoid a dilution of earnings per share if no up-front premium is paid to merge.

NBD Bancorp and INB

NBD (affectionately referred to as "No Bad Deals") has a fine reputation for its lending practices and superior asset quality. The bank's loan losses and nonperforming loans are less than half those of other large regional banks. However, NBD is facing a problem: Its earnings growth is likely to be minimal until the demand for loans picks up. This factor acted as a catalyst in NBD's search for a merger partner. In 1992, NBD agreed to acquire $6.6 billion INB Financial Corp. Detroit's NBD will be the largest bank holding company in Michigan and Indiana, with assets of $40 billion, and a member of the 20 largest bank holding companies in the United States. Following the acquisition, NBD will have a 17-percent share of the deposit market in both Michigan and Indiana. NBD is thought to have paid a steep price (almost twice book value) for INB, Indiana's largest independent banking company with a solid, but unspectacular, reputation. It is anticipated that NBD shareholders will face an estimated earnings dilution of 5 percent in 1992 and 2 percent in 1993 as their company "digests" INB. On the other hand, NBD should be able to shave $44 million in costs from its Indiana banks by 1994. Based on this figure, the long-term impact of the acquisition would be positive. While the merger does not represent an embarrassment of riches, it clearly should prove to be a good deal for NBD shareholders. NBD owns two other Indiana banks: Summcorp, with $2.5 billion in assets, and Gainer Bank, with $1.5 billion in assets. As of year-end 1991, NBD had a return on assets of 1.07 percent and a return on equity of 14.8 percent, with nonperforming assets of 1 percent; INB had a return on assets of 0.78 percent, a return on equity of 10.7 percent, and nonperforming assets of 1.9 percent. After the merger, the two banks' combined return on equity slipped temporarily to 10.4 percent at year-end 1992, while nonperforming assets were at 1.63 percent of loans. The combined return on equity was expected to rise to 15.5 percent in 1993.

All of the banks in the holding company ring Lake Michigan and have loan portfolios of reasonably high quality. Charles Fischer, chairman of NBD, is fond of saying, "We don't know how to run a troubled bank . . . and we don't want to learn how."[28] NBD is eyeing the Chicago, Ohio, and Wisconsin areas for additional acquisitions, as well as seeking meaningful stakes in Missouri, Tennessee, and Kentucky. The company also has a small presence in Florida, where it tries to serve midwestern retirees.

NBD's strategy includes avoiding heavy loan concentrations and megacredits syndicated by the money-center banks. Rather, it prefers to catch and deal with problematic loans early and to concentrate on middle-market loans and consumer loans (which have higher lending margins than most commercial loans to large corporations). In accordance with its strategy of pursuing the consumer, consumer deposits represent 70 percent of all deposits and 25 percent of all loans. NBD is also pushing for higher noninterest income, including fees from trust operations, deposit and mortgage services, and credit cards. The bank is also working hard to reduce its overhead ratio, that is, noninterest expenses as a percent of net interest income.

NBD likes to acquire banks with sound loan portfolios without overpaying. This allows the firm to eliminate any dilution in earnings per share created by an acquisition within 18 months. Following this strategy, NBD had an average return on equity of 14.8 percent over the past six years, compared with an average of 11.8 percent for 23 comparable regional banks.

National City Corporation Buys Merchants National Corporation

After being rebuffed in an attempt to acquire crosstown rival Ameritrust Corp. of Cleveland, National City Corp. agreed to buy Merchants National Corporation of Indianapolis. This acquisition boosted National City's assets to approximately $30 billion from about $24 billion and gave the bank 138 additional branches in Indiana. Buying Merchants helped National City reach its goal of increasing its fee-income operations, since Merchants has a contract with the Defense Department to offer banking services at 181 military bases throughout the world. While the acquisition may be a good long-term strategic positioning move, National City paid a handsome 50 percent premium over the previous day's market price for the shares of Merchants, which meant that the price of the stock was 16.2 times earnings per share. In sum, National City paid top price to acquire a mediocre bank with an average return on equity of about 8 percent and an average return on assets of 0.56 percent over the past decade. Prior to the acquisition, at year-end 1991 National City had a respectable return on assets of 0.93 percent and a return on equity of 13.2 percent. In addition, Merchants possessed an uninspiring nonperforming asset ratio of 3.7 percent, compared with only 1.7 percent at National City. Book value for National City will be diluted by about 7 percent. As part of the acquisition, National City expected to take a restructuring charge of $20 million in 1992 to cover the costs of cutting 600 of Merchants' 3,500 jobs. The acquisition diluted National City's earnings per share in 1992 by about 8 percent. However, National City had a return on equity of 15.3 percent and a return on assets of 1.16 percent in 1992. In response to the merger announcement, Moody's placed $975 million of National City's debt under review for a possible downgrading, while S&P placed $850 million of National City's debt and preferred stock and $165 million of Merchants National's debt on its CreditWatch.

KeyCorp

KeyCorp, a well-run multistate bank holding company that had less than $8 billion in assets when it began its acquisition campaign is expected to have close to $30 billion in assets by the end of 1993. Headquartered in Albany, New York, KeyCorp has diversified geographically in seven northern states from Alaska to Maine. Although more than half of its assets are in New York State, the bank had a presence in Oregon, Washington, Wyoming, Utah, Alaska, Maine, and Idaho. In fact, in 1992, KeyCorp announced the acquisition of Puget Sound Bancorp, with $4.9 billion in assets and 112 branches in Washington, along with the purchase of 48 branches of BankAmerica with $1.5 billion in deposits. These two acquisitions made KeyCorp the third largest bank in the state of Washington, with an 11-percent share of the market. In addition, in mid-1992, KeyCorp announced the purchase of a thrift headquartered in Albany, New York, with assets of almost $1 billion.

While KeyCorp's capital ratios are a notch below those of the best capitalized regional banks, they are far more than adequate to meet minimum regulatory requirements. In addition, other balance sheet ratios, such as the return on assets and the return on equity, were well above average, at 1.01 and 16.1 percent, respectively, at year-end 1991 and 1.02 and 16.7 percent, respectively, in 1992. Combined non-performing assets to total assets were 2.0 percent in early 1993, compared with a bank group average of 4.3 percent. This demonstrates a low-risk loan portfolio. However, after all of the announced acquisitions are closed, the company's exposure in commercial real estate will reach 23 percent of loans. KeyCorp concentrates on providing banking services to consumers and small businesses. The bank has no highly leveraged transactions or lending exposure to lesser developed countries and has less than $400 million in construction loans. As a precaution, it also has a lending limit of $25 million to any single customer, despite a capital position that would allow it to lend in excess of $100 million. Management is expected to continue to make acquisitions, but is also concerned with the bottom-line impact of future acquisitions on earnings per share. The major risk is that management will lose its discipline and pay too much for an acquisition. Some analysts expect KeyCorp to achieve a 1.2-percent return on assets and a 17.25-percent return on equity in 1993.

KeyCorp's management has indicated that acquisitions will remain important to the bank holding company as long as they do not dilute earnings per share. Management will not make acquisitions just for the sake of asset growth and would not be interested in buying banks with weak loan portfolios.

Mellon

Pittsburgh-based Mellon Bank, often referred to as the "J. P. Morgan of the Alleghenies," has begun to change from chiefly a blue-chip corporate lender and trust money manager to playing a role as a consumer lender with a large retail branch system. Mellon has also become a significant force in personal investment management, the management of cash for corporations, and the handling of data processing for smaller banks. These businesses now supply an estimated 40 percent of Mellon's profits.

This business shift has led to a shift in the mix of Mellon's $30 billion in assets. Consumer lending, which accounted for 20 percent of loans at the end of 1986, now accounts for 50 percent of loans, while lending to blue-chip corporations has fallen to 46 percent of assets from 50 percent over the same time frame. In addition, Mellon agreed to pay $1.5 billion to an American Express subsidiary to acquire Boston Company, an investment management company. Over two-thirds of Boston Company's revenues are derived from fees for administering mutual funds, managing institutional custody assets, and private banking. The acquisition will give Mellon a big boost in fee-based income and dovetails well with the bank's strong trust business.

Mellon's return on assets in 1991 was a highly respectable 0.96 percent, while its return on equity was a healthy 15.8 percent. In 1992, the return on assets jumped to 1.46 percent, while the return on equity reached 21.1 percent. These ratios represent a vast improvement over previous years, when Mellon suffered from poor management and troubled real estate loans. As a matter of fact, Mellon was one of the first banks to establish a "good bank/bad bank" strategy, allowing it to keep its performing loans intact, while swapping out $1.4 billion in troubled loans by selling them for a few cents on the dollar to a "bad bank" called Grant Street National Bank. Mellon closed the year 1991 with a nonperforming loan ratio of 4.78 percent, down from its peak of 8.01 percent in 1987, when rumors persisted that Mellon was in danger of failing.

Mellon has been busy buying banks with large retail deposits and good consumer and residential mortgage franchises throughout Pennsylvania. The bank acquired most of the suburban branches of troubled PSFS, a major savings bank in the Philadelphia area, in 1990, after having acquired the Philadelphia-based Girard bank in the mid-1980s. Girard had a strong branch network and large trust department. Mellon now has close to 30 percent of the deposits in the Pittsburgh area and a 17-percent share of the deposits in the Delaware Valley (including Philadelphia) following the acquisition of the deposits of Meritor Savings Bank with its 27 Philadelphia branches in December 1992.

Along with Northern Trust and State Street Bank, Mellon is one of the leading bookkeepers for thousands of corporate pension plans, executing trades on behalf of money managers, tracking the money managers' performance, and keeping account records for pension plan participants. Mellon is the nation's third largest "master trustee" and is in second place among banks offering corporate cash management services. Mellon also provides computer services to smaller banks ranging from the bookkeeping function and platform functions to processing credit card transactions and running regional automated teller networks. It is estimated that 1992 service revenue will exceed $800 million, or more than 40 percent of the bank's total revenue.

Mellon's management indicated that it would issue $250 million in common stock and $450 million in preferred stock in 1993. Some of these funds will be used to cover the costs related to the acquisitions of Meritor and Boston Company, while boosting the already strong capital ratios of the bank.

Integra Financial

In July 1992, Integra Financial, a $10.5 billion bank holding company based in Pittsburgh, announced a merger with crosstown rival Equimark, a troubled bank with $2.9 billion in assets. The merger will create a formidable banking company with about a 20-percent share of the Pittsburgh market, compared with a 30-percent share for Mellon, the largest bank in Pittsburgh, and a 25-percent share for PNC Financial, the second largest bank in Pittsburgh. This acquisition could enhance Integra's attractiveness as a takeover target, as Banc One, Society, National City Corp., NBD, CoreStates, Meridian, and Huntingdon Bancshares are said to be interested in a presence in the Pittsburgh market.

Integra officials are optimistic that they can easily combine Equimark's 53 branches with Integra's 233 branches. Mergers are not new for Integra. The company was originally created in the late 1980s from the merger of eight small banks. Integra expects to close about 25 branches and eliminate 500 jobs, including the jobs of the top management at Equimark. This should reduce Equimark's noninterest expenses by 35 percent.

Equimark showed a profit in the second quarter of 1992 after suffering losses in both 1990 and 1991. At the time of this writing, Integra had not decided what to do with Equimark's Liberty Savings (Philadelphia area) and Liberty Business Credit (northeastern region of the United States). The sale price for Equimark was close to twice Equimark's book value and should dilute Integra's earnings per share in 1993 by about 2 percent. However, Integra achieved a return on equity of 19.0 percent and a return on assets of 1.16 percent in 1992.

SUPERREGIONALS AND INVESTMENT BANKING ACTIVITY

Superregional banks have been slower than money-center banks to develop investment banking activities. In addition, they have retreated from international lending, retaining large interests in middle-market lending and consumer products and services. There should be greater inroads of superregionals into investment banking during the second half of the decade as more mergers create giant banks that can commit the capital and specialized skills to the task, as these banks develop more corporate business, and as they exhaust the greatest opportunities for profit growth in consumer banking with the completion of regional cost-cutting and integration programs. In addition, commercial banks entering into investment banking will enable these banks to diversify their revenues and generate greater fee income. Also, banks would not have to pay underwriting fees in securing their own loans or in raising external capital.[29]

MERGER ACTIVITY AND OTHER POTENTIAL MERGERS

"Eventually, the next wave of bank consolidations could see acquisitions of the current crop of acquirers by even bigger banks or mergers among regionals to create a truly national bank. . . . Bank and thrift managements that traditionally wanted independence or were acquirers themselves are rethinking that strategy in view of the rich premiums acquirers are paying."[30] As of mid-1992, the ratio of the acquisition price to the book value of banks acquired through mergers had risen to 1.85 from an average of 1.60 in 1991. Some banks have paid as much as 2.6 times book value to make an acquisition.

The search for efficiency and cost savings has been behind some of the recent bank mergers. The latest banking combinations are in sharp contrast to earlier mergers, in which managers sought to extend the influence of their banks into new geographic markets. Some of these market extension mergers generated disappointing returns, as the resources of the banks were stretched over a broad geographic territory, limiting cost savings. In addition, control of the quality of credit became difficult in less familiar regional markets. Furthermore, the franchise value that acquirers thought they had purchased in the form of customer loyalty and name recognition sometimes disappeared with the shift away from relationship banking toward commodity pricing or price sensitivity. When a bank raised its fees for customer services or lowered rates on certificates of deposit following a merger, it often lost price-sensitive customers, since they could readily compare the rates of different certificates or mortgages.[31]

Although bankers and investors expect large savings from announced bank mergers, there is much skepticism among researchers about the claims of major cost savings and high levels of profitability. A study by J. C. Linder and D. B. Crane of New England bank mergers between 1982 and 1987[32] and a study by A. Srinivasan and L. D. Wall, economists at the Federal Reserve Bank of Atlanta, of all bank mergers with assets in excess of $100 million from 1982 through 1986[33] found that mergers do not necessarily lower costs or raise profits significantly.

As a matter of fact, the Harvard Business School study concluded that, while merged banks had reduced their costs compared with other banks, the lower costs "were more than offset by the loss of business and revenue to competitors." The Atlanta study concluded that the acquiring banks were more efficient than banks in general before the mergers and that in the years following the mergers costs rose more rapidly for the combined banks than for the rest of the industry. Edward Ettin, deputy director of research at the Federal Reserve Board, has suggested that the earlier mergers were in an environment where bankers were not emphasizing cost control as they do now. For example, the top 25 banks eliminated 44,000 jobs in 1991 and trimmed about 100,000 jobs in 1992. In previous consolidations and mergers, the number of jobs eliminated was miniscule. Ettin also pointed out that some studies of bank mergers failed to point out differences in the quality of management between today's banking leaders and those in control in the early 1980s. Dwight B. Crane, coauthor of the New England merger study, indicated that the quality of management makes a huge difference in the outcome of a merger and that while expense savings are difficult to achieve, some banks proved that they were possible. Crane also felt that there were too many banks in this country and that that was one reason for their low profits. Lowell Bryan, a partner at McKinsey & Co., remained convinced that there were potentially great benefits from bank mergers "when they are done well." However, he warned that the benefits of spreading fixed costs over a larger asset base and the elimination of duplicate branches and redundant personnel could easily be overshadowed by poor management. He also warned that poor management can undermine the benefits of mergers by allowing revenues to fall.

While merger and acquisition activity reached record levels during 1991–1992, we can expect further consolidation during the rest of the decade. Other markets that may be ripe for a shakeout because of intense competition are Indianapolis, Chicago, Philadelphia, New Jersey, New York, Maryland, Michigan, California, and Florida. Chicago does not have the sophisticated middle-market lending of other regions, so it has become a marked area for acquisition-minded banks. Detroit's NBD Bancorp has acquired several Chicago and Indiana banks, as have Manufacturers National, Kalamazoo's First of America, and Grand Rapids' Old Kent. It is expected that there will be merger activity amongst CoreStates, First Fidelity, Meridian, Mellon, PNC Financial, Mid-Atlantic, and other New Jersey and Maryland banks. Managers at several mid-Atlantic banks have expressed an interest in extending their operations south into Maryland and Virginia, and consolidation is expected to continue in that region. The trend in the consolidation process during 1991–1992 seems to be to target turnaround banks, as the banks that acquire them strive to minimize the dilution of earnings per share to shareholders.

Oppenheimer & Co.'s banking analysts examined smaller banks with assets of between $500 million and $2 billion, to see whether they were attractive merger candidates. The company sought to find banks that

1. had at least a compound annual growth rate of 10 percent over the last four years;
2. had nonperforming assets below 2 percent of loans; and
3. traded at less than 1.5 times book value.

Only 15 banks satisfied these criteria, and most were located in the midwest. This small group appears to be more profitable, has better credit quality, and is more cheaply valued than most larger banks. The group had an average return on assets of 1.1 percent, return on equity of 14 percent, and price-to-earnings ratio of 10.3. The members of the group are Firstbank of Illinois, First Source Corp., First Merchants Corp., Irwin Financial Corp., Brenton Banks, Hawkeye Bancorp, Chemical Financial, First Michigan Bank, Capital Bancorp, BT Financial, Commonwealth Bancshares, FB&T Corp., Financial Trust Corp., First Western Bancorp, and Associated Banc Corp.[34]

In screening larger financially sound banks with assets of $3 billion to $25 billion for attractive acquisition candidates, Oppenheimer & Co. looked for institutions that had tangible equity-to-asset ratios of at least 6 percent, nonperforming assets below 3 percent, and reserve coverage of nonperforming loans above 100 percent. These companies also had to be trading at or below 140 percent of book value. The few banks that satisfied these criteria were Meridian, Amsouth, Trustmark, BB&T, Southern National, Union Planters, Key Centurion, Mercantile, Commerce Bancshares, West One, and First Security. It is likely that as the superregionals strive to build their empires, some of these medium-sized banks will be acquired at above-market prices. It is also possible that some of them will choose to remain independent.[35]

FOREIGN BANKING MERGERS

Another possibility is for a foreign bank to merge with or buy one of the money-center banks. A Japanese bank already had a 4.9-percent position in Manufacturers Hanover before its merger with Chemical Bank, while British, Canadian, Hong Kong, and Israeli banks have both a major retail and a wholesale presence in the U.S. banking market. Foreign banks already own Marine Midland, Harris Trust, and some west coast banks. Bank of Montreal, the owner of Harris Trust, is rumored to have an interest in Continental Illinois, which is also coveted by First Chicago. Credit Lyonnais, an aggressive French bank, and WestPac Banking, the huge Australian bank holding company, are also rumored to be seeking U.S. acquisitions.

The British banking system appears to be in the midst of a fundamental restructuring, with the chairmen of Midland and Barclays Bank, as well as the CEO of National Westminster, having been forced to resign. Following in the footsteps of their American counterparts, both Lloyds and Hongkong and Shanghai Banking Corp. made offers to merge with Midland Bank. Lloyds later withdrew its offer, leaving Hongkong and Shanghai as the apparent winner. The strategy of foreign banks would lead to the development of a global system with a strong presence in Asia, Europe, and the United States. Already, Spain's Banco de Balboa and Banco de Vizcaya have merged, as have Alemagne Bank Nederland and Amsterdam-Rotterdam Bank in the Netherlands. Most banking experts expect to see a wave of mergers take place among the smaller banks in Europe and among the building societies in Great Britain.[36]

FINANCIAL CONGLOMERATES OR "BOUTIQUES"

The breakdown of product market boundaries and conglomeration across product lines has led to the formation of some financial conglomerates. Institutions such as Sears, Citicorp, and American Express have implemented strategies that resemble financial supermarkets. Under the Sears umbrella reside Dean Witter, Coldwell Banker, a savings bank, Allstate Insurance, the Discover card, Sears credit card, a "nonbank bank," and, of course, the troubled retailer. American Express owns most of Shearson Lehman, part of an insurance company, an international bank, the American Express and Optima credit cards, and a traveler's check company, as well as the well-known travel company.

Other companies, such as Xerox and GE, have also become major players in the financial services industry. Even AT&T has made a major move into the industry with the distribution of over 5 million credit cards. The trend toward price banking, the erosion of traditional relationships, and the reduced regulatory interference with market transactions led companies to develop broader product lines and to make at least a first bid at competitive prices.

At the same time that some companies were pursing a strategy of becoming financial supermarkets, others were pursuing the status of a financial "boutique" or niche player. The 1980s saw financial investment bank "boutiques" (James D. Wolfensohn; Lazard Freres; Blackstone Group; Kohlberg Kravis Roberts; Wasserstein, Perella; and Forstmann Little & Co.) flourish, along with money market funds and some option players. The product market spectrum has been filled by financial conglomerates, "boutiques," and traditional players. A wide array of financial service firms compete actively in numerous market segments.[37] Strategy has assumed a much more important role, with the potential risks and rewards becoming so great that some firms have been unable to remain independent entities while others have generated riches.

Most of the financial supermarkets cannot offer better products than their more specialized competitors. Not many customers seem to care whether they buy insurance, stocks, or real estate in the same place. In addition, nationwide banking offers few economies and appeals to only a few.[38]

Both Sears and Xerox announced that they would undergo a major restructuring in 1993. Sears spun off part of Dean Witter and Allstate in public offerings, while Xerox is expected to sell off most of its empire in the financial services industry, with its management concentrating on the growth and expansion of the firm's core business. Xerox paid top dollar for its Crum & Foster subsidiary and then suffered through years of poor underwriting results in the property and casualty industry.

SPECIALIZED BANKING

Specialized banking is said to offer a number of advantages over universal banking at the macrolevel. Many observers feel that the lessened concentration of power and enhanced competition give the consumer greater choice. On the other hand, a certain amount of reduced competition results because the smaller size of companies keep them from offering some services and products. Many analysts also feel that government can more easily direct resources and that conflicts of interest are fewer in a world of specialized banking. Others disagree and claim that there are likely to be more conflicts of interest. For example, a commercial banker can suggest that a client borrow from the bank rather than float a debenture. Or the banker might recommend a particular underwriter in return for large demand deposit balances. Also, a bank that desires to have an unprofitable loan repaid can suggest that the customer issue securities through an underwriter. Some analysts claim that there are fewer tie-in sales and there is less favoritism shown to customers in a specialized bank. A bank that could offer any product or service (e.g., loans and insurance) might force its customers to purchase all their required items from that bank. A person who wants a mortgage loan might be required to purchase homeowner's and mortgage life insurance from the bank. If the potential mortgagor refused to buy the additional insurance coverage from the bank, the bank might deny the loan. There is nothing wrong with this practice if the bank does not overcharge its customers for the additional product, exploiting both its full market power and the consumer's ignorance.[39]

ENDNOTES

1. R. S. Litan,"The Revolution in U.S. Finance: Past, Present and Future," Frank M. Engle Lecture (Bryn Mawr, PA: The American College, April 30, 1991), pp. 26–27.

2. P. Thomas, "Regulators Seek Rules Allowing Interstate S&Ls," *The Wall Street Journal,* December 23, 1991, pp. A3–A4.

3. S. Greenbaum and J. B. Higgins, "Financial Innovation," *Dynamics of Banking,* eds. T. Havrilesky and R. Schweitzer (Arlington Heights, IL: Harlan Davidson, Inc., 1985), p. 122.

4. G. Hector, "Banking Finally Hits the Bottom," *Fortune,* April 6, 1992, p. 98.

5. H. E. Heinemann, "Fixing the Banks: Mispriced Risks," *Heinemann Economics* 7 (June 10, 1991), pp. 7–8.

6. M. Quint, "Giant Banks: Will Little Guy Pay?" *New York Times,* August 23, 1991, p. D1.

7. J. Meehan, S. Wooley, et al., "If Mergers Were Simple, Banking's Troubles Might Be Over," *Business Week,* April 22, 1991, pp. 77–79.

8. G. Hector, "Bank Reforms Won't Save the Bank," *Fortune,* April 8, 1991, pp. 67–69.

9. G. Hector, "Do Mergers Make Sense?" *Fortune,* August 12, 1991, pp 70–71.

10. K. Holland, "Why the Chemistry Is Right at Chemical," *Business Week,* June 7, 1992, p. 91.

11. Ibid., p. 92.

12. D. Rogers, *The Future of American Banking* (New York: McGraw-Hill, 1993), p. 246.

13. Ibid., p. 194.

14. C. Yang, G. Gleckman, and M. McNamee, et al., "The Future of Banking," *Business Week,* April 22, 1991, p. 76.

15. Rogers, p. 143.

16. S. Lipin, "Citicorp Sees Retail Banking as Growth Area," *The Wall Street Journal,* June 11, 1992, p. A3.

17. Rogers, p. 43.

18. Ibid., p. 30.

19. Ibid., p. 71.

20. Ibid., p. 299.

21. Ibid., p. 299.

22. Ibid., p. 300.

23. G. Gorton, "Mergers Alone Don't Cut Banks' Costs," *The Wall Street Journal,* January 24, 1992, p. A14.

24. T. McCardle, *Investors Business Daily,* September 26, 1991.

25. G. Stern, "Banc One Continues to Expand Across the U.S.," *The Wall Street Journal,* April 15, 1992, p. B4.

26. L. L. Freeman, "Society: Midwest's New Superregional Bank," *Investors Business Daily,* May 1, 1992, pp. 1–2.

27. Ibid.

28. C. T. Fischer III, "Banking in the '90s: The Superregional Challenge," *Game Plan for the '90s,* Annual Conference on Bank Structure, Federal Reserve Bank of Chicago, 1990, pp. 285–286.

29. I. Leveson, *Financial Services: The Next Era* (Marlboro, NJ: Author, 1991), pp. 76–77.

30. S. Lipin and M. Charlier, "As National Banking Nears, Mergers Sweep Across Border States," *The Wall Street Journal,* June 22, 1992, p. A9.

31. I. N. Spady, "Strategies for Success: Charting the Future of the Banking Industry," *Great Westerner,* December 1991, p. 7.

32. J. C. Linder and D. B. Crane, "Bank Mergers: Integration and Profitability," *Journal of Financial Services Research* 7 (February 1993), pp. 30–50.

33. A. Srinivasan and L. D. Wall, *Cost Savings Associated with Bank Mergers,* Working Paper No. 92-2, Federal Reserve Bank of Atlanta, February 1992.

34. C. Katowski, "Prospects for Value in Small Cap Bank Stocks," *Banking,* February 4, 1992, pp. 1–3.

35. C. Swaim, "Consolidation: Beyond the Top 30," *Banking,* March 9, 1992, pp. 1–4.

36. R. A. Melcher, "Whatever Happened to Genteel London Banking?" *Business Week,* May 11, 1992, pp. 53–54.

37. D. M. Meerschwam, *Breaking Financial Boundaries* (Boston: Harvard Business School Press, 1991), p. 253.

38. Spady, p. 7.

39. G. M. Benston, *The Separation of Commercial and Investment Banking* (New York: Oxford Press, 1990), pp. 180–208.

PART FOUR

Prospects for Reregulation and Deregulation in the Financial Services Industry

12 What Do the Experts Say About Reforming the Banking Industry?

An outmoded and inefficient structure, imposed by our laws and regulations, must change. . . . [Regulations] must allow [banks] to compete at home and abroad. . . . Competition will breed competitiveness. It will also breed safety, for competitive banks must also be strong banks. Competition and safety go hand in hand.

Paul J. Collins, *Competitiveness and Safety Go Hand in Hand*

While Congress passed legislation in 1991 that required risk-based deposit insurance premiums, tightened bank regulation, and eliminated the FDIC's "too big to fail" policy, it really only plastered over a leak without attempting to examine why there was a leak in the first place or to fix it properly so that there will not be another leak. Although Congress provided the FDIC with the ability to borrow up to $70 billion, it did not provide enough funding to handle the failure of even one giant money-center bank, along with hundreds of smaller ones that will likely be closed under the new regulations. In not granting additional powers, Congress will stifle the attempts of many banks to raise new capital. After all, investors will buy new stock only if, in doing so, they have an opportunity to obtain a good return on their capital. Congress has merely to look at the banking numbers over the last two decades to see that there has been a decline in market share, a decline in margins, a decline in credit quality, and a decline in overall profitability of the banking industry relative to other corporations. Congress should stop using the banking industry as a whipping post to make up for past congressional and regulatory sins and start instituting the kind of reforms that will allow the banking industry to grow and prosper. Strong, healthy banks can act as leaders in ensuring a healthy economy. In a scathing editorial, *Business Week* lambasted Congress:

> Washington's failure to pass a comprehensive bank-reform bill tops the list in legislative ineffectiveness. . . . The largest [excuse] is that the insurance companies, Wall Street firms, big banks, small banks, and just about anybody with a money stake and a political action committee bribed and cajoled to save their bacon. So what? Government is about resisting these pressures and making hard decisions in the national interest. . . . A bill ought not to be shaped by special-interest plead-

ing. . . . A bill limited almost exclusively to funding deposit insurance is a copout
that will cost taxpayers billions more than true bank reform.[1]

In early 1993, the FDIC signaled that the worst of the banking crisis was over
by slashing its projections for that year from 120 bank failures with assets of $76
billion to 70 to 90 bank failures with assets of $25 billion. The combination of a
slowdown in the bank failure rate and higher FDIC Bank Insurance Fund (BIF)
premiums should eliminate the BIF deficit in 1993. The 1.25-percent reserve target
for the BIF should be reached well before the year 2000. This could lead to a
cutback in bank depository insurance premiums before the end of the decade.

Some experts (e.g., Jacobs, Taylor, and LaWare), call for further deregulation,
while others (e.g., Schumer, Pierce, and Bryan) support regulation in terms of a
narrow or core bank. Still other experts (e.g., McCormick, Fischer, Leveson, and
Rogers) offer specific suggestions or strategies for improving bank earnings.

MICHAEL JACOBS

Michael Jacobs, former director of corporate finance at the U.S. Department of the
Treasury and author of *Short-Term America: The Causes and Cures of Our Business
Myopia*, has called on Congress to reform the banking system. He urges Congress
to stop "prescribing aspirin for a cancer patient."

Jacobs feels that German and Japanese banks have been so successful in part
because of the strong and deep relationship that exists between the financial and
corporate sectors in those countries. These banks offer more services and often own
stock in the companies of their corporate customers, which gives them a different
perspective from that of American banks. A key question that arises is, If lenders
were also owners, wouldn't they be more interested in the long-term success of
their customers? American banks have no extra reward or return (which comes from
capital gains on corporate stock ownership) if corporate customers succeed. If banks
were also owners of the stock of their customers, banks would be more concerned
about the survival of their customers. Owner-banks would have an additional incentive to help customers who were facing difficult times. Also, allowing banks to own
stock would make them less adventurous. Stock ownership may explain why fewer
German and Japanese companies go bankrupt, although they are highly leveraged:
"Corporations can take a longer-term perspective in developing strategies and
investing in new technologies knowing that they have a reliable source of capital.
Investors and corporations are partners, not adversaries, which is critical when
competing in a global economy."[2] Jacobs pleaded for Congress to allow banks to
offer more services and to have greater powers. He also encouraged Congress to
permit banks to own stock in their customers, because doing so would encourage
banks to build a long-term perspective. Finally, Jacobs called for the partial removal
of the safety net of depository insurance.

JEREMY F. TAYLOR

Jeremy F. Taylor, author of *The Process of Change in American Banking: Political Economy and the Public Purpose,* sees the failure of the FSLIC as symbolic of what could happen to banking with the erosion of profits, capital, loan quality, and liquidity. Taylor labeled the large increase in lending by regional banks to lesser developed countries unsound banking and the rush to lend in highly leveraged transactions a deterioration of lending standards. He felt that the foreign lending was partially related to the need to seek new loan outlets not available in the United States because of geographic restrictions and blamed lending for leveraged buy-outs on the Glass-Steagall restrictions on bank corporate underwriting activities.

Taylor supports nationwide bank branching without geographic limits, eliminating the dual banking system, and removing the antitrust challenge to mergers and acquisitions. He also suggests establishing a commission to recommend a national policy for setting up a system of strong national institutions that would be able to compete effectively on a global basis. (It is important to note, however, that the removal of geographic boundaries and the development of large international banking institutions are not necessarily incompatible with the dual banking system.) Taylor favors share drafts or direct participation in bank loans, as well as increased securitization to allow banks to offer yields that are more competitive with those available at mutual funds.[3]

SCHUMER PLAN

Charles E. Schumer, New York Democrat and member of the House Banking, Finance, and Urban Affairs Committee, has suggested a number of regulatory changes and ideas that appear to make a great deal of sense and that follow in the footsteps of the Pierce Plan. He would establish a core, insured bank for making small, less risky loans and investments and an uninsured bank for riskier lending practices. First, for banks offering FDIC insurance, there would be a lending limit of 3 to 4 percent of a bank's capital, instead of the current 15-percent limit. Second, no single equity investment of more than 5 percent would be allowed. Third, interest on all deposits would not exceed a floating-rate cap. Fourth, weak banks would not be allowed to offer ridiculously high interest rates to lure depositors and take advantage of their government-guaranteed depository insurance. Fifth, a floating-rate interest cap and a maximum loan limit would apply to core banking functions needed to serve small borrowers, individuals, and midsized companies. Riskier, higher yielding activities would be permitted in a separately capitalized uninsured bank. There would be strict fire walls between the insured bank and this uninsured affiliate. Core banking would coerce banks to become financially healthy and strong. Banks would raise needed funds in the money and capital markets to support their riskier lending and investment goals. The market would then act as a disciplinarian, denying capital to less worthy institutions.[4]

There are several problems associated with the concept of the core, or narrow, bank. First, the flow of funds to commerce and industry may be impeded. Second, the artificial partitioning of bank asset powers appears inconsistent with the underlying economics of business and banking. Finally, the imposition of narrow banking would not eliminate the issuance of risky demand debt and the concomitant dilemma of bank runs and would even appear to hinder financial disintermediation.[5]

PIERCE PLAN

In *The Future of Banking,* James L. Pierce suggests the creation of a new, insured, regulated entity: a monetary service company. This company could be in the form of a bank subsidiary, in the form of a stand-alone operation, or part of any other commercial grouping. It would hold only money market instruments, offer fully federally insured current accounts, and provide payment services. It would resemble an insured money market fund with unlimited checking privileges. The company would not be able to lend to its owners and would be completely insulated from the liability of its parents. All other activities that we currently associate with banking would become uninsured, and would be regulated only by company and securities law, not by banking supervision. Pierce's proposal resembles in part those of Schumer.[6]

McCORMICK PRESCRIPTION

James M. McCormick, president of First Manhattan Consulting Group, has made six salient observations about the banking industry:

1. For many banks, the profitability of core deposits subsidizes lending.
2. As a consequence, banks without strong core deposits must have advantaged loan or fee niches (e.g., credit cards on the loan side and securities processing or trust on the fee side), or they earn unattractive returns or take high risks.
3. The growth rate of attractive revenues in the banking industry is even less than the inflation rate. The industry was even shrinking in real terms during the mid- to late 1980s, when people thought that regional banking was growing.
4. Banks that attempted to raise the growth rates of their loans to a high level increased their risks substantially. As a consequence, many of these banks are now fighting for survival, having taken on ill-advised levels of risk.
5. Overcapacity is a problem for most of the banking industry.
6. The ability of banks to meet customers' needs with competitive operating and structural costs is the key to long-run soundness in the industry. If legislators and regulators do not allow banks to meet a broader set of customers' needs with more efficient structures, the banking industry will continue to shrink in

real terms, while nonbank competitors will continue to take away the banks' market share.[7]

Given this general scenario and the fact that a wave of consolidation is underway, the prime strategic issue for top management is how to play the acquisition game. Management must ask, Are we going to be an acquirer or a seller, and With whom? A second management issue is to determine what can be done to improve capital ratios and returns on equity and assets. Which low performance assets should be sold, and which activities should be discontinued? How should the loan mix be adjusted, and at what rates should loans grow? Should the bank downsize, readjust its growth expectations, reduce overhead, or seek a merger partner? Downsizing is required at many banks to help eliminate the overcapacity in their expense structure and in their balance sheet. Banks must realign balance sheets, expenses, growth rates, and capital to the realities of the marketplace.

Many banks would be better off with their assets invested just in Treasuries than they are with their current loan mix, adjusted for yields and operating expenses. The top quartile of the 200 largest banks have loans that earn about 80 basis points more than Treasuries. However, banks in the second quartile earn only 15 basis points more than Treasuries, while banks in the lower two quartiles earn considerably less than Treasuries. This seems to imply that only about a quarter of the largest banks have an attractive mix of loans with appropriate spreads on a risk-adjusted basis. According to McCormick, attractive revenues were growing at about 4 percent per year, while unattractive revenues were up 11 percent per year, during the 1984–1990 period. Excluding their acquisitions, the top 25 bank holding companies grew loans at 16 percent per year over this same time frame, with their commercial real estate loans growing at an annual rate of 29 percent. As a result, the fast-growing banks grew hot money sources at 18 percent per year, increasing their relative funding costs. According to McCormick, funding this rapid growth costs about five points of lost return on equity from the liability side of the balance sheet. It also pressures banks to seek higher returns on loans and, consequently, higher risks. Not surprisingly, nonperforming assets grew rapidly during the period.

Based on the First Manhattan Consulting Group's experience with successful banks, a bank must develop a profitability reporting system that shows risk-adjusted return on equity by business units. Banks can use such a management information system in strategic planning, budgeting, risk management, performance measurement, and incentive compensation. They can focus on ensuring that their business mix is attractive and has a potential for earning a return of 15 percent or more on equity. Banks can manage their day-to-day activities according to pricing, risk control, cost targets, and the like, while being mindful of earning an attractive return. The best banks utilizing management information systems and disciplined management appear to be moving away from the pack in terms of returns on assets and equity, as well as the price of their stock. These banks also have established credit-risk policies and procedures for transactions, while ensuring adequate diversification of their overall portfolios by type of loan, industry, geography, and fixed-versus variable-rate pricing. They are paying attention to interest rate risk and productivity and will selectively "outsource" technology functions if doing so reduces the time of their implementation and cost of their development. Duplicate and unprofitable branches are closed, the staff becomes leaner, and the overall organization becomes an efficient banking operator. Risk management practices must also be linked to market intelligence to help determine pricing, allocation, and rate of growth of assets.[8]

BRYAN'S BLUEPRINT

Lowell L. Bryan's suggestions for financial reconstruction take a complex set of issues and reduce them to two public policy goals:

1. "It places a flexible interest rate ceiling on deposits and other borrowed funds raised by an insured depository," and
2. "It lowers the lending limit for large insured banks."[9]

According to Bryan, a McKinsey & Company consultant, in order to stop the downward spiral in the banking industry and to reinstate market discipline and encourage innovation, flexibility, and market efficiency, Congress must repeal the McFadden Act, the Douglas Amendment, the Bank Holding Company Act, and the Glass-Steagall Act. Bryan would also permit industrial firms to own banks. He proposes to remove the riskiest assets from the insured "core" bank and confine them to a separately capitalized, uninsured bank or affiliate that is separated from the core bank legally and by financial fire walls. He acknowledges the need for a type of universal holding company to serve the full range of financial needs through separate affiliates. The "core" bank would lend to consumers and small to midsized corporate borrowers who are unable to access the securities markets directly. There might be 10 to 15 of these core banks or franchised monopolies throughout the country, each with $100 billion to $200 billion in deposits.[10]

The "noncore" affiliate would be typified by a money-center institution that would represent the United States without government guarantees in world capital markets. To help protect the core bank, insured-deposit interest rates and other borrowed funds would have a flexible deposit ceiling equal to the Treasury rate for comparable maturities. This would produce limited competition for deposits among insured banks. In addition, Bryan recommends that the maximum permissible loan to any one borrower be lowered from today's levels for large insured banks and that restrictions be imposed on lending to real estate developers. Further, he would essentially ban from the "core" portfolio any loan category that has not performed well in the last 10 years. A price for Bryan's system is the closure of at least 12,000 commercial banks and 2,000 thrifts, as well as the development of a new regulatory format to handle the "core" regional bank monopolies.

FEDERAL RESERVE BOARD GOVERNOR JOHN LaWARE

In a speech to the Banking Law Committee of the Boston Bar Association in March 1992, John LaWare, governor of the Federal Reserve Board, pointed out that recent studies have shown that large bank mergers have been less successful in reducing costs and improving earnings than previously thought. However, he cited the recent megamergers discussed in Chapter 11 as models for future consolidation in the industry.

According to LaWare, an essential element to future bank profitability would be the passage of legislation that would, among other reforms, remove barriers between banks and insurance companies, streamline the regulatory process, permit widespread interstate banking, and permit banks to underwrite securities. A weak attempt by the Bush Administration to push this legislation through Congress in 1991 failed, falling prey to competitive interests and public concern about giving added powers to a troubled industry. LaWare stated that "Congress has been preoccupied with short-term political considerations. . . . Unless Congress enacts drastic reform measures for our financial system within the next few years the U.S. will become a fading factor in world financial markets. . . . To prevent that from happening, a nongovernmental commission should be named to study the banking industry and recommend changes, without having to worry about a cacophony of demands from different industry interest groups."[11]

CHARLES T. FISCHER

Charles T. Fischer, chairman and president of NBD Bancorp, feels that credit quality is the major issue facing the banking industry in the 1990s. More attention must be paid to the process of managing risk in an economy with high corporate debt ratios and lower debt service coverage. In addition to having highly qualified lenders, "management must have information systems that provide fast, reliable credit information; a well-established process for regularly reviewing and analyzing costs; a discriminating rating system to identify and characterize developing problems; and a means to assure that top management receives this information promptly."[12]

Fischer advises banks to develop an acquisition strategy that deals with cost savings and limited dilution of shareholder value. He is also a proponent of developing a technological plan that enhances telecommunications systems, reduces costs for a given amount of computer power, and allows for the spreading of computer and telecommunications costs over substantially greater business volume as interstate banking restrictions are removed.[13]

According to Fischer, technology will also play a key role in asset and liability management: "The more sophisticated and timely management of net interest margins and interest rate risks exposure will require similarly sophisticated systems and the people to develop and manage them. I believe that the banks that have access to these management techniques and systems will be the ones to capture and hold a competitive advantage in the marketplace of the 1990s."[14]

IRVING LEVESON

In his book, *The Financial Services: The Next Era,* Irving Leveson drew the following conclusions:

1. During 1993–1995, the financial services industry will move out of the present era of adjustment and renewal to enter an era of resurgence that has the potential to last into the 21st century.
2. Profit opportunities will be limited in consumer financial services in the United States because of market saturation, high debt, low savings, and changed demographics, despite some strong individual liens on business.
3. Capital market businesses, corporate lending, and investing will rebound, but the biggest opportunities will be international, particularly in private-sector and government-assisted lending and investing. Strong financial market activities will be associated with globalization and the spread of strong economic development to more countries, as well as the renaissance of capitalism throughout the world.[15]

Leveson holds that the transition toward an era of resurgence will be made possible by (1) a decline in the worst problems in commercial real estate, banks, and thrifts; (2) improvements in noninterest costs; and (3) a global economic recovery. The era of resurgence should include the following elements:

1. Bank expansion into securities activities and merchant banking.
2. National banking in the United States, resulting from mergers of banks in different regions.
3. Extensive growth in global investing.
4. Strong capital demands for the growth of the third world and the revitalization of the Eastern European socialist bloc, following the collapse of Communism and the renaissance of capitalism.
5. A renewal of the international expansion of U.S. banks later in the decade.
6. The success of some technological financial services that did not take off earlier, including point-of-sale terminals, debit and smart cards, home banking, and videotex.
7. More networking, mergers, and acquisitions between U.S. and foreign financial firms.

8. Increased strategic alliances and cross ownership with foreign banks later in the decade.

9. Increased regulation of market and company behavior.[16]

DAVID ROGERS

David Rogers, professor in the Stern School of Business, New York University, and author of *The Future of American Banking,* feels that bad management is prevalent throughout the banking system and has contributed to many of the industry's problems. Also, the regulatory apparatus has contributed to industry problems in terms of capital forbearance. Some of the bad credit judgments that have led to high levels of nonperforming loans must be interpreted in a wider context as symptomatic of "macroweaknesses" of the entire industry. Rogers opines that there will be less likelihood of bank mismanagement in the future and less likelihood that U.S. banks will continue to lose out competitively to foreign banks when both the regulatory and banking industry structure change.[17]

Rogers feels that strategic focus is critical for survival. Banks must exit from or discard unprofitable businesses and should sell businesses that do not fit into their long-range strategic plans. Global banks must pare down to what they do best, concentrating on their areas of expertise. The leading banks of the future will be more focused, highly successful niche players that "stick to their knitting."[18] They will spend more time on strategic thinking and implementation plans and on thinking through merger strategies. Rogers also supports management expert Peter Drucker's suggestions on how to be big and competitive at the same time, namely, that the bank must set up various product units as separate companies with their own chief executives and boards of directors.[19] On the other hand, Rogers seems to disagree with Martin Mayer, another distinguished banking authority and author. Mayer asserts that big banks are unwieldy dinosaurs that should not be saved by regulators. He feels that if big banks are provided with more powers by bank regulators, this will only perpetuate banking problems at the money-center banks.[20] Rogers believes that there will be a continued trend toward "outsourcing," wherein banks contract out back office functions and other technological functions to data-processing firms, as well as contracting out training programs. The objective is to avoid performing too many in-house functions that can be done better and more cheaply outside the bank. There will also be more joint ventures that can be accomplished better and more cheaply outside the bank.

Rogers classifies future banks into four different categories. First, there will be efficient, low-cost, high-volume providers of consumer services, such as BankAmerica, Wells Fargo, Banc One, and NationsBank. These banks will provide profitable consumer banking at reasonable prices and are expected to become nationwide banks as regulatory barriers to interstate banking are removed. Second, there will be regional, middle-market banks that will focus on serving midsized corporations in large and middle-sized cities. Chemical Banking, Wachovia, PNC Financial, First Bank Systems, First Union, First Fidelity, First Interstate, NBD, Fleet, and Sun Banks fall into this category. Third, there will be small banks that provide quality service to retail customers on a first-name basis with a pleasant smile. Fourth, there will be the global merchant banks—for example, J. P. Morgan, Bankers Trust, Continental Illinois, and First Chicago in the United States; Deutsche Bank and some of the large Swiss, British, and French banks in Europe; and their counterparts in Japan. They will be the wholesale banks, serving corporations, governments, other financial institutions, and pension funds.[21]

To these four categories, we should probably add another: the niche players, such as State Street (featuring technology-driven custodial, trust, accounting, and information systems), Northern Trust, U.S. Trust, Wilmington Trust, Harris Trust (money managers), and CoreStates (with technology-driven debit and credit card systems).

ENDNOTES

1. Editorial, *Business Week,* December 9, 1991.

2. M. Jacobs, "A Failure of Nerve on Banking Reform," *New York Times,* December 8, 1991, p. 15.

3. J. W. Duggar, "Book Review of *The Process of Change in American Banking: Political Economy and the Public Purpose* by J. F. Taylor," *Business Economics,* October 1991, pp. 67–68.

4. C. E. Schumer, "The Best Way to Save the Banks," *New York Times,* July 19, 1991, p. A27.

5. R. J. Pozdena, "False Hope of Narrow Bank," *Weekly Letter,* Federal Reserve Bank of San Francisco, November 8, 1991, pp. 1–3.

6. Martin, *Financial Times,* August 1, 1991, p. 10.

7. J. M. McCormick, "Prescription for Reinvigorating the Ailing Banking Industry," *American Banker,* May 30, 1991, p. 8A.

8. Ibid.

9. L.L. Bryan, "Lowell Bryan Responds: Deposits Are Either Safe or Risky; You Can't Have It Both Ways," *Harvard Business Review,* July–August 1991, pp. 146–147.

10. L.L. Bryan, "A Blueprint for Financial Reconstruction," *Harvard Business Review,* May–June 1991, p. 74.

11. *Boston Globe,* March 11, 1992.

12. C. T. Fischer III, "Banking in the '90s: The Superregional Challenge," *Game Plan for the '90s,* Annual Conference on Bank Structure, Federal Reserve Bank of Chicago, 1990, p. 285.

13. Ibid., p. 288.

14. Ibid.

15. I. Leveson, *Financial Services: The Next Era* (Marlboro, NJ: Author, 1991), pp. 4–13.

16. Ibid.

17. D. Rogers, *The Future of American Banking* (New York: McGraw-Hill, 1993), p. 289.

18. C. Yang, G. Gleckman, et al., "The Future of Banking," *Business Week,* April 22, 1991, pp. 72–76.

19. P. Drucker, "How to Be Competitive Though Big," *The Wall Street Journal,* February 7, 1991, p. A14.

20. Rogers, p. 289.

21. Ibid., pp. 302–303.

13 Where Are We Headed?

Commercial banks are going through a period of cost cutting, of building up bad debt reserves, of attracting new capital, of consolidation, and of being the object of the most widespread and most far-reaching debate on bank restructuring and reform since the early 1930s.

Wray O. Candilis, *U.S. Industrial Outlook 1992*

Over the last decade we have witnessed major changes in the financial services industry, including the decline of the relative importance within the U.S. financial system of depository institutions and insurance companies. As a matter of fact, for the first time in 20 years, banks are allocating more of their asset portfolios to securities holdings than to business loans. As a percentage of bank financial assets, business loans have declined from about 34 percent in the early 1970s to less than 22 percent at year-end 1992. Another trend is the significant and steady rise in mortgage loans held by the banking system: At the end of 1951, mortgages were less than 10 percent of total bank assets; by the end of 1992, they had increased to over 25 percent.

Thrifts have been losing their market share of traditional residential mortgages and savings deposits. Full-line brokerage firms no longer depend for most of their revenue on commissions from the purchase or sale of equities; rather, they rely on trading activities and a variety of sources of services to derive fee income. Even staid, old life insurance companies have suffered a loss of market share and prestige following the collapse of the junk bond and commercial real estate markets. The insolvencies of a few well-known life insurance companies have frightened investors, policyholders, and Congress. And the insurance industry is accompanied in the "world of insolvency" by huge numbers of failed commercial banks and thrifts, as well as the insolvent FSLIC and the near-insolvent FDIC.

Within most sectors of the financial services industry, profitability has been highly volatile and, in some cases, invisible. Many customers have thrown away old school ties or relationship banking practices, which dominated commercial and investment banking, and have adopted price-sensitive, commodity-type relationships with their bankers. Banks have fought hard to recapture market share and to add new products and services, as have insurance companies and brokerage firms. Insurance companies have been establishing mutual funds and buying brokerage businesses to lock in distribution systems for their new products. Giant companies like Prudential, Equitable, Kemper, John Hancock, American Express, Travelers, and New England Life have sought to replace lost traditional business and to ensure a sales force for their products by entering the securities industry. The wealthy insurance companies have pumped substantial equity capital into their brokerage subsidiaries, which has resulted, overall, in better capitalized brokerage firms. There have also been increases in capital within the banking and insurance industries. All of these structural changes have taken place amidst changing regulations, changing distribution systems, changes in technology, the expansion of products into new lines of business, and a great deal of merger and acquisition activity. Banks, thrifts, securities firms, and insurance companies are moving into an environment of intensified competition, with a blurring of the traditional distinctions among the various players and among the services they offer. It is already difficult to distinguish between commercial banks and thrifts when it comes to services offered to the retail customer. The groundwork has been laid in the United States for the development of the universal bank or, should the regulators allow U.S. institutions to copy the European model, the establishment of the diversified financial holding company. With a relaxation of restrictive regulation, a number of money-center and super-regional banks could take advantage of synergies arising from an overlap of marketing systems and similarities among the services offered to customers.

In a speech before the New York State Bankers Association in January 1992, E. Gerald Corrigan, president of the Federal Reserve Bank of New York, stated that

> Many of the painful but necessary adjustments occurring today are laying the foundation for a stronger, a more efficient, and a more competitive banking system. . . . Perhaps the progress we are now seeking in the strengthening of the banking system suggests that some hard lessons have been learned. But even if that is true, we still have a very long way to go. . . . While progressive legislation and an improved environment will assist the banking industry in restoring the full measure of its strength, the fact remains that the lion's share of the burden for this adjustment lies with the banks and bankers themselves. . . . The historic dictates of (1) knowing your customer, (2) knowing how and when to say no, and (3) seeking strength through diversification must assume a still larger role in the banking marketplace. . . . Nothing would please me more than to see the U.S. banking system reemerge from these recent painful years as a true world-class leader in creativity and innovation, yes, but especially as the bedrock of confidence for the national economy and the international banking system.[1]

THE REST OF THE NINETIES

In the remainder of the 1990s, we can certainly anticipate a continuation of the trend toward consolidation and cost cutting within the banking and insurance industries, as decades of excessive overhead and ingrained inefficiencies are permanently removed. The desire to consolidate is driven by profit or survival. Banks must try to become as cost effective as the no-load mutual funds with the lowest expense ratios. In addition to chronic bank overcapacity and inefficiently used capital, too many banks are trying to expand their market share, which results in inadequate pricing of loans to cover the inherent risks. The same is true in the property-casualty industry. Also, bankers can no longer depend upon robust loan growth and have discovered that a good way to produce growth in earnings is through cutting costs on the expense side and generating fee income on the revenue side. Expense savings of 15–35 percent of an acquired bank are normal. Half of the savings come from the salaries and benefits of redundant employees, while the remainder comes from closing branches and reducing the cost of office equipment, systems, and rent. Therefore, consolidation has become a popular way to boost earnings at banks. Even banks choosing not to combine with others are shedding employees and closing unprofitable offices in order to become more productive. The big banks are attempting to restructure their way out of recession with large increases in the provision for loan loss reserves, massive cuts in spending, disposal of their nonstrategic assets, visits to the capital markets to raise the cash necessary to bolster capital ratios, and the increasing use of mergers to eliminate duplication of effort, excess capacity, back office, and administrative costs. However, cost cutting requires a level of planning and management skills that banks have not always displayed in the past decade. An important factor that has slowed down the merger process is the high acquisition cost of a bank and the potential for dilution of earnings per share. Banks must carefully examine what they do, identifying those lines of business that do not add value and then selling or eliminating them. The most successful banks will have a specific focus or series of niches where they can capitalize on their expertise or cost efficiencies. Banks must also develop first-class internal information systems and must emphasize and reward reductions in expense, because the push toward greater efficiency could help determine the survivors in the industry. Also, with increased competition, it has become more difficult to earn acceptable returns on some types of loans. If banks cannot price these loans at a higher markup over their cost of funds to produce a reasonable return, they will reduce their holdings of such loans or exit from that market altogether.

Costly loan problems and layoffs are likely to continue through at least 1993, but by the middle of the decade cost savings will be fattening the bottom lines of a "meaner and leaner" banking industry. Despite punishing loan losses over the last few years, the 50 largest banking companies increased their capital from 5.5 percent of assets in 1988 to 7.0 percent by the end of the third quarter of 1993, while simultaneously beefing up their loan loss reserves from 2.3 percent of loans to nearly 5.0 percent. The overhang of losses in commercial real estate, along with other problematic loans, will continue to be a significant drain on industry earnings over the next few years. In addition, falling market values for properties securing the loans could force banks to set aside greater reserves for losses than anticipated. Some banks have not yet established adequate reserves to cover potential losses, and this could have a major impact on their earnings and solvency.[2]

Banks, brokerage firms, and insurance companies are in the throes of a multiyear cost-cutting phase that should reduce overhead and make their operations more efficient and more profitable. For example, over 50,000 securities industry workers and more than 200,000 bankers have lost their jobs since the stock market "crash" of October 19, 1987.

By the turn of the century, we are likely to see megabanks with assets in the neighborhood of $400 billion and a shrinking of the present roster of 11,400 banks to well under 5,000. With about 50 banks per million persons, compared with 8 banks per million in France and 6 per million in both Germany and Great Britain, the United States has too many banks and too many underutilized branches. All of that excess capacity has created unnecessary expense. As a matter of fact, noninterest expenses have grown at close to 10 percent a year at U.S. banks and now stand at more than $120 billion. If the number of banks and branches were reduced, that figure could decline by $10 to $15 billion.[3]

Traditional thrift institutions that concentrate on originating and holding residential mortgage loans in their portfolios are likely to disappear. They simply are not needed any more: Commercial banks and other financial institutions already dominate this mortgage market. Instead, thrifts will probably emulate retail banks or mortgage bankers.

Superregional banks will continue to play a salient role in the consolidation phase because, currently, they are better capitalized and for the most part have fewer loan problems than money-center banks, which are suffering from inadequate capital and large portfolios of nonperforming loans. We can anticipate that, in order to strengthen their capital base and control ever-mounting costs, banks may have to downsize (by selling off assets or securitizing loans), consolidate, merge, or visit the capital markets. When this is done, we should have fewer, larger, and better capitalized banks that no longer have to compete with recklessly managed banks and thrifts that overpaid for deposits and compromised lending standards in the search for potential high-yield borrowers. A more soundly capitalized industry is emerging that should reverse the decades-old phenomenon of banks steadily losing the market share of their most creditworthy customers (those who seek commercial and industrial loans) to the commercial paper market and foreign banks and being forced to rummage among heavily leveraged corporate credits to bolster their loan base. The worst point in the cycle, the ballooning of nonperforming assets and the deterioration in asset quality, has passed with modestly better economic conditions. In addition, high-quality, well-capitalized regional banks have emerged that have bright prospects for continued growth and increases in market share within their regions.

Small community banks and start-up banks might share back office functions, legal services, accounting and bookkeeping services, computer hardware and software, and the training function with larger banks. This should lower unit operating costs for the small banks and provide fee income for the larger banks. In addition, many of the larger banks will eliminate costly and technologically inferior delivery systems. We are likely to see more outsourcing of information systems and data-processing systems when doing so would generate cost savings.[4] At the same time, banks must learn to sell annuities and mutual fund products. The sale of these products is another way of generating additional fee income.

According to Kenneth Wright, retired vice-president and chief economist of the American Council of Life Insurance,

It is quite apparent that the life insurance industry today is not as financially sound as it was a dozen years ago. The nature of the business has undergone radical changes over that period, which has reduced its profitability and heightened its exposure to financial risks. In contrast to the 1970s, life insurance and annuities in the 1980s have become investment-oriented products, sensitive as never before to movements in market interest rates. The industry now passes along a greater proportion of its investment return to contract holders while still providing guarantees. To maintain profitability, it has reached beyond its traditional limits of credit risk and interest rate risk and has begun to pay the price of so doing. Competition among companies has become more intense than ever before, with a larger share of products linked to investment returns, allowing buyers of annuities to shop and compare on the basis of interest rates, either implied or guaranteed.[5]

The capital base of life insurance companies has been eroded through junk bond defaults and the collapse of the commercial real estate market. A decade of poor underwriting, resulting from underpricing, has similarly affected property and casualty insurers. The property and casualty industry will have to discontinue its practice of cash flow underwriting. Many property and casualty insurance carriers are undergoing a slowdown in investment income growth and are having to pay off claims resulting from the devastating storms that hit the United States in 1992. Because of this, some insurers have announced their withdrawal from certain unprofitable commercial and homeowners lines of coverage, as well as from some geographical jurisdictions. While the mammoth hurricane and storm damage of 1992 led to the financial collapse of numerous small insurers, the situation may act as a catalyst in raising premiums in order to reduce underwriting losses.

The entire insurance industry is going through a crisis that is likely to result in more cost cutting and consolidation. This in turn should lead to the eventual shrinkage of the industry from more than 6,000 insurance companies to fewer than 4,000 by the turn of the century. There will probably also be a measurable shift from the mutual form of ownership to stock ownership, following the Equitable conversion process. Life insurers will modify their old ways and no longer offer fixed-rate permanent financing so far into the future to developers in commercial real estate projects. Also, long-term, fixed-rate guaranteed investment contracts are likely to be avoided, unless durations on both sides of the balance sheet can be married with a favorable spread. It is difficult to predict what legislation Congress will pass apropos of insurance companies and banks over the next few years. It is likely that Congress will again offer piecemeal legislation and come back in a few years to undo what hasn't worked and introduce further changes pointed toward a better and safer banking and insurance system. What is certain is that Congress will stand behind the FDIC bank insurance fund. While Congress has called for risk-based deposit insurance premiums, it has left it up to the regulators to determine the degrees or levels of risk that should exist within the loan and investment portfolios, as well as the off-balance-sheet items. Theoretically, banks with riskier loans and investments would be required to pay higher deposit insurance premiums, just as drivers who have caused automobile accidents have to pay higher car insurance premiums. Risk-based premiums would penalize banks for taking greater risks and maintaining lower levels of capital and would spread the cost of deposit insurance more fairly. A salient weakness of this approach is that it assumes that regulators can reliably measure the riskiness of bank portfolios. However, the inability of regulators to evaluate bank riskiness accurately is in some sense the source of the problem. The regulators also bowed to political pressure from Bush administration officials and bank trade associations to minimize increases in depository rate insurance premiums. Although we now have risk-based premiums, only 25 percent of the banks are paying premiums above the base level of $0.23 per $100 of domestic deposits.

Under a new proposal to require that debt be subordinated to FDIC claims, banks would have to finance a certain fraction of their lending by borrowing in the capital markets. The proposal would be an attempt to impose market discipline on banks by investors, who would have more incentive to monitor the bank than insured depositors would. This discipline would also prevent weak banks from expanding and would assist in aligning the interests of stockholders, bondholders, and regulators. To encourage the use of subordinated debt, we might allow it to count as part of tier I capital, but then, the minimum acceptable tier I capital requirements should probably be increased from 4 to 7 percent of risk-adjusted assets. We might also consider some form of deposit coinsurance, which would restore the incentive for depositors to keep an eye on bank lending and profitability. To make bank regulation more effective, we might consolidate the regulatory agencies or reorganize the various agencies supervising depository institutions in order to clarify the division of regulatory responsibilities. We might also improve accounting procedures to reflect more accurately the true economic value of bank assets. Market-value accounting would give bank owners, creditors, customers, and regulators better and more up-to-date information for making investment and regulatory decisions. Market-value accounting procedures should also be required of insurance companies, along with audited financial statements by mutuals. This would subject financial institutions to greater market discipline by providing more accurate information about the financial soundness of a company.

Congress is likely to allow further geographic deregulation of bank branching practices and additional bank corporate underwriting powers before the end of the decade. Interstate branching makes both economic sense and good common sense for commuters and travelers across state lines. Companies such as NationsBank could save millions of dollars annually if they were permitted to change all of their acquired regional banks to branches. Numerous boards of directors, financial and investment officers, comptrollers, and other officers would no longer be needed. The forced separation of commercial and investment banking, brought about by the Glass-Steagall Act, never really made economic sense: Before the passage of the Act, commercial and investment banking were done together.

Also, lending, credit guarantees, syndicating, and securitization, which are all current bank functions, involve monitoring, evaluation, and marketing expertise, which should be transferable to underwriting.[6]

It is less certain what Congress will do on the subject of regulating insurance companies. The outcome of the issue of federal versus state regulation could depend on how quickly the states can strengthen their supervision mechanisms. Perhaps a limited federal role would be best, with reinsurance, international activities, investment portfolio guidelines, minimum federal standards for solvency regulation, and state guaranty fund guidelines (if the National Association of Insurance Commissioners doesn't develop and implement them) as examples of appropriate areas of federal regulation. A prefunded guaranty system would be preferred to the usual postinsolvency assessment procedure. Recall that thrift regulators engaged in forbearance primarily because of insufficient funds to resolve failed savings and loans. While state regulation (especially with improvements such as those currently in process) can do a satisfactory job of detecting and acting against emerging insolvencies, liquidations and guarantees for large-scale general liability insolvencies should be managed at the national level. Regulators might even consider decreasing guaranty fund coverage in order to improve market discipline. In addition, it might be wise to phase out state rate regulation of property and liability insurance and rely instead on competitive forces to control prices.

If the present trend of banks affiliating with other types of financial firms continues, it will probably result in increased profitability for the banks. However, the fire walls separating the depository function and any underwriting or securities activities must be sufficiently strong and sufficiently insulated to deal with major losses on either side of the fence. There is nothing intrinsically wrong with permitting banks to affiliate with insurance companies. Underwriting powers should remain with the insurance companies, and joint marketing efforts should be a first step in effecting any combination. If banks would like just to sell insurance, then they would only need brokerage powers. Insurance powers would enhance the competitive position of banks by allowing them to offer a more complete menu of financial services. Again, the bank depository function (insured by the FDIC) must be insulated from the effects of failure of the insurance entity and vice versa. Therefore, the form of affiliation will probably be a holding company, with both the bank and insurance company subsidiaries separately and independently capitalized. Such a combination should provide efficiencies in the investment and distribution functions. The easy access of customers to bank branches gives banks an advantage over the typical insurance agent with regard to customer contact. It is likely that the average person visits a bank at least once a month, while direct personal contact with an insurance agent is substantially less frequent.

Liaisons between banks and insurance companies could prove quite profitable for all parties: the bank, the insurance company, and the customer. Certainly, some of the cost saved by the insurance company could be passed on to the customer in the form of lower premiums. Citicorp claims that it would be able to offer insurance coverage comparable to what is now offered, but for a premium 10–15 percent under currently available premiums. The insurance company would have many more prospects, while the bank would be in a position to earn fee income on insurance sales. Homeowner's insurance and life insurance related to bank mortgage loans appear to be natural products for such a combination. The same is true for automobile insurance when a car loan is obtained from the bank. It is reasonably certain that insurance companies' distribution costs could be cut if insurance could be sold through or by banks. Certainly, that would be in the best interests of consumers.

Ownership of banks by entities outside the financial services industry is a different story, however. The synergy provided by each half feeding from the other would not be present to anywhere near the same degree. Losses from commercial or industrial firms could spill over to the banking affiliate. There could be no guarantee that a huge diversified holding company would come to the aid of its troubled banking affiliate if the need were to arise. Also, a corporate parent or a commercial affiliate may place undesirable pressure on the bank to treat customers in a particular manner or to underwrite or lend to particular customers, countries, or local governments. Further, there is a danger in allowing commercial and industrial firms to have control over insured funds. Eventually, we may be able to work out the appropriate safeguards that would allow us to have bank ownership by commercial firms. For the time being, however, it seems safer to limit the intermingling of banks to insurance companies, securities firms, and other participants in the financial services industry and to prevent any affiliation with commercial or industrial enterprises. Risk-based capital and insurance premiums should lead ultimately to safer banks and should reduce the moral hazard problem substantially. After all, banking reform is really about creating an environment in which to provide financial services more efficiently, at the same time allowing banks to be able to increase their earnings, which affects their ability to attract fresh capital.

Continued underwriting losses of property-casualty insurers and the prospects for a prolonged period of depressed commercial real estate values suggest that both property-casualty and life insurance company solvency problems will be with us for some time.[7] While Congress has no wish to establish a federal guaranty fund for insolvent insurance companies, especially after the current problems with both the FSLIC and the FDIC, it may be desirable for the federal government or the National Association of Insurance Commissioners to establish uniform guidelines for states to follow in establishing guaranty funds and in regulating investment policies for insurance companies. Also, it makes sense to remove some of the artificial barriers to insurance company consolidation so that companies can become more efficient. State insurance commissioners seem to think it is part of their mission to protect existing managements. In addition, the demutualization process should be made easier, allowing companies access to the capital markets. As publicly held stock companies, they might become more disciplined and profit oriented.[8]

AN AGENDA FOR REREGULATION

We must return to the more prudent investment and lending practices formerly followed by the insurance industry, and we must establish better credit controls and higher loan underwriting standards in the banking industry. Too many lenders have forgotten (or never learned) some of the fundamentals of banking, such as the desirability of geographically and industrially diversifying the loan portfolio. Too many, too often, have failed to ask relevant questions such as "Is the risk commensurate with the reward?" or "Will I get my money back on this loan or investment?" The biggest need in banking today is to improve the quality of the lending process. When it comes to loans, quality must be given a higher priority than growth. There must be a disciplined credit policy throughout the banking organization. Bankers must not be afraid to turn down risky loans. There must strong credit controls, followed by a comprehensive loan review and preventative maintenance procedures, as part of a system of checks and balances. Too much lending authority must not be vested in any one person. Also, every bank must set lending limits for geographic, industry, and loan type exposures, as well as keeping single-borrower exposures well below the bank's legal lending limit.

Many banks have neglected the important "Six C's of Credit" in evaluating risk:

1. *Character.* The bank must be convinced that the customer has a well-defined purpose for borrowing and a responsible attitude and serious intention toward repayment of the debt.

2. *Capacity.* The bank must be certain that the customer requesting credit has the authority to request a loan and the legal standing to sign a binding loan agreement. The banker must also make a subjective judgment of the customer's ability to pay.

3. *Capital.* The bank must evaluate the financial strength of the borrower, as measured by financial ratio analysis and the borrower's tangible net worth. Does the borrower have the ability to generate sufficient cash flow to repay the loan?

4. *Collateral.* This is a fallback for the bank—the liquidation value of the assets offered by the borrower as security for the credit extended. The bank must ask, Has the borrower pledged assets of sufficient quality and value to back up the loan?

5. *Conditions.* The bank must assess the anticipated impact of general economic conditions on the borrower's line of work, industry, or collateral; indeed, it must examine *any* extrinsic factor that may affect the borrower's ability to pay the loan.

6. *Control.* Control centers on such questions as whether changes in laws and regulations could adversely affect the borrower and whether the loan request meets the bank's and the regulatory authorities' standards of quality. For example, the passage of the 1986 Tax Act eliminated tax deductions for certain passive losses of investors in real estate and of limited partnerships in oil and gas exploration. As a result, many borrowers seeking real estate or energy-related loans became less attractive customers.

During the 1980s, banks often lent real estate developers 100 percent of their acquisition and construction costs. As property values increased in the real estate boom, this type of lending was exceptionally profitable because real estate lending earned large up-front fees and generated interest rates higher than those typically available on other commercial loans. However, in their efforts to enhance their market share in real estate lending, banks permitted underwriting standards to deteriorate. Many banks accepted a developer's personal appraisal of the value of a project without questioning it or utilizing independent appraisals, audits, or other forms of confirmation. In some cases, the developer had no equity stake in the project. When real estate values plummeted, the banks lost billions on uncollectible loans.

In 1992, regulators acted upon a proposal by former Senator Wirth (D-CO) to reimpose the strict loan-to-value lending rules that were lifted when the Garn-St. Germain Act became law in 1982. As this book was going to press, federal regulators embraced a set of lending standards that would require banks and thrifts to hold real estate loans to a percentage of the underlying collateral, a so-called loan-to-value ratio. Unfortunately, the ratios established are more lenient and less rigid than what Wirth proposed and than what is needed to protect the banks, their depositors, and the Bank Insurance Fund of the FDIC. The 1992 guidelines recommend that banks and thrifts lend no more than 65 percent of the appraised value of raw land, 75 percent on land development products, 80 percent on nonresidential construction, and 85 percent on one- to four-family residential construction and improved property. In addition, the regulators suggested that permanent mortgages and home equity loans on owner-occupied one- to four-family properties with a loan-to-value ratio exceeding 90 percent be backed by private mortgage insurance or easily marketable collateral. Although the guidelines are perhaps weaker than they should be, this is a step in the right direction. The loan-to-value limitations suggested by the regulators, although suboptimal in some respects, should certainly help prevent a repeat of the lending mistakes made by bankers in the 1980s.

Another agenda item for reregulation is the maximum lending limit to any one borrower. To reduce the risk of failure of individual banks, lending to any one customer should be limited to no more than 5 percent of the bank's total tier I and tier II capital. Also, more discipline needs to be brought to commercial lending in terms of both pricing and credit quality.

There is also a real need to introduce market-based analytic tools (e.g., risk-based capital allocation models and discriminant analysis) into management's decision-making process. In addition, banks are going to have to develop more sophisticated systems and hire more knowledgeable people to manage interest rate margins and risk exposure. Banks will also have to search for better ways to manage and integrate their delivery systems (e.g., branches, automated teller machines, and telephone banking), while providing quality services with high value added for the customer. Successful banks will try and market the services in which they excel, thereby becoming niche players. Banks will continue to focus on fee income, realizing that they are no longer only lending institutions, but also service organizations. They will be brokers between money and the people who need it.[9]

According to former FDIC regulator William Seidman, the bulk of bad loans that contributed to the increase in bank failures during the 1980s were exactly the type of construction and development loans that were prohibited before Garn-St. Germain: "We looked at First Republic Bank, the largest loss to the government ever in Texas, and of the roughly 77 loans that broke the bank, 75 of them would have been illegal prior to 1982. . . . That is true for almost all of the big banks, and it was certainly true in the Bank of New England."[10]

We also need legislation that will help attract new capital to the banking industry. We must create an economic and legal environment that is hospitable to investment in banks. This means adopting regulations that will allow banks to increase their profitability—particularly, regulations that enable banks to generate more fee income, while reducing their dependence on interest rate spreads as a source of income.[11]

CONCLUSION

In this book we have called for continuing the trend toward geographic and product *deregulation*—allowing nationwide branching and the intermingling of commercial banking, investment banking, brokerage, and insurance products with appropriate safety or fire walls. On the other hand, there is a need for some *reregulation*. If we are to have government deposit insurance, there must be even higher risk-based premiums to help cover losses so that the taxpayer's involvement in bailing out insolvent banks and thrifts will be minimal. There is also a need to reimpose higher loan-to-value ratios in real estate lending and to reduce maximum lending limits to any one customer. These are all safeguards to help prevent bank failures. In addition, we need more federal involvement in the insurance industry in regard to uniform, safer investment guidelines, an improved private-sector safety net (i.e., improved guaranty funds), and issues involving insurance company solvency. This is not to say that the federal government should guarantee failing companies; that should be left to the private sector and state regulators, but clearly, greater uniformity and stricter guidelines to protect the insured are needed.

However, in addition to these suggested changes, and regardless of what new legislation is enacted by Congress, what we really need are *better bankers* and *better insurance company executives*. We need executives who understand their businesses; can improve investment performance without taking unnecessary risks; can trim waste, improve productivity, service, and image; and are actively engaged in planning—and more. But that is a story for another book.

ENDNOTES

1. E. G. Corrigan, "Rebuilding the Economic and Financial Fundamentals: The Cases for Vision and Patience," *Quarterly Review,* Federal Reserve Bank of New York, Winter 1991–1992, pp. 1, 4, 5.

2. P. Pae, "S&P Expects Few Upgrades in Earnings," *The Wall Street Journal,* May 26, 1992, p. A4.

3. L. Mendonca, "Done Right, Bank Mergers Can Save Money," *The Wall Street Journal,* May 13, 1992, p. A14.

4. T. W. Koch, "The Emerging Bank Structure of the 1990s," *Business Economics,* July 1992, p. 36.

5. K. Wright, "The Structure, Conduct and Regulation of the Life Insurance Industry," *The Financial Condition and Regulation of Insurance Companies,* Conference Proceedings, Federal Reserve Bank of Boston, June 1991, pp. 73–96.

6. R. T. Parry, "A Central Banker's Perspective on Bank Reform," *Business Economics,* July 1992, p. 17.

7. J. Cohen, "Discussion, 'Insurance Companies as Financial Intermediaries: Risk and Return,' by R. E. Randall and R. W. Kopcke," *The Financial Condition and Regulation of Insurance Companies,* Conference Proceedings, Federal Reserve Bank of Boston, June 1991, pp. 55–56.

8. R. E. Randall and R. W. Kopcke, "The Financial Condition and Regulation of Insurance Companies," *New England Economic Review,* May-June 1992, p. 43.

9. R. Scolari, "The Role of Nonbanks in Commercial Lending," *Game Plan for the '90s,* Annual Conference on Bank Structure and Competition, Federal Reserve Bank of Chicago, May 1990, p. 414.

10. R. Hylton, "New Curb on Bank Loans Expected," *New York Times,* August 5, 1991, p. D4.

11. J. D. Hawkes, Jr., "Politics, Alas, Still Taint Banking," *New York Times,* October 13, 1991, p. F3.

Appendix: Major Legislation Affecting U.S. Depository Institutions

National Banking Act of 1864   Created Comptroller of the Currency, which provided for the granting of federal banking charters and examination and supervision of national banks. Uniform currency was established in the United States and financing of the Civil War was accomplished.

Federal Reserve Act of 1913   Created the system of 12 Federal Reserve banks to be the lender of last resort to banks, to supervise state-chartered banks that are members of the Federal Reserve, to facilitate the payments system, and to provide for monetary policy and control of inflation and interest rates.

Edge Act of 1919   Allowed banks to have corporate subsidiaries in other locations besides their home state, to engage solely in international banking activities.

McFadden Act of 1927   Prohibited interstate expansion of banks, unless the affected states permitted out-of-state banks to enter. Permitted national banks intrastate branching if state's banks were allowed to do so.

Banking Act of 1933   Also called the Glass-Steagall Act, its major provisions were (1) to create deposit insurance and the FDIC; (2) to establish Regulation Q to set maximum interest rates that banks could pay on interest-bearing deposits; (3) to separate investment from commercial banking; and (4) to prohibit the payment of interest on demand deposits.

Banking Act of 1935   Provided more power to both the Federal Reserve and the Comptroller of the Currency to oversee banks and grant charters.

Bank Holding Company Act and Douglas Amendment of 1956   Gave the Federal Reserve authority to supervise the formation and expansion of bank holding companies. The Acts also dictated that holding companies with headquarters in one state could not acquire banks in other states, unless those states would allow the acquisition. The Acts allowed bank subsidiaries to operate across state lines.

Bank Holding Company Act of 1956, 1970 Amendment to   Extended Federal Reserve authority over one-bank holding companies, as well as multibank holding companies, and restricted holding companies to activities "closely related to banking."

Community Reinvestment Act of 1971   Required banks and thrifts to consider the needs of all their communities and constituencies in granting credit. This was to prevent redlining, in which depository institutions would systematically deny loans to communities deemed to be unworthy or risky, regardless of the individual borrowers' capabilities. Regulatory authorities were to consider banks' records in lending to all areas when approving holding company or branch expansions.

International Banking Act of 1978   Placed foreign banks operating in the United States on an equal footing with domestic banks. Like U.S. banks, foreign banks were to declare a home state and were subjected to the same laws regarding interstate branching. Foreign banks were also subjected to reserve requirements, deposit insurance, and regulation of their nonbanking activities.

Depository Institutions Deregulation & Monetary Control Act of 1980   Phased out Regulation Q and certain usury ceilings; authorized new deposit and asset products; allowed interest on transaction deposits; extended reserve requirements to nonmember banks and thrifts offering transaction accounts; offered nonmember banks and thrifts having transaction accounts access to Federal Reserve clearings and borrowings; increased FDIC insurance to $100,000.

Garn-St. Germain Depository Institutions Act of 1982   Permitted depository institutions to pay interest on money market deposit accounts without an interest rate ceiling. Also, permitted thrifts to compete with banks in lending to businesses, while ending the interest rate differential favoring thrifts. In addition, the Act allowed for the possibility of interstate and interinstitutional mergers; allowed federal, state, and local governments to open NOW accounts; permitted thrifts to switch between state and federal charters, between the mutual and stock forms of organization, and between S&L and savings bank charters; and allowed regulators to guarantee assets and liabilities of problematic institutions.

Competitive Equality Banking Act of 1987   Closed the "nonbank loophole" by subjecting every institution covered by depository insurance to banking laws. The Act also provided for emergency funding of the FSLIC and established maximum time limits on when deposited funds must be available.

Financial Institutions Reform, Recovery, and Enforcement Act of 1989   Abolished the FSLIC and placed deposit insurance under the FDIC. Also, abolished the FHLBB and placed the regulation of thrifts under the new Office of Thrift Supervision, within the U.S. Department of the Treasury. The Act mandated the liquidation of failing S&Ls and provided funds to do so; surviving S&Ls were subjected to higher deposit insurance premiums and tighter financial standards; raised capital requirements and restricted investment activities of S&Ls; created RTC and RefCorp to assist in closing failed thrifts.

Comprehensive Deposit Insurance Reform and Taxpayer Protection Act of 1991   Bolstered the failing bank insurance fund at the FDIC; tightened bank regulation; gave the Federal Reserve new authority to monitor and control the operations of foreign banks in the U.S.; gave brokerage access to the discount window; limited the FDIC's ability to reimburse uninsured depositors over $100,000 and proposed risk-based fees for depository insurance; and restricted the Federal Reserve's ability to keep banks alive with extended loans from the discount window.

Glossary

Acquisition   The taking over of one company by another.

Adjustable rate mortgage (ARM)   A mortgage with an interest rate that can be adjusted with changes in a base rate. The index usually varies with market interest rates.

Arbitrage   Simultaneous purchasing and selling of the identical item in different markets in order to yield profits.

Automated teller machine (ATM)   A machine capable of processing a variety of transactions, such as accepting deposits, providing withdrawals, transferring funds between accounts, and accepting instructions to pay third parties in transactions.

Bank holding company   A company that either owns or controls one or more banks.

Bank Holding Company Act   In 1956, the Bank Holding Company Act was passed to restrict the expansion of bank holding companies. It did, however, allow vigorous expansion by one-bank holding companies. In 1970, the Act was amended and gave the Federal Reserve the authority under Regulation Y to regulate and control the operations of bank holding companies. Generally, the Federal Reserve has the power to disallow mergers, acquisitions, or other business activities proposed by specific bank holding companies. However, the central bank usually allows bank holding companies to engage in lines of business that are closely related to banking, provided that such activities will not have an anticompetitive effect.

Banking syndicate   A group of banks created for the purpose of underwriting and selling an issue of securities.

Bank panic   The simultaneous failure of many banks.

Bankwire   A private computerized message system administered for and by participating banks through the facilities of Western Union. The system links about 250 banks in approximately 75 cities. It transfers funds and transmits information concerning loan participations, bond closings, payments for securities, borrowings of federal funds, and balances in corporate accounts.

Basle Accord   Pact agreed to by the United States, Canada, Japan, and nine Western European countries to establish common international capital standards for banks.

Best efforts   An arrangement between a securities issuer and an investment banking intermediary in which the intermediary uses its "best efforts" to sell all of the offered securities, but does not provide the standard guarantee of sale, referred to as a "firm commitment," that is normally at the center of an "underwriting" agreement.

Blue-sky laws   The laws of those states generally regulating the public issuance and sale of securities within the state and the transactions and activities of persons engaging in the securities business within state boundaries. The term "blue sky" is believed to have originated when a judge ruled that a particular stock had about the same value as a patch of blue sky.

Board of Governors of the Federal Reserve   A board with seven governors (including the chairman) that plays a salient role in decision making within the Federal Reserve System.

Bond   A written obligation of a corporation or municipality, either secured or unsecured, usually having a maturity of more than one year from its date of issuance and promising to pay specific sums of principal and interest to the holder or bearer.

Bond rating   An assessment of relative credit quality assigned to a company or municipality having outstanding or prospective bonds in the public market. Moody's and Standard & Poor's ratings are the two most frequently cited. Duff & Phelps and Fitch also have well-established analysts' rating groups.

Bought deal   In securities underwriting, a firm commitment to purchase an entire issue outright from the issuing company. In recent years, the term has been used to mean a firm commitment by one or a small number of investment banking firms.

"Boutique"   A small, specialized securities firm with a limited product line.

Branch banking   A banking system in which there are few parent institutions, each with branches operating over a large geographic area.

Bridge loan   A short-term loan made by an investment bank to facilitate a transaction. It is made in anticipation of a security issue that would repay the loan.

Broker   An intermediary in a secondary market that brings buyers and sellers together; an agent who handles the public's orders to buy and sell securities, commodities, or other property; a sales and service representative who handles insurance for clients, generally selling insurance of various kinds and for several companies.

Broker-dealer   A firm that retails mutual fund shares and other securities to the public; dealer firm acts as market maker by quoting bids and offers on securities.

Call provision   A provision in a bond that allows the issuer to redeem the bond, typically at a premium over par, prior to maturity.

CAMEL rating   A system that assigns a numerical rating to a bank based on an examiner's judgment regarding the bank's *c*apital adequacy, *a*sset condition, *m*anagement quality, *e*arnings record, and *l*iquidity position.

Capital   Funds subscribed to and paid for by stockholders representing ownership in a bank.

Cash management account (CMA)   An account developed by Merrill Lynch in partnership with Bank One of Columbus, Ohio. Affluent clients are offered a Visa card and a checking account to draw against their investment balances, which earn a money market fund interest rate.

Cash management services   Cash collections and disbursements handled by a bank for a business firm. Temporary cash surpluses are invested in interest-bearing securities.

Central bank   The bank that acts as the fiscal agent for the government and as a lender of last resort for financial institutions (primarily banks) suffering liquidity problems. In addition, a central bank (the Federal Reserve in the United States) may act to control the monetary base, reserve requirements, and discount rate and to regulate bank activity.

Certificate of deposit (CD)   A negotiable or transferable interest-bearing receipt for funds deposited with a bank, payable to the holder at some specified date in excess of seven days after issuance. The negotiable CD was first brought to market in 1962 by First National Citibank.

Charge-off   The act of writing off a loan to its present value in recognition that the asset secured by the loan has decreased in value.

Charter   A document that authorizes a bank to conduct business.

Churn   A practice alleged of certain securities brokers who use their influence or discretionary decision making with certain customers' accounts to cause frequent purchases and sales of securities for the purpose of generating large brokerage commissions.

Clayton Act   An antitrust law enacted in 1914 prohibiting (a) mergers that substantially lessen competition or tend to create a monopoly, (b) certain anticompetitive interlocking directorates, and (c) discriminatory or anticompetitive marketing practices.

Clearing House Interbank Payment Systems (CHIPS)   An automated clearing facility operated by the New York Clearing House Association which processes international transfers of funds among 100 New York financial institutions, mostly major U.S. banks, branches of foreign banks, and Edge Act corporate subsidiaries of out-of-state banks.

Collaterized mortgage obligation (CMO)   A security backed by mortgage bonds. The cash flows from the mortgage bonds are typically separated into different portions (e.g., they can be separated into short-term, intermediate, and long-term portions of the mortgages).

Commercial paper   A short-term debt with maturities ranging from 2 to 270 days, issued by corporations and other short-term borrowers.

Comptroller of the Currency   The federal government agency that awards charters for new national banks in the United States and also supervises and regularly examines all existing national banks.

Core capital   Tier I capital consisting primarily of stockholders' equity.

Core deposits   A stable and predictable base of deposit funds that is not highly sensitive to movements in market interest rates. Generally consists of transaction accounts, savings deposits, and small consumer CDs.

Correspondent bank   A bank that provides services to other banks.

Credit rating   Bond and commercial paper ratings assigned by Standard & Poor's, Moody's, or some other credit-rating agency.

Debit card   A plastic card that, when used, immediately reduces the balance in a customer's transaction account.

Debt   A security that indicates a legal obligation of a borrower to repay principal and interest on specified dates. "Debt" is a general name for bonds, notes, mortgages, and other forms of credit obligations.

Deficiency letter   A letter from a staff officer of the SEC to the registrant of a proposed security offering prior to the effectiveness of a registration statement, citing perceived failures of compliance with the requirements of the 1933 Glass-Steagall Act, requesting additional information, suggesting changes in form and style of the prospectus, or raising questions of adequacy of content.

Deficit units   Financial participants that obtain funds from the markets.

Demand deposit   Transaction account, payable on demand, that pays no interest to the depositor.

Depository ceiling rates of interest   Maximum interest rates under Regulation Q that could be paid on savings and time deposits at federally insured banks, savings and loan associations, savings banks, and credit unions.

Depository Institutions Deregulation and Monetary Control Act (DIDMCA)
Legislation passed in the spring of 1980, committing the government to deregulation of the banking system. The Act (1) provided for the elimination of interest rate controls for banks and savings institutions within six years; (2) authorized banks and savings institutions to offer interest-bearing NOW accounts; (3) overrode many state usury ceilings on mortgage, agricultural, business, and consumer loans; (4) required the Federal Reserve to open up its discount window to all depository institutions subject to reserve requirements and to make its funds transfer payments and clearing services available to all depository institutions at the same price; and (5) gave the Federal Reserve board new powers to control the money supply by establishing reserve requirements for all depository institutions.

Deregulation   A trend to relax the regulation of rules governing various aspects of commerce that began gradually and later accelerated. Deregulation is rooted in both politics and the rebirth of free enterprise economics. There was an underlying perception that an unfettered private sector could improve upon rigorous systems of governmental control.

Discount brokerage   A brokerage firm offering commission rates on stock and bond transactions that are considerably below the commission rates charged by the established, leading brokerage firms. Discount brokerages provide no research or advice to the customer, but only execute buy and sell orders at a discount from the old fixed-rate commission structure.

Disintermediation   The taking of money out of low-interest-bearing accounts at depository institutions for reinvestment at higher rates elsewhere.

Distribution   The selling channels through which investment securities are placed with investors.

Divestiture   The sale of a corporate asset, such as a division.

Douglas Amendment to the Bank Holding Company Act of 1956   An amendment that prohibits bank holding companies from acquiring out-of-state banks, unless the laws of the host state permit such entry.

Dual system of banking   System wherein banks may choose to operate under either a federal or a state charter.

Due diligence   The "reasonable investigation" referred to in section 11(b)(3) of the 1933 Glass-Steagall Act that permits a person (other than an issuer) to avoid liability for material misstatements or omissions contained in a registration statement when it becomes effective. Under section 11(b)(3), the defendant must prove that he or she made a reasonable investigation of, and had reasonable grounds to believe in, the accuracy of the nonexpert portions of the registration statement or, with respect to any part presented upon the authority of an expert other than the defendant, that he or she had no reasonable ground to believe and did not believe that there was a material omission or misstatement.

Dutch auction   A form of competitive bidding in which all bonds are awarded at a uniform price at the highest yield accepted once the full amount is spoken for.

Edge Act corporations   Subsidiaries of U.S. banks formed to permit banks to engage in international banking and financial activities. These corporations are allowed to open offices across state lines.

Electronic funds transfer systems   Computerized systems that process financial transactions, process information about financial transactions, or effect an exchange of value between two parties.

Equity multiplier   The ratio of a bank's total assets to its equity.

Eurodollars   Deposits denominated in U.S. dollars and placed in banks located in such countries as the United Kingdom, the Bahamas, the Cayman Islands, and Germany.

Federal Deposit Insurance Corporation (FDIC)   A federal regulatory authority that began operating in 1934 and that supervises insured state banks and provides insurance protection to both commercial banks and thrifts for deposits of up to $100,000 in separate insured funds: the Savings Association Insurance Fund (SAIF) for savings associations and the Bank Insurance Fund (BIF) for banks.

Federal Home Loan Bank   One of 11 regional banks established in 1932 to encourage thrift and home financing during the Great Depression. The banks are owned jointly by various savings and loan associations. The Federal Home Loan Banks lend both short-term and long-term money to member institutions under certain conditions.

Federal Reserve Bank   One of 12 banks created by and operating under the Federal Reserve System.

Federal Reserve Board   The seven-member governing body of the Federal Reserve System. Appointed for 14-year terms by the president, and subject to Senate confirmation, the members of the Board have jurisdiction over bank holding companies and uninsured state-chartered banks and also set national money and credit policy.

Federal Reserve System   The central banking system of the United States, as created by the Federal Reserve Act of 1913. The Federal Reserve System regulates the money supply, sets reserve requirements, oversees the mint, effects transfers of funds, promotes and facilitates the clearance and collection of checks, examines member banks, and discharges other functions. The system consists of 12 Federal Reserve Banks, their 25 branches, and various national and state banks.

Fedwire   A communication network that links Federal Reserve Banks, branches, and member banks and that is used to transfer funds and transmit information.

Federal Home Loan Mortgage Corporation (FHLMC; Freddie Mac)   A private corporation, operating with an implicit federal guarantee, that buys mortgages financed largely by mortgage-backed securities.

Financial "boutiques"   Banks and other financial service companies that offer a limited set of services to selected customer groups.

Financial "department stores"   Firms that offer one-stop shopping for all customer financial services in order to gain access to basic credit, savings, investment, payments, and insurance and brokerage services.

Financial institution   An institution that uses its funds chiefly to purchase financial assets as opposed to tangible property. Financial institutions can be classified according to the nature of the principal claims they issue. Nondeposit intermediaries include, among others, insurance companies, pension companies, and financial companies. Depository intermediaries include commercial banks, savings banks, savings and loan associations, and credit unions.

Financial markets   The money and capital markets of the economy.

Full-service bank   A commercial bank that is capable of meeting the total financial needs of the banking public.

Full-service broker   A broker that provides information and advice, in addition to executing transactions.

Glass-Steagall Act   The Banking Act of 1933 that was designed to establish depository insurance and to prevent commercial banks from engaging in investment banking activities. That is, a banking entity would be prohibited both from taking public deposits and making loans on the one hand and from underwriting issuances of corporate securities on the other.

Going public   The process of issuing securities to public investors for the first time.

"Grandfathered" activities   Nonbank activities, some of which would not normally be permissible for bank holding companies, but which were acquired or engaged in before a particular date and may be continued under the "grandfather" clause of the Bank Holding Company Act.

Guaranteed Investment or Interest Contract (GIC)   A financial instrument offered by an insurance company that sets forth a fixed maturity date and will guarantee the repayment of the amounts deposited under the contract plus credited interest at the maturity date.

Highly leveraged transaction (HLT)   A transaction in which a borrower's debt increases sharply after the exchange of assets. A leveraged buy-out (LBO) is an example of an HLT.

Holding company   A corporation that owns the securities of another corporation, in most cases with voting control.

Insider trading   Trades in the securities of a company by persons deemed to be affiliated with that company, either because of a formal relationship or because of possession of as yet undisclosed (insider) information.

Institutional investor   A professional manager with a pool of money lodged in a financial institution, such as an investment company, insurance company, trust company, or pension fund managed and supervised on behalf of savers, investors, or pensioners.

Insurance company   An organization chartered under state or provisional laws to act as an insurer. In the United States, insurance companies are usually classified by the kind of insurance they sell (e.g., property and casualty, health, life, or multiline insurance).

Interest rate risk   The probability that changing interest rates will erode a bank's net interest margin.

Interstate banking   The establishment of banks or bank branches across state lines by individual banking organizations.

Investment banking   The financing of the capital requirements of enterprises. The usual practice is for one or more investment bankers to buy outright a new issue of stocks or bonds from a corporation. The group forms a syndicate to sell securities to individuals and institutions. The investment banker is the underwriter of the issue.

Investment-grade bond   Typically, a bond with a credit rating of A or better.

Junk bond   A non-investment-grade bond with a rating of BBB or Baa or less.

Letter of credit   A legal notice in which a bank guarantees the credit of one of its customers who is borrowing from another institution.

Leveraged buy-out (LBO)   The purchase of a company, or part of a company, using borrowed funds that might amount to as much as 90 percent of the total cost of the acquisition. The target company's assets usually serve as security for the loans taken out by the acquiring firm. These loans are then repaid out of the acquiring firm's cash flows.

Liability management   The active adjustment of a financial institution's liabilities to help meet the demand for loans, minimize the cost of funds, and balance the maturity of liabilities with the maturity structure of assets.

Liquidity   Access to sufficient immediately spendable funds at reasonable cost exactly when those funds are needed.

Limited branching   Provisions that restrict branching to a geographic area smaller than an entire state.

McFadden Act of 1927   Federal statute that banned interstate banking.

Merchant banking   In Great Britain, the activities of an organization that underwrites securities, advises clients on mergers, and is involved in the ownership of commercial ventures. In the United States, a cluster of corporate finance-related activities interpreted to be permissible under the Glass-Steagall Act for non-commercial banks.

Money-center banks   Large commercial banks in cities such as New York, Chicago, San Francisco, and Los Angeles.

Money market funds   Mutual funds established in 1972 that invest in short-term, high-quality credit instruments and provide the equivalent of check-writing privileges.

Moral hazard   Hazard that depository institutions are subject to when they are encouraged to take risks when deposit insurance pricing does not penalize risk taking.

National Association of Security Dealers (NASD)   A trade association encompassing almost all of the securities firms that deal in the trading markets for corporate securities. The NASD is self-regulating, but subject to SEC jurisdiction and review.

National bank   A commercial bank organized with the consent of the Comptroller of the Currency and operated under the supervision of the federal government.

National banks must be members of the Federal Reserve system and must have federal depository insurance.

"Nonbank banks" Financial institutions that look like and act like banks, but do not offer either demand deposits or commercial loans. They were established by bank holding companies and nonbanks to avoid regulations pertaining to interstate banking.

Nonperforming loan Loan for which an obligated interest payment is past due.

NOW Account A savings account from which the account holder can withdraw funds by writing a negotiable order of withdrawal payable to a third party; an interest-bearing checking account that became effective in 1981.

Off-balance-sheet activities Commitments, such as loan guarantees, that do not appear on a bank's balance sheet, but that represent actual contractual obligations.

Point-of-sale transfer system (POST) A communication and data-capturing terminal located where goods or services are paid for. System that links stores' cash registers directly to bank computers. The terminal may operate as part of an authorization and verification system.

Preliminary prospectus A preliminary registration statement or prospectus, commonly called a "red herring," that is circulated to potential buyers before the offering date of a new security.

Primary market The first time a security is sold to investors.

Private placement Placement of securities directly with an institutional investor, such as a life insurance company, rather than sale through a public offering. Private placements do not have to be registered with the SEC.

Prospectus Document that accompanies all new issues of securities and that contains just about the same information that appears in a registration statement. Usually included in a prospectus are a list of directors and officers; their salaries, stock options, and shareholdings; financial reports certified by a CPA; a list of underwriters; the purpose and use of the funds to be provided from the sale of securities; and any other reasonable information that investors may need before they can invest their money wisely.

Prudent man rule Requirement that a fiduciary exercise discretion, prudence, and sound judgment in managing the assets of a third party.

Recapitalization A change in a corporation's capital structure, for example, when the corporation exchanges bonds for outstanding stock. Some companies have been recapitalized in this fashion to make them less attractive targets for takeover.

Registration Procedure whereby all offerings except government bonds and bank stocks that are to be sold in more than one state must be registered with the SEC. A registration statement must be filed 20 days in advance of the date of sale and must include detailed information similar to that which appears in the prospectus.

Regulation D   The regulation of the Federal Reserve Bank which defines and prescribes legal requirements of member banks.

Regulation Q   A Federal Reserve regulation that sets a maximum interest rate that banks can pay on time and savings deposits.

Reinsurance   Insurance by another insurer of all or part of a risk previously assumed by an insurance company.

Reserve requirement ratios   Percentages applied to transaction accounts and time deposits to determine the dollar amount of required reserve assets.

Reserve requirements   Percentage of customer deposits that banks must set aside in the form of reserves. The Board of Governors of the Federal Reserve can raise or lower reserve requirements for banks.

Retail banks   Consumer-oriented banks that sell the majority of their services to households and small businesses.

Retail distribution   A securities firm's distribution of securities to individual investors through retail brokers.

Return on assets (ROA)   Return on the total assets of a bank, measured by its ratio of net income after taxes to total assets.

Return on equity (ROE)   Return on equity capital invested in a bank by its stockholders, measured by after-tax net income divided by total equity capital.

Rule 415 (shelf registration)   An SEC registration filing by an issuer of securities to the public invoking the authorization to hold "on the shelf," over a maximum two-year period, all or part of the securities proposed to be offered for possible future sale at times deemed opportune by the issuer.

Run on a bank   Situation in which a large number of depositors of a bank lose confidence in the safety of their deposits and attempt to withdraw their funds from the bank.

Savings Association Insurance Fund (SAIF)   Fund that insures deposits at thrift institutions. SAIF replaced the FSLIC in 1989 and was placed under the jurisdiction of the FDIC.

Savings and loan (S&L) association   A mutual or stock organization chartered by state or federal regulators. The association competes for savings from consumers and uses most of its funds to finance residential mortgages.

Savings bank   A stock or mutual association that competes for consumer and corporate deposits and that makes mortgage loans, as well as a wider assortment of other loans and investments than most S&Ls.

Securities and Exchange Commission (SEC)   Agency established by Congress in 1934 to administer federal laws applying to securities. The SEC has five commissioners, each appointed by the president of the United States. The statutes they administer are designed to promote full public disclosure of material facts and protect the investing public against malpractice in the securities markets.

Securities Act of 1933   A law administered by the SEC and generally dealing with the public offering and sale of securities. The Act provides for dealing with fraud and full disclosure of material facts in the issuing of securities.

Securities Exchange Act of 1934   A law administered by the SEC and generally dealing with the trading of publicly outstanding securities.

Securities industry   The collection of investment banks and brokerage firms that deal in various types of outstanding securities.

Securitization   The act of setting aside a group of income-earning assets and issuing securities against those assets in order to raise new funds.

Sherman Act   First federal law specifically designed with the concept that the public interest demands competition; enacted in 1890, it prohibited agreements or acts in restraint of trade or commerce and monopolies generally.

Special-bracket firm   An investment banking firm that leads the bulk of securities underwritten in the United States (e.g., First Boston, Salomon Brothers, Goldman Sachs, Merrill Lynch, Morgan Stanley, and Lehman Brothers).

Standard & Poor   A leading U.S. securities research and evaluation organization, known for its independent ratings of the quality of publicly outstanding debt and equity issues.

State banking commissions   Boards or commissions, appointed by governors or legislators in each state, that are charged with the responsibility of issuing new bank charters and supervising and examining state-chartered banks.

Syndicate   A group of securities firms organized to undertake the specific offering and distribution of certain securities.

Term insurance   Life insurance payable to a beneficiary only when a policyholder dies within a specified period. The policy expires without cash value if the insured survives the stated period.

Thrift institutions   Institutions, such as savings banks and S&Ls, that accept consumer deposits and concentrate on mortgage lending.

Tombstone   An advertisement placed in newspapers and magazines by investment bankers to announce an offering of securities. It gives basic details about the issue and lists the underwriting group members in a manner that indicates the relative levels of their participation.

Transaction account   Deposit account on which checks can be written.

Trust (fiduciary) services   Management of a company's property in order to protect and increase the value of that property.

Truth in Lending Act   Congressional legislation passed in 1968 that promotes the informed use of credit among consumers by requiring full disclosure of credit terms and costs.

Underwrite investments   Securities firms: to assume the risk of buying a securities issue and then reselling the securities to the public, either directly or through dealers. Insurance: the process by which an insurance company determines whether or not it can accept an application for insurance.

Uniform bank performance report   A compilation of financial and operating information, periodically required to be submitted to the federal banking agencies, that is designed to aid regulators in analyzing a bank's financial condition.

Unit bank   Single, independent bank with one home office.

Universal life   A flexible premium life insurance under which the policyholder may change the death benefit and vary the amount and timing of premium payments. Premiums less expense charges are credited to a policy account from which mortality charges are deducted and to which interest is credited at rates that may vary from time to time.

Whole life insurance   A type of insurance policy continuing in force throughout the policyholder's lifetime and payable at death or when the policyholder reaches a certain age. The policy builds up a cash surrender value, has level premiums, and offers an option to borrow against the cash value at favorable rates. Whole life is often referred to as ordinary life.

Wholesale lenders   Banks that devote the bulk of their credit portfolios to large-denomination loans extended to corporations, governments, and other relatively "big" businesses and institutions.

Wirehouse   A national or international brokerage firm that has a large retail network of branch offices.

Bibliography

Auerbach, J., and Hayes, S. L. *Investment Banking and Diligence: What Price Deregulation?* Boston: Harvard Business School Press, 1986.

Banks under Stress. Paris: OECD, 1992.

Barth, J. L. *The Great Savings and Loan Debacle.* Washington, DC: AEI Press, 1991.

Benston, G. M. *The Separation of Commercial and Investment Banking.* New York: Oxford Press, 1990.

Benston, G. M., Eisenbeis, R. A., Horvitz, P. M., Kane, E., and Kaufman, G. G. *Perspectives on Safe and Sound Banking: Past, Present and Future.* Cambridge, MA: MIT Press, 1986.

Bowden, E. V., and Pilenski, R. *Modern Money and Banking,* 2d ed. New York: McGraw-Hill Book Co., 1989.

Brookings Institute. *The Rescue of the Thrift Industry.* Washington, DC: Brookings Institution, 1983.

Bryan, L. *Bankrupt: Restoring the Health and Profitability of Our Banking System.* New York: Harper Business Books, 1992.

Bryan, L. *Bankrupt: Why the Financial System Is Collapsing and How to Rescue It.* New York: Harper Business Books, 1991.

Caruso, V. P. *Investment Banking in America,* Boston: Harvard university Press, 1970.

Colen, M., and Ratner, E. *Financial Services: Insiders' Views of the Future.* New York: NYIF, 1988.

Compton, E. M. *The New World of Commercial Banking.* Lexington, MA: Lexington Books, 1987.

Dale, R. *International Banking Deregulation: The Great Banking Experiment.* Oxford, U.K.: Blackwell Publishers, 1992.

Eccles, R. G., and D. B. Crane. *Doing Deals.* Boston: Harvard Business School Press, 1988.

England, C., ed. *Governing Banking's Future: Markets vs. Regulation.* Boston: Kluwer Academic Publishers, 1991.

Fact Book, Property Casualty Insurance Facts. New York: Insurance Information Institute, yearly editions.

Francis, J. C. *Investments: Analysis and Management,* 5th ed. New York: McGraw-Hill Book Co., 1991.

Friars, E. M., and Gogel, R. N., eds. *The Financial Services Handbook.* New York: John Wiley & Sons, 1987.

Game Plan for the '90s. Proceedings of Conference on Bank Structure and Competition, sponsored by Federal Reserve Bank of Chicago, May 9–11, 1991.

Galbraith, J. K. *The Great Crash.* Boston: Houghton-Mifflin, 1961.

Gardner, D., and Mills, D. L. *Managing Financial Institutions,* 2d ed. Hinsdale, IL: Dryden Press, 1991.

Gart, A. *An Analysis of the New Financial Institutions.* Westport, CT: Quorum Books, 1989.

Gart, A. *Banks, Thrifts and Insurance Companies: Surviving the Eighties.* Lexington, MA: Lexington Books, 1985.

Gart, A. *The Insider's Guide to the Financial Services Revolution.* New York: McGraw-Hill Book Co., 1984.

Graddy, D. P., and Spencer, A. H. *Managing Commercial Banks.* Englewood Cliffs, NJ: Prentice Hall, 1990.

Havrilesky, T. M., Scweitzer, P., and Bookman, J. T., eds. *Dynamics of Banking.* Arlington, VA: Harlem Davidson Press, 1985.

Hawawini, G., and Swary, J. *Mergers and Acquisitions in the U.S. Banking Industry.* Amsterdam: North-Holland, 1990.

Hayes, S. L. *Wall Street and Regulation.* Boston: Harvard Business School Press, 1987.

Hayes, S., and Hubbard, P. M. *Investment Banking.* Boston: Harvard Business School Press, 1990.

Hayes, S., and Meerschwam, D. *Managing Financial Institutions.* Hinsdale, IL: Dryden Press, 1992.

Hayes, S. L., Spence, A. M., and Marks, D. V. *Competition in the Investment Banking Industry.* Boston: Harvard University Press, 1983.

Hempel, G., Coleman, A., and Simpson, A. *Bank Management: Text and Cases,* 3d ed. New York: John Wiley & Sons, 1991.

Howard, D. E. *Dynamic Planning and Management in the Securities Industry.* New York: NYIF, 1987.

Kane, E. J. *The Gathering Crisis in Federal Deposit Insurance.* Cambridge, MA: MIT Press, 1985.

Kane, E. J. *The S&L Insurance Mess: How Did It Happen?* Washington, DC: The Urban Institute Press, 1989.

Jacobs, M. J., *Short-Term America: The Causes and Cures of Our Business Myopia* Boston: Harvard Business School Press, 1991.

Kaufman, G. G., ed. *Restructuring the American Financial System.* Boston: Kluwer Academic Publishers, 1990.

Kaufman, G. G. *The U.S. Financial System: Money Markets and Institutions,* 4th ed. Englewood Cliffs, N.J: Prentice Hall, 1989.

Kidwell, D. S., and Peterson, R. L. *Financial Institutions, Markets, and Money,* 4th ed. Hinsdale, IL: Dryden Press, 1990.

Koch, T. *Bank Management,* 2d ed. Hinsdale, IL: Dryden Press, 1992.

Kohn, M. *Money, Banking, and Financial Markets.* Hinsdale, IL: Dryden Press, 1991.

Kopcke, R., and Randall, P. *The Financial Condition and Regulation of Insurance Companies.* Proceedings of conference sponsored by the Federal Reserve Bank of Boston, June 1991.

Kostens, M. H., and Meltzer, A. H., eds. *International Competitiveness in Financial Services.* Boston: Kluwer Academic Publishers, 1990.

Kramer, O. *Rating the Risks.* New York: Insurance Information Institute, 1990.

Lash, N. A. *Banking Laws and Regulation: An Economic Perspective.* Englewood Cliffs, NJ: Prentice Hall, 1987.

Leveson, I. *Financial Services: The Next Era.* Marlboro, N.J: Author, 1991.

Life Insurance Fact Book. Washington, DC: American Council of Life Insurance, yearly editions.

Madura, J. *Financial Markets and Institutions.* 2d ed. St. Paul, MN: West Publishing Co., 1992.

Meerschwam, D. *Breaking Financial Boundaries.* Boston: Harvard Business School Press, 1991.

Miller, R. and Pilenski, R. *Modern Money and Banking.* 2d ed. New York: McGraw-Hill Book Co., 1989.

Mishkin, F. *The Economics of Money, Banking and Financial Markets.* Hinsdale, IL: Dryden Press, 1992.

Pierce, J. L. *The Future of Banking.* New Haven, CT: Yale University Press, 1991.

Rogers, D. *The Future of American Banking.* New York: McGraw Hill Book Co., 1993.

Rose, P. S. *Commercial Bank Management.* Homewood, IL: Richard D. Irwin, 1991.

Rose, P. S., and Fraser, D. R. *Financial Institutions,* 3d ed. Plano, TX: Business Publications, Inc., 1988.

Scott, W. L. *Contemporary Financial Markets and Services.* St. Paul, MN: West Publishing Co., 1991.

Sinkey, J. F. *Commercial Bank Financial Management: In the Financial Services Industry.* New York: Macmillan Publishing Co., 1986.

Smith, R. C. *The Global Bankers.* New York: E.P. Dutton, 1989.

Taylor, J. F. *The Banking System in Troubled Times: New Issues of Stability and Continuity.* Westport, CT: Quorum Books, 1988.

Taylor, J. F. *The Keepers of Finance: U.S. Financial Leadership at the Crossroads.* Westport, CT: Quorum Books, 1991.

Taylor, J. F. *The Process of Change in American Banking: Political, Economic and the Public Purpose,* Westport, CT: Quorum Books, 1990.

Teck, A. *Mutual Savings Banks and Savings and Loan Associations: Aspects of Growth.* New York: Columbia University Press, 1968.

Wallison, P. J. *Back From the Brink.* Washington, DC: AEI, 1990.

White, L. J. *The S&L Debacle.* New York: Oxford Press, 1991.

Woerheide, W. J. *The Savings and Loan Industry: Current Problems and Hostile Solutions.* Westport CT: Quorum Books, 1984.

Index

accounting systems, bank, 157
acquisitions, 20-21, 23, 62, 391. *See also* mergers
adjustable rate mortgage, 64, 140, 391
adjusted surplus, 203
Aetna Life Insurance Company, 27, 195, 199, 208
agency-brokerage system, 225-229
AIDS, impact on insurance industry, 240
Alemagne Bank Nederland, 356
Alliance Capital Management, 21, 208
Allstate, 19, 104, 229, 357
Altman, Edward, 279
A.M. Best, 26, 198, 211-214, 218
AMBAC, 336
American Council of Life Insurance, 209, 378
American Enterprise Institute, 318
American Exchange (AMEX), 45
American Express, 5, 21, 25, 30, 137, 256, 271, 284, 290, 335, 351, 56, 376
American Institute for Property and Liability Underwriters, 224
American Institute of Certified Public Accountants, 109
American Insurance Association, 214
American Re-Insurance Co., 195
American Savings Bank, 337
Ameritrust Corp., 339, 344-345, 350
amortizing assets, 126
Amsterdam-Rotterdam Bank, 356
Anderson, Roger, 160-161
Angell, Wayne D., 144
annuities, 111-112, 182, 217, 242
antifraud provisions, 43-44
antitrust immunity, 206
arbitrage, definition of, 391
ARM. *See* adjustable rate mortgage
Armstrong Congressional investigation, 104
assets
    classification of, 126
    quality of, rating of, 150-151
    shares of, by type of institution, 5, 6f
    shifts in, 291-296
Astor, John Jacob, 250
ATM. *See* automated teller machine
AT&T, 25, 137, 290, 356
auto insurance, 27, 113, 206, 214, 232, 382
auto loans, 270, 291

automated teller machine, 22, 73, 291, 391
automation, 21-22
    of insurance distribution system, 224-225, 227-228, 230-231, 236-237, 243
    of securities industry, 76-77, 252, 255, 271, 281-283
Autry, Sandra, 111

Bache, 208, 256
Bacot, Carter, 338
bad banks, 166-167, 191, 332
Baird, Bruce, 262
balance sheet changes, 291-302
Baldwin United Corporation, 216, 238
Banco Nacional de Mexico, 344
Banc One, 130, 164, 307, 326, 342-344, 346, 352
BankAmerica, 28, 99, 137, 162, 164, 326-327, 331-333, 339, 350
bank(s)/banking. *See also* commercial bank(s); investment bank(s)/banking; savings bank(s); *specific bank*
    accounting systems, 157
    analogy with insurance industry, 26-28
    assets, 291-296
    bad, 166-167, 191, 332
    balance sheet changes, 291-302
    capital standards, 117-120, 128, 324
    commerce, controversy over, 133-137
    consolidation of, 21, 23, 25, 300, 321-359
        examples of, 328-333
    contemporary issues in, 117-146
    correspondent, 24, 394
    crisis in, factors contributing to, 325
    definition of, 89
    deregulation of, 81-101
    effects of deregulation on, 17-18
    employment in, 300
    federally chartered, 38
    foreign competition in, 307-315
    functions of, 13-14, 15f
    good, 166-167, 191
    hostility toward, 98
    insurance sales by, 16, 22-23, 86, 89, 133, 232-234, 237, 253
    interstate, 17, 60, 130-131, 380, 397
    lending practices, 24-25, 301, 301f

Note: Page numbers followed by *t* and *f* denote tables and figures, respectively.

bank(s)/banking (*Cont'd.*)
  liability shifts, 296-300
  liquidity, rating of, 152-153
  loan portfolios, 17, 25
    composition of, 291, 292f
    evaluation of, 153-154
    regulation of, 125-126
  management, rating of, 152
  mergers of. *See* mergers
  merging of, with commerce, 134-136
  multiple regulatory agencies involved in, 140-143
  number of, 289
  portfolios, composition of, 297, 297t
  price, 3, 315-316, 356
  problems in, 24-25
  profitability, 132, 300-302, 304, 304t, 307, 308t
  relationship, 250, 315-316
  returns on assets and equity, 303-307
  risk-based capital standards for, 120-130
  risk taking by
    excessive, 168, 173-174, 322
    regulation of, 122, 125-127
  role in securitization, 317-319
  role in U.S. financial system, decline in, 131-132
  runaway noninterest expenses in, 304, 304f
  specialized, 357
  state-chartered, 38, 56
    nonbanking activities for, state authorization of, 65, 68t-69t
  structural change in, 289-320
Bankers Trust, 5, 42, 96, 164, 273, 333-334
bank failures, 7, 23-24, 31, 34, 55, 148f. *See also specific failure*
  and deposit insurance, 94, 147-177
  potential, 163-166
  identification of, 147-154
  resolution of, process of, 158-160
Bank for International Settlements, 311
bank holding company, 15f, 86. *See also* holding company
  definition of, 391
  double umbrella concept for, 140
  forms of, 63
  nonbanking activities of, 16, 66t-67t, 86
Bank Holding Company Act of 1956, 60-61, 132, 233, 387, 391
  1966 Amendment to, 63
  1970 Amendment to, 64-65, 387-388, 391
  Douglas Amendment to, 60-61, 387, 395
Banking Act of 1864, 387
Banking Act of 1933, 31, 35, 39-40, 42, 60, 387. *See also* Glass-Steagall Act; Regulation Q
Banking Act of 1935, 51-55, 387
banking syndicate, 253, 391
Bank Insurance Fund, 8, 92, 117, 147, 165, 364
Bank Merger Act of 1960, 62

Bank Merger Act of 1966, 63
Bank of Boston, 162, 164, 326, 347
Bank of Credit and Commerce International, 95, 259, 312, 345
Bank of Japan, 128, 311
Bank of Montreal, 356
Bank of New England, 147, 151, 161-163, 328, 331, 347
Bank of New York, 130, 312, 326-327, 337-338
bank panic, 55, 391
bank run, 34, 55, 152, 155, 168, 400
bankwire, 143-144, 328, 391
Barclays Bank, 312, 337, 356
Barnett Banks, 130, 164, 345-347
Basle Accord, 113, 120, 124, 126, 311, 391
BB&T Financial Corp., 164
BCCI. *See* Bank of Credit and Commerce International
Bear Stearns, 163-164, 259, 280
Belth, Joseph, 112, 222
best efforts, definition of, 391-392
bidding
  de facto competitive, 84, 265
  noncompetitive, 84
Biddle, Thomas A., 250
BIF. *See* Bank Insurance Fund
Black, Robert P., 174
Blackstone Group, 256, 357
Blinder, Robinson, & Co., 76
blue-sky laws, 44, 47, 392
Board of Governors of Federal Reserve, 51, 62, 97-98, 119, 233, 392, 396
Boesky, Ivan, 46
bond rating. *See also* Moody's; Standard & Poor
  definition of, 392
bonds. *See also* junk bonds
  Brady, 313
  definition of, 392
  government agency-sponsored, 262-263
  investment-grade, definition of, 398
  municipal, 87-88, 192, 254, 278-279, 295
  non-investment-grade, elimination of, 90
  plain vanilla, 279
  registration of. *See* shelf registration
Boston Company, 351-352
bought deal, definition of, 392
boutiques, 270-271, 276-277, 283, 356-357
  definition of, 392
  research, 78, 257
Braddock, Richard S., 336
Brady bonds, 313
branch banking
  definition of, 392
  nationwide, 97-98, 130, 289, 321-322, 380
  outside the U.S., 61-62
  restriction of, 60-62
Brandeis, Louis, 36
Breeden, Richard C., 76, 262
Bretton Woods agreement, 4

bridge loans, 267, 278, 291, 392
Brobeck, Stephen, 199
broker, definition of, 392
brokerage, discount, 28, 78, 208, 264, 271, 395
brokerage firms. *See also* investment bank(s);
    securities industry
  automation of, 76-77
  diversification of, 18-19, 270-271
  failures of, 74-75, 271
  financial health of, monitoring of, 76
  functions of, 14
  going public, 255-256
  insurance for, 75-76
  size of, 284, 284t
broker-dealer, 261, 392
brokered deposits, 169
Brookings Institute, 98, 268
Brown, Alexander, 250
Bryan, Lowell L., 354, 368
Buffet, Warren E., 260-263
bulk transfer, 76
Burger, Warren, 87
Bush Administration, 91, 93, 97-98, 143, 170

California
  insurance regulation in, 105, 206
  Proposition 103, 113
California Credit Union Guaranty Corporation,
  173
call provision, definition of, 392
CAMEL ratings, 128, 129t, 149-153, 392
Candilis, Wray O., 375
capacity, 383
capital, 383
  adequacy, rating of, 118, 150
  deficiency, book-value measures of, 93
  definition of, 118, 123t, 392
  primary, 119
  risk-based, example of, 125t
  role in banking, 118
  tangible, 91
  total, 119
capitalization levels, classification of, 170
capital markets, 17, 118
capital ratios, 96, 118-119, 122, 124f, 128, 148
capital standards
  bank, 117-120, 128, 324
  risk-based
    for banks, 120-130
    for insurers, 112-113
cash flow underwriting practices, 27, 211
cash management account, 264, 270, 393
cash management services, definition of, 393
CBOT. *See* Chicago Board of Trade
CD. *See* certificate of deposit
CEBA. *See* Competitive Equality Banking Act
  of 1987
Celler-Kefauver Act of 1950, 62
central bank, definition of, 393

Central Liquidity Facility, 72
certificate of deposit, 3, 83, 290, 297, 316, 393
CFOs. *See* chief financial officers
character, 383
charge-off, definition of, 393
charitable organizations, 96, 156
Charles Schwab, 28, 78
charter, 38, 393
Chase Manhattan, 39, 164, 326-327, 333, 335
Chemical Banking Corporation, 326, 328-330,
  332, 339, 356
Chesson, John, 110
Chicago Board of Trade, 257
Chicago Mercantile Exchange, 257
Chicago Research and Trading Group, 342
chief financial officers, 266, 325
China, equity market in, 258
CHIPS. *See* Clearing House Interbank Payment
  Systems
Chrysler, 132, 134, 155, 341
churn, definition of, 393
Citibank, 335, 338
Citicorp, 3, 39, 96, 134, 164, 232-233, 275, 332,
  335-336, 356, 381
Clarke, Robert L., 163, 339
Clausen, A. W., 137
Clayton Act, 62, 251, 393
clearinghouse, 56
Clearing House Interbank Payment Systems,
  143-144, 393
CMA. *See* cash management account
CME. *See* Chicago Mercantile Exchange
CMO. *See* collaterized mortgage obligation
Coffee, John C., Jr., 259
Coldwell Banker, 19, 356
collateral, 383
collateralized loans, 270
collaterized mortgage obligation, definition of,
  393
Collins, Paul J., 363
Comerica, 326, 339, 348
commerce, merging of banking with, 134-136
commercial bank(s)
  assets and liabilities of, 5, 6f, 298, 299t
  balance sheet, compared to manufacturing
    firm, 303, 303t
  definition of, 85-86
  failures of. *See* bank failures
  federal income tax rate for, 90
  market share of, 5, 5t
  nonbanking activities of, 40-42, 251, 270
  permitted services of, 40, 65, 70t
  primary risks of, 302
  regulation and supervision of, 141f
  risk-based capital ratios at, 122, 124f
  separation from investment banks, 34, 252.
    See also Banking Act of 1933; Glass-
    Steagall Act
commercial loans, 86-87

commercial paper, 82, 291, 316, 323-324, 393
commercial real estate, 86, 165, 165f, 292
  insurance company involvement in, 199, 200f,
      203, 203t
commission(s)
  income from, 271-272
  insurance, 237
  minimum fixed-rate, 45
    elimination of, 28, 76-78, 256
  regulated rate structure for, 77
  soft-dollar, 257
Commission on Financial Institutions and
    Nation's Economy. See Fine Commission
Commission on Financial Structure and Regula-
    tion. See Hunt Commission
Community Reinvestment Act, 73, 322, 327, 388
Competitive Equality Banking Act of 1987, 88-
    89, 388
Competitive Strategy (Porter), 277
Comprehensive Deposit Insurance Reform and
    Taxpayer Protection Act of 1991, 94-97,
    170, 389
computers, 22, 154
  in insurance industry, 224-225, 227-228,
      231, 236
  in securities industry, 255, 281-283
conditions, 383
Congress. See also specific act
  role in regulation, 8, 31
Conn, Michael, 182
Connecticut National Bank, 161-163
Conover, Todd, 86
consolidation. See also mergers
  of banking industry, 21, 23, 25, 92, 300,
      321-359
    examples of, 328-333
  of insurance industry, 27, 113
  of securities industry, 256-258, 271-272, 286
consumer confidence, in insurance industry,
    187-190
consumer credit, protection legislation, 32, 72-
    73, 295
Consumer Credit Protection Act, 72
Consumer Federation of America, 199
consumer information, 32, 34
consumer loans, 82, 86, 292, 295. See also spe-
    cific type
contagion effect, 134. See also run on a bank
Continental Illinois Bank, 73, 147, 151, 153-155,
    158-161, 169, 331, 356
control, 383
Cooke, Jay, 250
Cooke, Peter, 234
core capital, 90, 394
core deposits, 152, 264, 394
CoreStates, 130, 326, 328, 344, 353, 355
corporate debt securities, 82, 254, 258
corporate finance, 290-291
  and commercial banks, 40, 42

corporate finance (Cont'd.)
  and securities firms, 252, 266-268, 271, 273
correspondent bank, 24, 394
Corrigan, E. G., 133-137, 289, 376
CRA. See Community Reinvestment Act
Crane, Dwight B., 354
credit
  consumer, 32, 71-73, 295
  six C's of, 383
credit cards, 22, 25, 82, 270, 295
credit rating. See also Moody's; Standard & Poor
  definition of, 394
credit substitutes, 120. See also off-balance-
    sheet activities
credit unions, 88
CreditWatch, 346, 350
Cross, Leonora, 99
cross-selling, 20, 208, 264
Crutchfield, Edward A., Jr., 346
C&S/Sovran Corp., 164, 339-341
currency exchange rates, 4, 313

daylight overdrafts, 143-144, 328
dealers, 276. See also broker-dealer
Dean Witter Reynolds, 19, 256, 269, 276, 280,
    285, 341, 356-357
debit cards, 82, 270, 394
debt
  definition of, 394
  foreign, 36
  as regulatory capital, 60, 120, 171
debt capital, 171
debt hangover, 301, 302f
deep discount assets, 126
deep discount brokers, 264
de facto competitive bidding, 84, 265
deficiency letter, definition of, 394
deficit units, definition of, 394
Delaware laws, concerning insurance activity,
    232-233
demand deposits
  decline of, 24, 83, 297
  definition of, 86, 394
  interest paid on, 42
    elimination of, 39. See also Banking Act of
        1933; Glass-Steagall Act
demutualization, 20-21, 219-220
  advantages and disadvantages of, 223
  example of, 220-224, 221f
Denmark, bank soundness policy in, 175
Department of Health, Education, and Welfare,
    71
Department of Housing and Urban Develop-
    ment, 92
Department of Justice, 233, 254, 263, 332
Department of Treasury, 91, 98, 143, 261-262
Depco. See Rhode Island Depositors Economic
    Protection Corporation
deposit(s). See also certificate of deposit;
    demand deposits

deposit(s) (*Cont'd.*)
 brokered, 169
 core, 152, 264, 394
 direct, 73
 time, 37, 39, 298
deposit insurance, 167-173. *See also* FDIC
 and bank failures, 94, 147-177
 establishment of, 5, 34, 38-39. *See also* Banking Act of 1933; Glass-Steagall Act
 moral hazard created by, 18, 41, 117-118, 168-169, 173-174
 opposition to, 37
 premiums, 95-96, 324
 private, 171-173
 risk-based, 41, 96, 117, 167-171, 322, 379-380
 for securities firms, 283
 state, 56
 system, reform of, 174-175
 voluntary, 172
Deposit Insurance Reform and Taxpayer Protection Act of 1991, 97-100
depository ceiling rates of interest, 37, 39, 64. *See also* Regulation Q
 definition of, 394
 elimination of, 16-17, 19, 82
depository institutions. *See also specific institution*
 diversification of, 18-19
 major legislation affecting, 387-389. *See also specific act*
 market share of, 5, 5t
 regulatory structure for, 140, 142t
 reserve requirements of, 51, 52f
 shares of assets, 5, 6f
Depository Institutions Deregulation & Monetary Control Act of 1980, 19, 42, 81-83, 388, 394
Depression, 31-37, 47-48, 51, 55, 252-253
deregulation, 8, 16-19, 23, 324-325, 385
 bank, 81-101
 impact of, 17-19
 definition of, 394-395
 of securities industry, 28-29
Deutsche Bank, 137
DIA. *See* Garn-St. Germain Depository Institutions Act of 1982
DIDMCA. *See* Depository Institutions Deregulation & Monetary Control Act of 1980
Dillon, Read, and Keystone Mutual Funds, 208, 253, 255, 279
Dingell committee, 107, 213-214
Dingell legislation, 109-112
direct-debit systems, 22
direct deposits, 73
direct marketing, 20
direct-response marketing system, 231-232
direct-selling marketing system, 230-231
direct-writing insurers, 104
discount brokerage, 28, 78, 208, 264, 271, 395

discounter, 277
discount window, 95, 100, 152, 300
disintermediation, 3, 16, 37, 42, 63, 82, 264, 290, 321
 definition of, 395
distribution, 19-20, 276
 definition of, 395
 insurance, 19-20, 104, 224-237
 retail, 400
diversification, 16, 18-19
 of insurance industry, 208
 of securities industry, 270-271
divestiture, definition of, 395
Dominion Bankshares, 345-346
Donaldson, Lufkin, & Jenrette, 208, 222, 254-256, 268, 280, 285
double umbrella, 139-140
Douglas Amendment, 60-61, 387, 395
Downe, Edward A., Jr., 259
Dresdner Bank, 137
Drexel Burnham Lambert, 46, 258-262, 265
dual system of banking, 38, 140, 395
due diligence, 37, 43-44, 253, 266, 395
duPont formula, 306
Dutch auction, 262, 395

early warning models, bank, 147-154
ECOA. *See* Equal Credit Opportunity Act
Edge Act corporations, 387, 395
E.F. Hutton, 208, 256, 261
EFTA. *See* Electronic Funds Transfer Act of 1978
Eisenbeis, Robert A., 147
Electronic Funds Transfer Act of 1978, 73
electronic funds transfer systems, 73, 395
elephant weddings, 301
employment, in financial industry, 237, 275, 300
Equal Credit Opportunity Act, 72
Equimark, 352-353
Equitable Life, 14, 21, 26-27, 109, 182, 208, 219-224, 256, 285, 376
equity capital market, 219-220, 256, 258, 279
equity investment departments, 268
equity multiplier, 118, 164, 298-299, 299f, 395
equity retention, 119
ethical standards, in securities industry, 46-47
Ettin, Edward, 354
Eurodollar, 4, 395
Eurodollar market, 3, 6, 258, 265, 282, 297-298, 316, 322
European American Bank, 161
European Community, 113, 313
 banking in, 137-138, 312-313, 356
 securities industry in, 257-258, 282
European investment, in U.S. insurance industry, 207
exchanges, 276. *See also specific exchange*
exclusive agency marketing system, 229-230

Executive Life, 107, 192-195, 199-200, 205, 209, 217-218, 238
  of California, 26, 182, 215
  of New York, 194, 204, 215

factoring, 65
Failed Promises (House Subcommittee on Oversight and Investigations), 109, 213
Fair Credit Billing Act, 73
Fair Credit Reporting Act, 72
Fannie Mae. *See* Federal National Mortgage Association
Farm Credit Administration, 71
Farmers Insurance Exchange, 229
FDIC, 83, 88, 95, 97, 119, 131, 143
  Bank Insurance Fund, 8, 92, 117, 147, 165, 364
  definition of, 395-396
  double standard, 154-158
  establishment of, 34, 40-42, 253. *See also* Banking Act of 1933; Glass-Steagall Act
  failure-to-quality rating model, 149-150
  losses, 2, 7, 55
  regulation of insurance premiums by, 95, 324
  responsibilities of, 41
FDIC Improvement Act of 1991, 126
Fearsome Foursome, 254
Federal Banking Regulator, 143
Federal Deposit Guaranty Administration, 71
Federal Deposit Insurance Corporation. *See* FDIC
Federal Financing Bank, 162-163
federal funds market, 283, 297
Federal Home Loan Bank Board, 37-39, 64, 91. *See also* Office of Thrift Supervision
Federal Home Loan Banks, 38, 92, 396
Federal Home Loan Mortgage Corporation, 38, 51, 123, 262, 396
Federal Housing Administration, 50-51
Federal Housing Finance Board, 92
federal income taxes, 51, 90
Federal Insurance Insolvency Act of 1992, 110-111
Federal Insurance Solvency Commission, 110-111
Federal Insurer Solvency Corporation, 110
federally chartered banks, 38
Federal National Mortgage Association, 51, 123, 262
Federal Open Market Committee, 51
Federal Reserve, 143, 233, 252
  and daylight overdrafts, 144
  definition of, 396
  depository interest rate ceilings set by, 64
  and discount window loans, 100
  foreign bank regulation, 95, 312
  margin requirements regulation, 34
  nonbanking activities regulation, 64-65
  risk taking regulation, 95, 125-127

Federal Reserve Act of 1913, 39, 387
Federal Reserve Bank
  of Atlanta, 354
  of Cleveland, 5
  definition of, 396
  interest rates, 51, 53f-54f
  of New York, 134, 260, 376
  of Richmond, 174
Federal Reserve Board, 51, 62, 97-98, 119, 233, 392, 396
Federal Savings and Loan Insurance Corporation. *See* FSLIC
Federal Trade Commission, 251
Fedwire, 143-144, 328, 396
fee income, 277, 280, 300, 307, 309f
fee-splitting, 74
FHA. *See* Federal Housing Administration
FHLBB. *See* Federal Home Loan Bank Board
FHLMC. *See* Federal Home Loan Mortgage Corporation
Fidelity Acceptance Corporation, 347
Fidelity Bankers Life Insurance, 190, 215
Fidelity Mutual Life Insurance Company, 199-201
fiduciary services. *See* trust services
financial boutiques. *See* boutiques
financial department stores, 270, 396
financial fragility, 117
financial institutions. *See also specific institution*
  definition of, 396
  distinctions between, blurring of, 18-19
  market share of, 5, 5t
  shares of assets by type of, 5, 6f
Financial Institutions Reform, Recovery, and Enforcement Act of 1989, 89-94, 163, 169, 174, 388
financial markets
  boundaries of, 29-30
  definition of, 396
financial services industry, 13-30
  deregulation of, 16-19
  distribution systems, 19-20
  diversification and regulation of, 16
  and insurance, 22-23
  mergers/acquisitions/demutualizations, 20-21
  problems in, 24-29
  prognosis for, 29-30
  technological change in, 21-22
  trends in, 23-24
financial supermarkets, 236, 283, 356-357
Fine Commission, 64-71
fire insurance, 104
firewalls, 89, 135
FIRRE. *See* Financial Institutions Reform, Recovery, and Enforcement Act of 1989
First American Metro-Corp, 345-346
First Bank System, 61, 164, 344
First Boston Corporation, 14, 39, 253, 258, 266-267, 276, 280

First Capital Life, 109, 190, 215, 217
First Chicago, 164, 326, 331, 338, 356
First City Bancorp, 147, 330
First Executive Life, 109, 238
First Fidelity, 326, 331, 355
First Interstate Bancorp, 61, 164, 326, 344
First Manhattan Consulting Group, 366-367
First Republic Bancorp, 147, 169, 341
First Republic Bank of Dallas, 156, 161
First Union Corp., 130, 327, 339, 342, 345-346
Fischer, Charles T., 349, 369-370
fixed-rate commissions, 45
  elimination of, 28, 76-78, 256
Fleet Financial, 130, 162-164, 326, 328, 344
Fogel, R. W., 260
Ford Financial Services Group, 136, 291, 335
foreign banks. *See also specific bank*
  advantages of, in U.S. market, 42, 65
  branch banking by, 61-62
  Federal Reserve regulation of, 95, 312
  loans made by, 291
  merger activity, 355-356
  permitted services of, 65, 70f
foreign competition
  for U.S. banks abroad, 324-325
  in U.S. market, 307-315, 309t-310t, 310f
foreign debt, 36
foreign exchange trading, 4, 313
foreign insurance companies, 111, 243
foreign securities firms, 270, 276
Foresman, Little, 277
Frank, Barney, 97-98
fraud laws, 43-44, 47-48
Freddie Mac. *See* Federal Home Loan Mortgage Corporation
Fredericks, J. Richard, 21
Freedom National Bank, 96, 156
FSLIC, 8, 38-39, 56, 88, 117
  elimination of, 89, 92
  Savings Association Insurance Fund, 92, 400
  warrants retained by, 93-94
FTC. *See* Federal Trade Commission
Fuchs, Victor K., 181
full-service bank, definition of, 396
full-service broker, definition of, 397
Furash, Edward, 98-99

GAO. *See* General Accounting Office
Garamendi, John, 192-194, 207, 217
Garn-St. Germain Depository Institutions Act of 1982, 20, 81, 84-86, 297, 384-385, 388
General Accounting Office, 108
General Electric (GE), financial services, 5, 25, 30, 256, 291, 335, 356
General Motors, financial services, 5, 25, 137, 291, 335
General Reinsurance Corporation, 173, 243
geographic deregulation, 16-17, 21, 44, 380
geographic restrictions, 60-62

Germany, banking in, 136-137
Gessler Commission, 138-139
GI Bill of Rights, 51
GIC. *See* guaranteed investment contract
Ginnie Mae. *See* Government National Mortgage Association
Girard, Stephen, 250
Glass, Carter, 37, 39, 44
Glass-Steagall Act, 31, 39-42, 44, 249, 267, 323, 380, 387. *See also* Banking Act of 1933; Regulation Q
  consequences of, 133, 252-253, 325
  repeal of, 89, 131-132, 264, 283, 313
globalization, 4, 6
  of financial services industry, 17, 23, 325
  of insurance industry, 207-208
  of securities industry, 139, 256-258, 282-283, 285
GM. *See* General Motors
going public, 255-256, 297
Goldman, Marcus, 250
Goldman Sachs, 14, 250, 256, 265-266, 268, 276, 280
good banks, 166-167, 191
Gorton, Gary, 339
Gourrich, Paul, 36-37
government agency-sponsored bonds, 262-263
government debt auctions, 261
government loan guarantees, 132. *See also* deposit insurance; FDIC
Government National Mortgage Association, 51, 122
grandfathered activities, definition of, 397
Grant, James, 221-222
Great Depression, 31-37, 47-48, 51, 55, 252-253
Greenspan, Alan, 81, 100, 130
guaranteed investment contract, 26, 182, 195-196, 206-207, 215, 220
  definition of, 397
Guarantee Security Life Insurance Co., 199, 207
guaranty funds, 215-224, 382
  national, 110
  state, 107, 191, 194, 215
Gutfreund, John H., 260-261

Halsey, Stuart, 254
Hamilton, Alexander, 337
Harrington, Scott, 219
Harris, Forbes, 39
Harris Trust, 39, 356
Havenmeyer, H. O., 35
health insurance, 28, 182, 199, 205, 238-240
Health Insurance Association of America, 239-240
Hector, Gary, 327
Heinemann, H. E., 98-99, 358
Heller, H. Robert, 140
highly leveraged transactions (HLT), 165f, 303, 397

high-margin products, 274
high-risk lending, growth of, 293-294
holding company. *See also* bank holding company
  definition of, 397
  good bank, bad banks spin-offs by, 166-167
  multibank, 6, 63
  one-bank, 6, 40, 63
home equity loans, 51, 294
Home Federal Corporation, 25
Home Life Insurance Company, 195, 204
Home Loan Owners' Act of 1933, 38, 50
Home Mortgage Disclosure Act, 73
home ownership, encouragement of, 50-51
homeowner's insurance, 232, 381
Homer, Sidney, 254
Hongkong and Shanghai Banking Corp., 356
Hoskins, W. Lee, 5
hostile mergers, regulatory acceptance of, 130
House Banking Committee, 40, 339, 365
House Committee on Energy and Commerce, 108-110, 213
House Subcommittee on Oversight and Investigations, 109-110, 213
Hughes, Charles Evans, 104
Hunt Commission, 64-71
Huntingdon Bancshares, 326, 353
Hutzler, Morton, 250
H.W. Wainwright, 78, 257

IAA. *See* Investment Advisers Act of 1940
ICA. *See* Investment Company Act of 1940
ICC. *See* Interstate Commerce Commission
INB Financial Corp., 349-350
income taxes, federal, 51, 90
Independent Bankers Association, 86
initial margin requirements, 45
insider, definition of, 46
insider's report, 46
insider trading, 46-48, 259, 397
Insider Trading and Securities Fraud Enforcement Act of 1988, 47
Instinet, 76, 286
Institute for Strategic Development, 98
Institutional Investor, 270
institutional investor, definition of, 397
Institutional Investor All-America Research Team, 255, 269
insurance. *See also specific type*
  agency-brokerage system, 225-229
  agents, 227-229
  classification of, 226-227
  depository. *See* deposit insurance; FDIC
  distribution systems, 19-20, 104, 236
    automation of, 224-225, 227-228, 230-231, 236-237, 243
    changes in, 224-237
  fraud, 108
  guaranty funds. *See* guaranty funds

insurance (*Cont'd.*)
  higher risk, 104, 111
  policy owners
    confidence of, 198
    rights of, 106
  rating agencies, mistakes made by, 198
  regulators, 108-109
  sold by banks, 16, 22-23, 86, 89, 133, 232-234, 237, 253
  sold by securities industry, 20, 208, 232-234, 281
insurance company(ies)
  auditing rules for, 109
  captive, 27
  and changing environment, 234-237
  definition of, 397
  diversification of, 19
  efficiency problems of, 235-236
  financial soundness of, statutory requirements concerning, 106
  functions of, 14
  market share of, 5, 5t
  mergers of, 204-205, 208, 243
  ratings for, 112-113
  risk-based capital requirements for, 112-113
  shares of assets, 5, 6f
  solvency regulation for, national system of, 108, 110-111
  stock, 205
  troubled, 108, 198-205
insurance industry
  analogy with banking industry, 26-28, 240-243
  annual rate of return, 187, 188t
  brokerage activity by, 208
  classification of, 181
  consolidation of, 27, 113
  consumer confidence in, 187-190
  diversification of, 208
  employment in, 237
  future of, 205-206, 243-244, 375-376
  globalization of, 207-208
  history of, 103-108
  insolvency in, 208-215
  problems in, 206-240
  regulation of, 103-114, 189
  reserves, 109
  state regulation of, 103-104, 106-107, 205
  structural change in, 181-247
  worldwide regulatory trends in, 113-114
Insurance Information Institute, 214
Insurance Regulatory Information System ratios. *See* IRIS ratios
Integra Financial, 352-353
interest rate ceilings. *See* depository ceiling rates of interest
Interest Rate Control Act of 1966, 63-64
interest rate risk, 109, 318
  definition of, 397
  measurement of, 125-127

interest rates, Federal Reserve Bank, 51, 53f-54f
Intermarket Trading System, 77
International Banking Act of 1978, 65, 388
international insurance companies, 111
international securities, 256-258
interstate banking, 17, 60, 130-131, 380, 397
Interstate Commerce Commission, 251, 254
interstate mergers, 85
Investment Advisers Act of 1940, 60, 252
investment bank(s)/banking, 249-287. *See also*
    brokerage firms; securities industry
  classification of, 276
  definition of, 249, 397-398
  deposit ban on, 40
  employment in, 275
  global, 139
  history of, 34, 249-252
  managerial issues in, 273-274
  mergers of, 251
  regulation of, 59-79
  separation from commercial banking, 34, 252.
     See also Banking Act of 1933; Glass-
     Steagall Act
  sources of revenue for, 277-281, 278t
  underwriting activities of, 89, 253
Investment Bankers Association, 44
Investment Company Act of 1940, 59-60, 111,
    252
investment-grade bond, definition of, 398
investment income, adequacy of, 203, 204t
investment tax credit, 88
Investors Equity Life of Hawaii, 199
IRCA. *See* Interest Rate Control Act of 1966
IRIS ratios, 209, 210t
Irving Corp., 130, 326
Isaacs, William, 86
ITS. *See* Intermarket Trading System

Jacobs, Michael, 364
Janney, Montgomery, Scott, Inc., 208, 269
Japanese banks
  capital standards, 128, 311, 313
  in U.S. banking markets, 307, 311-312, 355
Japanese ownership, of U.S. investment banks,
    256, 257t
Japanese securities industry, 252, 256-257, 259
JC Penney, financial services, 19, 87, 230
Jenrette, Richard H., 220
Jewish banking houses, 250
John Hancock Mutual Life, 21, 195, 208, 256,
    376
Johnson, Thomas S., 321, 326
Johnson Administration, 3
Joseph, Frederick H., 259
J.P. Morgan, 32, 39, 42, 98, 204, 234, 273, 326,
    334-337
jumbo commercial insurance accounts, 226-227
junk bonds, 25-27, 265, 270, 279-280, 291
  collapse of market, 107, 267, 279f

junk bonds (*Cont'd.*)
  definition of, 398
  purchase by insurance companies, 182, 199,
    202-203, 206, 215, 220, 241-242
  purchase by S&Ls, 86, 90
  ratio to net worth, for insurance industry,
    201, 201t
Justice Department, 233, 254, 263, 332

Kahn, Abraham, 250
Kane, Edward J., 31
Kaufman, Henry, 136, 254
Keating, Charles, 96
Keefe, Bruyette, and Woods, 336
Kemper Investors Life Insurance Company, 195,
    205, 376
Kennedy, Joseph, 45
KeyCorp, 326, 350-351
Kidder Peabody, 46, 99, 256, 259, 280, 285
KKR. *See* Kohlberg, Kravis Roberts & Co.
Kmart, financial services, 30
Kohlberg, Kravis Roberts & Co., 162, 195, 271,
    277, 357
Kohn, Meir, 130
Kopcke, R. W., 103
Kramer, Orin, 214
Kuhn, Loeb, and Company, 250, 253, 255

large-business insurance, 226-227
Law, William A., 59
LaWare, John, 98, 156, 339, 369
Lazard Freres, 139, 277, 357
LBO. *See* leveraged buy-out
LDC loans. *See* lesser-developed country loans
League of Savings Institutions, 88
legislation, affecting U.S. depository institutions,
    387-389. *See also specific act*
Lehman Brothers, 250, 254
Leibowitz, Martin, 254
Leshner, Martin, 237
lesser-developed country loans, 163, 202, 258,
    313, 314t-315t
letter of credit
  definition of, 398
  standby, 120, 318
leveraged buy-outs, 164, 266-267, 291, 297,
    307, 311
  definition of, 398
Leveson, Irving, 370-371
Levine, Dennis B., 46
Lewin, Kurt, 193, 217
Lewis, Michael, 261
liability insurance, 104, 111, 187
liability management, 296-300, 398
Liar's Poker (Lewis), 261
Liberty Mutual Insurance Corp., 14, 229, 330
life insurance, 181-182, 208

life insurance company(ies). *See also* insurance company(ies)
agency system, 19-20, 225-229
assets and premium receipts of, 181t, 183t-184t
commercial mortgage loan delinquency rate, 199, 200f
commercial real estate assets, 203, 203t
evaluation of, 203, 204t
failures of, 26, 182, 185f, 188-189, 208-217. *See also specific failure*
frequency of, 210, 211f
prediction of, 209, 210t
primary causes of, 211, 212t
ratings for, 112-113
downgrades in, 195-198
selected ratios of, 203, 204t
troubled, 198-205
Light, Michael, 163
limited branching, 60-61, 398
Lincoln National Corp., 199, 222
Linder, J. C., 354
lines of credit, 318
liquidation account, 222
liquidity
definition of, 398
rating of, 152-153
Litan, Robert E, 98-99, 268, 321
Lloyds, 356
loan. *See specific type*
loan guarantees, 132-133. *See also* deposit insurance
loan loss provisions, 151
loan-loss reserves, 87, 322
loan-to-deposit ratio, 24, 118, 148, 291-292
loan-to-value limitations, 384
Lockheed, 132, 155
Loeb, Solomon, 250
low-margin products, 274

Maine National Bank, 161-163
Maloney Act, 56
management
liability, 398
money, by securities firms, 265-266
rating of, 152
in securities industry, 272-275, 285
Manufacturers Hanover Corporation, 326, 328-330, 339, 355
Manufacturers National Corporation, 307, 339, 348, 355
margin requirements, 34, 45
Marine Midland Banks, 164, 326, 356
Market 2000 (SEC), 286
market-value accounting, 157, 380
Marshall, Buchan, 224
Maryland Casualty Co., 222
Maryland Savings Share Insurance Corporation, 172
Massachusetts, insurance regulation in, 105

mass marketing, 237
matched orders, 47
Mayer, Martin, 371
McCarran-Ferguson Act (Public Law 15), 104, 106, 113, 211
McColl, Hugh, 341
McCormick, James M., 289-290, 366-368
McCoy, John B., 343
McFadden Act of 1927, 60, 387, 398
McGillicuddy, John, 329
McKinsey and Company, 328, 354, 368
medical malpractice insurance, 104, 111
Medicare, 107
Medlin, John G., 167
Meehan, John, 275
megamergers, 326, 328-333
Mellon Bank, 39, 164, 326, 331, 343, 351-352, 355
merchant banking, 250, 278, 398
Merchants National Corporation, 339, 350
mergers, 7, 20-21, 23, 130-131, 291. *See also* consolidation; *specific merger*
foreign banking, 356
hostile, regulatory acceptance of, 130
impact of, 338-339
in insurance industry, 204-205, 208, 243
interstate, 85
of money-center banks, 326
potential, 353-355
regulation of, 62, 88
in securities industry, 251, 255, 266-267, 267f, 271-272, 284
success of, 330-331
superregionals, 130, 305, 339-353, 378
Meridian, 353, 355
Meriweather, John, 260
Merrill Lynch, 14, 76, 87, 208, 253-256, 258, 264-265, 269-270, 276, 280-281, 284
Merritt Commission, 104
Metropolitan Life, 190, 192, 197, 208, 216
Metzenbaum, Howard, 189
Metzenbaum legislation, 109-112
Michigan National Bank, 164, 326
MidAtlantic Bank, 164, 326, 355
Midland Bank, 356
Mid Ocean Reinsurance Company, 234, 244
Milanovich, Mike, 344
Milken, Michael, 46, 96, 259
Miller, G. W., 105
minimum fixed-rate commissions, 45
elimination of, 28, 76-78, 256
Mishkin, Frederic S., 100
Mitchell Hutchins, 78, 257
MMDAs. *See* money market mutual funds
MNC Financial, 164, 341
modified payoff transaction, 158
Monarch Life Insurance, 109, 190
money-center banks, 42, 270, 307, 323, 333-338
definition of, 398

money-center banks (*Cont'd.*)
  mergers of, 326
money management, by securities firms, 265-266
money market mutual funds, 3, 263-264, 298, 321
  definition of, 398
  development of, 2, 19, 42, 82, 84-86
  market share of, 5, 5t
  shares of assets, 5, 6f
Montgomery Ward, financial services, 30, 230
MONY. *See* Mutual Life of New York
Moody's, 26, 295, 350
  ratings for life insurance companies, 195-196,
    197t, 218
moral hazard, 168-169, 398
Morgan Stanley, 84, 253-254, 265-266, 268, 276,
  279-280, 343
mortgage(s). *See also* commercial real estate; real
  estate loans
  adjustable rate, 64, 140, 391
  commercial, loan delinquency rate, for life
    insurance industry, 199, 200f
  nonperforming, ratio to net worth, for insur-
    ance industry, 201, 201t
  pass-throughs, 270
  second, 51
mortgage-backed securities, 268, 317, 317f
mortgage insurance, 50-51, 232
Mozer, Paul, 261
multibank holding companies, 6, 63
multinational institutions, 307-315, 322
municipal bonds, 87-88, 192, 254, 278-279, 295
Mutual Benefit Life, 26, 107, 182, 190-192, 199-
  200, 202, 204-205, 238, 244
mutual funds. *See* money market mutual funds
Mutual Life of New York, 195-197, 199, 204

NAIC. *See* National Association of Insurance
  Commissioners
Naisbitt, John, 234
NASD. *See* National Association of Securities
  Dealers
NASDAQ system, 76, 281
National Association of Insurance Brokers, 113
National Association of Insurance Commission-
  ers, 105-106, 109, 111-113, 202, 205,
  209, 381-382
  Annual Statement, 108
  financial and other ratios used by, 209, 210t
National Association of Securities Dealers, 56,
  74, 398
national bank, definition of, 398
National City Corp., 32, 164, 326, 339, 344,
  350, 352
National Credit Union Administration, 71, 173
National Credit Union Share Insurance Fund, 71
National Deposit Insurance Corporation of
  Columbus, Ohio, 173
national health insurance, 238-240
National Housing Act, 38

National Insurance Guaranty Corporation, 110,
  218
national insurance guaranty funds, 110
National Insurance Protection Corporation, 110
National Market System, 76
National Organization of Life and Health Insur-
  ance Guaranty Associations, 193
National Reinsurance, 243
National Westminster Bank, 356
NationsBank, 130, 285, 339-342, 346, 380
nationwide branch banking, 97-98, 130, 289,
  321-322
Nationwide Insurance, 205, 229
natural disaster insurance, 107, 111, 187, 212,
  242-244
NBD Bancorp, 164, 326, 348-350, 353, 355, 369
NCNB, 339-341
NCUA. *See* National Credit Union Administra-
  tion
NCUSIF. *See* National Credit Union Share Insur-
  ance Fund
Nebraska Depository Guarantee Corporation,
  172
negotiable order of withdrawal account. *See*
  NOW account
New Deal legislation, 2, 35, 37-55
New England Mutual Life, 195, 376
New York, insurance regulation in, 104-105
New York Stock Exchange, 44-45, 269, 271, 286
  ban on public ownership, 256
  limited after-hours trading for, 49
  minimum fixed-rate commission requirement,
    45, 74
  regulated rate structure suggested by, 77
  trading volume increases in, 73, 255, 281, 283
NIGC. *See* National Insurance Guaranty Corporation
Nikko Securities, 257
Nippon Credit Bank Limited, 312
NMS. *See* National Market System
NOLHGA. *See* National Organization of Life and
  Health Insurance Guaranty Associations
Nomura Securities, 139, 257
nonamortizing assets, 126
nonbank banks, 18-19, 86-89, 135, 356
  definition of, 398-399
nonbanking activities. *See also specific activity*
  of bank holding companies, 16, 66t-67t, 86
  of commercial banks, 40-42, 65, 70t, 251, 270
  definition of, 64-65
  separation of, 40
  of state-chartered banks, state authorization of,
    65, 68t-69t
noncompetitive bidding, 84
non-interest-bearing deposits, decline of, 297,
  298f
nonperforming loans, 26-27, 182, 191, 195, 197,
  199-203, 220, 241-242, 293
  definition of, 399

Northern Trust, 164, 352
Norwest Corp., 61, 164, 344
NOW account, 2, 82-83, 297, 399
Nutter, Franklin, 113

Obermaier, Otto, 260
OCC. *See* Office of Comptroller of Currency
off-balance-sheet activities, 17, 120, 126
  credit conversion factors for, 122t
  definition of, 318, 399
  increases in, 318-319
off-budget guarantees, 132
Office of Administrator of State Banks, 71
Office of Comptroller of Currency, 62, 71, 91,
    118-119, 233, 393
Office of Thrift Supervision, 26, 90-91, 97,
    143, 322
offshore banking centers, 313
Ohio Deposit Guarantee Fund, 172
Old Kent, 326, 355
Olympia & York, 164, 336
one-bank holding companies, 6, 40, 63
originating firms, 276
OTC markets. *See* over-the-counter markets
OTS. *See* Office of Thrift Supervision
over-the-counter markets, 50, 56, 74, 77

P&A agreement. *See* purchase and assumption
    agreement
Pacific Mutual Life Insurance Company, 194,
    217
Paine Webber, 14, 256, 276, 280
passbook accounts, 83
payment system safety, issues of, 143-144
PBGC. *See* Pension Benefits Guarantee Corpora-
    tion
Peabody, Charles, 98-99
Pecora hearings, 33-34
Pennsylvania Insurance Department, 200-201
Pension Benefits Guarantee Corporation, 132,
    217
pension funds
  guarantee of, 217
  market share of, 5, 5t
  shares of assets, 5, 6f
personal insurance, 226, 236
Philadelphia Stock Exchange, 49
Phoenix Mutual Life Insurance Company, 204
Pierce, James L., 139, 366
plain vanilla bonds, 279
play or pay plan, 239
PNC Financial, 130, 164, 326, 344, 352, 355
point-of-sale transfer system, 22, 73, 399
pools, 45
Porter, Michael, 277
portfolio insurance, 285
Posit, 286
POST. *See* point-of-sale transfer system

Postal Savings System, 33
preauthorized payments, 73
preliminary prospectus (red herring), 50, 399
price banking, 3, 315-316, 356
price fixing, 104
price manipulation schemes, 45
primary capital, 119
primary market, definition of, 399
Primerica Corp., 30, 196, 284
principal bankers, 250
private deposit insurance, 171-173
private loan guarantees, 132
private placement, definition of, 399
product line separation, 32
profitability, bank, 132, 300-302, 304, 304t,
    307, 308t
property and casualty insurance, 27, 104, 184-
    187, 206, 237
property and casualty insurance companies
  annual rate of return, 187, 188t
  cycle combined ratio, 184, 186f
  failures of, 211-215, 212f, 213f
  investment of, 184, 185t
  1990 market share, 189t
  ratings for, 113
  underwriting results, 184, 186t
prospectus, 37, 42, 48, 50
  definition of, 399
  preliminary, 50, 399
Prudential, 30, 87, 208, 232, 256, 264, 269, 271,
    276, 280, 376
prudent man rule, definition of, 399
Public Law 15. *See* McCarran-Ferguson Act
    (Public Law 15)
public loan guarantees, 132
Public Utility Holding Act of 1935, 31-32, 252
Pujo Committee, 32
purchase and assumption agreement, 158

qualified thrift lender test, 96
quality, of investment, 43-44
Quotron, 336

railroads, 250-251, 254
Randall, R. E., 103
real estate loans. *See also* commercial real estate
  nonperforming, 26-27, 182, 191, 195, 197,
    199-203, 220, 241-242, 293
recapitalization, definition of, 399
recession, 7, 151, 163
red herring (preliminary prospectus), 50, 399
redlining, 73
Reed, John, 335-336
registered representatives, 276
registration, 42-43, 48, 50, 59
  definition of, 399
  shelf, 83-84
registration statement, 37, 43t, 50

regulation, 8, 16
  classification of, 32
  expert opinions on, 363-373
  history of, 31-58
  of insurance industry, 103-114, 189
  multiple agencies involved in, problems
    caused by, 140-143
  problems created by, 18
  of securities industry, 45, 47-48, 59-74
  stimulus for, 131
  urgency of, 7-8
Regulation D, definition of, 399
Regulation Q, 1-3, 16, 34, 39, 51, 264, 290,
    316, 321
  definition of, 399
  establishment of. *See* Banking Act of 1933;
    Glass-Steagall Act
  patch, 64
  repeal of, 19, 82, 85-86, 290, 321
reinsurance, 27, 108-111, 234, 400
Reinsurance Association of America, 113
relationship banking, 250, 315-316
relationship manager, role of, 274
reorganization, types of, 222-223
reregulation, 8, 385
research boutiques, 78, 257
research departments, shifting role of, 268-270
reserve requirements, 51, 52f, 400
Resolution Trust Corporation, 25-26, 90, 96-97,
    263, 322
Resolution Trust Corporation Refinancing,
    Restructuring, and Improvement Act of
    1991, 94-97
restructuring, 129, 266
retail banks, definition of, 400
retail distribution, definition of, 400
retail securities firms, 276-277
retirement benefits, 107
retirement funds
  guarantee of, 217
  market share of, 5, 5t
  shares of assets, 5, 6f
return on assets, 129, 148, 303-307, 306f
  definition of, 400
return on equity, 129, 303-307, 305f-306f
  definition of, 400
  securities firms, 281, 282f
Rhode Island, bank failures in, 96, 172-173
Rhode Island Depositors Economic Protection
    Corporation, 172-173
risk-based capital, example of, 123, 125t
risk-based capital ratios, at insured commercial
    banks, 122, 124f
risk-based capital standards
  for banks, 120-130
  for insurers, 112-113
risk-based deposit insurance, 41, 96, 117, 167-
    171, 322, 379-380
riskiness, of investment, 43

risk retention groups, 187
risk taking
  excessive, 168, 173-174, 322
  regulation of, 122
risk weights/categories, 121t, 126-127
risky asset ratio, 203, 204t
ROA. *See* return on assets
rocket scientists, 254, 266, 281
ROE. *See* return on equity
Roffman, Marvin, 269
Rogers, David, 336, 371-372
Roosevelt Administration, 31, 33-36, 40, 44, 104,
    167, 252
Rose, Sanford, 275
Rosenberg, Richard, 332
RTC. *See* Resolution Trust Corporation
Rule 415, 83-84, 400
run on a bank, 34, 55, 152, 155, 168, 400

SAIF. *See* Savings Association Insurance Fund
Salomon Brothers, 14, 84, 136, 139, 250, 256,
    258, 265-266, 276, 279-280, 334
  rise of, 253-255
  scandal of 1991, 259-263
savings and loan associations. *See also* thrift insti-
    tutions
  definition of, 400
  failures of, 25-26, 96-97, 132, 298, 321. *See
    also specific failure*
Savings Association Insurance Fund, 92, 400
savings bank(s)
  chartering and supervision of, federal-state
    system of, 38
  definition of, 400
  diversification of, 18
Schlesinger, Arthur M., Jr., 35
Schumer, Charles E., 365-366
Scott, William L., 13, 249
Scrimmegour Vickers, 336
SeaFirst, 147, 333
Sears, financial services, 5, 19, 21-22, 25, 30,
    87, 256, 271, 285, 290, 356-357
SEC. *See* Securities and Exchange Commission
secondary market trading, 281, 318
second mortgages, 51
securities, new types of, 270
Securities Act of 1933, 31, 35-37, 42-44, 48, 252-
    253, 400
  Rule 415, 83-84, 400
Securities Acts
  Amendment of 1964, 50
  Amendment of 1975, 9-10, 76-78
  consequences of, 252-253
Securities Enforcement Remedies Act of 1990,
    49, 94
Securities Exchange Act of 1934, 31, 35, 45-48,
    50, 56, 252-253, 401
Securities and Exchange Commission, 28, 47-
    50, 254

Securities and Exchange Commission (*Cont'd.*)
central security system mandated by, 77
definition of, 400
establishment of, 45, 48, 253
investment funds study by, 59
Market 2000 study, 286
organization of, 49, 49f
regulation of securities industry, 56, 73-74
rules 390 and 500, 286
securities firms. *See also* brokerage firms; investment bank(s)
classification of, 276-277
retail, 276-277
wholesale, 276-277
securities industry, 249-287
consolidation of, 256-258, 271-272, 286
and corporate finance, 266-268
definition of, 401
diversification of, 19, 270-271
ethical standards in, 46-47
future of, 283-286
geographic concentration of, 44
globalization of, 256-258, 282-283, 285
history of, 33-34, 47-48
insurance sales by, 20, 208, 232-234, 281
laws affecting, changes in, 262-263
managerial issues in, 272-273, 285
mergers in, 251, 255, 266-267, 267f, 271-
272, 284
money management by, 265-266
regulation of, 45, 47-48, 59-74
research departments, shifting role of, 268-270
sources of revenue for, 277-281, 278t
strategies of, 276-277
structure of, 271-272, 275-276
technological change in, 252, 255, 271, 281-
283
trends in, 28-29
and venture capital/real estate, 268
Securities Investor Protection Corporation Act of
1970, 75-76
securitization, 17, 23, 265
of credit card market, 295
definition of, 401
role of banking in, 318-319
Security Pacific, 164, 326, 331-333, 339
Seidman, L. William, 131-132, 156-157, 162, 384
self-designing organizations, 274
self-insurance, 187, 206
self-liquidating trust. *See* bad bank
self-regulation, 45, 56
Servicemen's Readjustment Act of 1944, 51
Shaw, Karen, 98-99
Shawmut Banking Corporation, 164, 347
Shea, Dennis, 343
Shearson Lehman, 21, 217, 256, 264-265, 268-
269, 276, 280, 284, 356
shelf registration, 83-84, 265, 400
Sherman Act, 74, 104, 251, 401

Shipley, Gordon, 329
Siegel, Martin A., 46
single-premium whole life insurance, 182
SIPC. *See* Securities Investor Protection Corporation Act of 1970
S&Ls. *See* savings and loan associations
small-business insurance, 226
small-business loans, 132
SNOW. *See* super-NOW accounts
social responsibility laws, 32, 72-73
Social Security, 107
Society Corp., 339, 344-345, 352
soft-dollar commissions, 257
source-of-strength policy, 139-140
South Carolina National Bank, 164, 339, 342
Southeast Banking Corp., 147, 164, 339, 345-346
special-bracket firm, definition of, 401
specialist firms, 266, 284
specialized banking, 357
Standard & Poor, 26, 198, 218, 295, 346, 401
standby letters of credit, 120, 318
state banking commissions, 38, 401
state-chartered banks, 38, 56
nonbanking activities for, state authorization
of, 65, 68t-69t
state demutualization statutes, 222
state deposit insurance plans, 172
State Farm, 14, 104, 229, 234
state insurance guaranty funds, 107, 191, 194,
215
state regulation, of insurance industry, 103-104,
106-107, 205
state risk pools, for high-risk uninsured, 238
State Street Management Co., 208, 352
Steagall, Henry, 40
Stewart, Richard E., 214, 217-218
stock(s)
buying on margin, 47
registration of. *See* shelf registration
stock exchanges. *See also specific exchange*
national system of, 76-77
stock insurance companies, 205
stock market crash of 1929, 31, 34-35
stock watering, 33, 44
storm insurance, 107
Strauss, Thomas W., 260
stripped securities, 270
SunTrust, 130, 164, 307, 344-346
super-NOW accounts, 85
superregionals, 130, 305, 339-353, 378
supervisory levels, classification of, 170
Supreme Court. *See also specific ruling*
rulings on Glass-Steagall Act, 40
rulings on insurance products, 104, 233-234
rulings on mergers and acquisitions, 62
rulings on nonbank banks, 87
surplus ratio, 203, 204t
surplus relief reinsurance, 108

sweetheart deals, 36
Switzerland, banking in, 137, 312-313
syndicate
    banking, 253, 391
    definition of, 401
systemic risk, 134-135, 143-144, 155

tangible capital, 91
Tax Reform Act of 1986, 51, 87-88, 279, 294-295
Taylor, Jeremy F., 365
TBTF. *See* too big to fail doctrine
technological change. *See* automation
telephone services/transfers, 22, 73
tenant migration, 201-202
term insurance, 207, 401
Texas Commerce Bancshares, 147, 330
Thalman, Ladenburg, 99
3–6–3 rule, 13
Thrift Depositor Protection Oversight Board, 97
Thrift Guarantee Corporation of Hawaii, 172
thrift institutions. *See also* savings and loan asso-
        ciations
    analogy with banking and insurance industries,
        26-28
    chartering and supervision of, federal-state
        system of, 38
    classification of, by capital ratios, 96
    collapse of, 5
    consolidation of, 92
    definition of, 401
    federal income tax rate for, 90
    functions of, 14
    and Garn-St. Germain Act, 85-86
    interest rate ceilings for, 64
time deposits, 37, 39, 298
Tobin, James, 275
Tokyo Stock Exchange, 128
tombstone, definition of, 401
too big to fail doctrine, 136, 154-158, 169,
        174, 300
tort law, 187
total capital, 119
trading hours, 49
trading practices, regulation of, 46
transaction account, definition of, 401
Transamerica Life Occidental, 217
Travelers Insurance Company, 27, 195-196, 199,
        208, 376
Treasury Department, 91, 98, 143, 261-262
Treasury securities, 82, 120, 256, 263, 282, 296
Trump, Donald, 269
Trust Indenture Act of 1939, 252
trusts, development of, 32-33
trust services, 82, 401
Truth in Lending Act, 72, 401
truth-in-savings provision, 96
truth in securities law. *See* Securities Act of 1933
Tucker Anthony, 21, 208, 256

underwrite investments, definition of, 401
underwriters
    consolidation among, 27
    future role of, 229
    leading, 280, 280t
    lower cost, 104
underwriting income, nature of, 29
underwriting losses, insurance, 27
underwriting practices, cash flow, 27
underwriting spreads, reduction in, 279
unemployment, 34
unemployment benefits, 107
unethical practices
    provisions for, 43-44
    in securities industry, 46-47
Uniform Bank Performance Rating system,
        153-154
uniform bank performance report, 153-154,
        402
uninsured, 205, 238-240
unit bank, definition of, 402
United Kingdom
    banking in, 137, 312-313, 356
    securities industry in, 257, 261
United States Building and Loan League, 37
United States National Bank of San Diego, 151
universal banking, 32, 42, 137-139, 283
universal life, 182, 208, 402
UNUM, 21, 199, 224
U.S. League of Savings Associations, 26
U.S. v. Philadelphia National Bank, 62

vacancy rates, 165
Vagley, Robert, 214
Valley National, 164, 343
valuation analysis, 266
variable universal life, 182, 208
venture capital, 268
videotex systems, 22
voice modulator, 231
Vojta, George J., 5
Volker, Paul, 86
volume discounts, 74, 77

Wachovia Corp., 130, 164, 167, 339-342
Wall, L. D., 354
Warren, Earl, 74
wash sales, 45, 47
Wasserstein, Perella, 139, 256, 277, 357
Wells Fargo, 14, 164-165, 326, 332
Whipple, Kenneth, 136-137
whole life insurance, 182, 402
wholesale lenders, 270, 402
wholesale securities firms, 276-277
Winans, R. Foster, 46
winner's curse, 262

wirehouse, definition of, 402
Wise, Warren, 218-219
worker's compensation, 27, 214
World Trade Bank, 165
World War I, economic growth after, 33
Wright, Elizer, 103

Wright, Kenneth, 378-379
Wriston, Walter, 134, 275, 336

Xerox, 30, 285, 356-357

Yamaichi Securities, 257